THE JACK ADJMI EDITION

לקדושים אשר בארץ

Aleppo

City of Scholars

FIRST EDITION *First Impression ... March 2005*

ARTSCROLL SEPHARDIC HERITAGE SERIES® / ALEPPO — CITY OF SCHOLARS

ISBN: 1-57819-056-8 (hard cover)

Typography by CompuScribe at ArtScroll Studios, Ltd.

Printed in USA by Edison Lithographing and Printing Corp. • Bound by Sefercraft, Quality Bookbinders, Ltd., Brooklyn NY 11232

The Jack Adjmi Edition

Aleppo

City of Scholars

by Rabbi David Sutton

based on *LiKedoshim Asher Ba'Aretz*
by Hacham David-Sion Laniado

Edited by Isaac Kirzner

Yad Yosef Torah Center
Birkat Yaakov
In Memory of Jack Adjmi

A Project of the Yad Yosef Torah Center

Jack *A"H* ***with some of the Rabbis he loved***

This volume is dedicated in loving memory of
a great man and an inspiring leader

Jack Adjmi A"H

יעקב בן נזירה ע״ה

May 17, 2003 / ט"ז אייר, תשס"ג

Recalling his youth, he said, "I told God that if I ever became rich, I would treat the wealthy and poor alike and see to the needs of everyone, no matter what his financial position." That is what he did, always, without fail. He loved people and they loved him.

Everyone felt comfortable and respected in his company. Someone's "status" did not matter to him. Rich man, poor man, professional or laborer — to him every man and woman were equally worthy of respect — and he made sure they knew it.

Although magnanimous, he was never content with his own giving. He encouraged others to give — and did it with his contagious smile and eminent charm. He helped those people feel grateful that they could help others and be a part of worthy causes. Jack looked for people who needed his help, and it was his pleasure to extend it to them.

He revered rabbis and teachers of Torah. He considered it a privilege to help them in their holy work, and he never believed that these servants of Hashem should feel beholden to him. That he could help them was a blessing, and he thanked them for giving him the opportunity. He helped build and maintain synagogues and yeshivot, even performing menial tasks when necessary.

How fitting that this man who had such enormous respect for rabbis be memorialized in such a publication. He would have loved this book because it will show our brethren the faces and lives of the great rabbis, teachers, and pious laymen who were the model for his life.

He was one of the most respected, loved, and admired people in the Syrian community. May his life be an example for everyone as it was for us, and may his memory be blessed in the merit of the good deeds this book will inspire.

From his loving wife and children

Rachel Adjmi

Elliot and Joy Mahana
Eric and Audrey Adjmi
Ronnie and Adele Adjmi
Joey and Terry Dwek
Mark and Corie Adjmi
Solomon and Kim Dabbah

A Father's Blessing

DIPLOMATE AMERICAN
BOARD OF DERMATOLOGY

JOSEPH D. SUTTON, M.D., P.C.
222 ROUTE 59
SUFFERN, NEW YORK 10901

Feb. 2005

It is a great pleasure and privilege to share my thoughts regarding my son's new book about Aleppo. When discussing my family history with some of the great Ashkenazi Rabbis of the past generation. I was always impressed with the reverence that they expressed when informed that I was of Aleppo- Syrian descent. As Rav Schach stated , "What a Yichus!! " What is special about Syrian Jewry?

Many human physical traits are determined by our genetic make-up. However, our spiritual development is strongly influenced by our ancestors growth in Torah over the generations. Aleppo is a city that was famous for its commitment to authentic Sephardic Torah tradition. This was incorporated into the spirit of the descendants who started the migration to America at the beginning of the 20th century. In their new community , the study of Torah and the observance of our laws continued.

On a personal note, my grandfather, Abraham D. Sutton, started a synagogue in Bensonhurst, known as *Knees Sithon*. Besides praying there, many of the hachamim gathered every morning to learn. Among them were Hacham Moshe Gindi, Hacham Moshe Dweck (Kassab), Hacham Yaacob Nahem, Hacham Yosef Mansour, and Hacham Selim Ashkenazi. They would study *Tur Bet Yosef* , and my grandfather, although a layman, held his own. Hacham Yaacob Kassin would arrive at 11:30 a.m. and get involved as well. These were the ways of laymen of our community - to spend their mornings learning before going to work. It comes as no surprise, therefore, to see my son continuing in our tradition of building synagogues and batei midrash. Furthermore, with this new book, I can appreciate who these rabbis were, who learned in my grandfather's shul. Of greater importance to the community is the ability to study our glorious past. This history is an integral part of our spiritual essence. May we merit to continue it in its authentic form as documented in this book.

May my son, David, continue to teach and spread Torah in the community. May he, his dear wife Chaya, and all his children be blessed from heaven with long life, health and much nachat. And we and our fellow members of the Syrian - Sephardic community merit to continue on the path set for us by our distinguished forebears.

Joseph D. Sutton

Joseph D. Sutton

ישיבת קול יעקב

YESHIVATH KOL YAAKOV • ע״ש הגר״י עדס זצוק״ל

עמותה מס׳ 580021806

בס״ד ירושלים עיה״ק תובב״א, ט׳ שבט תשס״ה

באתי בזה לברך על היוזמה של תרגום הספר החשוב "לקדושים אשר באר״ץ" לאנגלית. הרה״צ רבי דוד לניאדו זצ״ל עמל רבות לרכז בצורה חדשנית ומתומצתת את תולדות חכמי ורבני ארם צובא כאשר הביא בפני בני העיר ועם ישראל כולו את גדולתם ופעלם של חכמי העדה כפי שהדבר מתבטא בקצרה על מצבות קבורתם.

ומי לנו גדול מרבן של כל ישראל בכל הדורות שאחריו, הרמב״ם אשר העיד שביקר בקהילות ישראל ולא מצא תורה כי אם באחלב שבסוריה, עדות על מקומה המיוחד של קהילת אר״צ בעולם התורה היהודי, ואשר ע״י ספרו של הרב לניאדו זצ״ל אנו למדים על ההמשכיות במעלת העדה מאז ועד לדור האחרון.

ענין גדול יש בתרגום הספר לאנגלית להביא לידיעת הדור הצעיר של בני עדתינו הקדושה את ההיסטוריה ארוכת השנים של גדולי חכמי התורה של העדה. כאשר חלק נכבד מבני העדה מתגוררים בקהילה הנפלאה בברוקלין ואנגלית היא שפת האם שלהם. ובתרגום הספר לאנגלית פותחים בפניהם צוהר רחב להכירות בת מאות שנים עם פני העדה וחכמיה, דבר שיכול להדק את הקשר של הקוראים עם עברם המפואר. ויכול לתת את הדחיפה להידמות למעשיהם של הראשונים ולהתקרב אליהם.

ועל כן בואו ונחזיק טובה להרה״ג ר׳ דוד סיתהון שליט״א על העבודה המאומצת שעשה בתרגום הספר ועל ההארות החשובות שלו שמוסיפות נופך מיוחד לקירוב הספר ללב הקוראים. ויחד עמו יבואו על הברכה בני משפחת עג׳מי היקרה אשר הספר יוצא לאור בהוצאתם לע״נ אביהם היקר באדם ר׳ יעקב עג׳מי ז״ל.

ותפילתי להשי״ת שאכסניה זו של תורה של עדתינו המפוארת תמשיך להאיר לעדה בכל מקומות מושבותיהם ולהפיץ את אהבת התורה וכבוד חכמיה בעולם כולו.

ביקרא דאורייתא

יהודה עדס

הרב יהודה עדס

רח׳ דברי ירוחם 4, בית וגן, ירושלים 91061, ת״ד 6174, טל׳: TEL:02-6424152 פקס: FAX:02-6437081

4 DIVREI YERUHAM ST., JERUSALEM 91061, ISRAEL. P.O.B. 6174 U.S.A. ADRESS: 1879 EAST 2ND STREET, BROOKLYN, N.Y. 11223

ישיבת קול יעקב
YESHIVATH KOL YAAKOV • ע"ש הגר"י עדס זצוק"ל
עמותה מס' 580021806

Jerusalem, 9 Shevat 5765 (2005)

I herewith give my blessing to the project of translating the important book LiKedoshim Asher Ba'Aretz into English. The worthy Rabbi David Laniado of blessed memory worked many years to concentrate into a new and focused form the history of the scholars and rabbis of Aram Soba. In so doing he brought to the attention of the Jewish public the greatness of that community's scholars and their achievements, as succinctly expressed on their tombstones.

And who is there greater than the Rabbi of all Israel in all succeeding generations, the Rambam? It was he who bore witness to his search throughout the communities of Israel and to the fact that he could not find [scholars that were truly immersed in] Torah except for Halab in Syria. This was testimony to the unique position of the community of Aram Soba in the Jewish world. Through Rabbi Laniado's book we learn how the virtuous quality of this community has continued into the present time.

There is great value in translating this book into English in order to bring to the attention of our holy community's younger generation the long history of the community's great Torah scholars. A significant portion of the community lives in a wonderful congregation in Brooklyn where English is the common language. And by translating this book into English they have opened before them a wide window into the hundreds of years of the life of the community and its scholars. This has the potential of strengthening the bond of the readers with their glorious past. It can encourage them to emulate the behavior of their ancestors and to become nearer to them.

Therefore, let us give thanks to the worthy Rabbi David Sutton for his dedicated work of translating the book and for the important additions which he provided to make the book more attractive to its readers. At the same time may there be a blessing for the worthy Adjmi family who funded the printing of this book to be a merit for their dear father Reb Yaakob Adjmi, of blessed memory.

I pray to Hashem that this glorious Torah resource of our community will continue to cast light upon the community in all its dwelling places and that it will continue to spread the love of Torah and the honor of Torah scholars throughout the world.

With Torah blessings,
Rabbi Yehudah Ades

רח' דברי ירוחם 4, בית וגן, ירושלים 91061, ת"ד 6174, טל': TEL:02-6424152 פקס: FAX:02-6437081
4 DIVREI YERUHAM ST., JERUSALEM 91061, ISRAEL. P.O.B. 6174 U.S.A. ADRESS: 1879 EAST 2ND STREET, BROOKLYN, N.Y. 11223

בני שערי ציון
B'NEI SHAARE ZION

February 8th 2004

It is with mixed feelings that I write this approbation. My father, Hacham Baruch, may he live and be well, was planning on writing this letter before he became ill, and I am expressing his feelings on his behalf.

My father loved the book "Likdoshim asher Baretz"; in fact, he had the original printing on his table over the past few months and enjoyed reading it.

He was approached by Rabbi David Sutton, who was translating it, and by Ronnie Adjmi, and he said that although he does not usually write approbations he would do it out of the great love he has for Mr. Jack Adjmi, of blessed memory whose family is dedicating the book in his honor.

Rabbi David Sutton is beloved to my father as well, going back to the special relationship he has with Rabbi Sutton's father, Dr. Joe Sutton. Dr. Sutton was one of my father's first students.

We hope and pray that my father will have a full recovery and give his blessings to the project.

Yaacov Ben-Haim

Yaacov Ben-Haim

2030 Ocean Parkway, Brooklyn, NY 11223 718-376-0009 Fax 718-339-4072

THE SYNAGOGUE OF DEAL

Rosh Hodesh Adar I. 5765
February 10th 2005

After thousands of years of great erudition and spiritual contributions to Torah Study, Halab has closed down. There are no more minyanim, no more yeshibot, no more authors. At this critical juncture in our history, Rabbi David Sutton's 'Aleppo-City of Scholars,' is extremely valuable to preserve the history that was tilled over the centuries on its soil.

This book will awaken our pride in the rich heritage of the Syrian Community. This renowned city had a dynasty rich with spiritual giants – both among the leaders and the learned laymen. Because of this work, the English-speaking public can appreciate the glory and heights of their grandparents and the generations before them.

Although the Syrian community has adjusted comfortably to new surroundings, there is so much more we are able to gain through acknowledgement of the people and places that formed our foundations. 'Aleppo-City of Scholors,' is a monumental work- both in its scope and potential impact. Our progeny stands to benefit greatly from having access to the humbling lessons and saintly stories that occurred in our midst not so long ago.

Having spent my childhood years in Syria, I have distinct thankfulness to Rabbi David Sutton for, through this book, teaching the Jewish community about the Gedolim that have formed the linked chain from the times of the Second Beit Hamikdash until today. The awe of the Great Synagogue and the commitment the Aleppo community had towards Torah and Mitzvot is a tradition we could not have afforded to lose.

A special thank you to my devoted newest daughter-in-law Vickie Dwek for her significant contribution to this work.

This book was written in memory of my dear and beloved friend Jack Adjmi A'H, benefactor of Torah institutions at home and abroad. May he continue to serve as a model of Sedaka and chesed to his children, his illustrious family and our community for years to come.

I had the pleasure of working closely with Rabbi Sutton for many years at the Deal Synagogue and Yeshiva. Though I did not have the opportunity to review most of the manuscript, I know I can rely on Rabbi Sutton's scholarship and extreme diligence.

I wish our prominent author continued success in spreading Torah and knowledge of Hashem, in the Avenue J Torah Center and throughout our community, Amen.

Sincerely,
RABBI ISAAC DWEK

I. Dwek

128 Norwood Avenue • Deal, NJ 07723 • (732) 531-3200 • Fax (732) 517-0798

Rosh Yeshivat
Hevrat Ahavat Shalom
45 Arzei Habirah St. Jerusalem

דברי הסכמה וברכה

שמחתי לראות פעולת צדיק לחיים ספר "לקדושים אשר בארץ" בשפה האנגלית והוא תולדות הרבנים מגדולי חכמי ארם צובא על יסוד הספר בשם הנ"ל שחיברו בלשון הקודש הרב הגדול חסידא ופרישא כמהר"ר דוד לאנייאדו ז"ל. ועתה נערך מחדש ותורגם לשפה האנגלית על ידי ידידי וחביבי כמ"ע הרה"ג כה"ר דוד סתהון שליט"א אשר אני מכירו לשעבר משנות לימודו בשקדנות בירושלים ת"ו שהיה מבני עליה ממש. וגם עד היום לא זזה ידי מתוך ידו כאשר אני מלווה את פעליו החשובים לתורה ולתעודה בהרבצת תורה לתלמידים רבים המשכימים ומעריבים ל"מרכז התורה" לבעלי בתים קובעי עתים שמחבב עליהם לימוד התורה ודקדוק המצוות. וגם הינו מנקיי הדעת ועומד בפרץ לגדור פרצות התקופה וידו נטויה להעמיד ולחזק גדרי הדת על תילם ואינו זז מדרכם בקודש נהדר של גדולי חכמי הדור מרביצי תורה ויראה שליט"א. ובסייעתא דשמיא זכה וזיכה את הרבים שחפץ ה' בידו הצליח להוסיף ספסלים בבית המדרש ולהגדיל תורה ולהאדירה.

והנה עתה הולך מחיל לחיל בהוצאתו לאור מחדש בשפה האנגלית את הספר היקר והנחוץ "לקדושים אשר בארץ" והוסיף עליו במידה גדושה כהנה וכהנה מהני מילי מעלייתא תולדות חייהם ומעשיהם סיפוריהם ופעולותיהם של הצדיקים לחיים מגדולי חו"ר ארם צובה בצירוף הרבה תמונות נדירות לקיים מ"ש (ישעיה ל' כ'): והיו עיניך רואות את מוריך וכמ"ש חז"ל (ילקוט שמעוני תהלים ל"ט רמז תשל"ה): יהא דומה בעל שמועה כאלו עומד נגדו. וגם צילומי מסמכים נדירים ושטרות ושערי ספרים ודפי כתבי יד וחתימות הרבנים להמחיש ולתעד העובדות והמעשים. ושמחתי לראות שבאיזהו מקומן של שבחי"ם ליקט גם מתוך מאמרי תולדות שנרשמו על ידינו בהקדמות ספרים שיצאו לאור על ידי ישיבתנו הק'.

ואכן הספר מלא וגדוש בידיעות יקרות ונחוצות אשר בלי ספק ילהיבו הלבבות לעלות בסולם העליה במעלות התורה והיראה ללמוד ממעשיהם ועבודתם של צדיקי הדורות איך עבדו את ה' באמת ובתמים ואיך הגיעו למעלות רמות בידיעות התורה ובחיבורים שחברו ובתיקון מדותיהם ובדקדוק מצוותיהם וממלחמותיהם להעמיד גדרי הדת על תילם כדי שמהם ניקח ונלמד לעבוד את ה' אלהינו. ובפרט כי בעוונותינו הרבים הדור פרוץ מאוד בכמה נסיונות קשים ובלבול הדעת. ודעות פסולות וכפרניות אשר לכן חשוב מאוד ונחוץ לקיים מה שמפרשים על הפסוק (רש"י שיר השירים א' ח'): צאי לך בעקבי הצאן ללכת בתמימות ובדרכי רבותינו הראשונים בדרך הסלולה והכבושה לנו מדור דור במסילה העולה בית אל כי מהם ניקח לעבוד את ה' אלהינו וללכת בדרכיו ולדבקה בו כאשר נהגו ופעלו במסירות נפש חכמי הדורות ולא בדרכים חדשים מקרוב באו אשר לא שערום אבותינו.

ומלבד זה כמה עידוד הוא למשפחות המפוארות והמיוחסות שבישראל אשר בראותם "מאין באו" ר"ל מי היו אבותיהם וראשי שורש משפחותיהם למעלה בקודש. יבינו לאחרים- "לאן ילכו". את המעשה אשר יעשון ללכת בדרכם. כי כאשר יכירו את ייחוסם החשוב. ישתדלו להיות בנים אמון בם. ההולכים בדרכי אבותיהם. ולומדים ממעשיהם ומחנכים את בניהם לתורה וליראה ולמעשים טובים. כדי שלא יבושו ולא יכלמו לעולם שכולו טוב כאשר יעמדו בפני אבותיהם הקדושים. וישאלום "איכה". לאן הגעתם והתרחקתם.

ולכן אמרתי לחזק את ידי הרב המחבר שליט"א ולברכו ולעודדו על פעלא טבא זו. כי דבר גדול עשה לזכות את הרבים. ואין ספק שרבים יתעוררו מתוך לימוד דרכיהם של הצדיקים. להטיב מעשיהם ולשוב אל השם.

ושמחתי באומרים לי כי ספר חשוב זה יוצא לאור לעילוי נשמת המנוח היקר הנדיב הדגול. שהיה ידידי ומתומכי ישיבתנו הקדושה. מר יעקב אג'מי ז"ל. כי נתעוררו בניו היקרים להנציח שמו הטוב במצוה זו. וכאשר אני מתבונן על ההשגחה הפרטית הטמונה בזה אני נפעם ומתפעל. כי נדיר היה למצוא מי שיכבד ויחבב חכמים כמו המנוח הדגול הזה. כי ממש אהב את חכמי התורה בלב ובנפש. ולכן כמה מתאים הדבר שנבחר ספר "לקדושים אשר בארץ". להוציאו על שמו הטוב. כי זה מורה שמי שנזהר בכבוד התורה ולומדיה בחייו. הולך מחיל אל חיל במדה זו גם בהיותו בעולם האמת. ומזמינים לו הזכויות המתאימות לו בדיוק. ולזה אני מברך את כל יוצאי חלציו. שיזכו למעלה זו. להיות אוהבי תורה. ואוהבי חכמי ישראל. ויתמכו בהם בכל יכולתם בשמחה. ובכך ימשיכו במסורת הטובה שהנחיל להם אביהם ז"ל. ויזכו גם הם לדורות ישרים ומבורכים. לומדי תורה ומקיימי מצוות אכי"ר.

ויהי רצון שכל העושים והמעשים במפעל זה. יזכו לדובב שפתי הצדיקים נוחי עדן. שיהיו הם מליצי יושר עליהם. ועל כל ישראל ונזכה לגאולה קרובה ולתחיית המתים ואז יראו עינינו וישמח ליבנו בראותינו את פניהם המאירים והמזהירים של גדולי ישראל הקמים לתחיה ותמלא הארץ דעה את ה' כמים לים מכסים.

הכותב והחותם לכבוד התורה
ולכבודם של חכמי ישראל מרביצי תורה

הצעיר יעקב משה הלל יצ"ו

Rosh Yeshivat
Hevrat Ahavat Shalom
45 Arzei Habirah St. Jerusalem

16 Shevat 5765

I am very happy to see the recasting of the book, ***LiKedoshim Asher Ba'Aretz,*** into the English language. This new work contains the history of the scholars and rabbis of Aram Soba, based on the above book, which was written in Hebrew by the holy and pious Rabbi David Laniado, of blessed memory, and has now been completely re-edited and translated into English by my dear friend, the worthy Rabbi David Sutton, may he have a long and productive life.

I know Rabbi Sutton well from the years gone by when he was immersed in his studies in Jerusalem. We have continued to be in close contact to the present day. I have been personally involved in his noble efforts for the dissemination of Torah. His efforts have led to the spreading of Torah to multitudes of students, who come early in the morning and late at night to study in the Torah Center of Avenue J (Brooklyn). His efforts have also reached the pious workingmen who have set for themselves fixed times for the study of Torah. He caused them to love Torah learning and to be meticulous in the observance of *mitzvot.* He is of pure mind and stands in the breach to defend against the calamities of our era. His hand reaches out to support and strengthen those who defend the religion. He has not moved away from the sacred and glorious path of the great scholars of our time, those who teach the Torah and the fear of G-d (may they have long and productive lives). With G-d's help, he has been a benefactor to the public, so that Hashem has been gracious to him and he has succeeded in adding "benches in the *Bet Midrash*" and in magnifying the Torah and glorifying it.

And now he goes from strength to strength in bringing out anew in the English language the valuable and essential book, *LiKedoshim Asher Ba'Aretz,* and in adding to it a generous variety of important new material. He has provided valuable additional information concerning the pious scholars and rabbis of Aram Soba, including many stories of their life and their deeds, their books, and their works. He has also included many impressive pictures, to fulfill what is written, "Let your eyes see your Teacher" (*Yeshayahu* 30:20), and as our Sages have said, "Let the one who gives knowledge to you be as if he is standing before you" (*Yalkut Shimoni, Tehillim* 39:735). He has also provided the images of rare artifacts, including ancient documents, title pages, manuscripts, and signatures of rabbis. All of this is to make concrete and to authenticate the events and the deeds described in the book. I am also very gratified to see that he has complimented our holy yeshiva by including among the biographical notes the introductions to books which the yeshiva published.

Indeed the book is replete with valuable and essential knowledge, which will surely inspire hearts to ascend the spiritual ladder of Torah and the fear of G-d. It will inspire people to learn from the deeds and the dedication of the righteous men of old, how they served Hashem in truth and with total commitment, and how they reached great heights of Torah knowledge. From the scholarly works that they composed, the refinement of their character, the meticulousness of their observance of *mitzvot,* and their battles to defend the ramparts of the religion, we can take instruction as to how to serve Hashem, our G-d.

All of this is especially relevant today. Our generation has tragically succumbed to immoral behavior and to intellectual confusion, with people being vulnerable to false and heretical opinions. It is therefore very important and essential to fulfill what our

Sages comment on the verse, "Go forth in the footsteps of the flock" (*Shir HaShirim* 1:8). The commentators explain, based on *Rashi*, "Go with total commitment, following the paths of our rabbis of old, in the way that has been prepared for us from ancient times. This is the road that rises to the House of G-d. From them we can take guidance to serve Hashem our G-d, to go in His ways and to cleave to Him. Do as the scholars of old did and as they practiced with total commitment, and not with newly acquired ways which our ancestors did not set for us."

And besides this, how encouraging is it for the glorious and noble families of Israel to see "from where they came," that is, who were their forefathers, and the originators of their family lineage! They will then understand their destiny, "to where they will go." And they will understand the actions they will need to take to follow in the ways of their forefathers. When they understand their noble lineage, they will surely seek to be true sons of their forebears, to go in their ways and to learn from their deeds. They will educate their children in the Torah, the fear of G-d, and good deeds. Thus, they will not be embarrassed in the World to Come when they stand before their holy ancestors, asking, "How did you get to be so lost, so far away?"

I have therefore resolved to hearten the worthy author (may he have a long and productive life), to bless him, and to encourage him in this good work, because he has done a great thing for the benefit of the public, and there is no doubt that many will become inspired by learning about the righteous men of the past, so that they will do better and will return to *Hashem*.

I was deeply moved to hear that this important book will memorialize the beloved philanthropist ***Mr. Jack Adjmi*** *a"h*. He was a dear friend of mine and a staunch supporter of our yeshiva. I am amazed at the Divine Providence that has guided his family in linking this book to the respected name of Mr. Jack Adjmi. Rarely do we find someone who honored and loved rabbis as he did; he loved them with his heart and soul. How fitting it is that the book *LiKedoshim Asher Ba'Aretz* is being brought to a new generation in his name. This shows that someone who is careful to respect the Torah in his lifetime continues to do so while he is in the True World. The deeds of those who were inspired by him are now providing him with merits that match what he did in his lifetime. I give my sincere blessing to all of his family — that they may aspire to reach his level of devotion, to be lovers of Torah and lovers of rabbis, supporting them with joy. With this they continue the beautiful tradition that they inherited from their father so that they too will merit to have worthy children learning Torah and doing *mitzvot*.

For all who participate in this initiative, may *Hashem* grant that they merit the blessings of the righteous ones who dwell in Paradise. May they be good advocates for them and for all of Israel. And may we merit to the Redemption soon in our days and to the Resurrection of the Dead, and then our eyes will see and our hearts will rejoice at the shining faces of the great ones of Israel rising to life, and the whole world will be filled with the knowledge of *Hashem*.

Written and signed for the honor of the Torah and for the honor of the scholars of Israel who disseminate Torah,

Yaakob Moshe Hillel

הכותב והחותם לכבוד התורה
ולכבודם של חכמי ישראל מרביצי תורה

הצעיר יעקב משה הלל יצ"ו

SAUL J. KASSIN, CHIEF RABBI שאול י קצין, הרב הראשי

On Tu Bishbat, Rabbi David J. Sutton came to me with a precious book, an English translation of the Hebrew book LIKEDOSHIM ASHER BA'ARETZ — The Holy People of the Land, which was written by the pious Rabbi David Laniado *A"H*.

Rabbi Sutton, in addition to translating the book, spent two and a half years researching, investigating, and gathering historical data of famous, pious, and authoritive Rabbis. His 400-page book deals with three countries: Israel, Syria, and the United States. This book contains many rare pictures, holy places, synagogues, authors and their books, and various important documents.

Looking through the book reminded me of old memories of historical and holy places and great personalities of the past. I remember when I used to go with my father *A"H* and the *Mekubalim* Rabbis of *Porat Yoseph* to the *Kotel Hamaarabi* on the three holidays of Pesach, Shavuoth, and Succoth. At the *Kotel* they prayed *Musaf* and sang the *Keter* in a beautiful melody, which still rings in my ears. Another memory is when the Chief Rabbi Yaacob Meir *A"H* used to come escorted by two guards to *Ohel Moshe* where he visited my grandfather Rabbi Shalom Hedaya *A"H*. The entire neighborhood of *Ohel Moshe* used to come out to see the Chief Rabbi. It was an unforgettable scene.

Among the photographs in this book there is a picture of the old *Porat Yoseph* where we lived for a few years. In the wide courtyard my father *A"H* used to perform wedding ceremonies on Friday afternoons. I remember when I was a student in *Porat Yoseph*. Rabbi Ezra Attiah, *Rosh Yeshivat Porat Yoseph*, tested my class monthly on Gemara, as we had to know by heart one page of Gemara each week. Other noteworthy Rabbis mentioned in this book, include:

Rabbi Shaul Dweck HaCohen, the Head of *Mekubalim*, taught many Rabbis Kaballah. Rabbi Ben-Zion Hazan was appointed by Rabbi Yoseph Haim (the *Ben Ish Chai*) to supervise the synagogue of *Porat Yoseph*. Rabbi Yehudah Haddad was the principal in charge of the office and administration. The faculty included additional prominent Rabbis such as, Rabbi Yaacob Ades, Rabbi Moshe Ades, Rabbi Eliyahu Lofez, Rabbi Sharabani, Rabbi Yoseph Tawil, Rabbi Ezra Hedaya, and Rabbi Schechter (he taught grammar and arithmetic) to name a few. These Rabbis lived in poverty, drawing a monthly salary of 5 to 10 sterling pounds, equivalent to $20 to $40. They were devoted to Torah and Mitzvot and strived for attaining Spiritual accomplishments. In our generation, such people don't exist. Knowing and seeing these giants of the past generation made an everlasting impression on me which influenced me to this day.

The book contains rare and valuable images of the 20th-century ancestors of Aleppo, Damascus, Jerusalem, and New York. Rabbi Sutton traveled twice to Israel to collect information, pictures, documents, and data from many people and sources. This book is rich, elaborate, and splendid, especially for the Sephardic Syrian community. To the people who came recently from Syria, it will bring many memories of personalities and places. To the people here in Brooklyn, it will bring memories of the 20th century. I give Rabbi David Sutton credit and gratitude for the translation, additional supplements, and pictures. This book is a masterpiece and one of a kind.

I wish Rabbi David Sutton and his family heavenly blessings of long life, good health, and happiness, and spiritual and physical success in all his endeavors, Amen.

Rabbi Saul J. Kassin
Chief Rabbi

Congregation Bet Yaacob, Sao Paulo

Rabbi Ephraim Laniado

1 Adar 5765 \ February 2005

Dear Rabbi David Sutton,

We are overjoyed to hear that you are about to publish the English translation of the book "*LiKedoshim Asher Ba'Aretz*." This will surely be well received by the new generation of our beloved Aleppo community of the Diaspora.

Without a doubt, this important work will be a link between our generation and the generations which have preceded us. People will surely come to appreciate the source from which the important and respected Congregation Shaare Zion and the other Aleppo congregations worldwide draw their holiness and purity. They continue in the support of the three pillars of the world: Torah, *Avodah*, and *Hesed*. They are especially known for the strengthening of Torah learning in the *yeshivot* of *Eretz Yisrael* and the Diaspora.

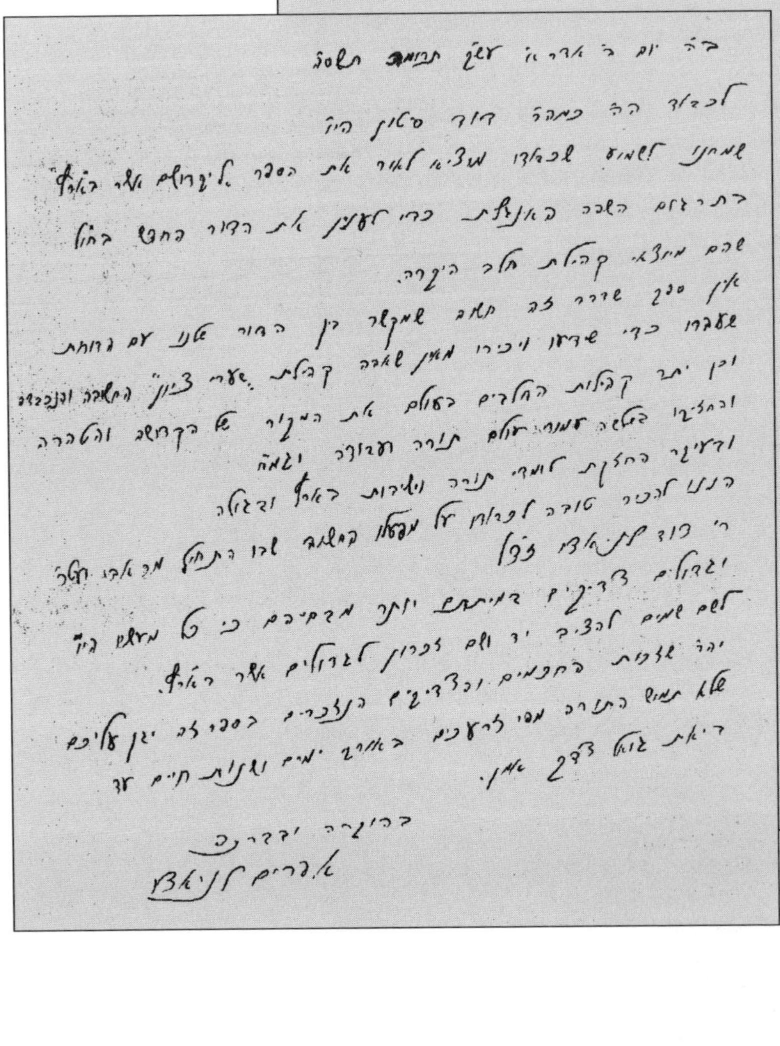

I greatly appreciate this monumental project that you have taken upon yourself, continuing what my father, my master, the crown of my head, Hacham David Laniado, of blessed memory, had started.

The righteous are greater after their death than when they were alive. All of my father's efforts for the sake of Heaven continue to serve as a monument and testimony for the great rabbis of Aram Soba.

May it be G-d's will that the merit of the rabbis and righteous people mentioned in the book guard those involved in the project. May Torah never leave them or their children , and may they live a long life until the coming of our Redeemer. Amen

With respect and blessings,

Rabbi Ephraim Laniado

YAD YOSEF TORAH CENTER

BIRKAT YAAKOV

In Memory of Jack Adjmi ז"ל

February 1st 2005

The Syrian Community began to immigrate to these American shores almost a hundred years ago.

They left behind in Aleppo a treasured legacy of outstanding scholars and sages. Over the decades we heard stories of their towering piety, humility, scholarly abilities and saintliness. However, only undocumented stories.

Rabbi David Sutton Shlita, has brought these luminaries to life through this monumental work. For the last two years I personally have witnessed Rabbi Sutton work tirelessly, translating, researching and reresearching every Rabbi's history, writings and story, for ultimate accuracy. Literally spanning the globe for information and photographs. Interviewing individuals too numerous to count.

שהחיינו וקיימנו והגענו לזמן הזה

This is a glorious day for our community – where we now have a documented text of our great and profound lineage.

The Rabbi's only interest in this Herculean project is to increase the glory of Hashem and Torah among our people.

It is a privilege and honor to work with Rabbi Sutton on a daily basis and I look forward to many years of spreading the Debar Hashem with him.

May Hashem shower him with all the blessings intended for those who heed His Glorious Name. Amen.

With Torah Blessings,

Rabbi David Ozeirey

Table of Contents

Publisher's Preface

We are proud to publish this work, Aleppo — City of Scholars, which will be a great service not only to the Syrian-Sephardic community that originated in Aleppo, but also to all Jewish communities. For centuries, Aleppo was a center of Jews who revered the Torah and adhered to the customs and traditions going back to the city's ancient origins.

Like so many capitals of Jewish life, Aleppo lost its Jews, as they left their traditional homeland, by choice or under duress. But large numbers of Aleppo's diaspora retained their love for their city of origin. They revered their past, even when its traditions began to fade.

Rabbi David Sutton is a proud descendant of Aleppo and a rising star in the burgeoning Syrian Torah community in Flatbush. He and Rabbi David Ozeirey are the spiritual leaders and teachers in the Yad Yosef Torah Center of Avenue J. In this comprehensive book, Rabbi Sutton takes us back to Aleppo, by chronicling its rabbis and pious laymen, their way of life, their teachings, their pronouncements, and their values. Over six hundred rabbis are represented in this volume. To read this book is to step back to the homeland where they were formed, flourished, and taught.

Most Jews, Sephardi or Ashkenazi, look to the past with much nostalgia and little realism. What they did in the "old home" was quaint, even inspiring, but what does it have to do with me?

Rabbi Sutton's answer is, "It has everything to do with me — and you!" He believes passionately that we must reconnect ourselves to our origins and learn from them. No one can read this book and not be inspired, as he learns about the rabbis — some little known and some famous — who lived lives of Torah study and holiness.

We are grateful also to the children of Rabbi David-Sion Laniado, who graciously permitted Rabbi Sutton to draw from "*LiKedoshim Asher Ba'Aretz*," their father's classic Hebrew work on the rabbis of Aleppo. Rabbi Sutton has not been content to rest on the laurels of Rabbi Laniado; he has done considerable research in America and Israel, unearthing nuggets of information and collecting a wealth of photographs, many of them never before published.

The families that have sponsored this book are amply rewarded, for they have made possible the creation of a work that will be respected and consulted for many decades, and that will bring pride and awareness to their children and grandchildren for generations to come.

We have worked with many authors, but none of them have been more zealous in producing a work of such impeccable accuracy and high quality. Rabbi Sutton's awesome expenditure of time, curiosity, and effort has borne amazing fruit in the form of this book. We congratulate him and commend this work to anyone who seeks entry into one of Judaism's most distinguished communities.

Rabbi Meir Zlotowitz Rabbi Nosson Scherman
I Adar 5765 / February 2005

ACKNOWLEDGMENTS

This book is about a timeless, living community. Many of its members participated in the book's creation by sharing their knowledge, their memories, and their support. I want to thank all of them individually, as well as the members of the larger Jewish community, who demonstrated their respect and affection for the spirit of Aleppo by helping us memorialize it.

But first I must thank *Hashem* for the tremendous *"Siyata D'Shmaya"* (Heavenly aid) that He graciously bestowed on this project.

The current initiative started with an audiotape series about the scholars of Aleppo, distributed by Mr. Rico Tousson. From there it became a monthly article in the Community magazine, written by Mrs. Victoria Dwek and edited by Mr. Jack Cohen. Finally, it became a full-fledged publishing effort under the guidance of the ArtScroll organization. My partner in this venture from the onset was Mr. Isaac Kirzner, who translated and edited the bulk of the material included in the book and directed the project in his quiet and unassuming way. He epitomizes the expression, "a gentleman and a scholar."

Four members of the Syrian community of New York joined to spearhead the initiative: Adam Azrak, Saul A. Kassin, Morris J. Levy, and Eddie B. Sitt. If not for their steadfast encouragement and persistence, the project would never have gotten beyond its initial phase.

The Adjmi family generously dedicated this project and named it "The Jack Adjmi Edition" in memory of Mr. Jack Adjmi *A"H* the patriarch of their family.

Special thanks go to the patrons of each individual section: Victor, Elliott and Adam Azrak, Barry and Marilyn Sitt and family, Mr. and Mrs. Steven S. Sutton, Eddie A. Betesh, the Haber family and Esther, N. Sam and Samantha Sasson and family, Dr. Joseph and Victor Sutton, Elie Sutton and family. May *Hashem* repay them for their generosity and may the merit of all the righteous people in this book invoke merit on their behalf.

A great amount of painstaking research went into verifying all the factual details presented in the book; Rabbi Abraham E. Ades gets the credit for that along with Rabbi Ephraim Levy.

The following individuals read drafts of the book and offered vital comments and corrections: Rabbi Isaac Dwek, Mr. Moshe Faham, Mr. Yosef Faham, Rabbi Edmond Nahum, Mrs. Alice Shalom, and Miss Ahuva Sutton.

The following people supplied information and details on their relatives or teachers mentioned in the articles: Rabbi Elie Abadie, Mr. David E. Ashear, Mr. Morris E. Ashear, Mrs. Sally Ashkenazi, Mr. Joseph Assa, Mr. David M. Betesh, Rabbi Shemuel Beyda, Rabbi Shelomo Churba, Mr. Shelomo Dayan, Mr. Lou M. Franco, Mr. Morris Gindi, Rabbi Asher Hamway, Mr. Sam N. Hamway, Rabbis Aharon and Moshe Harari-Raful, Mr. David Hidary, Rabbi Moshe Laniado, Mr. Joseph M. Levy, Mr. Irving Maleh, Rabbi Yosef M. Maslaton, Rabbi David Ozeri, Rabbi Shalom Raful, Mr. Joe E. Saff, Mr. Hy Serure, Mr. Elly J. Shamah, Mr. Jack D. Shamah, Rabbi Dvir Shrem, Mr. Leon S. Sutton, Mr. Miro Sutton, Mr. Ralph S. Tawil, and Hacham Yitzhak Zafrani.

Hacham Abraham Zafrani, of blessed memory, spent a great amount of time describing the Great Synagogue and other facts about Aleppo. Tragically, he passed on before having the opportunity to see the book come to print.

Special thanks are due to Mr. Gabe Zeitouni and Mr. Joe Mosseri for their information on the *pizmonim* and *hazzanim*.

Hacham Moshe Zafrani and his son Rabbi David Zafrani helped translate some of the documents from the old Syrian script, a very tedious job. Mr. Pinhas Nissim helped read some of the old script. Hacham Moshe Zafrani also helped with pronunciations and transliterating Arabic words and places.

A special thank-you goes to Dr. Yaron Harel for sharing the many title-page images collected in his work, "The Books of Aleppo." Also, thanks are due to Reb Chaim Reich of Renaissance Hebraica for supplying additional title-page images.

A great deal of effort went into enhancing the book with historical photographs of the scholars and places of Aleppo. Many kind people came forward to make their photos available: Mr. Morris S. Ashear, Mr. Ralph Attie, Mr. Joseph Cohen, Mr. Morris Cohen, Mr. Joseph S. Dwek, Mr. Charles S. Gammal, Mr. Joseph Gindi (*Magen David* business office), Mr. Morris Gindi, Mr. Manny Haber, Rabbi Harel of *Yeshivat Kol Yaacob*, Mr. Bert Hidary, Mr. Zaci Jarada, Mr. Sonny Laniado, Mr. Jack I. Maleh, Hacham Jack Maslaton, Mrs. Susan Menashe, Rabbi David Rabi, Mr. Joey Soffer, Mr. Steven S. Sutton, Mr. Nathan Tawil, and Mr. Saul M. Tawil.

I would like to thank Mr. Joe A. Esses and family for the use of their *Sefer Torah* case that is displayed on the cover of the book; Mr. Michael Strauss, who handcrafted the case; and Mr. Menachem Adelman for the photography.

I am happy to have this opportunity to thank Mr. David Shweky and Mr. Steven Shweky for their friendship and technical support throughout the project.

The following museums and institutions generously opened their archives:

- Beth Hatefusoth (the Diaspora Museum) of Israel. Special thanks to: Zippi Rosenne, Director, Visual Documentation Center; Pazit Shani-Schwarz, Client Services; and Neta Harel, Scanning.
- The Jewish National and University Library, Jerusalem. Special thanks to Mrs. Rosalind Duke, Deputy Director; Mr. Rafael Weiser, former Head of the Manuscripts and Archives Department; Ms. Rachel Misrati, current Head of the Manuscripts and Archives Department; and Ms. Diana Gliksman, Head of the Accounts Department.
- Moreshet Aram Soba Heritage Center. Special thanks to Mr. Menachem Yedid.
- Archives of the Sephardic Community Center, Brooklyn. Special thanks to Sheila Schweky.

I am also grateful to Ms. Amelia Keshet of the Israel Museum in Jerusalem for directing me to the correct archive departments in Israel.

Of course, among the many people to whom I owe gratitude, prominent recognition is fitting to the entire ArtScroll family, starting with Rabbi Meir Zlotowitz, who gave so much of his precious time and advice, and to my dear father-in-law Rabbi Nosson Scherman, who gave me moral support and encouragement throughout the project. I am grateful to Rabbi Sheah Brander for his involvement and guidance. I am also indebted to Mrs. Faygie Weinbaum for her painstaking and highly professional proofreading; Reb Avrohom Biderman and Reb Mendy Herzberg for overseeing the project; Reb Eli Kroen, a master in the world of graphics; Reb Hershy Feuerwerker for his innovation and design, Reb Yidi Siegman and Miss Esty Lebovits for their tireless scanning efforts; Miss Chaya Perel Teichman, who patiently laid out and paginated the book, never becoming overwhelmed by the complexity of the project; and Mr. Steve Blitz in Israel, who aided in acquiring many of the photos. These are the ArtScroll staff that I dealt with and I am sure there are numerous others working behind the scenes. I thank you all.

I would like to thank countless individuals in the Syrian community of Brooklyn, New York and Deal, New Jersey for showing interest throughout the project and giving encouragement.

No acknowledgment is complete without mentioning my family: first, my cherished parents, Dr. Joseph and Leila Sutton, for their direction and support and for instilling in me the pride of our heritage. A separate book could be written about their kindness and respect for Torah learning. I am most grateful to my in-laws Rabbi Nosson and Chana Scherman, who gave me the confidence to take on this project and see it through from start to finish, and last to my dear wife Chaya and our children for their understanding and for bearing with me during the development of this book. May it be *Hashem's* will that the objective of this project, to educate a new generation about our glorious past, be fulfilled.

Rabbi David Sutton
Brooklyn, New York
March 2005

A Special Thanks to the Laniado Family. We are deeply grateful to the children of Hacham David-Sion Laniado: his sons — Yitzhak, Yaakob, Abraham, Aharon, Ephraim, Eliyahu, Shemuel, Yisrael — and his daughters — Sarah, Rachel, Esther, Tziporah, and Rina — for permitting us to draw upon their father's copious sources and insights. Rabbi Laniado's work is a treasure-house of information for those who love the heritage of Aleppo, and it is our privilege to bring it to our English-speaking brethren.

In memory of **Shelomo Laniado**, eldest son of chacham david.
Shelomo ben Mazal *A"H*

We Need Your Help

This is the first edition of a book whose potential scope far exceeds the limits of time and space which governed its preparation. We ask the forbearance of our readers for any errors or omissions which they may encounter. We appeal to our readers to help us by communicating their suggestions, additional information, and photos to the publisher.

Introduction

Aram Soba is the Biblical name for Aleppo (Arabic: *Haleb*), the second-largest city in Syria and the center of northern Syria. The illustrious Jewish community of Aram Soba had deep roots, stretching into ancient times. The continuous Jewish presence in the city lasted until the end of the 20th century, when most of the remaining Jews left the city.

This was a vibrant center of Torah with its unique community of rabbis, scholars, and scholarly laymen, living a life of piety and devotion. They would rouse themselves each night, filling the study halls and synagogues in huddled groups to recite *Tehillim* and to continue studying Torah until morning.

Aleppo citadel, early 1900's

R' David Ben-Sion Laniado

Aram Soba no longer exists as a physical center for Jewish life, because the Jews who defined it have been dispersed. However, the spiritual Aram Soba continues to flourish in all of the Aram Soba Jewish communities around the world, where the holy books written by its scholars are studied, and their piety is remembered and emulated. These scattered but dynamic communities share a common legacy through the customs they practice, the *Nusach HaTefillah* (prayer format) they follow, and the *pizmonim* (hymns of worship) they sing to the ancient *maqam* melodies (see Traditional Music, sec. IV).

How This Book Came to Be

This book represents an effort to capture for a new generation the vibrant spiritual heritage of Syrian Jewry. It is based upon the monumental book, *LiKedoshim Asher Ba'Aretz*, written by R' David-Sion Laniado in the early part of the last century. Hacham David, as he was called, had a deep love for the pious and learned men who had preserved the unbroken tradition of Torah in Aram Soba over the years.

"If everyone leaves Syria," Hacham David reasoned, "who will remember these great people? Great-grandchildren won't know their great ancestors." He sensed that he had a duty "to publicize the names of these great people, because if you talk about them you invoke their *zechuyot* (the merits of their good deeds), and so their souls will rest in peace and their children will inherit their place in the world."

"If everyone leaves Syria," Hacham David reasoned, "who will remember these great people?"

Therefore he committed himself to the thankless task of gathering together everything he could find about Aram Soba's spiritual heritage. Although he lived in Jerusalem, he would periodically visit his parents in Syria. While there, he would spend countless hours at the old Aleppo cemetery, recording the inscriptions on each tombstone of the hundreds of Sephardic rabbis buried there.

He painstakingly assembled biographical details on hundreds of the most notable pious men who had lived in Aram Soba over the years. Besides the inscriptions on tombstones, he researched community records and the many old manuscripts of holy books that were kept in synagogues and private collections. He put all of this material into a book, which he titled *LiKedoshim Asher Ba'Aretz* after the verse in *Tehillim* (16:3): לקדושים אשר בארץ, "For the sake of the holy ones who are [interred] in the earth." (The word אר"ץ, *Aretz*, is a common abbreviation for "Aram Soba.")

The old Aleppo cemetery

The original volume appeared in 1932. Over the next two decades he managed to publish two additional volumes: one covering the scholars who had moved to Jerusalem and were buried there, and another, covering scholars buried in other Syrian cemeteries, in Damascus, Izmir, and Salonika. Finally, in 1952 he was able to combine all of his previous works into a single volume.

In 1965, he published a collection of over 40 pictures of Aram Soba scholars, which he had painstakingly gathered from a variety of sources in Aram Soba and elsewhere.

After his death, others took up the holy work, including R' David Sharikaz, R' Eliyahu Attiah, and R' Ephraim Levi. Together with Hacham David's sons they published a complete revision in 1980, which incorporated the pictures that Hacham David had assembled. Three years earlier his sons had arranged for the printing of *Likutei David* (Jerusalem 5737/1977), based on other manuscripts left by their father. This material included biographies of various great Torah scholars and anecdotes of Jerusalem.

In bringing *Aleppo — City of Scholars* to print, we have utilized all of the above sources, and many others, including unpublished materials kindly provided by R' Abraham Ezra Ades of Bnei Brak, who is in the process of preparing a new revision to *LiKedoshim Asher Ba'Aretz*, commissioned by the Laniado family. We are grateful to him and to various individuals who have shared their personal recollections of the pious scholars and laymen of Aleppo, Jerusalem, and New York — all the bearers of the Aram Soba legacy. We are also grateful to R' Ephraim Levi, who inherited his father's photo collection and permitted us to include the vintage photos that contribute so much to making the book come alive. A special thanks is due to Dr. Yaron Harel (Senior Lecturer in the Department of Jewish History, Bar Ilan University, Ramat Gan, Israel), who graciously allowed the use of the many title pages he collected in his work, "The Books of Aleppo" (Jerusalem 1997).

What This Book Contains

The primary section of this book is the biographical section (Section 6), in which we have provided 600 biographical entries for the pious men who carried the tradition of Aram Soba through the centuries. We have followed the example of *LiKedoshim Asher Ba'Aretz* in arranging the entries in alphabetical sequence and assigning each name a reference number. We have made generous use of these references to link fathers to sons, students to teachers, and colleagues to colleagues. All numbered references may easily be found by looking up the entries in the biographical section.

The other sections of the book are intended to set the scene, providing a historical and cultural context for the numbered biographies:

- **Section 1, Aram Soba Through the Ages,** traces the history of the city from its ancient beginnings to the modern day, emphasizing its spiritual roots and the contributions made by immigrants to Syria over the centuries. It should be noted that the names Aram Soba and Aleppo are essentially synonymous and are used interchangeably throughout the book.
- **Section 2, The Great Synagogue**, describes the ancient edifice which served as the beating heart of the community from its earliest times until the end of the 20th century.
- **Section 3, The Aleppo Codex (Keter Aram Soba),** describes the most treasured possession of the Aram Soba community over the generations. This is one of the earliest-known manuscripts containing the entire text of the *Tanach* (*Torah, Nebi'im, Ketubim*). It was stored in the Great Synagogue and jealously protected by the elders of the community.
- **Section 4, The Religious Life of Aram Soba,** explores the social and educational institutions of the community, showing how religious life was supported by the community's spiritual structures.
- **Section 5, Syrian Yeshivot in Jerusalem,** follows the trail of the Aram Soba scholars who immigrated to Jerusalem in the 19th century, to preserve and build upon their spiritual heritage, thereby preparing the way for the eventual re-creation of the Aram Soba community in other cities around the world.
- **Section 6, Biographies,** is the heart of this book, presenting the lives of 600 pious scholars and spiritually motivated laymen.
- **Section 7, Documents,** provides the reader with a sense of immediacy and reality by presenting actual documents which implemented the religious practices of Aram Soba.

One of the Seven Hechalot of the Great Synagogue

We have divided the book into the above seven sections corresponding to the seven *Hechalot* (Holy Arks for the Torah scrolls) of the great synagogue of Aleppo (see section IV for details on the seven *Hechalot*). This analogy is based on the following incident: Rav Saadiah Gaon immigrated from Egypt to Sura to become the *Rosh Yeshiva* of the new yeshiva that was being established there. He sent letters to his acquaintances asking them to help in the new building campaign.

Seven Sections — Seven Hechalot

A wealthy Egyptian Jew decided to donate a large sum toward the dedication of the *Hechal*. He set out on the journey with a pouch full of money, but when he arrived he was told that someone had already bought the dedication rights. He was greatly pained that he wouldn't have a part in the holiest part of the yeshiva. He came to Rav Saadiah Gaon and poured out his heart.

Rav Saadiah told him "You should know, my son, that our nation has a Written Law and an Oral Law. The Written Law is placed in the Holy Ark; the Oral Law, on the other hand, is transmitted from rabbi to student, from generation to generation. Every rabbi is a *Sefer Torah* and every student is a *Sefer Torah*. Therefore the place where a student stands and learns is considered a *hechal*, the bench he sits on is a *hechal*, his table is a *hechal*, the entire yeshiva is a *hechal*."

Each section of this book discusses a different aspect of the Syrian community, so each section is in essence a *hechal* containing the lives and ideals of these holy people.

The Goal of This Book

The goal of this book is that stated by *Rabbenu Yonah* in *Shaare Avodah* (*The Gateway to Serving Hashem*) — a person should know his own worth. *Rabbenu Yonah* explains that a Jew must recognize his own spiritual qualities and the great spiritual qualities of his forefathers, as well as the love that Hashem had for them. He will then be able to aspire to reach and to maintain the spiritual levels of those who preceded him. He should make an effort every day to add a little to his own spiritual level, so that he will get continually closer to his G-d. Progress may be slow, especially in the beginning, but in this way he will attain greatness. He should do this so that his ancestors in Heaven will not be embarassed by his behavior. In so doing, he will achieve self-control; whenever he desires something forbidden, he will think, *How can a special and important person, who has so many wonderful qualities and is the son of eminent and noble people of the past, behave in such a sinful way, becoming a sinner to my G-d and to my parents?* However, if Heaven forbid, a person does not recognize his own spiritual qualities and those of his forefathers, he will find it very easy to behave immodestly and to act like an immoral person, focusing himself on his physical desires.

These holy thoughts of *Rabbenu Yonah* capture the goal of this book. The more a person reads of his glorious past, the more he desires to emulate the ways of his ancestors, and the closer will he be to greatness. As the *Midrash* (*Tanna D'Vei Eliyahu*, Chapter 25) says: "Every person must ask himself, *When will my actions reach the [level of] the actions of my forefathers?*" May it be G-d's will that the goal of this book be fulfilled and that people realize where they came from and how special they really are.

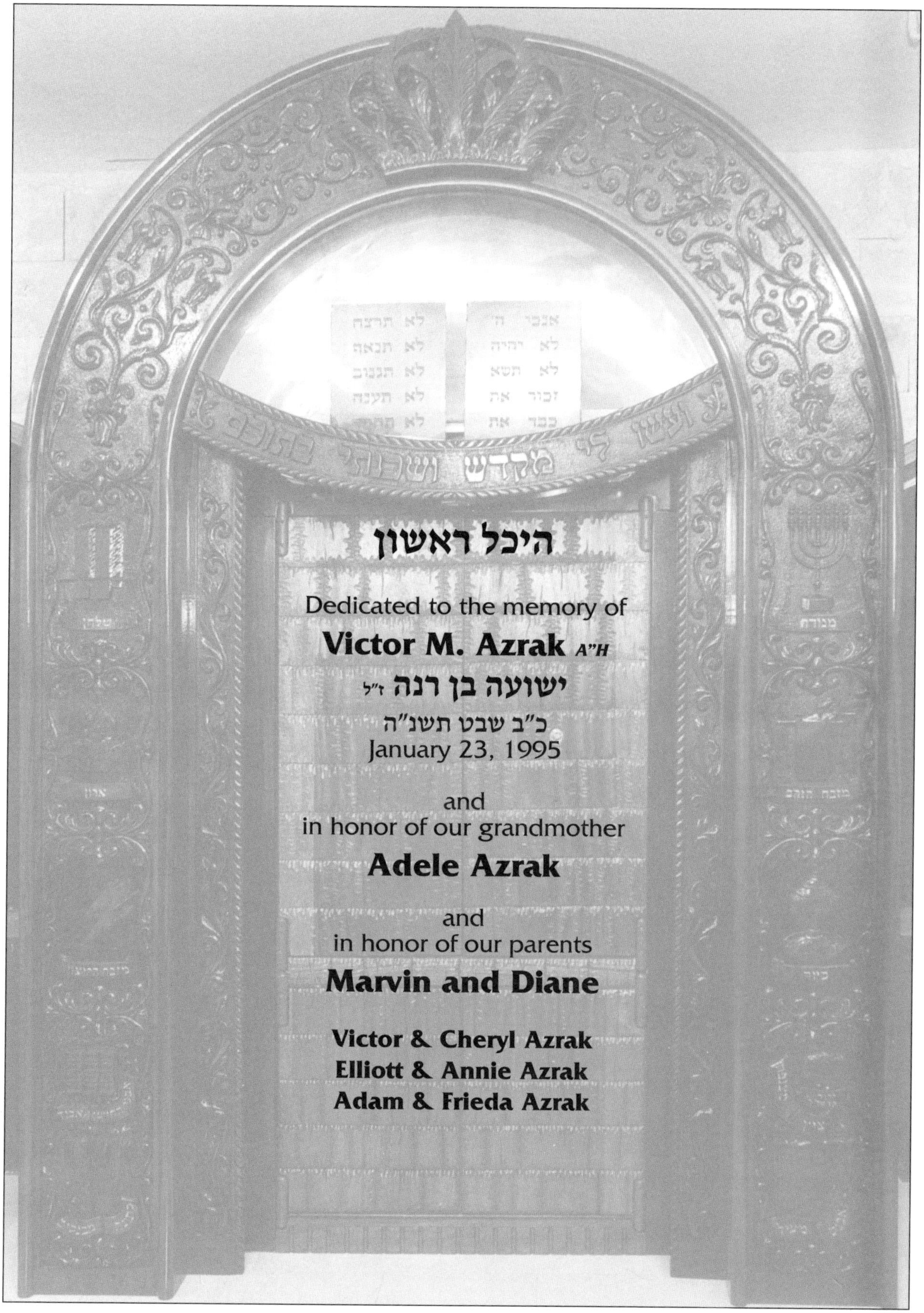

היכל ראשון

Dedicated to the memory of

Victor M. Azrak *A"H*

ישועה בן רנה ז"ל

כ"ב שבט תשנ"ה

January 23, 1995

and

in honor of our grandmother

Adele Azrak

and

in honor of our parents

Marvin and Diane

Victor & Cheryl Azrak

Elliott & Annie Azrak

Adam & Frieda Azrak

Section One

ARAM SOBA THROUGH THE AGES

Throughout its long history, Aleppo represented one of the foremost urban centers of western Asia, owing largely to its strategic location on a vital commercial crossroad. The town was located on the main caravan routes connecting the eastern Mediterranean region and Europe, at a location which also formed a link with Iraq, Persia, central Asia, and India. In its heyday, from the 15th to the 19th century, the size of Aleppo's population placed it among the major cities of the world; in 1517 it had 70,000 inhabitants (London by comparison had 80,000 in 1545). In this illustrious metropolis, the Jewish community thrived, both in terms of affluence and learning. It was a community which attracted immigrants from many countries; most notable among these were the Spanish expatriates (the Sephardim) and the merchants from Italy.

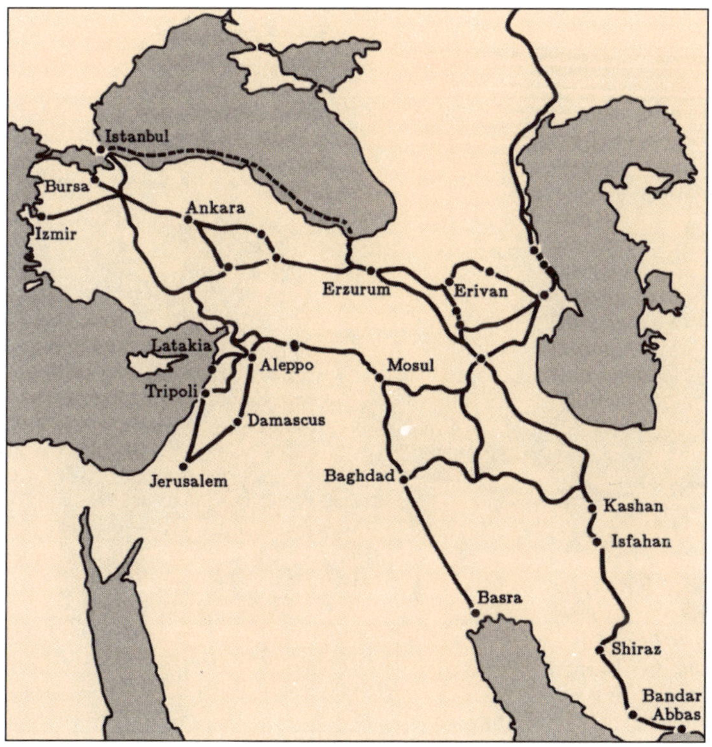

Map showing Aleppo and the trade routes on which it was situated

View of Aleppo, showing the citadel in the background

A Righteous People. R' Abraham Antebi (see #63), in the beginning of his work *Hochmah U'Mussar,* describes the Syrian community of old.

"On *Shabbat* most of the community would come after midday to the synagogue or *Bet Midrash* and gather into study groups. Some of them studied timely *halachot,* including the laws of the holidays at their proper times and the laws of *Shabbat* throughout the year; others studied *Aggadah* (teachings of inspiration and spiritual development from the *Gemara*), and others studied the holy *Zohar*.

"On Motza'e Shabbat (Saturday night) after Habdalah they again returned to the synagogue where many great Torah scholars would give classes."

"Some could not study on their own; they sat in front of a *Hacham* (learned scholar) and listened to a lecture on a timely topic, ending with words of *mussar* (spiritual development) that would capture the heart. Others would gather the children together to check on what they had learned the previous week. Parents and others constantly examined the children because they did not want to depend on the appointed teachers only.

Bab al Faraj (Gate of Salvation), a modern shopping district of Aleppo as it appeared in the early 1900's Note watchtower

"On *Motza'e Shabbat* (Saturday night) after *Habdalah* they again returned to the synagogue where many great Torah scholars would give classes on the *perashat hashavua* (weekly Torah reading) with words of *mussar* and practical *halachah*. Other scholars gathered on their own to learn *Gemara* and *halachah*. In this way they would escort the *Shabbat* Queen out with words of Torah. It was a favorable omen for the entire week, bringing the fear of G-d to their faces and preventing them from being tripped up by sinful temptations in their daily affairs. After the learning session they would join together in the recitation of *Tehillim*.Thus, they would bid farewell to the *Shabbat's* extra spirit with happinesss and joy.

"On Sunday, since the business district was mostly closed, they would leave their stores open till midday and they would then return to their studies.

"The benefits of these customs were many. The rabbi's lecture would influence at least some of the people and to some degree. Even if only one person became inspired to do better, it was worthwhile and the rabbi saved a soul of Israel. Most people transgress due to ignorance of the law and when they hear the truth they change; especially when they hear about punishments, they repent out of fear of the consequences. Another tremendous benefit is that the *Kaddish* recited after the rabbi's lecture has the power to forgive one's sins. What greater benefit could there be than starting off the week with a clean slate?

"There is no question that all these good practices described above helped our community greatly. It brought fear of G-d into their hearts and kept them from sin. They were continually being roused to repentance. The entire generation was meritorious and G-d had mercy on them. The proof is that as long as we kept these customs there was general peace and satisfaction, the economy was good, and the little work the people did supported their financial needs. We had many extremely old people in full health and people did not die before their time. On this generation I apply the verse, 'And all your people are righteous (*Yeshayah* 60:21).'"

See the box "The Power of Oil" in the biographical section for a description of the nightly learning groups [under the entry for R' Yedidyah Dayan (see #200)].

"There is no question that all these good practices described above helped our community greatly. It brought fear of G-d into their hearts and kept them from sin."

Suq (market), Aleppo, early 1900's

FOUNDATIONS OF ARAM SOBA

The earliest reference to the name Aram Soba dates from the time of our Patriarch Abraham.

Origin of "Aram Soba"

Rabbinical sources tell us that in his old age, Terah, the father of Abraham, took another wife by the name of Pelilah. According to *Seder HaDorot*, this occurred in the year 2083 after Creation, which is 1677 years before the Common Era (B.C.E.). Furthermore, we are told that Pelilah bore a son, named Soba. When Soba was 30, three sons were born to him, whom he named Aram, Achlin, and Marich. The family expanded quickly. Aram ben Soba had three wives, who gave birth to 12 sons and three daughters. *Hashem* blessed Aram and his brothers with great wealth. In their ongoing search of pasture for their expanding flocks, they came upon a distant valley, which they found suitable for their needs. The settlement that they established there was given the name Aram, which became the forerunner to the present city of Aram Soba (Aleppo).

The earliest reference to the name Aram Soba dates from the time of our Patriarch Abraham.

Subsequently, the name "Aram" came to refer to the entire region, approximating present-day Syria and Lebanon, whereas Soba was the designation for a particular city in that region. Damascus (Damesek) was another city in Aram and was sometimes referred to as Aram Damascus (*Shemuel II*, 8:6). In legal documents, such as marriage certificates and divorce papers, we often find Aram Soba being referred to simply as "Soba," since that is its original unique name.

In legal documents, such as marriage certificates and divorce papers, we often find Aram Soba being referred to simply as "Soba," since that is its original unique name.

Approximately 800 years ago, R' Petachiah of Regensburg traveled through the ancient Biblical lands and kept a journal of what he saw and learned.

Appearance of the Name "Haleb"

He describes passing through Nineveh (in present-day Iraq) and from there to Netzivin, a town with a Jewish population of 800. In Netzivin he found a synagogue built by Ezra HaSofer (Ezra the Scribe), containing a stone on which Ezra's name had been engraved. From there he continued to Haleb, which he identified as the current name for Aram Soba of old. He explains the origin of the name Haleb "because upon this mountain

He explains the origin of the name Haleb "because upon this mountain Abraham herded his sheep. There were steps leading down the mountain slope, which he descended in order to distribute milk — halab — to the poor."

Abraham herded his sheep. There were steps leading down the mountain slope, which he descended in order to distribute milk — *halab* — to the poor." The Arabic equivalent of *halab* is Haleb, which was written "Alep" in French and "Aleppo" in Italian. This has been adopted into English as well. Aleppo continues to be the largest city of northern Syria.

Yoab built a tower and fortress which form the foundation of the foundations of the ancient fortifications that can still be seen in Aleppo today. According to tradition, Yoab inscribed the following on a rock in the wall of the fortress, "I am Yoab ben Seruyah, I have conquered this fortress and city."

King David's Conquest of Aram Soba

According to tradition, when King David began to build the foundations of the Western Wall in Jerusalem, it was his habit to go out and watch the workers all day long. The general of his army, Yoab ben Seruyah, admired his devotion, and one day thought to himself, *O that I were a king, then I also would build a house for Hashem.*

That night King David had a dream in which he was informed that it was not for him to build the Temple because of all the blood that he had spilled in the course of his battles. Instead the Temple would be built by his son, Shelomo, but he should continue to follow his destiny of engaging in war against the enemies of *Hashem*. The city of Aram Soba was at that time occupied by Amalek, the ancient enemy of the Jewish people. And so it was that King David conquered Aram Soba, with Yoab ben Seruyah leading the army. Yoab built a tower and fortress which form the foundations of the ancient fortifications that can still be seen in Aleppo today. According to tradition, Yoab inscribed the following on a rock in the wall of the fortress, "I am Yoab ben Seruyah, I have conquered this fortress and city." In his 19th-century work *Zichron Dibrei Eretz*, R' Abraham Dayan (see #173) mentions the inscription and states, "I heard from old people that the rock has since been covered by a newer wall and can no longer be seen." The Seruya family has a tradition that their surname is traced back to Yoab ben Seruyah.

As a reward for his loyalty, the king gave the city to Yoab, who then realized that he finally had the opportunity to realize his desire of building a house for *Hashem*. That structure ultimately became the Great Synagogue of Aram Soba (see Section II).

Adjacent to the Great Synagogue there is a stone on which is engraved, "Burial Ground of Tanna'im and Amora'im (Scholars of the Mishnah and Talmud)."

The Courtyard of R' Asi in Aram Soba

There is a courtyard in Aram Soba, which has been referred to from time immemorial by its Arabic name, *"Hush d'Raav al Sif."* The tradition has been passed down through the centuries that this is the courtyard of R' Asi, one of the scholars of the *Talmud*. Until recent times there was a family in Aram Soba, named *"Beit Asi,"* and adjacent to the Great Synagogue there is a stone on which is engraved, "Burial Ground of *Tanna'im* and *Amora'im* (Scholars of the *Mishnah* and *Talmud*)."

The Aleppo citadel with part of the ancient wall

By tradition, Aram Soba had seven gates, all covered in iron. Each gate was reputed to have been the site of a wondrous event in ancient times. Additional information about the gates may be found in the book *Zichron Dibrei Eretz,* which is a history of Aram Soba, written by R' Abraham Dayan.

The Seven Gates of Aram Soba

In his book, R' Dayan writes, "I heard from an elderly Torah scholar, who has knowledge of ancient traditions, that each gate had a wondrous artifact from the days of old. He heard of three of them. The first had the tooth of large fish, about five feet long. This gate is known [in Arabic] as *Bab al Nasir* [Gate of Victory] and it may be seen to this day. Another gate has a fingernail from one of the *Nephilim* [the giants of Canaan mentioned in *Bamidbar* 13:33], which is the size of a pillow. Another gate has a jar of sand from the Sambatyon River, which seethes and churns all week and rests on *Shabbat*. [See *Targum Yonatan ben Uziel, Shemot* 34:10 and *Midrash Rabah, Bereshit* 11:5.] Once a non-Jew saw the jar and became resentful, saying it supports the Jewish religion's concept of *Shabbat*. He therefore broke it and destroyed it. Some foreign travelers who have wandered the world over did not come across the river and so denied its existence. However, the *Hida* (R' Haim Yosef David Azulai) writes about its existence at length."

זכרון דברי ארץ יע"א

אמרתי אלקטה לה קצת מדברי ומקרי עירנו ארם צובה יע"א
מה ששמעתי מפי אנשים חשובים שקבלו בידם
מהדבר הזה ואמרתי לחברו הנה כי יש בו תועלת לכמה דברים
ולענין דינא ארם צובה היא אשר כבשה אדונינו דוד המע"ה
על ידי שר צבאו יואב ן' צרויה וראיתי בס' כ"י
שכתב כי היו בה באותו עת עמלקים ומשו"ה נלחם בהם וקבלה
בידינו שהיה כתוב על אבן בכותל המגדל שקורין אל קלעה אני
יואב ן' צרויה כבשתי זה המגדל והעיר ושמעתי היום מזקנים
שמזה כמה שנים בנו כותל אחר לפני הכתיבה ונעלמה האבן
ההיא עד היום הזה ויש בעירנו חומה גבוהה בנין חזק וקדום
באבנים גדולות אבן לא נודע מאיזה זמן ויש שם שבעה פתחים
לעיר מצופים בברזל ושמעתי מזקן ת"ח אחד ז"ל שקבלה בידו
שבכל פתח ופתח היה שם דבר פלא במה שהיה מימי קדם ושמע
על ג' מהם אחד יש בו שן דג גדול אורך ב' אמות והוא פי באב
אל נציר ועד היום רואים אותו ובפתח אחר יש צפורן של אחד מן
הנפילים

Title Page of Zichron Dibrei Eretz

By tradition, Aram Soba had seven gates, all covered in iron. Each gate was reputed to have been the site of a wondrous event in ancient times.

R' Dayan continues, "I have seen some people, convinced of their own intelligence, who think that nothing exists beyond nature and don't believe what they haven't seen with their own eyes or in secular sources. Therefore, for those skeptics I cite a book, which quotes secular sources concerning the existence of ancient giants. He writes of scientific finds of the teeth of giants that are one hundred times the size of average human teeth. The book *Mikveh Yisrael* writes of a man in Lisbon, Portugal, who had a glass jar with sand from the Sambatyon River and every Friday afternoon he would go to the Jewish Quarter and show the sand stopping its restless motion. He would then tell them, 'Close your stores for it is time to welcome *Shabbat*.'

"I also heard from a reliable Jewish man whose friend had traveled to Rome. There a non-Jew showed him some grains wrapped in paper. These grains were in a state of agitation all week but became still on *Shabbat*.

"And concerning the giants, I have received written information from a scholar, who is a a good friend of mine. Besides his breadth of Torah knowledge he has extensive familiarity with secular books. He states that he has read of a gentile scholar who researched this topic and presented innumerable proofs of the large bones and teeth that were found, especially those of an ancient French king, whose shoulders were extremely wide. In this way he clearly demonstrated that all which is written in the holy books about the giants is true and correct. This is enough to close the mouths of the skeptics and scoffers."

OTHER HISTORIC VISITORS

Ezra HaSofer

An ancient tradition granting prestige to the community was the sojourn in the nearby village of Tedef and its connection to Ezra HaSofer and the Jews returning from exile in Babylonia. While they were there, a rabbinical dispute broke out regarding the exact wording of the Torah. Ezra was faced with the challenge of persuading the people to accept his Divinely inspired insight into the exact wording of the Torah. He prepared a Torah scroll in which the Name of *Hashem* was missing. He then announced that he would leave it in

An ancient tradition granting prestige to the community was the sojourn in the nearby village of Tedef.

a secure cave overnight.The next morning the scroll would be examined and if the Name was written where it should be, that would demonstrate the correctness of his interpretation. This was done and he was proven right by the miraculous appearance of *Hashem's* Name in every place that had been left blank. To celebrate this wondrous event, a beautiful synagogue was built in Tedef near the cave.

There was a custom that each year during the months of Elul and Tishrei Jews from Aram Soba would go out to that place to fulfill vows that they made during the year. They would pray and light candles there for the soul of Ezra.

Near the village there is a spring in which Ezra regularly immersed himself during his sojourn in Tedef. That place is called by the local Arab inhabitants *Al Azir* in recognition of its history. There was a custom that each year during the months of Elul and Tishrei Jews from Aram Soba would go out to that place to fulfill vows that they made during the year. They would pray and light candles there for the soul of Ezra.

In the Book of *Ezra* (8:15), the verse states, "I assembled them at the flowing river, at the Ahaba, and we encamped there for three days." There is a tradition in the rabbinical Kassin family that this refers to the river Dahab which runs near Tedef and the three-day encampment refers to the dispute mentioned above. Also, there is a nearby hill called Sheikh Waquil which has a monument to mark the burial spot of some of the bones of Yiftah HaGiladi. The death of Yiftah is described in the book of *Shoftim* (12:7), "Yiftah HaGiladi died and was buried in the cities of Gilead." The phrase "in the cities of Gilead" implies that he received more than one burial. The *Midrash* explains that his limbs atrophied and fell off one by one; each was buried in the place he happened to be at the time.

R' Saadiah Gaon (882–942) was the greatest scholar of his time and an important leader of Babylonian Jewry. He lived for a time in Aram Soba.

R' Saadiah Gaon

R' Saadiah Gaon (882–942) was the greatest scholar of his time and an important leader of Babylonian Jewry. He lived for a time in Aram Soba and was still there when he became embroiled in a major dispute related to the setting of the leap year.

In the year 922 R' Aaron Ben-Meir, head of the Jerusalem community, announced that the festival of *Pesah* that year would fall on Sunday, and not on Tuesday as accepted according to the Babylonian calendar, and therefore the following *Rosh Hashanah* would fall on Tuesday and not Thursday. These changes would also affect the fixing of the days of the other holidays during the following year.

The Rambam

While R' Saadiah was still in Aram Soba, he was informed by some students who came from Baghdad of R' Ben-Meir's intentions, and he attempted to dissuade him from implementing it. R' Ben-Meir, however, did not heed his advice. He sincerely believed in the *halachic* rightness of his acts. He upheld a tradition that recognized the sole right of Jerusalem to declare new moons and holidays. R' Saadiah, however, denied the validity of R' Ben-Meir's arguments and returned to Babylon to press his case with the leaders of the Jewish community there. R' Saadiah and the Babylonian leaders ultimately achieved victory, and he was considered one of the greatest authorities in the field of fixing the calendar.

In one of his letters dealing with this issue R' Saadiah writes, "Know that while I was still in Haleb, which is Aram Soba, a few disciples ... came and said that Ben-Meir is considering establishing this as a non-leap year, and I refused to believe it." In yet another letter he writes, "In the summer, when I was in Haleb I heard that Ben-Meir intends to announce Mar-Heshvan and Kislev as short months (29 days) and I wrote many letters to discourage him from doing that."

The Rambam admired and respected Aram Soba, as he indicated in a letter which he wrote to the scholars of Luniel, France.

The Emissary of the Rambam

From the 12th century, Aram Soba began to stand out as an important center of learning and its scholars were in contact with the leading rabbis of the other Torah centers of the region. The *Rambam* admired and respected Aram Soba, as he indicated in a letter which he wrote to the scholars of Luniel, France. In the letter he bewailed the deterioration of Torah study throughout the lands of the

East. The only bright spot that he could see was Aram Soba, "which still has a remnant of Torah scholars who are immersed in study."

The only bright spot that he could see was Aram Soba, "which still has a remnant of Torah scholars who are immersed in study."

One of the *Rambam*'s favorite students was R' Yosef bar Yehudah ben-Akanin who was born in Rabat, Morocco, but fled to Alexandria, Egypt, during a period of forced conversions. In Egypt, R' Yosef corresponded with the *Rambam*, who invited him to join him at his home in Fostat, the old city of Cairo. R' Yosef remained a year with the *Rambam* and became his avid student and follower. The *Rambam* was very fond of R' Yosef and dedicated his major philosophical work, *Guide for the Perplexed*, to him.

In 1186 R' Yosef went to Aram Soba, where he establish a *Bet Midrash* under the authority of the *Rambam*. He became a court physician to Salah al-Din (Saladin), who was at that time the prince of Aleppo. (Saladin was later to defeat the Crusaders and to become the ruler of Jerusalem, inviting Jews to settle there.) R' Yosef also wrote a medical book and a commentary on *Shir HaShirim* (Song of Songs).

R' Yehudah Al-Ḥarizi

In 1217 the noted Spanish poet R' Yehudah al-Harizi visited Aram Soba and described the spiritual beauty of the city in elaborate terms in his book, *Tahkemoni*. He referred to the *Rambam*'s emissary, R' Yosef bar Yehudah ben-Akanin, as "R' Yosef of the West ... who brought life with his wisdom to the sons of Soba and infused the spirit of his knowledge into their bodies."

In 1217 the noted Spanish poet R' Yehudah Al-Harizi visited Aram Soba and described the spiritual beauty of the city in elaborate terms in his book, Tahkemoni.

R' Levi ibn Habib (Ralbach)

R' Levi ben Yaakov ibn Habib (the *Ralbach*), one of the Spanish exiles in the 15th century, was the son of the *Ein Yaakob* (R' Yaakob ben Shelomo ibn Habib) and completed this classic work after his father passed away. The *Ralbach* ultimately settled in Jerusalem, where he became the Chief Rabbi. He also wrote an important book of responsa. In this book he describes a visit which he made to Aram Soba, where he was pleased to find a group of learned scholars, who studied together each day Chapter 3 of *Masechet Ketubot*. He writes that he was happy to learn with them in mutual goodwill.

R' Yeshayah Horowitz (Shelah)

R' Yeshayah Horowitz (the *Shelah*) was a renowned Kabbalist of the early 17th century. He was born in Prague and later traveled to Jerusalem where he was accepted as Chief Rabbi. He became famous as the author of the book *Shenei Luhot HaBrit*, which clarifies the basic concepts of Torah and *mitzvot*. In 1622, while traveling to *Eretz Yisrael* he passed through Aram Soba and described his visit in a letter. He writes that the fellowship and goodwill that he experienced in Aram Soba "cannot be described." He felt the same sense of sanctity and dignity as in the holy congregation of Prague. The *Shelah* was pleased at being able to communicate with the scholars of Aram Soba in Hebrew and he sensed a great hunger to hear his teachings.

R' Yeshaya Horowitz (the Shelah) writes that the fellowship and goodwill that he experienced in Aram Soba "cannot be described." He felt the same sense of sanctity and dignity as in the the holy congregation of Prague.

R' Mordechai ben Shemuel Yafeh Ashkenazi

R' Mordechai ben Shemuel Yafeh Ashkenazi of Poland traveled to *Eretz Yisrael* in about 1745. On his way he passed through Aram Soba, where he was impressed by the dedication and devoutness of its scholars. He took especial note of their faithful attendance in the *Bet Midrash* to study "half the night" in all weathers and all conditions. He writes of the brilliance of Chief Rabbi Shemuel Laniado and notes that wherever he went in this holy land he saw exceptional scholars who were surely "worthy that the Divine Presence [*Shechinah*] should rest upon them."

He took especial note of their faithful attendance in the Bet Midrash to study "half the night" in all weathers and all conditions.

HISTORICAL CURRENTS

Ancient Times

Jews have been living in Aleppo for thousands of years. During the time of the Second Temple, the Jewish communities in Syria formed a central link in the unbroken chain of Jewish settlement throughout the Fertile Crescent, which stretched from Egypt through *Eretz Yisrael* and Syria to Babylonia (Iraq). The Jewish community in Aleppo persisted even after the decimation of the Jewish population of *Eretz Yisrael* at the close of the Talmudic period at the end of the sixth century.

From the seventh century when Islamic caliphates began ruling the region until the end of Ottoman rule in the early 20th century, the Jewish community of Aram Soba was self-governed.

Arab Rule and the Mongol Invasion

From the seventh century when Islamic caliphates began ruling the region until the end of Ottoman rule in the early 20th century, the Jewish community of Aram Soba was self-governed. Thus, the Jews were entitled to freedom of religion and a separate court system to handle internal disputes.

During the 10th century, living conditions in Iraq deteriorated under the shaky Abbasid dynasty, so many of that country's Jews emigrated to Syria, a large number of whom settled in Aleppo.

In 1260 Syria was invaded by the Mongols from the north, led by Hulagu Khan. They laid waste the countryside and massacred a great number of Aleppo's residents, but it appears that the Jews suffered less than the Muslims. In the Arab historians' reports of the conquest it is related that many of the Jews found refuge in the Great Synagogue and that all the Jews who had escaped to this place were saved. There was no bloodshed in Damascus since the town surrendered to the Mongols. The two largest Jewish communities in Syria thus remained unharmed. However, in the course of a subsequent Mongol invasion in 1400, led by Tamerlane, many of the Jews were slaughtered or enslaved and the Great Synagogue was destroyed. It was not rebuilt until 1418.

Over the years the Jews of Aleppo were in continual danger of encroachment by the surrounding peoples upon their rights and property. Thus, for example, of the three synagogues used by the community in the 13th century, only one remained in Jewish hands. One synagogue was expropriated in 1327 and converted into a mosque (*Jame el-Hayat*, the Mosque of the Life, or some say, the Mosque of the Snake), and in this capacity, it has continued to function till this day. A wall in the building bears an inscription testifying to its Jewish origins.

Ottoman Rule and the Hacham Bashi

In 1516, Syria was conquered by the Ottoman armies and was placed under the dominion of the Ottoman sultan of Istanbul. With the inclusion of Syria in the Ottoman Empire, economic ties with the countries under the sultan's rule were strengthened. This resulted in a continued immigration of Spanish Jews to the towns of Syria.

In the 19th century, the community of Aram Soba numbered about 10,000, enjoying nearly total autonomy under the Turkish Empire and operating independent judicial, educational, and philanthropic institutions as well as tax collection.

In the 19th century, the community of Aram Soba numbered about 10,000, enjoying nearly total autonomy under the Turkish Empire and operating independent judicial, educational, and philanthropic institutions as well as tax collection. There were a large number of pious scholars and rabbis. People earned their livelihood as merchants and money changers. However, a severe economic crisis struck the community in 1869 with the opening of the Suez Canal, which removed Aram Soba entirely from international trade routes.

From the mid-19th century on, the Ottoman government appointed a chief rabbi (Hacham Bashi). This individual represented the Jewish community before government agencies and could be a powerful individual in the community in his own right.

From the mid-19th century on, the Ottoman government appointed a chief rabbi (*Hacham Bashi*). This individual represented the Jewish community before government agencies and could be a powerful individual in the community in his own right.

The *Hacham Bashi* was distinguished by the size and color of his turban and the long, wide sleeves of his outer garments. While it was customary for everyone to wear an ankle-length robe with a sash around the waist, the *Hacham Bashi* was a government official and wore a finer robe with ceremonial orders and medals, and gold and silver embroidery. The *Hacham Bashi* had two government-appointed bodyguards, known as Kawas [Turkish for Guard of Honor], who carried his staff of office and cleared the way for him.

Ancient Traditions and Leadership — the Dayan Family

For a great many generations prior to the 16th century, leadership of Aram Soba was centered in members of the Dayan family, who trace their origins to the house of King David. Many traditions and customs have adhered to this family, which symbolized the continuity of Jewish life in Aram Soba. [Refer to the Biographies section for additional information on the Dayan lineage.]

Influence of the Jews from Spain

At the beginning of the 16th century, exiles from Spain started to arrive in Aram Soba, among them outstanding rabbis and scholars. Since the Hebrew word for Spain is *Sepharad,* the Spanish exiles were known as the *Sephardim*. They did not reach Syria all at once but gradually. Generally, they passed through several places until finally settling in one of the Mediterranean countries like Syria. Many of them came to Syria from Italy and Turkey, where they had lived for a number of years. Once the number of Spanish Jews in the Syrian towns increased, various problems connected with the organization of the communities arose and the process of their assimilation with the native-born Jews raised considerable difficulties.

Once the number of Spanish Jews in the Syrian towns increased, various problems connected with the organization of the communities arose and the process of their assimilation with the native-born Jews raised considerable difficulties.

In contrast to the Sephardim, the native-born Jews were referred to as the *Mustarabim* (the Hebrew word for Arabs) because they generally spoke Arabic and read Hebrew with an Arabic accent. In contrast, the Spanish Jews spoke Ladino, a mixture of Hebrew and Spanish that was not understood in Aram Soba. Besides the language differences, the Sephardim differed in their way of life, habits, and outlook from that of Jews living in Arab countries. In the large towns — where they were in greater numbers — the Spanish Jews established their own communities, with independent synagogues, courts, and cemeteries. The wide erudition of their rabbis and the relatively large number of scholars among them favored the Spanish Jews, and it was not long before they assumed leadership positions in Aram Soba — a situation which also prevailed throughout the eastern part of the Mediterranean.

With the arrival in Aram Soba of of the Sephardim, the spiritual and economic development of the community reached new heights. This flourishing continued throughout the 16th century, during which time Syria was a part of the Ottoman Empire (since 1516). For some time, members of the Dayan family continued to serve as leaders of the Mustarabim and rabbis from the Laniado family led the community of Sephardim. In the course of time the descendants of the native Jews recognized the authority of descendants of the exiles from Spain and the community was reorganized, while still preserving certain customs of the Mustarabim and the privileges of the Dayan family.

For some time, members of the Dayan family continued to serve as leaders of the Mustarabim and rabbis from the Laniado family led the community of Sephardim.

It took several centuries, but eventually the two communities — the new Spanish Jews and the Jews indigenous to Aleppo — converged into one and the Ladino language of the Spanish Jews died out by the middle of the 18th century. Yet the surnames of the Spanish families — like Kassin and Labaton — have lived on into the 21st century.

One of the customs of Aram Soba which originated with the Spanish Jews was the addition of an extra candle when lighting the *Hanukah* lights. This was introduced as a sign of celebration for being saved from the horrors of the Inquisition. It is possible that the celebration was particularly associated with *Hanukah* because that is the time of year when this group fled from Spain. (Suggested by Hacham Yitzchak Chehebar [#152] in his book *Yitzchak Yeranen*.)

One of the customs of Aram Soba which originated with the Spanish Jews was the addition of an extra candle when lighting the Hanukkah lights.

Influence of the Francos

At the end of the 17th century, additional Sephardic Jews, mainly from Italy and France, began to settle in Aram Soba to participate in the extensive trade between Persia and Southern Europe in which Aram Soba served as an important station. These Jews, called Francos, did not establish a separate community, and they did not give up their European citizenship, and thus enjoyed the protection of the consuls of the European powers. From 1784 the Picciotto family served as consular representatives of a number of European countries, which, of course, gave them prestige within the Jewish community and beyond it. Other notable Franco family names are Altaras, Ankona, Belilios, Lofez, and Silvera.

From 1784 the Picciotto family served as consular representatives of a number of European countries, which, of course, gave them prestige within the Jewish community and beyond it.

The Francos liberally supported local communal institutions and even established new philanthropic ones, such as a fund for aiding the ill (*Kupat Bikkur Holim*) and a fund for teaching the children of the poor and orphans. However, as Europeans, the Francos refused to be subjected to local community regulations, including the payment of the regular communal taxes.

R' Shemuel Laniado (see #372), who was Chief Rabbi of Aram Soba in the first half of the 18th century, forcefully demanded that the Francos have the same obligations as all the other Jews of Aleppo and that all the rules should bind them. In the second half of the 18th century the dispute flared up again when Chief Rabbi R' Rafael Shelomo Laniado (see #363) tried to compel the Francos to accept the rules of the community and was opposed by R' Yehudah Kassin (see #331), who defended the Francos. The dispute had a social background, since the Francos were wealthy and learned, and were attached to the ideas and customs they brought from Europe. The dispute and *halachic* issues are treated at length in R' Kassin's book *Mahane Yehudah* and R' Laniado's book, *Bet Dino shel Shelomo*.

At the end of the 18th century, with the decline of trade between Aram Soba and Persia, the number of Francos dwindled.

Founders of the Magen David Synagogue and Talmud Torah, Brooklyn, 1921
Left to right: Haim Dalale Harari (who paid for the land), Hacham Moshe Ashear (see #88), unknown, R' Yosef Husney, Hacham Moshe Dweck (Kassab) (see #256), Mr. Habib Chalom, Hacham Haim Tawil (see #584), Mr. Joseph Sitt

Emigration from Aram Soba

From the late 18th century, European traders gradually began to prefer alternative avenues of commerce to the caravan routes that passed through Aleppo. This led to a gradual deterioration in the economic situation of the Jewish community, and conditions became even worse when the Suez Canal was inaugurated in 1869. Nevertheless, the Jewish population of Aleppo, which numbered roughly 5000 in the middle of the 19th century, continued to grow, reaching more than 10,000 on the eve of World War I and 18,000 in the early 30's.

This led to a gradual deterioration in the economic situation of the Jewish community, and conditions became even worse when the Suez Canal was inaugurated in 1869.

While the population was growing, the economic stagnation helped spur emigration from Aleppo. However, the initial impetus for departure of Jews from this fabled city was a spiritual one. Throughout the 19th century there was a pattern of selective emigration of scholars and rabbis to Jerusalem. These courageous pioneers were motivated by the potential for an elevated spiritual life in the holy city. In fact they exerted considerable influence on spiritual life in Jerusalem.

Emigration of the general Jewish population began in the 1880's as a result of deteriorating economic conditions, lack of hope for radical improvement of the legal and social status of the Jews in Syria, and the influence of western education. However, because of the economic hardships in Jerusalem, it was not regarded as an attractive goal for mass immigration. Consequently, communities of Aram Soba Jews developed in many other cities all over the world: Cairo, Manchester, New York, Buenos Aires, Mexico City, Sao Paulo, Panama, among others. These communities preserved their heritage tenaciously. Emigration from Aram Soba reached its height during the French mandate, between the two world wars; by that time *Eretz Yisrael* had become a suitable goal for the masses as well as for scholars and rabbis.

In 1908 the Young Turks, a rebel group responsible for the overthrow of the Ottoman sultan, began conscripting Jews into their army, spurring a mass emigration of Jews to the Americas. Many young men secretly fled Syria to avoid being drafted for service in the Balkan wars.

Emigration from Syria halted during World War I and many families were separated. After World War I, the French took control over Aleppo and it, along with Damascus, became a French Mandate. Travel required a French passport or travel papers. Jews who had passports from European countries were exempt from local taxation, which was a drain on the finances of the local Jewish community. Massive emigration from Syria occurred again during the period after World War I and continued until the mid-1920's, when the Great Depression began. The emigrés from the early 20th-century migration populate the Syrian Jewish communities of Brooklyn, New York and Deal, New Jersey.

Despite the continuing emigration from Aram Soba, the Jewish community of Aram Soba still had about 10,000 people in 1947 because of its natural population growth. The United Nations resolution on November 29 of that year to partition Palestine aroused deep resentment among Arabs around the Middle East. In an outbreak of violence against the Jews in December 1947, most of the synagogues were destroyed. Altogether, over 1500 Torah scrolls and countless books and manuscripts were destroyed in the flames. The great treasure of the community, the Aram Soba Codex (see Section III), was damaged, and part of it even disappeared. About 6,000 Jews fled the city, many of them secretly crossing the frontier into Turkey or Lebanon, where they settled, or continued to Israel, Europe, or America.

The United Nations resolution on November 29 of that year to partition Palestine aroused deep resentment among Arabs around the Middle East. In an outbreak of violence against the Jews in December 1947, most of the synagogues were destroyed.

The Final Years

With the declaration of the State of Israel in 1948 the Jews of Aram Soba became hostages in the hands of the Syrian authorities. They were subject to abuses by the government and by parts of the population who sought to express their hatred for the Zionist state by attacking the local Jews.

The government issued a number of anti-Jewish laws, including a prohibition on sale of Jewish property (1948) and the freezing of Jewish bank accounts (1953). Many had their property confiscated by the authorities, and Palestinian refugees were housed in the dwellings vacated in the Jewish quarters of Damascus and Aram Soba. Many Jews were put on trial because one of their relatives succeeded in escaping from Syria, others were obliged to visit the police station daily, and many were imprisoned without trial. In addition, various limitations were imposed on them, in particular one forbidding them to leave the country. Only after Hashimu l-Atasi came to power in 1950 were Jews allowed to leave Syria, on condition that they renounce their claim to their property. After the first group reached Turkey, however, in November 1951, the police forbade others to leave.

The government issued a number of anti-Jewish laws, including a prohibition on sale of Jewish property (1948) and the freezing of Jewish bank accounts (1953).

Immediately after the union with Egypt and the founding of the United Arab Republic in 1958, the prohibition on the exit of Jews was again canceled. However, shortly afterward the frontiers were again closed to them, and in 1959 trials of those accused of helping Jews to leave Syria began. In March 1964, a decree was enacted which prohibited Jews from traveling more than three miles beyond the limits of their hometowns.

After the trial of the Israel intelligence agent Eli Cohen, and at the time of his public hanging in Damascus (1965), attacks against Jews increased. They suffered even more during the Six Day War (1967) and afterward, when many were arrested and others assaulted by the Muslim population.

After the trial of the Israel intelligence agent Eli Cohen, and at the time of his public hanging in Damascus (1965), attacks against Jews increased. They suffered even more during the Six Day War (1967) and afterward, when many were arrested and others assaulted by the Muslim population. Jews were murdered in Damascus, Aram Soba, and in Qamishli, near the Turkish border, but because of the strict censorship no exact details are known. Jews made many efforts to leave Syria. Between 1948 and 1961, about 5,000 Syrian Jews reached Israel.

The 1,000 Jews living in Aram Soba in 1968 resided in two quarters: Bahsita, the old quarter, which was also known as Charrat El Yahud, the "Jewish neighborhood"; and Jamileyé, founded after World War I. Muslims, who had moved into these quarters after the departure of the Jewish residents, occasionally assaulted their Jewish neighbors and several cases of murder were recorded.

During the 1980's, a collection of Jewish holy objects was smuggled out of Syria after repeated requests for them to be taken out of the country were denied. The Chief Rabbi of Damascus, R' Abraham Hamra, devoted considerable efforts to see to it that the treasures of Damascus were safely transferred. The collection included nine ancient Bible manuscripts, known as the *Ketarim*, each between 700 and 900 years old. In addition, there were 40 Torah scrolls and 32 decorative cases in which the Torah scrolls were held. The collection was taken, via Turkey, in stages to the University Library of the Hebrew University in Israel.

Torah cases in the Great Synagogue, 1946

Never forgetting their brethren in Syria, community members from Brooklyn, New York often bribed Syrian government officials to help those relatives still in Syria get out of the country. Negotiations between America's President George H. Bush and Syria's President Assad, with heavy lobbying from the Syrian community of Brooklyn, resulted in exit visas to America as tourists being granted in the early 1990's for the families who remained, and thus for the first time in over two millennia, Aram Soba had almost no Jewish population.

Assad's demand that they not leave the country as emigrés gave the Syrian Jews who entered America yet another ten years of persecution. In the United States as tourists, they could not practice their chosen profession, obtain licenses, and apply for public assistance or travel outside the United States. In the year 2000, Brooklyn's Syrian community, led by the Council for the Rescue of Syrian Jews, was able to gain passage of federal legislation to change the immigration status of the immigrants. Their new legal status allows them to work legally in the United States, obtain working documents (green cards), and apply for citizenship.

Today, there are essentially no Jews left in Aleppo, but the Jewish heritage of this illustrious city continues to stand out among that of other Jewish communities of the world by virtue of the Jewish families who emigrated over the years but continued to maintain a spiritual bond with their roots.

Although the Jewish presence is no longer felt, the Magen David symbol is still seen on the border of the watchtower located at the Bab al Faraj shopping district.

A call for help! Rabbi Abraham Kalmanowitz, *Rosh Yeshivah* of the Mirrer Yeshiva received a secret note (dated Thursday, *Perashat Shemot*, 5708/1948) that had been smuggled out of Syria via Lebanon. It was signed: The rabbis and scholars of Aleppo. No names were mentioned out of fear of being detected. In the letter their trepidation with regard to the future virtually screams out. The following is a translation of the letter: To the loyal faithful people of Israel.

With a pained heart and tear-flowing eyes we reiterate our plea to publicize that our general situation is worsening daily. Our entire community is in great danger. The local newspapers are rousing the populace and its leaders to a frenzy. They write articles daily that make our ears ring. We have heard that there are most diabolical plans afoot , such as establishing internment camps for Jews, Heaven forbid. The situation is extremely tense. All the community leaders and close to a hundred of the middle class families have fled. The the hearts of those who remain tremble and are waiting for the mercy of G-d and their brothers. Please, you strong ones stand in the breach because it is a time of distress for Jacob. Please do everything in your power to arouse world public opinion in our favor. Petition your government to put an end to our terrible troubles. We can not be more specific in print than this, but wise men need no more than a hint. We are counting on the mercy of G-d and waiting for his salvation. May the merit of our forefathers bring you Divine assistance.

Signed The rabbis and scholars of Aleppo.

Rabbi Kalmanowitz sent a telegram to President Truman, saying:" Alarming reports from Arab countries portend mass murder of Jewish men, women and children by Arabs. Please do not repeat the error of the European tragedy. Please bring full diplomatic pressure to bear on the above countries to stop the murders and protect the Jewish population."

A call for help

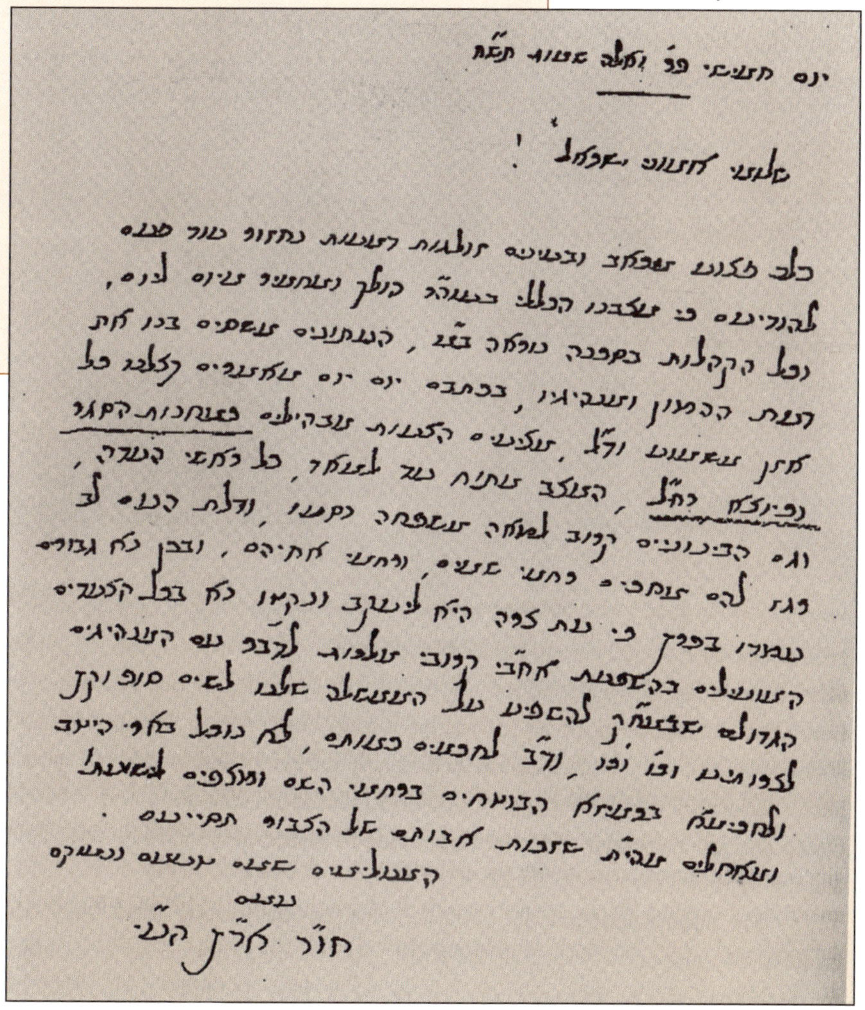

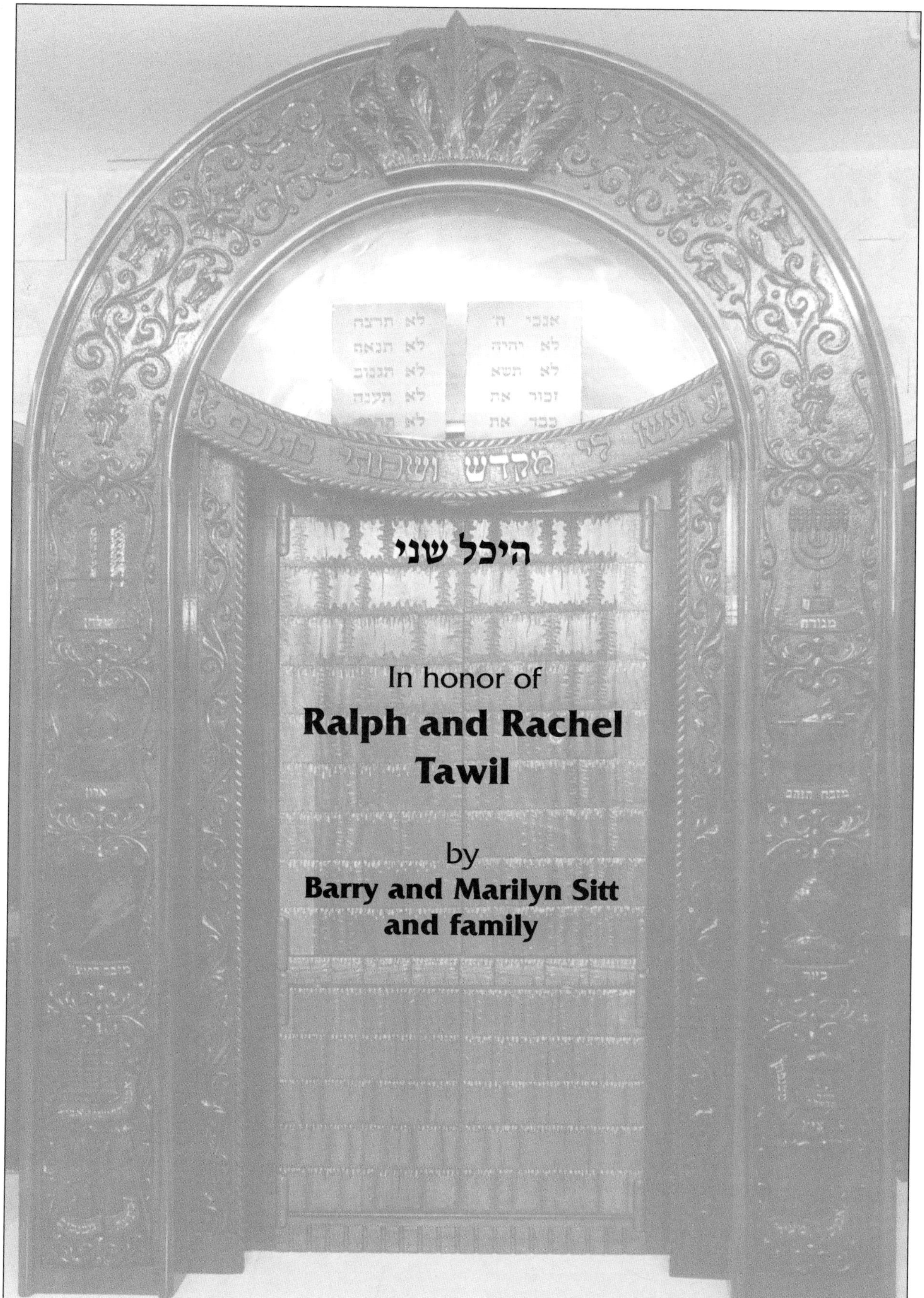

היכל שני

In honor of

Ralph and Rachel Tawil

by

Barry and Marilyn Sitt and family

Section Two

THE GREAT SYNAGOGUE

ORIGINS

The Rabbis of Aleppo. In the background is the Hechal of the Great Synagogue.
Bottom: left to right, R' Ezra Lofez (# 395), R' Moshe Harari (# 291), Chief Rabbi R' Yaakob Shaul Dweck (# 248), R' Reuven Ancona (# 61)

The Great Synagogue of Aram Soba, which had its roots in antiquity, was a grand building in a parklike setting. An aura of holiness and tradition pervaded the entire structure. It was lit with beautiful chandeliers, some of which were electrified in later years.

The Great Synagogue was already famous in the times of the *Rishonim* (early Sages) and was reputedly built well before the First Temple. According to tradition, after King David conquered Aram Soba, he gave the city to his victorious general, Yoab ben Seruyah, who then realized that he finally had the opportunity to realize his desire of building a house for *Hashem*.

He organized work crews and built the imposing structure which became known as the Great Synagogue of Aram Soba. However, Yoab did not just leave it up to the workers. He picked up the large stones on his shoulders and carried them up the ladder to be put in place into the new walls.

One day Yoab was overcome with emotion and he wept, saying, "Is it possible that *Hashem* will leave the great Temple which Shelomo is destined to build, and dwell in this house which I am building? At that point a Heavenly voice was heard, saying to him, "Yoab, Yoab, two Temples are destined to be destroyed, but your house will stand."

Interior view of the old western wing

Model of the summer courtyard, on permanent display at Beth HaTefusoth with the tebah in the center and the Hechal HaTekiah, with platform, on the right

A SACRED STRUCTURE

In the latter part of the 19th century there were 18 synagogues in Aram Soba. However, it was in the Great Synagogue, known by the local Jews as *"al-Safra"* (the yellow), that the most prized spiritual treasure of Aram Soba was kept — the *Keter Aram Soba* (the Aleppo Codex of the Bible).

The oldest section of the synagogue is the western wing, originally built in the form of three colonnaded aisles separated by rows of columns and arches. This section dates back to the fifth or sixth century, which made it the world's oldest functioning synagogue up until the end of the 20th century. After the de-

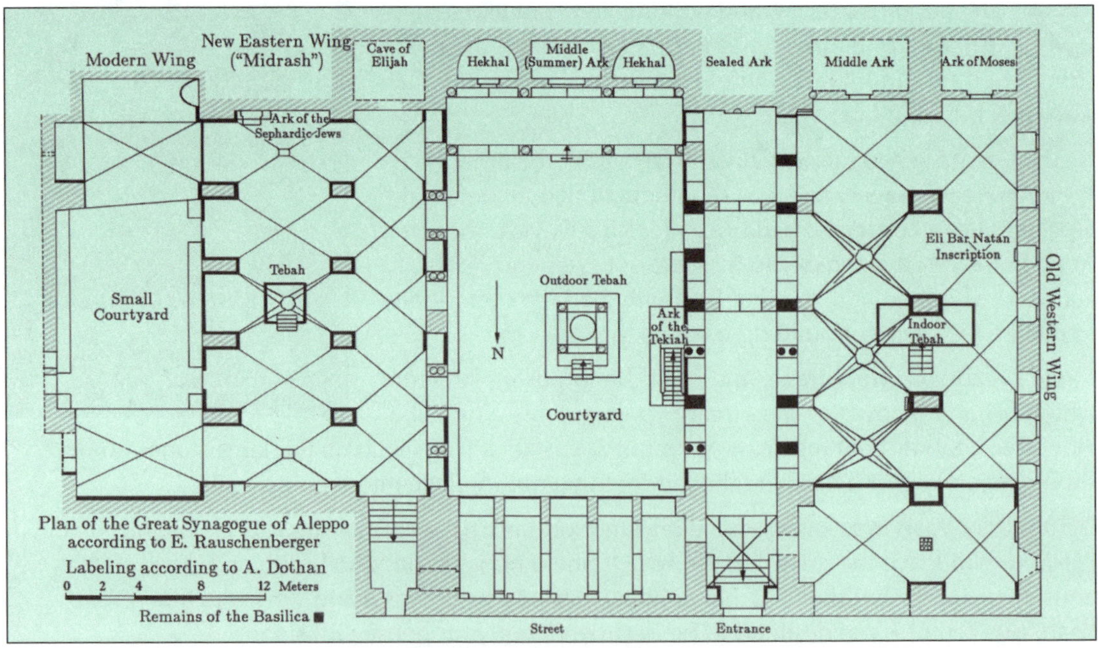

Plan of the Great Synagogue, showing the old western wing (right), the entrance corridor leading to the Sealed Ark (Hechal), the summer courtyard (center) with its outdoor tebah, the "Midrash" wing to the left of the courtyard, and the Cave of Elijah connecting to the Midrash

struction of the synagogue by the invading Mongols in 1400, reconstruction began in 1405 and was not completed until 1418. Having learned a bitter lesson, the community now changed the structure of the building to avoid attracting the attention of potential enemies; the main entrance and magnificient facade of the synagogue were scaled down; the prayer hall was reduced in size and reconstructed as two colonnaded aisles; the third (western) aisle became an entrance corridor. Light entered the building through seven differently shaped windows and the entrance corridor was surmounted by a women's gallery with arcades overlooking the prayer hall on one side and the central courtyard on the other.

Hechal HaTekiah

Seven *hechalot* (Holy Arks housing the Torah scrolls) were built along the southern wall of the synagogue, facing toward Jerusalem. [Note that the word *hechal*, literally: temple, actually refers to the recess in which the ark (*Aron HaKodesh*) stands.] Two of the *hechalot* were at the south side of the old prayer hall: the *Hechal Moshe* and the *Middle Hechal*. Around the central column of the prayer hall was the indoor *tebah (bimah)*, slightly raised and constructed of carved wood. Six steps led up to this platform on which public readings of the Torah took place. Wooden benches were arranged against the walls and around the columns. Located south of the entrance hallway was the structure now known as the *Sealed Hechal* (see box below, "The Hechalot").

During the hot summer days, services were held in the central courtyard and a permanent outdoor *tebah* (*bimah*) was built there. This featured four columns which supported an oriental-style dome. The courtyard, too, had its *hechalot* – three to the south and one to the west. The rectangular central southern *hechal* was known as the Middle (Summer) Ark. Flanking it were two small semicircular *hechalot*. The *hechalot* were separated from the courtyard by a portico of three pairs of arches mounted on columns.

The western *hechal*, the Ark of the *Tekiah* (*shofar* blast), was known by this name because the *Toke'a* (the person sounding the *shofar*) would stand on this raised platform and blow it to be heard by people in both the summer courtyard and the indoor sanctuary. The rabbi

Outdoor tebah in the summer courtyard, early 1900's (Washington, Freer Gallery of Art, Arthur M. Sackler Gallery Archives)

Outdoor tebah, showing destruction of 1947

Outdoor tebah as it appears today after reconstruction

would speak on the raised platform on the High Holy Days as well. This *hechal* comprised nine steps and an upper level, and decorated with carvings. Stone benches were placed around the courtyard and the central *tebah*. *Brit milah's* (circumcisions) were also performed on the raised platform.

On the northern side of the courtyard was a *bet midrash* (study room), which could only be entered via the main entrance, as there was no doorway in the wall which bordered on the street.

Part of the Midrash, recent photograph

With the influx of the Spanish Jews, who first began to arrive in the early 16th century, it became necessary to add another wing to the east of the courtyard, enabling the newcomers to pray according to their own *nusach* (ritual). This wing, named *Midrash*, was constructed of two aisles and had a separate entrance from the street. A wooden *tebah* stood on a stone foundation at the center of the *Midrash*. Opposite it, in the southern wall, was the relatively small Ark of the Sephardic Jews. An additional *hechal*, the Cave of Eliyahu HaNabi, was built to the south of the *Midrash*. This is where the treasured *Keter* was stored.

All of the *hechalot* were enclosed by richly decorated wooden doors and above these, Biblical passages were carved, in addition to the Ten Commandments.

There was an additional *bet midrash* (study hall), called the modern wing, consisting of a small courtyard and two study rooms,

The entire building was renovated in 1855. Justifiably the pride of the community, its unique beauty had been noted by many travelers at various times.

An outstanding example of one of its treasures was the pure silver case for a Torah scroll, which was kept in the *Middle Hechal* and because of its great value, was taken out only on *Yom Kippur*. Made by Joseph Laham in 1710, the case bears precise reproductions of several sections of the synagogue and ritual objects, together with fragments of poetry and Biblical passages.

Cave of Eliyahu HaNabi, where the Keter was kept, photographed by recent visitors to Aleppo

The Hechalot and the Cave of Eliyahu HaNabi. In his 19th-century work *Zichron Dibrei Eretz*, R' Abraham Dayan (see #173), writes, "The old synagogue has many *hechalot* (sacred cabinets for Torah scrolls), one in which the *Keter* is kept. Anyone who needs to make an oath does it at that *hechal* and no other.

"There is a cave near that *hechal*, and tradition has it that Eliyahu HaNabi (the prophet Elijah) appeared there, hence its name 'Cave of Eliyahu HaNabi.' Candles are lit there in times of distress. When a lady enters her ninth month [of pregnancy] she lights a candle there. On *Erev Yom Kippur* at the time of *Minhah* [afternoon prayer service] all the women come to light candles, walking through the men's section to get there. They are definitely causing the masses to sin [due to jostling in the crowded area] and Eliyahu is not happy with the honor he is receiving under such circumstances. Recently some G-d-fearing people stirred themselves and announced that the ladies should come to light the candles at an earlier time so that the *mitzvah* should not come about through sinning. Anyone attempting to revert back to the old practice will have the responsibility of the sin on his head. Even though the synagogue is losing some funds due to the new system, the community must not act out of poverty. Another option would be to widen the entrance to stop the crowded situation.

"One of the seven *hechalot* is known as the 'Sealed *Hechal*.' I heard the story behind the sealing of this *hechal* from an old man. Once on *Simhat Torah* they put seven Torah scrolls in front of each *hechal* all in silver cases and the people rejoiced with the Torah, and they danced with the Torah scrolls outside the synagogue as well. During this time a government minister happened to be passing by. When he saw the festivities and the beautiful ceremonies, he became jealous of the glory of the Jewish people and the beautiful edifice, and he wanted it for his religion. He stayed overnight in the synagogue with some of his advisers. In middle of the night a large snake came out of that *hechal* and coiled itself around the minister's neck. No one could come close because it was a poisonous snake. He screamed, but no one could help him. They called my grandfather (from the Dayan family) and he asked the minister, 'Tell me, did you have any evil plans for the synagogue?' He answered, 'Yes, but I regret it totally and in the future I will only benefit the Jews.' My grandfather then told the snake to return to its place and it went back into the *hechal*. From that point on they sealed the *hechal* because they decided it was no ordinary snake but rather an angel.

"Another explanation of why they sealed this *hechal* is that the young married men who used to sit there on *Shabbat* did not live out the year. It is not clear if this happened before the incident of the minister and the snake or afterwards. My theory is that it happened afterwards. Originally they planned to leave it open after the snake incident, but after the young men were seen to be dying, they decided to seal it."

THE TRAGIC EVENTS OF 1947

In an outbreak of violence against the Jews of Aram Soba in December 1947, most of the synagogues were destroyed. Although the Great Synagogue was left standing, it was vandalized and desecrated and then set aflame. The tragic events were described by R'

Moshe Tawil (see #586), the principal of *Midrash Degel Torah* at that time, and who later became Chief Rabbi:

"The decision to partition Palestine to establish a Jewish state was made on Friday. On Sunday, the Arabs did not bother us, but they closed the city of Aleppo and announced a rest day. We Jews decided to stay indoors. On Monday morning, soldiers were stationed outside the Great Synagogue to protect it. Two leaders of the Jewish community, Mr. Siahu Shamah and Mr. Rahamo Nehmad, went to visit the mayor of the city, who was also head of the police force. They asked for protection and security and he assured them that the community would be protected from any danger that might arise from unruly mobs. Upon their return, Mr. Shamah announced that he did not trust this promise, but Mr. Nehmad felt it was believable."

Ner Tamid as it looks today

The narrative is continued by R' Haim Levi, the author of *Vayizra Yitzhak*, a book devoted to the life of R' Yitzhak Chehebar (see #152), who was then the principal of the Talmud Torah of Aram Soba and was later to become the Chief Rabbi of Argentina:

"In the afternoon, an enraged crowd of Arabs assembled in the vicinity of the Great Synagogue, yelling, 'Palestine is our land and the Jews are our dogs.' These rantings elicited no reaction from the military personnel there. In the late afternoon and evening a rampaging mob attacked the synagogue and torched it. As for the soldiers, not only did they not prevent the ravages of the mob, they actively supported it and assisted in the destruction. This took place on 19 Kislev, 5708 (December 2, 1947), which became a fast day in Aleppo at that time.

"Hacham Moshe Tawil, who lived opposite a synagogue in the Jamileyé section of Aleppo, witnessed with his own eyes how the hooligans were lifted on the backs of the soldiers in order to enter the the courtyard of the synagogue.

"At the very same time Hacham Yitzhak Chehebar and his wife were observing the frightful events from their kitchen window, which faced the Great Synagogue. They also saw with their own eyes as the Arabs were climbing on each other's shoulders to get over the wall of the synagogue courtyard. They then broke open the doors of the synagogue and the mob poured in. They took out the Torah scrolls and ripped the holy parchments. After that some firemen came; they started a fire and poured diesel oil and kerosene on the holy books instead of using water to extinguish the conflagration.

"Over a period of 30 minutes, the wicked marauders took out 40 Torah scrolls and burned them in the courtyard with oil and kerosene. They then proceeded to burn a large collection of at least 2,000 pairs of *tefillin*. While all this was happening the Jews were afraid to step out of their houses because the Arabs threatened to slaughter anyone who stood in their way. The police discouraged the rioters from attacking Jews, but gave them free rein to destroy Jewish property. On that day, they set fire to all of the synagogues and study halls. The hellish riot lasted throughout the night. The mobs also attacked Jewish homes, looting them and setting them aflame. Only then did the soldiers come and disperse the crowds. Hacham Tawil recalls that on the following day, the head of the police, who had himself assured them of his protection, came by with a big smile on his face. His expression did not change when he saw the destruction. In fact, he was not disturbed by the scene but seemed pleased and continued to smile.

"That night Aleppo lost [a large part of] its Jews. The wealthy and all who had the means to escape did so immediately. With the absence of security and the removal of restrictions against leaving the country, they hastened to leave before new edicts could be passed. The community leaders who had been the primary supporters for Hacham Chehebar, like Rahamo Nehmad, Jabra Safdeyé, Abraham Cohen, Edmon Nehmad, and Siahu Shamah, left Aleppo for Beirut with their families. In Aleppo there remained only the families with limited means."

Although severely damaged by fire in 1947, the Great Synagogue was partially reconstructed. The dwindling Jewish community continued to function with vibrancy and schools were restarted. One wing of the Great Synagogue was repaired in 5752 (1992) and a plaque was placed in a prominent location to record the event.

Plaque recording the repair of the Great Synagogue in 5752 (1992)
Translation: Forty years after the burning of his holy house, the managing committee and Bet Din of Aram Soba (Aleppo) decided to renovate this holy house. Those involved were the blessed ones, Mr. F. Gindi, Mr. Abraham Nakash, and Mr. Jack Shacalo. May Hashem repay them (5752)

היכל שלישי

In memory
of
Albert D. Sutton *A"H*

Dedicated by
Mr. & Mrs. Steven S. Sutton

Section Three

THE ALEPPO CODEX (KETER ARAM SOBA)

HISTORY OF THE KETER

The Aleppo Codex is one of the earliest-known manuscripts containing the entire text of the *Tanach* (*Torah, Nebi'im, Ketubim*), and probably the most accurate. It is referred to as a "codex" to indicate that although it is an ancient manuscript, it is in book form (separate pages) rather than in the form of a scroll. The Codex has achieved a position of pre-eminence among Jewish manuscripts and is widely considered to be an authoritative source document for the text and punctuation of the *Tanach*. Besides showing the authoritative punctuation, the manuscript includes additional notations. Because of its unique aura of authority and holiness it is referred to as the *Keter* (crown). It received the name of "Aleppo Codex" because for over 500 years it was kept in the synagogue in Aleppo (from the 14th century to the 20th century).

First existing page of the Keter, two out of the three columns

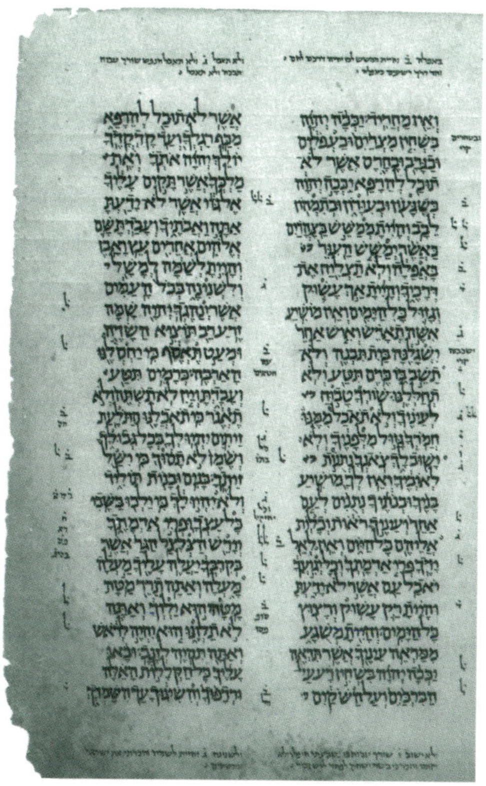

Its Origin

According to the colophon (record of the manuscript production details) appended to the *Keter*, the text was written by the expert scribe R' Shlomo Ben-Buya'a over 1000 years ago in the vicinity of Tiberias. This is where Jewish scholars developed the system of vowel pointing which was to become the standard Masoretic system of vocalization. The *Keter* was then carefully inspected and validated by R' Aharon Ben-Asher, a famous grammarian and scribe of the tenth century. It is believed that R' Aharon Ben-

Asher himself penned the vowel points and the marginal *Masorah* (a system of comments cross-referencing the spelling and the occurrence of particular words) in this manuscript. This was the manuscript consulted by the *Rambam* when he set down the exact rules for pointing, paragraphing, and formatting of the text in his *Hilchot Sefer Torah*.

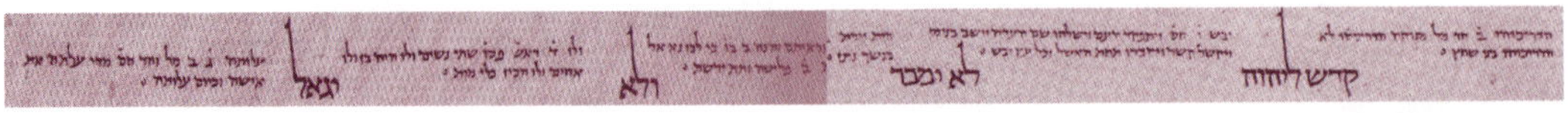

View of the Keter showing the message, "Holy to G-d, May not be sold, May not be redeemed"

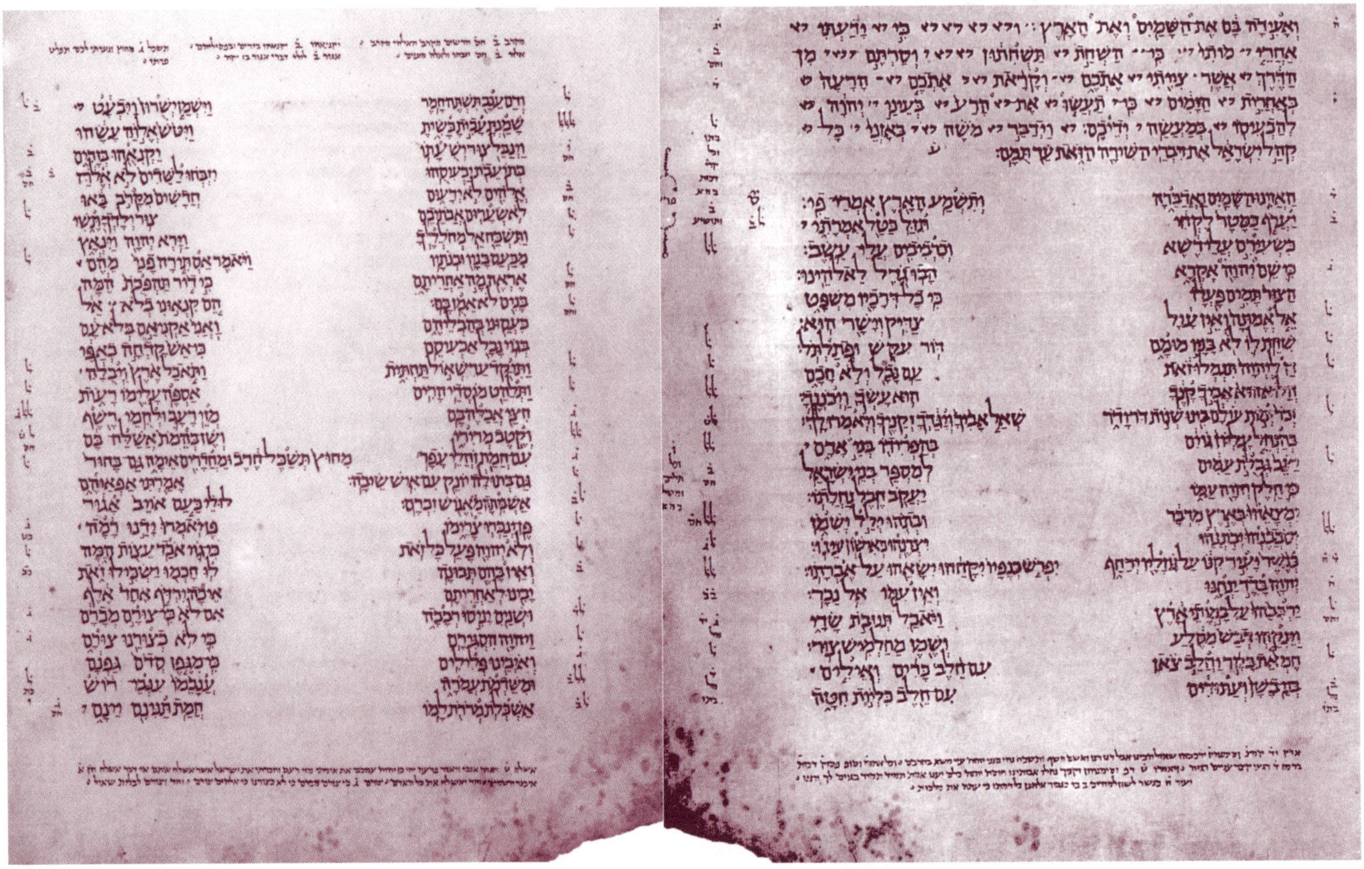

Ha'azinu

This was the manuscript consulted by the Rambam when he set down the exact rules for pointing, paragraphing, and formatting of the text in his Hilchot Sefer Torah.

In the Rambam's Words: "I have seen much fault in all Torah scrolls in these matters [the prescribed arrangement of lines and paragraphs]. Also the experts on the *Masorah*, who write guidelines to identify the *petuhot* [open paragraph endings having clear space to the end of the line] and *setumot* [closed paragraph endings in which the next paragraph starts on the same line], are in disagreement on which standard they should rely upon. Accordingly I have decided to write out all the paragraph endings of the Torah, the *setumot* and the *petuhot*, and the form of the lines, in order to use them as a standard to prepare every Torah scroll and to validate it. The manuscript of the Torah on which I have depended in these matters is the known manuscript in Egypt which comprises the 24 Books [of the entire *Tanach*] which were in Jerusalem for many years. It was this that [the most knowledgeable experts] followed, because it was checked with great care and annotated [with *nekudot* for pronunciation] by Ben-Asher over many years. And it was on this that I relied when I wrote a Torah scroll in accordance with the *halachah*" (*Hilchot Sefer Torah* 8:4).

Hechal where the Keter was kept

Cave of Eliyahu HaNabi

Coming to Aram Soba

In the 11th century, the *Keter* was stolen by the Seljuks (a Turkish warrior tribe) and taken from *Eretz Yisrael* to Egypt. There it was redeemed by the Jews of Cairo and placed in their synagogue. The *Keter* remained in Cairo for about three centuries and it was there that it was consulted by the *Rambam*.

In the 14th century the *Keter* was transported to *Aram Soba* by a direct descendant of the *Rambam,* who placed it in trust with the ancient Jewish community of that city. It then became known as the *Keter Aram Soba* (the crown of Aram Soba) and was kept in a vault in the Great Synagogue. However, the rabbis of *Aram Soba* traditionally referred to it as the *Keter of Ezra HaSofer* (Ezra the Scribe). This was apparently based on their conviction that the *Keter* was linked by a sequence of validated copies to the Torah written by Ezra during his stay in Tedef, near Aram Soba. (See Section I: *Other Historic Visitors.*)

Asher Baghdedi in front of the Great Synagogue shortly after the riot

In Aram Soba, the *Keter* was originally placed in the holiest of the seven *hechalot* (Holy Arks housing the Torah scrolls) in the Great Synagogue. Later it was transferred to a cabinet in a room known as the Cave of Eliyahu HaNabi.

The *Keter* was originally kept in a wooden cabinet, but after a fire broke out in the synagogue the decision was made to keep it in an iron vault. Over the generations, the community leaders of Aram Soba guarded the *Keter* jealously and refused access to almost everyone. In later years the cabinet was locked with two keys, which were never held by the same person. Thus, it could only be opened in the presence of the two keyholders.

בעזרת השי"ת

ספר

עמודי שש

שש אנכי על אמרתיך

Title page of *Amudei Shesh*

Researchers Over the Ages

Over the many centuries in which the *Keter* was in Aram Soba, there were periods when it was permitted to make manuscript copies and other periods when all access was denied. In the year 1559 R' Yosef Karo sent a certified copy from Safed to R' Moshe Isserles (the *Rama*) in Cracow, who used it as a guide in writing his own Torah scroll. The certified copy that had been sent from Safed was kept in the synagogue of the *Rama* in Cracow, where it remained until the Holocaust, when its trail vanished. Regarding this master copy, R' Yaakov Safir writes (*Even Safir*, 1866) that he traveled from Egypt to Syria to investigate the unique *Tanach* that is in Aram Soba. He felt unable to complete his investigations without consulting the findings of previous investigators who looked into a similar manuscript, "which is in the synagogue of the *Rama* in the community of Cracow, which the *Bet Yosef* sent from Safed, and which he had acquired for a large amount of money."

In 1753, an English researcher, Alexander Russell, visited Aleppo and was allowed to view the *Keter*. He described his investigations in a book, *The Natural History of Aleppo*, published in London in 1794 (second edition). He states that the Jews of Aleppo are of the opinion that the *Keter* was written in the era before the Roman general Titus, that is, before the destruction of the Second Temple. As evidence, he refers to a prayer for the preservation of the Temple, which appears at the end of the manuscript. He cites the argument that if the manuscript had been written later, the prayer would have been for the restoration of the Temple, rather than its preservation.

In his book *Amudei Shesh* (Jerusalem 1891), R' Shmuel Shlomo Boyarski of Grodno describes how he sent an emissary to Aram Soba to study the authoritative format for arranging poetic verses (such as the Song of the Sea in *Shemot*). He goes on to say that the mission was successful and he installed a copy of the Torah based on the Aram Soba model in the synagogue of R' Yehudah HaHasid in Jerusalem. He also speaks about writing two manuscripts of *Tehillim*, based on the *Keter Aram Soba*. One of these he sent to his brother in Brisk to put in the great synagogue of that town, so that public readings of *Tehillim* could be conducted there from a holy scripture.

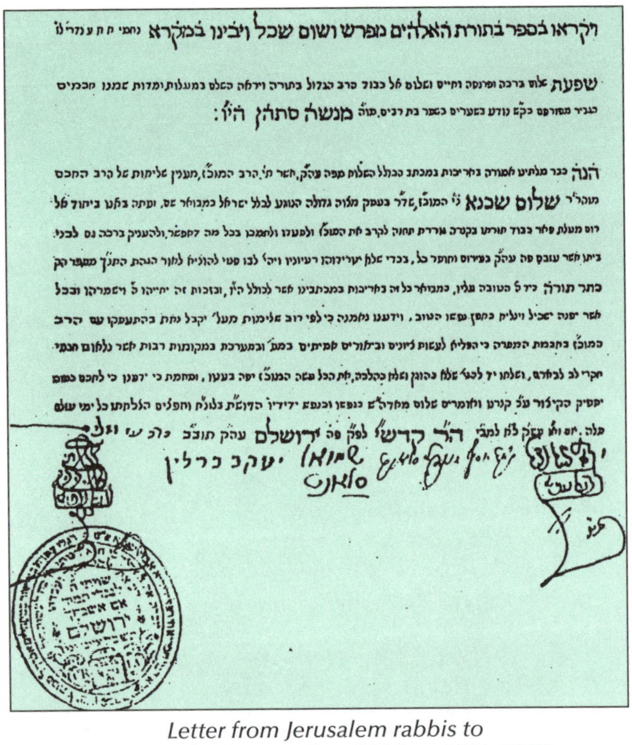

ויקראו בספר בתורת האלהים מפרש ושום שכל ויבינו במקרא

Letter from Jerusalem rabbis to R' Menashe Sutton, dated 23 Iyar, 5619 (1858)

In 1858, some of the most prominent rabbis of Jerusalem sent a letter to R' Menashe Sutton (see #551) requesting permission to copy parts of the *Keter*. The letter was signed by R' Haim Nissim Abulafia, who was Chief Rabbi of Jerusalem, R' Yosef Zundel of Salant, R' Shemuel of Salant, R' Yaakov Berlin, and R' Raphael Yedidyah Abulafia. R' Sutton was known to be an expert on the detailed issues related to the text of holy manuscripts.

One of the more recent researchers to gain access to the *Keter* was Moshe David Cassuto. Professor Cassuto came to Aleppo in 1943 from Jerusalem to study the *Keter* in the interest of publishing a definitive edition of the *Tanach*. Through the efforts of R'

Yitzhak Chehebar (see #152), who was then the principal of the Talmud Torah of Aram Soba, the professor was able to spend time studying the *Keter* and taking notes. However, photographing the *Keter* was strictly prohibited. After his death a new edition of the *Tanach* was published, reflecting his work. The professor also claimed to have found there some notes written in the previous century by the above-mentioned R' Menashe Sutton. These notes indicated specific differences between the traditional Torah scrolls of Aleppo (based on the Amsterdam *Humash*) and the *Keter*. [Editor's note: This would suggest that the scribes of Aleppo did not use the *Keter* as their text standard in writing Torah scrolls.]

It was believed that if the Keter were removed from the city, disaster would befall the community.

R' Ben-Sion Meir Hai Ouziel

The Keter at Risk

For generations it was believed that if the *Keter* were removed from the city, disaster would befall the community. The *Keter* remained safe until 1947 when terrible riots broke out, resulting in the torching of the Great Synagogue. The *Keter* itself was also damaged, but the members of the community were able to save most of it through a series of almost miraculous events.

After parts of the Great Synagogue were set aflame, the building was sealed off by the Syrian army, which did not allow Jews to enter. Because of the confused conditions of those fateful days, the exact sequence of events leading to the recovery of the *Keter* is shrouded in mystery. One researcher has been able to identify nine different versions of what might have actually happened (Amnon Shamosh, *The Story of the Aleppo Codex*, Jerusalem, 1987).

According to one notable version, Mr. Mordechai Faham, a prominent member of the community and an important figure in the history of the *Keter*, disguised himself as a Bedouin to gain entrance, thereby saving the *Keter* from immediate destruction in the fire.

However, others have reported that the *Keter* remained abandoned in the ruined building for four days, until Jews were permitted to enter. A key member of the first group to gain access was R' Moshe Tawil (see #586), *Rosh Yeshiva* of the yeshiva *Degel HaTorah* of Aram Soba and later Chief Rabbi of Aleppo after the passing of R' Moshe Mizrahi (see #424). Others in that group were R' Yitzhak Chehebar (see #152), who later became Chief Rabbi of Argentina, R' Sadek Harari, later to become Chief Rabbi of Mexico, R' Yaakob Attiah, later to become Rabbi of the Syrian and Lebanese Community of Bat Yam, and R' Attiah's father-in-law, R' Shelomo Zafrani (see #598), who was a *dayan* on the *Bet Din* of Aram Soba.

They found the *Keter* loose on a pile of ashes and debris, with many pages missing. They pulled the pages together and turned them over to the Chief Rabbi at the time, R' Moshe Mizrahi (see #424). (See also Document No. 16 for a detailed account of the above events, written by R' Yaakob Attiah with the concurrence of R' Abraham Zafrani.)

R' Yitzhak Chehebar, R' Moshe Tawil, and R' Shelomo Zafrani played a major role over the next 10 years in hiding the *Keter* in various locations.

Because of the great danger, the details of the Keter's survival were originally kept secret and the world was allowed to think that it had been destroyed in the fire.

The first hiding place was with a friendly Christian, who was the Austrian consul. After the riots ended, the *Keter* was hidden among the goods in a warehouse owned by the secretary of the community, Mr. Yaakob Hazan. During the 10-year period, the Syrian government often asked R' Moshe Tawil about the *Keter*, but he replied simply that it had been destroyed.

Because of the great danger, the details of the *Keter's* survival were originally kept secret and the world was allowed to think that it had been destroyed in the fire. However, in time the secret became known to the Israeli government. A concerted campaign of pressure and persuasion was directed at the rabbis of Aram Soba by the Israeli government, scholarly institutions, and Jewish organizations. An official letter issued in 1953 by the Sephardic Chief Rabbi, R' Ben-Zion Meir Hai Ouziel, admonished them to deliver the manuscript into the

To this day there are reports of people who possess single leaves from the Keter.

Part of a recovered missing leaf (Shemot 8:16)

hands of Israeli officials. Finally they did give up the *Keter*, or rather two-thirds of it. There has been no satisfactory account of what happened to the missing third, which includes most of the Five Books of the Torah and some other portions. It has been reported that the missing pages were burnt, but none of the surviving sections show signs of fire damage, suggesting that they may still exist. One missing leaf was turned over to the Jewish National Library in Jerusalem in December 1982 by a family of Jews who had moved from Aleppo to Brooklyn, New York, and to this day there are reports of people who possess single leaves from the *Keter*. One such person reportedly keeps it in his wallet as a good-luck omen.

In 1957, R' Moshe Tawil and R' Shelomo Zafrani turned the *Keter* over to Mr. Mordechai Faham, who smuggled it out of Syria to *Eretz Yisrael*, by way of Turkey, as described further below. Thus, the circle was completed and the *Keter* returned to the land of its origin. This was done only after R' Ouziel canceled the interdictions which had protected the Aleppo Codex from being taken out of Aleppo.

A New Home

In 1958, the *Keter* was presented to President Yitzhak Ben-Zvi, who had taken a personal interest in it. The *Keter* was first kept at the Ben-Zvi Institute in Jerusalem and was later moved to the Israel Museum, overseen by a board of eight trustees. However, of the original 487 leaves, only 295 leaves remain. Only the last six chapters of the *Humash* (the Torah) are accounted for. Also several chapters and even complete books are missing from the remainder of the *Tanach*. The first leaf that exists today is the leaf that contains the beginning of the Admonition (*Debarim* 28:15), describing the evil which will befall the Jewish people if they do not observe the Torah. The events surrounding the damage to the *Keter* are apparently a fulfillment of that dire warning.

The first leaf that exists today is the leaf that contains the beginning of the Admonition (Debarim 28:15), describing the evil which will befall the Jewish people if they do not observe the Torah. The events surrounding the damage to the Keter are apparently a fulfillment of that dire warning.

In a personal letter dated December 13, 1959, President Ben-Zvi expressed his deep appreciation to Mr. Faham, acknowledging the effort and sacrifice involved in rescuing the *Keter* at great risk, and without the expectation of material reward. A corresponding plaque was prepared for display with the *Keter*. The plaque summarizes the objective of Mr. Faham's mission as he understood it, simply "to bring it to the holy city of Jerusalem."

Controversy and Resolution

After the *Keter* was turned over to President Ben-Zvi, a storm of controversy broke out in the Aleppo community in Israel, many of whose leading members insisted that the *Keter* should have been placed in the hands of R' Yitzhak Dayan (see #208), a respected expatriate of Aram Soba. At the insistence of Hacham David-Sion Laniado (see #352) the following notice was issued in 1958 by three leading rabbis, who had been personally involved in safeguarding the *Keter* while it was still in Aram Soba:

> "Hear, O kings, and give ear, O lords, the representatives of the faithful of Israel. We certify that our holy *Keter* was originally sent [with the understanding] that it be turned over to the great rabbi, R' Yitzhak Dayan, only and to no one else, so that it would remain in fully qualified custody under [his] kingly authority. [Editor's note: The Dayan family traces its roots back to King David as described under *Tracing the Dayan Lineage*, in the Biographies section (page 155). Thus, R' Yitzhak was considered to bear the mantle of "kingly authority."]
>
> "No son of Israel is permitted to convey it to the custodianship of anyone else. Anyone who deviates [from this directive] is doing wrong. We resist and protest [such actions] with all our strength ...".

The notice was signed by R' Moshe Tawil (see #586), R' Shelomo Zafrani (see #598), and R' Yomtob J. Yedid (who was later to become Chief Rabbi after the departure of R' Moshe Tawil to Jerusalem). It was issued under the auspices of the *Bet Din* of the Aram Soba community and was sent out to leading rabbis in New York and Brazil.

Subsequently, a brief was filed with the official *Rabbinical Bet Din* of Jerusalem arguing that the *Keter* should be returned to representatives of the Aleppo community, who was its rightful owner. Mr. Menachem Yedid, youngest son of R' Yomtob Yedid (see #593), and founder of *Moreshet Aram Soba* (the Aleppo Heritage Center), who was involved in the case, related that the community was so sure of winning the suit that they had already built a concrete enclosure adjacent to the *hechal* in a synagogue of the Aleppo community in Tel Aviv. During this time R' Yitzhak Dayan, the previously designated custodian, left Israel to join his children in New York and Brazil. In his place the community designated the lawyer Meir Laniado, the president of the Aleppine community in Israel, to represent the community's interests in the litigation.

Subsequently, a brief was filed with the official Rabbinical Bet Din of Jerusalem arguing that the Keter should be returned to representatives of the Aleppo community, who were its rightful owner.

After close to three years of deliberation, a compromise was reached and a ruling was issued by the *Bet Din on* May 23, 1962. The ruling was signed by the head of the *Bet Din*, R' Eliezer Yehudah Waldenberg, and by the associate *dayanim* (judges), R' Ovadiah Yosef and R' Yosef Kappah. The document was also signed by President Yitzhak Ben-Zvi and Meir Laniado representing the two parties involved in the litigation.

It was agreed that although the *Keter* rightfully belonged to the Aleppine community, the interests of safety and security over the long term would best be served if the *Keter* remained where it was. To ensure that the interests of all affected parties were protected, the *Keter* would be held in the custody of the Israeli Museum Society, under the supervision of an eight-man committee, chaired by the president of Israel, and with the participation of the *Rishon LeSion*, the Sephardic Chief Rabbi of Israel (at that time R' Yitzhak Nissim). Of the remaining six members, four were to be of Aleppine descent. The original four were R' Abraham Antebi, head the *Bet Din* of Aram Soba in Jerusalem, Meir Laniado, R' Moshe Tawil, and R' Shelomo Zafrani. The original members have all since passed away and the current Aleppine members are Hacham Yehudah Ades, Hacham Yaakob Attiah, Mr. Edmond Cohen, and Mr. Menachem Yedid. In 1987 Moshe and Joseph Faham, the sons of Mr. Mordechai Faham, were added to the list of trustees, so that it effectively became a ten-man board, of which six members are of Syrian origin.

The participants committed themselves to the security of the *Keter* as a sacred object, never to be sold, redeemed, or exchanged, and never to be transferred out of the precincts of the Ben-Zvi Institute in Jerusalem. It was also agreed that any profits and proceeds arising from the exhibition of the *Keter* or the production of copies of the *Keter* would be assigned for the benefit of Aleppine organizations in Israel. [However, according to one source, no profits have ever been distributed.]

MR. MORDECHAI FAHAM, SAVIOR OF THE KETER

[Based on information provided by his sons Moshe and Joseph Faham]

Mr. Mordechai Faham

Mr. Mordechai Faham was an example of the worthy Syrian layman of yesteryear with a strong personality and even stronger *emunah* (faith). The verse, *"Na'aseh v'nishma,"* "We will do and we will obey" (*Shemot* 24:7), describes him best. Besides actually smuggling the *Keter* out of Syria, his sons relate that on the tragic day of Arab rioting in 1947, which destroyed many Jewish homes and synagogues, among them the Great Synagogue, he was the first to go out to check on the outcome of the riots. He dressed as a Bedouin and went into the synagogue, found the *Keter* on the floor, and saved it from the flames. He immediately gave it to the *shamosh* (caretaker) of the synagogue, Asher Baghdedi, who subsequently gave it to the Chief Rabbi at the time, R' Moshe Mizrahi (see #424).

He immediately gave it to the shamosh (caretaker) of the synagogue, Asher Baghdedi, who subsequently gave it to the Chief Rabbi at the time, R' Moshe Mizrahi (see #424).

In the 1950's, he was one of those in charge of the funds to be distributed for charitable causes. At one point, two men of the community wanted to use the money for their private use. Mr. Faham refused, and these unscrupulous men reported him to the authorities, claiming that he was smuggling Jews out of Syria to Israel. He was actually involved in saving many Syrian Jews at the time and many of their descendants have come to the Faham family in America to thank them.

As a consequence, he was put in prison and was tortured for a full week. The police wanted to know the names of the people he smuggled out and who else from the Jewish community was involved. He refused to talk and they tortured him mercilessly. Luckily, he had Iranian citizenship so they were afraid to kill him and in the end they dropped him off at his house, looking like a lifeless sack of bones.

After three months of constant care in the hospital, he was rehabilitated, but lost a major portion of his eyesight. The government wanted to exile him immediately but with the help of the Iranian ambassador in Damascus he managed to delay his departure for two years. Then one day, he and his wife were informed that they had 24 hours to leave the country. They packed their basic necessities, took their four children ages 4 to 12, and, accompanied by police detectives till they reached the border, were exiled to Turkey. Traveling through the snowy mountains of Turkey and Iran for four days, they reached Teheran, alone and penniless.

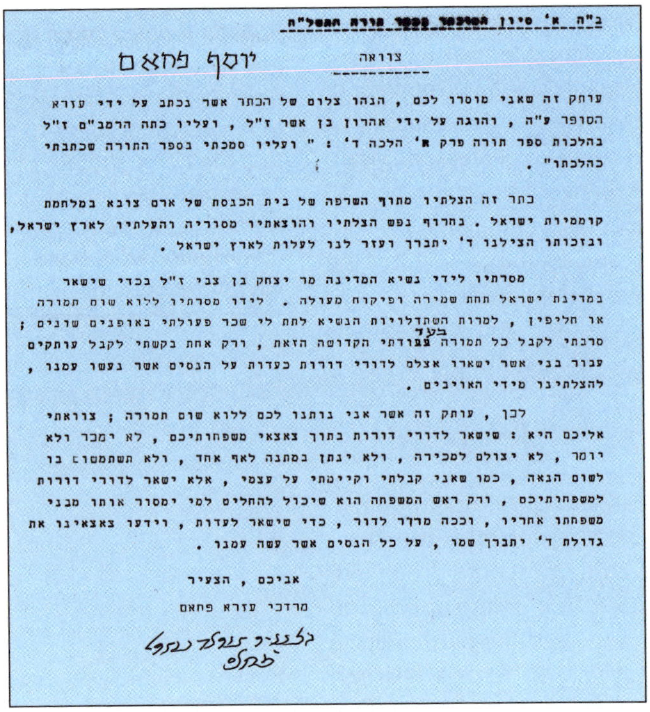

ב"ה א' סיון [illegible] התשל"ח

יוסף פחאם

צוואה

עותק זה שאני מוסרו לכם , הנהו צלום של הכתר אשר נכתב על ידי עזרא הסופר ע"ה , והוגה על ידי אהרון בן אשר ז"ל , ועליו כתב הרמב"ם ז"ל בהלכות ספר תורה פרק א' הלכה ד' : " ועליו סמכתי בספר התורה שכתבתי כהלכתו" .

כתר זה הצלתיו מתוך השרפה של בית הכנסת של ארם צובא במלחמת קוממיות ישראל . בחרוף נפש הצלתיו והוצאתיו מסוריה והעלתיו לארץ ישראל, ובזכותו הצילנו ד' יתברך ועזר לנו לעלות לארץ ישראל .

מסרתיו לידי נשיא המדינה מר יצחק בן צבי ז"ל בכדי שישאר במדינת ישראל תחת שמירה ופיקוח מעולה . לידו מסרתיו ללוא שום תמורה או חליפין , למרות השתדלויות הנשיא לתת לי שכר פעולתי באופנים שונים ; סרבתי לקבל כל תמורה בעד עבודתי הקדושה הזאת , ורק אחת בקשתי לקבל עותקים עבור בני אשר ישארו אצלם לדורי דורות כעדות על הנסים אשר נעשו עמנו , להצלתינו מידי האויבים .

לכן , עותק זה אשר אני נותנו לכם ללוא שום תמורה ; צוואתי אליכם היא : שישאר לדורי דורות בתוך צאצאי משפחותיכם , לא ימכר ולא יומר , לא יצולם למכירה , ולא ינתן במתנה לאף אחד , ולא תשתמשו בו לשום הנאה , כמו שאני קבלתי וקיימתי על עצמי , אלא ישאר לדורי דורות למשפחותיכם , ורק ראש המשפחה הוא שיכול להחליט למי ימסור אותו מבני משפחתו אחריו , וככה מדור לדור , כדי שישאר לעדות , ויודע צאצאינו את גדולת ד' יתברך שמו , על כל הנסים אשר עשה עמנו .

אביכם , הצעיר

מרדכי עזרא פחאם

Letter from Mr. Mordechai Faham with instructions on not taking personal benefit from the Keter

In Iran Mr. Faham was strongly advised to go to Israel or to America, but refused. He was adamant about returning to Syria to get the rest of his possessions. Finally, after 15 months of persistence and much hardship, he was granted a visa to return for three months. However, when he finally arrived in Syria, he was unable to find a buyer for his properties or collect his debts. The Syrian government had apparently defamed him as a Zionist traitor, therefore no one would buy from him.

Mr. Faham answered, "Now I understand why G-d put it in my head to return, seemingly for no reason. All that has happened to me is from Heaven. I realize the danger I am putting myself and family into, and I am ready and willing."

At the end of his stay in Syria, as he was preparing to leave, he was secretly approached by R' Moshe Tawil (see #586), the Chief Rabbi of Aram Soba at that time. R' Tawil explained that he had an important but highly dangerous mission involving the *Keter* of Ezra HaSofer. At the risk of his life, Mr. Faham was now being asked to smuggle the *Keter* to safety out of Syria. Mr. Faham answered, "Now I understand why G-d put it in my head to return, seemingly for no reason. All that has happened to me is from Heaven. I realize the danger I am putting myself and family into, and I am ready and willing." At this point R' Shelomo Zafrani (see #598) was called over and he agreed that the *Keter* should be entrusted to Mr. Faham for this mission.

To whom was Mr. Faham instructed to give the *Keter*? Years later when he recounted the story of this fateful day, he recalled that they left it up to his own discretion, saying, "You are free to give it to whomever you choose."

Mr. Faham eagerly took upon himself the dangerous mission of getting the *Keter* out of Syria. He brought the *Keter* home and Mrs. Faham wrapped it in cloth, hiding it among their household items. When they reached the border, the customs officer started to open up the baggage ropes and happened to choose the bale of household items containing the *Keter*. Immediately Mr. Faham approached the officer and grabbed his hand with such strength that the officer screamed in pain. The border police heard the commotion and the officer in charge came out to see what was happening. Mr. Faham said, "I came to Syria with permission to take out my personal belongings. How dare this officer search through my personal belongings?" The supervisor called the main office in Damascus and the reply was, "If you are referring to the infamous Faham the Zionist, send him out of the country immediately."

When Mr. Faham arrived in Israel, he presented the *Keter* to President Yitzhak Ben-Zvi for safekeeping. Mr. Ben-Zvi was a noted authority on Middle Eastern Jewry and had a lifelong obsession with the *Keter*. Mr. Faham felt that the *Keter* belonged to the entire Jewish people and that its security could best be assured with the president of Israel. The government offered him all kinds of financial benefits, including loans, housing, and job opportunities. They even wanted to name a street after him, but Mr. Faham refused everything. Years later the government presented each of his children with a copy of the *Keter*. At that time, he ordered them not to take any benefit directly or indirectly from the *Keter*. The trials and tribulations that he had experienced were all part of *Hashem's* ultimate plan to save the *Keter*, and were not meant for personal gain.

NEW EVIDENCE ON THE AUTHENTICITY OF THE KETER

Recently, in 2003, a commentary titled *Yesod Mishnah Torah* on the *Rambam* was printed for the first time from the manuscript by R' Yehudah Albotini of Jerusalem. The manuscript was written close to 500 years ago in the year 1515. In his commentary on the laws of *Sifrei Torah* (Torah scrolls) he writes:

"The *Rambam* left all other sources and depended on the *Tanach* that originated in Jerusalem. I, Yehudah the son of Moshe Albotini, have seen this *Tanach* in the synagogue of the community of Aleppo. It is a *sefer* (holy book) written on large parchment and it is written beautifully in *Ashurit* script. I saw many new points there. The leaders of the congregation told me that they have a tradition that Rabbi Abraham, the son of the *Rambam*, and his son, Rabbi David (who is buried in Aleppo), brought the *sefer* there, and with it a manuscript of the *Rambam*'s commentary on the *Mishnah*, together with five or six additional manuscripts of the *Rambam*. I saw all of this with my own eyes when I was in Aleppo. They were placed in one of the *hechals* [repositories for Torah scrolls] of that synagogue. That was the *sefer* the *Rambam* depended on. The entire Jewish nation worldwide, of which we have heard and seen, followed the *Rambam*'s custom on this concerning the opened and closed chapters of the Torah and concerning [the writings in] *tefillin* as the *Rambam* listed in his book so that nothing would be missing from it."

"The Rambam left all other sources and depended on the Tanach that originated in Jerusalem. I, Yehudah the son of Moshe Albotini, have seen this Tanach in the synagogue of the community of Aleppo."

Although most *halachic* authorities today agree to the authenticity of the *Keter* they do not agree that one should change the age-old customs of writing *Nebi'im* or *Ketubim* based on the *Keter*. In the year 2003 Rabbi Tzvi Goldberg of Jerusalem published a small book titled *Masoratenu* (*Our Tradition*), in which he goes on at length to prove the validity of the traditions other than the *Keter* and cites letters from many *halachic* authorities. See the Document Section (Document No. 16) for a letter on this issue by Rabbi Reuven Feinstein, *Rosh Yeshiva* of the Staten Island Yeshiva and son of Rav Moshe Feinstein.

Mission to Aram Soba

In the following extracts from the book *Amudei Shesh* (Jerusalem 1891), R' Shmuel Shlomo Boyarski of Grodno describes how he sent an emissary to Aram Soba to study the authoritative format for presenting the text of the *Ketubim* (*Writings* portion of the *Tanach*).

A similar mission is described by R' Yaakov Safir in his book *Even Safir* (1866).

R' Shmuel Shlomo Boyarski of Grodno describes how he sent an emissary to Aram Soba to study the authoritative format for presenting the text of the Ketubim.

> "My wife, who was childless, was tireless in her efforts to get me to come here to the Holy City of Jerusalem. With impressive dedication she wrote a beautiful *Sefer Torah, Nebi'im,* and *Ketubim*, to be a merit for her and to be an everlasting memorial. I myself helped her in everything, to fulfill the *Midrash* mentioned by the *Magen Abraham* (Section 155): "If a person does not do a *mitzvah* that he has put in place for the ages, what good is he?"

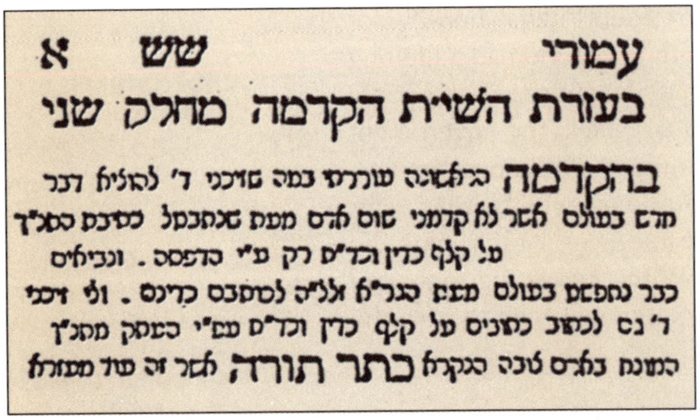

עמודי שש א
בעזרת השי"ת הקדמה מחלק שני
בהקדמה הראשונה שכתבתי במה שזיכני ד' להוציא דבר
חדש בעולם אשר לא קדמני שום אדם מעת שנתבטל כתיבת הנ"ך
על קלף כדין וכד"ת רק ע"י הדפוס . ונביאים
כבר נתפשט בעולם מעת הגר"א אליה לכתבם כדינם . ולי זכני
ד' גם לכתוב כתובים על קלף כדין וכד"ת עפ"י העתק מהנ"ך
המונח בארם צובה הנקרא כתר תורה, אשר זה עוד מעזרא

Introduction Page to Amudei Shesh, Volume II

"And then I got the idea of doing something innovative, something which no man has done since the printing press was invented and the practice of writing the *Tanach* on parchment as prescribed by Jewish law fell into disuse. In recent times (since the days of the *Vilna Gaon*) Jews again began writing the *Nebi'im* [Prophets] on parchment according to the law. The *Minhat Shai* [an expert on the *masoretic* traditions of the Scriptures] balanced and corrected the practices of scribes as to where to write *petuhot* [open paragraph endings having clear space to the end of the line] and *setumot* [closed paragraph endings in which the next paragraph starts on the same line], the *k'ri* [word pronunciations different from the text as written] and the *ketiv* [written version], and the like. Nevertheless, he refrained from correcting the *Ketubim* because in the *Gemara* (*Masechet Sofrim*) it states that the *Ketubim* are written as a song [text arranged in a visual pattern], but it was not known to him if the text is to be presented column by column [a nine-letter separation in the middle of each line forming a blank space down the center of the entire column] or tile on brick [nine-letter gaps spaced so that they appear like half bricks set over whole bricks].

"And then I heard that in Aram Soba there is a *Tanach* of the *Keter Torah* written by Ben-Asher, which the *Rambam* used as a proof-reading guide when writing a Torah scroll, and which goes back to Ezra HaSofer. (I have published information about it at length in the book *Shaarei Sion*, which can be acquired in Jerusalem, and I copied the introduction of the *Keter Torah* there and I added my own Torah thoughts.) Therefore, I took courage and sent a man to Aram Soba to copy instructions on how the *Ketubim* are written in song format, and thanks be to Hashem, the mission was successful. Thus, I wrote the text on parchment according to the *halachah* and I placed it in the great synagogue, which is in the ruin of R' Yehudah HaHasid."

Amudei Shesh, Introduction to Volume I

"And then I heard that in Aram Soba there is a Tanach of the Keter Torah written by Ben-Asher, which the Rambam used as a proof-reading guide when writing a Torah scroll, and which goes back to Ezra HaSofer.

Therefore, I took courage and sent a man to Aram Soba to copy instructions on how the Ketubim are written in song format, and thanks be to Hashem, the mission was successful. Thus, I wrote the text on parchment according to the halachah and I placed it in the great synagogue, which is in the ruin of R' Yehudah HaHasid."

"The *Minhat Shai* also explained in his introduction that he did not know exactly how the text for *Ketubim* should be written as a song [text arranged in a visual pattern]. Therefore, he did not make a distinction between *Ketubim* and other holy scriptures.

"Accordingly, I have considered it a matter of 'a time to act for Hashem' [that is, to act in a daring manner]. I only hope that when people see what I have done, they will accept it. And even though I already have *Tanach* copies needed for learning, I wrote out the *Sefer Torah, Nebi'im,* and *Ketubim* on parchment according to the *halachah*, consistent with the copy from the *Keter Torah*, which is in Aram Soba.

"The *Gemara* (*Moed Katan* 9a) cites the verse in *Mishlei* (5:6), 'Lest you weigh the path of life, so that its courses wander astray' [implying that when a person is presented with the opportunity to do many *mitzvot*, he should not pick and choose among them]. The *Gemara* explains that this is referring to a situation when no other qualified person is available to perform a *mitzvah* that needs to be done. Surely that applies to this *mitzvah* which others don't do at all ...

"The worthy and upright R' Moshe Yehoshua Kimhi of Bialistok was inspired to travel to Aram Soba with the *Tanach* that he had annotated and had been given to him by his father-in-law, the great grammarian of our generation, R' Shachna of Skidol, to proofread it against the *Keter Torah* from beginning to end. He wanted to know how many questionable points it contained in regard to *petuhot* and *setumot*, the separations between one section and another, writing the text as a song, and many other such issues, as it is written (*Yerushalmi Berachot* 86), '"*These are the mitzvot*" (*Vayikra* 27:34), You shall do them as they are commanded and if not, they are not a *mitzvah*.' The *Tanach* may be found in the Holy City of Jerusalem and anyone who has a question to ask about the *Masorah*, great or small, may apply in writing to the *Gaon*, R' Shmuel Salant, and his request will be fulfilled."

Amudei Shesh, Volume II, pages 2b-3a

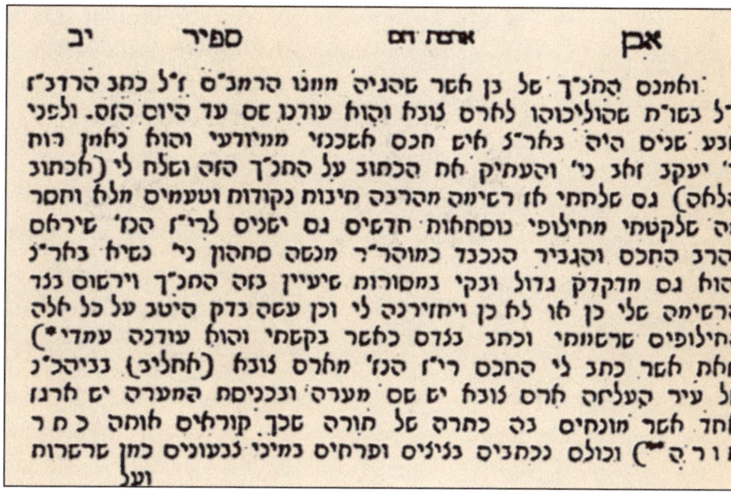
אבן ארחת חיים ספיר יב

ואמנם התנ"ך של בן אשר שהגיה ממנו הרמב"ם ז"ל כתב הרדב"ז
ז"ל בשו"ת שהוליכוהו לארם צובא והוא עודנו שם עד היום הזה. ולפני
שבע שנים היה באר"צ איש חכם אשכנזי ממיודעי והוא נאמן רוח
ר' יעקב זאב נ"י והעתיק את הכתוב על התנ"ך הזה ושלח לי (אכתוב
באלה) גם שלחתי או רשימה מהרבה תיבות נקודות וטעמים מלא וחסר
מה שלקטתי מחילופי נוסחאות חדשים גם ישנים לרי"ז הנז' שיראם
להרב החכם והגביר הנכבד כמוהר"ר מנשה סתהון נ"י נשיא באר"צ
והוא גם מדקדק גדול ובקי במסורות שיעיין בזה התנ"ך וירשום נגד
הרשימה שלי כן או לא כן ויחזירנה לי וכן עשה בדק היטב על כל אלה
החילופים שרשמתי וכתב נגדם כאשר בקשתי והוא עודנה עמדי*)
וזאת אשר כתב לי החכם רי"ז הנז' מארם צובא (אחלי"ב) בביהכ"נ
של עיר העליזה ארם צובא יש שם מערה ובכניסת המערה יש ארגז
אחד אשר מונחים בה כתרה של תורה שכך קוראים אותה כ ת ר
ת ו ר ה**) וכולם נכתבים בציצים ופרחים במיני צבעונים כמין שרשרות
ועל

Sample Page from Even Safir

"In the first Introduction I remarked that *Hashem* has granted me the merit of producing something new, something that no man has done since the practice of writing the *Tanach* on parchment according to the *halachah* fell into disuse and was replaced by printing. Indeed, the practice of writing the *Nebi'im* according to the law had already spread throughout the Jewish world since the time of the *Vilna Gaon*. But to me has fallen the opportunity from *Hashem* to write the *Ketubim* on parchment as proofed from the *Tanach* that lies in Aram Soba, the one called *Keter Torah*, which goes back to Ezra."

Amudei Shesh, Introduction to Volume II

"Indeed, with reference to the *Tanach* of Ben-Asher, which the *Rambam* used as a proofreading reference, the *Radvaz* wrote in his *Responsa* that they brought it to Aram Soba and it is still there until this very day. Seven years ago there was in Aram Soba an Ashkenazi scholar, by the name of R' Yaakov Zev, who was personally known to me as a trustworthy man of faith. He proofed the *Tanach* [which I am presenting here] against that reference. At that time I also sent to R' Yaakov Zev my notes concerning various alternatives of vowelization, cantillation, and pronunciation that I gathered from various formats new and old. I asked that he show my notes to the great and scholarly rabbi, the distinguished and respected R' Menashe Sutton [see #551], a leader of Aram Soba, who is also an accomplished grammarian and expert on the *Masorah*, that he should examine this *Tanach* and annotate my notes as to his agreement or disagreement with each point, and return it to me, and so he did. He carefully examined all these alternatives which I noted and wrote next to them as I asked and his response is still in my possession.

"I asked that he show my notes to the great and scholarly rabbi, the distinguished and respected R' Menashe Sutton [see #551], a leader of Aram Soba, who is also an accomplished grammarian and expert on the Mesorah, that he should examine this Tanach and annotate my notes as to his agreement or disagreement with each point, and return it to me, and so he did."

"And this is what the above-mentioned scholar R' Yaakov Zev wrote to me from Aram Soba: In the synagogue of the glorious city of Aram Soba there is a cave and in the entrance to the cave there is a cabinet in which the *Keter* rests. It is called the *Keter Torah* and is elaborately inscribed with blossoms and flowers in many colors and decorative emblems."

Even Safir, Volume I

In recent years, some secular scholars have raised questions about the authenticity of the *Keter Aram Soba* (the Aleppo Codex). In response, R' David Yitzhaki has written a book, titled *Nebiyei Emet V'Sedek,* to refute the arguments of the skeptics and to demonstrate the contrary. His work received a letter of approbation from two great rabbis of Aram Soba involved in the rescue of the *Keter*, including a description of its final days. A translation of the letter is provided below. (See Document Section, Document No. 15 for a translation of this letter.)

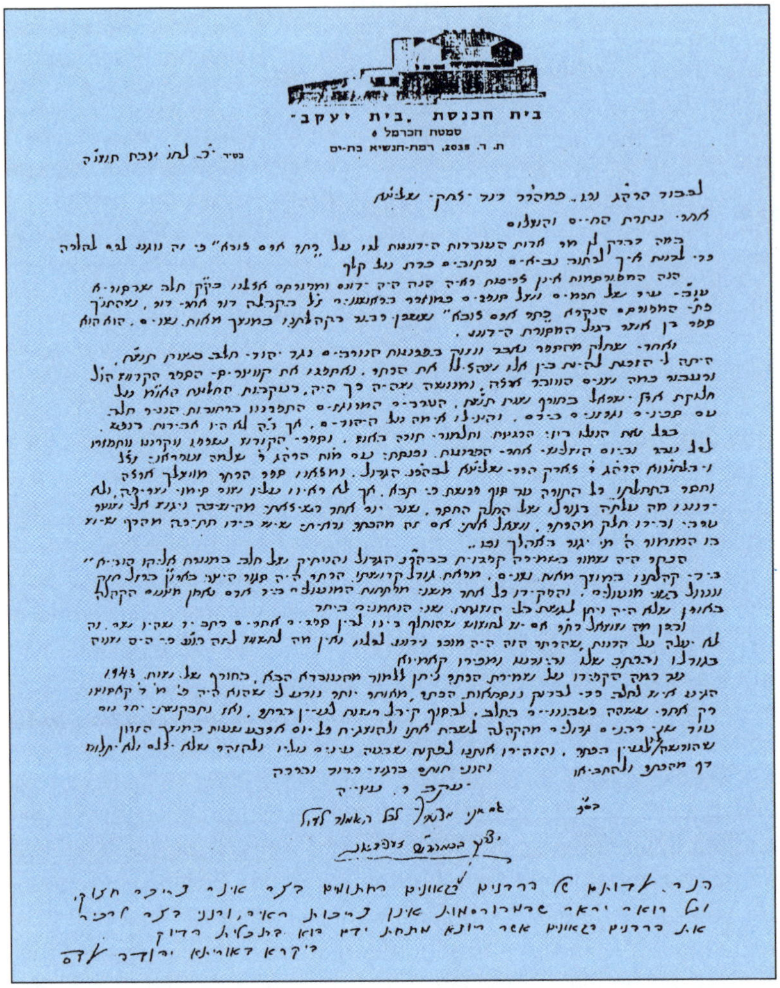
בית הכנסת "בית יעקב"
סמטת הכרמל 6
ת. ד. 2038, רמת-הנשיא בת-ים

Letter from Rabbi Yaakob Attiah on Authenticity of the Keter (1995)

The Curse of the Keter. Mr. Joseph A.D.Sutton in his work Aleppo Chronicles (page 472) quotes the following story concerning the *Keter*: "The Codex remained in safety and undisturbed in Aleppo for centuries. In recent years (circa 1946) a coup d'etat had taken place in Damascus, the national capital. One of the deposed cabinet officers was a Muslim Allepine, and fearful for his life he fled the country — with the *Keter*, which he had stolen. Subsequently an amnesty was declared, the cabinet member was assured of immunity and returned to Syria, with the *Keter*, which he restored to the Jewish community. However, he was speedily tried for treason, and soon hanged; fulfilling a part of the curse against possible theft of the *Keter*."

Mr. Amnon Shamosh in his book *The Keter* (page 45) quotes a response from Mr. Joseph Sutton concerning the source of the above story." All the information that I have concerning the *Keter* comes from the most reliable source possible — Mr Mordechai Faham."

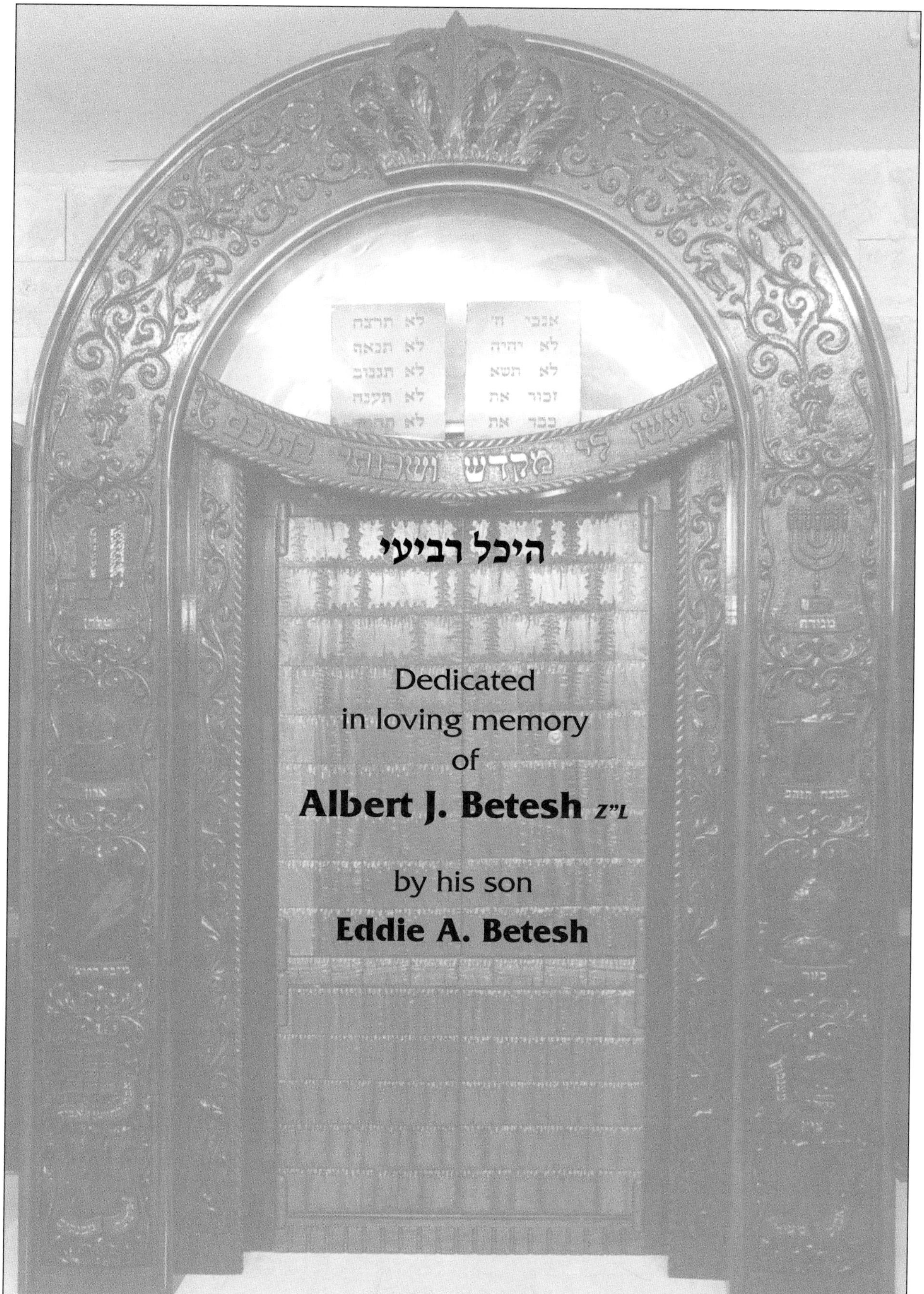

היכל רביעי

Dedicated
in loving memory
of

Albert J. Betesh *Z"L*

by his son

Eddie A. Betesh

Section Four

RELIGIOUS LIFE IN ARAM SOBA

SCHOLARS AND RABBIS

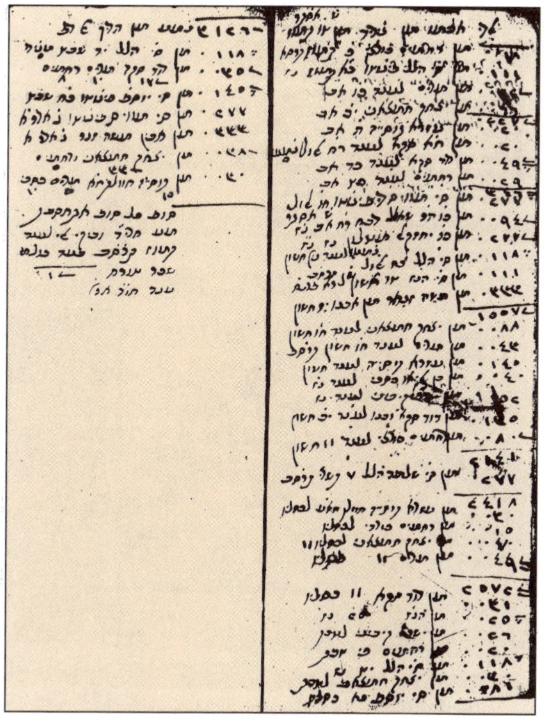

List of donors for stipends to scholars

The scholars and rabbis of Aram Soba were ranked in three major groupings. At the top were the Chief Rabbi and the *dayanim* (judges) of the *Bet Din* (religious court) at whose head was the *Av Bet Din* (senior judge). At times the Chief Rabbi and Av *Bet Din* were the same person. At other times, they were separate individuals, especially during those periods when the Chief Rabbi (*Hacham Bashi*) was appointed by the Ottoman governor.

The second group consisted of rabbis and administrators who were engaged by the community to perform various duties in the synagogues and study halls (*Batei Midrashim)* of the city. The third group consisted of individuals who devoted themselves to Torah study, but who did not have an official position.

Most of the scholars and rabbis in all three groups received some level of support from the communal budget, with the specific amount of their stipend depending upon the individual's position and scholarly abilities. These funds, which came from the taxes levied on the community, were often insufficient and many scholars existed in conditions of great hardship. For that reason, individual donors took it upon themselves to provide support to worthy scholars. In other cases, special charitable funds were set up to support designated numbers of scholars.

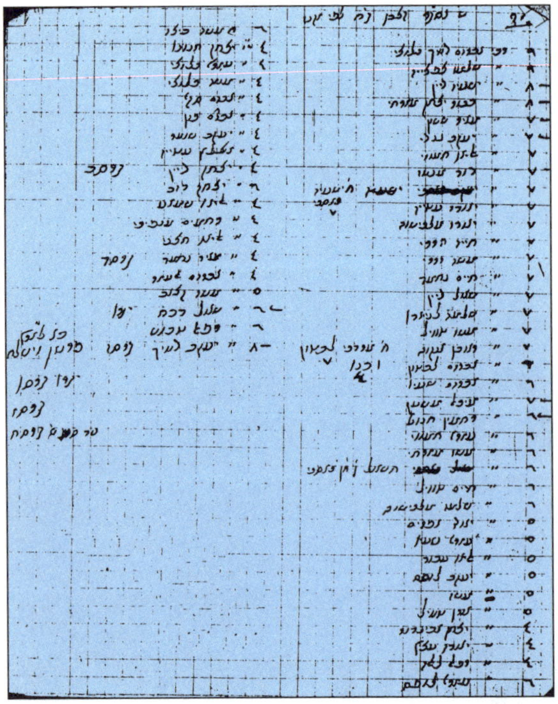

List of scholars receiving stipends See Document Section, Document #30.

Besides the central yeshiva of the city, individual philanthropists set up private *yeshivot* in their homes, where they provided libraries of holy books and financial support to scholars. In some cases a wealthy individual would engage a "court rabbi" to teach Torah and give spiritual guidance to the members of his family.

Notable rabbis from Europe, passing through Aram Soba, expressed astonishment at the extent and quality of Torah study in the community. According to some observers the high level of Aram Soba scholarship was attributable to the high level of respect that its scholars received from the general populace and especially to the financial support of its well-to-do citizens.

As a center of great Torah scholarship, Aram Soba's influence extended throughout the region and especially to the nearby towns: Tedef, Ein Tab, Kilis, Idlib, and Urfa.

BOOK PUBLISHING

The scholars of Aram Soba became attracted to the great benefits of book publishing almost as soon as the the first printing presses were invented in the 15th century. So many handwritten manuscripts had been lost over the centuries. Now, once the *hiddushim* (original Torah thoughts) of a scholar were captured on the printed page, they became immortal. The possibility of getting their intellectual creations published became a great incentive for books to be written and many scholars devoted their lives to authoring books and getting them published.

Arabic translation of Haggadah printed in Aleppo in 5656 (1895)

Until the middle of the 19th century Aram Soba's rabbis published their books abroad, primarily in Livorno (Italy), Salonika (Greece), and Constantinople (Turkey). This often involved dangerous travel over long distances and meant that the author might be away from home for years at a time. When the manuscripts were entrusted to others, they were often lost to such dangers as robbers and shipwrecks. The cost of printing a book also presented a great challenge to its author. Some authors were forced to sell all of their possessions to raise the necessary funds. Others were able to persuade generous individuals to help defray printing costs.

In 1865 R' Abraham Sasson (see #475) and his sons opened the first Jewish printing press in Aram Soba. From that time Aram Soba itself became an important center for printing Hebrew books. To help R' Sasson protect his investment, the rabbis of Aram Soba issued an official endorsement of the new venture, prohibiting anyone from starting a competing press over a period of 20 years. (See Document Section, Document No. 25.) However, despite the ambitious hopes of its founder, the Sasson printing house remained in operation for only eight years during which time 14 books were printed. Of these, seven were by Aram Soba authors.

R' Yeshayah Dayan (see #203) opened another printing press in 1887 but because of the difficulty in getting licensing, the publishing initiative was begun in secrecy without the blessing of the Turkish government. Accordingly, it was operated for a time on an intermittent basis because of the fear of discovery. For this reason, the name of the printer is missing from many of the books. Altogether 27 books were printed by the Dayan Press (original editions). Of these, eight were Arabic translations from the Hebrew.

From 1910 to 1933 R' Ezra Haim Jouegati of Damascus operated a press. He learned his craft over a four-year period with Eliezer Ben-Yehudah in Jerusalem. Production of books in this period was hampered by the departure of many scholars from Aram Soba to Jerusalem and elsewhere. The press continued on a small scale in secrecy during the 1980's. Altogether 14 books were printed, of which five were financial reports of the *Sedakah U'Marpeh* organization and two were prayer books.

Another printing press was founded by R' Ezra Bijou in 1924 and continued until 1925. In the 1940's an additional press was operated by R' Yosef Sutton. This was the first press in Aram Soba to use modern printing equipment. In fact, R' Yosef had to send his son to France to learn how to operate it. Both the Bijou and Sutton presses produced mainly prayer books and the financial reports of philanthropic organizations.

TALMUD TORAH SCHOOLS

[Based on the writings of R' Yitzhak Zafrani]

Introduction

There were many Talmud Torah schools in Aram Soba, but attendance was affected by economic conditions. Many parents not only couldn't pay school tuition for a child, they couldn't forgo the monthly income that his work would bring in. In many families, only one child received a full formal education while the others had to work to support the family.

The Orphanage Home of Aram Soba in the Bahsita neighborhood included a Talmud Torah (called *Kitab* in Arabic), which was under the direction of Hacham Rahamim Mizrahi (see #426).There was also a General Talmud Torah in the same neighborhood and another in the Jamileyé neighborhood. All of these worthy institutions were destroyed by rampaging Arab mobs during the riots of 1947 and 1948.

The Orphanage Home band

During the early 20th century, the General Talmud Torah of Aram Soba served about 1000 students, mostly from the middle-and lower-income groups. The principal was Hacham Moshe Safdeyé Bawabeh. He was succeeded in 1930 by R' Yitzhak Chehebar (see #152), who was later to become the Chief Rabbi of Argentina. In 1943 the school was visited by Janet Ben-Zvi, the wife of the second president of Israel. In her book, *BiShelichut LeLebanon VeSuria*, she gave a glowing description of the Talmud Torah and her impressions. The school was housed in a building of broad dimensions, surrounded by beautiful gardens and fruit orchards. The fragrance of the fruit blossoms pervaded the entire Talmud Torah. She described the principal, R' Yitzhak Chehebar, as a young man who had achieved his position through his own efforts. She found him to be both pious and intellectual. In the school she saw hundreds of students. The teachers were generally the product of local institutions. The course of study was that of the traditional *heder* (private school) system, with text of the Torah translated word by word into Arabic.

General Talmud Torah

In addition, there were a number of small private schools in nearby courtyards. Among these were the Talmud Torah of Hacham Yaakob Janani, the Talmud Torah of Hacham Aboud Ashkenazi-Kilzi, the Talmud Torah of Hacham Yosef Mamiyé, and the Talmud Torah of Hacham Eliyahu Antakli.

Smaller Schools

An additional Talmud Torah, called *Magen David*, existed in Aram Soba for a time. It was located in the Bahsita neighborhood and was established in memory of Señora Sarah Anzaroot. The first-grade class was taught by Hacham Yitzhak Dishi. Other grades were taught by Hacham Yosef Ashkenazi, Hacham Nissim Shasho, and Hacham Haim Turjeman. The highest class was taught by Hacham Yitzhak Chehebar (see #152).

Rules of the Talmud Torah, circa 1900

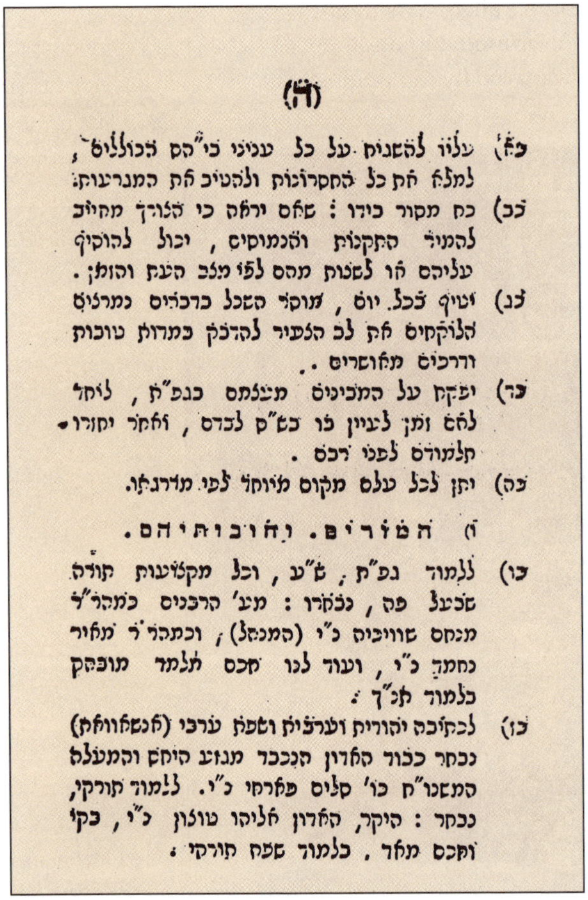

(ה)

כא) עליו להשגיח על כל ענייני בי"הס הכולליים, למלא את כל החסרונות ולהטיב את המגרעות:

כב) כח מסור בידו: שאם יראה כי הצורך מחייב להמיר התקנות והמנהגים, יוכל להוסיף עליהם או לשנות מהם לפי מצב העת והזמן.

כג) יטיף בכל יום, מוסר השכל בדברים נמרצים הלוקחים את לב הצעיר להדבק במדות טובות ודרכים מאושרים.

כד) יפקח על המכינים מעלתם כגפ"ת, לייחד להם זמן לעיין בו בש"ס לבדם, ואחר יחזרו תלמודם לפני רבם.

כה) יתן לכל אחד מקום מיוחד לפי מדרגתו.

ו) המורים. וחובותיהם.

כו) ללמוד גפ"ת, ש"ע, וכל מקצועות תורה שבעל פה, נבחרו: מע' הרבנים כמהר"ר מנחם שוויכה נ"י (המכהן), וכמהר"ר מאיר נחמד נ"י, ועוד לנו חכם תלמד מופלא בלמוד תנ"ך:

כז) לכתיבה יהודית וערבית ושפת ערבי (אנשאווחת) נבחר כבוד האדון הנכבד מגזע היחס והמעלה המשכו"ח כו' סלים פארחי נ"י. ללמוד תורקי, נבחר: היקר, האדון אליהו טובון נ"י, בקי וחכם מאד. בלמוד שפת תורקי:

Originally, the schools taught only religious subjects, including reading, *nekidah* (pointing of Hebrew vowel marks), writing, and a little Arabic. Writing was done in an ancient Syrian-Hebrew script, using a half-quill.

Curriculum

In later years the curriculum was expanded to include the Arabic and French languages. A consideration in making this change was to prevent students from being recruited by the Alliance Schools (see below). The Orphanage Home Talmud Torah also provided courses in bookkeeping and music for the older students. Girls were taught sewing, with each girl receiving her own Singer sewing machine. There were also separate dormitories for boys and girls.

Young children were introduced to the schools as soon as they were able to speak and maintain cleanliness. This was generally around the age of 2 or 3. They began with the letters of the *Alef-Bet*, each letter being drawn on a slate, accompanied by sweets. The sweets were then removed and the children were taught to recite the blessings aloud.

Alphabet chart of Syrian-Hebrew script

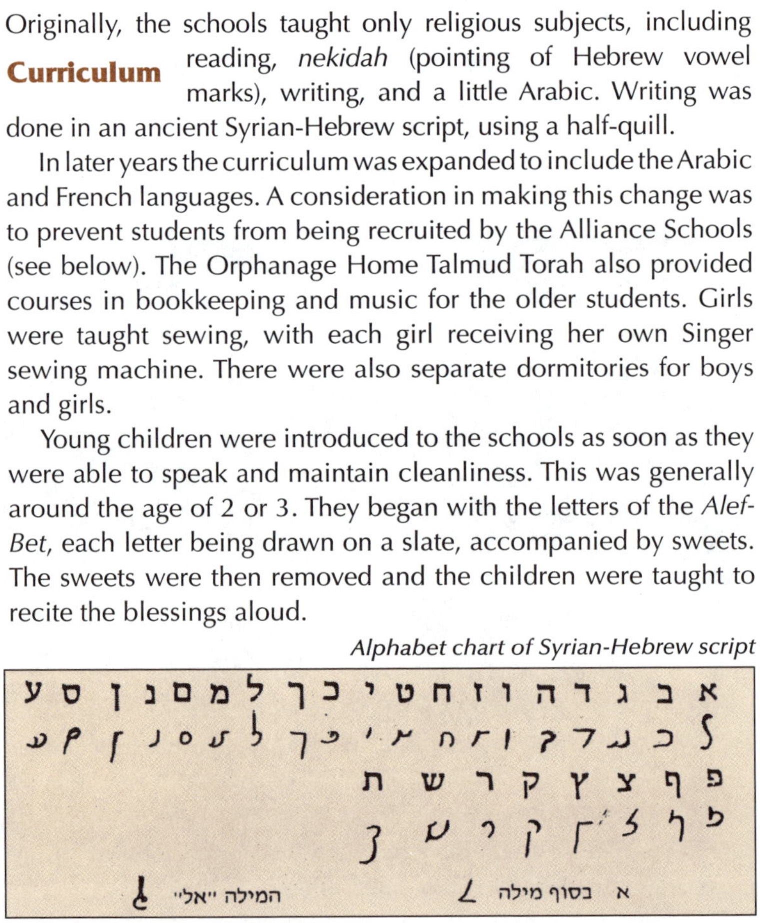

From the age of 7 or 8, children were taught verbatim Arabic translation (referred to as *"Sharah"*) of the Hebrew text. Originally, the translation used was that of R' Saadiah Gaon, who lived in the 10th century. However, R' Moshe Tawil (see #586), who was the principal of the *Degel Torah* yeshiva in Aram Soba, did not agree with this practice. He argued that since the children did not speak the ancient Arabic dialect used by R' Saadiah Gaon (called *"Nahabit"*), it did not help them understand the meaning of what they were reading. He instituted a change to the form of Judeo-Arabic commonly spoken in Syria. His student, R' Yitzhak Chehebar (see #152), continued this approach after he succeeded him.

בתי ספר
תלמוד תורה הכללי
ארם-צובה
مدارس تلمود توراة
حلب - سوريا
חשבון
ההכנסות וההוצאות לשנת
1943

Title page of the Talmud Torah's financial report

YESHIVA DEGEL TORAH

[Based on the writings of R' Yitzhak Zafrani]

Typically, at the age of 10, boys would enter the yeshiva *Degel Torah LeTalmidim*, which was headed by R' Moshe Tawil (see #586). The yeshiva, which he founded in 1921, was located in the building of the *Bet Nasi shul*. On the first floor there was the *Bet Din* (religious court) of the congregation. Above that was the yeshiva, which had about 150 boys. In the first class of the yeshiva, Hacham Shelomo Zafrani (see #598) taught *Gemara* to a group of 30-40 boys each morning. In the afternoon, the students reviewed what they had learned. In the second class, the boys studied *Gemara* in depth. The third-year class was taught by R' Moshe Tawil. Here the students went into even greater depth and covered all of the classic commentaries, including *Maharsha, Maharam, Maharam Shif, Rashba, Ramban*, and *Shitah Mekubetzet.*

All of the grades included studies of *halachah* (religious law) and the practice of writing Torah scrolls, *tefillin*, and *mezuzot*. Aram Soba had a reputation for maintaining the most rigorous standards in the writing of its Torah scrolls. In fact, in later years when over 20 such scrolls were brought to Jerusalem, they were all found to be free of errors.

On Fridays, the boys studied the *perashah* (Torah portion) of the week following the traditional practice of *Shenayim Mikra Ve'Ehad Targum* (reciting the Hebrew text twice and the Aramaic translation once). In addition, on Fridays, the classes were combined for a joint lecture on the week's *perashah* with *Rashi* given by R' Moshe Tawil.

On Friday nights, Hacham Yosef Ashkenazi brought a large group of students from the upper classes to join the *tefillot* in the Great Synagogue. The most qualified of the students were encouraged to give a lecture in which they expounded on a *hiddush* (original Torah thought) from the *perashah*.

The school day in the Talmud Torah and the yeshiva began at 7:30 or 8 a.m. and continued without a break for the entire day, except for lunch. Most boys brought their lunch with them in the morning. Lunch was served in the school to those who could not afford to bring their own.

On Fridays the school day ended two hours before sunset. On *Shabbat*, the boys came back to the school to be examined on what they had learned that week. The examinations began at 11 a.m. and ended late in the afternoon. Among the examiners in the Talmud Torah were R' Yosef Abadi-Shayo (see #507), R' Moshe Shamah, and his brother R' Ezra Shamah. In addition, R' Moshe Tawil came in to conduct examinations in *Talmud*, together with other rabbis.

The available hours on *Motza'e Shabbat* were used for review. The school program continued year-round with no provision for vacation or summer break. However, two days were given off before *Rosh Hashanah* and then again before *Sukkot*.

All students were expected to get up early each morning and participate in the first *minyan* (prayer service) of the day, which began 40 minutes before sunrise. During the days of *Selihot* (special supplications said before the *tefillah* during Elul and the period of the High Holy Days), the synagogue was filled with the Talmud Torah and yeshiva students, all of whom said *Tikkun Hatzot* (the midnight service) before the *Selihot* with great intensity and feeling.

There was no regular course of study in *mussar* (character development). However, during the festivals when the students had some free time, each student was required to commit to the learning of a complete inspirational book such as *Pele Yo'etz, Kab HaYashar, Mesilat Yesharim*, part of *Hovat HaLebabot* and *Shebet Mussar*, an Arabic translation of which had been published in Jerusalem by R' Abraham Dweck (see #216). Before *Rosh Hashanah* each student was required to commit to reciting the entire *Tehillim* over the course of *Rosh Hashanah*.

ALLIANCE SCHOOLS

[Based on the writings of R' Yitzhak Zafrani]

Irreligious Alliance Teachers

In 1869 the *"Kol Yisrael Haverim"* organization (Alliance Israelite Universelle) established a school for boys and in 1889, a school for girls, utilizing European teaching methods. These methods deemphasized religion, which was unfortunately not immediately apparent to all of the rabbis of Aram Soba.

Some rabbis, such as R' Abraham Haim Ades (see #37), realized that the appearance of Alliance leaders as devout Jews was merely superficial, and fiercely resisted their efforts, which were primarily to enroll young children into schools that deemphasized religion and diluted the Jewish identity while replacing spiritual thinking with cultural assimilation.

This course of study included the French language, European history, and other secular subjects. The school managed to attract a small number of students from upper-income families in the Jamileyé neighborhood. The net effect was to diminish religious observance in the members of the student body.

Initially, the school authorities declared that they were also concerned with teaching Torah. They installed six Torah scholars to teach *Tanach* and *Gemarah,* and many parents were optimistic about the new teaching methods. It was only after some years that the community leaders of Aram Soba realized the damage that was being done to their children.

The proportion of time assigned to Torah studies was gradually reduced over the years until it became almost insignificant. In 1901, R' Yaakob Dweck was installed as Chief Rabbi (see #248). He was especially sensitive to the importance of Jewish religious education and took every opportunity to denounce the Alliance schools and to warn parents against sending their children there.

The four schools of the Alliance Israelite Universelle were closed by the government in 1950, and thereafter most of the children studied at a Talmud Torah. As the community dwindled, this school was also closed.

TRADITIONAL EDUCATION

Jewish education in Aram Soba was traditionally conducted in Arabic, the language of the people. In the early 20th century various educators promoted the idea of conducting classes in Hebrew, especially in Argentina. The Syrian scholars and rabbis of Argentina were very much against this because Hebrew had become the means by which Zionists introduced antireligious ideas and vulgar language into common speech. At first they turned to R' Haim Shaul Dweck (see #228), the renowned Kabbalist and founder of the yeshiva *Rehovot HaNahar* of Jerusalem. R' Dweck agreed with what they were trying to do, but said he was already too old and weak to take a leading role in this fight. He suggested that they refer the matter to the *Bet Din* of R' Yosef Chaim Sonnenfeld. In the end they went to R' Yosef Yedid (see #594), the head of the *Bet Din* of the Aram Soba community in Jerusalem. R' Yedid took up the matter with all of his energy and fought vigorously to forbid the use of Hebrew as a teaching tool. Instead the Sephardic communities around the world were asked to keep to their ancient traditions and teach in the common language of the place in which they lived. (See Document Section, Document No. 8.)

Bnei Sion Talmud Torah

In 1926 the *Agudat Yisrael* organization sent an educator from Frankfurt, Dr. Auerbach, to lead the Talmud Torah *Bnei Sion* of the Sephardim in Jerusalem. This elicited strong objections from many of the Jerusalem rabbis who sent a letter of protest to the leaders of the *Agudat Yisrael*. In the letter they asked that every effort be made to cancel the appointment of Dr. Auerbach as that would be an opening to a change from traditional teaching methods. Furthermore, they objected to anyone with the West European title of "Dr." being appointed in a position of spiritual leadership. They were concerned that this might harm the souls of the students and implant the poison of the *Haskalah* (Enlightenment) and liberalism. Among the signers to this letter were R' Haim Shaul Dweck, the head of the yeshiva *Rehovot HaNahar* (see #228), R' Yosef Yedid, the head of the Sephardic *Bet Din* (see #594), R' Ezra Harari-Raful, founder of the Sephardic yeshiva *Ohel Moed* (see #304), and R' Yaakob Haim Sofer (the *Kaf HaHaim* (see #532). (See Document Section, Document No. 7.)

TRADITIONAL MUSIC

Syrian Jewry and particularly the community of Aram Soba long enjoyed a reputation as lovers of music and singing. In the course of eight centuries, they developed a characteristic style in their synagogue services and related activities. As early as the 13th century, the Spanish Hebrew poet R' Yehudah Al-Harizi, referring to Syrian personalities, mentioned a Syrian *hazzan* (cantor), saying his performance conquered "the hearts of the holy people by his delightful song." Almost all the *pizmonim* (hymns) sung outside the formal religious service were the work of distinguished Aram Soba rabbis such as R' Moshe Laniado (see #359), R' Raphael Antebi (see #87), R' Yaakob and R' Haim Mordechai Abadi (see #13 and #8), and R' Mordechai Labaton (see #336), who were poets as well as composers. Some of them may have modeled themselves after the poet R' Yisrael Najara of Damascus who was highly esteemed by composers of the period.

Manuscript of old book of pizmonim

This encouragement of the art of singing by the rabbis found strong support in R' Mordechai Abadi's introduction to *Mikra Kodesh,* a book of *bakashot* (Sephardic hymns) published in 1873. The melodic style of Aram Soba belongs to the Arabian-Turco-Persian musical family, but also shows other influences, mainly those of Sephardic Jews. Both in prayers and other songs, the *maqam* style (melodic pattern) prevail. For each *Shabbat* or Yom Tob (festival) prayer there is an appropriate *maqam,* and the various *zemirot* (hymns and songs) also conform to the *maqam* pattern.

Every week on *Motza'e Shabbat*, singers came to the Talmud Torah to sing holy hymns of R' Yisrael Najara and other rabbis. The songs were interspersed with inspirational lectures.

The singing of *bakashot* was conducted by choirs in the Great Synagogue and in the *Midrash Bet Nasi* early each *Shabbat* morning. Two choirs were used, responding to each other in harmony with alternating stanzas.

At one point, R' Moshe Tawil (see #586) introduced formal instruction in music so that the students of the Talmud Torah of Aram Soba would be able to properly sing the *bakashot*. However, he discontinued the lessons when a group of boys began singing the original Arabic lyrics of the songs on which the *pizmonim* and *bakashot* were fashioned. All singing of *bakashot* was then discontinued in the Talmud Torah.

Over the years many rabbis expressed concern with the negative effects of gentile music. R' Haim Palagi (see #449) mentions a strongly worded ban of Aram Soba on such music. (See Document Section, Document No. 22.) This is quoted by R' Yosef Yedid (see #594) in his introduction to the first printing of R' Moshe Ashear's book of *pizmonim* (hymns) titled *Hallel VeZimrah* (see #88).

Finding the Holy Spark. In the introduction to the book of *pizmonim* (hymns of devotion), R' Yaakob Kassin (see #330) presents a novel insight by R' Raphael Antebi (Tabush) (see #87) into the issue of Jewish lyrics being sung to non-Jewish melodies. He says that since a melody is a spark of holiness, when one sings love songs, the spark becomes defiled.

On the other hand, whenever a new melody is written by the gentiles, it is our obligation to set it to holy words, in order to draw out the spark from the side of impurity to purity. This is the same process that occurs when we bring sinners back in repentance. We are removing the pure from the impure, and drawing out the holy spark.

Along these lines, it is said that when Israel sings the melody of a gentile nation, we stir G-d to look at that nation and see that it is oppressing Israel. Thus, the poets of previous and current generations have often taken melodies from the gentiles and sanctified them by composing songs for G-d from those melodies. [For further discussion on this topic, see R' Yaakob Hillel's responsum in *Vayashev HaYam*, Vol. II, responsum 7.]

MUSIC FOR A NEW GENERATION

The Syrian *hazzan* (cantor) relies primarily upon ten *maqamat* (musical systems or melodies), each of which can be considered a parent *maqam* to one or more offspring *maqamat*. A *hazzan* must know all of these *maqamat* and their applications to the prayers. Certain *maqamat* are associated with certain themes and so the *hazzan* must have insight into the themes in the weekly *perashah* to apply the proper *maqam* on that *Shabbat*.

R' Raphael Antebi (Tabush) (see #87)

ספר
שירה חדשה
המה שירות ותשבחות מאשר
חנני ה' אלהי לשורר בקול
נעים ואלקים יודע כי לש"ש
נתכוונתי בכדי שלא יותן
לפושעים יד לשורר שירי
עגבים כי השירות של חשק
ונבול פה מפריד הנשמה
מצרור החיים ח"ו וי"י משמים
ישלח משיחנו בעג' ובז"ק כי"ר
ש' תר"מח

Title Page of Shirah Hadashah by R' Raphael Antebi (Tabush), 1888

R' Moshe Haim Ashear (see #88)

In 1888 a classic work of *pizmonim* based on the ancient *maqamat* and titled Shirah Hadashah was published in Aram Soba by R' Raphael Antebi (Tabush), an eminent poet, *hazzan*, and Kabbalist (see #87). All of R' Antebi's *pizmonim* were subsequently incorporated into a new book published in Jerusalem in 1905 by R' Raphael Haim Cohen. This work, which was reprinted with even more additions in 1921, was entitled *Shir U'Shevachah*.

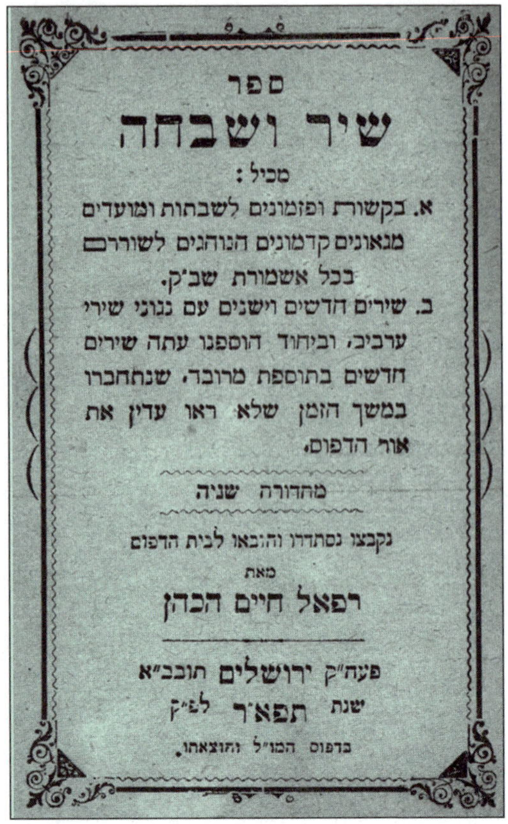

ספר
שיר ושבחה
מכיל:
א. בקשות ופזמונים לשבתות ומועדים
מגאונים קדמונים הנוהגים לשוררם
בכל אשמורת שב"ק.
ב. שירים חדשים וישנים עם נגוני שירי
ערביה, וביחוד הוספנו עתה שירים
חדשים בתוספת מרובה, שנתחברו
במשך הזמן שלא ראו עדין את
אור הדפוס.
מהדורה שניה
נקבצו נסתדרו והובאו לבית הדפוס
מאת
רפאל חיים הכהן
פעה"ק ירושלים תובב"א
שנת תפא"ר לפ"ק
בדפוס המו"ל ותוצאתו.

Title Page of Shir U'Shevachah which incororated the pizmonim of R' Antebi (1905-1921)

Although R' Antebi passed away in 1918, he had inspired a number of gifted students who carried on his holy work of preserving and invigorating the musical tradition of Aram Soba. Among those students was R' Moshe Ashear (see #88), the renowned *hazzan* of the *Magen David* Congregation in Brooklyn. In 1928 R' Ashear published his own compositions in the book, *Hallel VeZimrah*, which was destined to become another classic in the field of traditional Syrian music.

אז ישיר משה ובני ישראל
בס"ד בהנ"ו ספר עס"י קש"ו
הלל וזמרה
זה ספר, מלא אמרי שפר, זמרה והלל, ותשבחה
לסלל, בבי כנשתא, לחרווהה דשכינתא, וגם לרבות
לשמח הלבבות, וחתנים וכלות בתוך מקהלות,
להיות כל איש שורר בביתו, דבר בעתו, לאלהי
דשמייא, עזי וזמרת יה:
מאתי הקטן, בן לא"א היקר, ז"ל: עברא דרבנן,
ותלמידיהון,
ע"ה משה יוסף אשקר, הכהן, ס"ט
נדפס
פעה"ק - ירושלם תובב"א
שנת תפר"ח לפ"ק
בדפוס הר"ש. הלוי צוקרמן

Title Page of Hallel VeZimrah by R' Moshe Haim Ashear, 1928

R' Ashear continued his faithful service to the *Magen David* Congregation until his death in 1940. When he began to weaken in his old age, the managing committee of the synagogue became concerned about who would replace him as Chief *Hazzan*. He replied, "You have nothing to worry about; just get Nissim Franco to take my place."

R' (Nathan) Nissim Franco (1898-1977) had been R' Ashear's fellow student in Aleppo under R' Raphael Antebi. Coming to America in 1918, he served as the official *hazzan* of the Betesh Synagogue in Bensonhurst, before taking on R' Ashear's position at *Magen David*. He was to remain at *Magen David* until 1944 when he was asked to serve as *hazzan* in Congregation *Shaare Zion*, where R' Yaakob Kassin was the Rabbi (see #330). While still at *Magen David* he was assisted by R' Naphtali Tawil (1902-1963), who had emerged as R' Ashear's leading and most beloved student. After the departure of R' Franco for *Shaare Zion*, R' Tawil became the mainstay of the cantorial staff at *Magen David*, which he served for more than a decade, ultimately moving on to the *Ahi Ezer* Congregation of Brooklyn.

Another of R' Antebi's notable students in Aleppo was R' Eliyahu Menaged (1890-1964) who emigrated to America as a young man and served as an expert *hazzan* in various New York synagogues for half a century, generally gratis. For a number of years he served as *hazzan* at *Knees Sithon* (the Sutton Shul) and *Knees Betesh* in Bensonhurst. He was the premier *paytan* of the community and many people learned *pizmonim* from listening to him sing at happy occasions. R' Menaged kept alive the singing of *bakashot* (supplications to

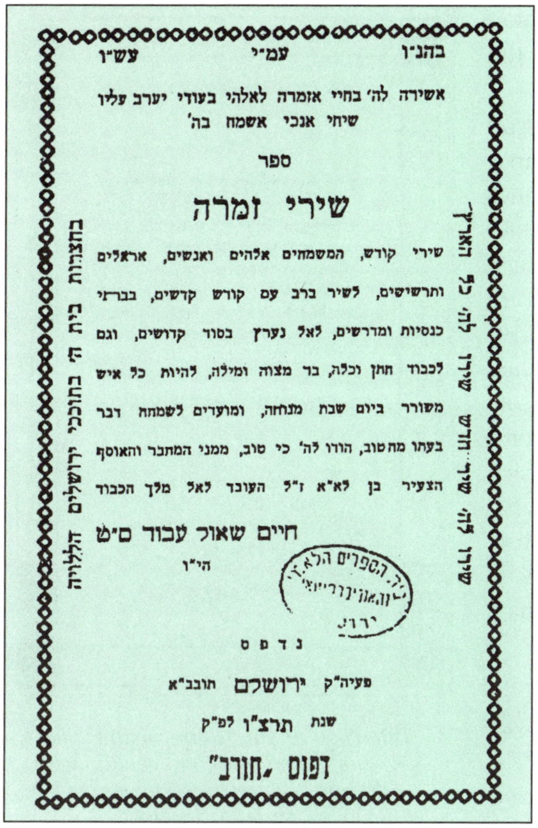

בהנ"ו　　　עמ"י　　　עש"ו

אשירה לה' בחיי אזמרה לאלהי בעודי יערב עליו
שיחי אנכי אשמח בה'

ספר

שירי זמרה

שירי קודש, המשמחים אלהים ואנשים, אראלים
ותרשישים, לשיר ברב עם קודש קדשים, בבה"כ
כנסיות ומדרשים, לאל נערץ בסוד קדושים, וגם
לכבוד חתן וכלה, בר מצוה ומילה, להיות כל איש
משורר ביום שבת מנוחה, ומועדים לשמחה דבר
בעתו מה טוב, הודו לה' כי טוב, ממני המחבר והאוסף
הצעיר בן לא"א ז"ל העובד לאל מלך הכבוד

חיים שאול עבוד ס"ט
הי"ו

נדפס

פעיה"ק ירושלם תובב"א
שנת תרצ"ו לפ"ק

דפוס „חורב"

Title Page of Shirei Zimrah
by R' Haim Shaul Aboud, 1963

Hashem) almost singlehandedly. He was remembered with fondness as a warm and friendly man, who taught youngsters *pizmonim* on *Shabbat* afternoons. He adopted as his beloved students the popular hazzanim, Meyer "Mickey" Kairey and Isaac Cabasso.

Another of R' Antebi's most influential students was the eminent composer and *hazzan*, R' Haim Shaul Aboud (see #30). R' Aboud became known for his efforts in making the traditional hymns of Aram Soba popular in Jerusalem. He also composed many *pizmonim*, which he published in 1936 in a book called *Shirei Zimrah*. This important work was subsequently reprinted in the 1950's and later again in the 1990's.

Through the devoted work of these pioneers, a new generation of *hazzan*im far removed from Aleppo continued to sing the inspiring *pizmonim* and *bakashot* in keeping with the ancient traditions.

In 1964 the *Magen David* Publication Society of Brooklyn under the leadership of its president, Mr. Sam Catton, issued an anthology combining the three classic works mentioned above. The expertise of Gabriel A. Shrem (1916-1986), the *hazzan* of the *Magen David* Synagogue, was critical to the success of this challenging task which took 15 years to complete. Among the other key participants were R' Raphael Elnadav (a student of R' Aboud), Mr. Isaac Cabasso (a student of R' Menaged), and Mr. Ezekiel Albeg of Baghdad.

R' Haim Shaul Aboud
(see #30)

The new book, *Shir U'Shevahah Hallel VeZimrah*, was highly successful and came to be known "The Pizmonim Book", and later as the "Red Book" because of its distinctive binding. The "Red Book" has gone though nine editions, the most recent of which was issued in 2002.

In 2004 modern technology and ancient tradition came together in a unique way: Over 300 *pizmonim* from the "Red Book" became available on a set of 11 CD's, as recorded by the *hazzan*, Gabriel A. Shrem.

After coming to the United States in 1930, Gabriel Shrem served the Brooklyn Syrian community for 45 years, starting in 1941 at the Betesh Synagogue in Bensonhurst. In 1945 he began his tenure at the *Magen David* Synagogue of 67th Street, where he faithfully served until 1963, as their senior cantor. In 1963 he moved on to the *Magen David* Synagogue of Ocean Parkway, and then on to the *Bnai Yosef* Syangogue, where he served for the remainder of his days.

In the 1970's he accepted a position as professor of Sephardic *hazzan*ut (cantorial arts) in the Cantorial Training Institute of Yeshiva University, where he taught classes every Monday night for four years.

ביאור שמות הנגינות האבות והתולדות
האב — והתולדה
ראשט
נהוונד — בוסליק
ביאת — עיראק אוג
חגאז
מוסתעאר — מיעורב

Handwritten list of maqamat written by R' Ezra Mishanieh (#421)

To prepare for his classes, he created cassette tapes representing all of the major *maqamat*.

Mr. David Betesh, a great-grandson of Gabriel Shrem, received these tapes as a *Bar Mitzvah* gift from his grandmother, Florence Zeitouni, the daughter of Gabriel Shrem, and resolved to pass on this treasured gift to the entire community. He re-released and upgraded both the published and the unpublished works of his great-grandfather to create an inclusive and wide-ranging recording of *pizmonim*. The CD set, which is distributed by the *Bnai Yosef* Synagogue, also includes an explanation of the origin of each *maqam*, as well as the *perashah* or occasion during which it should be used and why.

בהנ״י עמ״י עש״ו ויהי נועם ה׳ וכו׳

שירו לה׳ שיר חדש שירו לה׳ כל הארץ

ספר

שיר ושבחה הלל וזמרה

להנצחת זכרם של הפייטנים המפורסמים לתהלה ולברכה הראשון בקודש, הרב רפאל ענתבי טבוש ז״ל ושני לו נעים זמירות ישראל הרב משה אשקר הכהן ז״ל אשר זכו לחבר ברוח קודשם שירי קודש, מתוקים מדבש ונופת צופים. והרחיבו את גבול השירה, בהעמידם תלמידים חזנים, ומשוררים. יהי זכרם ברוך לנצח, אמן.

מהדורה תשיעית
נדפס בניו-יורק, ארצות הברית
הוצאת מורשת הספרדי בע״מ
ניו-יורק

2002

אז ישיר ישראל את השירה הזאת

Title Page of Shir U'Shevahah Hallel VeZimrah, the combined version with additions orchestrated by Hazzan Gabriel A. Shrem

Additional Hazzanim

The New York Syrian Jewish community was blessed with many other *hazzanim* and *paytanim* who inspired all who heard them and who made important contributions to the spirit of Jewish music in America.

Two of the most memorable *hazzanim* in the early part of the 20th century were David Shamula Mizrahi and David Shabot. Also, the sweet voice of Rafael Marcus could be heard in the early days of the *Shaare Zion* synagogue. In Bensonhurst, Ezra Tawil was the official *hazzan* of the Community Junior League.

Hazzan Gabriel A. Shrem

Hacham Ezra Mishanieh (see #421), a dedicated Talmud Torah teacher, was a prolific writer of *pizmonim* as well as a *hazzan* in the community. He was much sought after to officiate on the High Holy Days, especially in the *Bnai Yosef shul* where he also blew the *shofar*.

Another beloved community *hazzan* was Yehezkel Dweck-Khalousi, who was considered an expert in *maqamat*.

In some cases the musical tradition did not move directly from Aleppo to New York but came via Egypt. Typical of the *hazzanim* who came via this route were Isaac Salem and Joseph Hamaoui. They served for many years in *Shaare Zion*, as well as other community synagogues, bringing with them ancient tunes from Aram Soba that had been almost forgotten in New York, but which lived on in Cairo and are now thriving in America. Lately many old recordings and writings of all these *hazzanim* have been found and are being released to the public to ensure that their memories and their music will live on.

Commentary

Rabbi Moshe Douek of the Elberon Torah Center together with Rabbi Michael Haber of the Sephardic Press are releasing an English translation of the 250 most popular *pizmonim* and *bakashot*. Additionally, in a separate volume, Rabbi Douek is releasing a Hebrew commentary examining the sources for the *pizmonim* from the Torah and the writings of our Sages (*Gemara* and *Midrashim*). Vital historical background was provided by Rabbi Abraham E. Ades of Bnei Brak

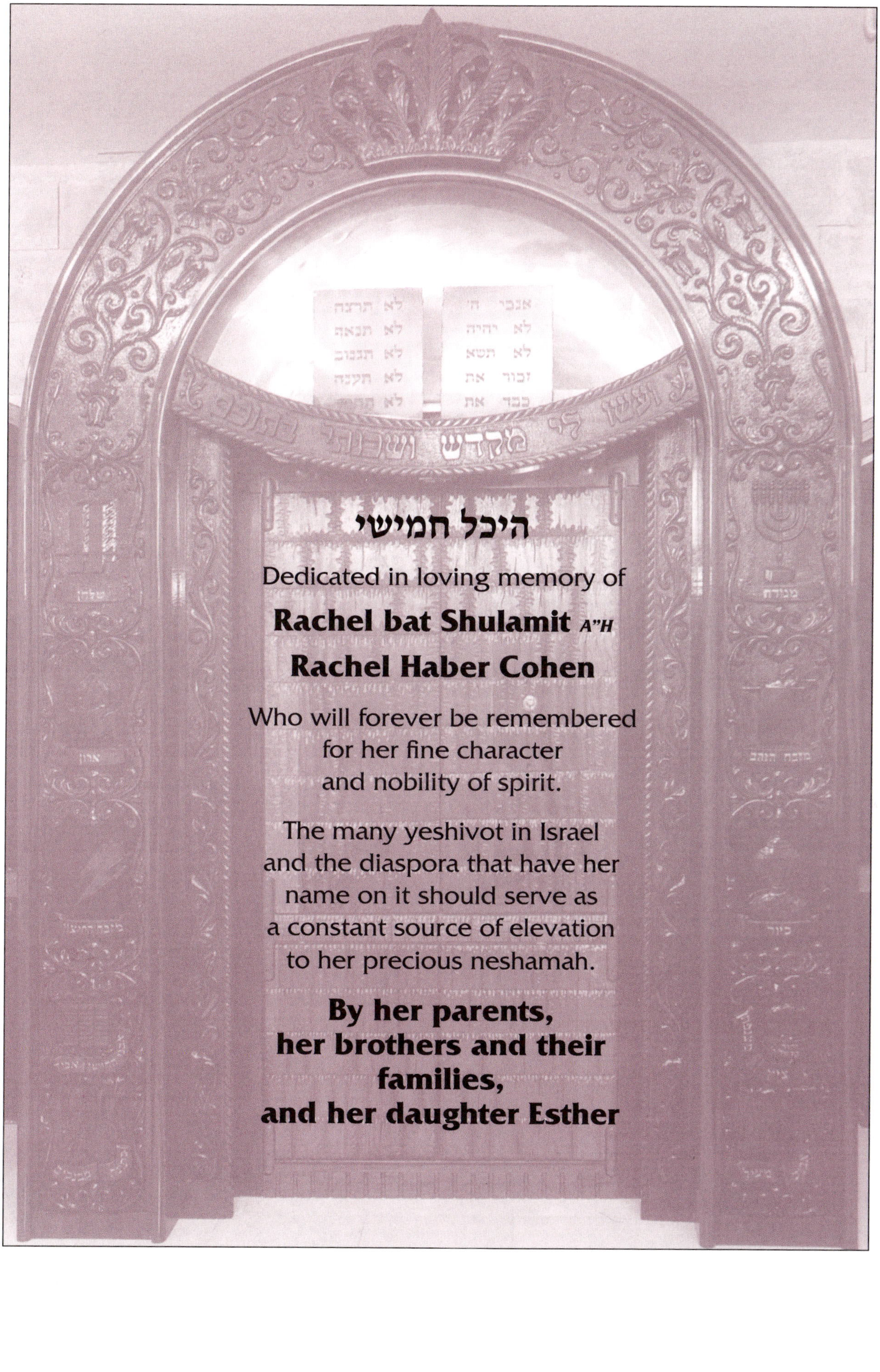

היכל חמישי

Dedicated in loving memory of

Rachel bat Shulamit ***A"H***

Rachel Haber Cohen

Who will forever be remembered
for her fine character
and nobility of spirit.

The many yeshivot in Israel
and the diaspora that have her
name on it should serve as
a constant source of elevation
to her precious neshamah.

By her parents,
her brothers and their
families,
and her daughter Esther

Section five

SYRIAN YESHIVOT IN JERUSALEM

After their departure from Syria in the late 19th century, many of the scholars of Aram Soba came to Jerusalem, where they found an opportunity to preserve and build upon their spiritual heritage. Despite great hardship they were instrumental in establishing and strengthening illustrious *yeshivot* in the holy city.

YESHIVA BET EL

The renowned yeshiva *Bet El* was founded in the Old City of Jerusalem in 1737 by the noted

Founding

Kabbalist R' Gedaliah Hayon of Constantinople. He organized the yeshiva around its *tefillot* (prayer services), which were designed to bring the scholars who studied there into mystical communion with *Hashem*. In this way the scholars might hope to be worthy to understand the secret teachings of Kabbalah. The *tefillot* were held in accordance with the *kavanot* (mystical meditations) of the *Ari'zal* (R' Yitzhak Luria) as transmitted through the works of R' Haim Vital, who was the *Ari'zal*'s outstanding pupil.

R' Obadiah Hedaya (#309) giving a class to Rabbis of Yeshivat Bet El

The Rashash

In 1751, R' Hayon passed away and was succeeded by the Kabbalist R' Shalom Sharabi, the *Rashash*. The *Rashash* did much for the yeshiva, initiating important regulations and arranging the order of the *tefillot*. He recorded his teachings in his *siddur* (prayer book) *Nehar Shalom* (Salonika, 5566/1806), also known as the *Siddur*

The last years of the 19th century witnessed an emigration of distinguished Kabbalah scholars from Aram Soba to Jerusalem.

HaRashash. This *siddur* is still used today by Kabbalists for prayer. In it, he included the *kavanot* (meditations) on the *tefillot* and on *mitzvot* for the entire year according to the *Ari'zal*'s approach to Kabbalah.

Aram Soba

After the *Rashash*, the yeshiva *Bet El* continued to be a magnet for scholars from far and wide who wished to immerse themselves in the study of Kabbalah. The last years of the 19th century witnessed an emigration of distinguished Kabbalah scholars from Aram Soba to Jerusalem. Among the outstanding scholars in this group were the following luminaries: R' Haim Shaul Dweck (see #228), R' Yomtob Yedid (see #593), R' Ezra Harari-Raful (see #304), R' Shaul Kassin (see #327), R' Yitzhak Shrem (see #517), and R' Abraham Ades (see #37). All of these scholars were drawn to the yeshiva *Bet El*, a place where they could dedicate themselves to spiritual growth.

The great rabbi burst into bitter tears. When his associates asked what was bothering him, he explained, "I don't understand what they are saying. Their words are over my head."

The level of scholarly achievement in the yeshiva *Bet El* is illustrated by a story about a great rabbi, R' Moshe ibn Sasson, author of the book *Shemen Sasson*, who was in the *Bet Midrash* of the yeshiva listening to a lively discussion of a topic in Kabbalah. Suddenly, the great rabbi burst into bitter tears. When his associates asked what was bothering him, he explained, "I don't understand what they are saying. Their words are over my head."

The 20th Century

With the fall of the Old City in in 1948, the *Bet Midrash* of the yeshiva was destroyed. However, in 1959 a new *Bet Midrash* was established in the New City and given the name *Bet El* to indicate continuity with the original. When the Old City was freed in 1967, R' Obadiah Hedaya (see #309) initiated the work of restoring the original *Bet Midrash* to its previous glory.

R' Abraham Kassin (see #319) was an active supporter of the yeshiva and it was primarily through his personal efforts that a new building was put up. Subsequently, R' Yosef Shayo (Abadi) (see #507) became *Rosh Yeshiva*.

Call for funds in three languages — Hebrew, English, Yiddish

YESHIVA REHOVOT HANAHAR

The Founders

In 1896, after six years of devoted study in *Bet El*, R' Haim Shaul Dweck (see #228) founded a new Kabbalist yeshiva in the Bukharan quarter of Jerusalem. This initiative was made possible through the generosity of the wealthy philanthropist R' Nissim Nahum (see #437). With the financial support provided by R' Nahum it became possible to pay each scholar a stipend that freed him from economic concerns. The new yeshiva had long been a dream of R' Dweck. It gave him an opportunity to apply Kabbalist teachings as he understood them.

R' Abraham Haim Ades (see #37), one of his colleagues from the yeshiva *Bet El*, became one of the co-founders of the new yeshiva.

The name *Rehovot HaNahar* appears in the Torah (*Bereishit* 36:37), where it refers to a geographical location. This name also happens to be the title that the classic Kabbalistic author, the *Rashash* (R' Shalom Sharabi), gave to the introduction to *Nahar Shalom*, his major work of meditations on the *tefillot*. Interestingly, the expression *Rehovot HaNahar* in the Torah is preceded by the name Shaul, a king who originated from that location. This offers a connection to the name of R' Haim Shaul Dweck, a name which will always be inextricably linked to the great yeshiva that he founded and headed.

R' Eliyahu Dweck (see #224) was the only son of R' Haim Shaul Dweck. After the passing of his father he served as *Rosh Yeshiva* (head) of *Rehovot HaNahar* for many years.

Rabbis of Rehovot HaNahar. From left to right: R' Eliyahu Dweck (#224), Harav Ouziel, R' Eliyahu Ma'arabi (#404), In background: R' Yosef Shayo (#507), R' David-Sion Laniado (#352)

The Scholars

In the book, *Tzvi LeSaddik*, R' Margolios writes, "I merited to see the sun in its brightness, the great holy yeshiva *Rehovot HaNahar*; here in Jerusalem, started by the father of all rabbis, my master, *HaKohen HaGadol*, R' Haim Shaul Dweck, and helped by the wealthy, generous, pious, Kabbalist R' Nissim Nahum." Among those who learned there, R' Margolios listed: "Hacham Abraham Haim Ades, Hacham Yomtob Yedid, and Hacham Shaul Kassin: the giants of Aram Soba, and the *Kaf HaHaim* from Baghdad." He also lists twenty or so other great rabbis from other Sephardic countries.

The Course of Study

R' Margolios continues to describe the schedule of the students of this yeshiva: "They were all married men who slept at the yeshiva the entire week. They would arrive Saturday night, go to the *mikveh* at midnight, and then pray *Tikkun Hatzot*, weeping on the floor of the *Bet Midrash*. After this, they would stay up all night learning, then pray *Shaharit* (morning services) at *netz* (sunrise) using the *Siddur HaRashash* and wearing two pairs of *tefillin* simultaneously [one in the format prescribed by *Rashi* and the other as prescribed by *Rabbeinu Tam*]. The *Siddur HaRashash* looks like a big *Gemara* — each page contains only a few words of the actual prayers, the rest of the space is filled with a detailed description of all the special *kavanot* (focused thoughts and meditations) one is expected to have in mind while praying. [A visitor related that he once came to the office of R' Yaakob Hillel, and was informed that he was inside saying *Sefirat HaOmer* (which is essentially two sentences). "I thought he would be out in thirty seconds. Twenty minutes later, he opened the door. When including all the proper *kavanot*, reciting *Sefirat HaOmer* takes twenty minutes."]

" It took four hours each morning for the students of the yeshiva to pray *Shaharit*. After eating breakfast, they would sleep for three hours before the afternoon *seder* (order of learning). After learning for several hours, they would pray *Minhah*, with *tefillin* and all the *kavanot*. [The *tefillin* worn at *Minhah* were known as *Shimusha Rabbah*.] They would learn again until later in the night, pray *Arbit* and then sleep for three hours before waking for *Tikkun Hatzot*. "Fortunate is the man who saw these people, the way they prayed, the way they pronounced every word slowly. Fortunate is the community — their *zechut* (merit) should guard this generation. There are no longer people like this," writes R' Margolios.

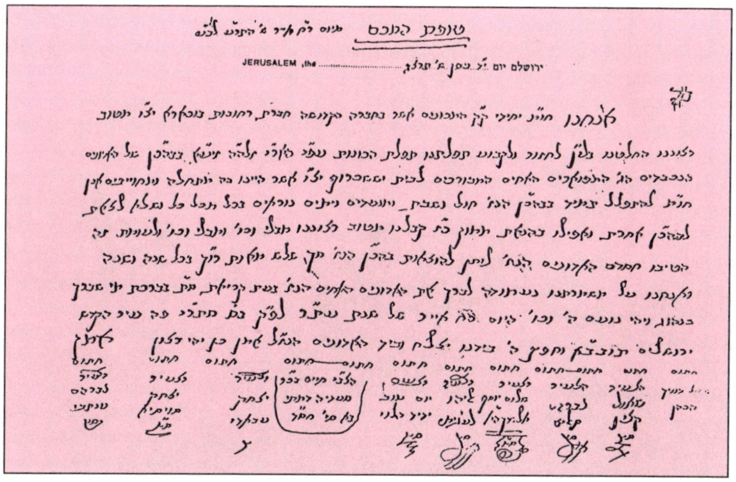

Shtar Hitkashrut of yeshiva — study group contract written by R' Yaakob Kassin (see Document Section, Document No. 32)

One might think that after years of adhering to such a taxing schedule, these students would be broken in their later years. "I knew the *Kaf HaHaim* [in his later years]," said Hacham Ben-Sion Abba Shaul (see #24), "and he was a happy, jubilant man."

Hacham Ben-Sion described the *Kaf HaHaim's* schedule during the later years of his life. "He prayed *Arbit* around 7 p.m. — and it took three hours. He then slept for a little before waking again for *Tikkun Hatzot*. Eating breakfast took an hour and a half because he ate everything with *kavanot*. During each meal, he would learn six chapters of *Mishnayot*, 18 in total each day. Then there would be *Pitum HaKetoret* (Torah verses describing the burning of the incense) because the meal would be like sending a *korban* (sacrifice) up to *Hashem*, followed by *Mayim Aharonim*, and *Bircat HaMazon* — it took an hour and a half." With this schedule, how did he have time to even write the *Kaf HaHaim*? Hacham Ben-Sion explains, "Because of their piety, their Torah learning stayed with them, they didn't forget anything and their livelihood was provided for ... they constantly served *Hashem*, but without any pressure." [Based on the *Gemara* in *Berachot* 32b: "Our Rabbis taught: The pious men of old used to wait for an hour and pray for an hour and then wait again for an hour. But seeing that they spend nine hours a day in prayer, how is their knowledge of Torah preserved and how is their work done? The answer is that because they are pious, their Torah is preserved and their work is blessed."]

Global Recognition

The yeshiva *Rehovot HaNahar* became recognized by all Kabbalists for its sanctity and for the greatness of its scholars. An indication of this is provided by the disclaimer which appears at the end of the *siddur Haim VeShalom*, published by the Kabbalist yeshiva *Shaar HaShamayim*. This disclaimer refers to a statement in the introduction of *the siddur* to the effect that the study of Kabbalah was neglected until the establishment of the yeshiva *Shaar HaShamayim*. That statement implied that there was no yeshiva where Kabbalah was being intensively studied and thus it appeared to malign the honor of the Sephardic *yeshivot* which had been studying Kabbalah for a very long time.

The disclaimer at the end of the *siddur* corrects that misinterpretation. It states that they were only referring to Ashkenaz *yeshivot* but they fully recognize that a yeshiva for the study of Kabbalah in the Sephardic world has existed from the time of the holy rabbi, R' Shalom Sharabi (the *Rashash*). He established the yeshiva *Bet El*, where the services are conducted with the *kavanot* of the *Ari'zal*, following the *siddur* of the *Rashash*. The disclaimer goes on to say that in "our time" there has been founded another yeshiva for Sephardic *hachamim* in the Rehovot neighborhood of the Bukharan quarter and its *bet midrash* is full of scholars who are learned in the knowledge of Kabbalah and for whom the ways of learning are illuminated like the public streets. There, the services are also conducted with the *kavanot* of the *Ari'zal*, following the *siddur* of the *Rashash*. "Happy is their portion."

YESHIVA PORAT YOSEF

The yeshiva *Porat Yosef* laid its cornerstone in 1914 in the Old City of Jerusalem at the outbreak of World War I, but due to the war, construction was delayed until much later. Initial funding came from the philanthropist Yosef Abraham Shalom of Calcutta, who dedicated his entire wealth to the yeshiva, under the direction of the *Ben Ish Hai*, R' Yosef Haim of Baghdad. The plaque on the front door mentions that the funds were managed by R' Moshe Sassoon of Calcutta.

Old Porat Yosef, pre-1948

Finally inaugurated in 1923, *Porat Yosef* was soon filled with young and eager pupils. In addition to the huge *bet midrash* where the younger yeshiva students learned, there were two other study halls for married men, plus fifty more rooms for dormitories, offices, and a library. The yeshiva was dedicated to the study of the revealed Torah, but also included an annex called *Oz VeHadar* for the study of Kabbalah. In the 1948 War of Independence the complex was destroyed only to be rebuilt on the same location after the Six Day War. During the intervening period, the yeshiva's students and scholars continued learning in small *shuls* and *batei midrash* throughout Jerusalem.

A forerunner to *Porat Yosef* was the yeshiva *Ohel Moed*, co-founded in 1904 by R' Ezra Harari-Raful (see #304) and R' Rafael Shelomo Laniado (see #364). Although successful for a while, *Ohel Moed* was forced to close due to lack of funds. R' Ezra then opened it again in 1918 with R' Obadiah Hedaya (see #309) as *Rosh Yeshiva*. It eventually joined with *Porat Yosef* in 1923. Ultimately, all of the students and rabbis associated with *Ohel Moed* moved to *Porat Yosef*.

Yeshivat Ohel Moed

Old Hechal of Porat Yosef, pre-1948

Yeshivat Ohel Moed 1905. From right: R' Yitzhak Shrem (#518), R' Raphael Shelomo Laniado (#364), R' Abraham Salem (#471), R' Yitzhak Abadi (#17), R' Yomtob Yedid (#593), a Yemenite rabbi (identity unknown), Mr. Ben Yaakob. Among the seated children are Yaakob and Moshe Ades

The official yeshiva *Porat Yosef* was dedicated in Nissan 5683 (1923). This became the first of its kind in the Sephardic communities of *Eretz Yisrael*, a yeshiva with a virtually "unlimited" capability of accepting new students. R' Nissim Nahum (see #437), who financed the founding of *Rehovot HaNahar*, was one of the five committee members involved in building *Porat Yosef*. The other four members were R' Eliyahu Shamah (see #500), R' Mashiach Borochov, R' Yaakob Meir, and R' Nissim Elyashar. All of their names were inscribed on the front door of the yeshiva. The role of R' Eliyahu Shamah was especially critical. There came a point where all of the original supporters abandoned the project because of a serious problem that had arisen. It was R' Eliyahu who came to the rescue

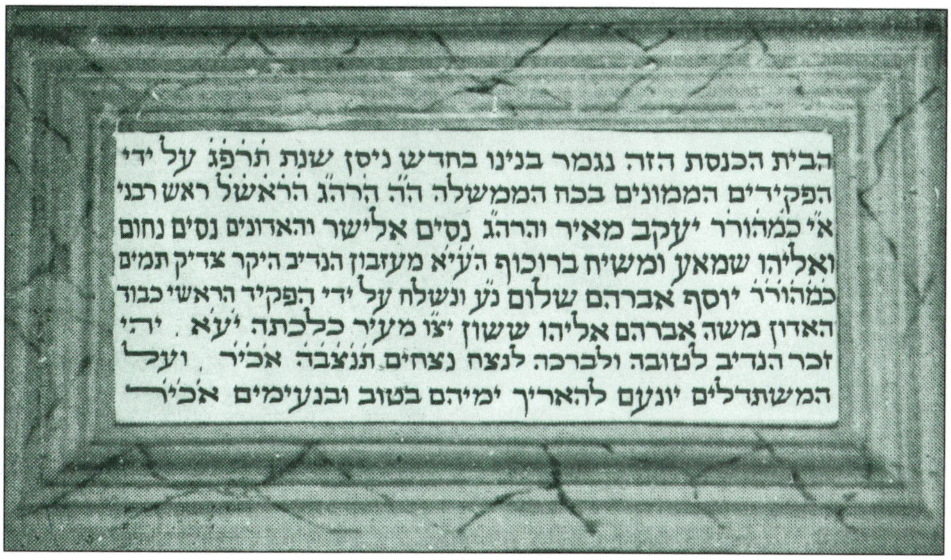

Sign on front door of yeshiva

R' Yaakob Ades (left) and R' Ephraim Cohen (right)

and took upon himself the responsibility for the continued existence of the institution.

In 1923, R' Raphael Shelomo Laniado (see #364) became the first *Rosh Yeshiva* of *Porat Yosef*, a position which he held until his untimely death in 1925. Among the senior lecturers were R' Obadiah Hedaya (see #309) and R' Eliyahu Lofez (see #394). R' Hedaya also led the *tefillot* in the Kabbalist annex *Oz VeHadar* in accordance with the *kavanot* of the *Ari'zal*. Among the other prominent scholars in *Oz VeHadar* were R' Mordechai Azran, R' Shemuel Azran, R' Ephraim Cohen, R' Eliyahu Aboud (see #29), R' Aharon Aboud (see #28), R' Yaakob Mounsa (see #435), R' Shalom Azulai, R' Eliyahu Ma'arabi, R' Eliyahu Lejimi, R' Yomtob Yedid (see #593), R' Yosef Shayo (see #507), and R' Moshe Ades (see #39).

Porat Yosef Wonder Class
Bottom row (from right): R' Ezra Shayo (see #506), R' Saadiah Lofez (#398), Hacham Baruch Ben-Haim (of the Brooklyn Syrian Community), Hacham Ovadiah Yosef (Rishon LeSion), R' Shabbetai Atoon (Rosh Yeshiva of Reshit Hochmah), R' Pinhas Vaknin of Jerusalem, R' David Levy (Rabbi in Tel Aviv)
Middle Row (from right): R' David Shalush (Rabbi of Netanya), R' Yosef Harari-Raful of Religious Ministry, R' Ezra Ades (son of R' Yaakob Ades) — Herzliyah, R' Eliyahu Shrem (#509), R' Raphael Ades (secretary of Rabbinical High Court, R' Yosef Elradav (killed in 1948)
Top row (from right): R' Aharon Aboud (Rabbi of Haifa), R' Moshe Yosef Ades (#40), R' Sion Levy (of the Panamanian Syrian Community), Hacham Ben-Sion Abba Shaul (#24)

After 1925 R' Ezra Attiah (see #102) served as *Rosh Yeshiva* until his death in 1970. During his tenure he was the focal point of the yeshiva, and through his brilliance at teaching Torah, young Sephardim chose to study there. Among his most famous students were R' Ovadiah Yosef, R' Yehudah Sadkah (see #468), R' Ben-Sion Abba Shaul (see #24),

An Arab woman on Rechov Bet El carrying three Sephardi Torah scrolls on her head during 1948

Hacham Baruch Ben-Haim, and R' Sion Levi. R' Sadkah was to become one of the most famous teachers of the yeshiva and later the *Rosh Yeshiva*. He was followed as *Rosh Yeshiva* by R' Abba Shaul. Another of its illustrious *Roshei Yeshiva* was R' Ezra Shayo (Abadi) (see #506).

Among the other renowned teachers were R' Ezra Ades (see #38), R' Moshe Ades (see #39), R' Yaakob Ades (see #41),R' Yosef Sasson (see #487), and R' Eliezer Yedid (see #590).

R' Ben-Sion Hazzan (right) and R' Yisrael Mintzburg in Jordanian custody, 1948

During the capture of Jerusalem's Old City by the Jordanian Legion in 1948, the yeshiva building was tragically destroyed. R' Ezra Attiah, the *Rosh Yeshiva* (see #102), and R' David-Sion Laniado (see #352), among the leading Kabbalists in the yeshiva, came to visit R' Ben-Sion Hazzan, who had remained in the Jewish Quarter until its fall.

During the capture of Jerusalem's Old City by the Jordanian Legion in 1948, the yeshiva building was tragically destroyed.

When they arrived at his home, the two rabbis sat on the ground and emotionally recited Chapter 137 in *Tehillim* that laments, "By the rivers of Babylon, there we sat and also wept as we remembered Sion." After they had calmed down a bit, R' Ezra asked, "The large library and its treasures, the books and the huge collections of manuscripts — what happened to them?" R' Ben-Sion informed him that they were all burned.

The two rabbis sat on the ground and emotionally recited Chapter 137 in Tehillim that laments, "By the rivers of Babylon, there we sat and also wept as we remembered Sion."

R' Ezra began reciting the *kinah* (lamentation), *Sha'ali Serufah Ba'Esh*, which was composed as a dirge over the burning of sacred books in France. He then asked, "And the *Batei Kenesset* (synagogues), what about them?"

"They too were destroyed."

They sat and wept, their tears flowing like rivers. R' Ezra asked about every building and was informed that everything was destroyed. Finally, he stood up, placed his hand on R' Ben-Sion's shoulder, and said, "You shall restore the foundations of old. We will build Jerusalem yet, and it will return to our hands, with Hashem's help."

R' Ezra placed his hand on R' Ben-Sion's shoulder, and said, "You shall restore the foundations of old. We will build Jerusalem yet, and it will return to our hands, with Hashem's help."

He immediately dedicated his efforts to the restoration project with the objective of rebuilding the yeshiva in the New City. Seven years later, the groundbreaking ceremony of the yeshiva building was held in the Geulah neighborhood. R' Ezra instructed that the invita-

Porat Yosef during the bombing,1948

tions and announcements of the event should begin with the verse, "Men from among you shall rebuild ancient ruins, you shall restore the foundations laid long ago, and you shall be called repairer of fallen walls, restorer of streets for habitation" (*Yeshayah* 58:12). He explained that this verse from the *haftarah* of *Yom Kippur* is a Divine promise to every individual who repents, and a promise to the community and nation at large, that everything that is destroyed, both physically and spiritually, can be rebuilt.

R' Ezra Attiah at Porat Yosef groundbreaking — prophecy fulfilled

R' Ezra Shrem (see #510) became one of the key administrators of the yeshiva, concerned with its development and success. After the War of Independence, the yeshiva needed to be reestablished outside the walls of the Old City and R' Shrem took an active role in this essential endeavor. Following this painful interruption, he saw the yeshiva grow and prosper, becoming a network of *yeshivot* connected by a common approach to Torah education.

Important Visitors

Visitors from Lithuanian *yeshivot* were impressed by *Yeshivat Porat Yosef* and its students. Rabbi Eliezer Silver visited in the year 1964 and gave a glowing report (see Document Section, Document No 34). Rav Aharon Kotler, the *Rosh Yeshiva* and founder of the Lakewood Yeshiva, came to visit accompanied by his father- in-law Rav Isser Zalman Meltzer. Rav Aharon asked one of the younger classes, "Is blood permissible to be eaten?" They all answered that it is not permitted. "Why not?" he asked. One boy answered, "Because the *pasuk* says, 'You must spill it on the ground like water.' "

He proceeded to ask, "Is liver permitted to be eaten?" "Yes," they answered in unison. "How could that be if the liver is an organ that's full of blood?" Nobody had the answer until one student said, "Because we know how to *kosher* it." Rav Aharon was pleased with the answer. That boy was none other than young Ovadiah Yosef who eventually became *Rishon LeSion* and Chief Rabbi of Israel.

In the year 1942 one of the committee members of Porat Yosef suggested teaching the English language as a subject in the yeshiva. He explained, "If we are to produce rabbis for the Diaspora they must be fluent in English." The rabbis of the yeshiva were strongly opposed. The committee member was insistent; he said "It will be taught in the evening and during lunch breaks. Rabbi Shalom Lofez (#399) got wind of the plans and he immediately took action. He wrote the text of a "*Kol Koreh* (proclamation)" voicing the opinions of the rabbis and had it signed by the leading rabbis of the yeshiva. (See Document Section, Document No. 37 for a translation of the document.)

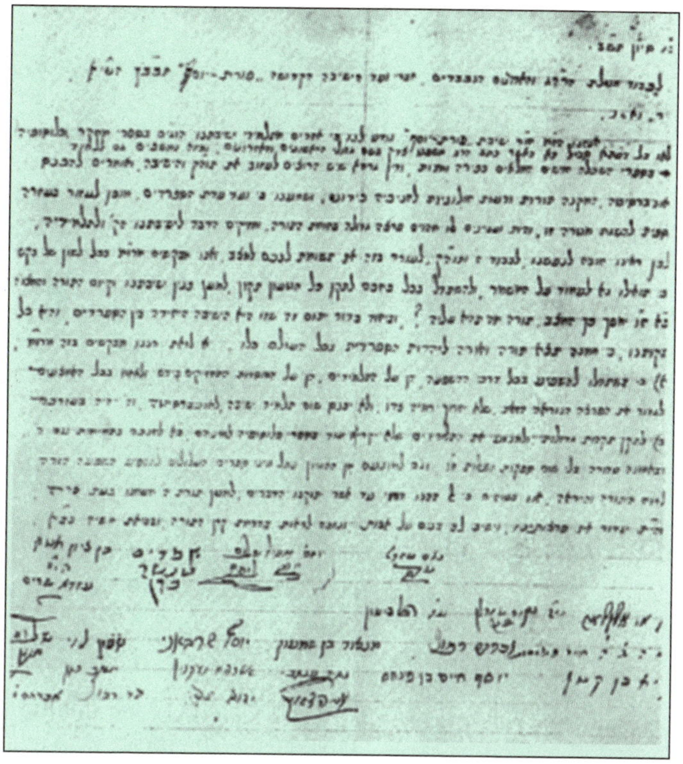

Letter from rabbis of Porat Yosef against the study of philosophy and college (1942)

SILVERA BET MIDRASH

A noteworthy Aram Soba contribution to Torah learning in Jerusalem was the *Silvera Bet Midrash* in the Mahane Yehudah section, founded by Señor Aharon Silvera (see #522). On the upper floor of a two-story apartment building he built a synagogue and *bet midrash*, open to all, day and night. The income from the rental of the apartments on the lower floor provided support for the *shamosh* (sexton) and the upkeep of the *Bet Midrash*, which was named *Zechut Aharon* after its founder. He spared no effort in embellishing the synagogue with beautiful furniture and books. The complex continues to serve the needs of scholars and is named *Bet Aharon*. For many years the position of *shamosh* was held by the eminent scholar, R' David-Sion Laniado (see #352).

During the period of 1936-1938 when Jerusalem experienced Arab rioting, it became dangerous for the students of yeshiva *Porat Yosef* in the Old City to walk to their homes in the New City. As a result, a learning group of *Porat Yosef* students was begun in the *Silvera Bet Midrash*. Subsequently, when the Old City fell to the Arabs in 1948, the *Porat Yosef* building was destroyed and all of the students were relocated to various *shuls* in the New City. A large group was temporarily placed in the *Bet Midrash* of Shelomo Sofioff in the Bukharan neighborhood and another group was placed in the *Silvera Bet Midrash*, where the *Av Bet Din* of Jerusalem, R' Yosef Babliki, conducted classes.

In the 1950's evening classes for young men were given in the *Bet Midrash* under the auspices of the *Hanoch LeNaar* organization, led by Mr. David Shalom. This was one of a network of such classes in *batei midrash* around the city sponsored by this organization, whose purpose was to provide a proper spiritual foundation for the Sephardic youth of the city.

In later years the *Bet Midrash* became the locale of the *Yeshivat HaMetzuyanim* of Brisk under the leadership of R' Haim Aharon Turchin, who was a close friend of the *shamosh*, R' David-Sion Laniado. It was also the study place of young scholars of the yeshiva *Sefat Emet* of the *Hasidei Gur*, which was located nearby. Today the *Kollel Darchei David*, named for R' David-Sion Laniado, is located in the building under the leadership of R' Shemuel Pinhasi.

TALMUD TORAH MAGEN DAVID JERUSALEM

The Talmud Torah *Magen David* of Jerusalem was founded in 1920 by R' Ezra Harari-Raful (see #304), a *dayan* (judge) of the Sephardic *Bet Din*, who was born in Aram Soba. It was run by his son, R' Aharon Harari-Raful (see #303), who was born in Jerusalem.

Magen David, Jerusalem 1941
R' Aharon Harari-Raful (see #303) in center of top row

The founding of the Talmud Torah was made possible by Mr. Eliyahu Franco (see #262), an eminent philanthropist, who was born in Aram Soba. Although he settled in the United States and lived there for many years, he had a lifelong dream of living in Jerusalem, which he was able to realize in his later years. Shortly after his arrival in Jerusalem he dedicated a large sum to finance the construction of a Talmud Torah for the children of the Aram Soba community in Jerusalem.

R' Aharon Harari-Raful operated the school on a shoestring budget. One of the teachers related that due to lack of funds they had a shortage of teachers. R' Aharon would teach three grades simultaneously. He would teach one group, have them review, then teach the next, and so on.

One teacher threatened to leave due to the lack of cleanliness because they couldn't afford a janitor. R' Aharon said, "No problem." He simply went into the classroom and instructed each boy to pick up two pieces of garbage a day.

Another important supporter was Señor Aharon Silvera (see #522), an eminent philanthropist, who devoted himself and his wealth to holy causes. The two major institutions that he favored were the Sephardic Old Age Home and the *Magen David* Talmud Torah of Jerusalem. The bequest to the Talmud Torah was conditional upon the school continuing to follow the holy traditions of Aram Soba.

The Talmud Torah continued into the late 60's. R' Shelomo Salem (see #473) of Aram Soba also served as a principal. A notable member of the managing board of the school was R' Ezra Shrem (see #510), who was the administrator and manager of the yeshiva *Porat Yosef.*

The last principal was R' Natan Salem (see #472), who initially taught in the Talmud Torah *Bnei Sion* and subsequently in the Talmud Torah *Doresh Sion.* However, when the latter Talmud Torah was placed under the auspices of the Jewish National Fund, he immediately resigned. He then moved to the Talmud Torah *Magen David*, and ultimately became its principal.

After *Magen David* closed down, the voices of children learning Torah continued in the building, which still stands today on *Rehov David Yellin*. The *Yeshiva Sucath David* of R' Menachem Basri currently occupies the building today together with part of *Yeshivat Meor HaTorah* founded by R' Abraham Salem, son of R' Natan. All of this is a continued merit for the original builder, Mr. Eliyahu Franco, and the founder, R' Ezra Harari-Raful.

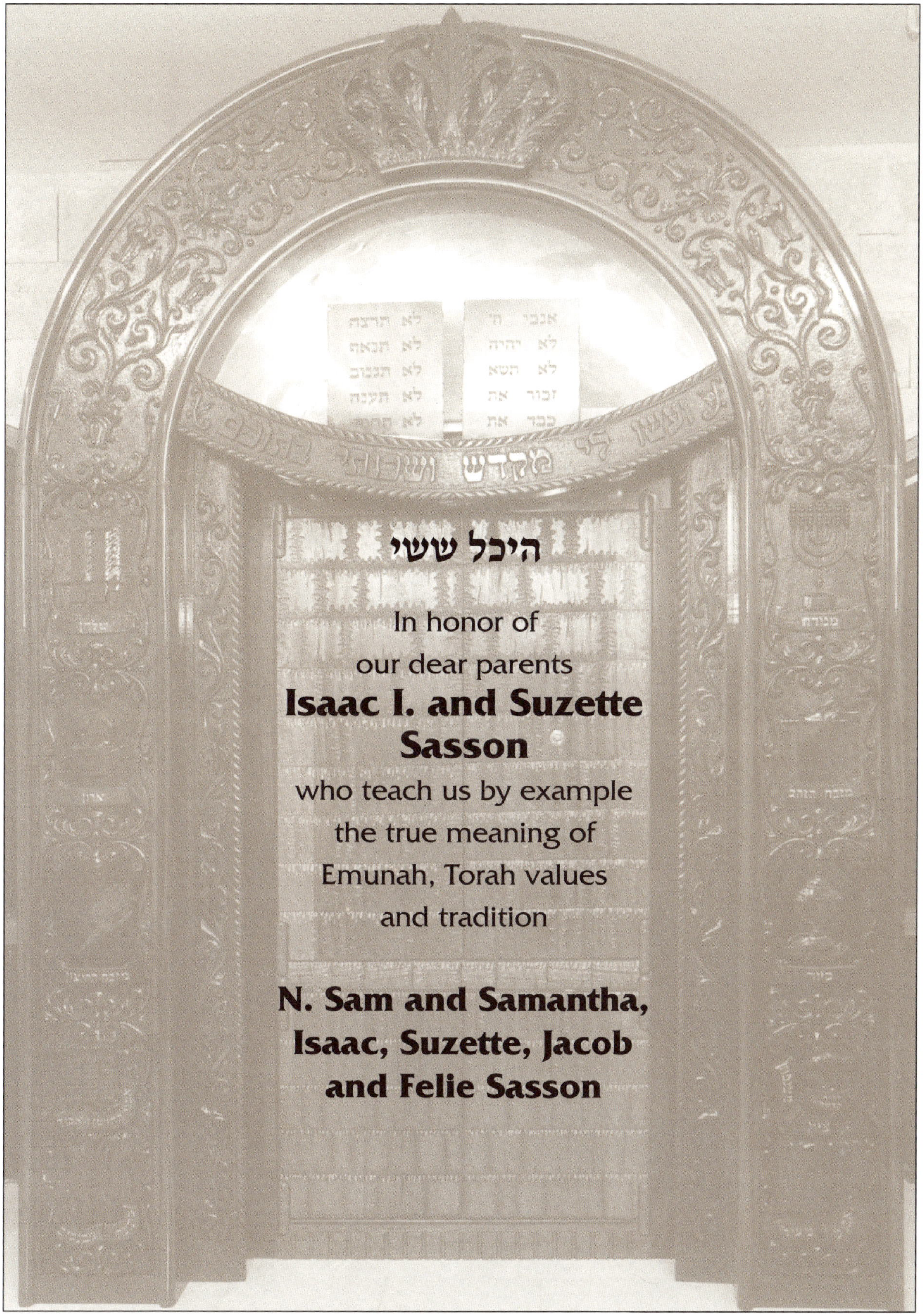

היכל ששי

In honor of
our dear parents

Isaac I. and Suzette Sasson

who teach us by example
the true meaning of
Emunah, Torah values
and tradition

**N. Sam and Samantha,
Isaac, Suzette, Jacob
and Felie Sasson**

Section Six

INTRODUCTION

Some types of speech are forbidden, some are permitted, but the *Rambam* writes (*Abot* 1:16) that there is talk which is beloved above all others. Recounting the greatness of our righteous ancestors is not only one of the most venerated activities, the *Hazon Ish* states, it is in fact a form of learning Torah. The *Midrash* explains, even after the *Tanach* was completed, the Torah continues to be written by the deeds of the *sadikim* (righteous people). The *Pele Yo'etz* takes this concept a step further, equating the praise of *tzadikim* to discussing the most revered and mystical subject of Torah, *maaseh hamerkavah* (the secrets of Hashem's heavenly chariot).

Stories of our great rabbis of old are the best *mussar* (spiritual inspiration), according to the *Hazon Ish* and to this end, the Biography Section presents the lives and ideals of the great Syrian rabbis of yesteryear.

Left to right: R' Ezra Attiah, unknown, R' Ephraim Cohen, R' Ezra Shrem, unknown, R' Ezra Ades, R' Yehudah Sadkah, R' Ezra Hedaya, R' Yosef Shayo

[1] ABADI, R' Abraham

רבי אברהם עבאדי

(— 1849 or 1859)

Eminent scholar and *dayan* (judge) of Aram Soba. His father's name was R' Yaakob Abadi. In approximately 1840 he moved to Tiberias, where he sat on the *Bet Din* together with the distinguished rabbis R' Haim Nissim Abulafia and R' Yehudah Nehmad (see #448). In 1843 the *dayanim* (judges) joined in signing the approbation for the book *Emet LeYaakob* by R' Yaakob Shaltiel Ninyo.

R' Eliyahu Chabieh Zeitoune, Mr. Isaac Sasson holding the sefer Torah

At the Ben-Zvi Institute there is an original document in which R' Abraham's name appears as the first signer, followed by R' David Kassin (see #322). The document is dated 27 Heshvan, 5599 (1831).

He passed away on 23 Adar in either 5609 (1849) or 5619 (1859).

[2] ABADI, R' Abraham

רבי אברהם עבאדי

(— 1880)

Worthy scholar and rabbi of Aram Soba. He passed away on 15 Kislev, 5641 (1880). Unfortunately, little else is known about him. The name Abraham was a common one in the renowned Abadi family, whose lineage of rabbis and scholars goes back several centuries to its origins in Spain and Provence. There was another rabbi of the 19th century with the same name, who passed away on 2 Adar, 5668 (1908).

R' Abraham Abadi (#3)

[3] ABADI (ABADIE), R' Abraham

רבי אברהם עבאדי

(1921 — 1988)

Distinguished rabbi, *dayan* (judge), and educator of Aram Soba, Beirut, and Mexico City. He devoted his life to serving the communities in which he lived and to inspiring the many students who were destined to follow in his footsteps. R' Abadie was the prototype Sephardic *hacham* who studied and practiced all the aspects of the Rabbinate, including *hazzanut*, *shehitah*, *brit milah*, and *safrut stam* (preparation of Torah scrolls, *tefillin*, and *mezuzot*). To avoid gaining personal benefit from his many community activities in Lebanon he supported his family there by working as an independent businessman and accountant.

He was born in Aram Soba in 1921 to R' Yaakob and Lulu Abadie. He studied under several prominent rabbis in Aram Soba, among them R' Moshe Mizrahi (see #424), who was the Chief Rabbi, and R' Moshe Tawil (see #586), who was *Rosh Yeshiva* of *Degel Torah* and later became Chief Rabbi. He studied together with R' Yomtob J. Yedid, who presently lives in Brooklyn, New York.

In 1950, at the age of 29, R' Abadie fled the persecution of Jews in Syria and settled in Lebanon with his wife Mazal Fortunée and their children. He continued his studies in Beirut under R' Eliyahu Chabieh Zeitoune, receiving his certification in *shehitah* and *brit milah*.

While in Lebanon he was asked by the community to become the principal of *École Nouvelle* (The New School), an Ozar HaTorah yeshiva that the late Mr. Isaac Shalom (see #497) had founded in Lebanon. All graduates of the yeshiva were well versed in *Mishnah, Gemara, Midrashim*, and *Halachah*. He was then appointed the Rabbi of the Bet Chabieh synagogue, named in memory of his teacher R' Eliyahu Chabieh Zeitoune. He was also elected to the *Bet Din* of Lebanon together with R' Shahud Shrem (see #515) and R' Yaakob Attiah.

After the Six Day War in 1967 many members of the Beirut community emigrated to Israel, among them several rabbis and providers of kosher food. R' Abadie and his wife took it upon themselves to provide kosher food to the community, including cheese, wine, and *Pesah* products. Many of the remaining Jews in Syria managed to escape during the years 1969 to 1971. R' Abadie helped them settle in Lebanon and then assisted them to immigrate to other countries around the world, including Israel, America, Mexico, Panama, and

Brazil. Among the notable individuals whom he helped in this way was R' Isaac Farhi of Deal, New Jersey.

The Jewish community in Lebanon was also dwindling during these years and the danger of persecution was increasing. Finally, in 1971 R' Abadie and his family left Lebanon for Mexico, where he was appointed to lead the *Shaare Shalom* congregation in Tecamachalco, the first Syrian synagogue in the suburbs of Mexico City. For the next 17 years, until his death, he continued to serve the Jewish community in Mexico in all his capacities as rabbi, *hazzan, shohet, mohel*, and *sofer stam*.

R' Abadie passed away on 9 Sivan, 5748 (1988). He left an undying legacy in the form of the many dedicated *talmidim* (students), whom he had nurtured over the course of his short but productive life. Many of those *talmidim* are serving Syrian communities around the world. R' Shelomo Attiah, R' Nissim Tawil, and several more are in Israel. In Brazil his students include R' Isaac Dishi, the Rabbi of the Syrian community in Sao Paulo. Among his *talmidim* in America are R' Isaac Farhi of Deal, New Jersey, R' David Jemal and R' Rahamim Harari of Congregation *Har HaLebanon* in New York. His student R' Tobeh is at *Magen David* of Vancouver, Canada. In Mexico his students include R' Ezra (Zouri) Ashkenazi and R' Shaul Chami. Among his other *talmidim* are Mr. Miro Sutton and Mr. Raphi Attie, both residing in Brooklyn. R' Abadie's own children are serving several communities. His son R' Mayer Abadie is the *hazzan* of the *Magen David* congregation in Mexico City and his youngest son, R' Dr. Elie Abadie, is the rabbi of the Edmond J. Safra Synagogue in New York City.

He also wrote many *hiddushim* (original Torah thoughts) that have not yet been published.

[4] ABADI, R' Eliyahu

רבי אליהו עבאדי

(late 18th century)

Worthy scholar and rabbi of Aram Soba. He was born in Aram Soba to R' Abraham Abadi and became a student of R' Yehudah Kassin (see #331), author of the book *Mahane Yehudah*. R' Eliyahu authored the unpublished book *Ben Abraham*. At the Ben-Zvi Institute [file no. 302] there is an original document in which R' Eliyahu's name appears as the second signer. The first signer is R' Yosef David Laniado (see #386) and the third signer is R' Ezra Sayagh (see #492). The document is dated 5 Heshvan, 5552 (1792).

[5] ABADI, R' Ephraim

רבי אפרים עבאדי

(19th century)

Worthy scholar and rabbi of Aram Soba. In 1865 he joined other rabbis of Aram Soba in signing the approbation for the first book-printing initiative of the city, which was introduced by R' Abraham Sasson and his sons (see #475). (See Document Section, Document No. 25 for the full text.)

[6] ABADI, R' Ezra

רבי עזרא עבאדי

(— 1876)

Worthy scholar and rabbi of Aram Soba. He is mentioned by R' Yitzhak Attiah (see #120) in his book *Vayikra Yitzhak*. R' Attiah had made a trip to Egypt and was gratified to find there a highly learned rabbi from his hometown Aram Soba, R' Ezra Abadi. He passed away on 4 Av, 5636 (1876).

R' Attiah had made a trip to Egypt and was gratified to find there a highly learned rabbi from his hometown Aram Soba, R' Ezra Abadi.

[7] ABADI, R' Haim

רבי חיים עבאדי

(1827 — 1866)

Eminent scholar and rabbi of Tiberias. He was born in Aram Soba and settled in Tiberias, where he gained a reputation as one of the eminent rabbis of the city. In 1857 he joined other rabbis of Tiberias in signing the announcement for the new yeshiva *Bet Yaakob*, which was established under the sponsorship of the wealthy benefactor R' Yitzhak Gouiatta.

R' Haim Abadi joined other rabbis of Tiberias in signing the announcement for the new yeshiva Bet Yaakob.

In 1864 he went to Iraq and Persia as an emissary of the Torah institutions of Tiberias. In 1866 he passed away in the town of Konjok, near Mosul, Iraq. He was blessed

R' Ezra Attiah attributes R' Matloub Abadi's effectiveness to the strong spiritual roots of his grandfather R' Mordechai Abadi.

with three scholarly sons: R' Eliyahu, R' Yitzhak (see #17), and R' Yehudah Abadi (see #14).

[8] ABADI, R' Mordechai

רבי מרדכי עבאדי

(1826 — 1883)

Distinguished scholar, Kabbalist, and *dayan* (judge) of Aram Soba. He was born in 1826 to R' Yaakob Abadi and he appears to have been a colleague of R' Moshe Swed (see #575). For a period of time he served as the rabbi of Kilis, a town in Turkey, north of Aram Soba.

He nurtured many students, including R' Yaakob Alfia (see #45) and R' Eliyahu Hamway (see #271). His student, R' Alfia, who later moved to *Eretz Yisrael*, wrote in a letter to R' Abadi, "I wish I had wings to fly back to you to hear your words of Torah." Other noteworthy students were R' Haim Shaul Dweck (see #228), the great Kabbalist of yeshiva *Rehovot HaNahar*; R' Yaakob Shaul Dweck (see #248), who became the Chief Rabbi of Aram Soba; and R' Yitzhak Dweck (see #250), who was a brother of R' Yaakob.

He fought against the European secularism of the time. He took an unusually strong stand in 1865 when he wrote a decision calling for the burning of all copies of the book Em LeMikra.

He fought against the European secularism of the time. He took an unusually strong stand in 1865 when he wrote a decision calling for the burning of all copies of the book *Em LeMikra*, written by Eliyahu ben Amozeg of Livorno. That author attempted to give a modern, scientific commentary to the Bible, making assumptions which were in conflict with Jewish tradition. The rabbis of Aram Soba called for rabbis of other communities to do the same and to excommunicate the author, but only the rabbis of Damascus agreed. The rabbis of Jerusalem accepted the arguments against Amozeg, but took less active measures. R' Abadi's decision was reprinted in *Ginzei Eretz* of R' Rahamim Shayo (Jerusalem 5761/ 2001). (See Document Section, Document No.9 for the full text.)

R' Ezra Attiah (see #102) writes about R' Matloub Abadi (see #9) and his achievements for the Jewish people. He attributes R' Matloub's effectiveness to the strong spiritual roots of his grandfather R' Mordechai Abadi, which were planted deep within the holy tradition of Aram Soba. He writes, "You come from a holy place, the holy of holies, you are a grandson to our master the rabbi, the *gaon*, the great one, a wellspring of knowledge, with no end to his depth, and with deep analytical abilities and tremendous sharpness, the crown of our head, the honorable and holy rabbi, Mordechai Abadi, whose fame extends from one end of the globe to the other." R' Ezra continues with two stories illustrating the greatness of R' Mordechai (See boxes: "When Brilliance Is Inspired" and "But Where Is Rabbah bar Nahmani?")

When Brilliance Is Inspired. R' Abraham Haim Ades (see #37) told of the time he was one of the students of R' Mordechai Abadi. They were studying an unusual *halachic* ruling of the *Ra'avad* (R' Abraham ben David of Posquieres). Based on all the accepted approaches to this issue, the *Ra'avad's* ruling did not seem to make any sense. However, R' Abadi instinctively came up with a whole new way of learning the underlying *Gemara* that revealed what must have been the *Ra'avad's* thinking. In fact, it resolved all of the questions that had been raised against his ruling.

R' Eliyahu Tawil (see #581), one of the students learning in the group, was a little skeptical. He admitted that the answer was brilliant and innovative, but doubted it was possible that R' Abadi could have recreated the *Ra'avad's* own thought processes. The next day, one of the rabbis was studying *Temim Deyim*, a book of responsa by the *Ra'avad*. In one of the responsa he discovered an explanation of the *Gemara* that had been discussed. Word for word, the approach that the *Ra'avad* had followed was the same as R' Abadi had given the day before.

When he arrived at the *Bet Midrash* in the middle of the night, there was only one man there — R' Mordechai Abadi. Before R' Tawil had a chance to say a word, R' Abadi suggested, "Drink something, you are fasting. I know why you have come. If you make a commitment not to tell anyone about your dream, I will explain the *Zohar* to you." R' Eliyahu immediately made the commitment and R' Mordechai explained the *Zohar* to him.

The above story was related by R' Ezra Attiah (see #102) who concluded that R' Abadi's soul had a spark of the soul of Rabbah bar Nachmani.

R' Abraham Salem (see #471) relates a story to show R' Abadi's greatness in Kabbalah. A great *gaon* from Europe visited Aram Soba and asked to see a great Kabbalist to clarify an issue that was bothering him for twenty years. They sent him to R' Abadi who gave a short answer. At first the rabbi didn't grasp how it answered the question, but R' Abadi said, "Take some time and think about it." He did and after a few minutes, he literally began to dance for joy.

R' Abadi was not afraid of stating his opinion, even when the listener might not like what he had to say. Once a wealthy man complained of the rabbis of late who make investments and are making money (as if to say, let them stick to Torah study and stay out of an area that belongs to businessmen). R' Abadi answered immediately. "G-d gives money to the wealthy as a *pikadon* (property held in trust) to give to the Torah scholars. To reward them for this holy mission they can keep some as well. However, when they don't fulfill their mission, G-d gives the money directly to the rabbis with no middleman."

He was not afraid of stating his opinion, even when the listener might not like what he had to say.

He was especially renowned for his many books and writings, among which were the following major works:

- *Dibrei Mordechai* (Aram Soba 5633/1873). This book was written during his tenure as rabbi of Kilis, when he discouraged the use of Arabic love songs as a basis for the tunes of synagogue prayers. He excuses it slightly on the basis that if they didn't have popular tunes with Hebrew words and concepts, people would sing the original Arab lyrics. However, the book offers support for a more authentic approach to the music of prayers by presenting a number of poetic *pizmonim* (hymns), set to the traditional musical scales known as *Maqamat*. [See also the analysis on this topic by R' Yaakob Hillel in his book of responsa entitled *Vayashev HaYam*.]
- *Mikra Kodesh* (Aram Soba 5633/1873). Special prayers that were said in Aram Soba before dawn and on Friday evenings. The book is introduced by an essay called *Shaar HaShir*, written by R' Abadi. It was published through the joint efforts of R' Mordechai Abadi, R'

Title Page of Dibrei Mordechai

Vikuach Na'im was written to counter the antireligious people who sought to undermine the Jewish faith by pointing to difficult passages in the Gemara and Midrashim.

Eliyahu Hamway (see #271), and R' Eliyahu Dahab.

- *Hen Mordechai* (Przemyel 5639/1879, Kracow 5652/1892). A guide to spiritual development based on the mystical approach to Torah. This volume also includes a commentary by R' Alter Noah HaCohen, called *Darkei Hen*.
- *Ma'ayan Mayim* (Jerusalem 5642/1882 and 5646/1886). Inspirational lectures on the *parashot* of the *Humash*, based on all aspects of the Torah *(Pshat, Remez, Drash, and Sod)*. The book was published in two volumes and was written in Aramaic. Volume II appeared after the author had passed away and was published by his two sons: R' Abraham and R' Shaul Raphael.
- *Melitz Na'im* (Jerusalem 5687/1927). Spiritual guidance in poetic form. It was published by the author's son R' Shaul Raphael Abadi (see #10), who wrote an introduction. This book and *Vikuach Na'im* were bound together in one volume.
- *Vikuach Na'im* (Jerusalem 5687/1927). This book was written to counter the antireligious people who sought to undermine the Jewish faith by pointing to difficult passages in the *Gemara* and *Midrashim*. The book explains these passages in a faith-affirming way. It was published by the author's son R' Shaul Raphael Abadi (see #10), who wrote an introduction. R' Abadi may have been prompted to write a book fighting for the belief in the *Midrashim* of our *Hazal* after he saw the damage being done to the "simple faith" of the community by the distribution of the book *Em LeMikra* in Aram Soba.
- *Ma'ayan Ganim* (Jerusalem 5718/1958 and 5721/1961). Volume I consists of responsa on *Orah Haim* and *Yoreh Deah*. Volume II consists of responsa on *Hoshen Mishpat*. Published by a grandson of the author, R' Shaul Matloub Abadi (see #9).
- *Na'im Zemirot* (Jerusalem 5722/1962). Commentary on *Tehillim*, based on all aspects of the Torah *(Pshat, Remez, Drash, and Sod)*. It begins with an essay on the nature of man.
- *Mei Ma'ayan* (Jerusalem 5726/1966). Commentary on *Pirkei Avot*. This book was published in the anthology *MeHalab Ha'Aretz* published by R' Yosef Shayo (see #507).

Title Page of *Vikuach Na'im*

R' Mordechai describes the difficulties he faced in getting his books printed.

In the introduction to *Ma'ayan Mayim* R' Mordechai describes the difficulties he faced in getting his books printed. On one occasion he received funds from the family of R' Ovadiah Ashkenazi to publish one of his books. As it happened a respected emissary of the institutions of Jerusalem was passing through the town of Kilis and R' Mordechai asked him to be his agent for the publishing effort. To that end he gave the visitor the manuscript and a sum of money to pay for printing. He heard nothing more from his agent after that. After four years had gone by, R' Mordechai finally gave up on his agent. Fortunately, he had made a copy of the book and so he was able to start the process of getting it printed, all over again.

Among the other major rabbinical authorities who spoke highly of R' Abadi in their books were R' Abraham Bik and R' Yaakob Shaul Elyashar. When he passed away in Beirut on 3 Sivan, 5643 (1883), he was eulogized by R' Yaakob Shaul Dweck (see #248), as recorded in the book *She'erit Yaakob* (Ch.1).

[9] ABADI, R' Shaul Matloub
רבי שאול מטלוב עבאדי

(1887 — 1970)

Distinguished scholar and rabbi of Aram Soba. He was born in Aram Soba on 2 Av, 5657 (1887), a grandson of R' Mordechai Abadi (see #8). His father's name was R' Abraham Abadi.

His Early Years

He studied Torah in Aram Soba under R' Ezra Shayo (see #505) and rapidly developed into a brilliant and learned scholar. He studied with R' Yitzhak Dayan (see #208) as well.

Because of the difficult economic circumstances in Syria, he thought to make his future in Jerusalem, where he married the daughter of the Kabbalist R' Nissim Nahum (see #437). With the founding of the yeshiva *Porat Yosef*, its trustees sought to appoint R' Abadi as *Rosh Yeshiva*, but he declined. Somehow he felt that Jerusalem was not for him and he returned to Aram Soba, where he established a Talmud Torah named *Magen David*.

Coming to America

Seeing the deteriorating conditions in Aram Soba and the continued Jewish emigration from Syria, he decided to move to the United States, which is where he lived out the remaining years of his life. He generally sought to avoid formal rabbinical positions, but wherever he went people honored him and readily accepted his spiritual guidance.

He was principal of the Talmud Torah in Brooklyn and conducted a class in *Rambam* for almost 40 years with many of the top students of the community. The teaching in the Talmud Torah at that time still followed the old style as practiced in Syria, with Hebrew and Aramaic text being translated into Arabic. R' Abadi strongly opposed this as the students of the new generation did not understand Arabic very well. He successfully fought for translating into Hebrew, that is, from the original text to a basic Hebrew that the students could understand.

R' Nissim Nahum

His Legacy

An American student of R' Abadi once visited R' Moshe Tawil (see #586), *Rosh Yeshiva* of the yeshiva *Zichron Moshe* of Tel Aviv, at his home in Israel. R' Moshe had studied under R' Abadi and he literally jumped for joy on hearing regards from his Rabbi. He told the visitor that he owed everything to R' Abadi, both in this world and the World to Come.

He wrote a noteworthy introduction to the book *Ma'ayan Ganim* of his grandfather R' Mordechai Abadi. In the introduction he included an extensive review of the historical background of Aram Soba, with a discussion of its illustrious rabbinical families and personalities.

He married the daughter of the Kabbalist R' Nissim Nahum.

He passed away in Brooklyn at the age of 83 on 23 Tevet, 5730 (1970). That was the same year in which his own *hiddushim* (original Torah thoughts) and responsa were published in the book *Magen Ba'adi* (Brooklyn 5730/1970).

He was unusually versed in the beauties of the Hebrew language, which he shared with his students. In the introduction to *Magen Ba'adi,* he wrote a poem that speaks of the glory of his ancestry in Aram Soba and mourns the spiritual damage done by the immigration to America. His expression of pain bespeaks of the glowing embers of holiness that he inherited from his grandfather, R' Mordechai Abadi. "In Aram Soba I was born and saw a blessing in my learning, which I owe to my parents who dedicated me to learning. On many nights the floor

R' Shaul Matloub Abadi

"On many nights the floor of the Midrash was my bed ... in my heart I cry, because I am in America and I should be in Jerusalem ..."

of the *Midrash* was my bed ... the bread fled from my basket. I traveled to Jerusalem hoping to build my future. Unfortunately, I encountered obstacles there and was forced to go to America ... I feel tremendous shame, in my heart I cry, because I am in America and I should be in Jerusalem ..."

He describes the status of Sephardic education in America before he and Isaac Shalom helped open *Magen David*. "The disgrace of Torah in our community is like an arrow in my liver. They are reading in a mechanical fashion. In understanding they are no different than the Italian and Irishman. The soul of the Syrian community cries out, 'America has pushed my nursing baby from my breast.' The public school system was built from my destruction. The ones that were supposed to guard my walls have attacked me."

"I wish children would continue on in Torah. We'll give you scholarships. We'll send you to Jerusalem to perfect yourself there. Go learn in Porat Yosef."

When the Syrian Jews first came to America, there were no *yeshivot* for their youth. A generation later, they had *Magen David* elementary school, but no high school. It wasn't until the next generation that their children had higher Torah education.

Nothing stopped him, neither physical weakness nor weather; nothing stopped him from his set learning times.

R' Matloub dedicated his energies to remedying the problems that he found and to foster higher Torah learning in the Syrian community. He spoke the following words in the course of an address, which he delivered at an elementary school graduation:

R' Matloub dedicated his energies to remedying the problems that he found and to foster higher Torah learning in the Syrian community.

"Even though there are people studying Torah today, their learning of *Gemara* is still only at a basic level. Although that is important, one must get to a higher level. Without it, the student doesn't reach his potential. It's a shame that only a few from our yeshiva continue to higher learning. Those that have done so were successful and we're proud of them . . . It's sad that parents are only pushing higher secular education, and not higher Torah education."

"Sending your children to a higher Torah education is a lifesaving mission."

In 1964 R' Matloub wrote in a letter, "Sending your children to a higher Torah education is a lifesaving mission. This will stop them from drowning in the mire of this city's abominations. There is no better defense to protect your youth from immodest behavior. The hard work of immersing themselves in the study of *Gemara* will keep them from being caught up in the inanities of the American culture."

He continues, "I wish children would continue on in Torah. We'll give you scholarships. We'll send you to Jerusalem to perfect yourself there. Go learn in *Porat Yosef* ... There is no greater kindness than supporting these young scholars. You will cause many to gain merit; you will be righteous and sit together with the *talmidei hachamim* (scholars) in the World to Come."

R' Yaakob Kassin (see #330) praised R' Matloub in a special journal, which was published in 1965 to celebrate his 40 years of dedication to teaching. These are his words: "Since our rabbis tell us you should only offer a portion of a person's praises while you are in his presence, I will only mention a few of his great qualities. Above all was his great loyalty to the job; nothing stopped him, neither physical weakness nor weather; nothing stopped him from his set learning times. At times in the winter the heat wasn't sufficient. [Editor's note: According to reliable sources this was due to lack of funds.] Nevertheless, R' Abadi was in his room teaching the students energetically and strengthening himself to overcome all obstacles, for the sake of teaching Torah to Jewish children."

[10] ABADI, R' Shaul Raphael
רבי שאול רפאל עבאדי

(19th century)

Worthy scholar and rabbi of Aram Soba. He was a son of R' Mordechai Abadi (see #8) and was responsible for preparing many of his father's books for printing. At the Ben-Zvi Institute may be found edited manuscripts of the books *Melitz Na'im* and *Vikuach Na'im* in R' Shaul's handwriting (file no. 4810). The title pages indicate that the editing was completed in 5649 (1889). In the National Library in Jerusalem there is a printed copy of the book *Mahane Yehudah* by R' Yehudah Kassin (see #331) with R' Shaul's signature, indicating that it had once belonged to him.

[11] **ABADI, R' Shelomo**

רבי שלמה עבאדי

(18th century)

Eminent scholar and rabbi of Aram Soba and Safed. His father's name was R' Gabriel Abadi. After establishing himself as a scholar in Aram Soba, he immigrated to Safed. However, severe economic conditions in Safed caused him to start a new settlement in the nearby town of Yassef. This became a very challenging initiative and he was forced to go abroad to seek funds to build a synagogue and *Bet Midrash*. He carried with him two letters of introduction explaining his mission. One letter was dated 1747 and was signed by various rabbis of Safed among whom was R' Shimon Dweck (see #246). A second letter, dated 1748, was issued by rabbis of Aram Soba including R' Shemuel Laniado (see #373) and R' Yosef Dayan (see #210). The letters are quoted in the book *Shibolim Bodedot* (Jerusalem 5675/1915, p. 26).

In 1741 R' Shelomo went to Salonika to arrange for printing of his books *Shaare Rahamim* and *Shaare Ratzon*. These works contain commentaries on the *tefillot* assembled from the writings of R' Haim Cohen (see #161), following the *Ari'zal* (R' Yitzhak Luria).

[12] **ABADI, R' Shimon**

רבי שמעון עבאדי

(1826 — 1892)

Eminent scholar and rabbi of Aram Soba and Tiberias. He was born in 1826 in Aram Soba to R' Abraham (see #1). In 1840 he moved to Tiberias together with his parents and rapidly became known as one of the leading personalities of the city. Like many of the rabbis of Tiberias he made a number of trips abroad to raise needed funds for Torah institutions. In 1857 he signed a document together with the rabbis of Tiberias, relating to the renewal of the yeshiva *Bet Yaakob* by the philanthropist, R' Yitzhak Gouiatta. In 1867 he was one of the signers to the announcement for the memorial to R' Meir Baal Haness in Tiberias.

Title Page of Shaare Rahamim

He authored many works of responsa and inspirational lectures but none were printed, except for his commentary on the Haggadah, *Sha'ah Tovah* (Jerusalem 5669), which also included a work about the month of Nissan, entitled *Nahal Eitan*.

He was a brother-in-law of R' Mordechai Abadi (see #8), with whom he maintained an active correspondence. In their letters, which consisted primarily of *hiddushim* (original Torah thoughts) , the two men addressed each other with great respect in a poetic style. Some of the correspondence is included in the book *Tov Re'i* (331) of R' Yosef Haim Yaluz (Jerusalem 5694/1934).

R' Shimon passed away in Tiberias on 5 Av, 5652 (1892). He was blessed with five scholarly sons-in-law, one of whom was R' Yitzhak Abo, who served as the French consul in Safed. One of R' Shimon's two sons was named Abraham after R' Shimon's father. When the second son was born, R' Shimon had passed away and so the child was named Abba-Shimon.

[13] **ABADI, R' Yaakob**

רבי יעקב עבאדי

(— 1876)

Eminent scholar and rabbi of Aram Soba. He was the son of R' Abraham Abadi. R' Yaakob composed a number of *pizmonim* (hymns), such as *"Yesh Mefazer Mamon,"* which is mentioned in the book *Peri Etz HaGan* of R' Yaakob Kassin (see #330). He passed away on the fifth day of Pesah 5636 (1876). He authored three unpublished works:

- *Kehillat Yaakob*, inspirational lectures on the Torah
- *Doresh Mishpat*, 14 eulogies
- *Tolaat Yaakob*, inspirational lectures

[14] ABADI, R' Yehudah

רבי יהודה עבאדי

(— 1903)

Worthy scholar and rabbi of Tiberias. He was born in Tiberias to R' Haim Abadi (see #7). In 1867 he was one of the signers to the announcement for the memorial to R' Meir Baal Haness in Tiberias. He passed away in Tiberias in 1903.

[15] ABADI, R' Yeshuah

רבי ישועה עבאדי

(19th century)

Eminent scholar and rabbi of Aram Soba. He was known for his book *Kol Rinah ViYeshuah* (Livorno 5613/1863), containing inspirational lectures on *Bereshit* and *Shemot*. In this book he also included an appendix entitled *Kuntras Shaare Yeshuah*, containing responsa related to the purchase of cheese from Moslems, as well as *hiddushim* (original Torah thoughts) on the tractate *Abodah Zarah*. He also included some of the *hiddushim* of his grandfather R' Yeshayah Dabbah (see #171). Among those who assisted him in getting his book published were his brother-in-law R' Matloub Rahamim, R' Matloub's son R' Ezra Haim, his own brother R' Shalom Abadi, as well as Señor Eliyahu di Picciotto (see #453) and his sons Señor Hillel and Señor Moshe di Picciotto (see #458).

ספר

קול רנה וישועה

ישועה עבאדי ס"ט:

פה ליוורנו

מדפיסים ומוכרי ספרים

Title Page of Kol Rinah ViYeshuah

In 1852 he joined other rabbis of Aram Soba in signing the approbation to the book *Kenisiyah Leshem Shamayim* by R' Menashe Sutton (see #551). (See Document Section, Document No.31 for the full text.)

He suffered much from poverty and from the burden of supporting a family with minimal income. This forced him to spend much time on earning a living so as to avoid depending on the generosity of others. However, he became embroiled in conflicts with non-Jews, from which he was rescued by R' Moshe di Picciotto (#458). To add to his other woes he agonized over not being blessed with sons to carry on his name.

[16] ABADI, R' Yitzhak

רבי יצחק עבאדי

(— 1847)

Eminent scholar and rabbi of Aram Soba. He was the father of R' Ephraim Abadi (see #5). One of his responsa was introduced with great respect in the book *Mar Ve'Ahalot* of R' Abraham Antebi (see #63) in the section on *Hoshen Mishpat* (no. 6). He is also spoken of with reverence in the book *Bet HaSimhah*, in which the author, R' Abraham Hamway (see #269), addresses a learned question that R' Abadi had raised. He passed away in 1847.

[17] ABADI, R' Yitzhak

רבי יצחק עבאדי

(— 1923)

Worthy scholar and rabbi of Tiberias. He was born in Tiberias to R' Haim Abadi (see #7). He passed away there in 1923.

[18] ABADI, R' Yosef

רבי יוסף עבאדי

(— 1866)

Eminent scholar and rabbi of Aram Soba. He is mentioned with great respect in the book *Rei'ach Sadeh* by R' Shimon Dweck (see #246) in the section on *Parashat Toldot* (p. 9) and similarly in the book *Hazon Obadiah* (p. 16c) by R' Obadiah Levy (see #392).

[19] ABADI (DAHAB), R' Eliyahu

רבי אליהו עבאדי (דהב)

(1898 — 1977)

Worthy scholar and scribe of Jerusalem. He was born in 1898 to R' Yitzhak Abadi (see #23). He was a brother of R' Ezra Abadi (see #20) and a son-in-law to the Kabbalist R' Rahamim Shrem (see #514). In his youth he studied in the *yeshivot* of Jerusalem and in 1914 received a certificate, identifying him as an expert scribe, qualified to prepare Torah scrolls, *tefillin*, and *mezuzot*. The certificate was issued by the master scribe R' Yihya ben R' Yosef Tzarom and endorsed by the Sephardic *Bet Din* of Jerusalem.

R' Eliyahu was one of the first residents of the new neighborhood of Bayit Vagan in the western suburbs of Jerusalem. He was actively involved in building the great Sephardic synagogue of Bayit Vagan, as well as the associated *mikveh*. He then served the synagogue as the *gabbai*, *hazzan* (cantor), and *baal koreh* (Torah reader) over a period of more than 40 years. In the last year of his life he suffered severe heart problems which required a number of hospital stays. He passed away on 20 Tevet, 5738 (1977).

He was actively involved in building the great Sephardic synagogue of Bayit Vagan, as well as the associated mikveh.

[20] ABADI (DAHAB), R' Ezra

רבי עזרא עבאדי (דהב)

(— 1914)

Worthy scholar and rabbi of Aram Soba. He was a son of R' Yitzhak Abadi (see #23) and a brother of R' Eliyahu Abadi (see #19). He was constantly immersed in Torah studies, to the extent that he was often unaware of what was happening around him.

R' Ezra married the daughter of the great Kabbalist R' Yehudah F'taya. They were blessed with only one child, a daughter. However, she gave them many scholarly grandsons, including R' Ezra Basri, named after his grandfather. R' Basri became a member of the Appeals *Bet Din* in Jerusalem. Other grandsons were R' Menachem Basri (the founder of the yeshiva *Sucath David* of Jerusalem) and R' David Basri.

R' Ezra Abadi suffered much from illness and passed away at a relatively young age on 4 Nissan, 5674 (1914).

[21] ABADI (DAHAB), R' Shaul

רבי שאול עבאדי (דהב)

(— 1884)

Worthy scholar and rabbi of Aram Soba. He was the father of R' Yitzhak Abadi (see #23). In his later years he moved to Jerusalem, where he passed away on 22 Heshvan, 5644 (1884). A eulogy delivered by R' Shaltiel Yaakob Ninyo appears in the book *Hen VeKavod* (lecture 18, page 69).

[22] ABADI (DAHAB), R' Shaul (Shehidyah)

רבי שחידיה עבאדי (דהב)

(19th century)

Worthy scholar of Aram Soba. He was a son of R' Eliyahu Abadi (see #19). His name also appears on the list of scholars receiving the weekly stipend (see #267).

[23] ABADI (DAHAB), R' Yitzhak

רבי יצחק עבאדי (דהב)

(— 1914)

R' Yitzhak Abadi (Dahab)

Eminent scholar and Kabbalist of Aram Soba. He was a son of R' Shaul Abadi (see #21). R' Yitzhak was known for his brilliance and his knowledge of all aspects of Torah. He authored an unpublished book of inspirational lectures on the Torah, called *Toldot Yitzhak*. He also contributed an important article to the Torah journal *HaMe'asef*, in Issue V of the third year, 5657 (1897). In addition some of his *hiddushim* (original Torah thoughts) were published in the book *MeHalab Ha'Aretz* (Jerusalem 5726/1966) of R' Yeshaya Dayan (see #203). Other *hiddushim* of his are included at the end of the book *Minhat Yehudah* of R' Yehudah Attiah (see #118).

In his later years R' Yitzhak moved to Jerusalem. He passed away on 8 Tevet, 5675 (1914) leaving four scholarly sons: R' Ezra (*see* #20), R' Eliyahu (*see* #19), R' Mordechai, and R' Yosef Abadi.

[24] ABBA SHAUL, R' Ben-Sion

רבי בן ציון אבא־שאול

(1924 — 1998)

Saintly *Rosh Yeshiva* of *Porat Yosef*, Jerusalem. Although not of Syrian descent, he is part of this work due to his status as *Rosh Yeshiva* of *Porat Yosef* and prize

> *R' Ezra said it was worth opening Porat Yosef just to produce a student like Hacham Ben-Sion.*

student of R' Ezra Attiah (see #102). R' Ezra said it was worth opening *Porat Yosef* just to produce a student like Hacham Ben-Sion.

His Parents

He was born in Jerusalem to R' Eliyahu and Benaya in 1924. His father had immigrated from Persia when he was a young boy and was the *gabbai* of the synagogue *Ohel Rachel*. He was a shoemaker by trade, but a dedicated scholar, who rose early to study Torah in a group of other pious workingmen.

R' Ben-Sion Abba Shaul

Although making due with only very limited means, R' Eliyahu and Benaya were anxious to own a home in Jerusalem. They learned of a parcel of land on Shmuel HaNavi Street, which was on the "green line" between Israel and Jordan. The land was relatively inexpensive because it was an extremely dangerous place to live in, but nevertheless the family lacked sufficient capital to make the transaction. When Benaya learned of the situation, she immediately took her jewelry and told her husband, "Sell all my jewelry so we can afford to buy the land."

When his mother was pregnant with the future R' Ben-Sion Abba Shaul, every time she met a *hacham*, she asked him, "Please pray that my son should eventually become a *talmid hacham* (Torah scholar)."

While still an infant, Ben-Sion Abba Shaul once had a high fever, but the family was poor and couldn't afford to take him to a doctor. His mother cried herself to sleep because she couldn't take care of her child. As she slept, she had a dream in which a man appeared to her and said, "I am Eliyahu HaNavi. This child will grow to be a great rabbi one day, and he has brought *berachah* (blessing) into your house. Because of this child, your husband's business will be successful. I have put a silver coin in his pocket and with this coin, he will be able to buy goods, and he will prosper."

When she woke up in the morning, her husband was returning home from early morning prayers. She told him about the dream, and he started to laugh. When he put his hand in his pocket, sure enough, there was a silver coin that he hadn't put there. With that coin, he bought goods, and indeed became successful.

His Early Years

Ben-Sion was the first of sixteen children and was named after his grandfather, R' Ben-Sion. There is a tradition of ten generations of "Ben-Sions'" that were *talmidei hachamim*.

As a young boy, during the war years in Jerusalem, the young Ben-Sion would give his bread to his sister telling her, "You're weaker, you need it more." He would fast and sustain himself with learning.

At the age of 11, he entered the yeshiva *Porat Yosef*, where he continued to progress until he became the *Rosh Yeshiva*. His first teacher there, Hacham Yehudah Sadkah (see #468), taught the young class of wonder boys — many of whom also became great rabbis — in great depth. Other members of the wonder class were Hacham Sion Levi, Hacham Ovadiah Yosef, and Hacham Baruch Ben-Haim. Ben-Sion continued on to the highest *shiur*, that of R' Ezra Attiah (see #102). The two enjoyed a special closeness and had a similar, intensive approach to learning.

Hacham Ben-Sion standing among his teachers
Left to right: R' Yaakob Ades, Hacham Ben-Sion, R' Ezra Attiah, R' Mansour Ben-Shimon, R' Yosef Ades, R' Moshe Porush

R' Eliezer Silver testing the boys of Porat Yosef. Hacham Ben-Sion is to his right, R' Ezra Attiah and R' Yehudah Sadkah are to his left.

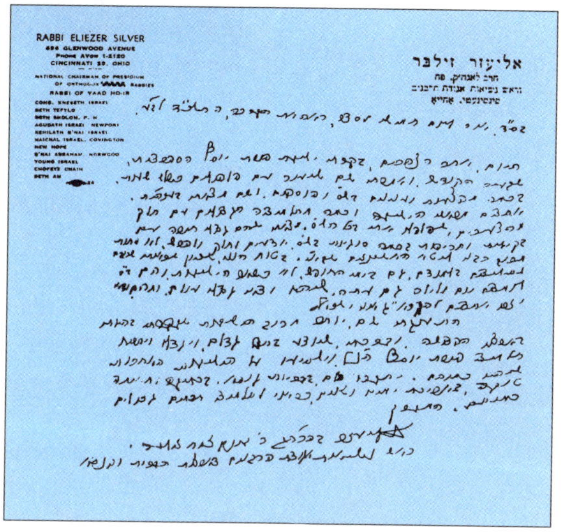

RABBI ELIEZER SILVER
694 GLENWOOD AVENUE
PHONE AVON 1-2120
CINCINNATI 29, OHIO

NATIONAL CHAIRMAN OF PRESIDIUM OF ORTHODOX RABBIES
RABBI OF VAAD HO-IR
CONG. KNESETH ISRAEL
BETH TEFYLO
BETH SHOLOM, P. H
AGUDATH ISRAEL NEWPORT
KEHILATH B'NAI ISRAEL
HAICHAL ISRAEL, COVINGTON
NEW HOPE
B'NAI ABRAHAM, NORWOOD
YOUNG ISRAEL
CHOFETZ CHAIM
BETH AM

אליעזר זילבר
הרב לאנהיק, פה
ראש נשיאות אגודת הרבנים
סינסינעטי, אהייא

Original letter from R' Silver describing Porat Yosef
See Document Section, Document No. 34.

From a very young age at *Porat Yosef*, R' Ben-Sion Abba Shaul was already known as the pride and joy of Hacham Ezra Attiah, the *Rosh Yeshiva* (see #102). When he was 20, a wealthy man from America came with Rabbi Eliezer Silver of Cincinnati, to test the boys of different *yeshivot*, in order to decide where to donate money.

R' Ezra Attiah, the *Rosh Yeshiva*, was nervous; he had heard from boys at other *yeshivot* that the test was difficult. R' Silver asked a complicated question from *Masechet Taharot*, which is not widely learned. Hacham Ben-Sion answered on the spot. R' Silver was impressed and commented that 40 years before, he had asked the question to R' Meir Simchah of Dvinsk, the *Ohr Sameach*, a great rabbi of the previous generation, and had received the same answer. When R' Silver went back to America, he sang the praises of a Sephardic boy named Ben-Sion. He also wrote a highly complimentary letter about what he had seen in the yeshiva. (See Document Section, Document No. 34.)

Later, Hacham Ben-Sion told Hacham Ezra Attiah that he also had a second answer to the question. But since one answer was sufficient to secure the donation for the yeshiva, he felt giving the second would amount to showing-off unnecessarily.

His Learning

Hacham Ben-Sion's first apartment was on Elkanah Street in Jerusalem, next door to that of Hacham Ovadiah Yosef. Every day, they would walk to the yeshiva *Porat Yosef* together and review a complete page of *Gemara* each way. During the Yom Kippur War, they sat together in a bomb shelter learning in darkness.

Even after he had a stroke, his wife would sit at his side as he would say over his *hiddushim* (original Torah thoughts) and she would write them down. When his vision further deteriorated, his students would read the *Gemara* to him.

> He would say over his hiddushim and she would write them down.

While learning *Masechet Nazir* (not a commonly learned section of *Gemara*), one student made a mistake while reading a *Rashi* (commentary) and Hacham Ben-Sion immediately corrected him from memory. His son had a similar experience while reading a *Rambam*. A student related that he once sat with him for half an hour, asking him questions of *Hilchot Niddah*, and Hacham Ben-Sion quoted the *Shulhan Aruch* by heart.

"There are no shortcuts," he told his students. "The only way to learn correctly is to constantly study and review."

When he met R' Chaim Kreiswirth, a rabbi from Antwerp who also had a remarkable memory, R' Chaim commented, "Abba Shaul is one of the names of the *Tannaim* (Rabbis of the *Mishnah*)." Then, in turn, each of the rabbis went on to quote all the instances where Abba Shaul is mentioned in the entire *Gemara*.

Hacham Ben-Sion often said, "A yeshiva boy should have one worry in life: How will I keep myself from thinking about Torah in places that it is forbidden to think about Torah?" When he went to the *mikveh*, he would rush, explaining that it was difficult for him to not be thinking about Torah during that time.

Hacham Ben-Sion's greatness is widely attributed to his dedication to the study of Torah. "There are no shortcuts," he told his students. "The only way to learn correctly is to constantly study and review." His *hatmadah* (diligence) knew no bounds. He spent the entire day, and a good part of the night, learning and reviewing tens of times until he knew most of *Shas* and *Poskim* by heart. When R' David Soloveitchik finished looking through the first volume of Hacham Ben-Sion's book, *Ohr LeSion,* he commented, "The *amelut* (effort) is recognizable in every piece." His teaching was also infused with effort; after giving a class, his clothing would be wet from perspiration.

Finding Torah Next Door. When *Ohel Rachel Shul* was locked early on Friday mornings, Hacham Ben-Sion would go to the *Navaradok* yeshiva next door and engross himself in a *Gemara*. People were amazed that they could almost bump into him yet he remained totally engrossed in the *Gemara*.

His Marriage

Hacham Ben-Sion was hand-picked by R' Yosef Shaharbani to marry his daughter Hadassah. He and his wife were tremendously devoted to each other. However, the most righteous men often endure difficult tests throughout their lives. Before having their only child, Hacham Ben-Sion's wife suffered ten miscarriages. Their only son, Eliyahu, was born after they received a blessing from the *Hazon Ish* and the Belzer Rebbe.

"If a man doesn't even know how to get along with his wife, how can he learn Kabbalah and get the title Mekubal (Kabbalist)?"

While his son Eliyahu was still young, Hacham Ben-Sion would bring the boy to recite *Kabbalat Shabbat* (prayers welcoming *Shabbat*) in the fields as taught by the great Kabbalist, *Ari'zal*. As they walked from his home to the fields and back, Hacham Ben-Sion would impart to his son words of *mussar*, often stressing the importance of respecting his mother.

Promoting the Study of Kabbalah

At one point he became aware that the knowledge of Kabbalah was diminishing. The people that were delving into it were not properly learned in other areas. He himself hadn't opened a book of Kabbalah until he completed the entire Talmud (*Bavli* and *Yerushalmi*). He thereupon gathered older *mekubalim* (Kabbalists) and started the yeshiva *Emet VeShalom* for learning Kabbalah at night.

He stressed the need for purification of character traits before learning Kabbalah. He said, "If a man doesn't even know how to get along with his wife, how can he learn Kabbalah and get the title *Mekubal* (Kabbalist)?"

His Power of Blessings

When R' Ben-Sion Abba Shaul was asked, "How do your *berachot* work?" He gave three reasons: "When you love *Klal Yisrael* (the Jewish nation), you can give blessings." Also, "*Hashem* told Abraham, 'I will bless the ones that bless you.' When people come to kiss my hand, they are blessing me. So when I bless them, it works." He also said, "If you guard your tongue, your blessings will work." If a person's tongue isn't used for lying, *lashon hara* (gossip), and improper speech, it will have the power to bless.

His Humility and Reverence

When R' Ben-Sion went to visit the Kabbalist HaRav Yisrael Abuchatzeira, he was asked what he does. Although he was the *Rosh Yeshiva* at the time, he simply said that he learns in the *Kollel* of *Porat Yosef*.

Once while visiting in the Israeli city of Ashdod, Hacham Ben-Sion heard of a man who passed away at a young age. Although he didn't know the family, he went to pay his respects. While there, he saw a young boy learning. The boy, an orphan of the deceased man, told him he was learning *Masechet Gittin*. Hacham Ben-Sion then learned with the young boy over the phone. The relationship continued for many years and the boy eventually became a *Maggid Shiur* (lecturer) in a yeshiva.

Hacham Ben-Sion once told his son Eliyahu that after his rebbi, Hacham Ezra Attiah, passed away, any time he was faced with a difficult question of *halachah* he would envision his rebbi and think how he would have decided. When a booklet was circulated, advising Sephardim to wear their *sisit* (fringes) out, he said, "I don't need to look at the booklet, I know what Hacham Ezra held on this matter. In the past, when a student in *Yeshivat Porat Yosef* was wearing his *sisit* out, Hacham Ezra told him, 'Tuck them in. You are causing the previous generations to look bad.'" (See *Ohr LeSion, Responsa,* Vol. 2, Ch. 2 for more details.)

Hacham Ben-Sion once said that he had such reverence for Hacham Ezra Attiah that not a week went by in which he did not picture his rebbi in front of him — sometimes he saw him in front of him every few hours. In his humility, Hacham Ben-Sion said in the eulogy for Hacham Ezra Attiah, "I merited one-fortieth of the *Rosh Yeshiva*'s depth in learning."

His Passing

He suffered much from painful illnesses in his later years and passed away on 19 Tamuz, 5758 (1998). R' Yehudah Ades said in his eulogy, "More than the purification process of his constant pain and suffering was his purification through toil in Torah." Hacham Ben-Sion always put special effort into explaining *Rashi*, feeling a special connection to *Rashi* because he was born on *Rashi's yahrzeit*. "Because of the effort I put into explaining *Rashi*," he believed, "he will come to greet me when I leave this world."

> *Hacham Ben-Sion always put special effort into explaining Rashi, feeling a special connection to Rashi because he was born on Rashi's yahrzeit.*

His Legacy

During his lifetime the following of his works were published:

- *Ohr LeSion*, *Responsa*, Parts 1 and 2.
- *Ohr LeSion*, *Commentary* on the tractate *Yebamot*.
- *Ohr LeSion*, *Topics* on the laws of the Sabbatical Year (*Shevi'it*).
- *Ohr LeSion*, *Topics* on Torah concepts and *mussar* (ethics).

Posthumously, the book *Tiferet Sion* was published, containing a collection of eulogies that he delivered for various Torah scholars, as well as eulogies that others delivered about him.

His other works are still in manuscript form.

> *Any time he was faced with a difficult question of halachah he would envision his rebbi and think how he would have decided.*

[25] ABIGDOR (BISTRIA), R' Yitzhak

רבי יצחק אביגדור (בסתריה)

(— 1918)

Humble scholar of Aram Soba. R' Yitzhak, whose father's name was Moshe, authored an unpublished book on the symbolic allusions to be found in Torah writings. He was a good and gentle man, who lived frugally within his limited means. R' Yitzhak passed away on 14 Adar, 5678 (1918).

[26] ABIYAD, R' Eliyahu

רבי אליהו אביץ'

(— 1900)

Deeply committed scholar of Aram Soba and *Eretz Yisrael*. He was born in Aram Soba to R' Shaul Abiyad (see #27) and moved to *Eretz Yisrael*, where he lived for the rest of his life. He passed away at a relatively young age on *Rosh Hodesh* Heshvan, 5661 (1900).

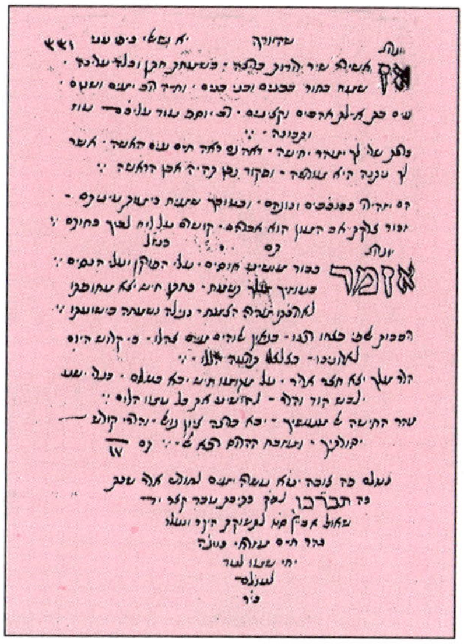

Handwrittten Pizmon of R' Shaul Abiyad (see #27)

[27] ABIYAD, R' Shaul

רבי שאול אביץ'

(— 1880)

Devoted teacher of *Gemara* in the Talmud Torah of Aram Soba. He was also a poet and composer of *pizmonim* (hymns). His son was the scholar R' Eliyahu Abiyad (see #26). He passed away on 26 Kislev, 5641 (1880).

R' Aharon Aboud

[28] ABOUD, R' Aharon

רבי אהרן עבוד

(— 1949)

Eminent scholar and Kabbalist of Jerusalem. He was a son of the Kabbalist R' Eliyahu Aboud (see #29) and studied in the yeshiva *Porat Yosef*. He was appointed to supervise and teach the students of the yeshiva *Oz VeHadar*, associated with *Porat Yosef*, but specializing in the study of Kabbalah. However, he passed away at a relatively young age on 28 Tishrei, 5710 (1949).

[29] ABOUD, R' Eliyahu

רבי אליהו עבוד

(1871 — 1936)

Eminent scholar and Kabbalist of Jerusalem. He was born in Aram Soba in 1871 and moved to Jerusalem as a young man. He was given a responsible position in the yeshiva *Porat Yosef,* where he excelled in both the revealed and mystical aspects of the Torah. He was known for his ability to comfort and nurture people with personal problems. He passed away in Jerusalem on 10 Shevat, 5696 (1936) and was buried on the Mount of Olives.

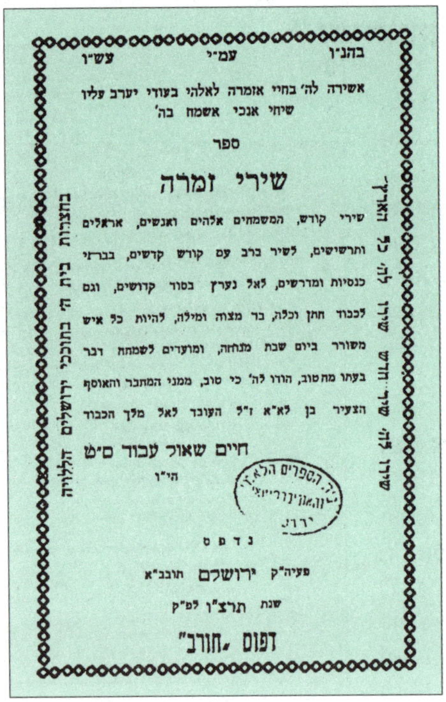

בהנ"ו עמ"י עש"ו

אשירה לה' בחיי אזמרה לאלהי בעודי יערב עליו

שיחי אנכי אשמח בה'

ספר

שירי זמרה

שירי קודש, המשמחים אלהים ואנשים, אראלים ותרשישים, לשיר ברב עם קורש קדשים, בבתי כנסיות ומדרשים, לאל נערץ בסוד קדושים, וגם לכבוד חתן וכלה, בר מצוה ומילה, להיות כל איש משורר ביום שבת מנוחה, ומועדים לשמחה דבר בעתו מה טוב, הודו לה' כי טוב, ממני המחבר והאוסף הצעיר בן לא"א ז"ל העובד לאל מלך הכבוד

חיים שאול עבוד ס"ט

הי"ו

נדפס

פעיה"ק ירושלם תובב"א

שנת תרצ"ו לפ"ק

דפוס „חורב"

שירו לה' שיר חדש שירו לה' כל הארץ

בחצרות בית ה' בתוככי ירושלים הללויה

Title Page of Shirei Zimrah

[30] ABOUD, R' Haim Shaul

רבי חיים שאול עבוד

(1890 — 1977)

Eminent composer and *hazzan* (cantor) of Aram Soba and Jerusalem. He was born in Aram Soba in 1890, the son of R' Abraham Aboud and the grandson of R' Eliyahu Aboud, who had been head of the *Hevra Kadisha* (Burial Society) in Ein Tab, a small town near Aram Soba. He was influential in preserving and invigorating the musical tradition of Aram Soba, especially working to make the traditional hymns of Aram Soba popular in Jerusalem. He composed many songs and hymns which he published in a book called *Shirei Zimrah*. He passed away in Jerusalem on 21 Sivan, 5737 (1977).

[31] ABOUD, R' Shelomo

רבי שלמה עבוד

(— 1911)

Worthy scholar of Aram Soba. He passed away on 22 Iyar, 5671 (1911).

[32] ABOUD, R' Yitzhak

רבי יצחק עבוד

(— 1903)

Chief Rabbi and *dayan* (judge) of the town of Maraas (near Aram Soba). He was born in Aram Soba and immigrated to Jerusalem, but returned to Aram Soba when he found the economic conditions in Jerusalem too difficult.

One of his responsa appears in the book *Et Sofer* (*Even HaEzer*, 3) of R' Ezra Tawil (see #582). The topic is the testimony of witnesses that can release a woman from her married state when her husband is believed dead. He passed away on 15 Tevet, 5663 (1903).

[33] ABOUD (KILSI), R' Yitzhak

רבי יצחק עבוד (קילזי)

(1876 — 1931)

Worthy rabbi and Talmud Torah teacher of Atlantic City and New York during the 1920's and 1930's. He was born in 1876 in the Turkish town of Kilis. After becoming a rabbi in Kilis he immigrated to Syria with his family and settled in Aram Soba. There, people called him "Kilsi" because of the town from which he came.

In Aram Soba he started a *Kitab* (Talmud Torah), beginning with a small class of young boys who were taught *Aleph Bet*. As the youngsters advanced he taught them to read the daily Hebrew prayers and, later, the *perashah* (weekly portion of the Torah) with its liturgical notes *(taamim)*. Each Thursday he taught them the portion which would be read the following week. He would also teach the corresponding *haftarah* with its proper tune.

After the students became proficient in reading he would teach *Shareh* (translating into Arabic the prayers, the *perashah,* and the *haftarah)*. Approximately three weeks before each Jewish holiday he would teach the proper readings and tunes pertaining to that holiday, in Hebrew and Arabic.

He also composed an Arabic translation of *Shir HaShirim* (Song of Songs).

After World War I, R' Yitzhak and his family moved to the United States. He originally taught Talmud Torah classes in Brooklyn, when he was offered a similar position by the Jewish community of Atlantic City. The results of his teaching in Atlantic City were spectacular. In one year's time the students went from *Alef Bet* to basic *Gemara*. Unfortunately, at the end of one year, there was a dispute with the local committee and he left his position.

He then moved back to Brooklyn and established his own small synagogue and Talmud Torah in the Sea Beach area at the corner of 65th Street and 21st Avenue. Over time, the *Kitab* grew to about 50 boys from 4 to 12 years of age.

R' Yitzhak was an excellent teacher and acquired a reputation as an outstanding *lomed tinokot* (teacher of young children). To this day, the boys who studied under him are recognized for their mastery of the Hebrew texts with their traditional melodies.

In the 1960's, two of R' Yitzhak's ex-students organized prayers for 90 young children during the High Holy Days (*Rosh Hashanah* and *Yom Kippur*). The prayers were held in the *Midrash* of the *Shaare Sion* Congregation and the two organizers were the chief *hazzanim* (cantors). This *minyan* (prayer group) continued to serve the community for many years during the High Holy Days.

It was common knowledge in the Syrian community of Brooklyn that his prize student in Syria was R' Ezra Mishanieh (see #421), who eventually became a rabbi in Brooklyn and became a top teacher in the local *Magen David* Talmud Torah.

R' Yitzhak passed away on 28 Adar, 5691 (1931) at the young age of 55. He was fondly remembered by his many students who had received their basic Hebrew foundation from him.

Title Page of R' Yitzchak Aboud's (#33) Arabic translation of Shir HaShirim (New York 1907)

[34] **ABOUD-ATTAR, R' Haim**

רבי חיים עבוד־עטר

(19th century)

Worthy scholar of Aram Soba. He is one of the two witnesses to a partnership contract dated 6 Tishrei, 5639 (1878), which is stored at the Ben-Zvi Institute (file no. 302). The parties are identified in the document as R' Haim Eliyahu Abadi and R' Yosef Raphael Attiah. The witnesses are R' Yedidya Dayan (see #201), who was the first signer, and R' Haim Aboud-Attar.

[35] **ABULAFIA, R' Yitzhak**

רבי יצחק אבואלעפייא

(1830 — 1910)

Distinguished scholar and Chief Rabbi of Damascus over a period of 34 years. He was the author of the six-volume book of responsa *Penei Yitzhak,* and was sometimes referred to as the *Penei Yitzhak*. R' Yitzhak was a scion of the illustrious Abulafia lineage, which consisted of five successive generations of pious scholars and rabbis. The patriarch was R' Haim Abulafia, author of the classic book *Etz HaHaim* and a descendant of the royal line of King David. R' Haim Abulafia founded the *yishuv* (settlement) in Tiberias.

R' Yitzhak Abulafia

His Early Years

R' Yitzhak Abulafia was born in Damascus in 1830 to R' Moshe Abulafia. His father was one of the rabbis of Damascus who were falsely accused and imprisoned during the infamous Damascus blood libel of 1840. His grandfather was R' Haim Nissim Abulafia, known by the acronym HANA. He was one of the great rabbis of Tiberias, and in his later years was appointed to the position of *Rishon LeSion* (Chief Rabbi) in Jerusalem.

His father was one of the rabbis of Damascus who were falsely accused and imprisoned during the infamous Damascus blood libel of 1840.

As a young boy in Damascus, Yitzhak Abulafia became known for his unusually sharp mind and so his grandfather R' Haim Nissim Abulafia invited him to come to Tiberias to study. Once he got the taste of learning Torah in depth he quickly advanced and it was not long before he exceeded his teachers.

His Missions Abroad

He became known as one of the most learned of the scholars of the fabled city of Tiberias and when the opportunity arose to send out an emissary to raise funds he was chosen for the mission. He made two trips to the cities of North Africa, visiting Tunis, Algiers, Tripoli, and others. The first trip was as an emissary of Tiberias. It was followed by a second trip, this time as an emissary of Safed. The Safed trip kept him on the road from 1860 to 1865. He was well received everywhere and asked to provide *halachic* rulings on issues that had come up over the years. He also provided approbation to books written by scholars in the cities which he visited.

R' Alfandri responded, "If there is such a great scholar, it is my duty to go there and learn from him."

His Return to Tiberias

Upon his return to Tiberias he became well known as an expert on complex *halachic* issues. He was consulted on a wide variety of questions, which he described in his six-volume work *Penei Yitzhak*. He also described there his discussions and correspondence with other rabbis, including R' Raphael Maman, R' Habib Sutton, the *Rishon LeSion* (Chief Rabbi of *Eretz Yisrael*) R' Haim David Hazzan, and the *Rishon LeSion* R' Abraham Ashkenazi. The first five volumes were published in Livorno (5631/1871) and in Izmir (5647/1887). Volume VI was published in Jerusalem (5665/1905).

R' Alfandri said, "I promise you that you will get up from this illness, but you must believe in the power of my promise, and with that power you will make a full recovery."

His Return to Damascus

In 1873 he was called to serve as the Chief Rabbi of Damascus, the city of his birth. He remained in this position until 1909. During his tenure in Damascus he governed with strength and dignity. He avoided showing favoritism to any person, no matter how rich or influential. He also gave public lectures on important occasions and many of these were later incorporated into Volume VI of his book *Penei Yitzhak*.

He was blessed with only one daughter, who was married to the eminent philanthropist, Señor Haim Moshe Laniado (see #356). In his book, R' Yitzhak praises his son-in-law, who was like a son to him, and thanks him for his help in publishing *Penei Yitzhak*.

In 1878 he published another book, *Lev Nishbar* (Izmir 5638), which was written to answer the arguments raised by R' Shalom Hai Gagin of Jerusalem against the rulings which he had published in *Penei Yitzhak*. He writes that he was surprised and saddened to see that R' Gagin had published his objections because on a trip to Jerusalem he had met with R' Gagin and was under the impression that all of the issues had been resolved.

The Saba Kadisha

In 1897 R' Shelomo Eliezer Alfandri (see #44) of Constantinople (known as the *Saba Kadisha*) received an official letter from the Ottoman government notifying him that he had been appointed as the Chief Rabbi (*Hacham Bashi*) of Damascus. The *Saba Kadisha* decided to travel to Damascus to present himself there. However, his friends sought to discourage him from going, as R' Yitzhak Abulafia, who was known as a brilliant man and a strong-willed community leader, would not take kindly to someone questioning his authority. However, R' Alfandri responded, "On the contrary, if there is such a great scholar, it is my duty to go there and learn from him."

For the first few months the two rabbis did not do anything together but after that each began to recognize the greatness of the other and they established an excellent working relationship to share in the responsibilities of governing Jewish affairs in the city.

On one occasion R' Yitzhak became deathly ill and was unable to move or speak. The doctors gave up hope for his recovery. When R' Shelomo Eliezer visited him, he said, "Hacham Yitzhak, I promise you that you will get up from this illness, but you must believe in the power of my promise, and with that power you will make a full recovery." To this, R' Yitzhak responded, "Amen."

After a few days, R' Yitzhak did in fact recover and went outside. Shortly thereafter, it became known that one of his close friends had become seriously ill and died, all within a short time. The deceased had lived in the neighborhood of the *Saba Kadisha* and so the *Saba Kadisha* went to the funeral, where he met R' Yitzhak. As they talked, R' Yitzhak reminded the *Saba Kadisha* about the time he had come to visit him on his sickbed. "After you left my house, this man (just now deceased) began to laugh and said to me, 'How is it possible that a man can recover from such a serious illness?' But when I did recover, through your blessing, he fell ill and passed away." R' Shelomo Eliezer responded, "Let this matter be silent and sealed. Don't tell anyone about it!"

His Final Return to Tiberias

In 1909 R' Yitzhak retired from his position in Damascus and returned to Tiberias, where he had grown up. He stayed in the house of his cousin, R' Rahamim Shelomo Abulafia, one of the respected rabbis of the city. It was there that he passed away on 16 Adar, 5670 (1910) at the venerable age of 80.

Ades Lineage. The illustrious Ades family was an offshoot of the ancient Antebi family. To distinguish between them and another Antebi family that lived in Aleppo, the two families were referred to as "Antebi-Saka" and "Antebi-Ades." Ultimately, Antebi-Ades became simply "Ades."

[36] ADES, R'Abraham Haim

רבי אברהם חיים עדס

(1920 — 1936)

Young scholar of Jerusalem. He was born in Jerusalem in 1920, the oldest son of R' Yaakob Ades (see #41) and a grandson of R' Abraham Haim Ades (see #37). He was an intensely committed student and showed promise of future greatness. However, at the age of 16 he suffered complications during a tonsillectomy, which resulted in his death on 18 Nissan, 5696 (1936).

[37] ADES, R' Abraham Haim

רבי אברהם חיים עדס

(1857 — 1925)

Distinguished scholar and *dayan* (judge) of Jerusalem, co-founder of yeshiva *Rehovot HaNahar*. He was born in Aram Soba in 1857 to R' Yitzhak Ades, a pious textile merchant (see #42). As a young, intensely committed student he showed signs of future greatness and at the age of 20 was taken as a son-in-law by the notable Chief Rabbi of Aram Soba, R' Moshe Swed (see #575). It is related that during this period, R' Ades studied so intensely that puddles of perspiration collected underneath the table at which he sat. After his marriage he devoted himself solely to Torah, studying with his colleague R' Yitzhak Shrem (see #517).

His Insight Into People

Among his other qualities, he was an extremely discerning person. On one occasion an emissary of the *Kol Yisrael Haverim* organization (Alliance Israelite Universelle) came to his synagogue to speak about the school they were introducing in Aram Soba. At the time the true nature of this organization was not yet apparent, but R' Ades immediately suspected that the visitor's intent was to plant an irreligious way of thinking in the minds of the people. And so he forcefully ejected the emissary from the synagogue.

R' Ades immediately suspected that the visitor's intent was to plant an irreligious way of thinking in the minds of the people. And so he forcefully ejected the emissary from the synagogue.

His Nurturing Role

While still a young man, R' Ades began to teach Torah in Aram Soba. Among his students were many men who were destined to become great rabbis. He imbued his students with a deep love of Torah, stressing the significance of devoting one's entire life to Torah study. Instilling such an ideal, however, was very difficult because of the harsh economic conditions that existed at that time. But R' Ades was not deterred. He not only taught the importance of such a goal, but he also arranged financial aid for his students so that they could continue to study undisturbed.

"One who wants to achieve the superlative level of total cleaving to Hashem cannot pamper himself with lavish food and clothes. He must keep his earthly needs to a minimum."

For eighteen years he guided the scholars who became the leaders of the next generation: R' Yosef Yedid (see #594), R' Ezra Hamway (see #37), R' Ezra Abadi Shayo (see #505), R' Ezra Attiah (see #102), and other scholars who taught in Aleppo and Jerusalem.

All the while, he himself continued to grow in his knowledge of revealed and mystical studies, ultimately becoming one of the great Kabbalists of the era.

His First Visit to Jerusalem

In 1890 he visited Jerusalem, staying at the house of R' Yaakob Shaul Elyashar, the *Rishon LeSion* (Chief Rabbi of *Eretz Yisrael*), who was very supportive. R' Elyashar was so impressed with his brilliance that he brought him water to wash his hands in the morning *(netilat yadayim)*. Despite his brilliance, R' Ades was extremely modest and humble and was generally silent. Some people remarked that he seemed to be a totally spiritual being.

R' Elyashar was so impressed with his brilliance that he brought him water to wash his hands in the morning.

His Return to Jerusalem

Because of the encouragement he received from R' Elyashar, R' Ades returned to Jerusalem five years later, this time to stay. The wealthy R' Shalom Musayof provided him with a rent-free apartment. He was quickly integrated into the community of scholars and rabbis of Jerusalem and joined the Sephardic *Bet Din*, where he presided alongside R' Yosef Yedid (see #594), his onetime student, and R' Ezra Harari-Raful (see #304). He also became one of the cofounders of the Kabbalist yeshiva *Rehovot HaNahar* in the Bukharan quarter.

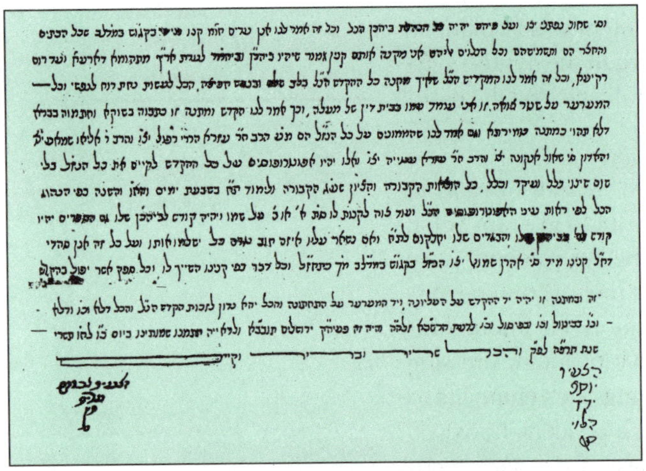

R' Abraham Ades handwritten will

He became renowned as a holy and saintly man, imbued with *ruach hakodesh* (the Divine spirit). Many inspiring stories are told about this remarkable man.

His Daily Regimen

R' Abraham's neighbor in Jerusalem, R' Raphael Meir, was like a member of his household. He once related that R' Abraham's daily diet consisted of coffee and a roll for breakfast, a roll and yogurt for lunch, and a little rice and soup for supper.

R' Raphael Meir asked him how he could have the vitality to study Torah day and night from such paltry nourishment. R' Abraham replied confidentially, "R' Raphael, I greatly longed to see Rav Yisrael Baal Shem Tov to ask him why he had merited such a sublime spiritual level. Finally I merited to see him in a dream and was able to ask him this. He quoted the verse, 'You who cleave to *Hashem,* your G-d, are all alive today' (*Devarim* 4:4), and explained that one who wants to achieve the superlative level of total cleaving to *Hashem* cannot pamper himself with lavish food and clothes. He must keep his earthly needs to a minimum."

His Involvement in Public Issues

In 1924, a B'nai B'rith office was established in Aram Soba. The Torah sages of the Aram Soba community who were living in *Eretz Yisrael*, among them R' Ades, disapproved of this organization. R' Ades was very close with R' Yosef Chaim Sonnenfeld and visited him frequently. When R' Ades learned about the founding of B'nai B'rith in Aram Soba, he, R' Yosef Yedid (#594), and R' Ezra Harari-Raful (see #304) asked R' Sonnenfeld for his opinion about it. When he heard that R' Sonnenfeld vehemently opposed it, R' Ades publicized R' Sonnenfeld's opinion and it was quoted in a proclamation entitled *Koshet Dibrei Emmet*, which publicly decried it. (See Document Section, Document No. 23.)

R' Ades was also greatly pained by the secular education that was gaining a foothold in *Eretz Yisrael* during his later years. At that time, there were a number of secular schools on Yeshayahu Street. When R' Ades had to be on Yeshayahu Street, he would avoid passing by those schools; instead, he took a roundabout, lengthier route to his destination. Fortunately, today those schools are Talmud Torahs.

He was blessed with four scholarly sons.

His Legacy

However, he also experienced many difficulties in his life. His oldest son, Yitzhak, a brilliant scholar, passed away as a young man. In 1914, when the Turks were drafting young men of Jerusalem into their army, R' Abraham's sons Ezra (see #38) and Moshe (see #39) escaped to Bukhara where they remained completely out of touch with their father for seven years. The life of R' Ades ended tragically in 1925, when he was struck by a bus. For three days the rabbi suffered in pain until he passed away on 28 Av, 5685 (1925).

His greatness is reflected in his students, some of whom came to rival his knowledge and depth:

- ***R' Yosef Yedid*** (see #594). R' Yedid was some 10 years younger than R' Ades and became the *Av Bet Din* (Chief Judge) in *Eretz Yisrael* for the Syrian and Bukharan communities.
- ***R' Raphael Shelomo Laniado*** (see #364). R' Laniado joined his teacher, R' Ades, in Jerusalem, and became the *Rosh Yeshiva* of *Ohel Moed* and *Porat Yosef*.
- ***R' Ezra Attiah*** (see #102). When R' Ades noticed the enormous potential in a young poor orphan boy, he took it upon himself to support and teach him. The boy turned out to be the great R' Ezra Attiah, who became the *Rosh Yeshiva* of *Porat Yosef* after R' Raphael Shelomo Laniado.
- ***R' Ezra Hamway*** (see #272). R' Hamway originally intended to become a business man. R' Ades recognized that the young man had tremendous promise and went so far as to personally arrange financial sponsorship, overcoming the misgivings of his student's father-in-law. R' Hamway went on to become the Chief Rabbi and *Av Bet Din* (Chief Judge) of Syria.
- ***The Baba Sali, R' Yisrael Abuchatzeira, from Morocco.*** The *Baba Sali* declared that he discovered the answers to many of his most perplexing questions on Kabbalah on his first visit to *Eretz Yisrael* in 1920 when he learned with R' Ades.
- ***R' Yaakob Kassin*** (see #330). R' Kassin, Chief Rabbi of Syrian Jews in New York, revealed that occasionally he would consult his teacher, R' Ades, on difficult topics of Kabbalah.

In addition to teaching great rabbis, R' Ades fathered giants of Torah as well. His sons, R' Ezra, and R' Moshe, each became heads of distinguished Torah institutions while his youngest son R' Yaakob (see #41), who was married to Esther Harari-Raful, had many sons who became Torah scholars, including R' Yehudah Ades, who founded the yeshiva *Kol Yaakob* with the help of his brother R' David Ades. R' Abraham Ades also had a daughter Rachel, who married R' Aharon Harari-Raful (see #303), father of Hacham Abraham and Hacham Yosef Harari-Raful of the Brooklyn Syrian community.

Living Memories

His grandson, Abraham Ades, was told by R' Ezra Attiah (see #102), "If this whole room were filled with books from the floor to the ceiling and we were to say that your grandfather knew everything in them, it would not be an exaggeration. But this was not the main point of his greatness; rather it was his extraordinary depth of thinking."

"If this whole room were filled with books from the floor to the ceiling and we were to say that your grandfather knew everything in them, it would not be an exaggeration."

Another time he said, "Just as the waves of the sea sometimes throw out a precious pearl, so R' Abraham came into our generation."

Baba Sali, R' Yisrael Abuchatzeira, in his youth

In later years R' Ezra related that for two years after R' Abraham passed away, every night when he recalled his image, he began weeping, thinking of his shining face and his deep Torah words.

R' Ezra also recalled, "Once he entered *Yeshivat Ohel Moed* to return a book to its place and saw us studying. He asked what *Gemara* topic we were dealing with and he immediately begain to explain our theme in three different and very profound ways, although he was not at the time involved in learning our tractate."

R' Shalom Harari-Raful once recalled that when he was young he used to enter the *Baba Tama* synagogue in the Bukharan quarter of Jerusalem early in the morning, as R' Abraham was diligently studying, and then again in the evening, where R' Abraham was still sitting in the same place.

His Final Days. The final chapter of R' Abraham Haim's life was both the most tragic and the most inspirational. In 1925, a wealthy man in Jerusalem imported several buses for use in the city. Fascinated by the huge machines, this man, who had never driven before, decided to take one of the buses for a ride around the city. As it happened, the bus struck R' Abraham as he was crossing the street, critically wounding him. For three days the rabbi suffered in pain until his soul left him.

Describing the final hours of his life, R' David Harari-Raful tells of how R' Abraham used his last vestiges of strength to recite *Shir HaShirim*, which discusses *Hashem*'s love for the Jewish people, while instructing those around him to do the same. He then summoned those around him to serve as witnesses and, in accordance with *halachah*, which requires that *mehilah* (forgiveness) must be said aloud, he proclaimed in a clear voice, "I fully forgive the man who drove the bus that struck me. This was an act of *Hashem*. May *Hashem* bless this man with a long and good life."

[38] ADES, R' Ezra

רבי עזרא עדס

(— 1959)

Eminent scholar and teacher of *Porat Yosef* in Jerusalem. He was born in Aram Soba to the saintly Kabbalist R' Abraham Haim Ades (see #37), and moved to Jerusalem at a young age together with his parents. R' Ezra studied in the *yeshivot* of Jerusalem and became one of the teachers at *Porat Yosef*, where he continued to inspire students throughout his life.

At the outbreak of World War I, when the Turks were drafting young men of Jerusalem into their army, he escaped to Bukhara in Central Asia, where he joined his brother R' Moshe Ades (see #39) and others in teaching and guiding the people.

R' Ezra Ades

He suffered from painful illnesses throughout most of his life, but always maintained a cheerful appearance, showing friendliness and goodwill to everyone. He passed away on 20 Kislev, 5720 (1959).

[39] ADES, R' Moshe

רבי משה עדס

(1893 — 1969)

R' Moshe Ades

Distinguished scholar, *dayan* (judge), and teacher of Jerusalem. He was born in Aram Soba in 1893 to the saintly Kabbalist R' Abraham Haim Ades (see #37), and named after his mother's father, the Chief Rabbi of Aram Soba, R' Moshe Swed (see #575).

When he was 2 years old his family moved to Jerusalem and he grew up in that holy city. He rapidly developed into a brilliant scholar in both the revealed and mystical aspects of Torah. With the opening of the yeshiva *Porat Yosef* in 1923, he immediately became one of its luminaries. His association with *Porat Yosef* as scholar and teacher continued for over 35 years, nurturing generations of students, many of whom would become great in their own right. R' Moshe was known for his unique in-depth approach to Torah study, squeezing the most meaning out of every subject and every text.

He studied Kabbalah with the great *hachamim* of his generation at the yeshiva *Oz VeHadar*, which was adjacent to *Porat Yosef* in the Old City of Jerusalem. Among his colleagues at *Oz VeHadar* were R' Eliyahu Aboud (see #29), R' Ephraim Cohen, and R' Obadiah Hedaya (see #309). It was said that his knowledge of Kabbalah was as thorough and clear as his understanding of the plain text.

At the outbreak of World War I, when the Turks were drafting young men of Jerusalem into their army, he and his colleague R' Ezra Attiah (see #102) escaped to Egypt by sea via the port of Jaffa. In Egypt at the time there happened to be some emissaries from Bukhara in Central Asia, who were seeking to persuade Torah scholars to come to their country and raise the level of religious observance. This seemed like an opportunity to do good and so after some difficulty, R' Moshe made his way to Tashkent, where he lived for seven years. During that time he taught Torah to the people and inculcated the love of *Eretz Yisrael*. A number of other Torah scholars, including his brother R' Ezra (see #38) and his brother-in-law R' Aharon Harari-Raful (see #303), were in a similar situation, having escaped the Turkish rule in Jerusalem to live in various towns of the Bukharan region for the duration. Together they had an important influence on the Bukharan Jews, which resulted in increased identification with Judaism and a significant immigration to *Eretz Yisrael*.

After the war, R' Moshe returned to his home in Jerusalem, where he became a member of the Sephardic *Bet Din*. He remained in that position for many years together with R' Ezra Attiah (see #102), R' Obadiah Hedaya (see #309), R' Abraham Philosoph, R' Binyamin Levi, R' Yehudah Shako, and others.

R' Moshe was a resident of the Old City of Jerusalem for about 20 years until the outbreak of the War of Independence in 1948. During that time he joined with R' Pinchas Epstein and R' David Jungreis in issuing timely edicts to preserve the sanctity of *Shabbat* among the citizenry.

He maintained his regimen of Torah study and his clarity of mind throughout the illnesses of his later years, until his passing on 23 Av, 5729 (1969). Some of his *hiddushim* (original Torah thoughts) were published posthumously.

At the outbreak of World War I, when the Turks were drafting young men of Jerusalem into their army, R' Moshe Ades escaped to Egypt by sea via the port of Jaffa. From there he made his way to Tashkent, where he lived for seven years.

[40] **ADES, R' Moshe Yosef**

רבי משה יוסף עדס

(1924 — 1993)

Eminent teacher of *Yeshivat Porat Yosef* of Jerusalem for over 40 years. He was born on *Sukkot* of the year 1924 to R' Yaakob (see #41) and Esther Ades. He was named Moshe after his great-grandfather R' Moshe Swed (see #574) and Yosef to commemorate Yosef *HaSadik*, on whose *ushpizin* (*Sukkot* guest day) he was born. People generally referred to him as Hacham Yosef.

Eminent teacher of Yeshivat Porat Yosef of Jerusalem for over 40 years.

His Early Years

He studied in *Porat Yosef* in the Old City of Jerusalem under the tutelage of R' Yehudah Sadkah (see #468), his uncle R' Moshe Ades (see #39), the *Rosh Yeshiva* R' Ezra Attiah (see #102), and his father R' Yaakob.

He married Rachel, daughter of R' Aharon Aboutbol and granddaughter of R' Yomtob Yedid (#593).

His Bond with R' Ezra Attiah

He developed a special closeness with R' Ezra Attiah, the *Rosh Yeshiva* of *Porat Yosef*. The following incident illustrates the high esteem in which R' Ezra held him. When Hacham Yosef was still a young man, R' Ezra asked him to perform a *pidyon nefesh* (special prayer to save a life by offering a monetary redemption) for someone who was gravely ill. It seems that R' Ezra provided for this purpose 160 pure silver coins that he had inherited from his grandfather, R' Abraham Ades. Hacham Yosef did not feel worthy of

R' Moshe Yosef Ades

> *"Hacham Yosef is a walking book of mussar (spiritual and character development)."*

such an important assignment and questioned him. R' Ezra answered, "Why do you ask me if there are older people who can do it? Your *pidyon* will make a greater impact in Heaven."

When R' Ezra was old and needed to regain his health in a resort area, it was Hacham Yosef who accompanied him. He was even chosen as one of the ten students to do the *taharah* (purification of the body) after R' Ezra passed away.

His Devotion to Teaching

Besides teaching in *Porat Yosef* for over forty years, he gave a *Gemara* class for workingmen at the *Kotel* before sunrise for twenty-five years. When asked why he chose to focus on *Gemara,* he explained, "If I teach them only *halachot* they will be satisfied if their children learn *halachot* in a *shul*. However, if I teach them *Gemara* and they taste the sweetness they will want their children to have the maximum pleasure and send them to *yeshivot*." He advised, "It is only with teaching *Gemara* that you will connect with the people and they will love you."

When one of the workingmen told him that his daughter was engaged, he asked if the boy was religious. The man answered, "Of course." Hacham Yosef then asked, "Does he have set times for learning Torah?" The man answered that he didn't. Hacham Yosef said, "Then he's not religious. If a person doesn't have a set time for learning, he can't possibly keep the Torah and *mitzvot* properly."

> *"If a person doesn't have a set time for learning, he can't possibly keep the Torah and mitzvot properly."*

His Humility and Benevolence

He was known for collecting money every morning at the *Kotel* almost like a beggar asking for handouts. One of his students once asked, "Isn't it beneath your dignity to ask for handouts?" He answered, "Should I worry about my dignity when yeshiva boys go around with torn shoes?"

> *"Should I worry about my dignity when yeshiva boys go around with torn shoes?"*

R' Binyamin Beinush Finkel, former *Rosh Yeshiva* of the Mirrer Yeshiva of Jerusalem, who also prayed every morning at the *Kotel netz* (sunrise) *minyan,* once remarked, "Hacham Yosef is a walking book of *mussar* (spiritual and character development). Learning from a *mussar* book would not bring someone to the same level of humility that could be learned from observing Hacham Yosef. It is instructive to see how he treats himself like dust as he collects money for poor yeshiva students." Once a fellow who didn't appreciate collectors knocked the money out of his hand. Hacham Yosef didn't react. He just bent down and picked the coins up.

In time, people began to realize the importance of his work and gave him larger donations. In fact, there were years that he collected over $200,000. However, he never gave any of the proceeds to relatives, even if they were in need, so as not to arouse suspicion that he was favoring his family and not properly distributing the funds. He was a genius at giving out the money, being careful not to embarrass anyone. He knew to whom to give cash and to whom to give goods. There was a certain fellow who would spend any extra money on *mitzvot* (e.g., a beautiful *etrog*) and not use it for his family; to this man he gave food and clothing.

Toward the end of his life when he was on his sickbed, his son came to visit him. He asked his son if he had given out all the money for the coming holiday. When he told him that he had not yet done so, Hacham Yosef said, "Don't visit me until you finish giving it out."

His Meticulous Observance of Mitzvot

He took great care in the performance of *mitzvot* so as to satisfy all *halachic* opinions. As a young boy, when his father bought him second-grade *tefillin* due to a lack of funds, he saved up enough money to upgrade them. This was extremely difficult for a young boy from a poor family, so he first upgraded one half of the set and then the second half. Now they didn't match, so he eventually upgraded to a perfect set. Later on he bought a new set of small *Rashi* and *Rabbenu Tam tefillin,* so that he could wear them together.

His *matzot* on *Pesah* were made from wheat that was ground by hand, and he would bake them *Erev Pesah* after midday. The wine that he used for the *mitzvah* of *Arba Kosot* (Four Cups) was home made, without any sugar.

His Wisdom

He never read newspapers, not even religious ones, so as not to waste time or get involved in gossip. A neighbor once bought him a radio and he didn't want to embarrass the man, so he accepted it. He intentionally left it on the table in a place where he knew his children would play with it and break it. When the man asked him if he used it, he answered that his children broke it. In that way he extricated himself from an awkward situation without causing ill will.

He was involved in matchmaking and in the associated financial agreements between the sets of parents. On one occasion the parents agreed to split the cost of the young couple's expenses. Hacham Yosef raised the price another $10,000 to help the couple live above poverty level. The father of the boy felt he couldn't afford it, but gave in after Hacham Yosef pressed him. Later he asked Hacham Yosef why he put him in such a spot, knowing that it was beyond his means. Hacham Yosef explained, "The other side can well afford it. I will give you $5,000 and the couple will end up with $10,000."

He passed away at exactly age 69 on 20 Tishrei, 5754 (1993).

[41] ADES, R' Yaakob

רבי יעקב עדס

(1898 — 1963)

Distinguished scholar, *dayan* (judge), and *Rosh Yeshiva* of *Porat Yosef* in Jerusalem. He was born there in 1898 shortly after the arrival of his father, R' Abraham Haim Ades (see #37), from Aram Soba.

His Early Years

He received his initial education from his father and in 1910, when he was 12 years old, his father enrolled him in the yeshiva *Ohel Moed*, which was the forerunner of *Porat Yosef*. R' Yaakob studied there under the *Rosh Yeshiva,* R' Raphael Shemuel Laniado (see #364), and under R' Yosef Yedid (see #594), until 1914 when World War I broke out. During the war period the yeshiva was forced to close because so many of its students and scholars had to flee in order to avoid being drafted into the Turkish army. Some went to Egypt and others went to Bukhara in Central Asia. However, R' Yaakob managed to stay in Jerusalem, despite the difficult conditions of those years. In 1918, after the war, the yeshiva students returned and tried to rebuild the yeshiva and renew their studies.

R' Yaakob Ades

R' Yaakob Ades addressing fellow judges

Torah Between the Lines. Because of the great poverty in his father's home, R' Yaakob Ades rarely ate supper as a youth. When he went to the home of his *havruta* (study partner), R' Ezra Harari-Raful (see #304), he was often invited to stay for supper. After he became engaged to R' Ezra's daughter he stopped coming to their home out of modesty, although the result was that he had to do without supper. In the week after their wedding *(Sheva Berachot)* he stayed at home all the time learning Torah without interruption. Due to their poverty he had almost nothing to eat the entire day. Another demonstration of their poverty, which today can hardly be imagined, is that among the many writings of Torah he left behind, he wrote a great part of them between the lines of wedding invitations and other pieces of paper he could find.

R' Yaakob looking over plans with R' Ezra Attiah.

In 1919, he married Haya Esther, the daughter of R' Ezra Harari-Raful (see #304), who had come to *Eretz Yisrael* from Aram Soba in 1890 and founded *Yeshivat Ohel Moed* in 1907. She was a very clever and worldly wise woman who joyfully bore the burden of livelihood so that her husband could devote himself to the study of Torah. The unanimity between them was outstanding and well known in the community. She passed away in Jerusalem on 4 Adar, 5748 (1988).

His Role as an Educator

His greatness in Torah was soon recognized and in the year 1920, when he was only 22 years old, he was made a *Maggid Shiur* (lecturer) in *Yeshivat Ohel Moed* at the side of R' Raphael Shelomo Laniado. He officiated in this position until Iyar 1923.

When *Yeshivat Ohel Moed* was closed in that year, its pupils and staff went with their *Rosh Yeshiva*, R' Raphael Shelomo Laniado, to *Yeshivat Porat Yosef*. Thus, R' Yaakob was appointed as *Maggid Shiur* in *Porat Yosef*, and later as *Rosh Yeshiva*. He gave daily *shiurim* (lectures) in the yeshiva: in the morning in *Gemara* and in the afternoon in *Halachah* — *Tur* and *Shulchan Aruch Hoshen Mishpat*. He continued in this position for 20 years, nurturing a generation of scholars and rabbis.

R' Yaakob was appointed as Maggid Shiur in Porat Yosef, and later as Rosh Yeshiva. He continued in this position for 20 years, nurturing a generation of scholars and rabbis. He had a talent for developing each student's potential.

His approach to Torah study was notable for its depth and for its completeness, linking the Talmudic give-and-take to the resulting *halachah* as determined by the various rabbinical authorities, such as the *Rambam* and the *Bet Yosef*. He made the studies come to life using stories and narratives to give insight into human behavior and ethics. He had a talent for developing each student's potential.

R' Yaakob would come home at 10 p.m., sleep for only a few hours and then leave at 2 a.m., to teach a class for workingmen until it was time for the *netz* (sunrise) *minyan* in the morning. Throughout the rest of the day he was so busy that his wife had no way of knowing if or when he was eating.

Preserving Torah in its purity was for R' Yaakob a part of Torah itself. Once, the Joint Distribution Committee (JDC) proposed that *Yeshivat Porat Yosef* organize a program called *Bet Hora'ah*, to train Torah scholars to become *dayanim* (judges). This program would require that the students devote two hours of each afternoon to the study of *halachic* civil law (*Shulhan Aruch Hoshen Mishpat)* and the laws of marriage and divorce (*Shulhan Aruch Even HaEzer)*. The "Joint" promised great financial support at a time when the financial situation of the Torah community was very bad, and such support could be very beneficial to the yeshiva. However, R' Yaakob was very strongly opposed to the program. He explained that never in the past generations had such an idea come up, to learn Torah toward a specific position. Jews learned Torah, grew with it, and naturally, whoever was found suitable for a position was appointed

He was very strongly opposed to the program. He explained that never in the past generations had such an idea come up, to learn Torah toward a specific position.

to it. But to study for a specific position was unacceptable. He argued that it was our duty to pass on Torah to the coming generations just as we had received it from our forefathers and teachers. It should be noted that when the proposal was brought before the *Rosh Yeshiva*, R' Ezra Attiah (see #102), he responded in the same manner without having spoken with R' Yaakob.

During the time R' Yaakob was a teacher in the yeshiva, an influential outside rabbi proposed that the study of foreign languages be introduced into the yeshiva curriculum with the noble purpose of enabling the scholars to officiate as rabbis in communities abroad. R' Yaakob and the *Rosh Yeshiva* deliberated how to quash this idea. A suitable opportunity arose on the *yahrzeit* of the yeshiva's patron, Yosef Shalom. It was customary for all the yeshiva students and rabbis to assemble on the anniversary, and R' Yaakob — after coordinating it with the *Rosh Yeshiva* — gave an inspiring address against the introduction of the study of languages in the agenda. His words had the desired effect. The program was removed from the agenda and it was made clear that any additional attempt to raise it would be rejected.

These ideas were subsequently expressed in a letter from the *Rosh Yeshiva* to R' Yaakob in which he addressed R' Yaakob as "a man of war, who overcomes any struggle." It might seem surprising that he described R' Yaakob in such terms, as anyone who had met him once could attest to the tenderness of his character and his great humility. And yet, here we find his great friend the *Rosh Yeshiva*, who undoubtedly knew him better than anyone else, characterizing him in such sharp terms. The answer is that, as we are aware, all the great rabbis in all generations, although humble and tender in their manner, demonstrated an unlimited strength and firmness when they dealt with *Kevod Shamayim* (the honor of *Hashem*). The source of their humility was *Hashem's* will and that same will was the source of their strength and firmness when there was a question of *Kevod Shamayim*. (See Document Section, Document No. 37.)

He argued that it was our duty to pass on Torah to the coming generations just as we had received it from our forefathers and teachers.

All the great rabbis in all generations, although humble and tender in their manner, demonstrated an unlimited strength and firmness when they dealt with Kevod Shamayim (the honor of Hashem).

Doing the Impossible. At the groundbreaking ceremony for *Yeshivat Porat Yosef* in the 1920's, R' Yaakob Ades spoke and related the story of R' Hanina Ben Dosa. According to the *Midrash*, R' Hanina Ben Dosa was a very poor man, who lived from *Erev Shabbat* to *Erev Shabbat* on one pound of carobs. But his piety was such that the entire world merited their *parnasah* (livelihood) because of him. R' Hanina saw people bringing sacrifices to the *Bet HaMikdash* in Jerusalem. He also wanted to bring a sacrifice, but didn't have any money for an animal. Instead, he decided to contribute what he could. He found a big rock, smoothed it out, and shined it so that it could serve as a bench for the people coming to visit the *Bet HaMikdash*.

The *Midrash* explains that once he was done with the rock, R' Hanina didn't know how he would transport it to Jerusalem. The first group of people he asked wanted too much money. Finally, a group of five strong men agreed to carry the rock for only a small fee, but on the condition that R' Hanina help in carrying the rock as well. R' Hanina placed his arms under the rock with the other men to lift it, and the next moment, he found himself in Jerusalem; the five men had disappeared. He then realized they were angels. Since he wasn't able to pay the men, he gave the fee he promised them to a yeshiva in Jerusalem.

R' Yaakob concluded, "We learn from R' Hanina, that although something might seem impossible to accomplish, all *Hashem* needs you to do is put your hand under it. You only need to start with the smallest effort, and he will send the angels. When we wanted to built a yeshiva in the midst of the poverty of the Old City in Jerusalem, people thought we were crazy. We put our hands under the rock and *Hashem* helped us accomplish it. When R' Hanina put his hands under the rock, it wasn't only the rock that went to Jerusalem; he went with it. We also aren't only building a yeshiva ... when the yeshiva comes up, we also move up to great places."

Porat Yosef's cornerstone dedication in Geulah; see box, previous page

His Role as Rabbi and Dayan

In 1935, being one of the senior lecturers of *Porat Yosef*, he was appointed by the *Rishon Le-Sion*, R' Yaakob Meir, to be a member of the Sephardic *Bet Din*, and officiated in this position until 1943.

In 1935, being one of the senior lecturers of Porat Yosef, he was appointed to be a member of the Sephardic Bet Din.

In 1944 he was appointed to a seat on the Sephardic *Bet Din* of Tel Aviv and at the same time he also became rabbi of the Tel Aviv Congregation of Syrian Jews (Aram Soba). He fulfilled this function with the greatest dedication and loyalty, leaving his Jerusalem home at the beginning of every week and returning only near *Shabbat*.

In 1945 he was appointed *dayan* (judge) in Jerusalem, and ten years later he was elected to the *Bet Din HaGadol* (Highest Religious Court), first as *dayan* and later as *Av Bet Din* (Senior Judge), together with R' Betzalel Zolty, Chief Rabbi of Jerusalem, and R' Yosef Shalom Elyashiv. He held this position until the end of his life in 1963.

It was his practice to fast so that he should not make errors in his judgments.

It was his practice to fast so that he should not make errors in his judgments. Every day that he needed to set up a *get* (divorce), he would fast to ensure that he would not make any mistake in his preparations, in order to avoid any error which would prevent the wife from being able to remarry.

He was always concerned with the dignity of the *Bet Din*. He made a point of asking the *dayanim* who sat with him in the *Bet Din* to wear a hat rather than just a *kippah* (skullcap), because this would inspire greater respect among the litigants.

On one occasion, when R' Ezra Attiah (see #102) was ill, he sent a messenger with money to R' Yaakob Ades in order to do *pidyon nefesh*, that is, paying a rabbi to pray for his recovery. His son asked him, "Why are you giving money to R' Ades to pray for you, when there are poorer people who need it more?" R' Attiah answered, "When you have a court case, you don't hire the poorest lawyer, you hire the best lawyer. I need someone whom *Hashem* loves to pray for me."

It was almost impossible to see R' Yaakob being angry. But his family remembers two cases in which he got terribly angry, and sent people out of his house. The first one occurred on the day before *Yom Kippur* as the family was eating the *Seudah Mafseket* (the last meal before the fast). During the meal, a man came to the house bringing a bottle of wine for the Rabbi. R' Yaakob became furious and rebuked him, saying: "Aren't you ashamed, to come at this time, on *Erev Yom Kippur*? Where is your fear of G-d?" It was only later that the family discovered the reason for R' Yaakob's anger: That man was scheduled to appear before R' Yaakob in the *Bet Din* that same week, and he wished to appease him with a bottle of wine. Although R' Yaakob did not accept the wine, he refused to deal with the man's case and transferred it to another *dayan*. A similar event occurred with another man who brought a golden watch as a gift, and again he was driven out of the house and his case brought before another *dayan*.

His Benevolence

One *Erev Shabbat* R' Yaakob came home later than usual, only an hour before *Shabbat*. That morning, he had seen an old man crying because he needed a doctor, but he didn't know where to go. R' Ades spent the day accompanying the old man, whom he didn't know, to the doctor, sitting with him there, and bringing him home afterwards.

Once, a poor rabbi came to Jerusalem to be tested for the position of *dayan*. He arrived at the house of R' Yaakob before going to the *Bet Din*. R' Yaakob noticed that the man was dressed shabbily, and he was concerned that someone might think he was a beggar when he arrived to be tested. R' Yaakob himself had only one suit, so he switched clothing with the poor rabbi, and wore the rags until he returned.

Once a writer brought his book for R' Yaakob to review. When he left, one of R' Yaakob's sons disrespectfully remarked that the writer emphasized his own name too prominently in the title of the book. R' Yaakob immediately responded, "Listen, my son. I give you my blessing to study Torah and compose scholarly books; you may even identify the books explicitly with your own name and add the title 'the great *gaon*.' You don't know how much this man toiled and invested in his writing until he succeeded in completing it. So how can you disdain his efforts in Torah study?" He then cited one of our Sages, who remarked that even one good idea in a book justifies its publication.

His Hatred of Gossip

Gossip and slander were never heard in his house. Although his noble soul prevented him from directly rebuking others talking gossip *(lashon hara)* in his presence, they immediately felt by the change in his facial expression that even the slightest hint of libelous talk distressed him very much. On the other hand, when he heard words of praise about somebody, particularly a Torah scholar, his face lit up. His sons attested that they could not remember any occasion in which he expressed words of criticism of any person, group or institution. On the contrary, he always strove to stress his approval.

His sons attested that they could not remember any occasion in which he expressed words of criticism of any person, group or institution.

When, nevertheless, he had to negatively comment about anything, it was done in a soft and quiet manner, with gentle words. He used to quote the verse, "All that does not pass through fire, make it pass through water" *(Bamidbar* 31:23), and interpret it to mean that even words of criticism, intended to guide a fellow man toward the way of Torah, should not be expressed in "fire," but in "water," softly and patiently.

His Meticulous Observance of Mitzvot

His strict adherence to *halachah* could often be seen between the lines of his writings, such as when he used the phrase, "Although one might be lenient about this, I could not dare to permit it."

He was especially conscientious about choosing the "Four Species" (*Arba Minim*) for *Sukkot*. He spent several hours to find the most outstanding *etrog*, and on the day after *Yom Kippur*, only after he had inspected hundreds of *hadass* twigs, did he decide which to take. It was characteristic of him that sometimes, he went out on the day before *Sukkot* to buy a new *etrog* after he had again examined his previous *etrog* and concluded that it was not sufficiently splendid.

He was especially conscientious about choosing the "Four Species."

Also, his strict observance of *Shemittah* (the Sabbatical year) was unique. When one of his sons accompanied him to the market to buy vegetables in the *Shemittah* year, he saw that R' Yaakob looked for a shop under rabbinical supervision, and asked him, "Isn't it better to buy from the Arab women who are here [as non-Jewish produce is not subject to the restrictions of *Shemittah*]?" He answered, "Look, I'll show you something." They went to one of the Arab women and asked her: "Where have you bought these vegetables?" and he added: "As I am one of the Jewish sages, you must tell me the truth, and it would not be in your interest for you to lie to me." She immediately took her vegetables and went with them to a Jewish shop. Pointing to the shop, she said, "He gave me the vegetables to sell for him."

He once remarked to his son that in his youth he had learned the entire book Hovot HaLevavot by heart.

His Humility

In 1953 it was proposed to R' Yaakob that he become Chief Rabbi of Israel. All those concerned were convinced that he would be unanimously elected. However, no one was surprised when he firmly rejected the proposal. In fact, his personality was so far removed from such an idea that it created an atmosphere in his home as if a great misfortune had occurred. Day after day, people visited R' Yaakob to influence him to the point that he asked his sons to stay at home to help him in resisting the pressure. When they finally heard that another candidate had been approached to accept the nomination, they all were relieved, and the family rejoiced.

In 1953 it was proposed to R' Yaakob that he become Chief Rabbi of Israel.

His Love of Mussar

He strongly believed in the importance of studying *mussar* (spiritual and character development). He once remarked to his son that in his youth he had learned the entire book *Hovot HaLevavot* by heart. He advised people to persevere in studying *mussar* every day, even if it is only for a short time, "as this is the special remedy for a Jew to rescue him from all diseases of the soul."

He used to make a point of observing the beauty of Creation, which aroused in him the greatest admiration and love for *Hashem*. On one occasion, when he came to a place of rare phenomena of nature, he excitedly announced, "Now I don't have to learn *mussar* for a whole month."

Prescription for a Troubled Soul. R' Yaakob Ades kept a special notebook in which he recorded everything that he encountered in the course of his studies which stirred his heart. In this notebook he wrote the following:

"A potion prescribed by the *Rambam* for people suffering from mental despair and depression, which he inserted at the beginning of a book he wrote. This was printed in Salonika and cited in *Midbar Kedemot* of the *Hida*.

"For an effective medicinal potion, take the roots of praise and thanksgiving, and the roots of happiness and faith, and remove from them the grains of sorrow and worry. Then take the flower of the pomegranates of knowledge and wisdom, and the roots of waiting and contentment, and crush all with the mortar of humility. Now, cook it in the vessel of modesty, season it with sweetness of the lips, and mix with the waters of favor and charity. Give it to those who are sick with despair to drink twice a day, in the morning and the evening, with three spoonfuls of water of thought. Clean up the waste of anger and small-mindedness, and then mix it with the extract of patience to please the Lord of praise and thanksgiving — Blessed be His Name — and give it to him to drink from the vessel of His praise, and the sick person will recover."

R' Yaakob added to these words of the *Rambam*: "One should learn these words, as they are like fresh water for a weary soul and like healing leaves for the health of the body."

The love of Torah dominated R' Yaakob's heart and mind. In the words of the *Rambam*, he "immersed himself in the waters of knowledge" (*Hilchot Mikvaot*). Among his writings we find the name of a book he wished to write: *"Hedvat Yaakob,"* and he explained that *Hedvat* means happiness, i.e., happiness with Torah; and it is also an acronym of *"Hiddushei Torah"* (original Torah thoughts) and very appropriate to the reality of his life, which was his happiness in Torah. His heart leapt with happiness whenever he managed to achieve a new understanding in Torah. His voice resonated with joy, and all those who surrounded him were swept up with a great desire to learn Torah. Whoever met him on the street, or at any occasion, always heard from R' Yaakob a problem or an answer to a question in Torah in which he was engaged at that time. The words were always said with sweetness and grace, making a full-time reality of the verse,"O how I love Your Torah! All day long it is my conversation" (*Tehillim* 119:97).

His Love of Torah

The love of Torah dominated R' Yaakob's heart and mind.

Once, when R' Yaakob was in Bnai Brak, he went to the *Kollel Hazon Ish* for *Arbit* services. When he saw that there were some minutes before prayer time, he told one of his sons to bring him any book from the bookshelves. Later he explained that when there is little time it is not worth while to waste time looking for a certain book, but to take any book and to learn wherever he chanced to open it. The book brought to him was *Responsa of the Radbaz*. He read one chapter and many years later, when he was writing a decision for the *Bet Din*, he showed his son that the problem in which he was currently engaged was mentioned in that very same chapter that he had read in the *Responsa of the Radbaz*. And he reminded his son that it was in those free minutes before *Arbit* in the *Kollel Hazon Ish* that he had seen the *Radbaz*.

Whenever a Torah scholar passed away, there was always a problem as to how to inform R' Yaakob, lest it endanger his health. When R' Tzvi Pesach Frank passed away, great sorrow prevailed in R' Yaakob's home. At the funeral, R' Yaakob sat bitterly weeping as the rabbis eulogized the deceased. When he heard about the passing of R' Ephraim Cohen, who was his *havruta* (study partner) for many years, he suffered piercing heartache and fainted. A doctor was immediately called to revive him.

His Love of Torah Scholars

Whenever a Torah scholar passed away, there was always a problem as to how to inform R' Yaakob, lest it endanger his health.

The true affection which prevailed between R' Yaakob and the *Rosh Yeshiva*, R' Ezra Attiah, was indescribable. Their close connection lasted for scores of years. During that time they felt the deepest esteem for each other and always reached full agreement, even in the most complex and intricate matters. R' Ezra once related that only one time did they separate with conflicting conclusions. However, the next day, R' Yaakob came to him and happily said, "I have found a convincing proof to your opinion."

The true affection which prevailed between R' Yaakob and the Rosh Yeshiva, R' Ezra Attiah, was indescribable.

During the course of his life, R' Yaakob experienced many hardships and tragedies. Even as a youngster he suffered from heart problems and was often confined to bed.

His Tragedies

He was sorely grieved when he lost a son and a daughter in their childhood to pneumonia. However, he did not allow himself to drown in the sorrow and continued with his Torah study, which was his only consolation.

In addition, on *Lag L'Omer* 1936 he lost his firstborn son, Abraham Haim (see #36), at the age of 16, who succumbed to a complication after a tonsillectomy. Abraham was a very diligent and promising Torah student, and his father had great hopes in his becoming an outstanding Torah scholar.

R' Yaakob could hardly be consoled after this loss. One night he saw in a dream an old man with a lustrous countenance who gave him a letter which read: "Why do you deal in things that the Compassionate has concealed?" [That is, do not try to understand G-d's hidden ways of justice.] After that R' Yaakob found consolation and added to his schedule a new series of daily

Torah lectures for laymen, which he carried on for many years. Many sons of those participating in these lectures later went on to become great Torah scholars as a result of the encouragement for Torah education which their fathers got from the lectures.

These Are Your Three Children. In 1936, after recovering from a heart attack, which he suffered after his firstborn son died, R' Yaakob Ades traveled to Tel Aviv to convalesce. He was accompanied by his son, R' Yosef. One day as they stayed in the hotel, a man — Peretz Damaskai — visited them with his three sons. When he saw R' Yaakob, he said to him, "These are your three children!" When R' Yosef asked Mr. Damaskai about the meaning of this declaration, the latter explained that he had been childless after ten years of marriage and had gone to pour out his heart before R' Yaakob, who officiated as rabbi in the Syrian synagogue. When Mr. Damaskai told R' Yaakob he was about to divorce his wife, R' Yaakob implored him to wait another year, as his father had dealt with similar cases and his prayers had borne fruit. R' Yaakob promised to go to his father's grave for prayer and surely *Hashem* would help. Mr. Damaskai did as the rabbi advised him and a year later he was blessed with the first son, and then the second and the third.

One of the workingmen who attended R' Yaakob's pre-dawn class was Mr. Eliyahu Abba Shaul, the father of Hacham Ben-Sion Abba Shaul (see #24).

"Believe me, my friend, without the holy Torah which grants me the strength to endure suffering, I should long ago have gone the way of all flesh."

Once, when a visitor complained about the hardships he had to endure, R' Yaakob told him, "Believe me, my friend, without the holy Torah which grants me the strength to endure suffering, I should long ago have gone the way of all flesh."

The Power of His Prayers

In 1942, during World War II, the German Army was relentlessly advancing eastward across North Africa toward Egypt and *Eretz Yisrael*. In a desperate hope of stopping the powerful German military machine, the small British Army built two great fortresses in Libya, one in Benghazi and the other in Tobruk. Even after the German Air Force destroyed the Benghazi fortress, the British counted on the very strong Tobruk line to stop the advance. But when this fortress also fell before the German onslaught, a curtain of fear descended upon the Jews of the Holy Land.

Everyone relied on the power and might of the British Army and their fortress, but when the "ring" of Tobruk was removed, all awoke to return to their G-d in Heaven.

R' Yaakob, who prayed and wept continually because of the terrible situation, arranged many *minyanim* (prayer groups) to pray for *Hashem's* help and deliverance. When the Germans bombed the fortress of Tobruk, he traveled with a group of rabbis to the graves of the righteous in Safed and Meron to pray for Israel's redemption. When he returned to Jerusalem, after many days of pouring his heart out to *Hashem*, he appeared quite happy, and when his sons asked him why the day before he was weeping and now he was happy, he answered: "Blessed be *Hashem*, the prayers were accepted," which was a great and welcome surprise for all.

At that time he cited the *Gemara* (*Megillah* 14a): "Greater is the removal of the ring [by King Ahasuerus to give authority to Haman] than forty-eight prophets and seven prophetesses who prophesized for Israel, as they all could not induce [the Jewish people] to return to G-d, whereas removal of the ring induced Israel to return." Similarly now, he said, everyone relied on the power and might of the British Army and their fortress, but when the "ring" of Tobruk was removed, all awoke to return to their G-d in Heaven.

After Tobruk fell, there was almost no significant military force to withstand the advance of the German army, and the danger to *Eretz Yisrael* was very great. However, Rommel's mighty army was unexpectedly defeated in the great battle of El Alamein on the Egyptian border, so that the danger of a German conquest of *Eretz Yisrael* passed.

Yeshiva Kol Yaakob cornerstone celebration

His Legacy

He passed away on 27 Tamuz (5723) 1963 after four and a half months of painful illness. His legacy continues today in the yeshiva named after him, *Kol Yaakob* in Jerusalem, founded by one of his younger sons, R' Yehudah Ades.

After R' Ades had passed away, the children asked R' Ezra Attiah (see #102) what they should do in his memory: Should they open a yeshiva or publish his manuscripts? R' Ezra advised, "You can publish the books later — seize the moment and open a yeshiva!" Although his own yeshiva, *Porat Yosef*, was the only Sephardic *Kollel* at the time, R' Ezra gave objective advice. To him, this wasn't inviting competition, but rather providing more Torah for more students. *Kol Yaakob* became the yeshiva named for R' Yaakob Ades, and his books were published later on as well. Recently, his children printed his responsa in a two-volume work called *Hedvat Yaakob*.

R' Ezra advised, "You can publish the books later — seize the moment and open a yeshiva!"

R' Yehudah Ades recalled one time when his father came home in a state of agitation. When asked what was wrong R' Yaakob explained that he had just come from visiting R' Yehudah (Aslan) Attiah (see #118), who was lying on his bed, deathly ill. R' Attiah's

Yeshivat Kol Yaakob, Jerusalem.

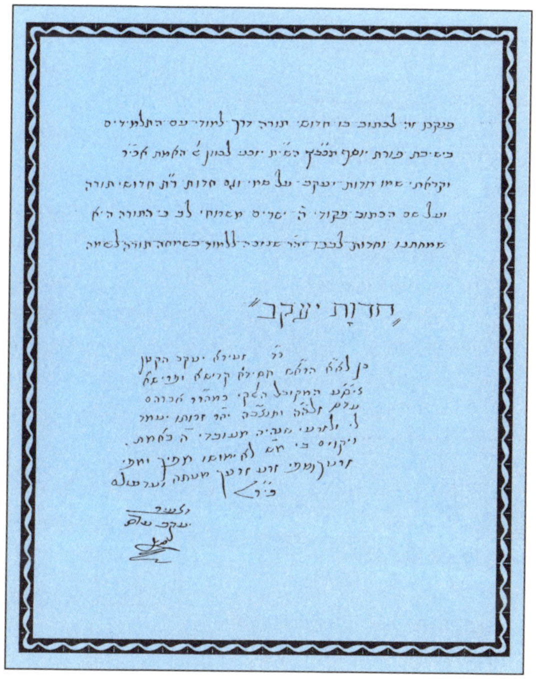

Hedvat Yaakob manuscript

flesh appeared to be falling away from his body and yet he was lying there, singing the *zemirot* (hymns) of *Shabbat*. R' Yaakob added, "If only I had the *zechut* (merit) of being buried next to him." When R' Yaakob passed away on a Friday, the funeral was on *Motza'e Shabbat* (Saturday night). Before the funeral, R' Abraham Shrem took the Ades family to see the gravesite, but it was dark and they couldn't see much. However, he assured them that he had obtained a good location. After the end of the *shivah* (seven days of mourning), they returned for the unveiling of the monument and they became aware that R' Yaakob's fervent wish had been fulfilled. He was buried right next to R' Aslan Attiah.

[42] **ADES, R' Yitzhak**

רבי יצחק עדס

(19th century)

Pious merchant of Aram Soba. He was the father of R' Abraham Ades (see #37) and other scholars. He earned his livelihood through the sale of textiles and made use of any available time to study Torah.

R' Yitzhak began his daily routine at midnight reciting *Tikkun Hatzot* followed by *Tehillim* until sunrise (*netz*), the ideal time for morning prayers. He would find time throughout the day to complete the reading of the entire *sefer Tehillim*.

R' Abraham Ades once explained that his father R' Yitzhak had merited such great children on account of his heartfelt, tear-filled prayers and consistent recitation of *Tehillim*. This devotion was apparent when in the final moments of his life, while barely conscious, R' Yitzhak lifted his head and called out, "Greetings, David HaMelech." He then lowered his head and passed away.

This devotion was apparent when in the final moments of his life, while barely conscious, R' Yitzhak lifted his head and called out, "Greetings, David HaMelech." He then lowered his head and passed away.

[43] **ADES, R' Yitzhak**

רבי יצחק עדס

(1884 — 1916)

Brilliant scholar of Aram Soba who did not live out his years. He was born in 1884, the son of R' Abraham Haim Ades (see #37). Even as a young man he was an unusually brilliant scholar. On one occasion he started to learn the tractate *Yebamot* and after three days he was up to folio page 90. A skeptical person in the yeshiva found it hard to believe that so much difficult material could be absorbed in so short a time. However, when questioned, R' Yitzhak was able to demonstrate total recall of what he had learned, which even included the commentary of the *Maharam Shif*.

On one occasion he started to learn the tractate Yebamot and after three days he was up to folio page 90.

When R' Ezra Attiah (see #102) approached R' Abraham Ades to ask for someone who would be his teacher, R' Abraham pointed to his son, R' Yitzhak, saying he was fully qualified, and so R' Yitzhak took on that role.

He wrote many responsa and *hiddushim* (original Torah thoughts) on *Gemara*. However, at the age of 32, while still unmarried, he became seriously ill and passed away on 9 Shevat, 5676 (1916).

[44] **ALFANDRI, R' Shelomo Eliezer**

רבי שלמה אליעזר אלפנדרי

(1826 — 1930)

R' Shelomo Eliezer Alfandri

Rabbinic authority of Constantinople and Chief Rabbi of Damascus and Safed. R' Alfandri was born in Constantinople (Istanbul) in 1826 to R' Yaakob Alfandri. He became known as the *Saba Kadisha* (holy elder) and as *Mercado* or *Maharsha* (**M**oreinu **HaR**av **S**helomo **E**liezer).

When he was about 25, he headed the yeshiva founded by a wealthy resident of Constantinople, named Foa, and among his pupils were many who subsequently became important rabbis. At the age of 30, he was elected a member of the general religious council *(Majlis)* of Constantinople. During the sultanate of Abdul Hamid, R' Alfandri opposed the conscription of Jews into the Turkish army, on the grounds that such conscription constituted interference with their religious practice, in violation of an agreement made by the Spanish exiles with the Turkish authorities as a condition for their settling in Turkey in the late 15th century. The order of conscription was finally rescinded.

In 1897 he received an official letter from the Ottoman government notifying him that he had been appointed as the Chief Rabbi *(Hacham Bashi)* of Damascus. He decided to travel to Damascus to present himself there. However, his friends sought to discourage him from going, as R' Yitzhak Abulafia (see #35), who had been Chief Rabbi since 1873 and was known as a brilliant man and a strong-willed community leader, would not take kindly to someone questioning his authority. However, R' Alfandri responded, "On the contrary, if there is such a great scholar, it is my duty to go there and learn from him." For the first few months the two rabbis did not do anything together but after that each began to recognize the greatness of the other and they established an excellent working relationship to share in the responsibilities of governing Jewish affairs in the city.

In 1897 he received an official letter from the Ottoman government notifying him that he had been appointed as the Chief Rabbi (Hacham Bashi) of Damascus.

Chief Rabbi Acceptance. This Acceptance Document was presented to R' Shelomo Eliezer Alfandri by the community leaders of Safed when they accepted him as their chief rabbi.

We the undersigned are the elders, rabbis, and prominent Jews of the city of Safed.

We have accepted as our chief in all sacred matters the venerable rabbi, the brilliant elder scholar, the revered man of holiness, Rabbi Shelomo Eliezer Alfandri, may *Hashem* preserve and protect him.

And we have accepted his rulings, even when he states *"that right is left and left is right,"* according to whatever comes from his mouth, in all matters, including financial affairs, conflicts between individuals, issues of what is forbidden and what is permissible, and nonmandatory matters.

Should he choose not to rule in any case but to delegate it to others who have been appointed to rule according to the *halachah*, with the consent of the community, he may do so, except for difficult cases where he is uniquely qualified to give a judicial ruling. He also has the option of not involving himself in community finances. However he has a holy obligation to appoint qualified individuals, under whose auspices the affairs of the community will be conducted.

Pursuant to the above, we the undersigned have fully committed ourselves in accordance with the ordinances of our sages to rent for him a residence that is fitting to his dignity and with an integral house of worship. This will be done from the funds of our community, immediately upon his arrival into our holy city. We have also committed to provide him with a permanent *shamosh* [sexton] to serve him in all of his requirements. These stipulations shall take effect from the day indicated above for a period of three years. We trust in *Hashem* Who ordains life and we trust in His mercies that it will be His will for our rabbi to be successful in raising the banner of Torah and elevating the circumstances of our impoverished community, Amen.

And we have accepted his rulings, even when he states "that right is left and left is right," according to whatever comes from his mouth, in all matters.

The *Saba Kadisha* continued in his position in Damascus until 1903. He then assumed the position of Chief Rabbi of Safed, which he held until 1918. In 1926 he settled in Jerusalem and remained there until his death in 1930.

R'Alfandri was accepted by both Sephardim and Ashkenazim and was visited by the rabbi of the Munkacs Hasidim, R' Haim Eliezer Shapira.

Regarded as one of the great scholars of his time, R' Alfandri was accepted by both Sephardim and Ashkenazim and despite his exceptional firmness, his responsa and rulings were honored without reservation. During the last years of his life, he was accepted by both Sephardim and Ashkenazim *and was* visited by the rabbi of the Munkacs *Hasidim*, R' Haim Eliezer Shapira, who was deeply impressed by his personality. After his death, the *Hasidim* of Munkacs dedicated to his memory *Masot Yerushalayim* (1931), a hymn in his praise.

R' Alfandri left many *hiddushim* (original Torah thoughts) and responsa in manuscript form, but most were lost. Some of his responsa were published in the periodical *Torah MiSiyyon, and* in the book *Kanah Abraham* by R' Abraham Hai Amozag, and in the works of his contemporaries. In 1932 a few of his responsa were published by R' Yitzhak Nissim, under the title *She'elot U'Teshuvot Maharsha*.

In 1973, his responsa were published in three parts under the title *She'elot U'Teshuvot HaSaba Kadisha*. In 1970 his responsum on the topic of marriage to a Karaite was published in the book *Gedolei Eretz Yisrael*. In 1974 his responsum *Limud Zechut* on the topic of grafted *ethrogim* was separately published. In the same year his commentary to *Dibrei Emet* by R' Yitzhak Bekhor David was published under the title *Esa Einai*.

R' Shelomo passed away after a long and full life at the venerable age of 104 on 22 Iyar, 5690 (1930).

[45] ALFIA (HADDAD), R' Yaakob Haim Yisrael Raphael [HaRei'ach]

רבי יעקב חיים ישראל רפאל אלפייה (חדאד)

(1858 — 1916)

Eminent scholar and *darshan* (lecturer), he became known as *HaRei'ach* [the fragrance], a name which is associated with his scholarly work *Rei'ach Le-Yitzhak*. He named this important book of *hiddushim* (original Torah thoughts) after his father R' Yitzhak Yeshayah Alfia (see #47). In this book he covers a wide range of topics, addressing both the plain meaning and Kabbalist interpretations. He includes texts for legal documents from the manuscripts of

בשם השם
עולה הוא אשה ריח ניחח לה'
ספר
ריח ליצחק
Adr. Rabbin ISAAC JACOB ALFIÉ JERUSALEM (Palestine).
ראה ריח בני כריח שדה אשר ברכו ה';

Title Page of Rei'ach LeYitzhak

Left to right: Three generations of Alfia scholars — R' Yitzhak Yeshayah (#47), R' Yitzhak (#46), R' Yaakob Haim Yisrael Raphael (#45)

R' Ephraim Laniado (see #355), concerning the topics of giving up legal rights, rentals, and marriage. He also includes a *derashah* (lecture) to be given on *Rosh Hashanah* before the *Tekiot,* and a lengthy responsum from R' Shelomo Eliezer Alfandri (see #44).

He left all of his writings in manuscript form. However, *Rei'ach LeYitzhak* was published by his son, R' Yitzhak Alfia (see #46), who wrote an informative introduction.

Like many other great scholars of Aram Soba, *HaRei'ach* focused much of his efforts on training younger scholars. In addition, he was a popular lecturer; whenever he spoke, crowds of people would flock to hear his words.

HaRei'ach was born in Aram Soba in about 1858. In 1880 he wrote a letter to his teacher and rabbi, R' Mordechai Abadi (see #8), in which he posed a learned question on the tractate *Me'ilah*. The letter was published by R' Yosef Shayo (see #507) in the anthology *MeHalab Ha'Aretz* (Jerusalem 5726/1966) (p. 180).

In about 1890 he immigrated to *Eretz Yisrael* together with his parents and his children (Yitzhak, Yeshaya Shaul, and Mordechai Moshe). In Jerusalem he studied in the Kabbalist yeshiva *Bet El*. Concerning his knowledge and great expertise in Kabbalah, his son R' Yitzhak Alfia tells the following story: Once when I was studying Kabbalah in the yeshiva *Bet El* in the year 1923, and I was having difficulty with a subject, the Kabbalist scholar R' Nachman Angel said to me, "If your father were here he would offer 60 answers to that" (quoted from the introduction to the book *Rei'ach LeYitzhak*).

HaRei'ach experienced pain and suffering during most of his years. In his last will and testament, which is published in his son's book *Si'ach Yitzhak*, he sought to write his epitaph, saying "This man experienced much suffering, too extensive to be described." He passed away on 23 Shevat, 5676 (1916).

[46] ALFIA (HADDAD), R' Yitzhak

רבי יצחק אלפייה (חדאד)

(1878 — 1955)

R' Yitzhak Alfia (Haddad)

Distinguished scholar, author, and community leader. He was born in Aram Soba in 1878 to R' Yitzhak, known as *HaRei'ach* (see #45). His mother, Salha, hailed from the Dayan family, whose lineage can be traced back to King David. She died when he was still a child and he grew up in the home of his grandfather, R' Yitzhak Yeshaya Alfia (see #47), remaining there until the age of 35, when his grandfather died. The grandfather was concerned about the grandson's education and he taught him *shehitah* (ritual slaughtering), which he later depended upon for his livelihood.

ויצא יצחק לשוח ואין שיחה אלא תפלה

ספר

שיח יצחק

חלק ראשון

רצב"י יצחק בכמהר"ח אלפייה הי"ו ס"ט

נדפס בירושת"ו בדפוס הר"ש צוקרמן

לעולם יקדים אדם תפלה לצרה

Title Page of Si'ach Yitzhak

In 1907, he moved with his father and grandfather to Jerusalem, where both became *dayanim* (judges) on the *Bet Din* (High Court). As for R' Yitzhak, he became widely known for his intense piety and for his self-denial. He lived a life of privation, barely supporting himself with the profession of *shehitah* and the examination of knives in the slaughterhouses.

In 1920 he started a yeshiva called *Ohr Hadash Ve-Semach Sedek*. At that time, the population of Jerusalem included the full gamut of people from the holiest rabbi to the common workingman, which constituted the vast majority. R' Alfia had a vision: to give the workingmen the opportunity to learn in the evenings. He raised money and hired rabbis to be available at night in the *Bet Midrash* where the great *Sedei Hemed* (R' Haim Hizkiah Medini) used to learn. He hoped that in the merit of the *Sedi Hemed* and the sanctity

R' Alfia had a vision: to give the workingmen the opportunity to learn in the evenings.

Sedei Hemed
(R' Haim Hizkiah Medini)

of the *Bet Midrash* where he wrote his holy books, the evening learning program would be a success. R' Alfia pasted posters all over Jerusalem, urging all men to come and learn. The classes grew steadily until the rooms were packed every night. Many men were learning two hours a night in the summer and three hours during the long winter nights. They learned six nights a week: *Gemara* two nights, *Halachah* (religious law) two nights, the *Zohar* one night, and on Thursday nights they stayed up all night and finished the entire book of *Tehillim*. In the months of Elul and Nissan, the men would visit Rachel's tomb and other graves of righteous Jews, and pray.

He initiated the "fast day of speaking" *(Taanit Dibur)*, in which his students would refrain from any talk that was not directly concerned with Torah and *mitzvot*. Instead *Tehillim* would be recited three times in one day. Thanks to his initiative, the *Taanit Dibur* has become standard practice in many communities throughout the world.

He initiated the "fast day of speaking" (Taanit Dibur), in which his students would refrain from any talk that was not directly concerned with Torah and mitzvot.

R' Yitzhak also started *Hevrat Oleh Regalim*, a group of men who would visit the *Kotel* on the *Shalosh Regalim* (the three festivals), just as all the Jews did in the time of the Holy Temple.

He passed away on 26 Elul, 5715 (1955). The history and achievements of R' Yitzhak are described at length in the introduction to the book, *Ohr Hadash VeSemach Sedek*, which was written about him by R' David Yehudioff (Jerusalem 5729/1969).

Ahavat Hashem contains essays seeking to strengthen traditional customs, and to avoid adulterating them with non-Jewish practices.

A list of his published works is provided below. However, many manuscripts of his *hiddushim* (original Torah thoughts) were tragically lost in the destruction accompanying the fall of the Old City in 1948.

- *Si'ach Yitzhak* (Jerusalem 5683/1923). Part I consists of various articles, teachings, prayers, and laws. Part II consists of inspirational lectures and collections of comments on the Torah.
- *Kuntras HaYiche'eli* (Jerusalem 5688/1928). Three parts: The House of *Hashem*, the House of Ages (the Temple), and the House of Man.
- *Rei'ach LeYitzhak* (Jerusalem 5696/1936). Topics on Kabbalah, lectures, and *halachic* (legal) rulings. Authored by his father R' Yaakob with contributions by R' Yitzhak himself.
- *Ya'ir Netiv* (Jerusalem 5699/1939, 5708/1948). A study on all aspects of Torah *(Pshat, Remez, Drash,* and *Sod)*, with a breakdown of all studies by hours and minutes (elapsed time of each study).
- *Ahavat Hashem*. Volume I (Jerusalem (5708/1948) contains the first of five parts. It contains essays seeking to strengthen traditional customs, and to avoid adulterating them with non-Jewish practices. (See Document Section, Document No. 5.) Special attention is given to the customs associated with accompanying the dead to the cemetery for burial. The book received approbations from 104 rabbis, including representatives of all Jerusalem communities. Among them was R' Haim Tawil (see #584) and R' Ezra Hamway (see #272). Volume II (Jerusalem 5732/1972) contains the four remaining parts, all of which were prepared from the author's manuscripts by R' David Yehudioff.
- *Ohr Hadash VeSemach Sedek* (Jerusalem 5632/1972). Articles on the virtues of the *Taanit Hadibur* ("fast day of speaking") and other topics. Published from the author's manuscripts by R' David Yehudioff.

[47] ALFIA (HADDAD), R' Yitzhak Yeshayah

רבי יצחק ישעיה אלפייה (חדאד)

(1827 — 1912)

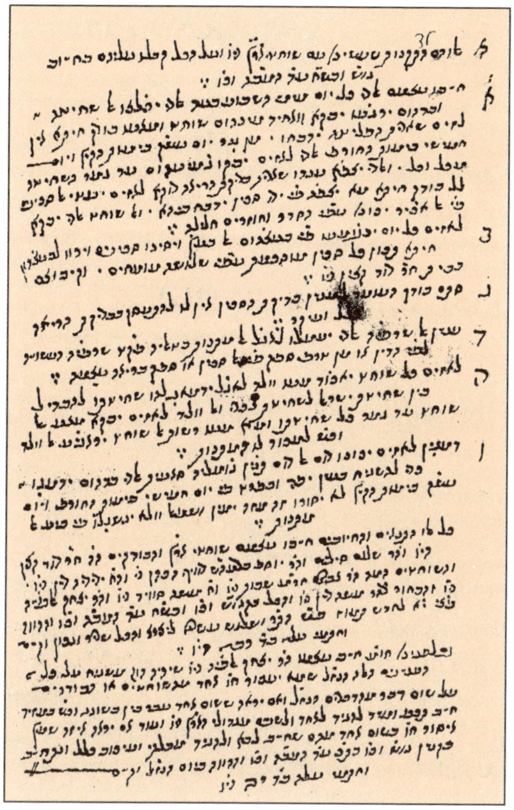

Takanot of Shohatim (see Document Section, Document No. 14)

Chief *shohet* (ritual slaughterer) of Aram Soba. He was born there in 1827. R' Mordechai Labaton, *Av Bet Din* (Chief Judge) of Aram Soba (see #336), used to call him "the trusted *shohet*" and refused to eat the meat of any *shohet* other than him. However, his primary function was to examine and certify the *shohatim* of the city. In about 1890 he settled in Jerusalem together with his son R' Yaakob and his grandchildren. There he studied in the Kabbalist yeshiva *Bet El*. He passed away in Jerusalem on 27 Nissan, 5672 (1912).

[48] ALFIA (HADDAD), R' Yosef

רבי יוסף אלפייה (חדאד)

(— 1926)

Worthy scholar of Aram Soba. He was born in Aram Soba to R' Menahem and, after spending time in Egypt, settled in Jerusalem. He passed away there on 21 Sivan, 5686 (1926).

[49] ALKABETZ, R' Moshe HaLevi

רבי משה אלקבץ הלוי

Worthy scholar of Aram Soba and father of R' Shelomo Alkabetz, author of the well-known hymn *Lechah Dodi*. He was born in Adrianople (Turkey). In the *Responsa HaMabit* by R' Moshe ben Yosef Trani (Part 3, Section 10:13), the author notes, "We have seen the legal ruling issued by the scholars of Aram Soba, the *dayan* (judge) HaRav Meir and the venerable rabbi R' Moshe HaLevi Alkabetz."

Father of R' Shelomo Alkabetz, author of the well-known hymn Lechah Dodi.

[50] ALTARAS, R' David

רבי דוד אלטראס

(18th century)

Pious philanthropist of Aram Soba. He was the oldest son of R' Shelomo Altaras (see #53). In his youth, he was a study companion of R' David Pardo. Later, their paths separated; R' David Altaras settled in Aram Soba, where he engaged in business. In contrast, R' David Pardo remained with his studies and after a time became known as one of the great Torah personalities of the age with his popular work *Shoshanim LeDavid*, published in Venice in 5512 (1752). When R' David Altaras saw that book, he was so overcome with emotion that he began to weep in regret over his truncated Torah studies. Even so, he followed the practice of many Aram Soba scholars, arising at midnight to apply himself to Torah study.

R' Mordechai Labaton, Av Bet Din of Aram Soba, used to call R' Yitzchak Yeshaya Alfia "the trusted shohet."

R' David Altaras was so overcome with emotion that he began to weep in regret over his truncated Torah studies.

The name of R' David Altaras is favorably mentioned in the introductions to the following contemporary works: *Bet Dino shel Shelomo* by R' Raphael Shelomo Laniado (see #363), *Beirach Yitzhak* by R' Yitzhak Berachah (see #129), and *Sedakah U'Mishpat* by R' Sadkah Houssin (see #313). He is known to have established 18 schools for Jewish children and two synagogues. In addition he addressed the needs of the teachers of Jewish children, providing them with financial compensation.

[51] ALTARAS, R' Raphael Yitzhak
רבי רפאל יצחק אלטראס

(19th century)

Worthy scholar and teacher of Jerusalem. He lived his early years in Aram Soba and then, in 1845, he settled in Jerusalem, where he wrote the book *Yitzhak Yeranen* (Jerusalem 5615/1855), containing sacred prayers, poems, and songs. R' Raphael was not blessed with surviving children; his daughters died at an early age. He devoted all his energies to teaching Jewish youth and sought to teach them songs of praise to be said before the break of day. In furtherance of this objective he founded a choral group called *Shomrim LaBoker*.

זה השער לה׳ צדיקים יבאו בו

יצחק ירנן

ירושלם

Title Page of *Yitzhak Yeranen*

[52] ALTARAS, R' Shabbetai
רבי שבתאי אלטראס

(18th century)

Brilliant scholar of Aram Soba. He was the second son of R' Shelomo Altaras (see #53). As are his brother R' David and R' Yitzhak (#50 and #55), he is favorably mentioned in the introductions to the following contemporary works: *Bet Dino shel Shelomo* by R' Raphael Shelomo Laniado (see #363), *Beirach Yitzhak* by R' Yitzhak Berachah (see #129), and *Sedakah U'Mishpat* by R' Sadkah Houssin (see #313). It appears that he was not blessed with children.

[53] ALTARAS, R' Shelomo
רבי שלמה אלטראס

(18th century)

Highly praised scholar of Aram Soba. He was born in Venice, but stopped off in Aram Soba while on his way to Jerusalem. He liked Aram Soba so much that he remained there for the rest of his life. Upon his death he was eulogized by the leading rabbis of Aram Soba: R' Raphael Shelomo Laniado (see #363), R' Yehudah Kassin (see #331), and R' Yeshayah Dabbah. He had three sons: David, Shabbetai, and Yitzhak, all acclaimed scholars.

[54] ALTARAS, R' Yaakob Moshe
רבי יעקב משה אלטראס

(— 1910)

Worthy scholar, teacher, and *darshan* (lecturer) of Jerusalem. He was known for having written books specifically designed to be useful to his fellow Sephardim. He passed away in Jerusalem on 9 Adar, 5679 (1910).

[55] ALTARAS, R' Yitzhak
רבי יצחק אלטראס

(18th century)

Worthy scholar and philanthropist of Aram Soba. He was the third son of R' Shelomo Alteras (see #53). As are his brothers R' David and R' Shabbetai (#50 and #52), he is favorably mentioned in the introductions to the following contemporary works: *Bet Dino shel Shelomo* by R' Raphael Shelomo Laniado (see #363), *Beirach Yitzhak* by R' Yitzhak Berachah (see #129), and *Sedakah U'Mishpat* by R' Sadkah Houssin (see #313). R' Yitzhak had three sons: Shelomo, Ezra, and Moshe. They are mentioned favorably in *Birchat Eliyahu* by R' Eliyahu Dweck (see #222), and described there as men who are active in Torah and charitable works.

[56] ALTARAS, R' Yitzhak
רבי יצחק אלטראס

(19th century)

Worthy scholar and civic leader of Marseilles. He became the head of the Jewish community of Marseilles. He is mentioned in the introduction to *Igeret HaTiyul* (Aram Soba 5632/1872), which was published by R' Moshe Mordechai Dayan (#191). R' Yitzhak had a scholarly son named R' Aharon, who, in turn, had three sons: Yitzhak, Nissim, and Moshe.

[57] ALTARAS, R' Yosef
רבי יוסף אלטראס

(16th century)

Worthy *hazzan* (cantor) and poet. Born in Damascus, he settled in Aram Soba. He was praised by the Hebrew poet R' Yisrael Najara as the "... highest of heavenly heights above all his contemporaries in the sweetness of his voice" (*Zemirot Yisrael*, 142–144, 147). R' Najara also praised his poetry. R' Yosef's son Nissim was also a poet. It may be assumed that the poems attributed to "Yosef" and "Nissim" scattered throughout the *Siddur* of Aram Soba (Venice, 1520, 1560) were written by these two. These poems are also included in the collection *Shirei Yisrael Be'Eretz HaKedem* (1921).

[58] ANHOURI, R' Moshe

רבי משה אנהורי

(— 1824)

Chief Rabbi of Aram Soba. He emigrated from the Sephardic countries of the west to Aram Soba in 1818. Upon his arrival in Aram Soba he was appointed Chief Rabbi in place of R' Abraham Sutton (see #535), who had recently died.

Owing to community politics, it was necessary for him to share the position with R' Moshe Dweck (see #256). In fact, he did not remain in Aram Soba for very long. In 1819 R' Anhouri was forced to leave his position and went to Egypt, where he was warmly received and was appointed rabbi. He passed away in Egypt on 18 Nissan, 5584 (1824). The story is told that during the Second World War, when the Jews of Egypt gathered to pray for Divine help at the graves of the righteous, they saw what appeared to be a living hand reaching out from one of the graves. This was determined to be the grave of R' Moshe Anhouri.

The events leading up to his forced departure from Aram Soba began when the *Bet Din* sent a summons to an officer of Señor Ezra Picciotto, the Austrian general consul in Aram Soba. The officer refused to come and R' Anhouri excommunicated him. Naturally, the consul became very angry at this and arranged for R' Anhouri to be banned from the city. In the month of Av 5581 (1821), the police came to his house and forced him, "barefoot and bareheaded," to leave Aram Soba for Latakia on the Mediterranean coast together with the members of his household. The people of Aram Soba were angry at the consul, but because of his position, they were powerless to act against him. However, the following year, 1822, Aram Soba was struck by a major earthquake in which many of the Jewish community lost their lives. Included among the fatalities was Señor Ezra Picciotto, who was struck in the head by a rock. The people of the city concluded that the terrible sin of banishing their rabbi was the cause of the calamitous earthquake. A description of the earthquake was recorded by R' Moshe Sutton (see #552) in his book *Kehillat Moshe*.

[59] ANCONA, R' Habib

רבי חביב אנקונה

(18th century)

Worthy scholar and rabbi of Aram Soba. His *hiddushim* (original Torah thoughts) are mentioned by R' Yosef Ergas in *Dibrei Yosef* (Sections 54 and 55). R' Eliyahu Dweck (see #225) in the introduction to *Birchat Eliyahu* speaks of him as the first in a series of members of the illustrious Ancona family. He fathered three sons, all of whom were venerable scholars: Halfon, Yosef, and Raphael.

[60] ANCONA, R' Halfon

רבי חלפון אנקונה

(— 1901)

Teacher of *Gemara* in the Talmud Torah of Aram Soba. In his later years he settled in *Eretz Yisrael*, where he passed away on 2 Tishrei, 5662 (1901).

[61] ANCONA, R' Reuven

רבי ראובן אנקונה

(— 1917)

Worthy scholar, *darshan* (lecturer), *shohet* (ritual slaughterer), and scribe. He was the son of R' Shaul Ancona. R' Reuven was a member of the council "*Isur VeHeter.*" One of his responsa was included in the book *Yisa Ish* by R' Yaakob Shaul Elyashar. He passed away on 11 Tamuz, 5677 (1917).

R' Reuven Ancona

R' Yosef Altaras was praised by the Hebrew poet R' Yisrael Najara.

When the Jews of Egypt gathered to pray for Divine help at the graves of the righteous, they saw what appeared to be a living hand reaching out from one of the graves. This was to be determined to be the grave of R' Moshe Anhouri.

[62] ANCONA, R' Yitzhak

רבי יצחק אנקונה

(19th century)

Worthy scholar of Aram Soba. He contributed to the journal *HaMe'asef* published by R' Ben-Sion Kouenka in the third issue of the first year 5655 (1895).

Antebi Lineage. The illustrious Antebi family originates from Ein Tab, a small village near Aleppo. Thus, the name Antebi indicates a person from Ein Tab.

[63] ANTEBI, R' Abraham

רבי אברהם ענתבי

(1765 — 1858)

Distinguished Chief Rabbi of Aram Soba. He was the second to hold the position of Chief Rabbi following the 11-generation Laniado dynasty, and served in that position for 40 years.

R' Antebi was born in Aram Soba in 1765 and studied Torah under his father R' Yitzhak Antebi (see #80), who was an eminent *dayan*. He was recognized as an impressive young scholar by R' Haim Nissim Abulafia, who contributed an introduction to his renowned book *Yoshev Ohalim*.

He became the Chief Rabbi of Aram Soba and his authority was respected by all the leading rabbis of his time, including those in Eretz Yisrael, Syria, Turkey, and Western Europe.

With the passing years his knowledge of Torah continued to grow in breadth and depth. He became the Chief Rabbi of Aram Soba and his authority was respected by all the leading rabbis of his time, including those in *Eretz Yisrael*, Syria, Turkey, and Western Europe. He continued to exert his leadership of Aram Soba for over 40 years. He was an uncle of R' Yaakob Antebi, the Chief Rabbi of Damascus (see #75), who was victimized during the infamous blood libel of 1840.

In the introduction to his book *Yoshev Ohalim* he describes the earthquake of 1824, which happened on the 27th of the month of Av. Most of the city was destroyed, especially the Jewish quarter. Close to 1000 Jews were killed and the survivors moved into the deserts in tents. Tradition has it that he named his book *Yoshev Ohalim*, which means "dwelling in tents," while he was living in a tent after the earthquake, and all that he wrote was from memory due to the lack of books.

A Timely Move. The story is told that R' Abraham used to frequently visit a particular man and stay the night. This man had a special room set aside for the Hacham. During one visit, Hacham Abraham asked that his bed be moved to the other side of the room — for some reason, he suddenly didn't like the bed in its particular spot. That night, Aram Soba was struck by the earthquake. Half of Hacham Abraham's room — the half where the bed used to be — was destroyed.

R' Abraham lived to the venerable age of 93 and passed away on 28 Tevet, 5618 (1858). He wrote the following books:

- *Yoshev Ohalim* (Livorno 5585/1825). Commentary on the Torah, interpreted according to the *halachah*. The subtitle is *Ohel Abraham*. This book was bound together with his father's book *Ohel Yitzhak* and with his own book *Penei Ha Bayit*. It was reissued in 1968 by R' Eliyahu Attiah.
- *Penei HaBayit* (Livorno 5585/1825). Analytic commentary on the teachings of the *Rashba* with regard to kosher slaughtering. This book was bound together with *Yoshev Ohalim*. It was subsequently republished in Jerusalem by R' Rahamim Shayo. Another book with the name *Penei*

HaBayit was published in 1849. It consisted of *hiddushim* (original Torah thoughts) on *Hoshen Mishpat*.

- *Mar Ve'Ahalot* (Livorno 5603/1843). Responsa on a variety of topics such as women who lost their *ketubah* (marriage contract) during the earthquake which struck Aram Soba in 1822. It was bound together with his father's book *Bet Av*.
- *Derech Hukecha* (Livorno 5610/ 1850). *Hiddushim* and rulings on the laws of *Pesah*. Bound together with *Hochmah U'Mussar*.
- *Penei Ohel Moed* (Jerusalem 5719/ 1959). *Shabbat* lectures for four key weeks in the year and for *Rosh Hashanah*. The book also contains two eulogies which were delivered on the death of the author. One of these was by R' Haim Mordechai Labaton (see #336).
- *Ohel Yesharim* (Livorno 5582/1822). Piercing exhortations for moral and spiritual development. Written in his later years. Hacham Mordechai Antebi said of his writings, "If you read these words, your whole body trembles, and all the words enter your heart."
- *Hochmah U'Mussar* (Livorno 5610/ 1850). Moral and spiritual guidance. This was the last of his books.

[64] ANTEBI, R' Abraham

רבי אברהם ענתבי

(1877 — 1967)

Distinguished Kabbalist and *Av Bet Din* (Chief Judge) of Aram Soba and Jerusalem. He was born in Aram Soba on 14 Nissan, 5637 (1877) to R' David Antebi. He applied himself to his studies and quickly became known as a brilliant young scholar. He was a colleague of R' Menahem Choueka (see #155) and R' Yehudah Aslan Esses (see #260). However he lived in extreme poverty, to the extent that he would often go outside at night to study by the light of the moon.

While he was still young he decided to study Kabbalah and formed a study group with R' Menahem Choueka (see #155) and R' Moshe Ezra Mizrahi (see #424) to focus intensely on Kabbalah for a full year. After that he continued with an austere life, fasting regularly on Mondays and Thursdays and getting up at midnight to study. He hardly ate all week long; his only regular meals were on *Shabbat*.

In approximately 1909 he moved to Jerusalem. Through the influence of R' Binyamin Alkasar, who had gotten to know him on one of his visits to Aram Soba, R' Abraham was accepted as a teacher at the yeshiva *Tiferet Yerushalayim*. He also continued to study at the yeshiva *Ohel Moed* and at the yeshiva *Shaare Zion*. People who saw him were amazed at the intensity of his studying, not lifting his head up for hours at a time.

He served as head of the *Bet Din* of Aram Soba in Jerusalem over a period of dozens of years. Despite his limited means he was known as a generous man who gave a helping hand to all, and especially to young men who needed help in getting married and setting up a home.

Some of his *hiddushim* (original Torah thoughts) appeared in the journal *HaMe'asef*, published by R' Ben-Sion Kouenka. He was blessed with a full life, in command of all his faculties until the age of 90 when he passed away on 6 Adar, 5727 (1967), leaving many worthy children and grandchildren.

ספר

חכמה ומוסר

תוכחת מגולה לאיש תועה מדרך השכל נתון כיד יקרו
ארי יתאסר · עודנו כאכו בן י"ג שנה נגהי ארכיסר ·
ישוב מחטאתו אשר הפליך אחרי גוו סתורה והמלוה
פתגמה דש' בשר · התאן לסיפא קונטרים קטן הכמות
ורב האיכות תקכן על יד דברי גדולים לענין דיכא מאיך
עיני חכמים טוס סר"י טוט אס"ר · זאת פעולת מעשה
ידי אמן זרוע המיומן הרב הגדול מעח ומגדול ר"מ ור"מ
כמהר"ר אברהם ענתיבי נר"ו האם על אר"ץ
רבה עליה טפסר · יהא רעוא ליתיב מר ארישא תדיר
ומקודש ואמר כל העם יחי המלך לעולם רועי אל יחסר :
אכי"ר :

פה ליוורנו יע"א

שנת אשרי תבחר ותקרב לפ"ק
בדפוס אליעזר מנחם אוטולינגי נ"ע
יורשיו מדפיסים ומוכרים ספרים

Con approvazione.

Title Page of Hochmah U'Mussar

R' Abraham Antebi (# 64)

R' Abraham Yaakob Antebi

[65] ANTEBI, R' Abraham Yaakob

רבי אברהם יעקב ענתבי

(— 1933)

Worthy scholar and rabbi of Safed. He was born in Safed to R' Yehudah Shabbetai Raphael Antebi (see #77). R' Antebi managed to earn his own living while committing his energies to Torah study. It was said of him that his prayers for the sick were quickly answered.

It appears that at some time during World War I he moved to Egypt. There he published, at his own expense, the book *Be'Ohr HaHaim* by R' Haim Kapusi, who was known as a saintly man, a performer of wonders.

He passed away on 17 Shevat, 5683 (1933) and was laid to rest in Egypt next to the grave of R' Haim Kapusi.

[66] ANTEBI, R' Bekhor Nissim

רבי בכור נסים ענתבי

(— 1824)

Worthy scholar and rabbi of Damascus. He passed away there on 26 Adar 2, 5584 (1824).

[67] ANTEBI, R' David

רבי דוד ענתבי

(— 1840)

Worthy scholar and rabbi of Damascus. He passed away there on 21 Sivan, 5600 (1840).

[68] ANTEBI, R' Eliyahu Rahamim

רבי אליהו רחמים ענתבי

(1852 — 1920)

Eminent scholar and *darshan* (lecturer) of Safed. He was born in Safed in 1852, the firstborn son of R' Yehudah Shabbetai Raphael Antebi (see #77). He wrote a number of books, all of which remained in manuscript form. According to references in the books of other scholars, he wrote the following:

Derachim. Commentary on *Tanach* and the book of *Esther*.

- *Tov Taam*. Commentary on the *mitzvot*.
- *Imrei Shabbat*. Commentary on the *halachot* of *Shabbat*; also eulogies.
- *Ar'ah DeRabanan*. Inspirational lectures.
- *Darash Eliyahu*. Eulogies. An original manuscript copy of this book is located in the Ben-Zvi Institute (file no. 477).

There is also an untitled manuscript of *hiddushim* (original Torah thoughts) (file no. 476), which is identified as having been written by R' Eliyahu Rahamim Antebi of Safed in 1880. On the first page he signs his name in three languages: Hebrew, Arabic, and English.

He passed away on 10 Adar, 5680 (1920) and was laid to rest in Safed next to R' Yosef Karo. In his eulogy his son R' Raphael Menashe Antebi spoke lovingly about his father's last years, describing his devotion to study Torah, to fulfill every *mitzvah*, and to say every *tefillah* in spite of painful weakness.

[69] ANTEBI, R' Haim

רבי חיים ענתבי

(— 1840)

Worthy scholar and rabbi of Damascus. He passed away there on 3 Shevat, 5600 (1840). He may have been a brother of R' David Antebi (see #67).

[70] ANTEBI, R' Moshe Haim

רבי משה חיים ענתבי

(— 1890)

Worthy scholar and rabbi of Damascus. He was the youngest son of R' Yaakob Antebi of Jerusalem. He passed away in Damascus on 28 Adar, 5650 (1890).

[71] ANTEBI, R' Ovadiah Moshe

רבי עובדיה משה ענתבי

(19th century)

Worthy scholar and teacher of Aram Soba. He is praised by R' Shalom Hedaya (see #310) in the introduction which R' Hedaya wrote to the book *Degel Mahane Ephraim* by R' Ephraim Laniado (see #355). R' Hedaya wrote of his deep gratitude to R' Antebi for his personal support.

[72] ANTEBI, R' Rahamim Haim David

רבי רחמים חיים דוד ענתבי

(— 1873)

Humble scholar and rabbi of Jerusalem. He was the father of R' Yitzhak Antebi (see #80). He was also one of the select members of the yeshiva *Bet El* and is described in the book *Ohr HaShemesh* (on the *Rashash*) as being one of the most eminent of the scholars in that yeshiva — a man of whom it may be said that his lips never ceased uttering words of Torah. One of his students appears to have been R' Abraham Shalom Hamway (see #269), who went on to became a distinguished and prolific author of holy books.

He joined other scholars of the yeshiva in signing on the last will and testament of the notable, Nissim Shemama. He passed away in Jerusalem on Friday, 6 Tevet, 5634 (1873).

[73] ANTEBI, R' Raphael Menashe

רבי רפאל מנשה ענתבי

(1883 — 1963)

Eminent scholar and *dayan* (judge) of Safed and Haifa. He was born in Safed in about 1883 to R' Eliyahu Rahamim Antebi (see #68). He studied Torah under his worthy father, under R' Yosef Yedid (see #594), and in the *Bet Midrash* of the *Radbaz* (R' David ben Zakai).

He was known as a truly holy man and an intensely committed scholar, a man with a photographic memory. He would get up at midnight every night and go to the *Bet Midrash* to say *Tikkun Hatzot*. He would then study *Zohar* for the rest of the night, dedicating the day to the study of *Gemara* and the works of the *halachic* (legal) authorities.

In 1937 he was asked to serve as a *dayan* (judge) in the *Bet Din* of Haifa. He also served as an influential and persuasive *darshan* (lecturer).

R' Antebi wrote many *hiddushim* (original Torah thoughts) and responsa. However, most remained as original manuscripts. An exception was the introduction which he wrote to the book *Be'Ohr HaHaim* by R' Haim Kapusi. In addition, two eulogies which he delivered are included at the end of that book, one on the passing of his father in 1920 and the second on the passing of his grandmother Kadoun, the widow of the *Yashar*, R' Yehudah Shabbetai Raphael Antebi, in 1916 (see #77).

He passed away in Haifa on 9 Shevat, 5723 (1963).

[74] ANTEBI, R' Yaakob

רבי יעקב ענתבי

(— 1826)

Worthy scholar and rabbi of Damascus. He passed away there on *Rosh Hashanah* 5586 (1826).

R' Raphael Menashe Antebi would get up at midnight every night and go to the Bet Midrash to say Tikkun Hatzot. He would then study Zohar for the rest of the night.

[75] ANTEBI, R' Yaakob

רבי יעקב ענתבי

(— 1846)

Distinguished Chief Rabbi and *dayan* (judge) of Damascus for over 30 years. He was a nephew of R' Abraham Antebi (see #63). During his tenure in the *Bet Din* of Damascus, a major controversy arose around the settlement of the inheritance of R' Haim Farhi (see #261), a wealthy man of Damascus. The complicated case involved the brothers of the deceased and the *Batei Din* of many major Jewish communities, including Aram Soba, Jerusalem, Tiberias, and Izmir. The affair caused a great deal of ill will and R' Yaakob's name was besmirched by those who disagreed with his judicial rulings. They even went so far as to complain about him to the governing authorities. However, R' Yaakob stood fast in his judgments and refused to compromise his integrity. The details of the legal rulings involved may be found in the book *Hukot Haim* (*Hoshen Mishpat*) of R' Haim Palagi (see #449).

R' Yaakob Antebi

He was also one of the select members of the yeshiva Bet El.

R' Yaakob Antebi endured imprisonment and torture during the infamous Damascus Blood Libel.

The Damascus Blood Libel. R' Yaakob Antebi endured imprisonment and torture during the infamous Damascus Blood Libel. The incident began on February 5, 1840 with the mysterious disappearance of a Catholic (Capuchin) monk and his Arab servant, Ibrahim Amara. The monk, whose name was Padre Tomas, had been involved in shady business, and the two men were probably murdered by tradesmen with whom he had quarreled. Nonetheless, the Capuchins immediately circulated the news that the Jews had murdered both men in order to use their blood in baking *matzot* for *Pesah*. Syria was then ruled by Muhammad Ali of Egypt but Catholics in Syria were officially under French protection, and so the investigation should have been conducted by the French consul. However, the consul allied himself with the accusers, and supervised the investigation jointly with the Egyptian governor-general; it was conducted in the most barbarous fashion. A barber, Solomon Negrin, was arbitrarily arrested and tortured until a "confession" was extorted from him, according to which the monk had been killed in the house of David Harari by seven Jews. A Muslim servant in the service of David Harari related under duress that Ibrahim Amara was killed in the house of Meir Farhi, in the presence of the latter and other Jewish notables.

The men who were named, including R' Antebi, were subsequently arrested and tortured to get them to "confess." They were held in tiny, infested cells and subjected to horrendous physical and verbal abuse. It was only after many months that a courageous individual managed to smuggle a letter out to R' Abraham Antebi, the Chief Rabbi of Aram Soba (see #63). He immediately took steps to arouse the Jewish world to press for intervention by the European powers. Among those who were instrumental in getting help were Solomon Rothschild, Sir Moses Montefiore, his secretary Louis Loewe, Adolphe Cremieux, and Solomon Munk. The liberation order was finally issued on August 28, 1840, and those prisoners who were still alive in Damascus were saved.

With his release into normal life, R' Yaakob resolved to leave Damascus and live in Jerusalem. He provided a detailed report of his experiences in a letter to Moses Montefiore. The narrative is also included in the book *Be'Ohr HaHaim* of R' Haim Kapusi in the edition published by R' Abraham Yaakob Antebi (see #65) and in an appendix to the book, *LiKedoshim Asher Ba'Aretz* by R' David-Sion Laniado (see #352).

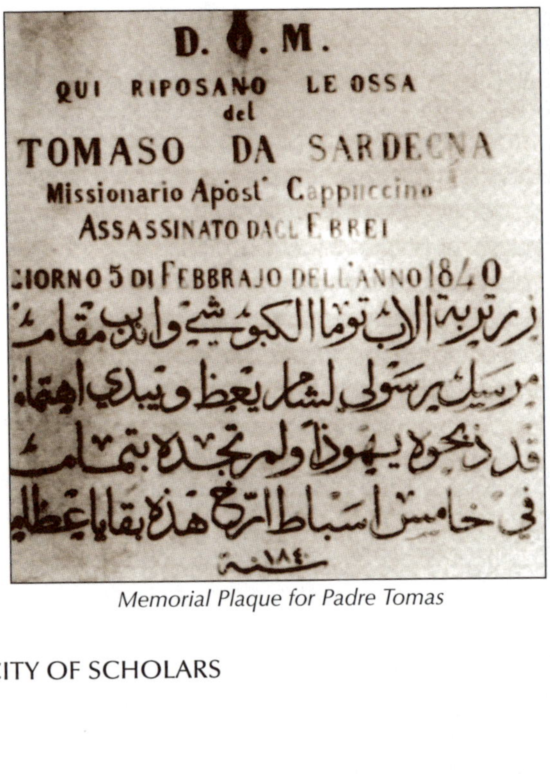

Memorial Plaque for Padre Tomas

Sir Moses Montefiore

A Sword on the Neck. During his months of captivity in Damascus R' Yaakob was tortured mentally and physically. One day the officer in charge ordered a soldier to decapitate him. The soldier pulled out his sword and struck his neck but used the blunt edge. R' Yaakob later related that the following thought entered his mind:

> The *Gemara* says, "Even if a sharp sword is on your neck don't give up hope for *Hashem's* mercy" (*Berachot* 10a). Why does the *Gemara* add the word "sharp"? Would it not have been sufficient to say, "Even if a sword is on your neck"? After my experience that day, I understand. The *Gemara* is telling us, not only if the blunt end is being used don't give up, but even if the sharp side is being used, count on *Hashem* to save you.

Shortly before R' Yaakob's arrival in Jerusalem, the *Rishon LeSion* (Chief Rabbi of *Eretz Yisrael*) had a dream in which he was questioned, "Our father Yaakob is coming to Jerusalem and you are lying in your bed?" He could not understand what this dream could possibly mean and so the next morning he told the scholars in the *Bet Midrash* about it. After some time, one of the scholars volunteered: "It means that R' Yaakob Antebi who suffered so much from the blood libel of that accursed Padre Tomas is coming to Jerusalem." When R' Yaakob came he was warmly greeted and embraced by the *Rishon LeSion* and the leading rabbis of the city. The *Rishon LeSion* took off his turban to put it on the head of R' Yaakob, but R' Yaakob refused saying that he had now fulfilled his rabbinical duty and that he thanked *Hashem* for bringing him in peace to Jerusalem. He felt that he was excused from bearing the painful yoke of office and could now experience the holiness of Jerusalem in tranquility.

Shortly before R' Yaakob's arrival in Jerusalem, the Rishon LeSion (Chief Rabbi of Eretz Yisrael) had a dream.

R' Yaakob passed away in Jerusalem on 7 Tishrei, 5607 (1846). One of his responsa was published in the book *Mar Ve'Ahalot* by R' Abraham Antebi (see #63). It was written in 1839 in Damascus, the year before the blood libel affair. In it he reminisces about his 30 years of having been a *dayan* (judge) in that city. Another of his responsa appears in the book *Poel Sedek* by R' Abraham Dayan (see #173).

[76] **ANTEBI, R' Yaakob**

רבי יעקב ענתבי

(— 1906)

Worthy scholar and rabbi of Damascus. He may have been a descendant of the earlier R' Yaakob Antebi (see #75). He passed away on 19 Shevat, 5666 (1906).

[77] **ANTEBI, R' Yehudah Shabbetai Raphael [Yashar]**

רבי יהודה שבתי רפאל (ישר) ענתבי

(1810 — 1888)

Saintly scholar and rabbi of Safed. People referred to him as the *Yashar*. He was born in approximately 1810, a nephew of R' Abraham Antebi (see #63).

In 1831, when he was only 21 years of age, he was sent out to the cities of Arabistan as an emissary of the Torah institutions of Safed. While on the way he composed a hymn in honor of the *Rashbi* (R' Shimon bar Yochai). The hymn may be found in the book *Be'Ohr HaHaim* by R' Haim Kapusi in the edition published by his son, R' Abraham Yaakob Antebi (see #65). In 1866 he went out again on another mission, this time to the cities of North Africa.

One of his inspirational lectures for *Shabbat HaGadol* was printed in the book *Be'Ohr HaHaim*. It was copied from his original manuscript by his grandson R' Raphael Menashe Antebi (see #73).

The *Yashar* passed away in Safed on 9 Tishrei, 5649 (1888) and was laid to rest in the burial vault of R' Moshe Alshich. His oldest son, Eliyahu, delivered a heartfelt eulogy at the end of the seven days of mourning and then again at the end of the first nine months. The eulogies, which appear in the book *Abir Yaakob* (p. 29), describe the *Yashar* as one of the 36 righteous men in whose merit our world exists.

He was blessed with eight worthy sons, seven of whom were mentioned in a eulogy delivered by a grandson on the occasion of the passing of R' Antebi's widow Kadoun in 1916. They are R' Eliyahu Rahamim (see #68), R' Abraham Yaakob (see #65), R' Yosef (see #86), R' Yitzhak, R' Yisrael, R' Yeshuah, and R' Shelomo. The eulogy was recorded in *Be'Ohr HaHaim*. The eighth son, R' Yomtob, passed away at a young age in 1903.

[78] ANTEBI, R' Yeshuah

רבי ישועה ענתבי

(19th century)

Chief Rabbi of Tiberias. His early years as a scholar and rabbi were spent in Aram Soba. In 1846 he joined other rabbis of Tiberias in signing a document detailing the ordinances of the yeshiva *Bet Yaakob*.

One of his grandchildren was R' Yomtob ben Shabbetai Antebi, who was born in Safed in 1880 and was known as a brilliant Torah scholar. However, while still a young man he died in the cholera epidemic that broke out in the year 1903.

[79] ANTEBI, R' Yisrael

רבי ישראל ענתבי

(— 1949)

Worthy scholar and rabbi of Tiberias. He passed away on the day before *Rosh Chodesh* Elul, 5709 (1949).

[80] ANTEBI, R' Yitzhak

רבי יצחק ענתבי

(1721 — 1804)

Eminent scholar and *dayan* (judge) of Aram Soba. He was born in 1721, a son of R' Shabbetai Antebi and had the merit of being the father of R' Abraham Antebi (see #63), the Chief Rabbi of the city. Among his contemporaries were R' Yehudah Yomtob Kassin (see #331), R' Raphael Shelomo Laniado (see #363), and R' Yeshayah Attiah (see #119).

He is known for his important book of inspirational lectures *Ohel Abraham Ve'Ohel Yitzhak* (Livorno 5585/1825), which was published by his son R' Abraham together with the commentary *Yoshev Ohalim*. R' Yitzhak also authored *Bet Av* (Livorno 5609/1849), a work of *hiddushim* (original Torah thoughts) on the *Rambam* and the *Bet Yosef*; and various responsa. This work was also published by his son, R' Abraham Antebi (see #63), together with R' Abraham's work *Penei HaBayit*.

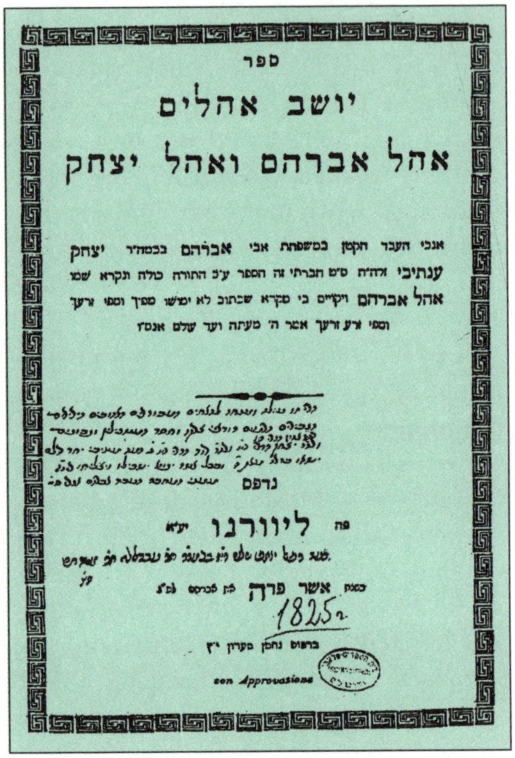
ספר

יושב אהלים

אהל אברהם ואהל יצחק

אנכי העבד הקטן במשפחת אבי אברהם בכמה"ר יצחק ענתיבי זהה"ה ס"ט חברתי זה הספר ע"ס התורה כולה תקרא שמו אהל אברהם ויקיים בי מקרא שכתוב לא ימושו מפיך ומפי זרעך ומפי זרע זרעך אמר ה' מעתה ועד עולם אנס"ו

נדפס

פה ליוורנו יע"א

בשנת אשר פרה

1825

con Approvazione

Title Page of Ohel Abraham Ve'Ohel Yitzhak

He signed along with R' Yeshayahu Attiah the approbations for the following works of R' Raphael Shelomo Laniado (see #363): *Bet Dino shel Shelomo* and *HaMa'alot LeShelomo*. He also signed along with other rabbis of Aram Soba the approbation for the work *Mahane Yehudah* of R' Yehudah Yomtob Kassin. At the Ben-Zvi Institute there is a hand-written document containing R' Yitzhak's signature as well as the signature of R' Raphael Shelomo Laniado (see #363), dated 20 Elul, 5616 (1855) [file no. 302].

The work *Bigdei Yesha* of R' Yeshayah Attiah (see #119) contains one of R' Yitzhak's responsa, as well as a responsum written by R' Yeshayah to him.

R' Abraham, his son, memorialized him in the introduction to his own work *Yoshev Ohalim* as a brilliant scholar and righteous man. He passed away on 20 Nissan, 5564 (1804).

[81] ANTEBI, R' Yitzhak

רבי יצחק ענתבי

(— 1823)

Worthy scholar and rabbi of Jerusalem. He passed away there on 4 Heshvan, 5584 (1823).

[82] ANTEBI, R' Yitzhak

רבי יצחק ענתבי

(— 1886)

Worthy scholar and rabbi of Jerusalem. He was also one of the select members of the yeshiva *Bet El*. His father was R' Rahamim Antebi (see #72). He passed away in Jerusalem on 11 Kislev, 5647 (1886).

[83] ANTEBI, R' Yitzhak

רבי יצחק ענתבי

(19th century)

Eminent scholar and rabbi of Aram Soba. He was a son of R' Abraham Antebi (see #63), the Chief Rabbi of Aram Soba. His father was also a talented composer of *pizmonim* (hymns). He composed the famous songs, *"Im Hacham Libecha"* on the occasion of the wedding of R' Yitzhak and *"Atah Ahuvi"* on the occasion of the birth of a grandson. His songs are sung to this day.

He wrote an unpublished book called *Hikekei Lev* (commentary on *Even HaEzer*). In addition, two of his responsa are included in his father's book *Mar Ve'Ahalot* (on *Hoshen Mishpat,* 34, and *Even HaEzer,* 13). Another of his responsa appears in the book *VaYosef Abraham* (sec. 4) by R' Abraham Dayan *(see* #173).

In 1852 he joined other rabbis of Aram Soba in signing the approbation to the book *Kenisiyah Leshem Shamayim* by R' Menashe Sutton (see #551). In 1865 he signed the approbation to *Hadar Ezer* by R' Yitzhak Shrem (see #517).

[84] ANTEBI, R' Yitzhak Shabbetai

רבי יצחק שבתי ענתבי

(— 1843)

Worthy scholar and rabbi of Damascus. He passed away there on 10 Tamuz, 5603 (1843).

R' Yosef Antebi

[85] ANTEBI, R' Yosef

רבי יוסף ענתבי

(1847 — 1919)

Eminent scholar and rabbi of Damascus. He was born in Damascus in 1847 to R' David Yitzhak Antebi. His grandfather was R' Yaakob Antebi (see #75). He was known for his book *Vayitzbor Yosef,* consisting primarily of inspirational lectures on *Bereshit*. In addition, there are two *Bar Mitzvah* lectures, one of which he delivered on the occasion of the *Bar Mitzvah* of his son David in 1879. The book also includes three *Shabbat HaGadol* lectures, which he delivered in the R' Yohanan ben Zakai synagogue in Damascus in 1914, 1915, and 1917. R' Mordechai Maslaton (see #411) was one of his students in Damascus.

He passed away on 26 Heshvan, 5679 (1919) and was laid to rest in the Mount of Olives in Jerusalem next to the burial place of his grandfather R' Yaakob Antebi. He was blessed with four worthy sons: R' David, R' Abraham, R' Raphael, and R' Eliyahu Yeshuah. R' David, the oldest, published *Vayitzbor Yosef* after his father's death and included the eulogy which he had delivered for his father.

R' Mordechai Maslaton (see # 411) was one of R' Yosef Antebi's students in Damascus.

R' Yitzhak Antebi (#83) composed the famous songs, "Im Hacham Libecha" on the occasion of the wedding of R' Yitzhak and "Atah Ahuvi" on the occasion of the birth of a grandson. His songs are sung to this day.

[86] ANTEBI, R' Yosef

רבי יוסף ענתבי

(— 1935)

Eminent scholar and rabbi of Safed and Beirut. He was born in Safed, the third son of R' Yehudah Shabbetai Raphael (the *Yashar*, see #77). During World War I he was forced to move to Beirut because of the difficult economic conditions in Safed. He took a rabbinical post in Beirut, where he remained for the rest of his life, passing away in 1935. He is spoken of highly in the book *Be'Ohr HaHaim* byR' Haim Kapusi in the edition published by R' Abraham Yaakob Antebi (see #65).

[87] ANTEBI (ADES) (TABUSH), R' Raphael

רבי רפאל (עדס) ענתבי (טבוש)

(1830 — 1918)

He had studied Kabbalah and many of his pizmonim contain allusions to its concepts.

Eminent poet, *hazzan* (cantor), and Kabbalist of Aram Soba. R' Antebi was born in Aram Soba in approximately 1830 to R' Yitzhak Antebi. He was a renowned composer of *pizmonim* (devotional songs or hymns), producing over 400 songs over the course of his life.

His book *Shirah Hadashah* (Aram Soba 5648/1888) consists primarily of *pizmonim*, many of which are still sung in synagogues on *Shabbat*, holidays, and on other joyful occasions. Originally limited to Syrian congregations, many have been adopted by the general Sephardic community. In 1905, R' Raphael Haim Cohen made additions and reprinted the book, in Jerusalem, under the title *Shir U'Shevahah*. Many of his *pizmonim* are also incorporated into the anthology *Shir U'Shevahah Hallel VeZimrah* (Jerusalem 5724/1964), which was published by the *Magen David* congregation of New York.

He had studied Kabbalah and many of his *pizmonim* contain allusions to its concepts. Although he was blind, his musical and

R' Raphael Antebi (Tabush)

ספר
שירה חדשה
המה שירות ותשבחות מאשר
חנני ה' אלהי לשורר בקול
נעים ואלקים יודע כי לש"ש
נתכונתי בכדי שלא יורתו
לפושעים יד לשורר שירי
עגבים כי השירות של חשק
ונבול פה מפריד הנשמה
מצרור החיים ח"ו ויי משמים
ישלח משיחנו בעג' ובק"ב כי"ר
ש' תר"מח

Title Page of Shirah Hadashah

poetic abilities were exceptional, and he was highly regarded by the scholars and rabbis of Jerusalem. As a worthy Torah scholar his name appeared in the 1901 list of Aram Soba scholars receiving a weekly stipend from the special fund that had been set up for the support of worthy individuals who dedicate their lives to Torah study.

While still in Aram Soba he taught musical and poetic skills to youngsters in the *Bet Midrash Aboud Harari*. Among his most gifted students were R' Murad Harari, Afrir Cohen, the renowned R' Moshe Ashear (see #88), and R' Haim Shaul Aboud (see #30), author of the book *Shirei Zimrah* (Jerusalem, 1933). Since R' Raphael was blind, he needed a scribe to record his compositions. Generally, his student R' Moshe Ashear filled this role and that is why most of R' Raphael's manuscripts display the elegant handwriting of R' Moshe.

His poetic talents were so profound that even when in conversation with someone he would find himself creating poetic stanzas from the subject matter of the discussion. On one occasion he and his students went for a walk in one of the parks outside Aram Soba, when they encountered Señor Mordechai Picciotto. Señor Picciotto, who was the consul of one of the European countries, was a man who loved songs and their composers. In the park there was a vertical irrigation water wheel which raised water from a stream by means of a series of buckets around the rim of the wheel. The buckets were filled by the motion of the wheel dipping them into the water below. As each bucket was raised by the turning wheel it was emptied out into an aqueduct. The irrigation wheel was driven by a second wheel arranged with a shaft, which was turned by a mule walking around in a circle. As the wheel turned, the water made a pleasant rhythmic sound. Señor Picciotto said to R' Antebi, "I will give you 100 golden lira if you compose a song for me, which has the same rhythmic beat as the water." And that is exactly what R' Antebi did, choosing the theme of a *brit milah* (circumcision) celebration. Señor Picciotto enjoyed the song and paid him on the spot. The song became well known and was traditionally sung in Aram Soba on the day of a *brit milah*, when the guests were assembling for the ceremony.

One evening he was invited to perform at a *Purim* party. Afterwards, one of the guests took his hand to guide him home. On the way they were accosted by an Arab beggar who was shaking a metal collection box and making a rhythmic jingling noise. R' Antebi's companion said to him, "I will give you 10 lira if you compose a song that matches the rhythmic sound of the beggar's box." And so R' Antebi immediately composed an appropriate song with the theme of *Purim*. The song was subsequently published in the book *Shirei Zimrah*.

In 1893 he visited Jerusalem and while he was there, R' Yaakob Shaul Elyashar was installed as the new *Rishon LeSion* (Chief Rabbi of *Eretz Yisrael*). In honor of the occasion R' Raphael had prepared a special *"Shir Zahav"* (Golden Song). When the *Rishon LeSion* came into the great synagogue of R' Yohanan ben Zakai in the Old City of Jerusalem, he was serenaded by two choirs of boys, one from the Talmud Torah *Doresh Zion* and the other from the yeshiva *Tiferet Yerushalayim*. The choirs sang under the direction of R' Raphael Antebi. At the end of the performance, the *Rishon LeSion* thanked R' Antebi profusely and as a token of his gratitude gave him 3 napoleons (valuable gold coins). The *"Shir Zahav"* is recorded in the book *Shir U'Shevahah* (p. 165).

Toward the end of his life he traveled to Egypt and he passed away there on 3 Kislev, 5679 (1918). He was blessed with two worthy sons: R' Zachi (Yitzhak) and R' Yedidyah. In addition, he had a brother, R' Abraham Ades, who was a talented singer. His brother's son, R' Yitzhak, edited the book *Shir U'Shevahah* and was also a composer in his own right. Another brother, R' Aboud Ades, was also a composer of *pizmonim*.

As a worthy Torah scholar his name appeared in the 1901 list of Aram Soba scholars receiving a weekly stipend from the special fund that had been set up for the support of worthy individuals.

His poetic talents were so profound that even when in conversation with someone he would find himself creating poetic stanzas from the subject matter of the discussion.

R' Yaacob Shaul Elyasher

The pizmonim (hymns) which he composed have won wide acceptance.

"Today, although I lost my buildings, I am indeed fortunate for I have you, my family."

[88] ASHEAR, R' Moshe Haim
רבי משה חיים אשקר הכהן
(1877 — 1940)

Worthy scholar, poet, and *hazzan* (cantor). The *pizmonim* (hymns) which he composed have won wide acceptance, especially those that are sung on Friday night. His book *Hallel VeZimrah* (Jerusalem 5688/1928) is still in use as a guide to Jewish liturgy. Many of his *pizmonim* are also incorporated into the anthology *Shir U'Shevahah Hallel VeZimrah* (Jerusalem 5724/1964), which was published by the *Magen David* congregation in Brooklyn. Many of his *hiddushim* (original Torah thoughts) may be found in the works of other authors of his period.

R' Moshe Haim Ashear

אז ישיר משה ובני ישראל
בס״ד בהנ״ו ספר עמ״י עש״ו
הלל וזמרה
זה ספר, סלא אמרי שפר, זמרה והלל, ושבחות למלל, בבי כנשהא, לחרווהה דשכינהא, וגם לרבות לשמח הלבבות, וההנים וכלות בהוך מקהלות, להיות כל איש שורר בביתו, דבר בעתו, לאלה׳ דשמייא, עזי וזמרת י״ה:
מאתי הקטן, בן לא״א היקר, ז״ל: עברא דרבנן, ותלמידיהן,
ע״כ משה יוסף אשקר, הכהן, ס״ט
נדפס
פעה״ק - ירושלם תובב״א
שנת תפר״ח לפ״ק
ברפוס הר״ש. הלוי צוקרמן

Title Page of Hallel VeZimrah

He was born in Aram Soba in 1877, a son of R' Yosef and Simchah Ashear. He was orphaned at a young age and was taken under the wing of the renowned *hazzan* and composer, R' Raphael Antebi Tabush (see #87), who recognized his musical talent and guided him in developing his skills. He also became a Torah scholar and effective *darshan* (lecturer).

At the age of 26 he was appointed to the prestigious position of *hazzan* and *baal koreh* (Torah reader) in the Great Synagogue of Aram Soba. He served in that capacity until the age of 35 when he immigrated to the United States together with many other members of the community. Arriving in New York, he began a 28-year career as *hazzan* of the congregation *Magen David* in Brooklyn. He and his brother R' Shehidyah Ashear devoted themselves to raising the caliber of Sephardic liturgical music in the United States.

He earned his livelihood as a bookkeeper at a textile company called Oriental Jobbers. As new immigrants arrived, with limited opportunities for employment, and no knowledge of the English language, he would provide them sample cases of products, encourage them to sell, and at day's end would balance their accounts.

Over time, R' Moshe got involved in buying and selling real estate, but lost all in the Great Depression of 1929. He came home that night, sat the family around the table, and told them of his financial loss. He said, "Today, although I lost my buildings, I am indeed fortunate for I have you, my family." In retrospect, his financial loss was a gain for the community, for now he spent more time on community work.

He was beloved by the community for his kindness of heart and his unselfishness as a public servant. Members of the community were encouraged to seek his counsel and services, whether it was in translating letters, matchmaking, *shalom bayit* (resolving family disputes), or settling business disputes. As a *Kohen* and a peacemaker he was a true descendant of Aharon HaKohen.

His legacy has been immortalized in song. On the occasion of a birth, *brit milah* (circumcision), *Bar Mitzvah*, or wedding, he would compose a *pizmon*, which included the names of the family members; these words were set to popular Jewish songs. On the day of the occasion, he would distribute the songs to the people, and would lead them in singing and rejoicing. The older men of the Syrian community still remember and cherish the uniforms he bought for them to sing in the *shul* choir.

In April 1940, R' Moshe's older children were apprised of their father's failing health. With a brief six months to live, he continued to serve as the *hazzan* through the High Holy Days. On *Yom Kippur*, he was so weak that he needed the support of the *tebah* (lectern) to stand upright.

Finally, at the age of 63, after twenty-eight years of devotion to his community, he passed away on *Hol HaMoed Sukkot*, 18 Tishrei, 5701. In an act of special consideration, Chief Rabbi Yaakob Kassin (see #330) ordered that his funeral be delayed to the next day to allow all the people a chance to attend. Rather than have a hearse transporting him, his loving community carried him from his home to the *shul*. The following *Shabbat*, R' Kassin officiated as the *hazzan* from his seat, leaving the *tebah* unattended, marking the loss they had all endured.

His family had deep respect for him and emulated his traits. His wife Salchah was a quiet modest woman, the daughter of R' Yaakob Shamah. They were blessed with five sons and a daughter. The oldest son, Yosef, became a community leader like his father. He also held the post of president of *Yeshivat Porat Yosef*. The second son, Albert (Amerique), was a *baal koreh* (Torah reader) and an accomplished musician. The third son, Seyah, was a gifted calligrapher, whose religious works can still be seen in local *shuls*. The two remaining boys, David and Eli, defined the humility and sensitivity which have become the hallmark of the Ashear family. His daughter, Allegra Franco, continued in the path of her mother, being a true *sadeket* (righteous woman) devoted to her family.

[89] **ASHKENAZI, R' Abraham**

רבי אברהם אשכנזי

(— 1825)

Eminent scholar and *dayan* (judge) of Aram Soba. His father was R' Gabriel Ashkenazi (see #93).

In 1822 R' Ashkenazi joined other leading rabbis of Aram Soba in signing the approbation for the book *Yoshev Ohalim* by R' Abraham Antebi (see #63).

He passed away in 1825 at the young age of 43 leaving two sons, both scholars, R' Michael and R' Ezra, and a son-in-law, R' Mordechai Ancona.

[90] **ASHKENAZI, R' David**

רבי דוד אשכנזי

(— 1847)

Rabbi and *dayan* (judge) of the Aram Soba *Bet Din*. He served on the *Bet Din* together with R' Abraham Antebi (see #63) and R' Haim Mordechai Labaton (see #336). R' Ashkenazi was the second son of R' Gabriel Ashkenazi (see #93). At the Ben-Zvi Institute there is an original document dated 22 Tamuz, 5600 (1840) in which his name appears under that of R' Haim Mordechai Labaton (see #336), reflecting his considerable stature and position in the community. He passed away on 20 Kislev, 5608 (1847) and was eulogized by R' Abraham Dayan (see #173).

[91] **ASHKENAZI, R' Eliyahu**

רבי אליהו אשכנזי

(1865 — 1936)

Humble scholar and teacher in Kilis and Aram Soba. He was born to R' Ezra Ashkenazi (see #92) in the town of Kilis in Turkey, north of Aram Soba. He began his career there, teaching *Tanach* and *Gemara*. When he came to Aram Soba he continued as a teacher in the Great Orphanage. He was known to love his students as a father loves his children and he concerned himself with all of their needs, both physical and spiritual.

After World War I he joined his children in Mexico City, and lived there for the remainder of his life. He passed away on 7 Iyar, 5696 (1936).

He was known to love his students as a father loves his children and he concerned himself with all of their needs, both physical and spiritual.

[92] **ASHKENAZI, R' Ezra**

רבי עזרא אשכנזי

(1821 — 1898)

Humble scholar and *darshan* (lecturer). He was the second son of R' Abraham Ashkenazi (see #89) and son-in-law of R' David Ashkenazi (see #90). In the eulogy which R' Abraham Dayan gave for R' David Ashkenazi in 1848, he praised R' Ezra Ashkenazi, who was his nephew. He was blessed with a long life and passed away at the age of 77 on 21 Adar, 5658 (1898).

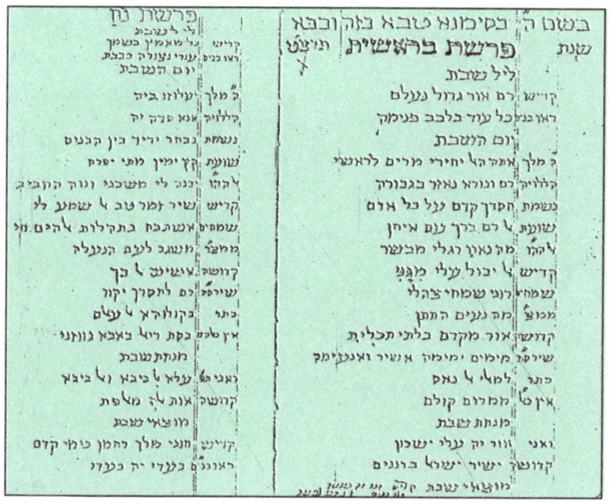

R' Moshe Ashear's handwritten notes of tunes for Shabbat prayer

[93] **ASHKENAZI, R' Gabriel**

רבי גבריאל אשכנזי

(1757 — 1810)

Eminent scholar and *dayan* (judge) of Aram Soba. He was born in Aram Soba to

R' Rahamim Ashkenazi. In his later years he left Aram Soba for *Eretz Yisrael* and while passing through the city of Shechem he decided to stay a while. He ended up spending the rest of his days there and was buried there in 1810, having lived only to the age of 53. When the news reached Aram Soba, the leading rabbis of the city, including R' Abraham Sutton (see #535), eulogized him (*Malel Le'Abraham*, 2). He was survived by two sons, both learned scholars: R' Abraham (see #89) and R' David (see #90).

He authored four collections of responsa and lectures, which he left in manuscript form. His *hiddushim* (original Torah thoughts) on *halachah* are referenced in *Korban Isheh* by R' Eliyahu Shamah (see #499) (*Hoshen Mishpat,* 32). One of his responsa was included in the book *Beirach Moshe* of R' Moshe Galante, the Chief Rabbi of Damascus (Section 16).

In 1985-1986, his responsa were published in two volumes in Jerusalem by R' Ezra Basri, working from the original manuscripts.

Even the gentiles in the area were in awe of him and gave him great respect. His name was associated with that "Sage's Orchard."

[94] ASHKENAZI, R' Haim

רבי חיים אשכנזי

(— 1890)

Chief Rabbi of Ein Tab and *dayan* (judge) of the Aram Soba *Bet Din*. Ein Tab was a small village near Aram Soba, whose Chief Rabbi had long been R' Shalom Chasky (see #149). After R' Chasky's return to Aram Soba in his old age, R' Ashkenazi went to Ein Tab to take his place. When his service there was completed he came back to Aram Soba, where he served on the *Bet Din* together with R' Moshe Swed (see #575) and R' Ezra Tawil (see #582). He was the second son of R' David Ashkenazi (see #90) and passed away on 15 Tishrei, 5651 (1890).

One of his *halachic* (legal) rulings was printed in *Maaseh Ish* (*Even HaEzer*, Section 1) of R' Yaakob Shaul Elyashar, the *Rishon LeSion* (Chief Rabbi of *Eretz Yisrael*). He also wrote lectures and responsa on the four parts of the *Shulhan Aruch*. His *hiddushim* (original Torah thoughts) were published under the title *Ginzei Haim* (New York 5702/1942) by his daughter's sons, Messrs. Abraham and Yitzhak Bijou. His poetic use of language was praised in the introduction to the book, written by the editor, R' Eliyahu Ezra Husney. The book was subsequently published again in Jerusalem in 5745 (1985).

In 1865 he joined other rabbis of Aram Soba in signing the approbation for the first book-printing initiative of the city, which was introduced by R' Abraham Sasson and his sons (see #475).

[95] ASHKENAZI, R' Michael

רבי מיכאל אשכנזי

(— 1889)

Eminent rabbi and *dayan* (judge) of Tedef, a town near Aram Soba. He was the first son of R' Abraham Ashkenazi (see #89). He conducted his office in a superior manner, with a firm and vigorous hand. Even the gentiles in the area were in awe of him and gave him great respect. At one time he owned a large orchard in the town of Tedef. It was cultivated and maintained by gentiles as a courtesy to the "Sage of the Jews," and his name was associated with that "Sage's Orchard" until recently.

In the eulogy which R' Abraham Dayan (see #173) gave for R' David Ashkenazi in 1848, he spoke of the brilliance of R' Michael Ashkenazi, who was his nephew.

In 1852 he joined other rabbis of Aram Soba in signing the approbation to the book *Kenisiyah Leshem Shamayim* by R' Menashe Sutton (see #551). (See Document Section, Document No. 31.) Subsequently, in 1865 his signature appears together with that of the rabbis of Aram Soba on the approbation for the Sasson printing initiative (see #475). (See Document Section, Document No. 25.) Later, in 1878 he signed the approbation for the book *Yashir Moshe* of R' Moshe Dayan (#192).

He passed away in Tedef on *Shabbat*, 18 Elul, 5649 (1889) and his grave is next to that of R' Shelomo Safdeyé (see #469).

[96] ASHKENAZI, R' Selim

רבי סאלם אשכנזי

(1878 — 1951)

Worthy scholar and Talmud Torah teacher of Aram Soba and New York. He was born in

Aram Soba in 1878 and gained experience as a *shohet* (ritual slaughterer) and as a teacher of boys in the Talmud Torah (*Kitab* in Arabic). He was a very kind, unpretentious person, and this showed in the way he related to his many students, whether he was teaching them *Alef Bet* or *Gemara*. He was an excellent pedagogue and his students remembered him fondly as a person who always wore a smile on his face.

He immigrated to America before World War I, and initially settled in Texas. In 1919, he relocated to the Lower East Side of New York and later moved to Brooklyn, where he lived the remainder of his life.

R' Selim Ashkenazi

His Talmud Torah in Brooklyn

In Brooklyn he started a *Kitab* in a small synagogue, located on 64th Street in the Sea Beach neighborhood, known as *K'nees Betesh*, founded by Shaul Betesh. In those years there was no Jewish day school for Sephardic children and so most of his students attended the *Kitab* in the late afternoon after a full day at the local public school. Traditionally, *Kitab* teachers used a small stick to maintain discipline. R' Selim's stick was very thin so that the child was not hurt too much when it was necessary to administer a *"sunta"* (a smack on the palm of the hand).

His fee was $5 per month per child. However, he would accept $2 from those who couldn't pay more. The hours were 9 a.m. to 5 p.m. for the younger children who did not attend public school. Older children's hours were from 3:30 p.m. to 6 p.m. On *Shabbat* the hours were from 1 p.m. to 4 p.m. and on Sundays from 9 a.m. to 3 p.m.

Each morning at about 11 a.m. he would peel a cucumber, make four slices, and put these in a glass of water. This served as his lunch. He would smoke a nargileh (a Turkish water pipe) two or three times a day. He had on his table a small metal box which contained assorted candies, which he sold to the students. Once two boys approached him to explain a passage in the *Gemara*. Since the *Gemara* was a large book, it covered the candy box and while one boy was receiving the rabbi's attention, the second boy sneaked a candy. A visitor was present in the classroom and noticed what was going on. When he mentioned it later, R' Selim said, "Let them take — they don't have money to buy."

Kaparot for Yom Kippur

Three or four days before *Yom Kippur* at about 6 a.m. he would start going to people's homes to slaughter their chickens for *kaparot* (atonement ritual). Later in the day he would go to the local kosher butcher shop run by Shaya Shalom to slaughter chickens for customers who came in.

In Brooklyn he started a Kitab and a small synagogue, located on 64th Street in the Sea Beach neighborhood.

Adviser to the Community

He had a reputation as a wise and knowledgeable man. People from the community would often consult him regarding their personal problems.

A Scholar Among Scholars

The revered scholar, R' Matloub Abadi (see #9), said, "Do not underestimate R' Selim Ashkenazi; he is a first-rate Talmudist." Nevertheless, he sought neither honors nor position.

Every *Shabbat* after lunch he would meet with R' Eliyahu Husney (see #314) and R' Yaakob Maleh *(see #402)* at the home of Mr. Ezra Safdya (father of Joe and Meyer Saff), and the four of them would study *Gemara* together until shortly before *Minhah*.

A Tragic Death

On his way to synagogue early one morning in 1951 he was beaten to death by a mugger. He was 73 years old and mourned by the entire community. His two sons and four daughters carried on his legacy.

[97] ASHKENAZI, R' Yeshayah

רבי ישעיה אשכנזי

(— 1892)

"I'm not a Hacham or a rabbi, I'm a regular man, just like anybody else."

Humble and dedicated scholar of Aram Soba. He was the elder son of R' David Ashkenazi (see #91). In his later years he settled in Jerusalem, where he passed away on 8 Kislev, 5653 (1892).

[98] ASSA, R' Yitzhak

רבי יצחק אסא

(1896 — 1996)

R' Yitzhak Assa

Eminent *mohel* and *shohet* of Damascus. He was born in Damascus in 1896 and excelled in his studies as a youth. The community was amazed at the depth and breadth of his *Bar Mitzvah derashah* (lecture), which he delivered under the guidance of his teacher, R' Yosef Dana, one of the elder rabbis of Damascus. Subsequently, he studied under R' Eliyahu Tarab Maslaton, together with his friend R' Nissim Huli.

In the 1930's there were about 60,000 Jews living in Damascus but there was a shortage of *mohalim* and *shohatim* (experts in performing circumcisions and kosher slaughtering). And so R' Yitzhak was chosen by the community leaders to become trained in these areas. He was sent to Tiberias and studied under the Chief Rabbi of the city, R' Meyer Waknin, for over a year. His dedication to his studies was so great that when he heard his wife in Damascus had given birth to twins he remained in Tiberias (after consulting with rabbis) and was not present at his own son's *brit milah*. At the end of his training, he received certification as a *shohet* and *mohel* from the heads of *shehitah* in Tiberias, R' Waknin and R' Yaacob Halpern. He later received *semichah* (rabbinical ordination) from the chief rabbinate of *Eretz Yisrael*.

R' Ezra Tarab-Maslaton - head of shehitah

He became integrated back into the Damascus community with the help of R' Nissim Indibo, the Chief Rabbi of Damascus (see #316), and R' Yosef Dana. In Damascus he worked as a *shohet* together with R' Ezra Tarab Maslaton, who was the head of *shehitah*. At first R' Maslaton was hesitant in giving full trust to the newcomer, but after a short time working with him all his suspicions were allayed.

He was also heavily involved in practicing *milah*. The pressing need for this essential service to the community became even greater when R' Dana moved to Israel in 1949. To help meet the demand, R' Yitzhak taught his son R' Yosef the art of *milah* as well as three other expert *mohalim: R'* Eliyahu Indibo, R' Yaakob Attar, and R' Nissan of Kamishli. He would at times travel to Lebanon to perform a *brit milah* and help in the *kashrut* there as well. His responsibilities became even heavier when the Chief Rabbi, R' Nissim Indibo, passed away.

When life became difficult for Jews in Damascus he was able to escape with his family after paying a large bribe to the local officials. He moved to *Eretz Yisrael,* first living in Haifa and then in Holon. He was well liked by the Iraqi community and gave *shiurim* (lectures) in their synagogue.

Among his many wonderful qualities, his humility was especially noteworthy. He never wanted to be noticed or to stand out. When someone referred to him as *Hacham* or *Rav* he would say, "I'm not a *Hacham* or a rabbi, I'm a regular man, just like anybody else."

He passed away on 17 Sivan, 5756 (1996), at the age of 100.

[99] ATTAR, R' Abraham

רבי אברהם עטאר

(1896 —)

Worthy scholar and rabbi of Aram Soba and Tiberias. He was born in Aram Soba in 1896 and moved to Tiberias, where he taught Torah. In 1917 he was sent as an emissary to India to raise funds for the institutions of Tiberias, accompanied by his wife. He passed away while in India.

Attiah Lineage. The origins of the illustrious Attiah family are believed to be among the Spanish Jews who were exiled from Castille in the 15th century. The various branches and offshoots of the family included rabbis, scribes, lecturers, teachers, poets, and community leaders. The spelling of the family name went through many variations over the years. The name is believed to have originated from the Arabic word meaning a gift or present. Another view is that the name originates from that of a Spanish city.

Rabbis with this family name have been identified in Israel, Italy, Hamburg (Germany), Lisbon (Portugal), Amsterdam (the Netherlands), London (Britian), North America, Egypt, and Syria. Among the noteworthy scions of the Attiah family were R' Menahem Attiah of Teatone (18th century), R' Moshe Attiah of Egypt, R' Shem Tob Attiah, a student of the saintly R' Yosef Karo of Safed, R' Shemuel Attiah (see #116), R' Shelomo ben Shem Tob Attiah of Lisbon (see #115), and R' Mordechai Attiah, author of the book *Mar Deror* (see #108), and later, R' Ezra Attiah (see #102), *Rosh Yeshiva* of *Porat Yosef*, Jerusalem.

[100] ATTIAH, R' Abraham

רבי אברהם עטייה

(— 1831)

Worthy scholar of Damascus. He appears to have been the son of R' Yitzhak Attiah (see #120). He passed away on 25 Tishrei, 5592 (1831).

[101] ATTIAH, R' Ezra

רבי עזרא עטייה

(— 1875)

Worthy scholar, rabbi, and poet of Aram Soba. He was a son of R' Yeshayah Attiah. Some of the *pizmonim* (hymns) which he composed may be found in the book *Shir U'Shevahah*, and many are still sung today in synagogues on Friday night. He is said to have composed altogether 150 *pizmonim* corresponding to the number of chapters in the book of *Tehillim.*

In 1852 he joined other rabbis of Aram Soba in signing the approbation to the book *Kenisiyah Leshem Shamayim* by R' Menashe Sutton (see #551). (See Document Section, Document No. 31.) He passed away on 9 Elul, 5635 (1875).

[102] ATTIAH, R' Ezra

רבי עזרא עטייה

(1887 — 1970)

Distinguished *Rosh Yeshiva* of *Porat Yosef*, Jerusalem from 1925 to 1970. He was born in Aram Soba in 1887 to R' Yitzhak Attiah, a tutor for children and a grandson of an earlier R' Yitzhak Attiah (see #120). He was also a descendant of Hacham Shem Tob Attiah, a student of the *Bet Yosef*. R' Yitzhak's wife, Leah, was a daughter of R' Michael Shammah, a descendant of the author of the *Korban Isheh*, R' Eliyahu Shammah (see #499).

In 1886, R' Yitzhak Attiah and his wife Leah traveled 20 miles by donkey — a one day's trip — from Aram Soba to a little town called Tedef. People visited Tedef to pray at the tomb of Ezra HaSofer. Although Leah had two children, Eliyahu and Frieda, she had suffered many miscarriages. As they beseeched *Hashem* for a healthy child, Leah promised that if it were a son, she would name him Ezra, after Ezra HaSofer, and dedicate him to Torah. Whether it was due to *zechut avot* (merit of their fathers) or their intense prayers, Leah was able to keep her promise. She had a son on the 17th of Shevat, a year after the visit to Tedef.

R' Ezra Attiah

His Early Years

As a young boy in Aram Soba he studied under the sainted R' Yehudah (Aslan) Attiah (see #118). When Hacham Aslan realized the precious vessel that had been entrusted to him, he started him off with *Gemara* at a very young age. Together the teacher and student began learning tractate *Ketubot* with the chapter *Elu Naarot*. And so the young Ezra received a solid grounding in an intensive, analytical approach to learning.

R' Ezra Attiah giving class
Left to right: R' Yitzhak Kaduri, R' Mansour Ben-Shimon, R' Ezra Attiah, R' Moshe Ades (see #39), R' Ben-Sion Atoon, R' Natan Salem (see #472)

However, the family's poverty in Aram Soba was severe and they moved to Jerusalem in search of a better life. In 1906, when R' Ezra Attiah was 20 years old and living with his family in Jerusalem, his father, R' Yitzhak, died because he couldn't afford medical care. Young Ezra was able to continue learning only because of the dedication of his mother and the commitment of R' Ezra Harari-Raful (see #304), R' Shalom Hedaya (see #310), and R' Abraham Ades (see #37), who supported him so that the boy would not have to go to work. R' Harari-Raful was enabled to support promising young scholars through the *maaser* (charitable contributions) sent to him by wealthy Syrian businessmen to allocate at his discretion.

His hatmadah (diligence) could sometimes set off sparks in those who saw him.

When R' Ezra Attiah was a young man learning in the yeshiva, his *hatmadah* (diligence) could sometimes set off sparks in those who saw him. When R' Yitzhak Nissim was a little boy, his older brother brought him to the *Bet Midrash*. He pointed to Ezra Attiah, and told the young Yitzhak, "Watch this person learn. If you learn with his diligence, you'll become a *talmid hacham*." In fact, R' Nissim became a Chief Rabbi of Jerusalem. He credits that moment in his life seeing Hacham Ezra as the source of his excitement and motivation to become a Torah scholar.

What kind of intense concentration did that young boy see? One night, Ezra's mother Leah placed a dip for his pita bread next to him while he was learning. Rather than sink his bread into the dip, Ezra kept dipping the bread into an empty plate. When his mother returned and saw the dip untouched, she realized what had happened. Ezra had been so engrossed in the *Gemara*, he hadn't even realized that he was eating plain bread.

A Pita a Day. Food was scarce when Hacham Ezra Attiah was a boy in Jerusalem. Young Ezra was learning 18 hours a day with different rabbis and yeshiva students, but would subsist on one piece of pita bread. On a good day, they could also buy an egg which he would split with his mother. Years later, when he could afford to eat more, Hacham Ezra kept to the same one pita-per-day diet. "See how *Hashem* blesses!" he told his son, "He gives us our livelihood. I have a day's worth of food, what else do I need? Now I can sit and learn."

R' Ezra Attiah speaking before Gedolei HaDor at meeting of Vaad HaYeshivot (1947)
From left to right: R' Yechiel Michel Tucazinsky, R' Isser Zalman Meltzer, R' Yitzhak Isaac Herzog, R' Yaakob Charlap, R' Ephraim Epstein, R' Eliezer Yehudah Finkel, R' Yechezkel Sarna, R' Meir Chodosh, R' Ezra Attiah, R' Chaim Elazar Alter

In 1907, he began to study in the new yeshiva *Ohel Moed* (which later became *Porat Yosef*) under the *Rosh Yeshiva*, Hacham Raphael Shelomo Laniado (see #364), and under Hacham Yosef Yedid (see #594), one of the *Gedolei HaDor* (great luminaries of the generation) and a member of the Syrian *Bet Din* in Jerusalem.

On one occasion, Hacham Yosef Yedid (see #594) was giving a *shiur* (Torah lesson) in the yeshiva *Ohel Moed,* when he posed a difficult question to the group. R' Ezra Attiah was the only one who volunteered a response — but his answer was refuted as Hacham Yosef Yedid answered him with a question that challenged his solution. This exchange sounded familiar to R' Raphael Shelomo Laniado, the *Rosh Yeshiva* (see #364). He ran to the library to find the *Mishmarot Kehunah sefer* that asked the same question posed in the *shiur*. In this *sefer*, the answer that was given was the same as Ezra Attiah's. The *sefer* also stated that although there is a question on this answer — the very one with which Hacham Yedid rebutted — it still remained the only answer.

When Hacham Laniado showed the *sefer* to Hacham Yosef Yedid, the latter instructed him to bring him the boy. This led to Hacham Yosef learning privately with young Ezra as *havrutot* (learning partners). R' Ezra developed under the tutelage of this Torah sage for many years.

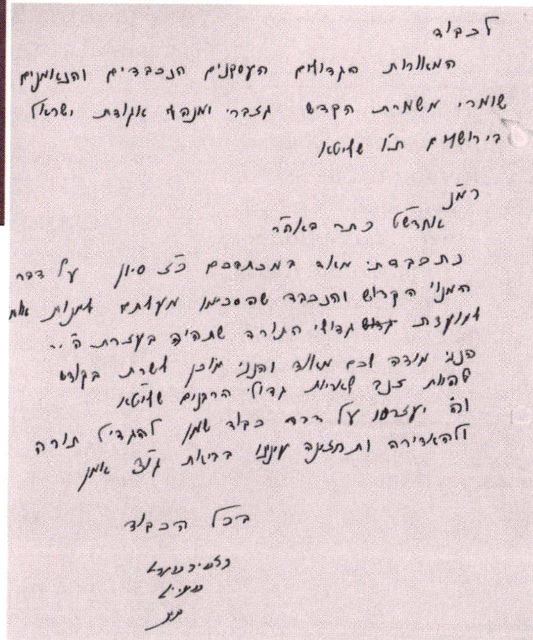

לכבוד
המאורות הגדולים העסקנים הנכבדים והנאמנים
שומרי משמרת הקודש גזברי ומנהלי אגודת ישראל
בירושלים תו"ב שליט"א

[illegible]
[illegible]

נתכבדתי מאוד במכתבכם כ"ג סיון על דבר
המנין הקדוש והנכבד שהסכימו מעלתם למנות אותי
למועצת גדולי התורה שתהיה בעזרת ה'..
הנני מודה לכם מאוד והנני מוכן לשרת בקודש
[illegible] גדולי הרבנים שליט"א
וה' יעזרנו על דבר כבוד שמו להגדיל תורה
ולהאדירה ותחזינה עינינו [illegible] אמן

[illegible]

[illegible]

R' Ezra's letter to Agudat Yisrael

His Marriage

In 1908 he married Bolisa Salem, the daughter of the Kabbalist R' Abraham Salem (see #471), and set up a household in Jerusalem. However, when World War I broke out, the Turkish army began drafting Jerusalem men and sending them to the front lines. Hacham Abraham Ades (see #37) urged R' Ezra, who was only 27 years old and a prime draft target, to leave the country. R' Ezra's brother R' Eliyahu had also fled, but when he returned briefly, he was drafted and sent off to fight. R' Ezra heeded the advice of his rabbi and fled to Cairo, Egypt, where he succeeded in building a flourishing Torah community between 1914 and 1922. Among other initiatives, he founded in Cairo the yeshiva *Keter Torah*, which was to nurture Jewish youth until 1948.

R' Ezra heeded the advice of his rabbi and fled to Cairo, Egypt, where he succeeded in building a flourishing Torah community between 1914 and 1922.

His Role as Rosh Yeshiva

Soon after Hacham Ezra's return to *Eretz Yisrael,* Hacham Abraham Ades appointed him *Rosh Yeshiva* upon Rabbi Laniado's passing. He also became a member of the Sephardic *Bet Din,* a position which he occupied for about 20 years.

When the boy saw that one can learn seriously, and still retain a sharp wit, he was no longer afraid of being serious.

"How many hours do you learn on Shabbat afternoons?" he asked his students. "One ... two ... three? In the summertime there are eight hours from the end of Musaf until Minhah time. Learn seven hours."

The Hazon Ish visited the yeshiva Porat Yosef and exchanged Torah insights with R' Ezra. When he returned to his students in Bnei Brak, he told them that R' Attiah's way of thinking was like that of a Rishon.

Many of his students went on to become great leaders in Israel and the Diaspora. Among them was R' Yehudah Sadkah (see #468) and R' Ben-Sion Abba Shaul (see #24), who remained in *Porat Yosef* all their lives and eventually became *Rosh Yeshiva*. Hacham Baruch Ben-Haim, Hacham Yosef, and Hacham Abraham Harari-Raful of the Brooklyn Syrian community were some of his prize students. Other distinguished students were Hacham Ovadiah Yosef, later to become Chief Rabbi of Israel, and R' Sion Levi of Panama.

A True Teacher

Although R' Ezra was primarily charged with teaching the top class in *Porat Yosef,* he knew every boy, tested each student personally, and made sure they were given the appropriate guidance. R' Shaul Kassin remembers being tested by this sage. His standards were high, but his words were gentle. When he saw one student wearing short sleeves, which he deemed inappropriate in that situation, rather than admonish him harshly, R' Ezra lovingly warned, "Be careful, you might get a sunburn!"

He once overheard two boys comparing some of the various *Rishonim* (rabbis from the medieval period). Who was greater, the *Rambam* or the *Ramban*? R' Ezra interpolated and answered their questions with a metaphor. "You can use a balance scale to measure very small things, but if you try to weigh bars of gold on the scale, it could break. The *Rishonim* are like boulders. You're going to weigh the *Rambam*, the *Ramban*, and the *Rashba*? The scale cannot hold such weight."

One student who began to learn with R' Ezra was a "class clown"; very bright and witty, but without the proper respect for learning. When the boy made a wisecrack one day in class, R' Ezra outwitted him with a quick response. The boy was taken aback, but answered with another quip and again R' Ezra responded with an even cleverer remark. The exchange continued until the boy ran out of things to say. After that day, he became a serious student. Before this incident, this boy thought that the life of a rabbi was boring and lacked any form of humor. When the boy saw that one can learn seriously, and still retain a sharp wit, he was no longer afraid of being serious. R' Ezra was able to see into this boy's psyche — and in one interaction, turn him onto a straighter path.

"How many hours do you learn on *Shabbat* afternoons?" he asked his students. "One ... two ... three? In the summertime there are eight hours from the end of *Musaf* until *Minhah* time. Learn seven hours." A group of boys, including R' Baruch Ben-Haim, R' Naim Ben Eliyahu, and R' David Shaharbani, approached him excitedly on Sunday. "We learned seven hours this *Shabbat*." Recognizing an opportunity to encourage the boys even more he told them, "This *Shabbat*? It should be every *Shabbat*!"

He once said, "How can you tell who is a serious and diligent student? After eating the *hamin* (hot *Shabbat* food), he is able to learn *Hoshen Mishpat* [a complex section of judicial laws]."

Important Visitors

After a visit to the *Kotel*, the *Hazon Ish* visited the yeshiva *Porat Yosef* and exchanged Torah insights with R' Ezra. When he returned to his students in Bnei Brak, he told them that R' Attiah's way of thinking was like that of a *Rishon* (great rabbi of medieval times). When a group of R' Ezra's students, including Hacham Baruch Ben-Haim, went to Bnei Brak, they sat down to learn in the *Bet Midrash* of the *Hazon Ish*. A crowd started to gather around their table, and watch them as if they were a spectacle. "Why are you watching us?" they asked the students that had surrounded them. The students replied, "We want to see the students of a *Rishon*."

When one of the Gerrer Rebbes, the *Bet Yisrael*, came to Jerusalem from Europe, R' Ezra went to greet him. When he returned, he told his students, "I had the privilege of meeting the Gerrer Rebbe." One of his students, who held his teacher in high esteem, responded, "Maybe he had the privilege of meeting you." R' Ezra saw this response as a lack of respect for the Gerrer Rebbe, and ignored the boy for a week to emphasize the lesson.

The *Moetzet Gedolai Torah,* the group of top Torah scholars of the generation, would meet regularly to discuss matters of the Jewish community at large. The group mostly spoke in Yiddish. Although he didn't understand the language, R' Ezra would attend these meetings. "I get spiritually uplifted to see all the great rabbis together," he would explain.

There was a poor man that habitually visited Hacham Ezra's home. Hacham Ezra would sit, chat with this fellow, and treat him with high regard. His students were perplexed as to why R' Ezra would spend so many of his precious minutes giving attention to this one simple man. He taught them, "There are men who need money for charity. Some people need a little bit of respect. That respect is like charity."

When R' Ezra became weak in his old age, the renowned Baba Sali, R' Yisrael Abuchatzeira from Morocco, came to visit. He told R' Ezra's son-in-law that he had a dream, where it was revealed to him that one righteous man's suffering was atoning for the entire generation: it was R' Ezra.

His Passing

On *Lag L'Omer* of his final year, students of Hacham Ezra Attiah stayed up next to him reading the *Zohar*. He was semicomatose, yet he recited it with them. In the final hours, he started listing the names of the *Mesechtot* (tractates of *Gemara*), "*Baba Kamma, Baba Metzia, Ketubot ...*" That was how he used the last of his strength before his passing on the following day, the 34th day of the *Omer*.

He passed away in Jerusalem on 19 Iyar, 5730 (1970). Approximately 2000 men and boys accompanied the body to its final resting place on *Har HaMenuchot* at the outskirts of the city.

His Legacy

He left six sons and one daughter. His youngest son, R' David, became a member of the *Bet Din* of the Rabbinate of Jerusalem and opened a *kollel* carrying his name, *Hechal Ezra*. Most of the manuscripts of his many *hiddushim* (original Torah thoughts) and responsa were kept in the great library of *Porat Yosef* in the Old City. When the Old City fell to the Arabs in 1948, all the manuscripts were tragically destroyed. Some manuscripts that remained outside the Old City were recently published through the efforts of R' David Zafrani of Lakewood, New Jersey, a grandson of R' Shelomo Zafrani (see #598). The book, titled *Aleh Ezra*, was published in the year 5759 (1999).

R' Ezra would attend these meetings. "I get spiritually uplifted to see all the great rabbis together," he would explain.

[103] ATTIAH, R' Haim

רבי חיים עטייה

(1751 — 1795)

Distinguished scholar and rabbi of Aram Soba. He was born in about 1751, the oldest son of R' Yeshayah Attiah (see #119). Haim was one of the great Aram Soba rabbis of his time and actively corresponded with other leading scholars on *halachic* (legal) issues. He was a devoted son-in-law of R' Yehudah Kassin (see #331) and edited his father-in-law's book *Mahane Yehudah* for publication.

R' Ezra taught them, "There are men who need money for charity. Some people need a little bit of respect. That respect is like charity."

He produced many responsa and *hiddushim* (original Torah thoughts), but only a small part of these have survived. Each of the following books contains one of his responsa:

- *Haim Sha'al* of the *Hida* (R' Haim Yosef David Azulai) (Vol. 2, 36-37).
- *Beirach Moshe* of R' Moshe Galante, the Chief Rabbi of Damascus (Section 2).
- *Korban Isheh* of R' Eliyahu Shamah (see #499).

A small part of his *hiddushim* appeared in the work *Artzot Haim* that was published as an appendix to the book *Ma'ayan Ganim* of R' Mordechai Abadi (see #8) (Jerusalem 5718/1958). In addition, some of his *hiddushim* were published in the book *MeHalab Ha'aretz* (Jerusalem 5726/1966).

R' Haim's oldest son, R' Bekhor Yeshayah Attiah, was also a great scholar and was highly praised in the eulogy which R' Gabriel Ashkenazi (see #93) delivered for R' Elazar Hai Dayan (see #177), who was a son-in-law of R' Haim.

R' Haim passed away at the age of 44 in the year 1795. Among the rabbis who eulogized him were R' Gabriel Ashkenazi (see #93) and R' Abraham Sutton (see #535). R' Sutton's eulogy was published in his book *Malel Le'Abraham* (no. 5).

[104] ATTIAH, R' Haim

רבי חיים עטייה

(1934 — 1962)

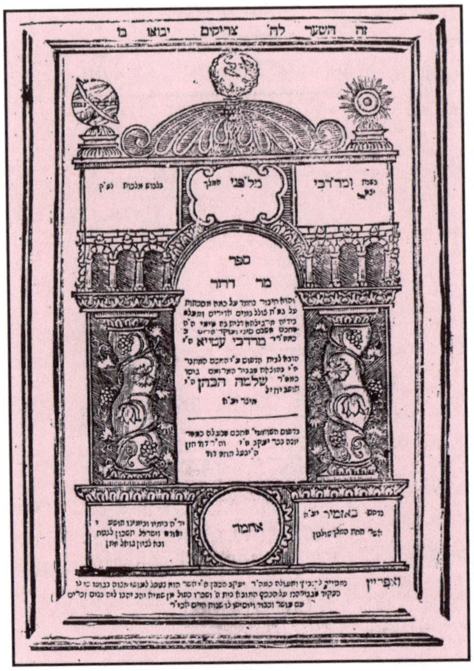

Title Page of Mar Deror

Promising young scholar of Jerusalem. He was a son of R' Mordechai Attiah (see #109) and a younger brother of R' Eliyahu Attiah, the editor of the second edition of *LiKedoshim Asher Ba'Aretz*. He was born on *Rosh Hodesh* Heshvan, 5695 (1934) in Mexico City. A few days before his birth his father had a dream in which he was visited by R' Haim Attiah (see #103) and was informed that the child would be a boy. Accordingly, when the boy was born, R' Mordechai named him Haim.

About a year later, the entire family moved to Jerusalem, where young Haim was able to study at the world-renowned *yeshivot Kol Torah* and *Ponevez*. A deeply committed student, R' Haim was rewarded with ordination to the rabbinate at a very young age. His ordination was certified by the Chief Rabbis Yitzhak Isaac Herzog and Ben-Zion Meir Hai Ouziel. Despite his youth he was drawn to mystical studies and devoted considerable effort to managing the publication of a series of books in this field.

Tragically, at the age of 28, R' Haim became seriously ill and after six months of painful suffering he passed away on 5 Tishrei, 5723 (1962).

[105] ATTIAH, R' Halfon

רבי חלפון עטייה

(— 1882)

Worthy scholar and rabbi of Aram Soba. He is believed to have been a grandson of the earlier R' Halfon Attiah (see #106). He passed away on 9 Tishrei, 5642 (1882).

[106] ATTIAH, R' Halfon

רבי חלפון עטייה

(early 19th century)

Eminent scholar and rabbi of Aram Soba. He was born in Aram Soba to R' Yeshayah Attiah (see #119) and before long became one of the great rabbis of the city. Together with his brother R' Yitzhak Attiah (see #120) he edited and published his father's book *Bigdei Yesha*. During the course of this effort he wrote a number of glosses which were incorporated into the published work.

He also wrote an introduction to the book *Zera Yitzhak*, which was written by his brother R' Yitzhak. R' Halfon also wrote many *hiddushim* (original Torah thoughts) himself, but unfortunately they were never published and most are now lost.

[107] ATTIAH, R' Menahem

רבי מנחם עטייה

(17th - 18th century)

Worthy scholar and rabbi of Aram Soba. He was the author of a work on *hilchot tereifah* (the laws of nonkosher meat) and inspirational lectures, which was printed as an appendix to the book *Ner Ma'arabi* (Jerusalem 5690/1930) of R' Yaakob ben Malkah.

[108] ATTIAH, R' Mordechai

רבי מרדכי עטייה

(17th - 18th century)

Worthy scholar and rabbi of Aram Soba. His father was R' Yitzhak Attiah. He was the author of the book *Mar Deror* (Izmir 5490/1730), containing *hiddushim* (original Torah thoughts) on the *Gemara*.

[109] ATTIAH, R' Mordechai

רבי מרדכי עטייה

(1898 — 1978)

Eminent scholar and rabbi of Jerusalem and Mexico. He was the father of R' Eliyahu Attiah, the editor of the second edition of *LiKedoshim Asher Ba'Aretz*. R' Mordechai was born in Aram Soba in 1898 to R' Yeshuah Attiah. His mother was the daughter of R' Yitzhak Labaton (see #340). When he was still a young child his family moved to Jerusalem and he was given the opportunity to study in the *yeshivot* of the Old City. However, his father passed away when he was only 6 or 7 years old and so the family suffered from extreme poverty.

At the outbreak of World War I he returned to Aram Soba to avoid being drafted into the Turkish army. He remained in Aram Soba a number of years, working with his cousin R' Yitzhak Hedaya (see #311) to organize study groups in the community.

R' Mordechai Attiah

In 1920 he married the daughter of R' Eliyahu Husney and two years later the young couple moved to Mexico City, which boasted a large population of immigrants from Aram Soba. However, in those years the city lacked most of the basic elements of Jewish community life. There was no Torah institution, no synagogue, no *mikveh*, and no kosher-slaughtering facilities. As the newly appointed rabbi of the community he saw it as his mission to awaken Jewish religious life in Mexico. Through his untiring efforts over a period of years a grand synagogue with a *mikveh* was built. This became the center of the spiritual life of the community. Besides daily morning and evening *tefillot*, the synagogue provided Torah-study classes for young and old, including a yeshiva for children. On *Shabbat* the entire day was occupied with well-attended classes and study groups, which were conducted in Arabic. In this way people who had strayed from their roots were brought back to authentic Judaism.

Throughout the years of his sojourn in Mexico he dreamed of returning to *Eretz Yisrael* and in 1936 he had the opportunity to make his dream come true, so he traveled to Jerusalem with his family of nine children. However, economic conditions in *Eretz Yisrael* proved to be very difficult and he was forced to travel abroad as a fund-raising emissary for various Torah institutions. This period of his life lasted until 1953. Life was difficult and frustrating; however, he did not allow himself to become depressed and continued to maintain a joyful attitude toward life. His main concern was that his children should be able to grow up in the holy city of Jerusalem. During the War of Independence in 1948, when Israel was fighting for its existence, R' Attiah was a leader in the spiritual battle, seeking *Hashem*'s salvation through special prayer assemblies in synagogues and public squares.

During the War of Independence in 1948, when Israel was fighting for its existence, R' Attiah was a leader in the spiritual battle, seeking Hashem's salvation through special prayer assemblies in synagogues and public squares.

In those days he printed and distributed thousands of copies of Chapter 34 of *Yeshayahu*, which begins, "Come near, you nations, to hear and listen." This chapter was publicly recited with great sincerity and emotion to invoke *Hashem*'s help against the Arab armies, which were besetting Israel from all directions.

In Elul 1948 he published a booklet called *Mahashavot Shalom*, which contains a collection of relevant thoughts from the *Gemara* and *Midrashim* to demonstrate that historical events are not random occurrences but are part of *Hashem*'s Divine plan. In subsequent years he published a number of other books and booklets in a similar vein. They are: *Artzot Haim* (Mexico City 5712/1952), *Simhat Olam* (Mexico City 5711/1951), *Mekor Haim* (Mexico City 5713/1953), *Mahasseh VeOz* (Mexico City 5715/1955), *Lech Lecha* (Jerusalem 5723/1963), *Sod HaShevuah* (Jerusalem 5725/1965), and *Bet Yosef* (Jerusalem 5729/1969).

He spoke in public and in private whenever he had the opportunity. His theme, always expressed with intense emotion, was to encourage people to travel to Eretz Yisrael and settle there.

He spoke in public and in private whenever he had the opportunity. His theme, always expressed with intense emotion, was to encourage people to travel to *Eretz Yisrael* and settle there. His enthusiasm was contagious and many people in many countries were persuaded to act on his words.

In 1967 he founded a yeshiva in Jerusalem for the study of Kabbalah. It was called *HaHaim VeHaShalom*, after one of his sons, R' Haim, who passed away at a young age, and in honor of a good friend from the United States, Mr. Isaac Shalom (see #497). Under the auspices of the yeshiva he taught Kabbalah to many young scholars and published many books on Kabbalah topics.

In his later years R' Mordechai was granted the joy of seeing many scholarly grandchildren from his sons R' Yeshuah and R' Eliyahu, and from his six daughters. He passed away on 14 Tamuz, 5738 (1978) after four months of painful illness and was buried on the Mount of Olives in Jerusalem.

In his memory, his son R' Eliyahu and his grandson R' Mordechai founded a yeshiva in 1979, called *Ateret Mordechai*. This yeshiva is oriented to the worthy goal of training young men who are relatively new to religious observance.

[110] ATTIAH, R' Moshe

רבי משה עטייה

(15th-16th century)

Worthy scholar and rabbi of Egypt. He is mentioned in the book *Tob Mitzrayim* (40:19) as having provided an approbation to a ruling of the *Maharikash* (R' Yaakob Kastro). He appears to have been a son or brother of R' Shemuel Attiah (see #116), who spent time in Egypt.

[111] ATTIAH, R' Moshe

רבי משה עטייה

Worthy scholar and rabbi of Damascus. In 1852 he joined other rabbis of Damascus in signing the approbation to the book *Kenisiyah Leshem Shamayim* by R' Menashe Sutton (see #551). (See Document Section, Document No.31.)

[112] ATTIAH, R' Moshe

רבי משה עטייה

(— 1918)

Pious scholar of Aram Soba. He was a son of R' Yaakob Attiah. His first wife gave birth to a number of daughters. It was not until he remarried that he was blessed with a son, but R' Moshe, an elderly man at that time, passed away shortly thereafter on 22 Elul, 5678 (1918).

[113] ATTIAH, R' Moshe

רבי משה עטייה

Worthy scholar and merchant of Salonika and Sufia. His name appears in one of the learned questions (no. 346) in the *Responsa of the Rashdam* (R' Shelomo D' Medini). He is described there as a resident of Salonika, a member of the community of Jews exiled from Spain.

After a bout of misfortune, he left Salonika for Sufia, apparenly to escape from his creditors. He then wrote to his wealthy brother, R' Yomtob Attiah, in France asking for assistance. His brother had pity on him and sent him some goods which he could trade and thereby support his family.

Unfortunately, R' Moshe then died in an epidemic, and his widow Plansisyanah, who was not privy to his business affairs, refused to acknowledge the debt. The matter was ultimately resolved with the aid of a mediator in Sufia. The mediator ruled that R' Yomtob's son R' Yosef should marry his cousin, the daughter of Plansisyanah, and that a specified amount should be given to the couple.

R' Moshe also had a son named R' Levi Attiah.

[114] ATTIAH, R' Nissim

רבי נסים עטייה

(— 1917)

R' Nissim Attiah was a proficient scribe, writing over 100 Torah scrolls during his lifetime.

Worthy scholar and scribe of Aram Soba. He was known as a righteous and humble man. He was a son of R' Ezra Attiah and the father of R' Yehudah Attiah (see #118). He was a proficient scribe, writing over 100 Torah scrolls during his lifetime. He passed away on 22 Tevet, 5677 (1917).

[115] ATTIAH, R' Shelomo

רבי שלמה עטייה

(15th-16th century)

Worthy scholar and rabbi of Spain. A son of R' Shem Tob Attiah, he was among those who were expelled from Spain in 1492. Initially he went to Patras, where he studied with R' Abraham Shamsolo. He then went to Salonika where he studied in the yeshiva of R' Yosef Passy. His next stop was Adrianople and the yeshiva of R' Levi ben Habib. R' Shelomo wrote a commentary on *Tehillim*, which was published in Venice in 1549. His father R' Shem Tob was also a worthy scholar. One of his responsa appears in the book *Avkat Rochel* (sec. 25) by R' Yosef Karo.

[116] ATTIAH, R' Shemuel

רבי שמואל עטייה

(15th-16th century)

Worthy scholar and rabbi of Lisbon. He was among those who were expelled from Spain in 1492. R' Shemuel appears to be the author of *Hamitpachot LeHaRambam* (Constantinople 5269/1509). One of his responsa appears in the book *Avkat Rochel* (sec. 152). Another appears in the *Responsa of the Mabit* (R' Moshe ben Yosef of Trani) (1:79).

[117] ATTIAH, R' Yehudah

רבי יהודה עטייה

(— 1905)

Eminent *darshan* (lecturer) and cantor of Aram Soba. He was a son of R' Ezra Attiah and a grandson of R' Yeshayah Attiah (see #119), the author of *Bigdei Yesha*.

He composed dozens of *pizmonim* (hymns), many of which were to be sung as special prayers on *Shabbat*. Some of his *pizmonim* were published in the book *Shir U'Shevahah*. He was also an expert in the art of *shehitah* and was a scribe of Torah scrolls, *tefillin*, and *mezuzot*. In 1852 he joined other rabbis of Aram Soba in signing the approbation to the book *Kenisiyah Leshem Shamayim* by R' Menashe Sutton (see #551). (See Document Section, Document No.31.) At the Ben-Zvi Institute (file no. 55), there is a manuscript book of his *pizmonim*, dated 5618 (1858). He passed away on 29 Shevat, 5665 (1905).

[118] ATTIAH, R' Yehudah (Aslan)

רבי יהודה (אצלן) עטייה

(1879 — 1962)

Saintly scholar and rabbi of Aram Soba and Jerusalem. He was born in Aram Soba to R' Nissim Attiah (see #114), and to Mazal of the Hedaya family.

He became renowned for his important work *Minhat Yehudah*. Volume I, which was published in Aram Soba in 1924, contains 87 chapters of *hiddushim* (original Torah thoughts) on all aspects of Torah: *Pshat, Remez, Drash, and Sod.* (Note that 87 is numerically equal to the word פז, which means pure gold.) Volume II, which was published in Jerusalem in 1929, contains inspirational lectures on the Torah, following the sequence of the *parashot*. He received approbations from many of the great scholars and rabbis of the day.

Le Grand Rabbin de l'Etat d'Alep
CH. BOHBOUTH
ספר
מנחת יהודה
ח"א
נסים עטיה
ס"ט
נדפס בארם צובה יע"א
שנת התרפ"ד לפ"ק.
ישעיה דיין

Title Page of Minhat Yehudah

His father had been a highly successful scribe. He tried to persuade his son to adopt this honorable and holy profession, but young Yehudah had an intense longing to immerse himself in the study of Torah. Therefore, as long as his father was alive, he dutifully obeyed his wishes by day, while devoting his nights to study. Then, when his father passed away, he "turned his days into nights" and completely dedicated himself to Torah.

In all seasons and in all weathers, even with a broken foot, he faithfully went to the *Bet Midrash* for *Tikkun Hatzot* (midnight service to mourn the destruction of the Temple).

He periodically received money from relatives in New York, from the Hedaya family. Even though the money was intended for him, he gave most of it away to poor people. Not only that, but when a particularly urgent need arose he went out himself to raise additional funds. To avoid any suspicion, he always took another person along on these expeditions to be able to testify

R' Yehudah (Aslan) Attiah

that all the proceeds went to the worthy cause in question. However, this precaution was really unnecessary because of his sterling reputation. In one instance, a storekeeper named Mr. Gida simply opened his cash register, saying, "Take what you need."

When he prepared to publish Volume I of his book, *Minhat Yehudah*, he was promised a sum of money by a wealthy individual. As it happened, the money arrived after the book went to press and it was no longer needed so he returned it. The donor then sent it back to him with a note saying that he could do with it as he liked, including covering his personal expenses. However, R' Attiah gave the money to the poor, since he did not wish to enrich himself from a *mitzvah*.

During the Second World War Aram Soba was in the middle of a war zone and many of its residents fled the city to avoid the bombing. However, Hacham Aslan refused to leave or change his regular routine.

During the Second World War Syria was controlled by Vichy France, which was allied with Germany. The British army, with its Jewish Legion, fought the French and invaded Syria. Aram Soba was in the middle of a war zone and many of its residents fled the city to avoid the bombing. However, Hacham Aslan refused to leave or change his regular routine. In fact, he was so highly respected by the local Arabs that many camped out next to his home and even stayed near him as he went to the *Bet Midrash*. They reasoned that as long as they were in the vicinity of this saintly man they would be safe.

He was known as a healer of the sick through his prayers and amulets.

The Attiah family lived in the old Jewish neighborhood of Aram Soba, but since most of the Jews had emigrated, their houses were occupied by Arabs. In those years Hacham Aslan said *Tikkun Hatzot* immediately upon waking and then went to the *Bet Midrash Señor Moshe Picciotto* for his regular learning. The dark of night was often dangerous for a lone pedestrian because of rowdy Arab youths who thought nothing of attacking a defenseless Jew. However, an Arab policeman became aware of his routine and took it upon himself to accompany him and see to it that he came to no harm. Upon safely arriving at the *Bet Midrash*, Hacham Aslan would give him a cigarette and the policeman would go on his way.

In 1946 he moved to Jerusalem, traveling via Beirut. While in Beirut he followed his regular practice of getting up at night for *Tikkun Hatzot*. His fervent prayers to *Hashem* woke up a neighbor, who was very unhappy about losing sleep and complained to the Hacham in a nasty way. The next day the neighbor became seriously ill and after fruitlessly seeking medical help, he remembered the incident of the *Tikkun Hatzot*. He immediately went to the Hacham to apologize and seek his blessing.

In Jerusalem the Hacham settled in the *Nahalat Ahim* neighborhood and renewed his dedication to intense Torah study. He soon became recognized as one of the eminent scholars of the city. Even in his declining years, he was among the first arrivals in the *Bet Midrash* and continued to exhibit the outstanding piety which characterized his entire life. His place of *tefillah* in Jerusalem was the Djermoklim synagogue. Each night he would jump up from his sleep at the call of Yaakob the *shamosh* (caretaker) and quickly go to *Tikkun Hatzot*. After the service he would study Kabbalah until shortly before the break of day, when he would focus on the study of *mussar* (character development).

He was known as a healer of the sick through his prayers and amulets. People in need came to him from the ends of the earth, seeking his blessings. It was not unusual for a person with a serious illness to wake him at night with a plea for his help. He would then accompany the individual to the hospital and give him his blessing. Before long, the person would be completely healed.

He passed away on 4 Nissan, 5722 (1962) after a bout of painful illness. While his mother was still alive in Aram Soba he purchased a cemetery plot in Jerusalem in her name. However, she died in Aram Soba and so it was necessary to bury her there. As he approached his own end he arranged to be buried in that plot so that it could be reckoned as though she herself was buried there.

R' Yehudah Ades, founder of *Kol Yaakob* in Jerusalem, recalled one time when his father, R' Yaakob Ades (see #41), came home in a state of agitation. When asked what was wrong R' Yaakob explained that he had just come from visiting R' Yehudah (Aslan) Attiah, who was lying on his bed, deathly ill. R' Attiah's flesh appeared to be falling away from his body and yet he was lying there, singing the *zemirot* (hymns) of *Shabbat*. He added, "If only I had the *zechut* (merit) of being buried next to him." (In the end he was buried there. See also #41.)

His youngest son, R' Abraham, became a notable scholar of the Kabbalist yeshiva *Nehar Shalom* in Jerusalem. He took it upon himself to publish Volume II of his father's book *Minhat Yehudah* and wrote a moving introduction. The financing for this initiative was arranged with the help of R' Yaakob Attiah, rabbi of the Aram Soba congregation of Bat Yam. The funds were provided through the generosity of the renowned philanthropist Mr. Edmond Safra (see #470), in memory of his parents Yaakob and Esther.

[119] ATTIAH, R' Yeshayah

רבי ישעיה עטייה

(1732 — 1792)

Distinguished scholar and author of Aram Soba. He was born in 1732 to R' Haim Attiah. Even as a youth he was known as one of the great scholars of his day. When he was 14, he was called upon to deliver a learned talk on the subject of *brit milah* (circumcision) at the occasion of the birth of the first son of R' Yehudah Kassin (see #331). At the age of 16 he delivered a eulogy on the passing of his grandfather, R' Yeshayah Attiah. Both are recorded in his book *Bigdei Yesha* (Livorno 5587/1827). In 1756, when he was 24, on his way back from a visit to *Eretz Yisrael*, he delivered a lecture to the main congregation of Damascus (*Bigdei Yesha*, p. 121).

In 1775 he joined R' Yitzhak Shabbetai Antebi (see #80) in signing the approbation to the books *HaMa'alot LeShelomo* and *Bet Dino shel Shelomo* by R' Raphael Shelomo Laniado (see #363).

His book *Bigdei Yesha* consists of responsa and lectures based on *halachah*. It was published through the efforts of his sons R' Yitzhak (see #120) and R' Halfon Attiah (see #106). He was blessed with five sons altogether. The others were R' Haim (see #103), R' Shimon, and R' David. He passed away in 1792. Some of his other *hiddushim* (original Torah thoughts) were included in the anthology *Otzarot Hachmei Aram Soba al HaRambam* (Jerusalem 5749/1989) that was published by the Aram Soba Foundation.

Title Page of Bigdei Yesha

R' Yeshayah was described as one of the greatest scholars of his generation by R' Haim Mordechai Labaton (see #336) in his book *Nochah HaShulhan*. In that book, R' Labaton cites a manuscript which gives R' Attiah's views on the topic of the laws of inheritance for daughters.

[120] ATTIAH, R' Yitzhak

רבי יצחק עטייה

(1755 —)

Distinguished scholar and author of Aram Soba. He was born in Aram Soba in about 1755, the third son of R' Yeshayah Attiah (see #119). He was recognized as one of the great Torah scholars of his day, writing many books of *hiddushim* (original Torah thoughts) , all of which were published during his lifetime in Livorno, Italy. R' Yitzhak traveled to Livorno and other distant places to promote the publishing effort, staying away from home over a period of many years. He recounts the details of his travels in the introduction to one of his books, *Vayikra Yitzhak*.

ספר
זרע יצחק
יקרא דחיי
פלפלת כל שהוא
כפרפראות
לחכמה
יצחק עטייה
ארם צובה
נדפס
פה ליוורנו יע"א
שמחה רבא
בדפוס המשובח של השותפים
יעקב נונים ואיס
רפאל מילדולה
Con Approvazione

Title Page of Zera Yitzhak

In the introduction to his book, *Zera Yitzhak*, R' Yitzhak describes some of the many afflictions and problems which he suffered during his lifetime. His first wife, Leah, the daughter of R' Menahem ben Shabbetai, bore him three daughters, two of whom died as small children. His wife died as she was giving birth to their third daughter, who also died after a short time. He then married his second wife Sabatya, the daughter of R' Abraham Sutton (see #535), but she soon became deathly ill. After many prayers and after exerting every effort, including a change of name and a change of place (to promote a change of *mazal*), she recovered. Her new name was Simhah. However, in 1791 Aram Soba experienced a terrible epidemic, in which close to 300 children died. Tragically, R' Yitzhak's wife also succumbed to the epidemic. He, himself, was deathly ill for a period of six months, a period which he remembered as having a "body without a soul." However, *Hashem* had mercy on him and he recovered.

In the year 1822 Aram Soba was struck by a major earthquake in which many of the Jewish community lost their lives, including his young son Moshe. He mentioned this loss during the course of a eulogy which he delivered for Señor Ezra di Picciotto, who passed away in the same earthquake. (The eulogy was published in the book *Zera Yitzhak*.)

Despite all his tribulations, he was blessed with four scholarly sons and a son-in-law. He speaks of his sons in the introduction to his book *Vayikra Yitzhak*. Their names were R' Abraham (see #100), R' David, R' Yaakob, and R' Eliyahu. R' Eliyahu accompanied him in some of his travels. He also had a fine son-in-law, R' Abraham Mizrahi, whom he mentioned during the course of the eulogy cited above.

R' Yitzhak passed away while in Livorno. The date is not known, nor is the location of his resting place. However, he is well remembered by the holy books which he worked so hard to write and publish. A brief review is provided below.

- *Zera Yitzhak* (Livorno 5553/1793 and 5554/1794). Analytical lectures on topics in *Bereshit* and *Shemot* (two volumes). Volume I also contains two additional books (named *Yakra De-Hayeh* and *Palpelet Kol Shehu*) with various eulogies and *hiddushim*. Both volumes were reissued in Jerusalem in 1977, together with an introduction giving a biography of the author, by R' Eliyahu Attiah, the editor of the second edition of *LiKedoshim Asher Ba'Aretz*. Approbations were given by the *Bet Din* of Livorno, R' Yisrael Sasson of Aram Soba (see #483), and R' Yaakob Noniss Weiss of Livorno. In addition, two brothers of the author, R' Haim and R' Halfon, provided their approbations.
- *Zechut Avot* (Livorno 5581/1821). Commentary on *Pirkei Avot*.
- *Rov Dagan* (Livorno 5578/1818). *Hiddushim* on the *Gemara*, supplemented with a book of responsa and *hiddushim* on *halachah*, called *Ot LeTovah*.
- *Vayikra Yitzhak* and *Doresh Tov* (Livorno 5586/1826). The first part, *Vayikra Yitzhak*, contains inspirational lectures on *Vayikra*, *Bamidbar*, and *Debarim*, arranged as a continuation to *Zera Yitzhak*. Also included are commentaries on *Shir HaShirim*, *Ruth*, *Eichah*, and *Kohelet*, as well as a lecture for *Shavuot*. The second part, *Doresh Tov*, contains additional lectures on *Bereshit*, *Shemot*, and *Vayikra*. Another appendix, *Eikev Anavah*, treats the topic of humility.
- *Tanna VeSha'yer* and *Penei HaMayim* (Livorno 5591/1831). *Hiddushim* on *Rashi* and *HaRe'em* (R' Eliyahu Miz-

rahi), responsa, inspirational lectures, and eulogies. The book received the approbation of the *Hida* (R' Haim Yosef David Azulai) and also contains a learned question which R' Yitzhak posed to the *Hida* in 1790. The response of the *Hida* may be found in the book *Yosef Ometz* (104) and in the book *Haim Sha'al* (Vol. 2, 14).

- *Mishrat Moshe* (Livorno 5583/1823). Commentary on the *Rambam*.
- *Eishet Hayil* (Livorno 5581/1821). Commentary on the chapter in *Mishlei* (31:10-31) praising woman's virtues.

Some of his other *hiddushim* were included in the anthology *Otzarot Hachmei Aram Soba al HaRambam* (Jerusalem 5749/1989) that was published by the Aram Soba Foundation.

In the book *Sedei Hemed* by R' Haim Hizkiah Medini (Appendix *Klalim, Lahash*, Sec. 117), there is a question as to whether it is permissible for a Hacham to offer an incantation (mystical prayer) to heal a non-Jew who requests his help. To answer this question the author quotes from the work *Ot LeTovah* (Sec. 45) of R' Yitzhak Attiah (see #120). In that work, R' Yitzhak recounts an incident in which a critically ill non-Jewish child was brought before the saintly Hacham Yehudah Kassin (see #331). The Hacham pronounced an incantion and the child recovered, resulting in a *Kiddush Hashem* (sanctification of the Name of *Hashem*).

[121] **ATTIAH, R' Yosef**

רבי יוסף חלפון עטייה

(— 1891)

Worthy scholar and rabbi of Damascus. He is believed to have been a son of R' Halfon Attiah of Aram Soba (see #105). He passed away on 15 Adar, 5651 (1891).

[122] **ATZBAN, R' Mordechai**

רבי מרדכי אצבאן

(— 1750)

Eminent scholar and rabbi of Livorno (Leghorn) and Aram Soba. His father, R' Yitzhak Atzban, and grandfather, R' Mordechai Atzban, were both notable scholars. He was born in Meknes, Morocco, and immigrated to Livorno in 1697, where he served as a rabbi. Following a *halachic* (legal) dispute in Livorno with R' Abraham Rodriguez, author of the book *Orah LaSadik* (Livorno 5540/1780), he left to go to *Eretz Yisrael*. However, he stopped off in Aram Soba and took up residence there, joining the community of scholars and rabbis of the city. He passed away in the year 5510 (1750).

In the introduction to his work, *Zovei'ah Todah* (Constantinople 5493/1733), he emphasizes the importance of focusing one's thoughts when performing *mitzvot*. He authored the *Viduy HaGadol* (Long Confession) said on *Yom Kippur* by the Syrian community, based on the words of the *Sefer Haredim*. It was included in his book, which is the earliest-known source of the *Viduy*. This section was later reprinted by R' Habib David Haim Sutton (see #544).

It was reprinted again by R' Yeshayah Dayan (see #203) in Aram Soba with the *piyut* (hymn) for *Yom Kippur*, lamenting the death of Aharon HaKohen's two sons. It was again reprinted by R' Yitzhak Moshe Dayan (see #207) in 1895, by R' Nissim Dayan (see #195) in 1925, and finally by R' Ephraim Dweck (see #226) in 1928 at the printing press of Ezra Bijou with an additional stanza of the *piyut* written by R' Ezra Hamway (see #272).

Among his other works is *Yisa Berachah* on the *Orah Haim*. He disputed matters of *halachah* with R' Abraham Rodriguez.

R' Mordechai was also known for his expertise in the mystical aspects of the Torah and is highly praised in that regard by R' Haim Abulafia in *Hanan Elokim*. That book includes a *halachic* ruling against eating

ספר
זובח תודה
בקושטאנדינא

Title Page of Zovei'ah Todah

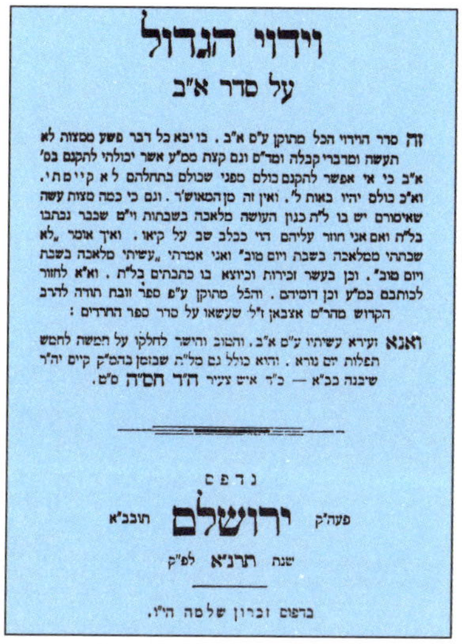
וידוי הגדול
על סדר א"ב
ירושלם

Title Page of Viduy HaGadol Published by R' Habib David Haim Sutton

Viduy HaGadol with addition by R' Hamway

grape leaves because of the incidence of worm infestation. (See Document Section, Document No. 13.) R' Mordechai was a signatory, together with other scholars of Aram Soba.

The *Hida* (R' Haim Yosef David Azulai) speaks highly of R' Atzban in his books *Shem HaGedolim* and *Medaber Kademot*.

Rabbi Abraham Ben-Asher was a brilliant scholar and rabbi of Aram Soba. He was a student of R' Yosef Karo.

[123] BAR NATAN, R' Moshe
רבי משה בר נתן

Worthy scholar of Aram Soba. R' Ovadiah HaLevi mentions him in his book *Hazon Ovadiah* (*Parashat Vayera*, 19) in the following terms: "In my younger years I heard an explanation of this *Tosafot* from the consummate scholar, the pious and holy man, R' Moshe Bar Natan ...".

[124] BATLAN, R' Moshe
רבי משה בטלן

Worthy scholar of Aram Soba. His name appears in the list of Aram Soba scholars receiving a weekly stipend from the special fund that had been set up for the support of worthy individuals who dedicate their lives to Torah study. His position within the list indicates that he was among the more notable scholars of the city. (For more information on the fund, see R' Yaakob Gindi-Daknish, #267.)

[125] BELILIOS, R' Abraham
רבי אברהם בליליוס

Well-to-do scholar and rabbi of Aram Soba. He is described as the venerable rabbi, Señor Abraham Belilios, in the introduction to the book *Hazon Ovadiah* by R' Ovadiah HaLevi.

[126] BELILIOS, R' Emanuel
רבי עמנואל בליליוס

Well-to-do scholar and rabbi of Aram Soba. He is described as our revered teacher and rabbi, Señor Emanuel Belilios, in the introduction to the book *Hazon Ovadiah* by R' Ovadiah HaLevi. His scholarly sons, Shelomo, Yaakob, and Yosef, are also mentioned there in very positive terms.

[127] BEN-ASHER, R' Abraham
רבי אברהם בן־אשר

(16th century)

Brilliant scholar and rabbi of Aram Soba. He was a student of R' Yosef Karo, the author of the *Shulhan Aruch,* and he was a colleague of R' Moshe Alshich, R' Yitzhak Mishan, and R' Haim ben R' Yitzhak HaChaver. R' Abraham wrote a commentary on the Midrash, called *Ohr HaSechel*. Elements of this commentary have been published under the name ABe'A (Abraham Ben-Asher) in some printings of *Bereshit*, positioned opposite the commentary of *Rashi*.

R' Abraham's name appears as an entry in *Shem HaGedolim* (1:24) by the *Hida* (R' Haim Yosef David Azulai). The *Hida* mentions that one of R' Abraham's responsa may be found in R' Yosef Karo's book *Avkat Rochel* (72), where it is made clear that he was a rabbi in Aram Soba. Approbations for this contribution are given by his colleagues, in addition to that of, R' Yosef Karo. One of his colleagues, R' Moshe Alshich, recalls fondly the days of his youth when he and R' Abraham studied together under the master, R' Yosef Karo.

R' Abraham speaks of Aram Soba when he describes the circumstances in which he made the *halachic* ruling referred to above: "At the time I was passing through the edge of Aram Soba, with one foot in the ford of the stream and the other on dry land. I was clearly in great discomfort and it was then that I was asked to make a ruling ...".

[128] BERACHAH (BRAHA), R' Ezra
רבי עזרא ברכה

Worthy scholar and dedicated teacher of young children. He was a grandson of R' Yitzhak Berachah (see #129). R' Moshe Dweck (see #256), author of the book *Kanah HaMidah* on *Tehillim*, included an explanation which he had heard from R' Ezra on a verse in *Tehillim*.

[129] BERACHAH (BRAHA), R' Yitzhak

רבי יצחק ברכה

(— 1772)

Distinguished scholar of Aram Soba. He was the son of R' Yaakob Berachah and became known for his important book *Beirach Yitzhak* (Venice 5523/1763). This work consists of homiletical interpretations of the Torah, based on a *halachic* (legal) approach. He passed away in in Aram Soba on 16 Adar 2 5532 (1772).

A dedicated scholar, he was supported in his studies by R' Eliyahu Silvera (see # 524). His scholarly abilities were highly praised by the rabbis of Venice in the introduction to his book *Beirach Yitzhak*. Four rabbis of Aram Soba also wrote a preface to the book in which they spoke of his greatness in Torah: R' Yehudah Kassin (see #331), R' Raphael Shelomo Laniado (see #363), R' Yisrael Dilubin (see #215), and R' Yeshayah Dabbah (see #171).

Many of his responsa were published in the book *Bet Dino shel Shelomo* (*Orah Haim*, 5, 17; *Hoshen Mishpat,* 2, 23) of R' Raphael Shelomo Laniado (see #363). On one of the responsa (*Orah Haim*, Sec. 17), his signature is accompanied by those of R' Moshe Harari (see #288) and R' Gabriel Cohen (see #160).

Upon his death, R' Abraham Sutton (see #535), who was one of his students, delivered a eulogy that was subsequently published in R' Abraham's book *Malel Le'Abraham* (under *Perashat Lech Lecha*). He was also eulogized by R' Yeshayah Attiah (see #119), as recorded in his book, *Bigdei Yesha* (p. 106b).

Title Page of Beirach Yitzhak

[130] BETESH, R' Chiya

רבי חייא בטיש

(18th century)

Senior rabbi in the town of Kilis in Turkey, north of Aram Soba. He was the son-in-law of R' Yitzhak Harari (see #295), who speaks about him in his book *Zechor LeYitzhak* (p. 117). R' Harari describes an occasion in which R' Betesh gave a ruling on an issue that arose in the Kilis synagogue.

R' Yitzhak Berachah's scholarly abilities were highly praised by the rabbis of Venice.

A Visit to Kilis. In 1764, R' Yitzhak Harari visited the town of Kilis in Turkey, north of Aram Soba, where his son-in-law, R' Chiya Betesh, was the senior rabbi. He subsequently gave the following account of the visit in his book *Zechor LeYitzhak* (p. 117):

"I was witness to an event in which the proper course of action was unclear and I decided to investigate what the *halachah* would be in that case. It happened when I was passing through the town of Kilis in the year 5524 (1764).

"While reading the Torah on *Shabbat*, an error was found in the Torah scroll, which was serious enough to necessitate taking another Torah in its place. This happened during the third portion of the reading (*Shelishi*). Unfortunately, there was no other Torah available, so the portion was read through to its end. Because of the error, the person who had been called up did not say the customary blessing. Instead, he waited until the *haftarah* was read and said the blessings then.

"I objected, arguing that this was wrong. However, there was present a scholar who was the senior rabbi of the town. He was my respected son-in-law, the consummate scholar, our revered teacher and rabbi, Chiya Betesh HaLevi, may his light shine brightly. He answered my objection, saying that since the Torah had been read in public, the number [of portions read] was not critical. I did not have my reference books with me at the time to verify this ...".

The author then concludes: "Anyone who reads a Torah, even when it is invalid, is permitted to say the *haftarah* with its blessings, in accordance with the ruling of the rabbi, my respected son-in-law, may his light shine brightly."

He was instrumental in founding a number of charitable organizations, including a Talmud Torah.

[131] BETESH, Señor Menashe Abraham
סי' מנשה אברהם בטיש

Wealthy British businessman and philanthropist. In his home city of Manchester, England, he was instrumental in founding a number of charitable organizations, including a Talmud Torah. Subsequently he donated the funds to build the magnificent *Ohel Moed* synagogue in Tel Aviv. In addition, he built a synagogue in the *Nahalat Sion* section of Jerusalem, which is named after him — the Betesh Synagogue. In the orphanage home on the Mount of Olives, he placed a beautiful entranceway, the entrance to "the Cave of the Righteous."

He passed away in Manchester and was brought to Jerusalem for burial on the Mount of Olives. He was eulogized by many of the eminent rabbis of Jerusalem, among whom was the *Av Bet Din* (Chief Judge), R' Yosef Yedid (see #594). R' Yosef included appropriate words of appreciation and praise in his book *She'erit Yosef* (Lectures, 12).

R' Haim Beyda

[132] BEYDA, R' Haim
רבי חיים ביצ'ה הכהן

(1830 — 1930)

Worthy scholar and rabbi of Jerusalem. He immigrated from Aram Soba to Jerusalem where he became the rabbi of the congregation of people from Aram Soba, located near the Damascus Gate. He passed away at the age of 100 on 21 Shevat, 5690 (1930).

[133] BIJOU, R' Shalom
רבי שלום ביג'ו

Worthy scholar of Aram Soba. His name appears in the same list of Aram Soba scholars as that of R' Moshe Batlan (see #124).

[134] BOHBOUT, R' Shabbetai
רבי שבתאי בוחבוט

(1870 — 1948)

Chief Rabbi of Beirut after serving in key rabbinical positions in Jaffa and Aram Soba. He was born in Jaffa on 23 Shevat, 5630 (1870) to R' Shelomo Bohbout. When he was 19 years old, the entire family moved to Jerusalem. There, he married the daughter of R' Azaryah di Biton, a man of substance in the city. One of the conditions that the families agreed to was that he would continue his Torah studies after the wedding, so R' Shabbetai attended the yeshiva of his father-in-law for 15 years. During this time he studied Gemara and the writings of the rabbinic authorities in company with the brilliant scholar R' Yaakob Meir. During this time he also acquired a knowledge of the Arabic, Turkic, and Spanish languages.

In 1906 he returned to the city of his birth and accepted a position as *dayan* (judge). However, when World War I broke out, he was forced to leave the country to avoid the Turkish military draft. He settled in Kilis, a town in Turkey, north of Aram Soba. The people of Kilis took him as their rabbi and he remained in that position until 1921, when he was invited to a rabbinical position in Aram Soba. In 1924 he was invited to serve as Chief Rabbi of Beirut.

After a full and long life, R' Shabbetai passed away in Beirut on 17 Iyar, 5708 (1948). He was reburied in Jerusalem on 27 Adar II, 5711 (1951).

One of his lifelong objectives was to promote peace and unity among the various factions within the Jewish people. His many lectures are imbued with the importance of peace and the love of one's fellow Jews.

R' Shabbetai Bohbout

One of his *hala*chic (legal) rulings on the laws of a deserted wife (*agunah*) was published in the book *Am Mordechai* by R' Mordechai Esran. The author R' Mordechai endorsed the ruling together with R' Yosef Orouats.

In the book *Simhat Yomtob* (Part 5, *Bigdei Yomtob*), there is a eulogy on the death of R' Yomtob Yedid, which was delivered by R' Shabbetai in the Great Synagogue of Aram Soba. The words of R' Shabbetai are exceptional in style and content, and are seasoned with erudite remarks touching upon all aspects of Torah learning (*Pshat, Remez, Drash,* and *Sod*).

[135] BOKA'I (KANE), R' Abraham

רבי אברהם בוקאעי

(— 1914)

Worthy scholar and rabbi of Damascus. He was a brother of R' Yosef Boka'i (see #141). He passed away on 20 Adar, 5674 (1914).

[136] BOKA'I (KANE), R' Bekhor Haim

רבי בכור חיים בוקאעי

(— 1842)

Worthy scholar and rabbi of Damascus. He passed away on 23 Av, 5602 (1842).

[137] BOKA'I (KANE), R' Mordechai

רבי מרדכי בוקאעי

(— 1903)

Worthy scholar and rabbi of Damascus. He passed away in 1903.

[138] BOKA'I (KANE), R' Nissim

רבי נסים בוקאעי

(19th century)

Worthy scholar and rabbi of Damascus. In 1868 he joined other rabbis of Damascus in signing the approbation to the book *Kenisiyah Leshem Shamayim* by R' Menashe Sutton (see #551). (See Document Section, Document No. 31.)

[139] BOKA'I (KANE), R' Yaakob

רבי יעקב בוקאעי

(— 1899)

Rabbi and teacher of Beirut. In 1852 he joined other rabbis of Aram Soba in signing the approbation to the book *Kenisiyah Leshem Shamayim* by R' Menashe Sutton (see #551). He passed away on 9 Tevet, 5660 (1899).

[140] BOKA'I (KANE), R' Yitzhak

רבי יצחק בוקאעי

(— 1871)

Worthy scholar and rabbi of Damascus. He passed away on 28 Iyar, 5631 (1871).

[141] BOKA'I (KANE), R' Yosef

רבי יוסף בוקאעי

(— 1942)

Worthy scholar and *darshan* (lecturer) of Aram Soba. A brother of R' Abraham Boka'i (see #135), he was born in Damascus and settled in Aram Soba. His lectures were delivered in the Great Synagogue of Aram Soba and attracted large crowds. Among his other duties was that of administering the charity fund for the poor. He passed away in 1942.

[142] CHABOT, R' Abraham

רבי אברהם שבות הלוי

(— 1884)

Worthy scholar and *shohet* (ritual slaughterer) of Aram Soba. He was the father-in-law of R' Yeshayah Dayan (see #203), who mentions him with great respect in his book *Zeh Ketav Yadi*. He passed away on 25 Kislev, 5644 (1884).

[143] CHABOT, R' Aharon

רבי אהרן שבות הלוי

(1797 — 1873)

Worthy scholar and rabbi of Aram Soba and Tiberias. He was born about 1797 in Aram Soba and in 1813 he settled in Tiberias, where he stayed the rest of his life. R' Chabot was the grandfather of R' Habib David Haim Sutton (see #544) and the father-in-law of R' Haim Sutton, who passed away at a young age childless. He passed away in Tiberias on 13 Adar, 5633 (1873).

[144] CHABOT, R' Moshe Menahem

רבי משה מנחם שבות הלוי

(18th century)

Worthy scholar and *dayan* (judge) of Aram Soba. He sat on the Aram Soba *Bet Din* together with R' Ezra Yeshuah Cohen and Yitzhak Dayan. In 1822 he joined other rabbis of Aram Soba in signing the approbation for *Yoshev Ohalim* of R' Abraham Antebi (see #63). In the Ben-Zvi Institute there are two original documents containing his signature, one from the year 1802 in which he is joined by R' Ezra Yeshuah Cohen (see #159) and Yitzhak Dayan (see #205), and the other from the year 1814 in which he is joined by R' Haim Harari (see #281).

[145] **CHASKY, R' Eliyahu David**

רבי אליהו דוד כאסכי

(1861 — 1921)

Worthy scholar and *darshan* (lecturer) of Aram Soba. He was the son of R' Shalom Chasky (see #149). He moved to Jerusalem and from there to Egypt, where he passed away at the age of 60 on 4 Av, 5681 (1921). At the Ben-Zvi Institute there is a manuscript Bill of Sale (file no. 302) from Eliyahu Chasky to R' Yeshayah Dayan (see #203), dated Nissan 5654 (1894).

R' Eliyahu David Chasky

He married one of the many daughters of R' Shelomo Harari-Raful, a man who was not blessed with sons. The latter's friends in Aram Soba used to ask him in jest whether he was confident that all of his daughters would marry Torah scholars. As it happens, he did achieve this worthy goal. Among his other sons-in-law were R' Meir Laniado (see #358), R' Moshe Harari (see #291), R' Abraham Salem (see #471), and R' Mordechai Harari-Raful.

[146] **CHASKY, R' Ezra**

רבי עזרא כאסכי

(— 1868)

Worthy scholar and rabbi of Aram Soba. He was the son of R' Halfon Chasky (see #147) and the brother of R' Shalom Chasky (see #149). In 1852 he joined other rabbis of Aram Soba in signing the approbation to the book *Kenisiyah Leshem Shamayim* by R' Menashe Sutton (see #551). (See Document Section, Document No. 31). In the Ben-Zvi Institute there are two original documents containing his signature: one from the year 1840 in which he is joined by R' Haim Mordechai Labaton (see #336) and R' David Ashkenazi (see #91), and the other from the year 1849 in which he is joined by R' Moshe Cohen (see #164). He passed away on 17 Heshvan, 5629 (1868). (See Document Section, Document No. 31.)

[147] **CHASKY, R' Halfon**

רבי חלפון כאסכי

(19th century)

Eminent scholar and rabbi of Aram Soba. He was the father of R' Shalom and R' Ezra Chasky (see #146 and #149). After a near-death experience in Aram Soba, he decided to move to *Eretz Yisrael*. He settled in Tiberias and that is where he passed away. When word of his death arrived in Aram Soba, he was eulogized by the rabbis of the city, among whom was R' Abraham Sutton (see #535), as recorded in his book *Malel Le'Abraham* (lecture no. 9).

R' Shelomo Harari-Raful's friends in Aram Soba used to ask him in jest whether he was confident that all of his daughters would marry Torah scholars. As it happens, he did achieve this worthy goal.

A Timely Sneeze. R' Abraham Hamway (see #269) relates the following story in his book *Bet El* (p. 92): "R' Halfon Chasky was a great rabbi in Aram Soba, the city of his birth. It happened that he became deathly ill and was visited by his friends. They were assembled to pay their last respects, as was the custom among Torah scholars. Suddenly he sneezed and sat up in bed, and said to his son R' Shalom Chasky, 'Shalom, Shalom, don't be afraid! I went up to the Heavenly Yeshiva and I said I will not give up my soul except in *Eretz Yisrael*.' And so he revived from his illness and immediately went to Damascus, and from there to Tiberias, where he found his honorable resting place."

At the Ben-Zvi Institute there is a hand-written document dated 8 Adar 2 (1807) containing the signature of R' Halfon Bekhor Abraham Chasky (third signer), together with that of R' Shelomo Sutton (first signer), and R' David Kassin (see #321) (second signer) [file no. 302].

[148] CHASKY, R' Moshe

רבי משה כאסכי

(— 1927)

Worthy scholar and expert *shohet* (ritual slaughterer) of Aram Soba. He worked as a *shohet* for most of his life, and then settled in *Eretz Yisrael* where he passed away on 26 Tishrei, 5688 (1927)

[149] CHASKY, R' Shalom

רבי שלום כאסכי

(— 1872)

Distinguished Chief Rabbi of Ein Tab and head of its yeshiva over a period of many years. He was born in Aram Soba and returned there to continue with other rabbinical duties after completing his service in Ein Tab, a small town near Aram Soba. R' Shalom was the main teacher of R' Nissim Harari-Raful (see #305).

He was a son of R' Halfon Chasky (see #147) and a brother of R' Ezra Chasky (see #146). His son-in-law was R' Hillel David Sutton (see #546).

He was known as a saintly person who observed all the restrictions described in the book *Reishit Hochmah* of R' Eliyahu di Widash. Because of his great piety he would not look at the face of any young man whose beard had not yet grown.

One of his *halachic* (legal) rulings was published in the book *Kapei Aharon* of R' Aharon Ezriel (*Hoshen Mishpat*, page 111a). R' Ezriel writes that he received the document in 1846 while he was passing through Ein Tab.

In 1861 he signed on a tax matter with R' Haim Mordechai Labaton (see #336) and R' Raphael Shelomo Nehmad, as recorded later in R' Labaton's book *Nochah HaShulhan*, *Even HaEzer* 16. In 1868 he signed the approbation to *Nochah HaShulchan*, and also to *Hadar Ezer* of R' Yitzhak Shrem (see #517).

He passed away on 5 Elul, 5632 (1872), leaving many of his *hiddushim* (original Torah thoughts) in manuscript form. Some of them were posthumously published by R' Saadiah Manir under the title *Shalom Le'Am* (Jerusalem 5742/1982). Others were included in the anthology *Otzarot Hachmei Aram Soba al HaRambam* (Jerusalem 5749/1989) that was published by the Aram Soba Foundation.

R' Shalom Chasky was known as a saintly person who observed all the restrictions described in the book Reishit Hochmah.

[150] CHASKY, R' Yaakob

רבי יעקב כאסכי

(early 19th century)

Worthy scholar of Aram Soba. At the Ben-Zvi Institute there is a Bill of Sale of the property of the deceased, R' Yedidyah Choueka, dated 8 Tamuz, 5570 (1810), signed R' Yedidyah Dayan (see #200) and R' Yaakob ben David Chasky.

[151] CHASKY, R' Yeshayah

רבי ישעיה כאסכי

(— 1910)

Eminent scholar and rabbi of Aram Soba. In 1865 he joined other rabbis of Aram Soba in signing the approbation for the first book-printing initiative of the city, which was introduced by R' Abraham Sasson and his sons (see #475). (See Document Section, Document No. 25.)

At the Ben-Zvi Institute there is a manuscript (file no. 259), which relates the events of Jewish life in Aram Soba and reports that in 5670 (1910), "the Holy Ark was burned," that is, R' Yeshayah Chasky passed away. His death is also mentioned by R' David Laniado. He writes (item 120) that "before his death, he sat up and recited Psalm 103. Then he stretched out on his bed and gave up his soul."

"Before his death, he sat up and recited Psalm 103. Then he stretched out on his bed and gave up his soul."

Chehebar Lineage. Tradition has it that the Chehebar's family's original name was Laham. Many years ago, all the children of an important Laham family member died at a young age, some right before their *Bar Mitzvah*. When he finally had a child that lived past his *Bar Mitzvah*, he changed his last name to commemorate the event. The name that he chose was *"chehai"* (who lived) — *"bar"* (to *Bar Mitzvah* age).

[152] CHEHEBAR, R' Yitzhak

רבי יצחק שחיבר

(1912 — 1990)

Distinguished scholar, educator, and rabbi of Aram Soba, Damascus, and Argentina. R' Yitzhak was known to be a highly dedicated person, devoting as much as 18 hours a day to Torah study.

Distinguished scholar, educator, and rabbi of Aram Soba, Damascus, and Argentina. He was born in Aram Soba in 1912 to R' Moshe ben Ezra Laham Chehebar. He studied in the Talmud Torah, which was headed by Hacham Moshe Safdeyé (Bawabe), and then in the yeshiva *Degel Torah* under R' Moshe Tawil (see #586), becoming one of R' Tawil's best students. After completing his course of study in 1930, he was appointed to a position as head of the Talmud Torah, which he successfully managed with great insight and understanding. He then moved to Damascus where he founded a Talmud Torah, which quickly showed his unique imprint.

R' Yitzhak Chehebar

R' Yitzhak was known to be a highly dedicated person, devoting as many as 18 hours a day to Torah study. As a result, he developed a phenomenal knowledge of *Gemara* and the works of the *halachic* (legal) authorities. (See Section II — "Tragic Events of 1947" — and Section III for his involvement in rescuing the *Keter*.)

In 1946 he married Jamilah, the daughter of R' Moshe Silvera (whose other son-in-law was R' Sadek Harari, the Chief Rabbi of Mexico).

His final stage was Buenos Aires, where he was called to officiate as Chief Rabbi of Argentina and the Sephardic congregation Yesod HaDat.

His final stage was Buenos Aires, where he was called to officiate as Chief Rabbi of Argentina and the Sephardic congregation *Yesod HaDat*. He worked tirelessly in that capacity and succeeded in provoking a spiritual revolution. He specifically focused on the quality of Jewish education and the ongoing battle against mixed marriage.

He passed away in Argentina on 27 Av, 5750 (1990) and was succeeded by his son R' Yosef Haim. He was also blessed with a son named R' Abraham. Many of his *hiddushim* (original Torah thoughts) and responsa were posthumously published by R' Yosef Haim in the book *Yitzhak Yeranen* (Buenos Aires 5751/1991). Among the responsa that he dealt with were questions of going bareheaded and of transporting Torah scrolls from the defunct synagogue in Sidon (Lebanon) to Brazil. In addition, his biography can be found in the book *Vayizra Yitzhak* that was written in his memory by R' Haim Halevy.

[153] CHOUEKA, R' Aharon

רבי אהרן שוויכה

(— 1881)

Eminent scholar and rabbi of Aram Soba. He nurtured many students and authored a book of responsa in manuscript form. R' Choueka was a highly respected man with a sterling reputation.

In 1869 his name appeared in the list of Aram Soba scholars receiving a weekly stipend from the special fund that had been set up for the support of worthy individuals who dedicated their lives to Torah study.

He joined other rabbis of Aram Soba in signing the approbation to the book *Zeh Ktav Yadi* (Aram Soba 5632/1872) of R' Yeshayah Dayan (see #203). He also signed on the *halachic* (legal) ruling published in the book *Imrei No'am* (Aram Soba 5658/1898) by the same author.

He passed away at a relatively young age on 15 Tamuz, 5641 (1881), while on the road to Tedef, a town near Aram Soba.

[154] CHOUEKA, R' Aharon

רבי אהרן שוויכה

(1896 — 1978)

R' Aharon established a number of yeshivot, among which were Segulah, Keter Torah, and Ahabah Ve'Ahvah.

Distinguished rabbi and educator of Egypt, Tel Aviv, and Jerusalem. He was born in Aram Soba in 1896 to his father R' Menahem Choueka (see #155), and was named after his grandfather R' Aharon Choueka (see #153). He began his Torah studies under his father and then went to Egypt, where he studied under R' Ezra Attiah (see #102). As a young man in Egypt he became active in organizing learning programs for Jewish youth. To that end he established a number of *yeshivot*, among which were *Segulah*, *Keter Torah*, and *Ahabah Ve'Ahvah*.

He held the position of *Rosh Yeshiva* of *Ahabah Ve'Ahavh* from its founding in 1930 until the year 1956, when he left Egypt. The *yeshivot* attracted thousands of students, from a wide variety of backgrounds, including those who had attended secular universities. R' Choueka paid special attention to the quality of the teaching staff, in which he himself participated.

In about 1950 he visited Jerusalem, spending time with his old teacher, R' Ezra Attiah. Following the advice of R' Attiah, he brought back with him to Egypt one of the brightest of the students of the yeshiva *Porat Yosef* to assume the position of *Av Bet Din* (Chief Judge) of Egypt. This was R' Ovadiah Yosef, who was destined to become the Sephardic Chief Rabbi of Israel. R' Ovadiah took a leadership role over the many Torah institutions of Egypt. He and R' Choueka worked as a team to raise the level of Torah education in Egypt. Many of the high-caliber graduates resulting from their efforts immigrated to *Eretz Yisrael* and went on to spread Torah throughout the land.

The home of R' Choueka in Egypt was a key destination for the emissaries of Torah institutions who regularly came from *Eretz Yisrael* to raise funds. R' Choueka was glad to be able to serve as their host and provide them with contacts and introductions to the wealthy Jews of Egypt.

R' Choueka was also known as an outstanding orator and people came from far and wide to hear his learned and inspirational lectures. Because of his outstanding reputation he was offered rabbinical posts in many key cities, including Aram Soba, all of which he declined because of his love of education. However, in 1956 he accepted a short-term position in the United States.

Two years later he moved to *Eretz Yisrael*, first to Jerusalem and then to Tel Aviv. He became a member of the Chief Rabbinate, responsible for promoting *Shabbat* observance and dealing with religious conversions. These were momentous years for R' Choueka, in which he was occupied with many communal activities, especially the delivery of lectures. In addition he managed to found the beautiful synagogue dedicated by David Mishan in the Kiryat Yovel section of Jerusalem. The synagogue included a *Bet Midrash* called *Imrei No'am*, over which he presided until the last day of his life.

In 1974 he moved back to Jerusalem and focused his time in giving lectures in the *Bet Midrash* which he had founded. His approach to Torah study was that which he had received from his teacher, R' Ezra Attiah.

R' Choueka also delved into the mystical approach to Torah and left a brief introduction to this topic in manuscript form. He also left a manuscript with *hiddushim* (original Torah thoughts) on *Masechet Berachot*. It is unfortunate that there is only a limited record of the extensive material that he developed for his lectures. However, some of his *hiddushim* were posthumously published by his grandchildren under the title *Minhat Aharon*.

Despite a severe and painful illness in the last year of his life he maintained a cheerful outlook and accepted his suffering with grace. He passed away in Jerusalem on 4 Shevat, 5738 (1978) and was laid to rest on the Mount of Olives. He left three worthy sons: Abraham, Yitzhak, and Yaakob.

In about 1950 he visited Jerusalem, spending time with his old teacher, R' Ezra Attiah. Following the advice of R' Attiah, he brought back with him to Egypt one of the brightest of the students of the yeshiva Porat Yosef to assume the position of Av Bet Din (Chief Judge) of Egypt. This was R' Ovadiah Yosef.

R' Aharon Choueka (#154)

R' Menahem Choueka

[155] CHOUEKA, R' Menahem

רבי מנחם שוויכה

(1873 — 1934)

Eminent scholar and rabbi of Aram Soba and Egypt. He was born in 1873 to R' Aharon Choueka (see #153), but was only 8 years old when his father passed away. He got married in 1891, at the age of 18.

R' Choueka excelled in his studies as a youth and quickly became one of the notable rabbis of Aram Soba. He was reputed to be an expert in all four volumes

R' Aharon Choueka moved to Tel Aviv, where he became a member of the Chief Rabbinate, responsible for promoting Shabbat observance and dealing with religious conversions.

of the *Shulhan Aruch* and was a colleague of R' Abraham Antebi (see #64). However he declined offers of rabbinical positions, preferring to earn his own livelihood.

Shortly before the outbreak of World War I he left Aram Soba and moved to Egypt. There he earned a livelihood in business while devoting his energies to serving *Hashem* by delivering inspiring lectures.

R' Rahamim would study continuously for hours, typically from early in the morning until the late hours of the evening. During his study periods he would not answer phone calls or accept visitors.

When the *Kaf HaHaim,* R' Yaakob Haim Sofer (see #532), visited Egypt, he was pleasantly surprised to find a large collection of volumes on Kabbalah in R' Choueka's personal library. Thereupon the two scholars engaged in extensive Torah discussions.

R' Choueka passed away on 11 Kislev, 5694 (1934).

CHREM, see SHREM

[156] CHURBA-COHEN, R' Rahamim
רבי רחמים שורבה־כהן

(1897 — 1987)

Distinguished spiritual leader of the Syrian Community in Brooklyn. He was born in 1897 in Aram Soba to R' Abraham Churba-Cohen, who sent him to study under the most distinguished rabbis of the city. Throughout his life, until his passing at the age of 90, he would reminisce about his formative years in Aram Soba.

R' Rahamim Churba-Cohen

He was blessed with a photographic memory, comparable to that of R' Eliezer ben Hyrcanus, who was described by the *Mishnah* in *Pirkei Avot* as a "cemented cistern that loses not a drop." His mind absorbed every word he ever learned from his teachers and his unfailing memory soon became legendary. Once, soon after undergoing major surgery, he received a phone call from Mr. Saul Kassin, himself an accomplished scholar with a thorough knowledge of *Tanach,* who asked where in *Tanach* a certain verse appeared. Despite his discomfort and malaise after surgery, R' Rahamim responded without hesitation and named the chapter and verse from the book of *Shemuel.*

His extraordinary memory was matched only by his power of concentration. He would study continuously for hours, typically from early in the morning until the late hours of the evening. During his study periods he would not answer phone calls or accept visitors. This remarkable intensity enabled him to achieve mastery over a wide range of Torah knowledge, including *Tanach, Talmud,* the *Poskim (halachic* authorities*), shehitah* (kosher slaughtering), and *hazzanut* (music of religious devotion). Even as a young man he distinguished himself as a talented and gifted public speaker.

His teachers quickly recognized his talents and ensured that he received the training he needed to become a religious leader of the next generation. Indeed, at the young age of 20, his mastery of *Gemara* and *Poskim* earned the respect and awe of the rabbis of Aram Soba, who, despite his youth, conferred upon him the title of *Hacham.*

The economic turmoil that struck the city of Aram Soba in the late 1920's forced him to leave the city together with his wife, Adele. He spent a number of years serving as spiritual leader for the Sephardic communities in Cuba and Rochester, New York, before settling in Brooklyn. There he established himself as a community leader of the city's Syrian community, with a mission of preserving the ancient Orthodox tradition of Aram Soba.

He devoted his six decades in America to the dissemination of Torah and the Syrian tradition in New York. On one snowy *Shabbat,* Hacham Shaul Matloub Abadi (see #9) took advantage of R' Rahamim's absence to speak in praise of the community and attributed its firm commitment to our ancestral tradition to R' Rahamim's influence and inspiring leadership. R' Rahamim earned the respect and admiration of the local Ashkenazic rabbinate, as well. He engaged in scholarly discourse with the *Roshei Yeshiva* of such prestigious institutions as the *Mirrer Yeshiva* and *Torah Vodaath*, as well as with other leading rabbinic figures in the Coney Island area of Brooklyn. When he lectured in these *yeshivot*, his *shiurim* were warmly and enthusiastically received.

Although R' Rahamim carried his title with dignity and respect, he never aspired to higher positions of honor and authority. His sole desire was to serve, to give, to lend assistance, and to oversee the religious development of the growing Syrian community in the United States.

The Sages describe Aharon, the first *Kohen Gadol*, as a person who "loved people and brought them closer to Torah." R' Rahamim Churba-Cohen was a worthy descendant of Aharon and a loyal follower of his example. He passed away on 4 Tishrei, 5748 (September 27, 1987), leaving behind a legacy of Torah instruction and leadership whose impact can be felt throughout the Syrian Jewish community that he was so instrumental in building.

His son R' Shelomo Churba opened a synagogue in Brooklyn carrying his father's name, *Shaare Rahamim,* and continuing his traditions.

[157] **COHEN, R' Abraham**

רבי אברהם הכהן

(— 1768)

Worthy scholar of Aram Soba. He was a colleague by R' Sadkah Houssin (see #313). In the book *Rei'ach Sadeh* (p. 10c) of R' Shimon Dweck (see #246), the author writes that R' Abraham Cohen and his colleague R' Sadkah Houssin have answered his question.

One of his responsa was published in *Hazon Obadiah* by R' Obadiah HaLevi (see #392) (p. 214b). It is believed that he passed away in approximately 1768. He left a manuscript of *hiddushim* (original Torah thoughts) on the *Rambam,* which is currently in the possession of the the Grand Rabbi *(Admor)* of Karlin.

[158] **COHEN, R' Abraham**

רבי אברהם הכהן

(19th century)

Worthy scholar of Aram Soba. His name appears in the list of Aram Soba scholars receiving a weekly stipend from the special fund that had been set up for the support of worthy individuals who dedicated their lives to Torah study. (For more information on the fund, see R' Yaakob Gindi-Daknish, #267.)

[159] **COHEN, R' Ezra Yeshuah**

רבי עזרא ישועה הכהן

(— 1846)

Eminent scholar and *dayan* (judge) of Aram Soba. He was one of the first to sit on the new *Bet Din* that had been established in his time. R' Ezra was a brother of R' Haim Cohen (see #162) and a student of R' Yisrael Sasson (see #483), the author of *Kenesset Yisrael*. He passed away on 7 Kislev, 5607 (1846).

In 1822 his name appears as the first of the signers on the approbation to the book *Yoshev Ohalim* by R' Abraham Antebi (see #63). At the Ben-Zvi Institute there is a hand-witten document dated 29 Shevat, 5562 (1802) containing R' Ezra's signature together with that of R' Moshe ben Abraham HaLevi (first signer) and R' Yitzhak Dayan (third signer) [file no. 302].

[160] **COHEN, R' Gabriel**

רבי גבריאל הכהן

(18th century)

Worthy scholar and rabbi of Aram Soba. His father was R' David Cohen. He was a colleague of R' Moshe Harari (see #288) and R' Yitzhak Berachah (see #129) and he joined them in signing a *halachic* (legal) ruling in the book *Bet Dino shel Shelomo* of R' Raphael Shelomo Laniado (see #363) (*Orah Haim* 10-17). He also signed together with other rabbis of Aram Soba on the *halachic* (legal) ruling against eating grape leaves because of worm infestation, as recorded in the book *Hanan Elokim* by R' Haim Abulafia. (See Document Section, Document No. 13.)

[161] COHEN, R' Haim

רבי חיים הכהן

(— 1655)

Title Page of Torat Hacham

Distinguished scholar, Kabbalist, and rabbi of Aram Soba. He was born in Egypt to R' Abraham, a descendant of the Jews who were driven out of Spain in the 15th century. In the introduction to his book *Torat Hacham* he traces the lineage of his family back to Don Yosef Cohen. From Egypt he went to *Eretz Yisrael* and studied Kabbalah under R' Haim Vital. In 1579 he was accepted as a rabbi in Aram Soba.

Even in his earliest days he had the habit of responding to questions from people who were drawn to whichever synagogue he happened to be sitting in. Every *Shabbat* he would teach *halachot*, concentrating on those *halachot* which were pertinent to that time of year.

Title Page of Migdal David

He was a prolific author of holy books, but the challenges of getting access to a printing press at that time were very great. The main printing facilities were in Italy, so a long dangerous sea voyage was necessary. R' Haim made this voyage, accompanied by a son, and described his experiences in the introduction of *Torat Hacham* (see below). He never made it back to Aram Soba and passed away in Livorno (Leghorn) on 25 Nissan, 5415 (1655).

In describing his trip to Italy, R' Haim wrote: "I had decided to send the commentary on *Megillat Esther* first ... However, from the time that I sent it there was a delay of many years without reason ... and so I finally decided to go myself. I set out from Aram Soba and boarded a ship, and after a day's sailing we entered a port, which was marked for catastrophe. We were held there for five days because of a violent storm. Then, on the sixth day we were attacked and overcome by pirates from Malta. When I saw that all hope was lost I threw myself into the turbulent waters and it seemed that I would drown. However, *Hashem* caused me to drift slowly to dry land and so I was miraculously saved from drowning and from being captured by the pirates. After that I endured many tribulations from hunger and wild animals so that all the books I had with me were lost. For a time I wept bitterly and bewailed their loss, which represented the destruction of 20 years' work. When I could no longer bear thinking about the loss, I decided to try and to write afresh. And so I pulled bits and pieces together and put them into the book *Torat Hacham*."

"Then, on the sixth day we were attacked and overcome by pirates from Malta."

The major published books which he authored are listed below:

- *Torat Hacham* (Venice 5414/1654). Commentary on the Torah based on both its revealed and mystical aspects.
- *Mekor Haim* (Amsterdam 5415/1655). *Halachot* following the *Shulhan Aruch*, but based on the mystical approach. Initially only the first part of the volume on *Orah Haim* was published. In the introduction to this volume he explains that he composed three volumes on each of the four parts of the *Shulhan Aruch*. The three volumes on *Orah Haim* were published separately, with the subtitles: *Tur Barakat* (Amsterdam 5514/1654)), *Tur Yahalom* (Livorno 5415/1655), and *Tur Pitedah* (Livorno 5415/1655). They were reprinted in the 19th century (Pietrkov 5639/1879). The *Hida* (R' Haim Yosef David Azulai) wrote that he had seen part of the volume on *Yoreh Deah* in printed form.

In addition, he left a number of manuscripts, including the following:

- *Ateret Shalom* — A commentary on *Shir HaShirim*.
- *Meginat Lev* — A commentary on *Megillat Eichah*.
- *Ateret Zahav* — A commentary on *Megillat Esther*.

- *Migdal David* — A commentary on *Megillat Ruth*. The original manuscript was lost and was subsequently found by R' David Lida, who published it (Amsterdam 5440/1680), but without giving credit to its author. This action earned sharp criticism from later authorities.
- *Mifshar Halmi* — A commentary on *Sefer Daniel*.
- *Menorat Zahav* — A commentary on *Kohelet*.
- Commentaries on *Iyob* and *Yeshayahu*.

[162] **COHEN, R' Haim**

רבי חיים הכהן

(— 1807)

Eminent scholar and Kabbalist of Aram Soba. He nurtured many students and achieved a reputation as an expert in the mystical aspects of Torah. He was a brother of R' Ezra Cohen (see #159) and the father-in-law of R' Aharon Nehmad (see #442). He passed away on 9 Heshvan, 5568 (1807) and was eulogized by R' Eliyahu Abadi (see #4), as recorded in the book *Ben Abraham*. He was blessed with one son, R' Meir, who was also his student.

[163] **COHEN, R' Mordechai**

רבי מרדכי הכהן

(17th century)

Eminent scholar and rabbi of Aram Soba. He was the son of R' Yitzhak Ashkenazi. R' Mordechai lived for 10 years in the house of his father-in-law, R' Shemuel Laniado (see #376), the *Baal HaKeilim*, who mentions him often in his books. He came to Aram Soba from Safed where he studied under R' Yisrael Di Koriel.

He authored *Rosh Mar Deror* (Venice 5375/1615), a book of inspirational lectures on the Torah, and also appears to be the author of *Siftei Kohen*, a commentary on the Torah, which was published in Venice at about that time. The preface to that book indicates that the author was R' Mordechai Cohen, a student of R' Yisrael *Di* Koriel of Safed.

[164] **COHEN, R' Moshe**

רבי משה הכהן

(— 1882)

Chief Rabbi of Aram Soba. He was a greatly learned and well-spoken man who was respected by government officials and by the community. R' Moshe was the son of R' Ezra Yeshuah Cohen (see #159) and a son-in-law of R' Shemuel Dweck (see #244). He passed away on 8 Nissan, 5642 (1882).

R' Shelomo Eliezer Alfandri, the Chief Rabbi of Damascus and Safed (see #44), once told R' David Laniado (#352) that when R' Moshe Cohen died, he left behind an expensive robe, ornamented in gold, that had been sent to him by the Turkish sultan. R' Alfandri said that he had the opportunity to buy the robe and did so, but only because it had belonged to R' Moshe Cohen.

Title Page of Rosh Mar Deror

R' Moshe left behind many responsa in manuscript form. One of them was included in the book *Holech Tamim U' Poel Sedek* (sec. 1) by R' Abraham Dayan (see #173). In 1865 he joined other rabbis of Aram Soba in signing the approbation for the first book-printing initiative of the city, which was introduced by R' Abraham Sasson and his sons (see #475). (See Document Section, Document No. 25.) Later, in 1878, he signed the approbation for the book *Yashir Moshe* of R' Moshe Dayan (#192). At the Ben-Zvi Institute there is a hand-witten document containing R' Moshe's signature together with that of R' Ezra Chasky, dated Adar 5609 (1849) [file no. 302].

[165] **COHEN, R' Pinehas**

רבי פנחס הכהן

(— 1250)

Worthy scholar of Aram Soba. He passed away in the month of Av in the year 5010 (1250). His gravestone indicates that his father's name was Elazar. According

According to tradition, he became known as "Sadik Rimoniyah."

to tradition, he became known as *"Sadik Rimoniyah"* and prayers said at his grave would be answered immediately. Since his grave is next to a pomegranate tree (*rimon* in Hebrew), the nickname may have been a way to direct people to his gravesite.

Title Page of Ner Mitzvah

[166] **COHEN, R' Shemuel**

רבי שמואל הכהן

(— 1601)

Chief Rabbi in the Spanish (Sephardic) community of Aram Soba. He was a descendant of the Jews exiled from Castille and is mainly known for his book *Minhat Kohen*. In the introduction he describes his lineage through three generations of highly respected rabbis. He says that his father was R' Yosef Cohen, and his grandfather, who is buried in Safed, was R' Shemuel Cohen. He adds that his great-grandfather, R' Judah Cohen, is buried in Jerusalem. He especially notes the praises heaped on his great-grandfather by R' Levi ben Habib. He passed away in the year 5362 (1601).

The book *Minhat Kohen* consists of four volumes. The first is *Ner Mitzvah* (Venice 5358/1598), which contains seventeen inspirational lectures on the elements of faith and belief. The second part is *Torah Ohr* (Venice 5369/1600), containing lectures on *Bereshit*, based on the revealed approach. The other two volumes may not have been printed. *Derech Haim* is a compilation of the *mitzvot* and *Tochehot Mussar* is a guide to behavior.

Title Page of Torah Ohr

[167] **COHEN, R' Yaakob**

רבי יעקב הכהן

(— 1662)

Worthy scholar of Aram Soba. He was a son of R' Haim Cohen (see #161) and passed away on a Tuesday, the 23rd day of the month in the year 5422 (1662). (The month is not known.)

[168] **COHEN, R' Yitzhak**

רבי יצחק הכהן

(— 1902)

Worthy scholar and rabbi of Aram Soba. He succumbed to the epidemic of cholera which broke out in 1902, and died on *Shemini Atzeret* of that year (5663).

[169] **DABBAH, R' Eliyahu**

רבי אליהו דבח

(— 1832)

Worthy scholar of Aram Soba. He is believed to have been a son of R' Yitzhak Dabbah (see #172). He passed away in 5592 (1832) and was praised by R' David Ashkenazi (see #90) in the course of a eulogy delivered on the passing of R' Yeshayah Dayan (see #202).

[170] **DABBAH, R' Moshe**

רבי משה דבח

(19th century)

Worthy scholar of Aram Soba. His name appears on the list of scholars receiving the weekly stipend. (For further information on the fund, see R' Yaakob Gindi-Daknish; #267.)

[171] **DABBAH, R' Yeshayah**

רבי ישעיה דבח

(— 1772)

Eminent scholar and *dayan* (judge) of Aram Soba. He was the son of R' Yitzhak Dabbah, a composer, whose name is associated with many Aram Soba *pizmonim* (hymns). R' Yeshayah became one of the most knowledgeable experts in the lunar calendar and in the *halachot* (laws) pertaining to Hebrew scribes (for Torah scrolls, *tefillin*, and *mezuzot)*.

Some of his *hiddushim* (original Torah thoughts) have been published in the 20th century by R' Yosef Shayo (see #507) in the anthology *MeHalab Ha'Aretz* (Jerusalem 5726/1966) and in the book *Shaare Rahamim* (Jerusalem 5722/1962).

He joined other rabbis of Aram Soba in signing the introduction to the book *Beirach Yitzhak* (Venice 5523/1763) by R' Yitzhak Berachah (see #129), as well as the approbation to the book *Hanan Elokim* by R' Haim Abulafia.

He passed away in the year 5532 (1772) and was eulogized by R' Raphael Shelomo Laniado (see #363), R' Yehuda Kassin (see #331), and R' Ovadiah HaLevi (see #392) (*Hazon Ovadiah*, 4:186).

[172] DABBAH, R' Yitzhak

רבי יצחק דבח

(— 1814)

Eminent scholar and rabbi of Aram Soba. He was a son of R' Yeshayah Dabbah (see #171). He was known to be an expert in the *Shulhan Aruch*, as well as in the lunar calendar. He passed away in 5574 (1814). He was highly praised by R' Gabriel Ashkenazi (see #93) at the funeral of R' Mordechai Dayan (see #186).

Dayan Lineage. According to ancient tradition, the illustrious Dayan family is descended from King David. The family's origin can be traced to a branch of the house of Yoshiyah Hasan ben Zakkai, brother of the *Reish Galuta* David (d. 940). One of his descendants, Shelomo ben Azariah, settled in Aram Soba, and his family there occupied the position of *Nasi*, the title of the House of David. The first to be known with the family name is R' Moshe ben Saadyah Dayan in the 16th century. His son, R' Mordechai (b. 1541), was a member of the *Bet Din* (religious court) of R' Shemuel Laniado. Even after many Spanish refugee scholars settled in Aram Soba, the Dayan family continued to be held in great esteem. Some of them held key positions in religious and communal life.

One of the most important members of the family in Aram Soba was R' Abraham Dayan (see #173), the author of many works including *Shir Hadash* (1841), a commentary on *Tehillim*. His son R' Moshe Dayan (#192) wrote *Yashir Moshe* (1879), an inspirational commentary on *Shir HaShirim* (*Song of Songs*); in the introduction to this work he traced the Dayan family lineage.

R' Yeshayah ben Mordechai (#203) was head of the *Bet Din* in Aram Soba. In 1888 he founded a Jewish press, which was administered after his death by his sons R' Shaul, R' Shelomo, and R' Yitzhak, and later by his grandson R' Yosef ben Ezra. R' Aharon (d. 1893) was Chief Rabbi of the community of Urfa, Turkey, during the 1880's. He was also a merchant and acted as the Persian consul. He wrote a book of inspirational lectures, *Beit Aharon* (unpublished).

The best-known member of the branch of the family which moved to *Eretz Yisrael* was R' Hiya ben Yosef Dayan (late 17th century), scholar and emissary. His grandfather had immigrated from Damascus to Jerusalem where R' Hiya was born and educated. He later moved to Hebron. As emissary of that community he traveled to North Africa (1665, 1669) and Italy (1673). While in Mantua he met R' Moshe Zacuto who recommended him to his pupil R' Benjamin ben Eliezer Cohen of Reggio. Both wrote poems dedicated to him. In Italy he strongly opposed the Shabbatean movement. [This was a messianic movement centered around the personality of Shabbetai Tzvi, who claimed to be *Mashiach* and won many adherents among people who desperately wanted to see the redemption in their lifetimes. However, Shabbetai Tzvi was ultimately discredited after he renounced Judaism and converted to Islam.]

R' Hiya also went to Turkey and Persia as emissary for Jerusalem (1680–96). In 1696, while returning from Persia, he was attacked by robbers near Baghdad who took from him, besides his money and clothes, the manuscript of his book *Adderet Eliyahu*. However, he found another copy he had made in Aram Soba, which he took with him on his last mission to Morocco. In the introduction there is a description of his travels and an autobiography. One of his pupils in Meknes was R' Haim ben Moshe Attar the Elder.

According to ancient tradition, the illustrious Dayan family is descended from King David.

"It is known in Judah and Israel that we of the Dayan family are descendants of King David and that we can trace our lineage from ancient times."

Tracing the Dayan Lineage. In the introduction to his book *Yashir Moshe* (Aram Soba 5638/1878), R' Moshe Dayan traces the lineage of the Dayan family back to King David. The accompanying text is as follows:

"It is known in Judah and Israel that we of the Dayan family are descendants of King David and that we can trace our lineage from ancient times. From the earliest times, every community leader of the people of Aram Soba was a member of the Dayan family and it was for that reason that our family was referred to as *Mishpahat HaNasi* (the family of the community leader). This leadership role was originally associated with the descendants of David after Yehoyakim. At a later point the name Dayan was applied to the family, referring to the *dayan* (judge) who makes *halachic* rulings for the spiritual welfare of people. The presiding *dayan* or rabbi of the community was given the necessary authority to carry out his role and this authority was passed down to his descendants. He received his salary from the proceeds of money pledged in the synagogue by those who were called up to the Torah (but not from individual offerings so as not to show favoritism to the wealthy).

"After the death of the presiding *dayan*, his oldest son would be raised to his position in accordance with the ruling of the *Rambam* (*Hilchot Klei HaMikdash,* 5). That ruling is based on the verse dealing with the death of Nadab and Abihu, the elder sons of Aharon. The verse states, "and they had no sons, but Elazar and Itamar ministered" (*Bamidbar* 3:4). The implication is that if Nadab and Abihu had sons, the sons would have had precedence in assuming the role of *Kohen Gadol*, even though Elazar and Ithamar were older than those sons.

"We find the same thing with the rules of royal succession. The *Rambam* (*Hilchot Malachim*) states that the oldest son inherits the kingship, as it is written, 'but he gave the kingship to Yehoram for he was the firstborn' (*Divrei HaYamim II* 21:3). This applies to all matters of hereditary authority. Thus, if the rightful heir is still young, the kingship is held for him until he becomes an adult. And if he is not as knowledgeable as the position requires, they would assign to him a Torah scholar who is suitable to be a spiritual guide to the people.

"The traditional duties and privileges of the presiding *dayan* of the community are outlined below:

- He is responsible for executing all contracts and legal documents relating to betrothal, marriage, and the Sabbatical year, as well as for administering legally binding oaths.
- He also has the right to assign the privilege of providing the different cloaks for the Torah scrolls on the various holy days. In return, he receives an honorarium according to the financial ability of the donor.
- He has the duty of saying the *Kol Nidrei* prayer in the main synagogue each *Yom Kippur* and *Habdalah* at the conclusion of *Shabbat*.
- He sets aside an *eruv tavshilin* prior to *Yom Tov* for the benefit of anyone who may have forgotten to do so.
- He is called up to the Torah for the special portions, such as the *Shirah* (*Song at the Sea*), the Ten Commandments, and the *Hatan Torah* (on *Simhat Torah*).
- He sends out *ethrogim* and *lulabim* to all towns in the vicinity of Aram Soba.
- On *Simhat Torah* he leads the seventh *hakafah* (circuit of the *bimah*), which is in honor of King David.

"When Jews were driven from Spain, many of the people came to Aram Soba and formed their own congregation because of differences with the existing community. They established their own chief rabbi to make halachic rulings and judgments. At the same time the hereditary *dayan* continued make rulings for the indigenous (Arabic-speaking) community as in times past. Each rabbinical leader maintained control over his own congregation.

"In time, more and more people with *halachic* questions and legal issues presented their cases before the rabbinical leader of the Sephardim (Spaniards). Thus, over time, the Torah knowledge in the Dayan family diminished and in some generations there was not even one Dayan who was qualified to make *halachic* rulings. And so everyone in the Arabic speaking community turned to the Sephardic rabbi for *halachic* rulings.

"Ultimately, the communities were effectively united in terms of religious practices. Nevertheless, each rabbi continued to serve the needs of his own community. Thus, the Sephardic rabbi continued to prepare betrothal contracts, *ketubot*, and *prosbols* for the Sephardic congregation and the rabbi of the Dayan family would write these contracts for the Arabic-speaking community. The same applied to pressing claims based on the contracts and to receiving the various honors, such as being called up to the Torah. However, the administration of oaths and the distribution of *lulabim* and *ethrogim* has remained with the Dayan family until this very day. Furthermore, the Dayan rabbi receives a salary from the proceeds of the people called up to the Torah. It is many years now that this state of affairs has been in place and the elder of the family, whether a scholar or a simple person, occupies himself with the said services and all the people of the community can testify to this.

"Now, there is a danger that if in the course of time a self-interested person without the fear of Heaven appears on the scene, he may confuse the people and lead them to violate the Torah's laws. He may hide some betrothal or marriage document from the affected family and when his disgraceful behavior is revealed, the *Bet Din* of that time will vigorously rebuke him. The conflict will necessarily be repugnant in the eyes of the populace, because all holy congregations would wish to protect this family like a lofty wall, as it is written: 'then their sons too, forever and ever, shall sit upon your throne' (*Tehillim* 132:12). And since our claim to royal ancestry has faded over the years and been renewed, and there may be 'evil mice' who wish to take advantage, and there is a concern that it will not be possible to substantiate the lineage, I have decided to bring the facts to light in this book, until Mashiah, the descendant of David, will come 'and raise the pride of his anointed one' (*Shmuel I* 2:10), and 'make great the salvations of His king and do kindness for His anointed, to David and his descendants forever' (*Tehillim* 18:51)."

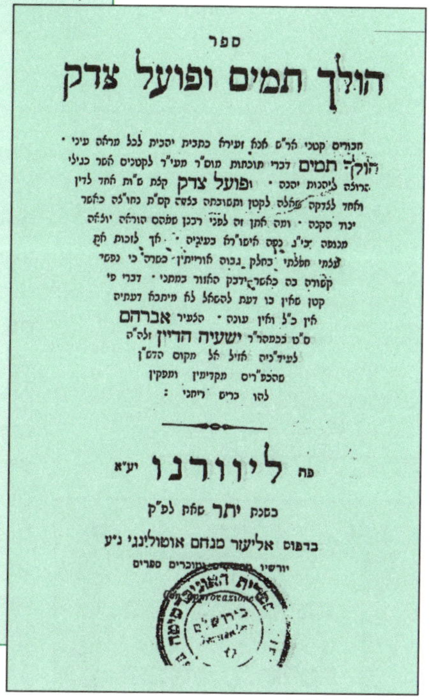
ספר
הולך תמים ופועל צדק
פה ליוורנו יע"א
בדפוס אליעזר מנחם אוטולינגי נ"ע

Title Page of Holech Tamim U'Poel Sedek

[173] DAYAN, R' Abraham

רבי אברהם דיין

(— 1876)

Distinguished scholar and rabbi of Aram Soba. He was a son of R' Yeshayah Dayan (see #202) and, according to family tradition, was a member of the 84th generation of the House of David. The lineage of the Dayan family was traced back to King David by R' Moshe Dayan (see #192). He also wrote an interesting historical essay on this ancient family, which he included in his book *Yashir Moshe* (see box on previous page).

R' Abraham Dayan was a leader of the native community of Aram Soba. This community was referred to as the *Mustarabim* — Jews who are native to an Arab country. He passed away on 18 Heshvan, 5637 (1876). Among those who eulogized him was R' Moshe Swed (see #575). He left two

He was a leader of the native community of Aram Soba — the Mustarabim.

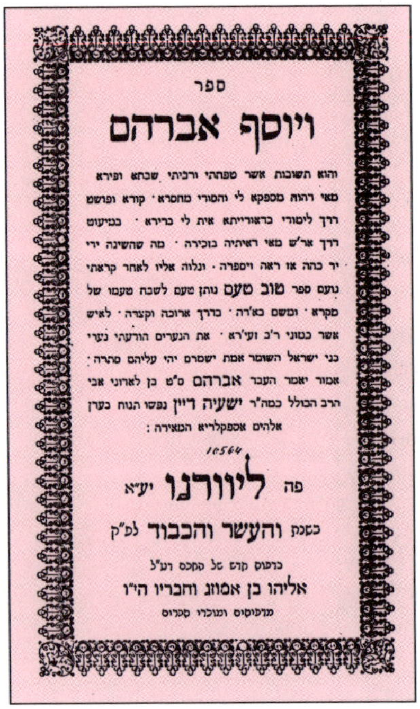

ספר

ויוסף אברהם

והוא תשובות אשר טפחתי ורביתי שבתא ופירא
מאי דהוה מספקא לי והסודי מחסרא· קורא ופושט
ודרך ליסודי כדאורייתא אית לי ברירא · כמיעוט
ודרך אר"ש מאי ראיתיה בוכירה · מה שהשיגה ידי
יד כהה אז ראה ויספרה · ונלוה אליו לאחר קראתי
נועם ספר טוב טעם נותן טעם לשבח טעמו של
מקרא · ומשם כא'רה · כדרך ארוכה וקצרה · לאיש
אשר כטוני ר"כ ועי'רא · את הנערים הורעתי נערי
כני ישראל השומר אמת ישמרם יהי עליהם סתרה:
אמור יאמר העבד אברהם ס"ט בן לאדוני אבי
הרב הכולל כמה"ר ישעיה דיין נפשו הנוח בעדן
אלהים אספקלריא המאירה :

10564

פה ליוורנו יע"א

בשנת והעשר והכבוד לפ"ק

בדפוס קדש של הקכס דע"ל
אליהו בן אמוזג וחבריו הי"ו
מדפיסים ומוכרי ספרים

Title Page of VeYosef Abraham

This was in regard to the practice of some Torah scholars in Aram Soba dedicating a portion of their learning on Shabbat to the memory of someone deceased and then being paid for the consideration on Sunday.

ב"ה בס"ד

מעשיות

צורת כסא שלמה

המלך ע"ה בלשון ערבי

והנמלה עם שלמה

המלך בלשון הקודש

ונלוה להם

שבראו אליהו הנביא

בלשון ערבי

נדפס פה ירושלם בשנת

וה' נתן חכמה לשלמה

השתדל בהדפסתו החכם אברהם דיין

בדפוס של שלמה ישראל שירזלי

Title Page of "Stories of King Solomon"

worthy sons, R' Moshe (see #192) and R' Shaul (see #198).

Despite his scholarly abilities and his royal lineage, he lived in great poverty. Still, this did not prevent him from a productive life of Torah scholarship. He wrote approximately 10 books of *halachic* (legal) responsa and inspirational lectures. The ones that were published are as follows:

- *Shir Hadash* (Livorno 5601/1841), commentary on *Tehillim*, with many words explained in Arabic. The same volume includes two songs, which were composed in honor of Sir Moses Montefiore and his wife Judith on their successful efforts to save the Jews of Damascus from the consequences of the infamous blood libel, which occurred in 1840.
- *Zichron LeNefesh* (Livorno 5602/1842). Essays on *mussar* (spiritual development), organized by the alphabet. This book is unusual in that it was published without approbations. Apparently, the author felt that since it is basically not a book of *halachic* rulings or interpretations, approbations would be unnecessary. However, at the end of the book, R' Dayan included his first *halachic* ruling. This was in regard to the practice of some Torah scholars in Aram Soba dedicating a portion of their learning on *Shabbat* to the memory of someone deceased and then being paid for the consideration on Sunday. The question raised was whether this practice should be forbidden as earning wages on *Shabbat*. After a lengthy discussion, R' Dayan chose the path of leniency, to which he received the approbation of his colleague, R' Abraham Baruch Pifirni of Livorno.
- *Holech Tamim U'Poel Sedek* (Livorno 5610/1850). The *Holech Tamim* part of the book contains essays on *mussar* (spiritual development) organized by the alphabet; the *Poel Sedek* part contains responsa on various topics, such as whether women have a duty to live in *Eretz Yisrael*. An Appendix, *Zichron Dibrei Eretz,* contains a history of Aram Soba and Tedef. Much of the information in the early parts of the present book are based on R' Dayan's research. This book has been reprinted in Jerusalem (5739/1979) through the generosity of Mr. Abraham (Albert) Missry and the efforts of R' Yitzhak Chehebar, Chief Rabbi of the Sephardic community in Argentina (see #152). Additional material was provided by R' Yitzhak Zafrani, the chairman of *Keter Torah,* from a manuscript written by his father R' Shelomo Zafrani (see #598).
- *VeYosef Abraham* (Livorno 5624/1864). Responsa on various topics, such as matchmaking and inheritance.
- *Tuv Taam* (Livorno 5624/1864). Four parts describing the reasoning and deeper meaning of various events, *mitzvot*, and *halachot*. A song written by his son R' Moshe is included at the end of the book.

Others that are still in manuscript form include:

- *Bet HaZohar*, commentary on the *Zohar*.
- *Vayigash Abraham*, responsa and inspirational lectures.
- *Vayisa Abraham*, responsa and inspirational lectures.

[174] DAYAN, R' Abraham

רבי אברהם דיין

(— 1916)

Worthy scholar and scribe of Aram Soba. He was a son of R' Shaul Dayan (see #198) and a grandson of the earlier R' Abraham

Dayan (#173). He is mentioned favorably in the book *Yashir Moshe* by his uncle, R' Moshe Dayan (see #192). He passed away on 12 Nissan, 5676 (1916). He published a book of "Stories of King Solomon" (Jerusalem 1910), based on an ancient manuscript found in the Great Synagogue of Aram Soba. Some of the stories are in Hebrew; others are in Judeo-Arabic. He also added a *pizmon* (hymn) from his father, entitled, *Shachran Eliyahu HaNabi*.

[175] **DAYAN, R' Aharon**

רבי אהרן דיין

(— 1893)

Eminent scholar and *dayan* (judge) of Aram Soba. He was the son of R' David ben R' Yedidyah Dayan. R' Aharon served as rabbi of the congregation *Ur Kasdim* and wrote the book *Bet Aharon* (Aram Soba 5647/1887), containing a variety of responsa on contempory issues, such as wearing a watch on *Shabbat,* making an *eruv* to permit carrying on *Shabbat*, laws of interest, and laws of *Bishul Akum* (prohibition against eating food cooked by non-Jews). He also included a list of directives that he instituted for the community. He passed away on 14 Tishrei, 5654 (1893).

[176] **DAYAN, R' David**

רבי דוד דיין

(— 1680)

Learned scholar of Aram Soba. He was a member of the 78th generation in the line of descent from King David. He passed away on 8 Heshvan, 5441 (1680).

[177] **DAYAN, R' Elazar Hai**

רבי אלעזר חי דיין

(— 1787)

Respected scholar, community leader of Aram Soba, and elder of the Dayan family. He was the oldest son of R' Mordechai Dayan (see #184) and a son-in-law of R' Haim Attiah (see #103). According to family tradition, he was a member of the 82nd generation of the House of David. In the book *Yashir Moshe* by R' Moshe Dayan (see #192) and other sources he is referred to as Elazar Haim, a name that he was apparently given to assure a long life. With the passing of his father, he inherited the traditional functions (*hazakot*) which were the heritage of the glorious Dayan family. These involved directing the affairs of the congregation in matters relating to religious prohibitions, marriage, matchmaking, marital certificates (*ketubot*), and registry of *britot* (circumcisions).

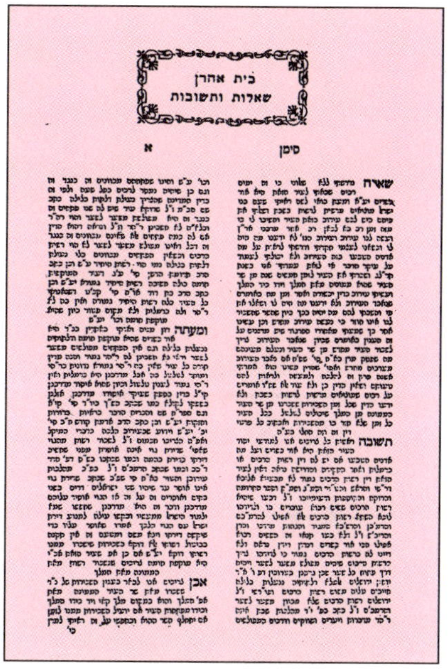
בית אהרן

שאלות ותשובות

סימן א

Title Page of Bet Aharon

It is interesting to note that many of the birth dates of the rabbis listed in this book were established through the painstaking research of R' David Laniado (see #352), R' Mordechai Attiah, R' Ephraim Levi, and R' Abraham Ezra Ades who pored through the tiny script in the registry of *britot* and subtracted eight days. Of course, the system is not always accurate if the *brit* was delayed for some reason.

In 1787, R' Elazar Hai succumbed to an epidemic, leaving behind two young sons, Mordechai (see #185) and Yeshayah (see #202). The two boys were too young to fill their father's position in the community, and so R' Yedidyah Dayan (see #200), younger brother of the deceased, assumed all of the *hazakot.* This situation continued for about 11 years until 1798, when R' Mordechai, the first of the two children, was old enough to claim his rights as the first-born son of his father. The conflict between R' Mordechai and R' Yedidyah, his uncle, was brought before the rabbis of the community, who decided on a compromise and divided up the various *hazakot* between the two parties. Sadly, R' Mordechai did not live long and died three years later without sons. At that point his younger brother R' Yeshayah claimed his brother's share of the Dayan family *hazakot*. This dispute is described in the book *Mar Ve'Ahalot* of R' Abraham Antebi

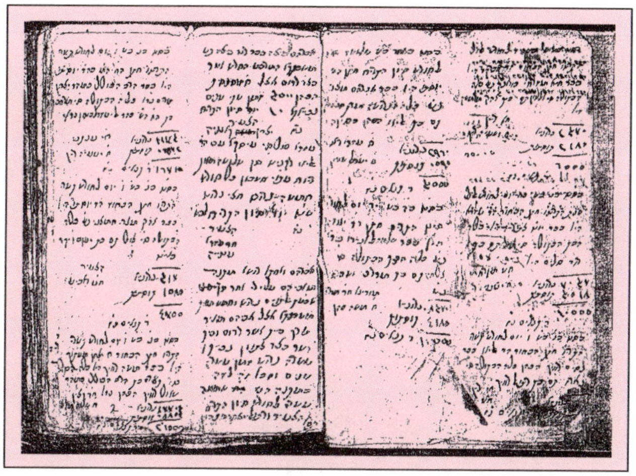

Registry of Ketubot

He inherited the traditional functions (hazakot), which were the heritage of the glorious Dayan family.

(see #63) and in the book *Poel Sedek,* written by R' Abraham Dayan (see #173), grandson of R' Elazar Haim. The grandson's version of the story indicates that the primary decisor in resolving the dispute was the *Maharshal,* R' Raphael Shelomo Laniado (see #363).

[178] DAYAN, R' Ephraim

רבי אפרים דיין

(18th century)

Eminent scholar of Aram Soba. He is mentioned in in the book *Ahavat Sion* (Jerusalem 5647/1847) by R' Simhah ben Yehoshua Mezalin. The author describes an incident that happened on a trip to *Eretz Yisrael* in 1765. "In Safed I saw a man from Aram Soba named R' Ephraim Dayan. This man, who was a direct descendant of King David, had two wives. He was a decent, upright man, who was very handsome, with a high forehead. I asked him, 'How many generations are you from King David?' He responded, 'I am 84 generations from King David.' People said to me that since he is called Ephraim Dayan [*Dayan* means "judge"], once he signs his name to a *halachic* (legal) ruling, even the Turkish sultan would not oppose it out of respect for King David."

'How many generations are you from King David?'

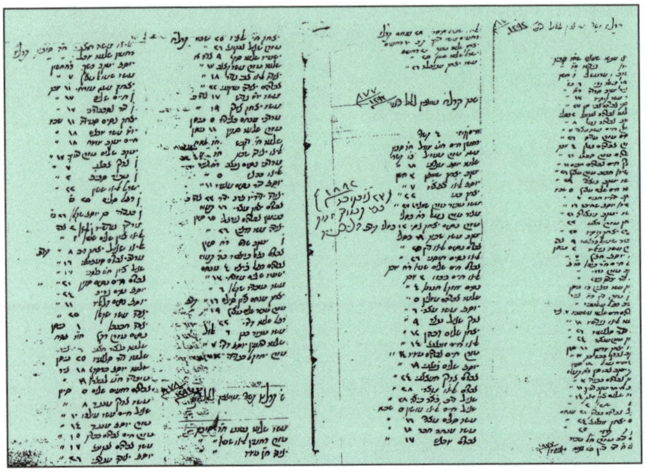

Registry of Britot (5638/1878)

[179] DAYAN, R' Ezra

רבי עזרא דיין

(1820 — 1905)

Outstanding scholar of Aram Soba. He was born in 1820 to R' Mordechai Dayan (see #186). Despite his marked abilities in learning, this kind and gentle scholar chose to earn his own living and finally passed away in 1905 after a long and productive life.

R' Meir Rahamim Dayan

[180] DAYAN, R' Haim

רבי חיים דיין

(20th century)

Expert *mohel* and *hazzan* (cantor) of Aram Soba. R' Haim earned his living as a merchant of Judaica. He was also a noted *darshan* (lecturer) and actively sought to increase Torah knowledge among ordinary working-men. He was a son of R' Moshe Dayan (see #191). In his later years he immigrated to the United States, where he died.

[181] DAYAN, R' Meir Rahamim

רבי מאיר רחמים דיין

(1889 — 1973)

Worthy scholar and rabbi of Aram Soba. He was born in 1889, a son of R' Moshe Dayan (see #192) and, according to family tradition, a member of the 84th generation of the House of David. He had the distinction of linking this illustrious rabbinical lineage into the modern age. In his later years he moved to *Eretz Yisrael* and settled in Tel Aviv. He passed away on *Shabbat,* 4 Tevet, 5734 (1973).

[182] DAYAN, R' Mordechai

רבי מרדכי דיין

(1541 — 1617)

Eminent scholar and *dayan* (judge) of Aram Soba. He was born in 1541, a son of R' Moshe HaNasi Dayan and, according to family tradition, a member of the 76th generation of the House of David. He was a contemporary of R' Shemuel Laniado, the *Baal HaKeilim* (see #376), and sat with him on the *Bet Din* of Aram Soba. He left one son, R' Natan Dayan (see #194). He passed away in 5377 (1617).

[183] DAYAN, R' Mordechai

רבי מרדכי דיין

(— 1733)

Worthy scholar of Aram Soba. He was a son of R' Yosef Dayan (see #209) and, according to family tradition, a member of the 79th generation of the House of David. He passed away in the epidemic which broke out in 1733. The book *Yashir Moshe* lists his date of death as 11 Tamuz, 5493

(1733). Later that year he was eulogized by R' Obadiah HaLevi (*Hazon Obadiah*, page 32).

[184] **DAYAN, R' Mordechai**

רבי מרדכי דיין

(1757 — 1773)

Young scholar and community leader of Aram Soba. He was born to R' Yosef Dayan in 1757. According to family tradition, he was a member of the 81st generation of the House of David. He lost his father while he was still a small child and he himself lived only to the age of 17. During his short life he held the residual rights (*hazakot*) to the traditional community functions of the illustrious Dayan family. He passed away on 24 Kislev, 5534 (1773) and was survived by two sons, R' Elazar Hai (see #177) and R' Yedidyah (see #200).

[185] **DAYAN, R' Mordechai**

רבי מרדכי דיין

(— 1801)

Worthy scholar and community leader of Aram Soba. He was the firstborn son of R' Elazar Hai Dayan (see #177) and, according to family tradition, a member of the 83rd generation of the House of David. Since both he and his younger brother, R' Yeshayah Dayan (see #202), were youngsters at the passing of their father, neither was able to take upon himself the traditional community functions (*hazakot*), which were the heritage of the glorious Dayan family. The *hazakot* were initially taken over by his uncle R' Yedidyah Dayan (see #200) and after 11 years, R' Mordechai sought to claim his rights. The matter was resolved by the rabbis of Aram Soba and the *hazakot* were divided between R' Yedidyah and R' Mordechai in 1798. Sadly, R' Mordechai did not live long and died three years later without sons. At that point his younger brother R' Yeshayah (#202) claimed his brother's share of the Dayan family *hazakot*. (For more information on the dispute between R' Yedidyah and his brother's sons, see #177.)

R' Mordechai was a son-in-law of R' Haim Attiah (see #103). He passed away on 13 Av, 5561 (1801) and was survived by an only daughter.

R' Mordechai Dayan (#185) was a member of the 83rd generation of the House of David.

[186] **DAYAN, R' Mordechai**

רבי מרדכי דיין

(— 1847)

Eminent scholar and rabbi of Aram Soba. He was the firstborn son of R' Yedidyah Dayan (see #200) and, according to family tradition, a member of the 83rd generation of the House of David. He was about 50 years old when he passed away on 15 Adar, 5607 (1847). He left four scholarly sons: R' Yedidyah (see #200), R' Ezra (see #179), R' Moshe (see #191), and R' Yeshayah (see #203).

At the Ben-Zvi Institute there is an original lease agreement dated Nissan 5586 (1826), with his signature and that of R' Haim Mordechai Labaton (see #336). There is also a bill of sale dated Tevet of the same year with his signature and that of R' Bekhor Yehudah Kassin and another document from the year 5593 (1833). [All are in file no. 302.]

R' Mordechai Dayan (#186) was a member of the 83rd generation of the House of David.

[187] **DAYAN, R' Mordechai**

רבי מרדכי דיין

(19th century)

Worthy scholar of Aram Soba. He was a son of R' Ezra Dayan (see #179) and grandson of R' Mordechai (see #186). He earned his living as a workingman of Aram Soba.

[188] **DAYAN, R' Moshe**

רבי משה דיין

(17th century)

Worthy scholar and rabbi of Aram Soba. He was a son of R' Saadyah Dayan (see #196) and, according to family tradition, a member of the 75th generation of the House of David.

[189] **DAYAN, R' Moshe**

רבי משה דיין

(17th century)

Worthy scholar and rabbi of Aram Soba. He was a son of R' Obadiah Dayan and, according to family tradition, a member of the 73rd generation of the House of David.

[190] DAYAN, R' Moshe

רבי משה דיין

(— 1723)

Worthy scholar and rabbi of Aram Soba. He was a son of R' Natan Dayan (see #194) and, according to family tradition, a member of the 78th generation of the House of David. He passed away in the terrible epidemic which struck Aram Soba in the year 1723. R' Moshe had a son named R' Yosef, who passed away in the same epidemic. His brother, also named R' Yosef (see #209), succumbed to the epidemic as well.

Title Page of Yashir Moshe

[191] DAYAN, R' Moshe

רבי משה דיין

(1829 — 1879)

Eminent scholar and rabbi of Aram Soba. He was born in 1829, the son of R' Mordechai Dayan (see #186). He was greatly respected for his wide-ranging knowledge and assumed responsibilty for the affairs of the community. The date of his death is uncertain, but may be 11 Shevat, 5639 (1879).

He published the book *Igeret HaTiyul* of R' Haim ben Betsalel, brother of the *Maharal* in the year 5632 (1872). He added his own inspirational remarks in an alphabetical system.

Title Page of Igeret HaTiyul

[192] DAYAN, R' Moshe

רבי משה דיין

(— 1901)

Distinguished scholar and rabbi of Aram Soba. He was a son of R' Abraham Dayan (#173) and, according to family tradition, a member of the 85th generation of the House of David. He passed away on 2 Nissan, 5661 (1901).

R' Moshe was known for his important book *Yashir Moshe* (Livorno 5639/1879), which is a commentary on *Shir HaShirim*. At the beginning of the book R' Moshe traces the lineage of the Dayan family back to King David. He includes an interesting historical essay on the lineage of the family (see page 4.3). The rest of the book is divided into three parts:

- *Peirush*. A brief explanation of the difficult words in *Shir HaShirim*. He provides an Arabic translation of some of the most difficult words.
- *Yashir Moshe*. Commentary on *Shir HaShirim* using homiletic interpretations (*drash* and *remez*).
- *Pirkei HaShir*. Symbolic interpretations (e.g., *gematria* and mystical allusions) to be found in *Shir Ha-Shirim*.

He received an approbation for his book from eleven of the most worthy rabbis and scholars in Aram Soba: R' Mordechai Abadi (see #8), R' Moshe Sutton (see #552), R' Moshe Cohen (see #164), R' Shaul Abadi (see #10), R' Moshe Swed (see #575), R' David Kassin (see #322), R' Eliyahu Mishan (see #418), R' Michael Ashkenazi (see #95), R' Raphael Sasson (see #480), R' Shalom Mizrahi (see #428), and R' Aharon Choueka (see #153).

(193) DAYAN, R' Moshe

רבי משה דיין

(1931 — 1979)

Chief Rabbi of Sao Paolo. He was born in 1931 in Cairo, Egypt, a son of R' Abraham Dayan. He studied at the yeshiva *Ahabah Ve'Ahvah*, ultimately becoming one of the senior students of *HaGaon* R' Obadiah Yosef, the head of the Cairo *Bet Din* at that time. In 1952 he went to Paris, France to study for the rabbinate, receiving his *semichah* (rabbinical certificate) from R' Yaakob Kaplan, the Chief Rabbi of France.

For a number of years he served as Chief Rabbi of Northern France and of the French Army's Jewish chaplains. At that time he also served as Chairman of the Regional Board of the World Jewish Congress for Northern France.

In 1963 he moved his family to Israel and settled in Holon, where he worked to spread Torah and *mitzvot* in the framework of the

Pirhei Kehunah organization founded by *HaGaon* R' Ben-Zion Hai Ouziel. He also continued with his studies in the Mesivta of the *Rishon LeSion* (Chief Rabbi of Israel) in Jerusalem, focusing on the knowledge needed to become a *dayan (*judge*)*.

In 1972 he accepted a position as Chief Rabbi of Sao Paulo, Brazil, which was offered to him by the congregation *Mekor Haim,* the community of Egyptian Jews. R' Moshe then pitted all his efforts into strengthening the Torah life in Sao Paulo. Among other things, he established a Talmud Torah, built a *mikveh*, and introduced kosher slaughtering. He promoted peaceful cooperation among all the rabbis of the city, encouraging them to work together in partnership for Torah and Judaism.

R' Moshe Dayan

He was a man of great charm who attracted large crowds to his inspiring lectures. Under his influence, most of the Jews of Sao Paulo began to take *maaser* (tithes) from their income for the support of charities and the *yeshivot* of Israel.

In 1978 he was elected as a member of the standing committee of the Congress of the Rabbis of South America. He also began working on a *kollel to* train rabbis and spiritual leaders in Sao Paulo. Tragically, his holy work was interrupted at its peak when he began to show signs of a serious illness. He endured a full year of painful suffering, which he accepted with love and calmness. On 21 Iyar, 5739 (1979) he passed away in Switzerland and was buried on the Mount of Olives in Jerusalem two days later. He left 10 children. Two of his daughters were married to young scholars: one to R' Shaul Mizrahi who translated the first volume of his father-in-law's book into Spanish, and one to R' Meir ben Ezra Ades.

He published his *hiddushim* (original Torah thoughts) in *halachah* in a book called *Likutei Hemed* (Vol. I, Tel Aviv 5736/1976, Volume II, Jerusalem 5737/1977). He received an approbation from R' Obadiah Yosef, his old mentor.

R' Moshe Dayan served as Chief Rabbi of Northern France and of the French Army's Jewish chaplains.

Under his influence, most of the Jews of Sao Paulo began to take maaser (tithes) from their income for the support of charities and the yeshivot of Israel.

[194] **DAYAN, R' Natan**

רבי נתן דיין

(— 1668)

Worthy scholar and rabbi of Aram Soba. He was a son of R' Mordechai Dayan (see #182) and, according to family tradition, a member of the 77th generation of the House of David. He passed away on 5 Adar II, 5428 (1668) and was survived by two sons, R' Yosef (see #209) and R' Moshe (see #190), both destined to lose their lives in the epidemic of 1723.

[195] **DAYAN, R' Nissim**

רבי נסים דיין

(1868 — 1942)

Worthy scholar and teacher of Aram Soba. He was born in Aram Soba 1867 to his father R' Moshe Dayan (see #191). His vocation was to teach *Gemara* in the Talmud Torah of Aram Soba. However, he also managed the printing of *Viduy HaGadol* (Aram Soba 5685/1925), which is the long penitential confession of the Syrian community. (For more information, see #122.)

R' Nissim Dayan's vocation was to teach Gemara in the Talmud Torah of Aram Soba.

In 1934 he settled in Jerusalem, where he earned his livelihood selling Judaica. He passed away at the age of 74 in Jerusalem on 18 Tishrei, 5703 (1942), leaving four sons and a daughter.

[196] **DAYAN, R' Saadyah**

רבי סעדיה דיין

(17th century)

Worthy scholar and rabbi of Aram Soba. He was a son of R' Moshe Dayan (see #189) and, according to family tradition, a member of the 74th generation of the House of David.

[197] DAYAN, R' Shalom

רבי שלום דיין

(1844 — 1868)

Worthy scholar and rabbi of Aram Soba. He was born in Aram Soba in about 1844, a son of R' Yitzhak Dayan, and got married on 14 Nissan, 5623 (1863).

[198] DAYAN, R' Shaul

רבי שאול דיין

(— 1903)

Worthy scholar and rabbi of Aram Soba. He was a son of R' Abraham Dayan (see #173) and a brother of R' Moshe Dayan (see #192). In the introduction to the book, *Yashir Moshe*, his brother praises his knowledge of Torah and expresses gratitude for the help he gave in preparing the book for publication. He passed away on 13 Nissan, 5663 (1903), leaving a son R' Abraham, who was also spoken of in the book.

He published the book *Shivhei Ha'Ari* (Aram Soba 5632/1872) dealing with the life and miracles of the *Ari'zal*. In the introduction he discusses the value of recounting stories of righteous men. In the back of the book he adds short thoughts and *Tikkunim* (special penitential prayers for designated sins and circumstances).

ספר

שבחי האר"י

ארם צובה

התרל"ב

Title Page of Shivhei Ha'Ari

He joined other rabbis of Aram Soba in signing the approbation to the printing initiative of R' Abraham Sasson in 1865 (see #475). (See Document Section, Document No. 25.)

[199] DAYAN, R' Shemuel

רבי שמואל דיין

(— 1722)

Eminent scholar of Aram Soba. He passed away in 1722 and was eulogized by R' Sadkah Houssin (see #313) in conjunction with the eulogy of R' Hanan Navon, who had passed away in Jerusalem the same week. (R' Navon was the father of R' Yonah Navon who authored *Nehpeh Bakesef* and who was one of the teachers of the famous *Hida*, R' Haim Yosef David Azulai.)

[200] DAYAN, R' Yedidyah

רבי ידידיה דיין

(— 1820)

Community leader, *dayan* (judge), and chief *mohel* of Aram Soba. R' Yedidyah was a son of R' Mordechai Dayan (see #184) and a younger brother of R' Elazar Hai Dayan (see #177). R' Elazar Hai had been the senior member of the Dayan family at the time. When he died, his two sons were too young to fill their father's position in the community. And so R' Yedidyah initially assumed all of the traditional functions (*hazakot*), which were the heritage of the illustrious Dayan family. At a later point, the *hazakot* were divided between R' Yedidyah and R' Yeshayah, the younger of R' Elazar Hai's two sons. (For more information on the dispute between R' Yedidyah and his brother's sons, see #177.)

At the Ben-Zvi Institute there is a Bill of Sale of the property of the deceased, R' Yedidyah Choueka, dated 8 Tamuz, 5570 (1810), signed R' Yedidyah Dayan and R' Yaakob ben David Chasky. R' Yedidyah passed away in approximately 1820 and left two sons: R' Mordechai (#186) and R' David.

The Power of Oil. R' Abraham Antebi (see #63) describes the memorable deeds of R' Yedidyah Dayan in the beginning of his book, *Hochmah U'Mussar*. "I will relate what I saw as a young man, that *Hashem* stirred the spirit of a man from the House of David [referring to the Dayan lineage, which is traced back to King David] whose name is Yedidyah Dayan. He gathered his strength to arise before midnight and he would take with him the *shamosh* (sexton) of the synagogue and he would bang on the people's doors to wake them to come and learn. G-d was with him and people did not turn him down, I could say that most of our community was there nightly.

"They would gather into various groups, one of which consisted of young yeshiva boys studying *Gemara* and *Tosafot*. I was one of those boys. Some studied *Shulhan Aruch*, the section of *Orah Haim* [dealing with daily *halachah*], with a rabbi to enlighten the subject for them. Another group studied the holy *Zohar* and yet another group studied the *mussar* classics, such as *Reshit Hochmah* or *Kad HaKemach*, in a way that every group of ten had *Hashem's* Divine Presence dwelling among them. Every Thursday night there were people who came to study the entire night following a set learning program known as '*Tikkun Semach*.'

"Hacham Yedidyah would prepare the oil on Friday afternoon for the [many] candelabra in the synagogue and the entire room would be full of light. Nearly all the people would come Friday night to recite the entire *Tehillim* from beginning to end, word for word. Then they would recite the entire *Shir HaShirim*. He would do this on *Erev Rosh Hodesh* as well.

"On Friday night and *Erev Rosh Hodesh* the people would come on their own due to their great desire to come to the synagogue that was so resplendent with lights, and as the verse states, 'A multitude of people is the King's glory' (*Mishlei* 14:28).

"When Hacham Yedidyah went around gathering the people he would chant a verse that describes the success of King Hizkiyahu in overpowering the mighty Sanherib through the merit of his Torah learning, 'The yoke was broken because of the oil' (*Yeshayah* 10:27). [As explained in *Sanhedrin* 94b, the yoke of Sanherib was broken on account of the oil of King Hizkiyahu, which burned in the synagogues and schools. When Sanherib attempted to attack Jerusalem, his 180,000 troops died miraculously. The force behind this miracle was 'the power of our oil by which we learn Torah.']

"This practice of Hacham Yedidyah to light up the night was quite expensive and Hashem helped him in that the community assisted him with the financial burden. There was a certain individual named Moshe who helped greatly; this *mitzvah* was dear to him and he got the nickname 'Moshe, man of G-d.' I heard from my master, my holy father, that Hacham Yedidyah, who was stirred to do this *mitzvah*, without a doubt possessed a spark of the ancient king Hizkiyahu, who followed the same practice.

Hacham Yedidyah, who was stirred to do this mitzvah, without a doubt possesed a spark of the ancient king Hizkiyahu, who followed the same practice.

"I can testify that as long as this good custom was part of our community there was always light in the dwellings of the Jewish people with no sadness or worries or harm. On that generation we can apply the verse, 'One who observes *mitzvot* shall know no evil.' This can be proven from Queen Esther, as the Midrash tells us, the night before she entered the palace of Ahasuerus to make her request was the evening of *Pesah* and she involved herself with the *mitzvah* of searching for the *hametz* and that protected her from the evil plan of Haman. [Editor's note: The *Hida* says we commemorate this by putting out ten pieces of bread that correspond to Haman's ten sons, who were hanged the next day.] If the *mitzvah* of an individual has such protective powers, how much more so the merit of the entire community, unified in the work of G-d."

[201] **DAYAN, R' Yedidyah**

רבי ידידיה דיין

(1818 — 1897)

He was a shohet (ritual slaughterer) and an expert in the removal of nonkosher fats and veins from slaughtered animals.

Community leader, *dayan* (judge), and chief *mohel* of Aram Soba. He was born in 1810, a son of R' Mordechai Dayan (see #186) and a grandson of R' Yedidyah Dayan (see #200). After the death of his father in 1847 he assumed all of the traditional functions (*hazakot*), which were the heritage of the Dayan family. Among other things, he was a *shohet* (ritual slaughterer) and an expert in the removal of nonkosher fats and veins from slaughtered animals. He trained many students in this difficult and important procedure. R' Yedidyah passed away on 24 Heshvan, 5658 (1897) and was survived by only one daughter.

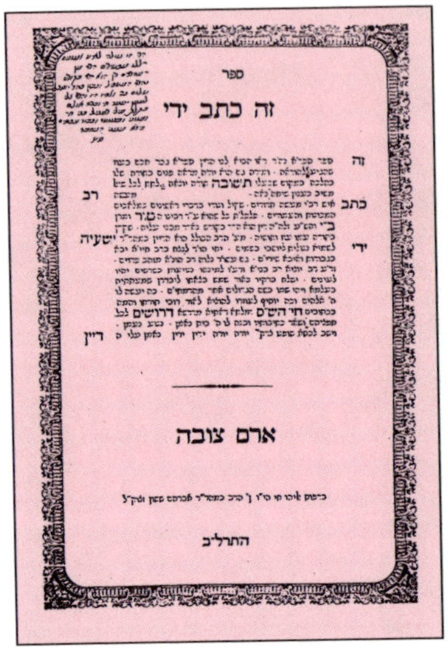
ספר
זה כתב ידי
ארם צובה
התרל"ב

Title Page of Zeh Ketav Yadi

[202] **DAYAN, R' Yeshayah**

רבי ישעיה דיין

(— 1830)

Eminent scholar and community leader of Aram Soba. He was the second son of R' Elazar Hai Dayan (see #177). Since both he and his older brother, R' Mordechai Dayan (see #185), were youngsters when their father died, neither was able to take upon himself the traditional functions (*hazakot*), which were the heritage of the glorious Dayan family. The *hazakot* were initially taken over by his uncle R' Yedidyah Dayan (see #200) and after a time were divided between R' Yedidyah and R' Mordechai. When R' Mordechai passed away, R' Yeshayah was able to take posssession of those *hazakot*. (For more information on the dispute between R' Yedidyah and his brother's sons, see #177.)

R' Yeshayah had a son, R' Abraham (see #173), who praises his father in the introduction to his book *Shir HaShirim*. In the same book R' Abraham also mentions a brother of his, R' Yosef, who passed away at a young age, shortly after the passing of their father. In the Ben-Zvi Institute there is a legal affidavit that is dated Sivan 5579 (1819) and is signed R' Yeshayah Dayan (file no. 302). He passed away on *Shabbat,* 22 Iyar, 5590 (1830).

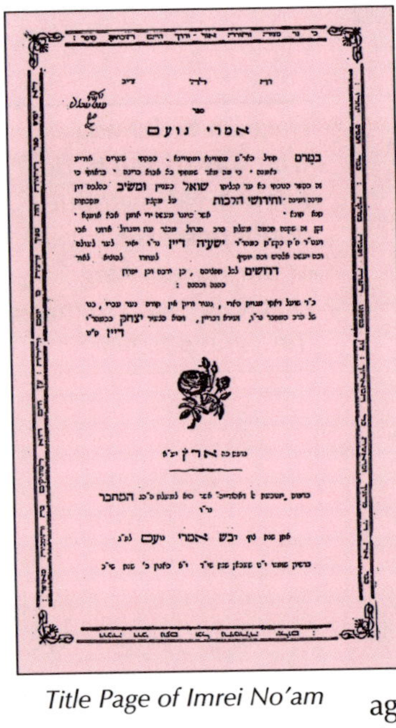
אמרי נועם

Title Page of Imrei No'am

[203] **DAYAN, R' Yeshayah**

רבי ישעיה דיין

(1833 — 1903)

Eminent scholar, publisher, and *Av Bet Din* (Chief Judge) of Aram Soba. He was born in 1833 to R' Mordechai Dayan (see #186), but his father passed away while Yeshayah was still a young boy. He was a studious lad and immersed himself in his studies throughout the week at the *Bet Midrash*. Every *Shabbat* he would stay with his brother, R' Yedidyah (see #201), who supported him. In the introduction to his book of responsa, *Zeh Ketav Yadi* (Aram Soba 5632/1872), R' Yeshayah thanks his brother for taking care of him.

He became a *dayan* (judge) in the *Bet Din* of Aram Soba and ultimately served as *Av Bet Din* together with the *dayanim* (judges) R' Shelomo Safdeyé (see #469) and R' Yitzhak Bekhor Mizrahi (see #432). He mentions the laws of divorce contracts in their name in his work *Imrei No'am*.

In 1852 he joined with his friend and *habruta* (study partner) R' Yaakob Dweck (see #248) to produce their first work, *Yaday Aseta Zot* [the word **ידי**, **Y**a**D**a**Y**, contains the initials of the two authors]. They explained that the reason for their book was to teach other students to write down *hiddushim* (original Torah thoughts), following the principle, *"Kinat sofrim tarbeh hochmah"* (competition among scribes increases knowledge). This publication was printed as an appendix to his book *Imrei No'am* (Aram Soba 5658/1898), which contains responsa on a variety of topics such as renting the city from the government for the purpose of an *eruv* to permit carrying on *Shabbat*. Some of his *hiddushim* were posthumously published by R' Yosef Shayo (see #507) in the anthology *MeHalab Ha'Aretz* (Jerusalem 5726/1966).

Another of his manuscripts, *Hazon Yeshayah*, has recently been published by R' Rahamim Shayo (Jerusalem 5758/1998).

In 1888 R' Yeshayah established a printing firm in Aram Soba, after waiting until the ban against competing presses had expired. (See Document Section, Document No. 25.) With the new press he produced dozens of holy books. In order to get it going, he brought in a professional printer from Jerusalem, R' Haim Pinehas Cohen. However, because of the difficulty in getting licensing, the publishing initiative was begun in secrecy without the blessing of the Turkish government. Accordingly, it was operated for a time on an intermittent basis because of the fear of discovery. For this reason, the name of the printer is missing from many of the books.

R' Yeshayah finally did receive official permission to open a press, subject to government regulations. R' Ezra Lofez (see #395) worked with him in developing books for printing.

In 1903 a terrible cholera epidemic broke out in Aram Soba, taking many victims, among whom was R' Yeshayah. In the Ben-Zvi Institute there is a manuscript describing the events of that time. It records that he passed away on 19 Elul, 5663 (1903).

After R' Yeshayah's death, his sons continued to operate the printing press until 1926. Altogether 27 books were printed by the Dayan Press (original editions). Of these, eight were Arabic translations from the Hebrew.

[204] **DAYAN, R' Yisrael**

רבי ישראל דיין

(— 1875)

Worthy scholar and rabbi of Damascus. He passed away in Damascus on 9 Av, 5635 (1875).

[205] **DAYAN, R' Yitzhak**

רבי יצחק דיין

(— 1870)

Worthy scholar of Aram Soba. He was a son of R' Yeshayah (see #202) and a brother of R' Abraham (see #173). He joined other rabbis of Aram Soba in signing the approbation to the printing initiative of R' Abraham Sasson in 1865 (see #475). (See Document Section, Document No. 25.) He passed away in 5630 (1870).

[206] **DAYAN, R' Yitzhak**

רבי יצחק דיין

(18th-19th century)

Worthy scholar and *dayan* (judge) of Aram Soba. At the Ben-Zvi Institute there is a handwritten document containing R' Yitzhak's signature as well as the signatures of R' Moshe ben Abraham HaLevi and R' Ezra Yeshuah Cohen, dated 29 Shevat, 5562 (1802) [file no. 302].

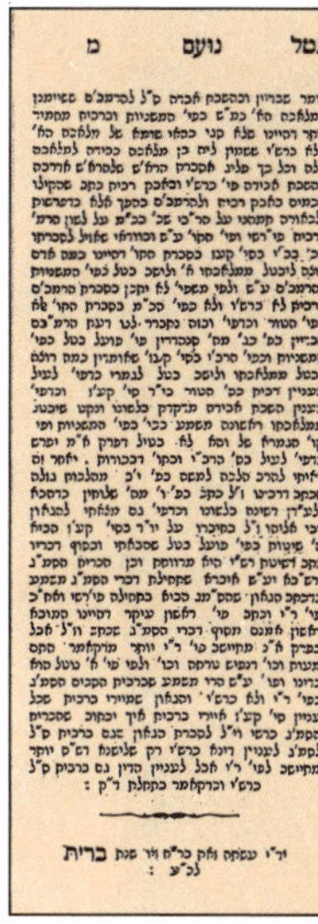

Title Page of Yaday Aseta Zot

[207] **DAYAN, R' Yitzhak**

רבי יצחק דיין

(— 1903)

Eminent scholar of Aram Soba. He was the chief *mohel* of Aram Soba and an expert scribe. He also had expertise in the printing arts. In time he came to Jerusalem and succeeded in publishing a number of holy books there, including a *Selihot* (5645/1885) according to the Syrian custom, with the *Viduy HaGadol*. He added a commentary and explanation to the *Selihot*. He also added *Hatarat Nedarim* (Release of Vows) according to the Syrian custom.

Title Page of Selichot Published by R' Yitzhak Dayan

Another of his achievements was to publish a *Shir HaShirim* with *Shareh* (Arabic translation). In it he describes the Syrian custom of going Friday night to the Cave of Eliyahu HaNabi and reciting *Shir HaShirim*. The congegation then learned *Mishnayot*, said *Kaddish*, and made pledges to pay for the oil for lighting the synagogue.

Upon his return to Aram Soba he continued with this initiative and worked to publish books in the printing establishment of his uncle, R' Yeshayah Dayan (see #203).

R' Yitzhak was a son of R' Moshe Dayan (see #191). He passed away on 18 Elul, 5663 (1903), leaving four sons: Moshe, Ezra, Yaakob, and Abraham. R' Abraham immigrated to Mexico City where he went into business. One of R' Abraham's sons, R' Haim, subsequently settled in Bnei Brak, where he devoted himself to Torah studies.

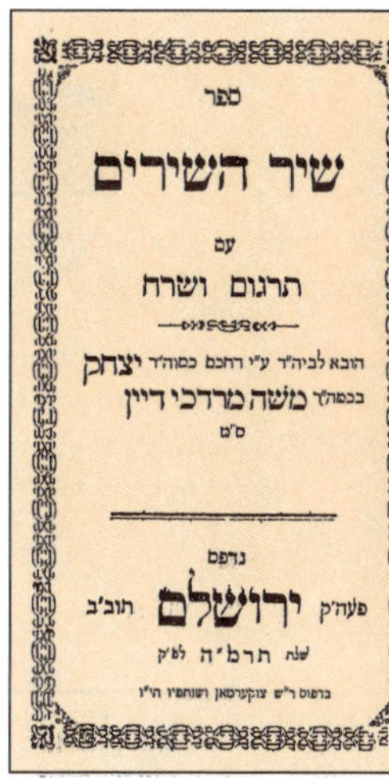

Title Page of Shir HaShirim with Arabic Translation

R' Yitzhak Dayan

[208] **DAYAN, R' Yitzhak**

רבי יצחק דיין

(1878 — 1964)

Distinguished scholar of Aram Soba. He was born in 1878, a son of R' Yeshayah Dayan (see #203), and earned his livelihood by working in his father's print shop.

R' Yitzhak was an expert in the treasures hidden within the Hebrew language, its grammar, its poetry, and its beauty of thought. He made a trip to New York in 1958, where he made a strong impression on R' Shaul Matloub Abadi (see #9). R' Abadi included one of R' Yitzhak's responsa, on the topic of shaving by mourners, in his book *Magen Ba'adi* (p. 66).

He made a trip to New York in 1958, where he made a strong impression on R' Shaul Matloub Abadi.

R' Yehudah Attiah (see #118) chose one of R' Yitzhak's essays to serve as the introduction to his book *Minhat Yehudah,* Vol. I (Aram Soba 5684/1924). The essay, *Torat Yisrael Ve'Am Yisrael*, discusses the bonds between the people of Yisrael and their holy Torah.

R' Yitzhak Dayan addressing a gathering in honor of Mr. I Shalom (# 497); R' Yaakob Ades (# 41) and Mr. I Shalom on the right. R' Ezra Attiah (# 101), R' Obadiah Hedaya (# 309), on the left.

R' Yitzhak passed away on *Shabbat*, 2 Kislev, 5725 (1964), while in Brazil. He was brought to Tel Aviv for burial.

[209] **DAYAN, R' Yosef**

רבי יוסף דיין

(— 1668)

Eminent scholar and *dayan* (judge) of Aram Soba. His father was R' Natan Dayan. According to family tradition, he was a member of the 78th generation of the House of David. He sat on the Aram Soba *Bet Din* together with R' Shelomo Laniado, the Elder (see #368). They both signed the approbation to the book *Hevel Bnai Yehudah* of R' Yehudah Habilio in 1695.

He was a member of the 78th generation of the House of David.

R' Yosef passed away in the terrible epidemic that struck Aram Soba in 1723, leaving one son, R' Mordechai Dayan. The same epidemic took R' Abraham Missry, R' Yosef Cohen together with his wife Simhola and daughter Sultana, R' Abraham Heifetz with his sister Sultana, R' Nissim Missry with his son R' Yaakob, R' Moshe Sutton, and two young men: Obadiah and Moshe Hamway. He was eulogized by R' Shemuel Laniado (the father of R' Raphael Shelomo Laniado, see #363), R' Moshe Harari (see #288), and R' Shemuel Dweck (see #243).

[210] **DAYAN, R' Yosef**

רבי יוסף דיין

(— 1757)

Eminent scholar and *dayan* (judge) of Aram Soba. According to family tradition, he was a member of the 80th generation of the House of David. He was a son of R' Mordechai Dayan (see #183). He signed together with other rabbis of Aram Soba on the *halachic* (legal) ruling against eating grape leaves because of worm infestation, as recorded in the book *Hanan Elokim* by R' Haim Abulafia. (See Document Section, Document No. 13.) He passed away on Monday, 6th day of *Hanukah*, 5518 (1757) and was survived by one son named R' Mordechai (#184).

[211] **DAYAN, R' Yosef**

רבי יוסף דיין

(— 1811)

Worthy scholar of Aram Soba. He passed away in 1811 and was eulogized by R' Yisrael Sasson (#297). In the eulogy, R' Yisrael also mentioned his worthy father-in-law R' Bekhor Abraham Amon.

[212] **DAYAN (HANONO) R' Rahamim**

רבי רחמים דיין (חנונו)

(— 1929)

Eminent scholar and rabbi of Aram Soba. He was a son of R' Abraham Dayan (see #174) and practiced *shehitah* together with his brother R' Yitzhak (see #213). R' Rahamim was the son-in-law of R' Yaakob Dweck (see #248). He passed away on 27 Shevat, 5689 (1929) and was survived by a son, R' Abraham.

On one of his visits to Jerusalem he met with the Kabbalist R' Moshe ibn Sasson, author of *Shemen Sasson*, and engaged in a challenging discussion on issues related to Kabbalah. At one point R' Rahamim was able to inform R' Moshe of certain thoughts of the *Ari'zal* (R' Yitzhak Luria) that he had not been aware of [that had been hidden from him]. R' Sasson was pleased and responded by quoting the verse, ועלמות אין מספר, *"and countless maidens"* (*Shir HaShirim* 6:8), which can be read as *"and countless hidden things."* In other words, R' Moshe was aware that many things were still hidden from him and he had much to learn.

In 1906, together with other scholars and rabbis of Aram Soba, he signed a *halachic* (legal) ruling directed against those who desecrate *Shabbat*. (See Document Section, Document No. 28.)

[213] DAYAN (HANONO), R' Yitzhak

רבי יצחק דיין (חנונו)

(— 1926)

Worthy scholar of Aram Soba. He was a son of R' Abraham Dayan (see #174) and practiced *shehitah* together with his brother R' Rahamim (see #212). In 1804 he left Aram Soba and settled in Cairo, where he became a teacher in the "Señor Sasson" Talmud Torah. He passed away in Cairo on 24 Iyar, 5686 (1926).

[214] DELLA ROSA, R' Rahamim

רבי רחמים דילה רוזה

(— 1890)

Worthy scholar and *darshan* (lecturer) of Aram Soba. He was known for his intense commitment to Torah study and for his effective lectures. He passed away on 16 Iyar, 5650 (1890).

[215] DILUBIN, R' Elisha

רבי אלישע דילובין

(— 1802)

Distinguished scholar and *dayan* (judge) of Aram Soba. He sat on the *Bet Din* together with R' Yehudah Kassin (see #331) and R' Raphael Shelomo Laniado (see #363). In 1763 he joined other rabbis of Aram Soba in signing the preface to the book *Beirach Yitzhak* of R' Yitzhak Berachah (see #129). He passed away in about 5562 (1802).

R' Abraham Dweck

[216] DWECK, R' Abraham

רבי אברהם דוויק הכהן

(— 1929)

Eminent scholar, *darshan* (lecturer), merchant, and civic leader of Aram Soba. His father was R' Yitzhak Dweck (see #250). He was the chairman of the board of the General Talmud Torah of Aram Soba, as well as the president of the Shevet Ahim organization. One of the objectives of the organization was to lend money at no interest to small business owners so that they could get through financial difficulties without becoming a burden on the community (similar to *Gemachs*, free loan funds of today).

He was the chairman of the board of the General Talmud Torah of Aram Soba, as well as the president of the Shevet Ahim organization.

Every *Shabbat* hundreds of people would gather to hear his lectures, which extended the entire afternoon until nightfall. R' Abraham earned his livelihood through his work as a bookkeeper/accountant and as a merchant. He passed away in Aram Soba on 6 Heshvan, 5690 (1929).

ספר
שבט מוסר
עצאית אלאדב
האדא אלמצחף מתרגם בלג׳ה אלערביה
האדא אלמצחף ידל עלא גמיע אלטראיק אלדי
ימשי בהם אלאנסאן לכי ינאל אלכיר פי האדי
אלדניא ויזכא לגן־עדן. מתל מא קאלו גאוני עולם.
ר׳ שאול הכהן דוויך נ״י
Rabbi Haim Saul Cohen Dwek for Yeshivat Rehovoth Hanahar
P.O.B. 285 — JERUSALEM (Palestine).
פעה״ק ירושלם תובב״א
שנת תרפ״ה לפ״ק
SHEBET MOUSSAR
ZION Printing — JERUSALEM

Title Page of Atzait al Adav (Arabic translation of Shevet Mussar)

He translated into Arabic the book *Shevet Mussar* of R' Eliyahu Cohen of Izmir and gave the resulting work the title *Atzait al Adav* (Jerusalem 5685/1925). This book was published through the efforts of the Kabbalist R' Haim Shaul Dweck (see #228).

His son Selim became the father of many respected community members, among them R' Isaac Dwek, Rabbi of the Deal, New Jersey Synagogue.

[217] DWECK, R' Abraham

רבי אברהם דוויק הכהן

(20th century)

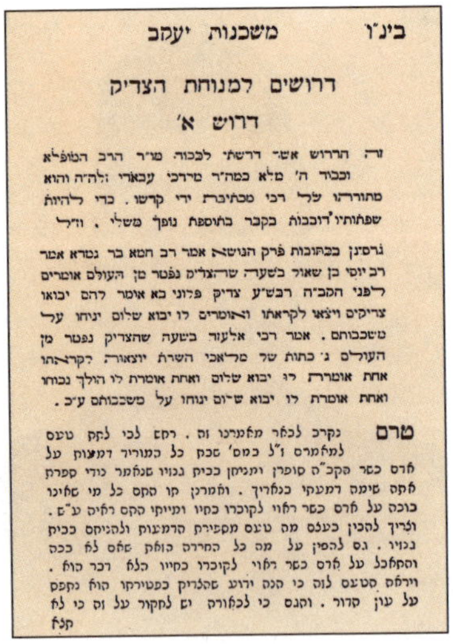

Title Page of Mishkenot Yaakob

Notable scholar of Aram Soba. He was a son of R' Yaakob Shaul Dweck (see #248) and was responsible for publishing his father's work *She'erit Yaakob* (Aram Soba 5685/1925). At the end of the book, R' Abraham added his own work entitled *Mishkenot Yaakob*, containing essays in honor of past sages. The first is in honor of R' Mordechai Abadi (see #8). R' Abraham was praised in the eulogy delivered by his brother-in-law, R' Moshe Dweck (Kassab) (see #256), at the funeral of R' Abraham's father, as recorded in *She'erit Yaakob*.

He was a strong proponent of studying Kabbalah, and was instrumental in forming the Etz Haim organization.

He was a strong proponent of studying Kabbalah, and was instrumental in forming the *Etz Haim* organization in 1919. Its objective was to provide financial support for students of Kabbalah and to promote the study of the works of the *Ari'zal* (R' Yitzhak Luria).

[218] DWECK, R' Abraham Gabriel

רבי אברהם גבריאל דוויק הכהן

(— 1874)

Eminent scholar and rabbi of Tiberias. He was born in Aram Soba, but in his younger years he moved to Tiberias, where he was raised in the house of R' Yehudah Nehmad (see #448). In 1833 he traveled to Morocco to obtain financial assistance for the Torah institutions of Tiberias. At that time such missions were undertaken only by the most eminent rabbis and scholars.

Title Page of Birchat Eliyahu

In his later years he lived in Peki'in (a town in Upper Galilee), but shortly before his death he had to move to Safed for health reasons. He passed away in Safed in 5634 (1874). He was survived by three sons, all rabbis: Haim Ezra, Mordechai, and Moshe Shelomo.

In 1836 his name appears as a signer of the approbation for *M'Ohr VaShemesh*, a book by R' Yehudah Koreit. Similarly, he signed the approbations for *Penei Yitzhak* by R' Yitzhak Abulafia (see #35) and *Ma'aseh Rokei'ach* by R' Masoud Hai Rokei'ach.

In 1857 he signed together with the rabbis of Tiberias on a matter relating to the yeshiva *Bet Yaakob*, which was founded by the philanthropist R' Yitzhak Gouiatta.

[219] DWECK, R' Aharon

רבי אהרן דוויק הכהן

(— 1884)

Worthy scholar and rabbi of Damascus. He passed away in Damascus on 2 Kislev, 5645 (1884).

[220] DWECK, R' Bekhor Haim Ezra

רבי בכור חיים עזרא דוויק הכהן

(— 1938)

Worthy scholar and rabbi of Tiberias. His father was R' Abraham Gabriel Dweck (see #218). His signature appears together with that of the rabbis of Tiberias on a publication of the yeshiva *Bet Yaakob*, which was sponsored by the philanthropist Yitzhak Gouiatta. He passed away in 1938.

[221] DWECK, R' David

רבי דוד דוויק הכהן

(18th century)

Worthy scholar of Aram Soba. His father was R' Shemuel Dweck (see #243). His name is found in a lecture delivered by his brother, R' Shimon Dweck, on the completion of the first year since the death of their mother, which was in 1726. This lecture was published in R' Shimon's book *Rei'ach Sadeh* in the chapter on *Perashat Ha'ye Sarah*.

[222] DWECK, R' Eliyahu

רבי אליהו דוויק הכהן

(— 1795)

Notable rabbi and *dayan* (judge) of Aram Soba. His father was R' Nissim Dweck (see #236). On his mother's side he was a grandson of R' Shemuel Pinto (see #462). He is especially known for his book of responsa and commentaries on the Torah, *Birchat Eliyahu* (Livorno 5553/1793). An earlier printing of the book in Constantinople (5545/1785) was an incomplete version.

He passed away in 1795 and was eulogized by R' Abraham Sutton (see #535), as recorded in the book *Malel Le'Abraham*. He was survived by four sons — Yeshuah, Raphael, Nissim, and Yisrael — whose names he mentioned in the introduction to his book, *Birchat Eliyahu*.

R' Eliyahu signed, together with the rabbis of Aram Soba, the approbation for *Mahane Yehudah* of R' Yehudah Kassin (see #331).

[223] DWECK, R' Eliyahu

רבי אליהו דוויק הכהן

(— 1903)

Worthy scholar and rabbi of Aram Soba. He was the son of R' Shaul Dweck (see #239) and father of the Kabbalist, R' Haim Shaul Dweck (see #228). R' Eliyahu was a signatory, together with the rabbis of Aram Soba, on the approbation for the Sasson printing initiative in 1865 (see #475). (See Document Section, Document No. 25.) He passed away in Jerusalem on 3 Shevat, 5663 (1903).

[224] DWECK, R' Eliyahu

רבי אליהו דוויק הכהן

(— 1949)

Kabbalist and *Rosh Yeshiva* of the yeshiva *Rehovot HaNahar* in Jerusalem. He was the only son of R' Haim Shaul Dweck (see #228). He learned the mysteries of Kabbalah from his father and came to know the hidden meanings of the prayers, essentially by heart.

After the passing of his father he served as head of *Rehovot HaNahar* for many years. He had an impressive library of holy books, which included the libraries of his father and his grandfather, R' Eliyahu Dweck (see #223). In his later years he endured severe and painful illnesses.

He passed away on 27 Adar, 5709 (1949). Owing to the war conditions at that time, he was laid to his rest in the temporary cemetery in the settlement of Givat Ram.

His son was R' Moshe Dweck (see #232), who wrote a book on his father's greatness.

[225] DWECK, R' Eliyahu

רבי אליהו דוויק הכהן

Worthy scholar of Aram Soba. His father, R' Yaakob (Shaul) Dweck (see #248), spoke of him in glowing terms in the introduction to his book *Derech Emunah*. Similarly, his brother, R' Abraham (see #217), mentioned him in the introduction to the book *She'erit Yaakob*. He died at a young age during his father's lifetime.

[226] DWECK, R' Ephraim

רבי אפרים דוויק הכהן

(— 1938)

Eminent scholar of Aram Soba. He was the only son of R' Yehudah Dweck (see #249). He was continually engaged in Torah study, but was dependent on his own efforts for his livelihood, which was in the sale of Judaica. At one point he attempted to settle in Jerusalem, but the problems of making a living at that time forced him to return to Aram Soba.

During the bloody events which occurred in *Eretz Yisrael* in the period 1936-1939, he was accosted by an inflamed Arabic mob, which was demonstrating against the Jews in Aram Soba. The frightening experience shook him up so badly that he died shortly thereafter, leaving behind young children. He passed away on 28 Heshvan, 5699 (1938).

R' Eliyahu Dweck

He published the following works (Aram Soba 5688/1928): *Viduy HaGadol* (the long confession said on *Yom Kippur* by the Syrian community), *Reshut LeBaruch She'amar*, and a liturgical poem *Al Mot Shenei Bnei Aharon* (which is read on *Yom Kippur*). (See #122 for earlier sources of *Viduy HaGadol*.)

[227] DWECK, R' Haim

רבי חיים דוויק הכהן

(— 1776)

Worthy scholar and rabbi of Tiberias. He joined other rabbis of Tiberias in signing the approbation to the book *Gedulat Mordechai* by R' Mordechai Galante (Section 16).

He is also mentioned in the book *Hasdei David* of R' David Pardo. He passed away in 5536 (1776).

[228] **DWECK, R' Haim Shaul**

רבי חיים שאול דוויק הכהן

(1857 — 1933)

R' Haim Shaul Dweck

Renowned Kabbalist and founder of the yeshiva *Rehovot HaNahar* of Jerusalem. He was born in Aram Soba in 1857 to R' Eliyahu Dweck (see #223). He was named after his grandfather, R' Shaul Dweck (see #239), author of *Emet Me'Eretz*.

Formative Years

In his youth he demonstrated an aptitude for intense Torah study. His primary teachers were R' Mordechai Abadi (see #8) and R' Ezra Tawil (see #582). However, he also began to delve into the mysteries of Kabbalah under the guidance of R' Eliyahu Mishan (see #418) and R' Nissim Harari-Raful (see #305).

He married Rachel, the daughter of R' Abraham Cohen, and his father-in-law was pleased to provide the financial support that enabled the young scholar to completely immerse himself in his studies. During these formative years he did not limit himself to the wisdom available in Aram Soba, but corresponded by mail with R' Bekhor Moshe Sasson, the senior rabbi of the Kabbalist yeshiva *Bet El* in Jerusalem. R' Dweck's extensive and wide-ranging knowledge of Kabbalah was considered phenomenonal. It extended to all the works of the *Ari'zal* (R' Yitzhak Luria), R' Haim Vital, and the *Rashash* (R' Shalom Sharabi).

In 1890, at the age of 32 R' Dweck was able to fulfill his fervent dream of moving to Jerusalem.

Joining Yeshiva Bet El

In 1890, at the age of 32 R' Dweck was able to fulfill his fervent dream of moving to Jerusalem by joining the great emigration of scholars from Aram Soba. Among the outstanding scholars in this group were R' Yomtob Yedid (see #593), R' Ezra Harari-Raful (see #304), R' Shaul Kassin (see #327), R' Yitzhak Shrem (see #517), and R' Abraham Ades (see #37). All of these scholars were drawn to the yeshiva *Bet El*, a place where they could dedicate themselves to spiritual growth in the company of fellow seekers.

Founding Yeshiva Rehovot HaNahar

In 1896, after six years of devoted study in *Bet El*, R' Dweck founded a new yeshiva in the Bukharan quarter of Jerusalem. This venture was made possible through the generosity of the wealthy philanthropist R' Nissim Nahum (see #437), who had recently arrived from Tripoli (Libya). At first, R' Nahum did not wish to be recognized. He put aside his expensive garments and spent a number of days studying in the *Bet Midrash* of the yeshiva *Bet El*. He approached various scholars asking for help but was turned down because his level of accomplishment was so minimal. However, R' Dweck had pity on him and befriended him, teaching him the basic concepts of Kabbalah over a six-month period.

In gratitude and love for the bond that had grown between them, R' Nahum offered to help R' Dweck achieve his ambition of establishing a new Kabbalist yeshiva, to be called *Rehovot HaNahar*.

His Loss of Sight

About 10 years after arriving in Jerusalem, his eyesight began to fail but no reliable treatment was available in *Eretz Yisrael* for his condition. His doctors urged him to travel to Vienna, where an appropriate operation had been perfected. However, R' Dweck refused to leave *Eretz Yisrael* even temporarily, so the operation was performed locally. Tragically, the operation failed and he lost his eyesight completely. According to one version of these events, R' Dweck was the victim of medical malpractice, committed intentionally by a Christian doctor affiliated with a missionary hospital.

Although he was unable to see for the last 30 years of his life, this did not prevent him from continuing with his studies and his lessons with students, which he did from memory. Because of the clarity of his mind he was able to continue authoring holy books, dictating the text to one of his students who would write it out, word for word. Among the students who sat with him for this holy work were R' A. Ma'arabi, R' Yaakob Mounsa (see #435), and R' Suleiman Eliyahu (author of the book *Kerem Eliyahu*).

However, his inability to learn new material caused him much anguish. Whenever there was spare time between classes he would ask anyone he could find — even a younger student — to read to him. As the years went by he became more and more desperate to learn. On occasion he would even stand at the door listening for the sound of a passerby to persuade the person, whoever it might be, to read to him.

Visit of the Munkacs Rabbi

In 1930 the venerable rabbi of the Munkacs *Hasidim*, R' Haim Elazar Shapira, visited R' Dweck at his home in the Bukharan district. The two sages treated each other with great respect and courtesy. The Munkacs Rabbi was highly impressed by the austere piety of R' Dweck and memorialized him in his classic book *Minhat Elazar*.

His Piety

R' Dweck's piety and devotion were evident to anyone who watched him pray, especially when he led the *tefillot* as the *hazzan* (cantor). During the repetition of the *Amidah* prayer, he would hold onto each individual word and pronounce it with utmost intensity. R' Abraham Harari- Raful (see #302), a student of R' Dweck, described the scene in the *Bet Midrash* of the yeshiva *Rehovot HaNahar* during the High Holy Days prayers. Surrounded by all the *hachamim* dressed in white, he felt as though he were in Paradise amid the ministering angels. As R' Dweck uttered the blessing "Who restores His Divine Presence to Sion *(HaMahazir Shehinato LeSion),*" he would weep with such feeling that streams of tears would flow down his cheeks. The floor on which he stood would actually become wet from his tears. On one occasion the emotional intensity of this prayer caused him to completely collapse and fall down.

Every Friday afternoon, R' Dweck would lead a procession of *hachamim*, all dressed in white, out to the fields surrounding his neighborhood. The holy assemblage would welcome the *Shabbat* Queen. At their head R' Dweck would joyfully sing the *Shabbat* hymn, *"Come, My Beloved (Lechah Dodi)."* Everyone who witnessed this sight was overwhelmed by the sense of holiness.

R' Dweck had a favorite phrase, which he repeated frequently throughout the day: *"Ein Od Milvado"* (There is none besides Him) (*Debarim* 4:35). One of his students, R' Yisrael Yitzhak Reisman, testified that R' Dweck was so spiritually elevated that even in his sleep, his lips would utter those words, *"Ein Od Milvado."*

R' Dweck had a favorite phrase, which he repeated frequently throughout the day: "Ein Od Milvado" (There is none besides Him). Even in his sleep, his lips would utter those words, "Ein Od Milvado."

As a *Kohen*, R' Dweck was unable to go to cemeteries to pray at the graves of the holy rabbis of previous generations. However, in those cases where a great sage was not buried in a cemetery, he followed the opinion that permits a *Kohen* to go to it. In such cases he prostrated himself upon the grave and focused his mind on all the relevant *kavanot* (meditations) prescribed by the *Ari'zal*.

His Meticulous Observance of Mitzvot

R' Dweck took great care in ensuring that his every action was consistent with both the *halachah* and the principles of Kabbalah. He put on two sets of *tefillin* simultaneously to satisfy the two major interpretations of how *tefillin* should be made, *Rashi* and *Rabbeinu Tam*. Both were constructed with meticulous attention to every detail, as specified by the *Ari'zal*. He was also concerned that the Scriptural passages contained in the *tefillin* be written by a fully qualified scribe who would keep in mind the *kavanot* (meditations) prescribed by the *Rashash*. In searching for a capable scribe, fully versed in every detail of the *halachic* requirements and with the proper background in Kabbalah, he was able to find only one elderly Yemenite scholar. Sadly, this individual suffered from paralysis and was

As R' Dweck uttered the blessing "Who restores His Divine Presence to Sion," he would weep with such feeling that streams of tears would flow down his cheeks.

Surrounded by all the hachamim dressed in white, he felt as though he were in Paradise amid the ministering angels.

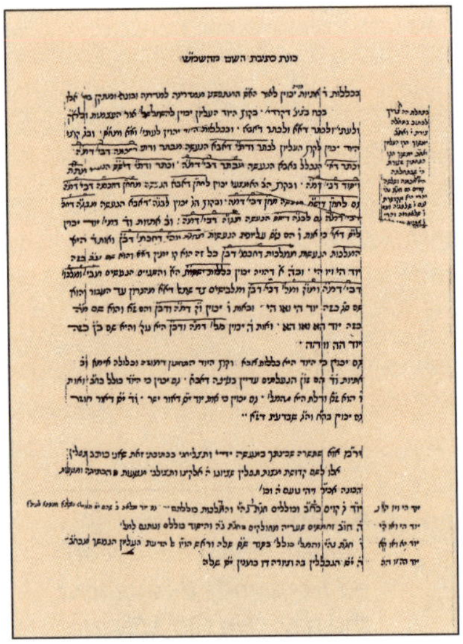

Directions for making tefillin given by R' Dweck to his personal scribe

able to move his hand only with great difficulty. Furthermore, in order to extend the scribe's knowledge to every last particular of the *mitzvah*, R' Dweck sat with him for many hours to instruct him in the *kavanot* of writing the passages and in constructing the boxes.

At the end, the scribe summarized all of this knowledge in a document which he wrote in accordance with the *kavanot* of the *Rashash*. The document was then enhanced by the comments and glosses of R' Dweck. After satisfying himself with the planning and instructional part of the process, R' Dweck gave his permission for the *tefillin* to be made. However, before beginning the work, the scribe was immersed in a *mikveh* (ritual bath) to ensure that the work be done in a state of purity. Because of his disability this required the assistance of a few strong men who gently lowered him into the *mikveh*.

Before beginning the work, the scribe was immersed in a mikveh (ritual bath) to ensure that the work be done in a state of purity.

The instructional document written by the scribe under R' Dweck's direction was ultimately used by the *Kaf HaHaim*, R' Yaakob Haim Sofer (see #532), as the underlying text for the book *Kol Yaakob*, a definitive text on the the laws of *tefillin, mezuzot*, and *Sifrei Torah*.

R' Dweck had a total grasp of the kavanot of the Rashash, not as unrelated details, but as a comprehensive whole.

The meticulous observance of *mitzvot* was a characteristic of R' Dweck's entire household. His worthy and righteous wife, the *Rabbanit*, supported her husband in all aspects of his sacred service, by day and by night. Since the family followed the Sephardic custom of eating rice on *Pesah*, she had a habit of carefully checking the rice for wheat kernels. She started doing this immediately after *Sukkot* and continued checking it over and over again whenever she had a few spare moments throughout all of the months until *Pesah*.

His Musical Ability

R' Dweck and his colleague R' Shaul Kassin (see #327) were known for their technical virtuosity in the vocal arts. They were blessed with unusually sweet voices combined with masterful control. Thus, they were able to prolong each word of the *tefillah* in order to have time to concentrate on the lengthy *kavanot* for each word, while simultaneously imbuing it with meaning and beautiful sound, and not becoming short of breath.

His Learning

Despite his blindness, R' Dweck forgot nothing of the Torah that he had learned and the words of the *Ari'zal* and the *Rashash* were engraved upon his mind in all of their detail. Thus, he was able to articulate all of the words of the prayers by heart accompanied with all of the elaborate *kavanot* specified in the *siddur* of the *Rashash*. This caused wonderment among those who observed him, especially those who understood the almost unbelievable complexity and depth of the *kavanot*. His student, R' Suleiman Moussafi, once asked him how he was able to do this. In answer, R' Dweck pointed to a window and asked, "What is this?" R' Moussafi answered, "It is a window." R' Dweck then remarked, "Have you ever thought how many hundreds of details it is composed of, and yet you say it is a window! So it is that when a person recognizes something as a whole, he simultaneously has a sense of all the parts that make it up." So it was that R' Dweck had a total grasp of the *kavanot* of the *Rashash*, not as unrelated details, but as a comprehensive whole, whose elements were clearly related to one another and to the whole concept of *tefillah*.

Although he practiced deep humility, R' Dweck could get fiery when it came to defending or asserting the truth of the Torah on any point of *halachah* or principle. The Kabbalist R' Suleiman Moussafi once went into the small *shul* next door to his home and saw him sitting alone by himself deeply immersed in learning. On the other side of the room he saw R' Dweck's only son, R' Eliyahu (see #224), who was also a great scholar, deeply engrossed in his own learning. R' Suleiman respectfully approached R' Eliyahu and asked why he was not studying together with his father. He answered, "He is a burning flame and I am a burning flame, so we cannot study together."

"He is a burning flame and I am a burning flame, so we cannot study together."

His Teachings

R' Dweck was successful in helping young students master the *kavanot* required by the Kabbalist approach to prayer. He advised the novice not to attempt to grasp everything at once but to focus on one part of the *tefillot* at a time. The student should not feel inadequate about not having mastered everything. If he has patience he will build up his ability over time. R' Suleiman Musafi, a student of R' Dweck, related that despite having heard this advice he attempted all the *kavanot* from the beginning and after a few weeks of the demanding regimen he weakened and became ill.

His approach to the study of Kabbalah was penetrating and original. He was not afraid to interpret the teachings of the *Ari'zal* and the *Rashash* in new and revolutionary ways. This caused some turmoil among those scholars who failed to grasp his thinking and who were concerned that he was overturning accepted wisdom. One such issue had to do with the proper *kavanot* in the *Amidah* prayer, during the *Shemittah* (Sabbatical) year. Just before the *Rashash* passed away in 1777 (which was during a *Shemittah* year), he had issued a new ruling which differed from the position he had taken in the previous *Shemittah* years. In the following *Shemittah* year, many scholars preferred to revert to the earlier position of the *Rashash*. Others found a compromise between the two positions and this compromise became generally accepted. It was followed by most Kabbalists, including those in the yeshiva *Bet El*, until R' Dweck came along and issued a new ruling, adopting the final position of the *Rashash*, without compromise. This aroused some resistance since it changed a practice that had been in force for close to 200 years. In fact, it was one of the reasons for his departure from *Bet El* and his starting a new yeshiva of his own. That was in 1896, which was also a *Shemittah* year, and enabled him to practice the interpretation that he had taught.

R' Dweck's independent approach led to a fierce challenge which threatened to hold up the printing of his major work, *Eifah Sheleimah*. One day, two scholars who were opponents of R' Dweck approached R' Nissim Nahum, who was managing the publishing process, and strongly criticized R' Dweck and his teachings. They told R' Nahum that R' Dweck had no authority to overthrow the teachings of those who had gone before him and that it would be a sin to print the new book. These remarks shook up R' Nahum and he became distraught and confused. He reacted by drastically slowing down the production process. Since R' Dweck knew nothing about this he was surprised and disturbed by the unexplained delay. Finally, R' Nahum decided to send samples of the manuscript to two respected Kabbalists in the *Galut* (diaspora), the *Darkei Teshuvah* (R' Hirsh Shapiro of Munkacs) and the *Leshem Sh'vo Ve'Ahlamah* (R' Shlomo Elyashiv). These two luminaries immediately recognized the worthiness of the work and sent back their enthusiastic approbations, filled with glowing words of praise for the author and his work. As soon as the approbations reached Jerusalem, R' Nahum immediately regained his courage and resumed the production process, thereby pleasing R' Dweck who never did get an explanation for the delay.

Printing the Siddur of the Rashash

The yeshiva *Rehovot HaNahar* was organized around the approach to *tefillah* established by the *Rashash* and documented in his classic *siddur*. Although the *siddur* of the *Rashash* had been in use for over a hundred years the full descriptions of the *kavanot* existed only in manuscript form. Someone who wished to study them would need to make his own copy or hire a scribe to make one for him at great expense. This naturally led to mistakes and there were many versions of the *siddur* as a result of the varying capabilities of the copyists, many of whom were not proficient in Kabbalah.

R' Dweck had in his possession authentic copies of the *siddur*, copied by his teachers R' Eliyahu Mishan (see #418) and R' Nissim Harari-Raful (see #305). He was also in possession of original manuscripts,

R' Dweck's independent approach led to a fierce challenge which threatened to hold up printing of his major work, Eifah Sheleimah.

He advised the novice not to attempt to grasp everything at once but to focus on one part of the tefillot at a time. The student should not feel inadequate about not having mastered everything.

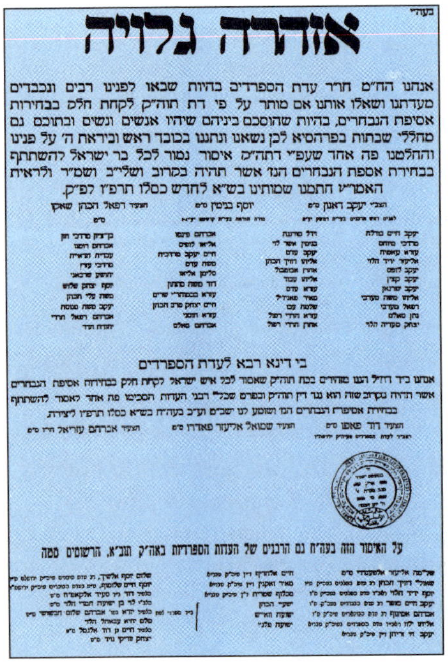

בעז"י

אזהרה גלויה

אנחנו הח"מ חר"ר עדת הספרדים בהיות שבאו לפנינו רבים ונכבדים מעדתנו ושאלו אותנו אם מותר על פי דת תוה"ק לקחת חלק בבחירות אסיפת הנבחרים, בהיות שהוסכם ביניהם שיהיו אנשים ונשים ובתוכם גם מחללי שבתות בפרהסיא לכן נשאנו ונתננו בכובד ראש וביראת ה' על פנינו והחלטנו פה אחד שעפ"י דתה"ק איסור גמור לכל בר ישראל להשתתף בבחירת אספת הנבחרים הנז אשר תהיה בקרוב ושלי"ב ושמ"ר ולראית האמו"ץ חתמנו שמותינו בש"א לחדש כסלו תרפ"ז לפ"ק.

Proclamation against association with political parties (See Document Section, Document No. 24)

written by the personal scribe of the *Rashash* himself, R' Yosef Deri. In addition, he had obtained other authentic manuscripts from the scholars of the yeshiva *Bet El*. With all of this material, R' Dweck felt that he had a sacred mission to see to the printing of an authentic version of the *siddur*. This he set about doing, with the help of R' Reuben Haz and scholars of the Kabbalist yeshiva *Shaar HaShamayim*. In 1911 he managed to produce the first volume of the new *siddur* covering the *tefillot* from the *Birkot HaShahar* until *Baruch She'amar*. It included R' Dweck's own commentary, which he called *Hesed Ve'Emet*.

However, after the first volume was published, R' Dweck withdrew from the project and refused to have any further part in publishing this material. He objected to the fact that the printers were using metal plates for typesetting, a method which enabled them to produce the book in unlimited quantities. Despite R' Dweck's natural inclination to disseminate Torah knowledge and to make it accessible to Jews all over the world, he was convinced that it was very wrong to mass-produce a mystical work of the Kabbalah. He was afraid that copies of such a book might come into the possession of unworthy people. Such people, who were not trained in Kabbalah, might treat the sacred text with its many renditions of the ineffable Name of *Hashem* with disrespect.

Despite R' Dweck's natural inclination to disseminate Torah knowledge and to make it accessible to Jews all over the world, he was convinced that it was very wrong to mass-produce a mystical work of the Kabbalah.

He preferred that a more restricted, paper-based method of reproduction be used, with a sharply limited pressrun, for the benefit of only those few Kabbalists who would actually practice the *kavanot* in their devotions. However, after R' Dweck withdrew from the project, the publishers decided to proceed without his cooperation and they published the entire work in nine volumes, with footnotes and commentaries by R' Yomtob Yedid (see #593) and his son R' Eliezer Yedid (see #590).

R' Dweck was extremely sensitive to any re-

Social Issues

duction in the standards of Jewish society, especially in the relationships between men and women. He was always among the first to join the other rabbis of his time in condemning such practices as the lack of a proper partition between men and women at weddings and immodest dress among women. (See Document Section, Document No. 19, for the text of such a proclamation.)

In fact, it was reported that the primary factor motivating him to leave Aram Soba for Jerusalem was his displeasure at the fall-off in traditional standards. When many women took advantage of a lenient ruling by one rabbi and started to allow some of their hair to show from under their kerchiefs, R' Dweck spoke out strongly against the practice. In fact, he threatened to leave Aram Soba if it was not stopped. Ultimately he did leave, causing great concern, and urgent appeals to return. In fact, shortly after he left, a great fire broke out and it was attributed to the deterioration in modesty. However, his mind was made up and he refused to return.

It was reported that the primary factor motivating him to leave Aram Soba for Jerusalem was his displeasure at the falloff in traditional standards.

In 1920, R' Dweck signed a proclamation against shaving with a razor. The announcement noted that while shaving with a depilatory is permitted by the *halachah* [electric shavers had not yet been invented], the pious people who follow the way of the *Zohar* and the *Ari'zal* avoid reducing their beard in any way.

R' Dweck also objected to participation in political events organized by the Zionists because of the involvement of women and irreligious Jews. (See Document Section, Document No. 24.) In 1926 he signed a proclamation against association with political parties and warning against being drawn into the schemes of the Zionists. The proclamation compared the situation to the capturing of an elephant, whereby two hunting teams stage a mock combat. One of the teams pretends to attack the elephant and the other pretends to defend it, thereby earning its trust. When the elephant, trusting its defender, lets down its guard, the defending team suddenly becomes the aggressor and takes the elephant into captivity.

He was also sensitive to the anguish of Jewish communities in lands such as Russia and Yemen where Jews were subject to violent attacks and pogroms. In 1932 he signed a proclamation which announced that 72 Kabbalah scholars would fast and pray for three consecutive days (72 hours) while the rest of the community would give money to rescue funds and other charities. In the merit of these actions, *Hashem* would take pity and allow His attribute of *"hesed"* (lovingkindness) to overcome His attribute of *"din"* (justice). The number 72 was emphasized because the *gematria* (numerical value) of the letters in the word *"hesed"* is 72.

His Healing Powers

The house of R' Dweck was a refuge for people suffering from grief and illness. Learned scholars and ordinary people, all came to him for help and healing. It was well known in Jerusalem that his prayers and his blessings were never rejected. However, he made a point of not using any amulets or charms. In this he followed the view of the *Ari'zal* who strongly opposed making practical use of Kabbalah. One time, though, as he was descending the stairs of the synagogue, he inadvertently stepped on a small child who was sitting at his feet. The child became very ill, causing great anguish to the rabbi. In this one instance he wrote an amulet and prayed tearfully to *Hashem* until the child recovered.

His Final Years

During the last few years of his life, R' Dweck moved his residence from the Bukharan district to the Mahane Yehudah district of Jerusalem and taught his classes there in the *"Zechut Aharon"* Silvera *Bet Midrash*. As a *Kohen*, R' Dweck was often called to perform the *mitzvah* of *Pidyon Haben* (redemption of the firstborn). He always put the silver coins, which he received from the father of the child, into a box that was dedicated for this purpose. As he lay on his deathbed he asked that the contents of this box be used to purchase his gravesite. Because he knew the Dweck family lineage of *Kohanim* was untainted, he was confident that the money was justly acquired and that it would therefore be appropriate for his final resting place.

He passed away on 4 Tevet, 5693 (1933) and was laid to rest on the Mount of Olives in Jerusalem. However, the location of his grave became lost as a result of the destruction of graves by marauders in 1943.

Shortly before his death, the financial condition of R' Dweck's household had become so bad that there was no money to buy the food needed for *Shabbat*. When asked what could be done, R' Dweck replied simply, *"Ein Od Milvado."* As it happened, the Munkacs Rabbi had chosen that week, which was the week of *Hanukkah*, to send R' Dweck a money order for 500 gold crowns and it arrived on Friday, in time to make the necessary purchases for *Shabbat*.

That Friday, as the Munkacs Rabbi began to kindle the *Hanukah* lights, he found no problem with the first seven lights. But when he lit the eighth light, it immediately went out. He tried again and it went out again. It was only after repeated attempts that he managed to get it to stay lit. However, later that night during the *Shabbat* meal, all the lights on the *menorah* went out. It was at that point that the Munkacs Rabbi said to his assistant, "I wonder how the holy R' Haim Shaul Dweck is faring in Jerusalem." On Tuesday, three days later, R' Dweck passed away.

His Legacy

He trained many students, both Sephardim and Ashkenazim, in the knowledge of Kabbalah and in the elaborate *kavonot* taught by the *Rashash* (R' Shalom Sharabi) and the *Ari'zal* (R' Yitzhak Luria). He also authored many books, among which are the following:

- *Eifah Sheleimah* (Jerusalem 5667/1907), a commentary on R' Haim Vital's Kabbalist book *Otzrot Haim*. This book, which is considered his most important legacy to future generations, was written after he lost

He was also sensitive to the anguish of Jewish communities in lands such as Russia and Yemen where Jews were subject to violent attacks and pogroms.

When asked what could be done, R' Dweck replied simply, "Ein Od Milbado."

The house of R' Dweck was a refuge for people suffering from grief and illness.

He always put the silver coins, which he received from the father of the child, into a box that was dedicated for this purpose.

ספר

אוצרות חיים

נדפס

פעה"ק ירושלם תובב"א

Title Page of
Eifah Sheleimah

ספר

כונות פרטיות

נדפס

פעה"ק ירושלם תובב"א

שנת תרע"א לפ"ק

Title Page of
Kavanot Peratiot

ספר

שר שלום

נדפס

פעה"ק ירושלם תובב"א

שנת תרע"ב לפ"ק

Title Page of
Sar Shalom

his sight. He created it by dictating the text to his students R' Yehudah Fetaya and R' Yaakob Haim Sofer (see #532). They sat with him many hours of the day over the course of a year, painstakingly writing out the words as he spoke them. R' Nissim Nahum, the co-founder and administrator of *Rehovot HaNahar,* took an active role in expediting the production process. Each day he carried the proof pages from the printer to R' Dweck and carried the corrections back to the printer. Through this process, R' Dweck kept up the pressure on all members of the production team, ensuring that no time was lost in getting the pages checked and resolving any questions. However, the process was almost stopped by a controversy about the content (see "His Teachings," above).

- *Benayahu ben Yehoyada* (Vol. I, 2, Jerusalem 5671/1911). Guide to various spiritual devotions such as *Tikkun Hatzot*. Co-authored with R' Eliyahu Yaakob Lejimi.
- *Kavanot Peratiot* (Jerusalem 5671/1911). Comments on the teachings of the *Rashash* (R' Shalom Sharabi), addressing the appropriate meditations while performing certain *mitzvot*. Co-authored with R' Eliyahu Yaakob Lejimi.
- Commentary on the book *Alei Nahar* of R' Nissim Harari-Raful (see #305) (Jerusalem 5663/1903 and 5736/1976).
- Commentary on the book *Sefat Emet* of R' Eliyahu Mishan (see #418) (Jerusalem 5664/1904 and 5736/1976).
- *Sar Shalom* (Jerusalem 5672/1912). Guide to the appropriate *kavonot* while performing certain time-related *mitzvot*, such as at the *Pesah Seder*.
- Glosses on the book *Ohr HaLevanah* of R' Yaakob Kassin (see #330) (Jerusalem 5686/1926).
- *Shaare Rahamim* (Jerusalem (5688/1928). Various *hiddushim* (original Torah thoughts).
- *Saakat Benei Yisrael* (Many editions). A call for *Tikkun HaBrit* (holiness in areas of immorality), accompanied with *Selihot* (penitential prayers) and stories of the *Ari'zal* in Hebrew and Arabic. It also includes a proclamation against shaving with a razor, signed by many rabbis, including R' Dweck, R' Abraham Ades (see #37), and R' Yosef Yedid (see #594). The 1920 edition was funded by the *Agudat Ahim* synagogue of the Brooklyn Syrian community.

He issued many approbations on books that were published during his lifetime, including many which were authored by Ashkenazi scholars of Kabbalah in Jerusalem.

[229] **DWECK, R' Meir**

רבי מאיר דוויק הכהן

(— 1838)

Worthy scholar and rabbi of Damascus. He passed away in 1838.

[230] **DWECK, R' Menahem**

רבי מנחם דוויק הכהן

(1690 — 1728)

Eminent scholar of Aram Soba. He was the son of R' Shemuel Dweck and brother of R' Shimon Dweck (see #246), author of *Rei'ach Sadeh*. R' Menahem partnered with his brother, R' Shimon, in writing the first part of the book, called *Zeman HaGet — Shevet Ahim*, which consisted of *halachic* (legal) rulings related to divorces. He passed away in 5488 (1728) at the young age of 38, while he was in Izmir, Turkey, during his father's lifetime.

[231] **DWECK, R' Mordechai**

רבי מרדכי דוויק הכהן

(— 1878)

Worthy scholar and *dayan* (judge) of Damascus. His father was R' Abraham Gabriel Dweck (see #218). In 1857 he signed a document together with the rabbis of Tiberias, relating to the renewal of the yeshiva *Bet Yaakob* by the philanthropist, R' Yitzhak Gouiatta. He passed away on 8 Shevat, 5638 (1878) at a young age, only four years after the death of his father.

[232] **DWECK, R' Moshe**

רבי משה דוויק הכהן

(20th century)

Born in Jerusalem. He was a grandson of R' Haim Shaul Dweck (see #228), the head of the Kabbalist yeshiva *Rehovot HaNahar*. He authored the book *Eder HaYikar* (Jerusalem 5709/1949) consisting of a eulogy and biography of his father R' Eliyahu Dweck (see #224).

[233] **DWECK, R' Moshe**

רבי משה דוויק הכהן

(— 1819)

Eminent *dayan* (judge) of Aram Soba. He served in the *Bet Din* of Aram Soba together with R' David Shelomo Sutton and R' Eliyahu Shamah (see #499), who was the Chief Rabbi of the city. At the Ben-Zvi Institute there is an original *halachic* (legal) ruling (file no. 302) with all three signatures, dated 1807.

After the death of R' Abraham Sutton (see #536) in 1816 there was a disagreement among the scholars and rabbis of Aram Soba as to who should be appointed in his place. Finally, when R' Moshe Anhouri arrived in Aram Soba four years later (see #58), it was decided to appoint them both together. However, R' Dweck passed away in the month of Tevet, 5580 (1819) during a cholera epidemic.

One of his responsa is included in the book *Vayikra Yitzhak* of R' Yitzhak Attiah (see #120).

[234] **DWECK, R' Moshe**

רבי משה דוויק הכהן

(— 1875)

Worthy scholar and cantor of Aram Soba. He was the oldest son of R' Shaul Dweck (see #239). R' Moshe passed away at a young age on 17 Av, 5635 (1875) only one year after the death of his father.

[235] **DWECK, R' Moshe**

רבי משה דוויק הכהן

(— 1911)

Worthy scholar and medical practitioner of Aram Soba. He was an expert in the medical arts and treated people at no charge. R' Moshe was the oldest son of R' Yaakob Dweck (see #248). He was a son-in-law of R' Meir Laniado and a grandson on his mother's side of R' Moshe Swed (see #575), after whom he was named.

His father mentions him in his book *Derech Emunah* (p. 63, Jerusalem edition), quoting his explanations of two verses in *Tanach*.

He passed away at a young age on 26 Tamuz, 5671 (1911), during his father's lifetime. His father talks about the tragic loss in *Derech Emunah*. R' Yitzhak Alfia (see #46) reports in his book *Kuntras HaYiche'eli* that at the funeral in the Great Synagogue of Aram Soba the mourners engaged in two hours of singing hymns of praise to *Hashem* before the start of the eulogies. This was done in keeping with the old Aram Soba custom of invoking merit for the deceased through the singing of tuneful songs, which has the power of suppressing evil forces and negative spirits. To this day, some of the more recent immigrants from Syria follow this custom at a funeral.

At the funeral in the Great Synagogue of Aram Soba the mourners engaged in two hours of singing hymns of praise to Hashem before the start of the eulogies.

[236] **DWECK, R' Nissim**

רבי נסים דוויק הכהן

(18th century)

Worthy scholar and Kabbalist of Aram Soba. He was a son of the distinguished *dayan* (judge) R' Shemuel Dweck (see #242). His son, R' Eliyahu Dweck (see #222), speaks highly of him in the introduction to his book, *Birchat Eliyahu*.

[237] **DWECK, R' Raphael**

רבי רפאל דוויק הכהן

Worthy scholar of Aram Soba. At the Ben-Zvi Institute there is an original document dated Kislev 5608 (1847), which is the "Will of the venerable Rabbi Raphael Dweck."

אֶדֶ"ר הַיְקָר

[רבי אליהו דוויק]

אדר היקר אשר יקרתי מעליהם (זכריה יא, יג)

מי יתנני כירחי קדם, אזכרנו ואהמיה. בהלו נרו עלי ראשי...

פה בן... אשר יצק מים על ידי אליהו! (מלכים ב, ג')

Title Page of Eder HaYikar

[238] DWECK, R' (Raphael) Abraham

רבי (רפאל) אברהם דוויק הכהן

(— 1776)

ספר
אמת מאר"ץ
נדפס
פעה"ק ירושלם תובב"א
Saül Cohen Dwek. Rabbi
Rehobot Boucharlim
Jerusalem (Palästina)

Title Page of Emet Me'Eretz

Eminent scholar and *dayan* (judge) of Safed. It is believed that the name Raphael was added at some point as a result of a life-threatening illness. He was the son of R' Shemuel Dweck (see #243).

He settled in Safed, where he became one of the *dayanim* (judges) of the city. He passed away in Tiberias on 18 Tevet, 5536 (1776).

R' Dweck is mentioned in the responsa section (p. 62) *of Rei'ach Sadeh* by his brother, R' Shimon Dweck (see #246). He is also mentioned in the same book, in the chapter dealing with *Perashat Ha'ye Sarah* (p. 7b).

In the book *Gedulat Mordechai* by R' Mordechai Galante (p. 149) the signature of a R' Raphael Abraham Dweck appears together with those of the rabbis of Tiberias. A number of responsa from the same R' Raphael Abraham Dweck appear in the book *Bet Dino shel Shelomo* by R' Raphael Shelomo Laniado (see #363) and in the book *Bigdei Yesha* by R' Yeshayah Attiah (see #119).

His name appears in 1758 among the signatories to *Bet Din shel Shelomo* (*Hoshen Mishpat*, Section 18) in Safed. Also signing there were the *dayanim* R' Masoud Bonan and R' Shelomo Saba.

> *He contributed to Torah education in many ways, including a regular Tehillim haburah (learning group).*

[239] DWECK, R' Shaul

רבי שאול דוויק הכהן

(— 1874)

Eminent scholar, *dayan* (judge), and philanthropist of Aram Soba. His father was R' Ezra Dweck (see #254). Besides being a productive scholar, he was a wealthy man of great influence. He contributed to Torah education in many ways, including a regular *Tehillim haburah* (learning group), which he personally conducted. For four to five hours every *Shabbat* afternoon, a large group of boys would assemble in the *Bet Midrash* and recite the entire *Tehillim* in unison. After the session they would pray *Minhah* and then have *Seudat Shelishit* (third meal of *Shabbat*) in the *Bet Midrash*.

He was a student of R' Abraham Antebi (see #63) and a brother of R' Abraham Dweck-Khalousi (see #257), the Chief Rabbi of Aram Soba.

He had five sons, all of whom became worthy scholars: R' Shemuel (see #245), R' Yosef (see #252), R' Eliyahu (see #223), R' Shelomo, and R' Moshe (see #23).

He wrote a number of scholarly works, including *Emet Me'Eretz* (Jerusalem 5670/1910), which was posthumously published by his grandson, R' Haim Shaul Dweck (see #228). This is a book of responsa on a variety of topics such as the tax levy in the town of Ein Tab and a dispute between the town of Antioch and the Chief Rabbi. In his grandson's introduction, he mentions many other works of his grandfather, which he had seen in his youth in the possession of his uncle R' Shaul Yosef Dweck. These included responsa and commentaries on *Gemara, Shulhan Aruch*, and *HaRe'em* (R' Eliyahu Mizrahi). Sadly, none of these works survived. He also wrote approbations for *Hadar Ezer* of R' Yitzhak Shrem (see #517) and *Ben Yair* of R' Haim Mordechai Labaton (see #336).

He passed away on 4 Shevat, 5634 (1874).

> *R' Shaul and his wife Kamar recognized the special qualities of their youngest son Yaakob and spared no expense in getting him the best teachers.*

[240] DWECK, R' Shaul

רבי שאול דוויק הכהן

(19th century)

Worthy scholar of Aram Soba. He was the father of R' Yaakob Dweck (see #248), the future Chief Rabbi and *Av Bet Din* (Chief Judge). R' Shaul was an unusually humble and pious man, who was blessed with five scholarly sons: R' Yitzhak, R' Nissim, R' Raphael, R' Shabbetai, and R' Yaakob. R' Shaul and his wife Kamar recognized the special qualities of their youngest son Yaakob and spared no expense in getting him the best teachers, even while he was still very young. Kamar had an extensive knowledge of *Tanach* and *Gemara*, which enabled her to give all of her children the best possible preparation for life.

[241] DWECK, R' Shehidyah

רבי שחידיה דוויק הכהן

(19th century)

Worthy scholar of Aram Soba. His name appears in the list of Aram Soba scholars receiving a weekly stipend from the special fund that had been set up for the support of worthy individuals who dedicate their lives to Torah study. (For more information on the fund, see R' Yaakob Gindi-Daknish, #267.)

[242] DWECK, R' Shemuel

רבי שמואל דוויק הכהן

(— 1725)

Distinguished scholar and *dayan* (judge) of Aram Soba. In 1715 he signed a *halachic* (legal) ruling together with other rabbis of Aram Soba concerning the validity of Kabbalah and the writings of the *Ari'zal*. (See Document Section, Document No. 10.) The ruling was published in the book *Dibrei Yosef* of R' Yosef Ergas. He is also mentioned there in reference to dissolving certain community agreements with which people were unable to comply.

He passed away in about 1725 in the town of Idleb, which is near Aram Soba. When news of his passing reached Aram Soba, he was eulogized by a number of major rabbis, including his student R' Shemuel Laniado (see #373), his brother-in-law R' Shemuel Dweck (see #243), and his sister's son R' Shimon Dweck (see #246). R' Yehudah Kassin (see #331) spoke of him with admiration in *Minhat Yehudah*, as did his nephew R' Shimon in his own book.

[243] DWECK, R' Shemuel

רבי שמואל דוויק הכהן

(— 1732)

Worthy scholar of Aram Soba. It appears that he had four scholarly sons: R' Shimon Dweck (author of *Rei'ah Sadeh*, see #246), R' David, R' Abraham, and R' Menachem. He signed an approbation for *Rei'ah Sadeh*). It is believed that he passed away on 10 Av, 5492 (1732).

[244] DWECK, R' Shemuel

רבי שמואל דוויק הכהן

(— 1868)

Distinguished scholar and *dayan* (judge) of Aram Soba. He was apparently the son of R' Moshe Dweck (see #233). Up to the age of 40 he was engaged in business, with fixed times set aside for studying Torah. His primary time for studying was from midnight until dawn. However, once he reached 40, he gave up his business activities and devoted himself completely to Torah. In this way he was able to develop his learning abilities and became one of the *dayanim* (judges) of Aram Soba. He joined with other rabbis of Aram Soba in 1852 in signing the approbation on *Kenesiyah Leshem Shamayim* of R' Menashe Sutton (see #551) concerning sacrifices to demons. (See Document Section, Document No. 31.)

He wrote commentaries on *Tanach*, on the *Mishnah*, as well as a book of responsa, called *Mishpatim Yesharim*. He also wrote a book of *hiddushim* (original Torah thoughts), called *Tenuvat HaSadeh*. All of these books remain in manuscript form.

He passed away on 3 Tevet, 5628 (1868). At his passing he was eulogized by many great rabbis among whom was his son-in-law R' Moshe Cohen who was the Chief Rabbi of Aram Soba at the time (see #164).

Once he reached 40, he gave up his business activities and devoted himself completely to Torah.

In 1715 R' Dweck (#242) signed a halachic (legal) ruling together with other rabbis of Aram Soba concerning the validity of Kabbalah and the writings of the Ari'zal.

[245] DWECK, R' Shemuel

רבי שמואל דוויק הכהן

(— 1900)

Worthy scholar and rabbi of Aram Soba. He was the son of R' Shaul Dweck (see #239). He passed away on 26 Adar, 5660 (1900).

[246] DWECK, R' Shimon

רבי שמעון דוויק הכהן

(17th-18th century)

Distinguished rabbinical authority of Aram Soba. He was the oldest son of R' Shemuel Dweck (see #243). He wrote the important book *Rei'ah Sadeh* (Constantinople 5498/1738) which contains various responsa, commentaries on the *Rambam*, and lectures on *Bereshit*. This book is bound with the work *Zeman HaGet — Shevet Ahim*

ספר
ריח שדה
נדפס
בקושטנדינא

Title Page of Rei'ah Sadeh

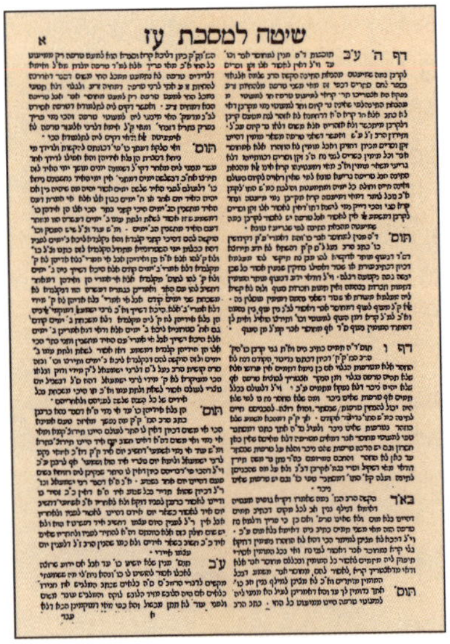

שיטה למסכת עז

Title Page of Commentary on the Tractate Avodah Zarah

containing *halachic* (legal) rulings related to divorces, which was co-authored with his brother, R' Menahem Dweck (see #230). Also, bound in the same volume is a commentary on the tractate *Avodah Zarah*, including dialogues with R' Abraham Cohen (see #157) and R' Sadkah Houssin (see #313). In the year 2004 it was reprinted by Machon HaKtav of R' Ezra Basri and sponsored by R' Shimon's descendants, Jack C. Azar, Irwin L. Azar, Nat Cheney, Morris Cheney Cohen and Irwin Shamah.

R' Dweck engaged in a *halachic* dispute with R' Shemuel Laniado (see #372). R' Raphael Shelomo Laniado (see #363) (the son of R' Shemuel) writes in his book *Bet Dino shel Shelomo* (on *Orah Haim 14*): "I have a response to the rabbi of *Rei'ah Sadeh*, who wrote opinions disputing with our teacher, our holy rabbi, Shemuel Laniado, and I can answer his issues. However, I have written responses here to only three of them so as not to allow selfish motivations to influence my learning."

Among the colleagues with whom he was close was R' Sadkah Houssin (see #313). He corresponded extensively with other rabbis of his time, especially R' Raphael Shelomo Laniado (see #363). In his book, R' Shimon mentions with admiration R' Yosef Abadi (see #18).

R' Yaakob Dweck

[247] DWECK, R' Yaakob

רבי יעקב דוויק הכהן

(— 1855)

Worthy scholar, merchant, and philanthropist of Aram Soba. He established a *Bet Midrash* for scholars in his house. He passed away in 1855 leaving four worthy sons, two of whom have been identified as R' Ezra and R' Yitzhak. He also had two sons-in-law, R' Ezra Harari and R' Eliyahu Dweck.

[248] DWECK, R' Yaakob (Shaul)

רבי יעקב דוויק הכהן

(1828-1919)

Distinguished Chief Rabbi and *Av Bet Din* (Chief Judge) of Aram Soba. He was a man of principle who devoted his life to the struggle against the waves of spiritual laxity and antireligious modernity, which washed over Aram Soba in the second half of the 19th century.

His Background

Sometimes referred to as R' Yaakob Shaul Dweck, he was a son of R' Shaul Dweck (see #240) and a brother of R' Yitzhak Dweck (see #250). R' Yaakob was a student of R' Mordechai Abadi (see #8) and a colleague of R' Yeshayah Dayan (see #203) and R' Nissim Lofez (see #396). His mother was named Kamar. In his book, *Derech Emunah* (p. 122), R' Yaacob talks about filtering vinegar to remove any bugs or worms. He mentions that in his youth he tried three times to filter the worms to no avail until his mother advised him to use a *tarboosh* (felt hat), which is made of a very thick material.

Teaching the Sons of the Wealthy

In his younger years he was a teacher of *Gemara* to the sons of the wealthy in Aram Soba. He was extremely conscientious about this role. As he later stated in his book *Derech Emunah*, any time wasted in class was like a merchant stealing from his customers by shortweighting them. He saw such a sin as being multiplied by the number of children in the class. (An hour lost for 40 students is equivalent to the loss of 40 hours.) Throughout his life he agonized over the neglect of traditional Judaism by individuals and blamed their teachers. He also blamed those parents who failed to give the payment of monthly Talmud Torah tuition the same sense of urgency as any other important debt.

He also blamed those parents who failed to give the payment of monthly Talmud Torah tuition the same sense of urgency as any other important debt.

Jerusalem and Hebron

In 1877 he visited *Eretz Yisrael* to pray at the graves of the righteous and to arrange for the publication of his writings. While there he studied with R' Aharon Ezriel, author of *Kapei Aharon* and head of the Sephardic *Beit Din* of Jerusalem. Also, during this trip he obtained the approbation of the *Rishon LeSion* (Chief Rabbi of *Eretz Yisrael*), R' Abraham Ashkenazi, on his important book *Derech Emunah*.

From Jerusalem he went to Hebron where he had the opportunity to study with the great Kabbalist, R' Eliyahu Mani, the Chief Rabbi of Hebron. They discovered that they shared common views on such matters as the risk that a rabbi's involvement in community affairs can bring him to sin.

A Position in Kilis

In those years his old teacher, R' Mordechai Abadi, was serving as the rabbi of Kilis, a small town in Turkey, north of Aram Soba. R' Abadi struggled mightily against the antireligious, modernizing influences affecting the Jews of Syria. With his passing in 1883, R' Yaakob was called to fill his position as rabbi of the community and carry on the struggle. In Kilis, and later in Aram Soba, R' Yaakob fought bitterly against immodest behavior such as attending non-Jewish parties, listening to Arab love songs in coffeehouses, mixed dancing, and ladies going without hair coverings. R' Yaakob did his best to set a good example by maintaining a modest lifestyle. He even refused an increase in salary which the leaders of the community offered out of concern for his poverty.

Chief Rabbi of Aram Soba

In 1901 R' Abraham Dweck-Khalousi, the Chief Rabbi of Aram Soba (see #257), passed away and R' Yaakob was invited by the community to fill this role. One of his major challenges was the secular school system of the *"Kol Yisrael Haverim"* organization (Alliance Israelite Universelle). This organization was begun in 1869, but its intentions of undermining religious beliefs and practices were not immediately apparent. The school authorities had pretended that they were also concerned with teaching Torah. They had originally installed six Torah scholars to teach *Tanach* and *Gemara* and many parents were optimistic about the new teaching methods. It was only after some years that the community leaders of Aram Soba realized the damage that was being done to their children. The proportion of time assigned to Torah studies was gradually reduced over the years until it became almost insignificant. R' Yaakob, who was especially sensitive to the importance of Jewish education, took every opportunity to denounce the Alliance schools and to warn parents against sending their children there.

He was especially sensitive to the importance of Jewish education, took every opportunity to denounce the Alliance schools and to warn parents against sending their children there.

Possibly as a result of the influence of the Alliance schools, Aram Soba began to experience a deterioration of religious standards in the late 19th century, especially with regards to the observance of *Shabbat*. At first the desecration of *Shabbat* was done in private only, but with the passage of time, it became open and blatant. R' Yaakob took up his sword against this calamitous situation. At his initiative, the scholars and rabbis of Aram Soba joined forces and in 1906 they formally adopted strong measures against the *Shabbat* offenders. Their decrees were published in all the synagogues and *Batei Midrashim* of the Aram Soba and Damascus regions. Subsequently, their resolutions were also adopted by the leading scholars and rabbis of Tiberias, Hebron, and Jerusalem, which were the main Jewish population centers of *Eretz Yisrael* at that time. (See Document Section, Document Nos. 28, 29.)

At his initiative, the scholars and rabbis of Aram Soba joined forces and in 1906 they formally adopted strong measures against the Shabbat offenders.

He fought bitterly against immodest behavior.

Loss of Position

At the outbreak of World War I in 1914, the threat of being drafted into the Turkish army loomed over Jewish young men. An aggressive person who could speak Turkish fluently was needed in the role of Chief Rabbi to press the government for draft deferments, especially for Torah scholars. R' Yaakob realized that he was not suited for this, and so he resigned from that position in favor of R' Hizkiah Shabbetai (see #495), a skilled diplomat who was able to ingratiate himself with the Ottoman authorities and exert a strong influence upon them. However, R' Yaakob continued in the role of *Av Bet Din* (Chief Judge) in Aram Soba and was recognized as the senior *halachic* (legal) authority until his dying day.

ספר
שארית יעקב
אברהם כמהר"ר יעקב
דוויך הכהן
נדפס בארם צובה יע"א
תפר"ה לפ"ק
ישעיה דיין

Title Page of She'erit Yaakob

R' Isaac Dwek of Deal, New Jersey (a grandson of R' Yaakob's brother, R' Abraham), relates that the primary reason for R' Yaakob's resignation was that a member of an influential family, who was a *Shabbat* desecrator, died and R' Dweck,

Stamp and signature of R' Yaakob Dweck

in accordance with the proclamation, refused to bury him. Out of spite, the family submitted false charges against him to the authorities and the Ottoman official in charge of the position of *Haham Bashi* (Chief Rabbi) removed him from his position. R' Yaakob continued as the true leader in the eyes of the people, although not in an official capacity.

The story is told (in the name of Mrs. Tera Hakim) that after R' Yaakob was deposed from his position as Chief Rabbi, he was walking in the street alone without the security protection he used to have. At the same time, R' Hizkiah Shabbetai was being inaugurated with much pomp and ceremony. A woman saw R' Yaakob from her porch and taunted him over his loss of prestige. At that moment the porch caved in and she fell to her death. People immediately understood the connection and renewed their respect for R' Yaakob, even though he no longer held the official position of Chief Rabbi.

His Tragedies

His life was a series of hardships and tribulations, which followed one another without letup. He talks about some of these problems, such as the death of three wives in succession, in the introduction to the book *Derech Emunah*. After the death of his first wife Sarah, the daughter of Joseph Sitt, he married Geraz, the daughter of R' Moshe Swed (see #575). It was not long before Geraz passed away and he married her sister Rachel, but not long after, she also was taken from him.

His Blessings

R' Yaakob was blessed with three sons and two daughters (that we know of), but two of his sons, R' Moshe (see #456) and R' Eliyahu (see #225), died during his lifetime. The other son, R' Abraham Dweck (see #217), survived him and edited his manuscripts. His two sons-in-law were R' Rahamim Dayan (see #212) and R' Moshe Dweck (Kassab) (see #256), both worthy scholars.

His Passing

R' Yaakob passed away on *Shabbat,* 2 Sivan, 5679 (1919) at the age of 91. He was buried in the "Cave of the Righteous" near Aram Soba's Great Synagogue. His resting place there is adjacent to that of R' Abraham Antebi (see #63), who had been Chief Rabbi in the early part of the 19th century. It had been R' Yaakob's lifelong wish to be buried in the Cave of the Righteous, which had provided the final rest for scholars and rabbis of Aram Soba since the time of the *Mishnah*. However, that possibility seemed to be closed to him because the limited space there had already been occupied by the righteous of previous generations. Only one plot was still available and that was owned by a wealthy man who refused to give it up. As it happened, it was *Hashem*'s will that the wealthy man should pass away on the same day, *Shabbat*, as R' Yaakob. The man happened to be out of town at the time and legal restrictions of the time prevented his body from being transported. And so it was necessary to bury him where he happened to be. Under these circumstances, the rabbis of Aram Soba decided to award the open plot to R' Yaakob so that his wish could be fulfilled.

That night, which was *Motza'e Shabbat*, R' Yaakob appeared in a dream to a good friend, saying that the decision about the burial plot was found to be a correct one in Heaven. It became a tradition in Aram Soba that each year on the day before *Yom Kippur* groups of people would gather at his graveside to pray.

His Legacy

He was a prolific author of holy books, but sadly only a fraction of his writings reached printed form. The rest appear to have been lost. His published works are described below.

- *Derech Emunah* (Aram Soba 5674/1914). This important work consists of inspirational topics arranged in alphabetical sequence. The material is based on the lectures that he regularly delivered between *Pesah* and *Shavuot*. The approbations which were received on this book included those of R' Hizkiah Shabbetai who was the Chief Rabbi of Aram Soba (see #495), and the *Bet Din* of Aram Soba. The book was subsequently reprinted in New York by R' Wieder and in Jerusalem by Albert Massry and Joe Dayan.

- *She'erit Yaakob* (Aram Soba 5685/1925). This book consists of inspirational lectures related to the four seasons of the year. The book was published by the author's son R' Abraham Dweck. At the end of the book, R' Abraham added an appendix entitled *Mishkenot Yaakob*, containing essays in honor of past sages. The book was subsequently reprinted in Jerusalem by the yeshiva *Ahavat Shalom*.
- Other Works. In 1852 R' Yaakob wrote *hiddushim* (original Torah thoughts) on the tractate *Betzah* and on the topic of an idle worker. These were published at the end of the book *Imrei No'am* of R' Yeshayah Dayan (see #203).

[249] **DWECK, R' Yehudah**

רבי יהודה דוויק הכהן

(— 1908)

Eminent scholar, Kabbalist, and rabbi of Aram Soba. A son of R' Ephraim Dweck, he was a student of R' Abraham Ades (see #37) and a colleague of R' Yosef Yedid (see #594). His customary practice was to get up at midnight and study Torah together with the local business people until dawn. By day, he taught *Gemara* in the *Bet HaMidrash*, but still managed to earn his livelihood as a merchant of Judaica.

He was an expert on Hebrew grammar and wrote *hiddushim* (original Torah thoughts) on the *halachot* (laws) pertaining to Hebrew scribes (for Torah scrolls, *tefillin*, and *mezuzot*) as well as on the *Gemara*.

In 1906, together with other scholars and rabbis of Aram Soba, he signed a *halachic* (legal) ruling directed against those who desecrate *Shabbat*. (See Document Section, Document No. 28.) He ultimately moved to Jerusalem and was warmly received by the rabbis of that city. However, he passed away in Jerusalem at a relatively young age on 27 Nissan, 5688 (1908), leaving behind an only son (see #226).

A eulogy which he delivered at the death of a mother in childbirth was published in the book *Minhat Yehudah* of R' Yehudah Attiah (see #118). The woman mentioned, Sheffia, was the wife of the notable scholar R' Hillel Meir Menashe Sutton.

[250] **DWECK, R' Yitzhak**

רבי יצחק דוויק הכהן

(— 1905)

Eminent scholar of Aram Soba. R' Yitzhak was especially talented as a counselor and adviser. When quarrels arose among the merchants, he found ways to make a compromise, and his compromises were generally accepted with understanding and appreciation. R' Mordechai Abadi (see #8) used to say that R' Yitzhak was an expert in the fifth volume of the *Shulhan Aruch*. [Since the *Shulhan Aruch* only contains four parts, he was referring to R' Yitzhak's ability to find imaginative, common-sense solutions to everyday challenges.]

He was a son of R' Shaul Dweck (see #239) and a brother of R' Yaakob Dweck (see #248). He was blessed with two scholarly sons, R' Abraham and R' Yosef (see #216 and #253). He passed away in 1905.

[251] **DWECK, R' Yosef**

רבי יוסף דוויק הכהן

(18th century)

Worthy scholar and *dayan* (judge) of Aram Soba. He was apparently a son of R' Shimon Dweck (see #246), the author of *Rei'ah Sadeh*. His signature appears on a manuscript document dated in late Nissan, 5551(1791). The original document is stored at the Ben-Zvi Institute (No. 302).

[252] **DWECK, R' Yosef**

רבי יוסף דוויק הכהן

(— 1883)

Worthy scholar and cantor of Aram Soba. He was the second son of R' Shaul Dweck

Alberto Sutton, on a recent trip to Syria, praying at the grave of his great-grandfather Hacham Yaakob located in the "Cave of the Righteous" of the old synagogue

R' Mordechai Abadi (see #8) used to say that R' Yitzhak was an expert in the fifth volume of the Shulhan Aruch.

R' Yehudah Dweck ultimately moved to Jerusalem and was warmly received by the rabbis of that city.

בס"ד

בהג"ו עמ"י עש"ו

לק"י ספר לס"י

בן דוד

הקונטרים הזה, בו לקטתי, מרז"ל ומהמפרשים אחרונים וראשוני' כמלאכים כאשר עיני הקורא תחזינה מישרים, מאשר השיגה ידי יד כהה, למען ימצא הקורא כשולחן ערוך לפניו, על כל פסוק ופסוק, בלתי שיפנה אנה ואנה וגם פרפראות, וקצת חדושים, על מאמרי רז"ל, ומעט כמכחול בשפופרת, בתוך אבני הקודש ז"ל. הם דברי איש צעיר

ע"ה משה דוויך הכהן הי"ו

[בן לאדוני אבי איש צדיק תמים וירא אלהים

כה"ר דוד זצ"ל וזיע"א]

נדפס

בעיה"ק ירושלם תובב"א

שנת שער"י דיצ"ה לפ"ק

רפוס "אביב" Imp. AVIV Jerusalem

Livre BEN DAVID

Title Page of Ben David

His customary practice was to get up at midnight and study Torah together with the local business people.

R' Moshe Dweck (Kassab)

(see #239). He is favorably mentioned in the eulogy that R' Mordechai Abadi (see #8) delivered upon the death of his father, R' Shaul, but he passed away only nine years later on 22 Tishrei, 5643 (1883).

[Note: Another scholar by the name of R' Yosef Dweck lived about the same time in Damascus. He passed away on 22 Tevet, 5618 (1858), but not much else is known about him.]

[253] DWECK, R' Yosef
רבי יוסף דוויק הכהן

(— 1933)

Worthy scholar of Aram Soba. His father was R' Yitzhak Dweck (see #250). His customary practice was to get up at midnight and study Torah together with the local business people. From midday until evening he would study in the *Bet HaMidrash* with his colleagues, the rabbis. He was an expert in the calendar, especially with regard to the setting of the leap year. In order to earn a livelihood, he engaged in business.

In about 1930 he visited the United States, but while he was there his head was tragically injured in a road accident. Upon his return to Aram Soba he sought treatment in Beirut, but it was not successful and he passed away there in 1933.

[254] DWECK (KASSAB), R' Ezra
רבי עזרא דוויק (קצאב) הכהן

Worthy scholar of Aram Soba. He was the father of R' Shaul Dweck (see #239) and an uncle of R' Yaakob (Shaul) Dweck (see #248). R' Yaakob praises him in his book *Derech Emunah* (p. 23, Jerusalem edition). R' Ezra was also one of the signers of the *halachic* (legal) ruling against those who desecrate *Shabbat*, which is included in the same book. (See Document Section, Document No. 28.)

(255) DWECK (KASSAB), R' Meir
רבי מאיר דוויק (קצאב) הכהן

(— 1925)

Worthy scholar and teacher of children in Aram Soba. He immigrated to the United States and passed away on 8 Shevat, 5685 (1925).

[256] DWECK (KASSAB), R' Moshe
רבי משה דוויק (קצאב) הכהן

(— 1949)

Notable scholar, *darshan* (lecturer), and senior *shohet* (ritual slaughterer) of Aram Soba. He was a son of R' David Dweck (Kassab) and a son-in-law of R' Yaakob Dweck (see #248). He authored a commentary on *Tehillim*, which he named *Kanah HaMidah* and which was published in Aram Soba in 1926. He dedicated the income from the book to the "Students Association" in which many of the Aram Soba students were educated.

He also wrote *Ben David*, a book of Torah lectures, which he named after his father R' David Dweck. The book was published in Jerusalem in 1929. In the introduction he apologizes for the relatively small size of the book, but notes that people of the Brooklyn community who commute to work on trains will find the small size to be an advantage. This is an amazing insight into the sincerity of the Syrian businessmen at the turn of the century, who took holy books with them to learn on the train rather than waste valuable time when they could be studying Torah. He was one of the rabbis who signed a proclamation in 1935 against accepting converts to the Syrian community. (See Document Section, Document No. 3.)

Later in life he joined his children in the United States, where he also occupied himself with service to the Aram Soba community. He passed away in New York on 18 Kislev, 5710 (1949).

R' Moshe named it in honor of his father, a righteous man, who was so pious that he never slept through midnight.

Memories of a Righteous Man. In the introduction to his book *Ben David*, R' Moshe explains that he named it in honor of his father, a righteous man, who was so pious that he never slept through midnight. R' David was extremely careful not to talk in the synagogue even when there were no prayers being said. R' Moshe recalled that when he was a young boy he would often come back from yeshiva at night and would go to the synagogue to see his father. He was sure that he would find him there and would come with questions for him. However, his father would completely ignore him, even when he cried. This is even more amazing considering that R' Moshe was at that time a young boy, born to his father in his old age.

When R' Moshe reminisced about those times, he was amazed at how R' David found the strength of character to control himself from talking to his beloved son. He concluded that it could only be his great connection to holiness, which made him unconcerned with wordly issues.

Another example of his unusual self-control was that he didn't talk at all on *Shabbat* and holidays; he only involved himself in Torah. This was especially difficult because many great rabbis who were relatives from his wife's side would come to visit him or he would go and visit them, and he would greet them only with a wave of his hand or the nodding of his head. His wife would often discuss his behavior after they left, expressing her view that it showed a lack of respect for the guests not to talk. However, as his son remembered, he stayed with his practice and didn't even answer her.

Another example of his unusual self-control was that he didn't talk at all on Shabbat and holidays.

[257] **DWECK-KHALOUSI, R' Abraham**

רבי אברהם דוויק הכהן (כלוצי)

(— 1901)

Chief Rabbi and *Rosh Yeshiva* of Aram Soba. He was the son of R' Ezra Dweck (see #254) and the brother of R' Shaul Dweck (see #239).

In his younger years he served as rabbi, *shohet* (ritual slaughterer), and *mohel* in the city of Antioch, Syria. After the death of R' Moshe Cohen, Chief Rabbi and *Rosh Yeshiva* of Aram Soba (see #164), he was appointed to serve in his place. He fulfilled his role in a superior manner and earned the respect of the community and the officials of the surrounding towns who treated him with distinct admiration. As was the custom of the dignitaries of the time he customarily went about riding on a white mule, preceded by an attendant. He was known as a strong leader, who feared no one. He was able to meet personally with the Turkish king, the famous Sultan Abdullah, who treated him with the greatest respect.

He was known for the benefits he was able to obtain for the downtrodden and oppressed Jewish community. He put extra effort into getting Jews released from service in the Turkish army, which was known for its disgraceful conditions. He had a regular practice of assisting Torah scholars and worthy poor people through secret donations of money and food on a weekly basis.

His relationship with the sultans continued until his final days. After a long and productive life, he passed away on 12 Tammuz 5661 (1901).

Although he was a scholar, he did not leave behind any *hiddushim* (original Torah thoughts) in his own name. However, he corresponded regularly with R' Yaakob Shaul Elyashar, the *Rishon LeSion* (Chief Rabbi of *Eretz Yisrael*), and there is a responsum in the latter's book *Ma'aseh Ish* (*Even HaEzer*, 1) in which he praises R' Abraham's scholarly abilities.

R' Abraham Dweck-Khalousi

R' Abraham Dweck-Khalousi had a regular practice of assisting Torah scholars and worthy poor people through secret donations of money and food on a weekly basis.

[258] **ELAZAR, R' Abraham**

רבי אברהם אלעזר

(— 1923)

Humble scholar of Aram Soba. He moved to the United States and passed away there in the year 5683 (1923).

[259] **ESSES, R' Siman Tob**

רבי סימן טוב עציץ

(— 1923)

Worthy scholar and community activist of Aram Soba. He was an effective organizer and was known for the charitable institutions which he founded. He passed away at a young age, approximately one month before the passing of R' Yomtob Yedid (see #593). When R' Shabbetai Bohbout (see #134) eulogized R' Yedid he reminded the congregation about the loss of R' Esses a few weeks earlier. He described R' Esses as a very wise *hacham* who pursued righteousness and improved the spiritual well-being of the community. R' Esses passed away on 4 Sivan, 5683 (1923).

[260] **ESSES, R' Yehudah**

רבי יהודה עציץ

(— 1908)

Worthy scholar and teacher of Aram Soba. He was also the rabbi of Kilis for a number of years, filling the position previously occupied by R' Yaakob Dweck (see #248).

He was apparently a son of R' Abraham Esses and the brother of R' Moshe Esses. In addition, he was a colleague of R' Abraham Antebi (see #64) and R' Menahem Choueka (see #155).

He was known for the intensity of his Torah learning and for the positive influence he had on his students. Tragically, he became seriously ill while still a young man and passed away shortly thereafter. He passed away on 5 Nissan, 5668 (1908).

Farhi Lineage. The wealthy Farhi family flourished in Damascus during the 18th and 19th centuries. What the Rothschilds were to European Jewry the Farhis were to Sephardic Jewry for close to a hundred years. As was the case with other wealthy Jewish families, the Farhis also played a role in the fostering of the spiritual life of the community. They established family religious trusts for the benefit of *yeshivot,* supported scholars, assisted the needy, and arranged for employment in their offices. They had great love for the Kabbalists of the yeshiva *Bet El* of Jerusalem and were its main supporters.

Members of this family served as officials in the financial administration of the province of Damascus and during the 1790's the bookkeeping of the provincial treasury was entrusted to them. The status and power of the Farhis reached its climax during the 19th century, when the responsibility for the affairs of the treasury of the provinces of Damascus and Sidon — the center of which was in Acre (*Acco*) — was handed over to Señor Haim Farhi.

The first Farhi to consolidate his position in Damascus was Shaul Farhi who lived there in the 18th century. He allied himself with the pasha of Damascus and in 1742 sent a message to R' Haim Abulafia, the founder of the *yishuv* (settlement) in Tiberias, not to back the local sheikh in his war against the pasha.

Two of his five sons, Raphael and Yosef, inherited his position in Damascus and their cousin Shelomo (Salmon) Farhi also shared their importance. The third son, Haim Farhi (see #261), became the most famous member of the family. He was a particularly generous donor to synagogues both in Damascus and in Acre.

[261] **FARHI, Señor Haim**

סי' חיים פרחי

(1760 — 1819)

Powerful financier and philanthropist of Damascus and Acre (*Acco*). He was born in Damascus in 1760. Señor Haim became a particularly generous donor to synagogues both in Syria and in *Eretz Yisrael.*

He entered the service of Ahmed al-Jazzar Pasha, the governor of the province of Sidon who had established his residence in Acre in about 1790. Ahmed al-Jazzar Pasha was a ruthless man (Jazzar means *butcher* in

Arabic) and Haim Farhi remained in his position primarily to help his fellow Jews. After an earlier earthquake in Safed, the pasha believed that bringing Jews to settle there would bring blessing. Haim Farhi brought *hasidim* from Europe to live in Safed. Among them were R' Yisrael Polatchek and R' Shlomo Segal. As an inducement, R' Haim gave them a tax-free status. R' Yisrael of Shklov describes the kindness of R' Haim and said that without him there would have been no Jewish settlement in Safed.

One day, in a state of rage the pasha lashed out at his loyal servant and ordered that Haim's eye be gouged out and that he be banished. After this occurred, the pasha calmed down and he reinstated Haim to his former position. The English historian Wilson provides the following version of what happened. The pasha told Haim, "You have such a nice personality and demeanor. When people come to visit they are more impressed by you than by me. I wanted to remove you from your position but I like you too much. I have a plan. I will gouge out your eye so you won't be so handsome anymore." After that, Haim wrapped his turban so that it covered his bad eye. When the pasha saw that, he said, "I see my plan isn't working; the only option I have is to cut off the tip of your nose." And that is what he did.

In 1799 Napoleon's armies attacked the Ottoman Empire and besieged Acre, the seat of the pasha's power. Haim Farhi was an adviser to the Ottoman Army and with the help of his brother, Moshe, helped them fight off the French. When Napoleon heard of the pasha's adviser he sent a secret messenger to persuade Haim to join him, but he refused.

In 1804 Haim was imprisoned by the pasha, but on the death of al-Jazzar he was set free. He immediately joined in the struggle for al-Jazzar's succession, supporting Suleiman Pasha. Suleiman achieved the position of governor in 1805 due to the assistance of Haim who intervened in his favor in Constantinople.

Suleiman had complete confidence in Haim and he gave him a free hand in the administration and its finances. The Suleiman period (until 1818) was one of consolidation for Haim and the family in general, especially after Suleiman was also appointed governor of Damascus. Haim Farhi also chose Suleiman Pasha's successor in Acre, a younger man named Abdallah Pasha. However, Abdallah Pasha ruled with an iron hand and treated his subjects harshly. When Haim reprimanded him, Abdallah realized that Haim would be a thorn in his side and looked for an opportunity to remove him from power.

Abdallah, with the advice of a French engineer, wanted to widen the walls of Acre and strengthen them. Haim was opposed on two accounts: The Turkish government wouldn't look with favor at the project and it would require increasing taxes. Abdallah finally decided that he had had enough of the interfering Jew and hired men to slander Haim, accusing him of treason. Moslems loyal to Haim told him the end was near and advised him to escape but he refused to do so out of fear of negative repercussions against his fellow Jews.

On *Ereb Rosh Hodesh Elul* 1819 Haim fasted as was his custom (he fasted every *Erev Rosh Hodesh,* which is known as *Yom Kippur Katan*), when a government official suddenly arrived at his house leading a squad of armed men and announced his death sentence, to be carried out immediately. Haim was strangled to death on the steps of his own house and the killers threw his body into the ocean without a burial. The next day his possessions in Acre were confiscated and his wife and family escaped to Damascus. His widow died on the way, a victim of her great anguish. His three brothers, Shelomo, Raphael, and Moshe, were enraged and persuaded the pashas of Aleppo and Damascus to go to war with Abdallah of Acre. Arriving at Acre six months later, their armies lay siege to the city. However, after a year, Shelomo Farhi was assassinated by someone loyal to Abdallah. This

One day, in a state of rage the pasha lashed out at his loyal servant and ordered that Haim's eye be gouged out and that he be banished.

Abdallah finally decided that he had had enough of the interfering Jew and hired men to slander Haim, accusing him of treason. Haim was strangled to death on the steps of his own house and the killers threw his body into the ocean without a burial.

broke the morale of the attacking forces and the army abandoned the siege.

When news of the death of Haim Farhi reached Aram Soba, he was eulogized by all the prominent rabbis of the time. Among them were R' Yaacob Shaul Elyashar and R' Yisrael of Shklov, leader of the Safed community. In addition, he was eulogized by R' Yitzhak Attiah (see #120), as recorded in his book *Vayikra Yitzhak* (Sermons, page 111). He emphasized that all of Haim's actions and those of the other members of the family were inspired by the desire to serve *Hashem* and help their fellow Jews. Many lamentations were written including one by R' Tzvi Hirsch Katzenelenbogen of Vilna.

Haim left no sons, only daughters. As a result, his extensive possessions were the cause of a bitter dispute between his brothers and their children. For many years this dispute occupied the *Batei Din* of Damascus, Aram Soba, Tiberias, and Jerusalem. The details of the legal rulings involved may be found in the book *Hukot Haim* (*Hoshen Mishpat*) by R' Haim Palagi (see #449).

One of Haim's four brothers, Menahem, had passed away during his lifetime and Haim had appointed his brother Moshe to serve as executor of Menahem's estate and as guardian of his small children. Moshe had been close to Haim in Acre and believed he had Haim's full confidence. And so, after Haim's death, Moshe assumed control of Haim's family and all his possessions, and conveyed them to Damascus. When Haim's widow died in transit, Moshe took ownership of her extensive jewels and ornaments.

Because of the confusion of the times, no one took issue with this until 1833 when Raphael Farhi and some of his nephews asked Moshe to clarify the basis of his claim on Haim's estate. However, Moshe refused to respond even when a case was brought against him in the *Bet Din*. He ignored R' Yaakob Antebi, the *Av Bet Din* (Chief Judge) of Damascus, R' Shemuel Laniado (see #374), the Chief Rabbi, and the *Rishon LeSion* in *Eretz Yisrael*. Instead, Moshe took the matter to the local government court of law and obtained a ruling which undercut R' Yaakob Antebi and caused him much pain. The dispute continued for many years. It was still alive in 1857 when R' Yehudah Navon, who was in Damascus at the time, issued a strong ruling against Moshe for refusing to accept the earlier judgments against him. However, Moshe let it be known that he had received a favorable ruling from the *Bet Din* of R' Haim Nissim Abulafia of Tiberias and that is why he felt free to disregard conflicting rulings. This matter was finally brought to the attention of R' Haim Palagi (see #449) to bring clarity.

The Egyptian conquest of Syria at the beginning of the 1830's struck a decisive blow at the Farhi family, both in relation to its financial matters and its influence in the town. In 1834 the family lost its positions in the financial administration and only a few of its members remained on the staff of the treasury and in the leadership of the Jewish community. However, with the return of the Ottoman rule in Syria in 1840, one of the members was again appointed to the direction of the treasury administration, even though the family could not regain its former financial power.

[262] **FRANCO, Mr. Eliyahu**

מר אליהו פרנקו

(— 1927)

Eminent philanthropist of New York and Jerusalem. A native of Aram Soba, he became known for his love of learning and for his benevolence. He settled in the United States, where he lived for many years. In his old age he fulfilled his lifelong dream of living in Jerusalem, leaving behind his entire family, including many children and grandchildren. Sadly, he passed away on 15 Adar, 5687 (1927), only a short time after arriving in Jerusalem. Before his death he dedicated a large sum to finance the construction of a Talmud Torah for the children of the Aram Soba community in Jerusalem. This institution became known as the *Talmud Torah Magen David*.

The Talmud Torah continued into the late '60's. The last principal was R' Natan Salem (see #472). Even after it closed down, the voices of children learning Torah continued in the building. The yeshiva *Succat David* of R' Menahem Basri occupies the building today together with part of *Yeshivat Meor HaTorah* founded by R' Abraham Salem, son of R' Natan. All of this is a continued merit for the original builder, Mr. Eliyahu Franco.

One of his sons was Mr. David Franco, a notable Brooklyn philanthropist who became known for the support he gave to institutions of Torah and charity in Jerusalem. The names of his other children were Moshe, Nissim, Abraham, Rahamim, Yitzhak, Aboud, Yaakob, Rachel, and Bolisa.

[263] **FRANCO (HALAK), R' Ezra**

רבי עזרא פרנקו (חלאק)

(— 1904)

Worthy scholar and scribe of Aram Soba. Over the course of his life he painstakingly wrote dozens of Torah scrolls, as well as *tefillin* and *mezuzot*. He passed away on 6 Adar, 5664 (1904).

[264] **FRANCO (HALAK), R' Yehudah**

רבי יהודה פרנקו (חלאק)

(— 1917)

Worthy Talmud Torah teacher of Aram Soba. A faultless, upright man, he passed away on 20 Shevat, 5677 (1917).

[265] **GABBAI, R' Meir**

רבי מאיר גבאי

(19th century)

Wealthy scholar of Aram Soba. He opened a yeshiva in his house with a large collection of holy books, which he made available to anyone who wished to come and study or do research. This was especially important to the development of Torah study in Aram Soba because of the great expense involved in acquiring holy books. R' Abraham Dayan (see #173), in the introduction to his book *VeYosef Abraham*, praises him for his good works and states, "If not for him, Torah would have been forgotten because of the difficulty in purchasing holy books. In the contract of commitment by members of a study group (see Document Section, Document No. 32), this yeshiva is mentioned as one of the three well-known learning spots of Aleppo in the mid-1800's.

The yeshiva Succat David occupies the building today together with part of Yeshivat Meor HaTorah. All of this is a continued merit for the original builder, Mr. Eliyahu Franco.

[266] **GINDI, R' Moshe**

רבי משה גנדי

(1888 — 1954)

Eminent Torah scholar and Kabbalist of Aram Soba and New York. He was born to Yaakob and Sarah Gindi in 1888 in Aram Soba. In 1907, at the age of 19, he traveled to America to earn enough money to get married and start a family in Aram Soba. After working as a peddler in places as far away as Chicago and New Orleans, he returned in 1908 with $1,000 in his pocket — a very large sum at the time.

Hacham Moshe Gindi

His Entry into the Scholarly Life

Arriving in Aram Soba as a "rich" man, he wanted to marry a rabbi's daughter. R' Yitzhak Dweck (see #250) had recently passed away, and his son R' Abraham Dweck (see #216) was now the head of the family. Moshe Gindi approached R' Abraham several times for permission to marry his sister, Nizha Dweck. But R' Abraham turned him down because Moshe's wealth was not enough of a qualification for his saintly sister. She would not marry anyone who was not a Torah scholar.

Moshe Gindi promised that he would learn Torah; he even promised that he would devote twenty years to learning Torah, but R' Abraham still declined. The young man who brought home money from America was not the Torah scholar who should marry Nizha Dweck.

One night R' Yitzhak Dweck visited his son, R' Abraham, in a dream. R' Abraham had many daughters, but only one son, Selim. [Selim was the father of R' Yitzhak Dwek, currently Rabbi of the Syrian Synagogue in Deal, New Jersey.] In the dream, R' Yitzhak told his son, R' Abraham, that he must allow Moshe Gindi to marry Nizha, or

"If not for him, Torah would have been forgotten."

he'd take away R' Abraham's only son, Selim. (Later it was learned that Nizha Dweck had a similar dream on the same night that her brother did. Her father had come to her also, saying that she was to marry Moshe Gindi.)

The next day, R' Abraham went to Moshe Gindi to say that he could marry Nizha Dweck. They were married in 1910, and Moshe Gindi proceeded to keep his promise of learning Torah. He sought out rabbis to study with, studying first with R' Moshe Mizrahi (see #424), who would come to his house six days a week, for six hours a day. In addition, while alone, Moshe Gindi would study by candlelight every night, late into the early hours of the morning.

After a few years, he began studying Kabbalah. This became his specialty, and he came to devote most of his time to its study.

Running a Business

In Aram Soba, the scholarly Hacham Moshe Gindi had a business that sold spices and homemade camel-soap. He and his brother Selim were partners in two stores that were directly across from each other in the marketplace. However, Hacham Moshe was hardly ever at the stores — he was home learning Torah. His wife would tell him, "Go to work. You have six children. They need food." His brother Selim helped keep the stores open while Hacham Moshe was learning Torah — they both knew that the Torah learning was their only true source of success.

His brother Selim helped keep the stores open while Hacham Moshe was learning Torah — they both knew that the Torah learning was their only true source of success.

Marrying Off a Daughter

In 1924, Hacham Moshe married off his oldest daughter, Sarina, to Murad (Mordechai) Faham. Murad seemed to be just like Hacham Moshe had been. He worked for a living, but was not an ordained rabbi. He promised that he would learn Torah, so Hacham Moshe agreed to the marriage. Then he told his 16-year-old daughter, Sarina, about it. Sarina was playing in her room on the floor with her friends, when her father opened the door to announce, "*Mabrook,* Sarina! You're engaged!" Sarina burst out crying, "Who's the *areece* (groom)?"

Mordechai Faham was later to become famous as the "savior of the *Keter*." It was he who smuggled the *Keter Aram Soba* out of Syria to *Eretz Yisrael* in 1957. (See the section on the *Keter Aram Soba* for further details.)

Sojourn in Beirut

In 1929, Hacham Moshe decided to move his growing family to America. The Arabs were getting more repressive toward the Jews in Syria and he felt that it was time to move on. He arranged for transportation to Beirut, and from there, passage on a ship bound for America. Traveling with Hacham Moshe and his wife were nine of their ten children, ages 17 to 1-year old: Adele, Julia, Yaakob, Yitzhak, Olga, Abraham, Yosef, Gita, and David. His married daughter Sarina stayed behind. Sponsorship from America came from *K'nees Betesh* (the Betesh Synagogue).

Arriving in Beirut, Hacham Moshe found that his documents were missing one signature. And so he sent them back to Aram Soba for that one signature, while the family waited in Beirut. They had to wait for three months for their papers to come back correctly and in the meantime, Hacham Moshe was sought out in Beirut as an important *Hacham* from Aram Soba.

While he was learning in the local *Bet Midrash*, a disturbed, fidgety, young man was brought to Hacham Moshe to see if he could help him. Hacham Moshe realized that the young man's body was being occupied by another spirit. He brought the young man into a room and laid him on a table. He then proceeded to read from his holy Kabbalah books. Periodically, he asked the spirit in the young man some questions, such as, "Who are you?"

He asked the spirit, "How did you get permission to move into this young man's body?" The spirit answered. "The man got angry and he threw something and broke it. It was then that I was able to get in." After some more readings from his books, Hacham Moshe succeeded in convincing the spirit to leave the young man's body, insisting that the exit be through his big toe. Hacham Moshe held the young man's foot,

He asked the spirit, "How did you get permission to move into this young man's body?"

and a small hole burst open in his big toe. Blood spurted out and at once the young man seemed to calm down. He gained his composure, and after realizing where he was and what had happened to him, he thanked Hacham Moshe profusely.

Life in America

Arriving in New York in September 1929, the family was detained at Ellis Island for a month while the authorities quarantined them because of a lesion on the face of one of the children. However, this proved to be nothing more than a "water boil" and the family was finally admitted.

In Brooklyn, Hacham Moshe continued his learning, and was quickly recognized as someone who should be teaching. He regularly taught Kabbalah to a group of rabbis in the Sutton Shul *(K'nees Sutton)* on 67th Street (between 21st and 22nd Avenues). Some of his study partners were Hacham Yaakob Kassin (see #330), Hacham Yaakob Maleh (see #402), and Hacham Baruch Ben-Haim.

To support the family, Hacham Moshe would go to homes and offices collecting donations for the 67th Street *Magen David Congregation*. To supplement his meager earnings, he would buy and sell ties, squeezing out a few pennies profit from each.

His main occupation was Torah study — he would always be seen with a book in his hand. He had a special chair by the window in his home from where he could wave a hello and quickly get back to his studies.

He was one of the rabbis who signed a proclamation in 1935 against accepting converts into the Syrian community. (See Document Section, Document No. 3.) Other signers were R' Yaakob Kassin (see #330), R' Haim Tawil (see #584), R' Moshe Dweck (Kassab) (see #256), and R' Mordechai Maslaton (see #411).

Hacham Moshe Gindi and his wife Nizha had three more children in America, Eva, Esther, and Ralph. Eva passed away when she was 8 years old. Murad and Sarina Faham moved to America in the early 1960's, after Hacham Moshe had already passed away. Sarina did not realize that the goodbye that she said to her father in 1929, over thirty years earlier, was the last time she would see him.

Hacham Moshe passed away at the young age of 66 in Heshvan 5715 (1954).

[267] GINDI-DAKNISH, R' Yaakob

רבי יעקב גנדי־דקנס הכהן

(— 1911)

Renowned *darshan* (lecturer) of Aram Soba. He delivered lectures for over 35 years, speaking with great passion. His lectures extended over many hours and covered all aspects of Torah.

He was in charge of the distribution of a weekly stipend to needy scholars. (The community chest was funded by charitable donations, as well as by a 2 percent tax that was imposed on out-of-town merchants who came to Aram Soba to buy merchandise. The weekly stipend was paid only to those scholars who regularly attended the *Magen Giborim Bet Midrash* and had no other sources of income.)

He was a member of the association, *Ohr HaTorah*, which included among its functions the promotion of *halachic* (legal) behavior within the community, even to the extent of punishing offenders. Every Friday he had the habit of going out into the streets of the city to remind the storekeepers and merchants to close their businesses early, as *Shabbat* was approaching. He passed away on 18 Shevat, 5671 (1911). One of his students, R' Yaakob Alfia (see #45), was there to eulogize him upon his passing.

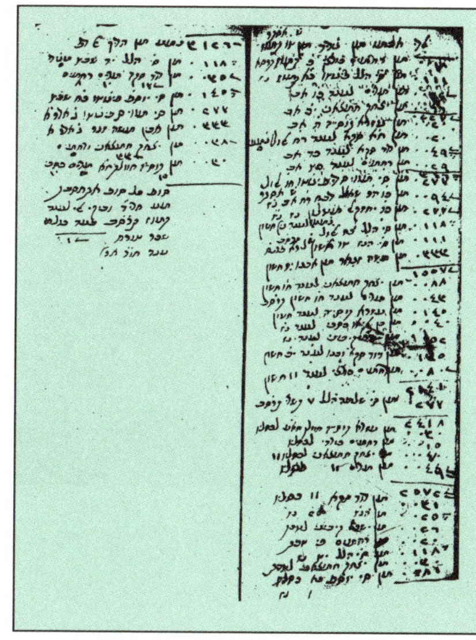

List of Donors for Weekly Stipend

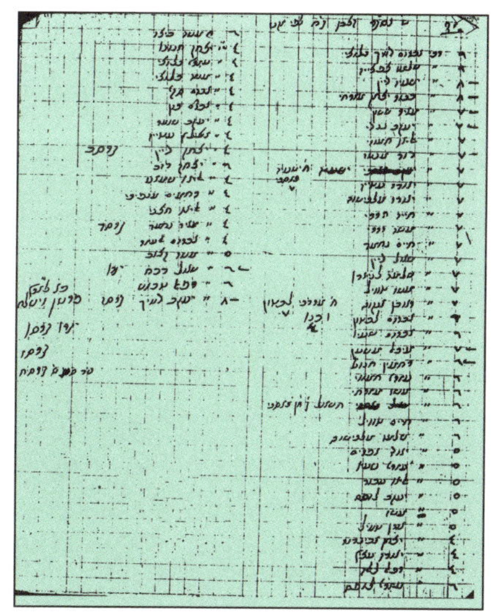

Weekly Stipend List for Torah Scholars (1901)

[268] HABOBA, R' Netanel

רבי נתנאל חבובא

(1839 — 1917)

Distinguished *Av Bet Din* (Chief Judge) of Damascus between 1880 and 1903. He corresponded with the great rabbis of his generation, including R' Yitzhak Abulafia *(see #35)*, R' Ezra Maslaton, R' Moshe Peretz, and R' Yaakob Shaul Elyashar.

He was born in 1839, a noble descendant of an ancient Damascus rabbinical family.

R' Netanel Haboba

However, his father, HaRav HaHasid Moshe Haboba, passed away when he was only a year old and he was brought up by his maternal grandfather, R' Yitzhak Maslaton-Tarab. R' Netanel studied under the great Damascus rabbis of his generation, R' Yaakob Peretz, R' Shelomo Sukri, R' Aharon Yaakob, and R' Meir Mishan. He was a brilliant student and at the age of 17 he was awarded the title of Hacham. At the age of 19 he married the daughter of R' Nissim Sukri. R' Netanel was appointed *Av Bet Din* at age 41.

In 1903, at the age of 64, he retired from the *Bet Din* and settled in Jerusalem where he joined a group of Kabbalist scholars under the leadership of R' Haim Shaul Dweck (see #228). R' Netanel passed away in Jerusalem on 9 Shevat, 5677 (1917) and was buried on the Mount of Olives.

R' Netanel's *hiddushim* (original Torah thoughts) were posthumously published in the book *Korban Netanel* through the efforts of his son, R' Eliyahu Haboba of Haifa (apparently in 1968). His son writes in the introduction that his father had visited *Eretz Yisrael* in his earlier years and had been persuaded by the Chief Rabbi of Hebron, R' Eliyahu Mani, to remain in Hebron for a full year to complete his studies. Later, when R' Eliyahu Mani visited Damascus he established a regular study session with R' Netanel for as long as he was there.

Hamway Lineage. The modern Hamway family originated in the city of Hama, which is 140 kilometers south of Aram Soba. (Hama became notorious as the site of a massacre in 1982 in which 20,000 residents were reported to have been killed by order of Hafez Assad, the president of Syria.) However, some of the illustrious Hamway lineage can be traced all the way back to the Davidic house of royalty. R' Abraham Harari-Raful (see #302) notes, referring to R' Ezra Hamway, that the verse "A sprout will come from the trunk of Yishai, and a shoot will blossom from its roots ..." (*Yeshayahu* 11:1) hints to this. The initials of the verse's first five words, scrambled, spell the name Hamway (**ויצא חטר מגזע ישי ונצר** משרשיו יפרה).

The earliest-known mention of the Hamway family name was in 1667 when a R' Abraham Hamway wrote a book on the *halachot* (laws) of *Shehitah* (ritual slaughter). Later, in 1723, there was an epidemic in Aram Soba among whose victims were the young men Obadiah and Moshe Hamway. The family grew over the years and many branches were formed. To distinguish the different branches, additional names were added to the Hamway root, such as Chasky and Beyda. In 1827 the government ordered the expulsion of all Jews from Hama and most went to Aram Soba.

[269] **HAMWAY, R' Abraham Shalom**

רבי אברהם שלום חמווי

(1839 — 1888)

Eminent scholar and prolific author of Aram Soba. He was born in Aram Soba in 1839 to R' Raphael Hamway. After receiving his education there and getting married, he was struck by a series of bitter tragedies over a relatively short period of time. These included the death of his wife and many close family members. He accepted all of these sad events as the will of *Hashem* and prayed that his suffering should serve as atonement for his sins. He found solace by immersing himself in Torah study and the writing of holy books. He saw it as his mission to share with others the lessons and insights that he gained from his bitter experiences.

He found solace by immersing himself in Torah study and the writing of holy books.

R' Abraham realized that if he stayed in Aram Soba he would not have an opportunity to raise the funds that he would need to publish his books. And so he became a wanderer, traveling throughout the Middle East and as far as India and Europe. During the course of his travels he continued with his writing and wherever he stayed he asked for access to the local repositories of printed books and manuscripts. Many of these libraries were jealously guarded and he needed all of his persuasive powers to obtain entrance.

At one point in his wanderings he lived in Jerusalem and studied under R' Rahamim Antebi (see #72). When word got back to Aram Soba of his stature in Jerusalem, the scholars there were amazed because he had not progressed anywhere near that level when he lived in Aram Soba.

Finally, in 1870 after about 10 years on the road he arrived at Constantinople, Turkey, where was able to get the sponsorship to print his first book. This was *Ha'ach Nafsheinu*, containing a wealth of information about various *segulot* (healing powers and remedies), arranged according to the *Alef Bet*. The printing of this book was a great consolation to him and he realized this would be his destiny. In fact, many of the books which he authored were published during his lifetime.

His first book was very successful because of the many illnesses that people were subject to in those days and the limited medical care that was available. However, his confidence was soon shattered when he was attacked by bandits while on the road to his next destination. Not only did the robbers take all of his possessions, they beat him unmercifully. Despite all of the physical abuse which he took in that experience, he found even worse the abject poverty in which he was left.

However, life had taught him how to keep going and so he recovered from his injuries and continued with his travels. He declined attractive offers of rabbinical positions in many of the cities which he passed through, notably in Baghdad and Sanaa (Yemen). He ultimately came to Livorno, Italy, and there his fortune took a turn for the better. He found a sympathetic philanthropist from Tunis, Shelomo Shamama, who took care of all his physical needs, providing him with food, clothing, and lodging so that he could devote himself to his holy work.

Sadly, he passed away while on his travels, without children and not yet having reached the age of 50. Despite his abbreviated and difficult life he was a prolific author of books. Altogether it is believed that he wrote as many as 45 books, covering a wide range of topics, but especially *halachot* (laws) and *segulot*. Knowing that people would be drawn to his *segulot*, he made a point of including reminders about ethical and moral behavior, wherever it seemed appropriate. He became known as the *Baal HaBatim* (master of the houses) because the titles of his books tended to feature the word *bet* ("house of").

He received approbations for his books from many of the greatest rabbis of his generation. Especially noteworthy among these was R' Haim Palagi, the distinguished Chief Rabbi of Izmir (see #449), and the *Rishon LeSion* (Chief Rabbi of *Eretz Yisrael*), R' Abraham Ashkenazi. His work was also praised by R' Suleiman Mani who was *Av Bet Din* (Chief Judge) of Hebron.

ספר
בית אל
פה ליוורנו יע"א
אליהו בן אמוזג וחברו הי"ו

Title Page of Bet El

ספר
בית דין
פה ליוורנו יע"א
אליהו בן אמוזג וחברו הי"ו

Title Page of Bet Din

The Miracle of Marrakesh. The rabbis of Marrakesh in Morocco had a special reason to respect R' Abraham Shalom Hamway and to be grateful to him. The incident occurred in 1881 after three years of drought. The community came together in fasting and prayer, but nothing seemed to help. However, when R' Abraham was within half a day of arriving in Marrakesh, two of its notable scholars were visited in a dream by the spirits of the city's deceased *dayanim* (judges). The *dayanim* said that the next day a *hacham* would arrive and that they should press him to pray for the city. If they did, *Hashem* would answer those prayers with rain, and that would inaugurate a blessed year.

Upon R' Abraham's arrival he was besieged with entreaties, "Father, give us rain!" R' Abraham felt he had no choice and so he decreed a day of intense public prayer in the local cemetery. A circumcision was scheduled that day and he used some of the blood of the circumcision to write the holy Name of *Hashem*. They then prayed the afternoon prayer *(Minhah)* together. All of this occurred on Thursday, the 18th day of Adar I in the year 5641 (1881). That *Shabbat* on Friday night the heavens opened up and the blessed rains fell, creating great joy among both Jews and non-Jews alike. They called R' Abraham, "*Hacham* of the Rains."

They called R' Abraham, "Hacham of the Rains."

That year the government decided to impose a harsh decree on the Jews of Marrakesh. R' Abraham went to the palace to plead that the decree be lifted. He used all his power of advocacy and he was successful — the decree was rescinded.

R' Bekhor Shalom Hamway

Title Page of Peh Eliyahu

Some of his more notable published books are the following:

- *Ha'ach Nafsheinu* (*Izmir* 5630/1870). *Segulot* (healing powers and remedies), arranged according to the *Alef Bet*.
- *Abeyah Hidot* (Livorno 5639/1879). *Mussar* (spiritual development) and *segulot*.
- *Bet El* (Livorno 5635/1875). *Halachot* (laws) related to prayers.
- *Bet Din* (Livorno 5613/1853). Commentary on the prayers of *Rosh Hashanah*.
- *Bet Hashem* (Livorno 5635/1875). *Halachot* related to *Shavuot*. Bound together with *Bet HaBehirah*, dealing with *halachot* related to *Pesah*.
- Bet *HaKaporet* (Livorno 5639/1879). *Halachot* related to *Yom Kippur*.
- *Bet Simhah* (Jerusalem 5721/1861). *Halachot* related to *Succot*.
- *Dabak Me'*Ach (Livorno 5634/1874). *Mussar* and *segulot*.
- *Zecher Asah* ((Izmir 5637/1877). *Segulot*, arranged according to the *Alef Bet.* Written in Ladino.
- *Yimalet Nafsho* (Calcutta 5644/1884). *Segulot*.
- *Lidrosh Elokim* (Livorno 5639/1879). Analysis of dreams.

[270] **HAMWAY, R' Bekhor Shalom**

רבי בכור שלום חמווי

(— 1934)

Worthy scholar of Aram Soba. He passed away on 11 Tishrei, 5695 (1934). His son, R' Shaul Emil Hamway, was a civic activist in Givatayim, who was known for building a synagogue and *Bet Midrash* by the name of *Vatitpalel Hanah*. The son also managed the publishing of the book *Bet Simhah* by R' Abraham Shalom Hamway (see #269).

[271] **HAMWAY, R' Eliyahu**

רבי אליהו חמווי

(1840 — 1915)

Av Bet Din (Chief Judge) of Aram Soba from 1894 to 1915. He endured great privation during much of his life and his scholarly abilities went largely unrecognized until he reached the age of 54. He is known for his important book *Peh Eliyahu* (Aram Soba 5674/1914), whose two volumes were published in one binding. The book contains *hiddushim* (original Torah thoughts) on the *perashot* of the Torah, as well as descriptions of customs and practices related to cemeteries. He received an approbation from R' Hizkiah Shabbetai (see #495), who was at that time the Chief Rabbi of Aram Soba, as well as from the *Bet Din of* Aram Soba.

He was born in about 1840 to R' Ezra Hamway, who passed away while his child was still young. His mother Sarah supported the family with great difficulty, but it was not long before she also passed away. He then went to live with relatives, but continued to suffer from great poverty. This did not prevent his commitment to Torah, which he studied under R' Mordechai Abadi (see #8). The first two responsa in the book *Ma'ayan Ganim* by his teacher were written by R' Eliyahu.

At the age of 20 he married Geraz, the daughter of R' Yitzhak Swed. The young couple lived in dire straits and continually experienced tragedy as their children died at a young age. Their economic hardships forced them to move to Kilis (a small town in Turkey, north of Aram Soba) where he became a teacher of Jewish children and ultimately rabbi of the town. He finally was granted surviving children, a daughter Sarah and a son Ben-Sion Hai. He also merited to see grandchildren.

At the age of 54 he was called back to Aram Soba as the head of the *Bet Din* and remained at this post until his death. He passed away on *Rosh Hashanah* 5676 (1915). He was eulogized by the greatest rabbis of his generation among whom was his colleague on the *Bet Din*, R' Ezra Hamway (see #272). That eulogy appears at the end of *Minhat Yehudah* (Vol. I) of R' Yehudah Attiah (see #118).

Besides his important published book, R' Eliyahu wrote two other books, which were not printed. They are *Ben Yayin* (*halachah* and inspirational lectures) and *Shir Mizmor* on *Tehillim*. In one of his more controversial responsa he permitted the use of soap on *Shabbat*. That ruling, in 1882, was addressed to R' Shalom Hedaya (see #310). He received support on it from R' Yitzhak Abulafia (see #35) who at that time was Chief Rabbi of Damascus. This responsum was also printed in the book *Maaseh Ish* of the *Rishon LeSion* (Chief Rabbi of *Eretz Yisrael*), R' Yaakob Shaul Elyashar. Some of his responsa were made available in the journal *HaMe'asef*. There is also one responsum which he wrote together with R' Hillel David Sutton (#546) in the book *Shaare Rahamim* of R' Rahamim Yosef Franco (on *Orah Haim*, Section 1).

[272] HAMWAY, R' Ezra

רבי עזרא חמווי

(1859 — 1945)

Distinguished *Rosh Av Bet Din* (Chief Judge) of Aram Soba. He presided over the *Bet Din* over a period of 45 years. The *Bet Din* dealt justly with a variety of cases. Even non-Jewish neighbors who had heard of the *Bet Din's* righteous verdicts would respectfully come to R' Ezra for adjudication. He also founded a yeshiva in Aram Soba and taught a generation of future rabbis and leaders.

R' Ezra Hamway

His Childhood

He was born in Aram Soba in 1859 R' Yitzhak Hamway (who was also known by the nickname Khabaz —"baker"), and Senyar. His parents lived in the Bahsita neighborhood, which was also known as *Charrat El Yahud*, the "Jewish neighborhood." This was the crowded neighborhood where the poorer Jews lived. Those who were more affluent lived in the Jamileyé, a wealthier neighborhood located in the suburbs of Aleppo.

R' Eliyahu Hamway was eulogized by the greatest rabbis of his generation among whom was his colleague on the Bet Din, R' Ezra Hamway (see #272).

He received his initial education in the General Talmud Torah of Aram Soba (called *Kitab* in Arabic). Among his teachers there were R' Mordechai Abadi (see #8), R' Abraham Tawil (see #579), and R' Mordechai Yedid (see #591).

In the *Kitab*, R' Ezra learned the art of writing *"nus alem"* — with a half-quill. The children learned calligraphy, writing both *Lashon Hakodesh* and Arabic. Destitute parents took pride in their sons who could write with a half-quill. This was a skill in which usually only the rabbis and the scholars were versed.

A Developing Scholar

R' Ezra's primary mentor and teacher was the saintly R' Abraham Haim Ades (see #37). He felt immense love for his select student, and their relationship was as close as that of a father and a son.

By the time R' Ezra was ready to marry, he had gained a reputation as a youth of outstanding spiritual stature and it was obvious that he was slated for greatness. The match suggested for him was the modest and righteous Rachel, the daughter of R' Ezra Marcus. Immediately after the wedding, R' Abraham offered to study daily with R' Ezra. This unexpected offer was extremely tempting, and without thinking twice, R' Ezra consented. However, his father-in-law, R' Ezra Marcus, who was present during the discussion, intervened and asked, "And what about living expenses? How will R' Hamway provide for his home?"

R' Abraham concluded the matter by saying, "All of R' Ezra's needs and livelihood will be on me."

R' Abraham was not surprised at the question, and it appeared that he had in fact prepared for it. He concluded the matter by saying, "All of R' Ezra's needs and livelihood will be on me." He didn't explain how he would be able to support his *havruta* (study partner), but who would question whatever came out of his holy mouth?

His Life as a Dayan

He received his initial appointment as a *dayan* (judge) of the Aram Soba *Bet Din* in 1887 at the young age of 28.

He remained on the Bet Din until he left for Eretz Yisrael in 1935, outliving many of his contemporaries on the Bet Din, including R' Yeshayah Dayan (see #203), who passed away in 1903, R' Shelomo Safdeyé (see #469), who passed away in 1904, R' Eliyahu Hamway (see #271), who passed away in 1915, and R' Yaakob Dweck (see #248), who passed away in 1919.

He placed particular importance on his students' character development.

His brilliance was evident during his sessions in the *Bet Din*. After he had sat many years in the *Bet Din*, and deliberated on thousands of cases in complete harmony with his colleagues, the spiritual leadership of Aram Soba appointed him as the *Rosh Av Beit Din* (Chief Judge) of the Aram Soba community, a distinguished role which he filled until the day he immigrated to the Holy Land in 1935. In the *Bet Din* over which he presided, his colleagues were R' Yomtob Yedid (see #593), R' Moshe Mizrahi (see #424), and R' Ezra Abadi Shayo (see #505).

For 45 years, Hacham Ezra presided over the *Bet Din* and judged righteously. The *Bet Din* had wide jurisdiction to decide on matters affecting the Jewish community, both in family affairs and civil jurisprudence. The *Bet Din's* verdicts also received legal recognition from the pasha, the Ottoman governor who ruled until the end of 1917, when the Turks were expelled from Syria and authority passed over to the French.

While dealing with the financial and domestic affairs of Halab Jews, Hacham Ezra frequently had to deal with what is called the "Fifth Section" of the *Shulhan Aruch* (since the *Shulhan Aruch* only contains four parts, it is a reference to one's ability to find imaginative, common-sense solutions to everyday challenges). In addition to his encompassing knowledge and mastery of Torah, he was well versed in worldly affairs, and the lifestyle of both Jewish and non-Jewish city and village dwellers.

R' Ezra resolved cases within a short period of time. He sorted out convoluted cases and complicated solutions with great wisdom. Litigants were interrogated without favoritism or sanctimony until he could arrive at a just verdict.

His Students

Despite his occupation with the *Bet Din*, R' Ezra founded a yeshiva in Aram Soba. Many students streamed to his *Bet Midrash* to learn from his Torah teachings and his sterling character. Hacham Ezra's influence was pivotal in founding a generation of exceptional Torah scholars. He placed particular importance on his students' character development. His approach was also to nullify the materialistic world outside the yeshiva walls. Many of his students went on to serve holy communities and themselves founded new generations of Torah scholars. Among his notable disciples was R' Raphael Shelomo Laniado (see #364), who was to become the first *Rosh Yeshiva* of *Porat Yosef.* Other notable students were R' Yehudah (Aslan) Attiah (see #118) and R' Yitzhak Chehebar (see #152).

It was only to be expected that R' Ezra would take an active role in his students' marriage arrangements. R' Ezra would sit together with the parents, and first discuss their financial state. When a prospective offer was made, he guided the financial negotiations, and with great skill expedited matters so the match could be closed quickly.

His Other Talents

In addition to his prowess in Torah he was an effective *darshan* (lecturer). He was also known for his sense of humor, which he displayed as a *badhan* (singing humorist) on festive occasions.

His Final Years

In 1935 he moved to Jerusalem and lived out the last 10 years of his life there. He had lost his eyesight while still in Aram Soba. However, he never lost his clarity of mind, especially the insights expressed in his humorous songs and conversations. In Jerusalem he became well known quickly and many of the rabbis of Jerusalem enjoyed visiting him to engage in stimulating and delightful Torah discussions. He passed away on the fourth day of *Hanukah*, on 28 Kislev, 5706 (1945) and was buried on the Mount of Olives.

In his eulogy, R' Yaakob Elmaleh compares the loss of R' Hamway in a way to that of our Patriarch Abraham. He quotes the *Gemara* (*Baba Batra* 91a), which speaks of the eulogy given on the passing of our Patriarch Abraham and mentions the following line, "Woe to the generation that loses its leader, woe to the ship that loses its captain." R' Yaakob explains that the choice of the ship captain as a metaphor is very specific. The doctor plays the role of savior for his patient; however, despite his total devotion to his patient's recovery, he still cannot feel the pain and suffering of his patient as if it were his own. By contrast, the ship's captain, when facing a perilous encounter, will throw his very life into the task of righting his ship and saving the lives of its passengers. The realization that his own life is also at stake drives him to extraordinary lifesaving efforts, beyond his natural capabilities.

His Family

Hacham Ezra left behind three sons, Sam E., Jack and Albert, and six daughters, Senyar, Gilsom, Rena, Adela, Sarah and Jemila.

His Legacy

He left behind many writings in *halachah* and inspirational lectures, most of which remained in Aram Soba and are now presumably lost. However, some of his *hiddushim* (original Torah thoughts) were printed in the book *Vayisa Yaakob* (Jerusalem 5716/1956) writtten by his son-in-law R' Yaakob Elmaleh, also known as Jacob Maleh (see #402). That book consists mostly of inspirational essays and also contains two of the eulogies that were delivered after his death. One is by R' Yaakob Kassin (see #330), the rabbi of the congregation *Magen David* in Brooklyn. The other is by R' Yaakob Elmaleh.

In the year 1988 the *Shaare Ezra Synagogue* of Deal, New Jersey was established in his memory. It was dedicated by his children Albert and Freida Hamway and his grandchildren Ezra (Zourie) and Paula Hamway.

His great-grandson R' Asher Hamway, son of Marvin, recently published a collection of all his writings and his history, titled, *Yismah Ezra*. He did this with the help of his uncle Sam N. Hamway and sons.

נצחו אראלים את המצוקים ונשבה ארון הקודש

ארץ במרר תבכה וירושלם תתן קולה

על פטירת הגאון המפור' אב בית דין מקודש לעדת אר"ץ בירושלם
והוא שפט את עמו בתום לבבו ובתבונות כפיו באר"ץ מ' שנה

מרן עזרא חמווי זצ"ל

הלוי' תצא מביה"ח „שערי־צדק" (ואלאך) בשעה שתים אחה"צ
היום, יום ב', כ"ח כסלו תש"ו.

מטעם בית הדין ורבני העדה, הוכרז על בטול מלאכה בשעת הלוי'.

בית־דין הצדק ורבני עדת החלבים
בירושלם תובב"א

Poster announcing his funeral, signed by Syrian Bet Din

Some of R' Hamway's responsa were made available in the journal *HaMe'asef*, published in Jerusalem by R' Ben-Sion Kouenka. There is also a responsum from him in the book *Asher Yisa Ish* by the *Rishon LeSion* (Chief Rabbi of *Eretz Yisrael*), R' Yaakob Shaul Elyashar (*Even HaEzer,* 13). One of his responsa on the laws of renting was found in the handwriting of R' Mansour ben Shimon who had received it by dictation from R' Ezra (after his eyesight was gone).

He was also responsible for contributing a stanza to the *piyut* (poem) "On the death of the two sons of Aharon," which is recited on *Yom Kippur* before the reading of the Torah in congregations that follow the customs of Aram Soba.

In *Minhat Yehudah* (Vol. I) by R' Yehudah (Aslan) Attiah (see #118), there are two eulogies which R' Ezra delivered, one on R' Yeshayah Dayan (see #203) and the other on R' Eliyahu Hamway (see #271). In addition there is a eulogy on R' Ezra Harari Raful in *LiKedoshim Asher Ba'Aretz* by R' David-Sion Laniado (see #352).

His Involvement in Community Affairs

In 1906, together with other scholars and rabbis of Aram Soba, R' Ezra signed a *halachic* (legal) ruling directed against those who desecrate *Shabbat.* (See Document Section, Document No. 28.)

In 1924 he was the main impetus in fighting the B'nai B'rith organization, which was seeking to make new inroads in Syria. Eventually, he sent the matter to the Aram Soba *Bet Din* in Jerusalem to get a *halachic* opinion. (See Document Section, Document No. 23.)

Besides his involvement in community life in Syria he took a stand on global issues as well.

Besides his involvement in community life in Syria he took a stand on global issues as well. In the city of Sanaa, Yemen, a group began questioning the validity of the *Zohar*. In 1914 he gathered twenty rabbis of Aram Soba and issued a proclamation against them. In it he writes, "As long as they don't correct their ways, they have no portion in the Jewish people." (See Document Section, Document No. 11.)

In 1938 he joined R' Haim Tawil (see #584) and R' Ezra Shayo (see #505) in providing an approbation to the ruling of R' Shaul Sutton (see #558) of the Syrian community of Argentina not to accept converts due to the lack of religious sincerity on the part of the converts. (See Document Section, Document No. 4.)

Even after moving to Jerusalem he took a strong stand against any breaches of tradition. Between 1932 and 1936 a *Hevra Kadisha* (Burial Society) in Jerusalem started to change funeral customs and copy the ways of the gentiles. R' Ezra wrote strongly against those new practices and was joined by R' Haim Tawil (see #584) in issuing a proclamation against them. (See Document Section, Document No. 5.)

תרגום
מגלת אסתר בלשון ערבי
מאת רב קדמון
רבי יוסף אל שמסא זל"הה
הוציאו לאור ראשונה
על פי כ"י ישן אחד ואין שני
הח' הש' כמה"ר שבתי נ"י בכמה"רר
משה חמווי הכהן ביצ"ה ז"ל
ארם צובה
ש' האסת"ר

Title Page of Arabic Translation of Megillat Esther

In 1944 he was involved in the issuance of a letter concerning the appropriation of funds donated in memory of Rav Meir Baal Haness. The issue was whether the funds must go to schools in Tiberias only or should be sent all over *Eretz Yisrael*.The Syrian rabbis argued that the custom in Aleppo over the generations had been to use the money donated for Rav Meir Baal Haness for local causes, whereas Tiberias causes had a separate *kupah* (collection box) marked Tiberias. (See Document Section, Document No. 2.)

He also signed on a request to R' Yaakob Moshe Toledano to help in the building of a synagogue for Syrians who had immigrated to Israel. He was joined by R' Ezra Attiah (see #102), R' Yaakob Ades (see #41), and R' Aharon Harari-Raful (see #303).

[273] HAMWAY, R' Shimon

רבי שמעון חמווי

(— 1832)

Worthy scholar and rabbi of Aram Soba. In 1828 he was the third among nine signers by a contract dealing with a guarantee for a fund in support of scholars. He passed away in 5592 (1832).

[274] HAMWAY, R' Yomtob

רבי יום טוב חמווי

Worthy scholar of Aram Soba. The Chief Rabbi, R' Shemuel Laniado (see #372), writing in the approbation to *Ha'ach Nafsheinu* by R' Abraham Hamway (see #269), speaks of R' Yomtob's death as the tragic loss of a learned and pious scholar. He had been informed of the passing of three worthy scholars at the same time. The other two were R' Haim Mordechai Labaton (see #336) and R' Ezra Chasky (see #146).

[275] HAMWAY (BEYDA), R' Moshe

רבי משה חמווי (ביצ'ה)

(— 1905)

Worthy scholar and rabbi of Aram Soba. He passed away on 15 Tamuz, 5665 (1905).

In 1901 his son, R' Shabbetai, published a translation and elucidation in Arabic of *Megillat Esther* based on the writings of R' Yosef el Shamsa, an unknown rabbi of earlier generations. At the end of the book he lists other manuscripts available to be printed, some of them from rabbis of Aram Soba.

[276] HAMWAY (CHASKY), R' Shaul

רבי שאול חמווי (כאסכי)

(— 1916)

Worthy scholar and scribe of Aram Soba. He was a son of R' Nissim Hamway and passed away on 24 Nissan, 5676 (1916).

[277] HAMWAY (CHASKY), R' Yaakob

רבי יעקב חמווי (כאסכי)

(— 1858)

Worthy scholar and *dayan* (judge) of Aram Soba. In 1852 he joined other scholars and rabbis of Aram Soba in signing the approbation for the book *Kenesiyah Leshem Shamayim* by R' Menashe Sutton (see #551). (See Document Section, Document No. 31.) He passed away on 20 Shevat, 5618 (1858). At the Ben-Zvi Institute there is a manuscript (file No. 302) containing the signature of a R' Yaakob Bekhor David Chasky (second signer), who may be the same as our R' Yaakob Hamway. He signed together with R' Yedidyah Hai Dayan (first signer) on 8 Tamuz, 5570 (1810).

[278] HANAN, R' Eliyahu

רבי אליהו חנן

(— 1696)

Worthy scholar of Aram Soba. He passed away at a relatively young age on the day before *Rosh Hashanah* 5457 (1696), the only son of his father Yaakob (see #279), who mourned him bitterly.

[279] HANAN, R' Yaakob

רבי יעקב חנן

(— 1706)

Worthy scholar and rabbi of Aram Soba. He was known as a man of substance, whose only son Eliyahu (see #278) died tragically during his lifetime. He passed away on 14 Av, 5466 (1706).

[280] HARARI, R' Abraham

רבי אברהם הררי

(18th century)

Worthy scholar of Aram Soba. He is mentioned in the introduction to the book *Zechor LeYitzhak* written by his grandson Yitzhak Harari (see #295).

[281] HARARI, R' Haim

רבי חיים הררי

(19th century)

Worthy scholar of Aram Soba. His signature appears together with that of R' Moshe HaLevi on a hand-written document dated 1814. The original document is stored at the Ben-Zvi Institute (file no. 302).

[282] HARARI, R' Hiyya

רבי חייא הררי

(18th century)

Worthy scholar and rabbi of Aram Soba. He wrote the introduction to the book *Zechor LeYitzhak* written by his father, R' Yitzhak Harari (see #295).

[283] HARARI, R' Hiyya

רבי חייא הררי

(— 1904)

Worthy scholar and rabbi of Aram Soba. He was a son of R' Yitzhak Harari and a brother of R' Moshe Harari (see #291), R' Yosef Harari, and R' Aboud Harari (a well-known philanthropist). In 1895 he joined other rabbis of Aram Soba in signing the approbation to the book *Shalom Le'Am*, of R' Shalom Hedaya (see #310).

In 1903 he left Aram Soba for Egypt, with the intent of ultimately settling in Jerusalem. However, he passed away in Egypt the following year on 10 Adar, 5664 (1904).

[284] HARARI, R' Michael

רבי מיכאל הררי

(18th century)

Worthy scholar and rabbi of Aram Soba. He was the father-in-law of R' Abraham Shemuel Laniado (see #347). R' Michael is mentioned with high praise during the course of a eulogy delivered in 1746 on the death of his son-in-law, who had died at a young age.

R' Michael Harari (#284) joined other rabbis and scholars of Aram Soba in signing on the halachic (legal) ruling against eating grape leaves.

He joined other rabbis and scholars of Aram Soba in signing on the *halachic* (legal) ruling against eating grape leaves because of worm infestation, as recorded in the book *Hanan Elokim* written by R' Haim Abulafia. (See Document Section, Document No. 13.)

[285] **HARARI, R' Michael**

רבי מיכאל הררי

(— 1852)

Worthy young scholar of Damascus. He passed away in his youth on 19 Kislev, 5613 (1852).

[286] **HARARI, R' Michael**

רבי מיכאל הררי

(19th century)

Worthy scholar and rabbi of Aram Soba. He was the son of the renowned R' Yitzhak Harari (see #295). He joined his brothers, R' Moshe and R' Hiyya, in writing an introduction to their father's book, *Zechor LeYitzhak*.

[287] **HARARI, R' Moshe**

רבי משה הררי

(— 1649)

Worthy scholar and philanthropist of Aram Soba. He was known for the support that he gave to poor scholars and families. R' Moshe had a good position as a tax collector with the local government. However, he was murdered by gangsters, who hanged his body in the Bureau of Taxation. This tragic event occurred on *Rosh Hodesh* Adar, 5409 (1649).

R' Moshe Harari (#288) got out of bed, got dressed, washed for bread, and ate with the proper kavanah.

[288] **HARARI, R' Moshe**

רבי משה הררי

(— 1723)

Eminent scholar and Kabbalist of Aram Soba. His daughter's son was R' Yitzhak Harari (see #295), author of the famous book, *Zechor LeYitzhak*. R' Yitzhak praises him in the introduction to the book. He passed away on 24 Heshvan, 5484 (1723). His daughter's husband was R' Moshe Harari (see #289).

In 1715 R' Moshe's name appears as the first of the signers to a *halachic* (legal) ruling together with other rabbis of Aram Soba concerning the validity of Kabbalah and the writings of the *Ari'zal*. (See Document Section, Document No. 10.) The ruling was published in the book *Dibrei Yosef* written by R' Yosef Ergas. Other signers to that ruling were R' Shemuel Pinto (see #462), R' Shemuel Dweck (see #242), R' Sadkah Houssin (see #313), and R' Yosef Elisha Nawi (see #439).

In 1691 he signed an approbation to the book *Hevel Bnai Yehudah* written by R' Shimon Habilio. He joined other rabbis and scholars of Aram Soba in signing on the *halachic* (legal) ruling against eating grape leaves because of worm infestation, as recorded in the book *Hanan Elokim* written by R' Haim Abulafia. (See Document Section, Document No. 13.) His name also appears among the signatories to the book *Bet Din shel Shelomo* by R' Raphael Shelomo Laniado (see #363) (*Orah Haim*, Section 17).

R' Mordechai Atzban (see #122) writes about his dedication to *mitzvot* in the introduction to his book *Zovei'ah Todah*. R' Mordechai relates that one year on the first night of *Sukkot*, when R' Moshe Harari was lying in bed, he suddenly realized that when he ate his festive meal in the *Sukkah* earlier that evening, he did not have the proper *kavanah* (conscious attention) of fulfilling the *mitzvah* of eating a *kezayit* (olive-sized amount) of bread in the *sukkah*. He got out of bed, got dressed, washed for bread, and ate with the proper *kavanah*. This story is mentioned by the *Hida*, as well, in his book *Simhat HaRegel*.

The *Hida* (R' Haim Yosef David Azulai) also mentions him in his book *Shem HaGedolim* (40), remarking that R' Moshe is an expert in the mystical knowledge concerning lotteries and other practical implication of Kabbalah. He notes that he had heard about him from R' Aba Mari, who was advised by R' Binyamin Tawil that he could attest to R' Moshe Harari's mystical knowledge.

[289] **HARARI, R' Moshe**

רבי משה הררי

(18th century)

Eminent scholar and rabbi of Aram Soba. He was the son of R' Abraham Harari (see #280) and the father of R' Yitzhak Harari (see #295), author of the renowned book *Zechor LeYitzhak*. His father-in-law was the

Kabbalist, R' Moshe Harari (see #288). He is believed to be the contributor of a long responsum (on *Hoshen Mishpat*, section 35), which appears in the book *Korban Isheh* by R' Eliyahu Shamah (see #499).

[290] **HARARI, R' Moshe**

רבי משה הררי

(— 1817)

Worthy scholar and rabbi of Aram Soba. He was responsible for writing the introduction to the renowned book *Zechor Le-Yitzhak* written by his father R' Yitzhak Harari (see #295). It appears that he passed away on 6 Elul, 5577 (1817).

[291] **HARARI, R' Moshe**

רבי משה הררי

(— 1917)

Eminent scholar and *dayan* (judge) of Aram Soba. He was a son of R' Yitzhak Harari and a brother of R' Hiyya Harari (see #283), R' Yosef Harari, and R' Aboud Harari (a well-known philanthropist). R' Moshe was a member of the *Bet Din* of Aram Soba, but in his later years he settled in Jerusalem. He passed away on 11 Kislev, 5678 (1917).

R' Moshe signed the approbation for the book *Shalom Le'Am* (Aram Soba 5655/1895) by R' Shalom Hedaya (see #310). One of his responsa was included in the book *Yisa Ish* by R' Yaakob Shaul Elyashar (the *Rashal*).

[292] **HARARI, R' Shelomo**

רבי שלמה הררי

(— 1842)

Worthy scholar and rabbi of Damascus. He is believed to have been the father of R' Yaakob Harari (see #293) and R' Yitzhak Haim Harari (see #298). He passed away on 12 Adar, 5602 (1842).

[293] **HARARI, R' Yaakob**

רבי יעקב הררי

(— 1888)

Worthy scholar and rabbi of Damascus. It appears that he was the son of R' Shelomo Harari (see #292). R' Yaakob passed away on 29 Adar, 5648 (1888).

[294] **HARARI, R' Yeshayah**

רבי ישעיה הררי

(— 1915)

Worthy scholar of Aram Soba. He passed away on 9 Tevet, 5676 (1915).

[295] **HARARI, R' Yitzhak**

רבי יצחק הררי

(— 1810)

Distinguished scholar of Aram Soba. He is known for his important book *Zechor LeYitzhak* (Livorno 5578/1818), which continues to be used by rabbis as a guide to *halachic* (legal) decisions.

He was descended from the scholarly Harari family, both on his father's side and his mother's side. His father was R' Moshe Harari (see #289), son of R' Abraham Harari (see #280). His mother's father was also named R' Moshe Harari (see #288), an important Kabbalist, who had been a descendant of the scholar R' Yehudah Rozanis, author of *Mishneh LeMelech* on the *Rambam*.

R' Yitzhak had a lifelong desire to go to *Eretz Yisrael* and later in life he did manage to settle in Safed, despite many difficulties. He passed away in Safed in the year 1810. Among those who eulogized him was R' Abraham Sutton (see #535), the eulogy being included in his book *Malel Le'Abraham* (eulogy no. 10). He was blessed with three scholarly sons: R' Moshe (see #290), R' Michael (see #286), and R' Hiyya (see #282).

He received approbations for his book *Zechor LeYitzhak* from R' Abraham Sutton, R' Eliyahu Shamah, author of *Korban Isheh* (see #499), and R' Yisrael Sasson (see #483). He also received an approbation from R' Moshe Sosin, who happened to be in Aram Soba at the time as an emissary of the rabbis of *Eretz Yisrael*. His three scholarly sons joined together in writing an introduction to the book. R' Eliyahu Shamah also speaks highly of R' Yitzhak in his own book *Korban Isheh* (*Yoreh Deah*, 16).

R' Yitzhak himself signed with other rabbis of Aram Soba on the approbation to the book *Beirach Moshe* written by R' Moshe Galante, the Chief Rabbi of Damascus. He

שות

זכור ליצחק

חלק א"ח

פה ליוורנו יע"א

שנת שלום רב

שמואל סערון

Title Page of
Zechor LeYitzhak

R' Moshe Harari

also contributed a responsum to that book together with his colleague Eliyahu Shamah.

[296] **HARARI, R' Yitzhak**

רבי יצחק הררי

(— 1866)

Worthy scholar of Aram Soba. He is apparently a grandson of the R' Yitzhak Harari (see #295), who wrote the book *Zechor LeYitzhak*. He passed away on 25 Adar, 5626 (1866), as indicated by his gravestone.

R' Abraham Harari-Raful

[297] **HARARI, R' Yitzhak**

רבי יצחק הררי

(19th century)

Worthy scholar of Aram Soba. He is apparently another grandson of R' Yitzhak Harari (see #295), who wrote the book *Zechor LeYitzhak*. He passed away on 25 Adar, the same date as another grandson with the same name (see #296), but the year of his death is not clear from his gravestone.

[298] **HARARI, R' Yitzhak Haim**

רבי יצחק חיים הררי

(— 1859)

Worthy scholar and rabbi of Damascus. It appears that he was a son of R' Haim Shelomo Harari and brother of R' Yaakob Harari (see #293). R' Yitzhak passed away at a relatively young age on 9 Nissan, 5619 (1859).

[299] **HARARI, R' Yosef**

רבי יוסף הררי

(— 1770)

Worthy scholar and rabbi of Aram Soba. He passed away on 2 Shevat, 5530 (1770).

[300] **HARARI, R' Yosef**

רבי יוסף הררי

(— 1854)

Worthy scholar and rabbi of Damascus. He passed away on 2 Adar, 5614 (1854).

[301] **HARARI (NAHEM), R' Yaakob Yosef**

רבי יעקב יוסף הררי (נאעם)

(— 1937)

Worthy scholar and *dayan* (judge) of Damascus. He passed away on 15 Tevet, 5697 (1937).

[302] **HARARI-RAFUL, R' Abraham**

רבי אברהם הררי־רפול

(1895 — 1992)

Eminent scholar, *dayan* (judge), and senior lecturer of *Yeshivat Porat Yosef* in Jerusalem. He was a son of R' Ezra Harari-Raful (see #304) and was born in Jerusalem in 1895, after his family had moved from Aram Soba.

His Early Years

He was raised in a special home. As a young boy he was once spending a lot of time shining his shoes on *Erev Shabbat*. His father, R' Ezra, noticed this and became concerned that the boy was being overly involved in wordly matters. He told his son, "Shine your soul, not your shoes." Years later R' Abraham remarked, "Whenever I shine my shoes I think of that comment from my father."

"Shine your soul, not your shoes."

He studied in *Yeshivat Ohel Moed* under the tutelage of R' Raphael Shelomo Laniado (see #363). His teacher for Kabbalah was R' Haim Shaul Dweck (see #228). He also studied under R' Ezra Attiah (see #102).

His First Marriage

He married Sarah, daughter of R' Yosef Zakai, in the year 1914. She revealed her great respect for his Torah knowledge when his eyesight became impaired, hindering his learning ability. She said, "If I could, I would give him my eyes."

He and his wife remained in *Eretz Yisrael* during World War I and lived in extreme poverty. In fact, it was so bad that they were forced to eat animal food. To add to his tribulations, he was forced to go into hiding to avoid being drafted into the Turkish Army. During one period he feigned illness and lay in a hospital bed. He later told someone that he finished *Tehillim* six times while under the covers. At other times he hid in the attic of R' Haim Shaul Dweck, his teacher of Kabbalah, and would learn with his teacher whenever he could. However, most of his time was spent in the dark attic and this took its toll on his vision.

His Second Marriage

After his first wife passed away in 1969, R' Abraham remarried, but his second wife passed away eight years later. He told someone, "Imagine if *Hashem* told me, 'I'll give her to you for only eight years.' Would I have said 'No, thank You'?"

A Respected Scholar

He became a senior lecturer in the *Yeshivat Porat Yosef* and was appointed to a postion as *dayan* on the Sephardic *Bet Din* of Jerusalem. The great respect that other Torah scholars had for him is illustrated by the following story. When Salhah, the wife of R' Abraham Ades (see #37), was deathly ill, R' Ades gathered ten outstanding scholars to say the entire *Tehillim* with the proper *kavanah* (meditation) on *Hashem's* name. R' Abraham Harari-Raful was one of them.

His Influence on Others

When he saw someone wasting time from learning Torah, he would tell him a *devar Torah* (Torah thought). If the person didn't show interest, R' Abraham would say, "You are passing up on gems." He would always end his remarks with a question to keep the person thinking afterwards.

In 1982 he published his father's book *Hechin Ezra*. At the end he included stories of great rabbis of old. He explained that through hearing stories of the righteous, people want to emulate them. He also used stories of *gedolim* (great rabbis) as an educational tool. Many of the stories of the great Syrian rabbis in the present book were told by him.

When his children misbehaved he didn't rebuke them directly. He would wait a day and tell them a story related to the topic.

His Feeling for Others

A person once came to him for a *berachah* (blessing) for his wife, who was depressed. R' Abraham asked, "Do you have a car?" The man didn't understand the connection to his request for a *berachah*. R' Abraham said, "Take me to your home." He went with the man and spent a few hours talking with the woman and giving her encouragement and strength.

Whenever he heard about a tragic situation it would bring him to tears. He said, "Wouldn't I cry if it was my child?"

A photographer once came to take his picture. At first, in his humility, he refused, saying he was not a *gadol*. However, after thinking a bit more about it, he said, "It's the man's livelihood," and agreed.

His Piety

R' Abraham Mounsa recalled what the rabbis of the previous generation said of R' Abraham, "He isn't classified as one who has fear of sin; rather, he doesn't know what sin is."

On one occasion it was late and he hadn't come home yet. His wife was nervous and sent a grandson to check on him. He found him in a synagogue with many *minyanim* (prayer groups), going from *minyan* to *minyan* answering *Amen*. He explained, "The time will come when I won't be able to answer *Amen*. I am taking advantage of the opportunity." He used to say his name was *Amen* (Abraham Mordechai Nissim).

> **A Caged Lion.** R' Abraham Harari-Raful once went to a zoo, and burst out crying when he saw a lion in a cage. The *Zohar* says that while the Jews are in exile, *Hashem* is like a caged lion; a king confined in a foreign place. When R' Abraham saw that image in life, the tragedy of exile and the destruction of the Temple brought him to tears.

His Memory

R' Abraham made a deliberate effort to use mnemonic devices to remember where topics in *Gemara* were located. For example, in *Masechet Hulin* the *daf* (folio page), which is numbered *Kaf-Bet* (22), discusses different types of kosher doves, so Hacham Abraham associated the initials *Kaf-Bet* with *"Kasher BeTorim"* (Kosher Doves). On *daf Lamed-Gimel* (33) of *Masechet Nazir*, there is no

When Hacham Abraham had brain surgery in his 80's, the doctor said, that in all his years, he had never seen a brain that was so vital at that age.

Gemara text, just a long *Tosafot* commentary, so for Hacham Abraham *Lamed-Gimel* stood for *"Lo Gemara"* (No *Gemara*). When Hacham Abraham had brain surgery in his 80's, the doctor said, that in all his years, he had never seen a brain that was so vital at that age.

His Passing

When R' Abraham's sister, *Rabanit* Esther Ades, passed away, his family tried hard to conceal her death from him. When he asked to visit, they would tell him, "It's not a good time. She's weak. She's not up to visitors now." He was near the end of his life, and they were afraid the news would upset him and compromise his well-being. On his deathbed, he asked, "How is Esther? Is she o.k.? Is she well? I think she passed away. All my family that have passed to the next world are coming to greet me now, and I see her."

R' Abraham Harari-Raful in his last years

R' Abraham passed away in 1992 at the age of 97.

[303] HARARI-RAFUL, R' Aharon

רבי אהרן הררי־רפול

(1891 — 1961)

Eminent scholar, educator, and *dayan* (judge) of Jerusalem. He was a son of R' Ezra Harari-Raful (see #304) and was born in Jerusalem in 1891 after the family had moved from Aram Soba. R' Aharon was known as an outstanding Torah scholar and became a son-in-law of R' Abraham Ades (see #37). After *Yom Kippur*, he and his brother-in-law, R' Yaakob Ades, would continue to sing the songs of *Yom Kippur*, because they didn't want the day to end.

R' Aharon Harari-Raful

He passed away in 26 Av, 5721 (1961) leaving two sons who are engaged in holy vocations with the Syrian community in Brooklyn — R' Abraham of the *Keter Torah* congregation and R' Yosef of *Ateret Torah* — as well as a third son, Shaul Harari-Raful.

Interlude in Tashkent

When World War I broke out, he was forced to leave the country to avoid the Turkish military draft. He left behind his wife Rachel and two children, a boy Ezra and a girl Simchah. He ended up in Tashkent (Bukhara) where he taught *Gemara* for six years. Upon his return to Jerusalem in 1920 he was informed that both his children had passed away due to the hunger and disease that ravaged Jerusalem during World War I. Subsequently, his wife gave birth to six daughters.

A Bukharan Jew once met one of R' Aharon's sons and told him of his father's impact on the Bukharan community during his short stay there in World War I. During the short time he was there he built a *mikveh* (ritual bathhouse) in a town that had lacked one.

Life in Jerusalem

In Jerusalem he continued in his teaching vocation and began to work with R' Eliyahu Shamah (see #500) to help the Aram Soba emigrant community in Jerusalem, especially the needy families with minimal resources. To relieve the community's desperate economic conditions, they set up a market in Jerusalem, which came to be called the Shamah Market.

From time to time he went out to other cities as an emissary of the Torah and *hesed* institutions of Jerusalem. Then, with the founding of the Talmud Torah *Magen David* by the Aram Soba community of Jerusalem he was appointed its director. In his later years he became a member of the Rabbinical Court of Tel Aviv.

His Bond with the Saba Kadisha

R' Aharon served and waited on the *Saba Kadisha*, R' Shelomo Eliezer Alfandri (see #44). His wife Rachel pleaded with her husband to ask the *Saba Kadisha* for a *berachah* (blessing) for a son to fulfill the commandment *P'ru u-R'vu* (procreation). Even though R' Aharon had a close relationship with the *Saba Kadisha*, he was afraid to ask for a *berachah*. (Great rabbis are sometimes upset when people view them as magical genies to give blessings.)

However, Rachel was persistent. One day she followed her husband to the *Saba Kadisha's* house and she entered his room. The *Saba Kadisha* picked up his head, and seeing her, he asked R' Aharon who had let the woman in. (Women were not usually allowed.) R' Aharon answered that she was his wife. The *Saba Kadisha* then asked, "What does she want?" R' Aharon answered, "She wants a *berachah* for a baby boy." At that the *Saba Kadisha* said, "And you don't have a mouth?" and blessed them. The next year, she gave birth to a boy and they named him Avraham Shelomo — Avraham after Rachel's father, R' Abraham Ades (see #37), and Shelomo using the *Saba Kadisha's* first name as a tribute to the rabbi whose blessing brought the child.

Not long after, they were blessed with a second boy whom they named Yosef Eliezer — Yosef after his grandfather, Yosef Raful (his father's father), and Eliezer using the *Saba Kadisha's* second name. (It is interesting to note that the *Saba Kadisha* had no children of his own.) A few years later they were blessed with a third son, whom they named Shaul. R' Aharon attributed the birth of his three sons to the blessing of the *Saba Kadisha*.

Finding Joy in an Oil Spill

R' Aharon took everything in stride. R Abraham Zafrani related the following story, which he had witnessed. R' Aharon came to Syria to the Great Synagogue and went to light candles at the cave of Eliyahu HaNabi. He bent down to light the candles, not realizing that a big oil candelabrum hung from the low ceiling. When he stood up, he bumped his head on it and the oil poured all over him. Instead of becoming upset or agitated, he broke into a jubilant dance and started to sing the verse in *Tehillim*, "Like the good oil that goes down the beard, the beard of Aharon" (133:2).

Instead of becoming upset or agitated, he broke into a jubilant dance and started to sing.

His Benevolence

As the aide to the *Saba Kadisha* he used to shop for his household needs, stocking the house with fruits and vegetables from the local market. Once R' Aharon was not available and someone else did the shopping. The *Saba Kadisha* gave him the same few dollars that he always gave R' Aharon and the fellow brought back a small basket with hardly enough food. The *Saba Kadisha* told him that he must have gone to an expensive store because R' Aharon always came back with much more. Subsequently, the man asked R' Aharon for the location of this discount store. He replied, "You add your money and you bring more."

Magen David Jerusalem 1941, R' Aharon Harari-Raful in center, top row

The above is but one example of his hidden *hesed* (benevolence). His brother-in-law, R' Yaacob Ades, had a position in the Tel Aviv *Bet Din* and R' Aharon was on the Jerusalem *Bet Din*. When he heard that R' Ades had a heart condition and the traveling was difficult for him he offered to switch and spent the week away from his family. By the time he came home each week most of his weekly salary had already been distributed to the needy.

His Position with Yeshivat Magen David, Jerusalem

He was the principal of *Yeshivat Magen David* and ran it on a shoestring budget. One of the teachers related that due to lack of funds they had a shortage of teachers. R' Aharon would teach three grades simultaneously. He would teach one group, have them review, then teach the next group, and so on.

One teacher threatened to leave due to the lack of cleanliness because they couldn't afford a janitor. R' Aharon said, "No problem." He simply went into the classroom and instructed each boy to pick up two pieces of garbage a day.

A Lesson from Water

His wife Rachel was a special person in her own right. Although she had no formal schooling, she was infused with the greatness and faith of her father's house. Her children relate that when she was going through hard times, she would drink a lot of water. Someone once asked her why she did that. She explained, "When I drink I make the *berachah, 'shehakol nihe'yeh b'dvaro'* [all was created with His word]. The glass of water was created by *Hashem*, the entire world was created by *Hashem*, and the problem was created by *Hashem*. And if it was created by *Hashem*, He knows what He is doing."

A Voice in the Night

There was a man who had a difficult life and would come to R' Aharon for advice and encouragement, and would pour his heart out to him. He would come at all times of the day and night. More often than not, he would come at the wee hours of the morning and stand in the street calling out "Hacham Aharon, Hacham Aharon," until R' Aharon would be awakened and go to him. After this went on for some time, his wife Rachel decided enough was enough, and told the fellow to stop waking them up. Hacham Aharon told the man, "If you need me at night, call for Hacham Shimon and I will know who you mean."

[304] HARARI-RAFUL, R' Ezra

רבי עזרא הררי־רפול

(1857 — 1936)

R' Ezra Harari-Raful

Eminent *dayan* (judge) of the Sephardic *Bet Din* in Jerusalem and founder of *Yeshivat Ohel Moed*. He was born in 1857 in Aram Soba to R' Yosef ben Yeshayah. He studied the revealed approach to Torah under R' Yaakob Shaul Dweck (see #248). His other notable teachers were R' Mordechai Labaton (see #336), R' Mordechai Abadi (see #8), and his uncle, R' Nissim Harari-Raful (see #305).

In 1890, at the age of 32, he left his parents to raise his family in Jerusalem, becoming one of the first of the Aram Soba community of his generation to make the move. On the way the boat stopped in Beirut and the townspeople came to greet him and invite him for lunch but he refused to leave the boat out of fear that they would convince him to stay.

In Jerusalem, he studied Kabbalah under R' Haim Shaul Dweck (see #228) in the yeshiva *Rehovot HaNahar*.

R' Ezra was active in opening institutions of learning in Jerusalem. In 1904 he became one of the founders of the yeshiva *Ohel Moed*, which was to be the forerunner of *Porat Yosef*. After *Ohel Moed* was closed at the outbreak of World War I, he opened another yeshiva in 1918 which eventually joined with *Porat Yosef* in 1923. In 1920, he started an elementary school in Jerusalem called *Magen David*. The building still stands today on Rehov David Yellin; it was run by his son, Hacham Aharon Harari-Raful (see # 303).

He was a founder of the Council of the Aram Soba Community in Jerusalem and was active in improving the material and spiritual circumstances of the members of that community who came to Jerusalem during his lifetime. He was especially concerned with arranging for the support of scholars who had dedicated themselves to the study of Kabbalah.

He was instrumental in forming the *"Bet Din* of the Aram Soba Community in Jerusalem" and served on it as a *dayan* (judge), together with R' Abraham Ades (see #37) and R' Yosef Yedid (see #594). In one of their more notable actions they issued a *halachic* ruling against the B'nai B'rith organization in 1924. (See Document Section, Document No. 23.) R' Ezra earned his own living as an accountant and was one of the builders of Jerusalem. Through his influence a number of houses were built in the Ruhamah district of Jerusalem.

He passed away on 10 Sivan, 5696 (1936) and was eulogized by the leading rabbis of Jerusalem, among whom were R' Ezra Hamway (see #272) and R' Shalom Hedaya (see #310). He left five sons: R' Aharon (see

It's the Thought that Counts. Each month, R' Ezra would give his son an envelope with money to pay for tuition for yeshiva. As he handed him the envelope he would say, "I am now fulfilling the *mitzvah* of teaching my son Torah."

#303), R' Abraham (see #302), R' Shalom, R' Eliyahu, and R' David.

He also had one daughter, Haya Esther, who became the wife of R' Yaakob Ades (see #41). When R' Ades spoke at the funeral of his mother-in-law Simchah Harari-Raful, he gave a wonderful picture of the great house which he had been privileged to enter. "I remember when I was very young, before I merited to be attached to them as to the *Shechinah* (Divine Presence), the greatest joy and spiritual inspiration I had at that time was to visit their home and to listen to their holy talk and stay close to them. Even at that time I felt the greatest inspiration and holy elation that I received from their pure spirit. That was the feeling of spirituality everyone — who entered that holy house — got. Only words of ethics and fear of G-d could you hear in that house. Instead of idle talk, you heard only holy words from *Hovot HaLevavot* or *Reshit Hochmah*. You felt as if you were transferred to a long-past era and atmosphere of the *Simhat Bet Hasho'evah* on *Sukkot* at the time of the Holy Temple, where you absorbed purity and holiness. This is no exaggeration, but the whole truth as I observed with my eyes."

R' Ezra also found time to write a book of *mussar* (morality and ethics) which was posthumously published by R' Saadyah Manir,with the help of R' Ezra's son R' Abraham under the title *Heichin Ezra* (Jerusalem 5742/1982).

[305] HARARI-RAFUL, R' Nissim
רבי נסים הררי־רפול

(— 1870)

Distinguished scholar and Kabbalist of Aram Soba. He was a son of R' Yeshayah Harari-Raful (see #306). R' Nissim signed together with other scholars and rabbis of Aram Soba in 1852 on the approbation to *Kenesiyah Leshem Shamayim* of R' Menashe Sutton (see #551). (See Document Section, Document No.31.)

His Way of Learning Torah

He went to the *mikveh* every day to be able to study Torah with holiness and purity. He studied together with R' Nissim Lofez (see #396). They studied from midnight until daybreak and he would tell his learning partner, "I have no greater pleasure in the world than the Torah knowledge we were worthy enough to learn tonight. We were blessed with an understanding of the truths of the Torah and we also came to an understanding of the great sages, such as the *Rashba*, the *Ritba*, and the *Ran*."

"I have no greater pleasure in the world than the Torah knowledge we were worthy enough to learn tonight."

His colleague in the study of Kabbalah was R' Eliyahu Mishan (see #418), author of the book *Sefat Emet*. The story is told that when the two friends went to Jerusalem for a visit, the Kabbalist R' Moshe ibn Sasson (author of *Shemen Sasson* on *Etz HaHaim*) heard them engaged in a discussion of Kabbalah. He was disconcerted by the depth of their reasoning and cried out, "I was not able to follow what they were saying!"

ספר
עלי נהר
פעה"ק ירושלם תובב"א

Title Page of *Alei Nahar*

Before he began to study, he would say the prayers of "*Tikkun Hatzot*." When he studied, he sat in fear and trepidation, as if in front of a king. Even in the hottest weather he did not remove his hat and jacket. In his great humility he never asked anyone to bring him a book. When testing younger students he never told them they made a mistake; rather, he would say, "Listen to the way I learned the topic," and they would realize the fallacies on their own.

When testing younger students he never told them they made a mistake.

סדר
תקון חצות
פעה"ק ירושלם
שנה קיבוץ גליות לפ"ק

Title Page of *Tikkun Hatzot*

With all his humility, he held firm on issues of *Bitul Torah* (wasting valuable Torah-study time). Once, one of the students accidently spilled the oil lantern on a seat in the synagogue and when the man who sat there saw what happened he started to reprimand the young man. R' Nissim got involved and told the upset fellow, "Even if they spilled oil on my clothes I wouldn't say anything as long as they are learning. Aren't you afraid that by yelling at the boy you would extinguish his enthusiaism for Torah learning? Just as the reward for learning outweighs all *mitzvot*, the punishment of interrupting learning outweighs all sins."

His Piety

Even at a young age he was very pious. At the age of 14 he learnt the entire *Seder Mishnayot* of *Taharot* (dealing with laws of purity) so that when he got married he would be able to think about them in the proper times.

Although he was busy with his Torah learning and also served on the *Bet Din,* he and his colleague R' Abraham Shabbetai (see #494) would fast the entire week during *Shobabim* [acronym for six weeks from *Perashat Shemot* to *Perashat Mishpatim].* The fast extended for six days, from Sunday to Friday. (See box #313, "The Spiritual Heights of Aram Soba," for a lengthy discussion on these weeklong fasts.)

The full measure of his great piety became evident only after his death.

The full measure of his great piety became evident only after his death. When the burial society purified his body they found that it was dressed in sackcloth, which he had been wearing his entire life. He passed away on 15 Shevat, 5630 (1870).

His Writings

Many of his *hiddushim* (original Torah thoughts) on Kabbalah were posthumously published in the book *Alei Nahar* (Jerusalem 5663/1903). In the introduction, written by Kabbalist scholars of Aram Soba in Jerusalem, R' Nissim and the brilliance of his work were highly praised. He also wrote the book *Tikkun Hatzot* (Jerusalem 5658/1898), a treatise on the inner meaning of rising at midnight to pray to *Hashem* and to lament the exile of the *Shechinah* (His Divine Presence).

Siddur written in original handwriting of R' Nissim Harari-Raful

Most of his works remained in manuscript form. One of his responsa was published in the book *Peh Eliyahu* of R' Eliyahu Hamway (see #271). Another appeared in the book *VeYosef Abraham* by R' Abraham Dayan (see #173). R' Haim Shaul Dweck (see #228) considered him one of his teachers in Kabbalah and prayed from the *siddur* that R' Harari-Raful wrote to pray from.

His Mystical Powers

One *Erev Rosh Hashanah,* Hacham Nissim went to buy a gourd from the market. He paid the gentile grocer with a large coin and waited for his change. The gentile just smiled for he had no intention of returning the money. Hacham Nissim went home and the gentile was left paralyzed in that position. His friends who saw Hacham Nissim leaving the store around the time of the paralysis realized the connection and went to the rabbi's house in his name to beg for forgiveness and to ask that he should pray for the man's recovery. Hacham Nissim agreed and, not long afterward, the man recovered and G-d's name was publicly sanctified.

The French consul in Aleppo also came to feel the impact of Hacham Nissim's mystical powers. Two Jews worked for a certain wealthy gentile, who happened to lose a large sum of money and suspected his Jewish workers. The wealthy man had French citizenship and was protected by the French consul, who allowed these Jews to be unjustifiably tortured. When Hacham Nissim heard this he went to the synagogue, opened the *heichal,* and put the French consul in *herem* (excommunication), using the text in the book *Kol Bo*. At that very moment the French consul was out riding on his large and powerful horse, followed by his aides on their horses. Suddenly the consul's horse went wild and threw him to the ground. The horse began to trample him and the consul cried out with heart-wrenching screams, but to no avail. He died a short while later. People understood it was a direct result of the torture he allowed to be inflicted on the two Jews.

[306] HARARI-RAFUL, R' Yeshayah

רבי ישעיה הררי־רפול

(19th century)

Worthy scholar and community leader of Aram Soba. He left two sons: R' Nissim (see #198) and R' Yosef. He appears to have been the father-in-law of R' Shelomo Nehmad (see #447).

HARARY (see HARARI)

Hedaya Lineage. The earliest-known member of the Hedaya family of Aram Soba was R' Moshe Haim Hedaya (see #308), who lived in the 19th century. However, tradition traces the lineage back to R' Saadiah Gaon, who was the head of the Babylonian community in the 10th century. In fact, the name Hedaya is believed to be the Arabic translation of the name Saadiah. R' Moshe Haim was the father of R' Shalom Hedaya (see #310), the *Av Bet Din* (Chief Judge) of the Sephardic *Bet Din* of Jerusalem and the head of the *Bet El* yeshiva. R' Shalom had four sons, one of whom, R' Obadiah Hedaya (see #309), re-established the yeshiva *Bet El* after it had been destroyed by the Arabs in 1948.

[307] **HEDAYA, R' Ezra**

רבי עזרא הדאיה

(1910 — 1980)

Worthy scholar and *dayan* (judge) of Haifa. He was born in Jerusalem in 1910, a son of R' Shalom Hedaya (see #310) and a brother of R' Yitzhak Hedaya (see #311) and R' Obadiah Hedaya (see #309). R' Ezra moved to Haifa where he served as a member of the regional *Bet Din*. He also wrote a manuscript, *Nahalat Ezra*, which was published after his death in Jerusalem (5744/1984) by the Machon HaKtav. He passed away on 14 Nissan, 5740 (1980).

[308] **HEDAYA, R' Moshe Haim**

רבי משה חיים הדאיה

(19th century)

Rabbi and *dayan* (judge) of Hebron. The book *Yehudei HaMizrach Be'Eretz Yisrael* (Vol. II, page 218, item 3) mentions him as having signed the letter of authorization for the mission of R' Menahem Burla, an emissary of the rabbis of Hebron in 1839. His son was the famous Hacham Shalom Hedaya (#310).

[309] **HEDAYA, R' Obadiah**

רבי עובדיה הדאיה

(1890 — 1969)

Distinguished scholar, rabbi, and *dayan* (judge). Besides being a prolific author, he occupied many noteworthy rabbinical positions, among which were: Chief Rabbi of Petah Tikvah, *dayan* (judge) of the Senior Appeals *Bet Din* in Jerusalem, and a member of the Council of Chief Rabbis of Israel. Despite all of the honors bestowed on him throughout his life he remained an intensely pious Jew, observing the *Tikkun Hatzot* (midnight service) every night and daily immersion in the *mikveh*. Until the age of 49 he served as the regular *hazzan* (cantor) at the Kabbalist yeshiva *Oz VeHadar* adjacent to *Yeshivat Porat Yosef* in Jerusalem. He continued to serve as *hazzan* on special occasions after that, applying the interpretive meanings to the prayers as specified by the *Ari'zal* (R' Yitzhak Luria), while still managing to complete them in time with the congregation. He was always an extremely pleasant and friendly man, with a smile on his lips in every circumstance.

R' Obadiah Hedaya

R' Ezra Hedaya

His Childhood

He was born in Aram Soba in 1890 to R' Shalom Hedaya (see #310), who was to become the head of the Sephardic *Bet Din* of Jerusalem. On his mother's side he was a grandson of R' Yitzhak Labaton (see #340), a respected member of the *Bet Din*.

His parents moved to Jerusalem when he was 5 years old and there he joined other children of his generation as a student of the *Talmud Torah Doresh Sion*. However, his father knew that the child was meant for greatness and sought an outstanding scholar to be his tutor. He cast his eyes on R' Shalom Bohbout, a respected Kabbalist, who was very poor, but devoted himself to Torah studies and to earnest prayers accompanied by the *kavanot* (meditations) specified by the *Ari'zal* (R' Yitzhak Luria).

R' Obadiah Hedaya giving shiur to rabbis of yeshiva Bet El in Medrash Matalon Jerusalem. From right: R' Mordechai Attiah (see #109), R' Ezra Hedaya (see #307), R' Yissachar Abu Aziz, R' Abraham Naim Shahror, R' Yitzhak Hedaya (see #311), R' Mordechai Sharabi, R' Yosef Shayo (see #507), R' Shaul David Hai, R' Ezra Ades (see #38), R' Reuven Zamir

Even when saying the most mundane prayer (such as *"Asher Yatzar,"* which is recited after attending to physical needs), he was careful to read the prayer from a *siddur*, together with all of the required *kavanot*.

Since R' Bohbout was in desperate straits, R' Hedaya was able to persuade him to learn with his young son for a month in exchange for a gold coin. During that short time R' Bohbout bonded with the child, setting the basis for a continued relationship. In fact, when the boy was only 7 years old, he had already acquired the rudiments of Kabbalah from his tutor, but without his father's knowledge.

As he grew older, the young Obadiah also received instruction from R' Yitzhak Shrem (see #518) and R' Yitzhak Alfia (see #46), both members of the *Bet Din*. The boy was especially attracted to Kabbalists and spent as much time as he could at the Kabbalist yeshiva *Bet El*. There he attached himself to R' Moshe ibn Sasson, the author of the book *Shemen Sasson*, who served as the *hazzan* in *Bet El*, following with the *kavanot* of the *Rashash* (R' Shalom Sharabi). In his later years, his father, R' Shalom, was to become head of *Bet El*, a position which he held until his death in 1945, and R' Obadiah was to become one of its most dedicated scholars.

The boy was especially attracted to Kabbalists and spent as much time as he could at the Kabbalist yeshiva Bet El.

R' Obadiah returned to Syria at the age of 24 to avoid the Turkish military draft in World War I. After spending the war years immersed in Torah studies in the land of his birth, he returned to Jerusalem and before long he was appointed as a *dayan* (judge) at the Sephardic *Bet Din*. With the opening of the yeshiva *Porat Yosef* in 1923 he was asked to serve as a senior lecturer (*Resh Metivta)*.

The Kabbalah section of the yeshiva was named *Oz VeHadar*. The *tefillot* there were conducted in accordance with the the *kavanot* of the *Ari'zal*. R' Obadiah led these *tefillot* as the *hazzan*.

In 1939 he was asked to take the position of Chief Rabbi in Petah Tikvah. In 1948, while he was still in Petah Tikvah, the world of Kabbalah scholarship was struck a catastrophic blow with the destruction of the *yeshivot Bet El* and *Porat Yosef* in the Old City of Jerusalem. And so, when R' Obadiah returned to Jerusalem in 1951 to take a judgeship on the Senior Appeals *Bet Din*, he immediately set to work on schemes to renew the study of Kabbalah in the Sephardic community. To that end he formed small groups of Kabbalah scholars to maintain continuity with the spirit of *Bet El*, which had been the classic Kabbalist yeshiva of the Sephardim.

Yeshiva on the Roof. R' Obadiah Hedaya recounted that he had a dream in which he saw his father, the great Kabbalist R' Shalom Hedaya, in a Heavenly council with other great scholars, debating whether it would be necessary to build a temporary home for the yeshiva *Bet El* in the New City and whether there was anyone suitable for this task. In the dream he saw himself standing up and announcing that he was ready to take on the assignment and to establish the yeshiva on the roof of his house on Rashi Street. A light shone on the gathered Kabbalists and they wished him success.

In 1959 he succeeded in establishing a new *Bet Midrash* to carry the name and the legacy of *Bet El*. He founded an associated yeshiva called *Shalom Avdo* for the study of the revealed Torah. When the Old City was freed in 1967, R' Hedaya initiated the work of restoring the original *Bet Midrash* of *Bet El* to its previous glory.

The Son Will Iluminate. R' Obadiah Hedaya's drive to write books led him to pore through ancient manuscripts, searching for unpublished books of earlier scholars. When he was still a young man he came across the manuscript for a book of lectures that his great-grandfather, R' Haim Mordechai Labaton (see #336), had written over a hundred years ago, but which had never been published. He prepared it for publication and wrote an introduction in which he describes his personal interest in the work. He explains that in the book *Tekufat Haim* of the illustrious R' Haim Palagi of Izmir (see #449) he learned that someone who is childless should publish a book and in that merit he will be blessed with male children. Since he had not yet been blessed with a son, he decided to publish that book, and titled it *Ben Yair*. That was a uniquely appropriate name for his purpose since it means, "the son will illuminate." This stratagem was successful, and even before the work was completed, his wife was expecting a boy.

His Legacy

Throughout his life he was a prolific author of books dealing with the entire range of Torah knowledge, including *halachah*, inspirational lectures, and Kabbalah. In addition to his books, he authored numerous articles, responsa, and essays in various Torah journals. In fact, in recognition of his creativity and productivity he received a number of awards over the course of his life including the prestigious *"Prass Yisrael"* and *"Itur Kabod shel Yekirei Yerushalayim."*

ספר
בן יאיר
דרושים
הצעיר עבדיה בהרה"ג שלום הדאיא הי"ו
נדפס פעה"ק ירושלם תובב"א
ובחר'ת בחיי'ם

Title Page of Ben Yair

The Book Fell to the Floor. R' Obadiah Hedaya passed away at the age of 79 on *Shabbat* afternoon, 20 Shevat, 5729 (1969). The Torah portion for that *Shabbat* was *Yitro* and he had been called up to read the *Aseret HaDibrot* (Ten Commandments) in his normal manner. In the afternoon he sat down to learn, but suddenly the book fell to the floor. He immediately got up and went to his bed to rest a bit, and it was then that his sublime soul left his body. He was survived by one son, the Kabbalist R' Shalom Mordechai Haim, who had helped his father reestablish *Bet El* and who took on the leadership of the institution in his father's later years.

Some of his more notable published works are summarized below:

- In 1902 at the age of 18 he wrote his first book, *Eved HaMelech* on the *Rambam*. This was subsequently published (Jerusalem 5701/1941) together with Volume I of his *Avda D'Rabanan* on *Gemara* and with Volume II of his *Vayikah Obadiahu* (inspirational lectures). Volumes 3 and 4 of *Vayikah Obadiahu* were published in 1962 (Jerusalem 5722) combined with another book of his lectures, *Shalom Avdo*. Volume V came out in 1965 (Jerusalem 5725). Volume II of *Avda D'Rabanan* was also published in Jerusalem in that year.

- In 1926 he edited and prepared for publication the book *Simhat Kohen* of R' Masoud Alhadad, Chief Rabbi of *Bet El*, and supplemented it with four responsa (Jerusalem 5686/1925). In the same year he edited and prepared for publication a book of inspirational lectures by his great-grandfather, R' Haim Mordechai Labaton (see #336). He combined this book, *Ben Yair*, with Volume I of his own book of lectures, *Vayikah Obadiahu* and with the book *Oseh Hayil* of his grandfather, R' Yitzhak Labaton (see #340).
- In 1928 he edited and prepared for publication the book *Debar Shaul* of R' Shaul David Sutton (#558), Chief Rabbi of Buenos Aires.
- In 1932 he published the first volume of another collection of his works (Jerusalem 5692), including *Yaskil Abdi* (responsa) and *De'ah Ve'Haskil* (responsa on Kabbalah). At intervals throughout the remainder of his life he published six additional volumes in the series. An eighth volume was published posthumously from his manuscripts by his only son R' Shalom. Included with Volume 4 (Jerusalem 5708/1948) was the work *Kuntris Shaalat Shalom* consisting of 24 responsa which his father R' Shalom Hedaya had published in the journal *HaMe'asef*.
- In 1962 he wrote a commentary on the *Zohar Bereshit*, as translated into Hebrew by R' Barchiel (Petah Tikvah 5706/1946).

Signing His Name. The word Obadiah is a composite of two Hebrew words, עבד י־ה, meaning the servant of *Hashem*. R' Obadiah was very conscious of the meaning of his name and in his youth he wrote his signature with a space between the two words. However, at some point in his life he stopped doing this and signed with a single word.

When asked about this, he explained that his great-grandfather, R' Haim Mordechai Labaton (see #336), author of the book *Nochah HaShulhan*, had appeared to him in a dream on *Shabbat* and had said to him, "There is an uproar in Heaven regarding 91."

When he woke up the next morning he was disturbed because it made no sense to him. He told the dream to various Kabbalists, but none of the interpretations that he received satisfied him. Finally, he went to his father to see if he could help.

After some thought, his father said, "My son, I will reveal the interpretation of the dream." He explained that the *gematria* (numerical value) of the name Obadiah is 91. That number also happens to be the sum of the values of the two words signifying the Name of *Hashem* — א־ד־נ־י and י־ה־ו־ה — corresponding to His attributes of Absolute Existence and Lordship (26 + 65 = 91). "Because you have been signing your name as two words you have caused a separation where there should be union, and that has caused an uproar in Heaven." And from that time on he signed his name as one word.

Contacts with Other Rabbis

R' Obadiah was in regular correspondence with many of the great rabbis and *dayanim* (judges) of the day, both Ashkenaz and Sephard. Copies of his letters, mostly on *halachic* issues, may be found in his book *Yaskil Abdi*. Among the names of Chief Rabbis to be found there are: R' Tzvi Pesach Frank, R' Yosef Chaim Sonnenfeld, R' Yitzchak Herzog, and R' Ben-Sion Meir Ouziel.

He had a special bond with R' Isser Zalman Meltzer, head of the yeshiva *Etz Chaim*, who lived nearby. R' Isser Zalman had a huge library of holy books, which he had inherited from R' Chaim Berlin. Whenever R' Obadiah would come over to look for a particular book, R' Isser Zalman would insist upon getting it for him, which often meant climbing up and down the bookshelves on a ladder. Their mutual respect and affection was evident to all.

He also exchanged holy books with the great rabbis of Lithuania and Poland, sending his own books and receiving their approbation. They in turn sent him what they had written. R' Baruch Ber Leibowitz of Kamenitz sent a particularly glowing approbation on two of his books, thanking *Hashem* for keeping His promise to provide learned Torah scholars in all the places where Jews live.

He also exchanged holy books with the great rabbis of Lithuania and Poland, sending his own books and receiving their approbation.

[310] HEDAYA, R' Shalom

רבי שלום הדאיה

(1864 — 1945)

Av Bet Din (Chief Judge) of the Sephardic *Bet Din* of Jerusalem and *Rosh Yeshiva* of the *Bet El* yeshiva. He was a prolific author, who campaigned tirelessly to raise the public's awareness of their responsibility to support Torah scholars and Torah institutions.

His Younger Years

He was born in Aram Soba in 1864 to R' Moshe Haim Hedaya (#308), the son of R' Ezra Hedaya. His mother was Sabtiah, the daughter of R' Obadiah and Rachel Shamah. Through the illustrious Shamah lineage she was related to R' Eliyahu Shamah (see #499), the author of the important book *Korban Isheh*. Sabtiah's mother, Rachel, was a daughter of another Sabtiah and her husband, R' Yitzhak Attiah (see #120), who was the author of *Zera Yitzhak* and other important books. That grandmother Sabtiah, in turn, was the daughter of R' Abraham Sutton (see #535), a Chief Rabbi of Aram Soba. He had two brothers: R' Yehudah Aslan and R' Ezra.

His father passed away while he was only 3 years old, and he was raised by his widowed mother Sabtiah and his grandmother Rachel. They lived in extreme poverty and when he was 7 years old his mother was no longer able to earn enough to pay their meager needs. It was necessary for the young child to put aside his studies and help support the family. This situation would have become the norm had not some generous benefactors came to their aid. Over the years he was fortunate enough to receive help of one kind or another from R' Shelomo Safdeyé (see #469), R' Ovadiah Moshe Antebi (see #71), R' Shemuel Silvera (see #529) and the latter's son, Señor Aharon Silvera (see #522). He offers profuse expressions of gratitude to these kind people in his books *Shalom Le'Am* and *Degel Abraham*.

In 1884, at the age of 20, R' Shalom married Sarah, the daughter of R' Yitzhak Labaton (see #340). She gave birth to 15 children, but only six survived, four boys and two girls. His son R' Yitzhak Hedaya (see #311) served on the *Bet Din* of Aram Soba. A second son, R' Obadiah Hedaya (see #309), helped publish his books and re-established the yeshiva *Bet El* after it had been destroyed by the Arabs in 1948. He became Chief Rabbi of Petah Tikvah, *dayan* of the Senior Appeals *Bet Din* in Jerusalem, and a member of the Council of Chief Rabbis of Israel. His other two sons were R' Moshe Hedaya and R' Ezra Hedaya (see #307). R' Ezra became a *dayan* on the regional *Bet Din* in Haifa.

R' Shalom Hedaya

R' Shalom's daughter Mazal married R' Yaakob Kassin (see #330), who became rabbi of the *Congregation Shaare Zion* in Brooklyn. His daughter Rina married R' Moshe Ezra Mizrahi (see #424) after his first wife died. She herself passed away at the young age of 28, but not before giving birth to R' Shalom Yitzhak Mizrahi (see #429), who was brought up in the house of his grandfather and became a *dayan* (judge) in the Appeals Court in Jerusalem.

He was a prolific author, who campaigned tirelessly to raise the public's awareness of their responsibility to support Torah scholars and Torah institutions.

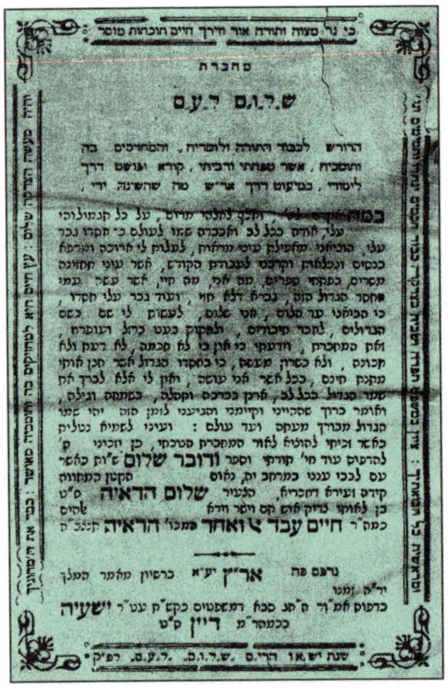
כי נר מצוה ותורה אור ודרך חיים תוכחות מוסר

מחברת

ש.ל.ום ל.ע.ם

הדורש לכבוד התורה ולומדיה, והמחזיקים בה
ותומכיה, אשר עפרתי ודכיתי, קורא ופושט דרך
ליסודי, כמיעוט דרך אר"ש מה שהשיגה ידי,

Title Page of *Shalom Le'Am*

For the first three years of married life, R' Hedaya had a golden period during which he was supported by his father-in-law, R' Yitzhak Labaton. He was forever grateful to R' Labaton for giving him the opportunity to totally immerse himself in Torah studies.

His Teachers and Colleagues

Among his teachers as a young man in Aram Soba were the eminent Kabbalist R' Moshe Swed (see #574), the *Av Bet Din* R' Yitzhak Bekhor Mizrahi (see #432), and R' Yitzchak Alfia (see #46). He was also close to the Chief Rabbi of Aram Soba, R' Shelomo Safdeyé (see #469), and R' Shaul Sutton (see #558), who was to become *Av Bet Din* (Chief Judge) of Buenos Aires. Toward the end of his life, R' Sutton published some manuscript responsa of Maharam ben Habib, which he obtained from R' Shalom Hedaya and which he included in his book *Diber Shaul*. In that book he mentions that these manuscripts were kept over the years by R' Haim Mordechai Labaton, *Av Bet Din* of Aram Soba (see #336), and are currently in the possession of his grandson, R' Shalom Hedaya.

In 1882, when he was 18, he was in correspondence with R' Eliyahu Hamway (see #271), a later *Av Bet Din* of Aram Soba. In a letter that R' Hamway wrote to R' Yitzhak Abulafia of Damascus (see #35), he mentions a *halachic* question which was posed to him by R' Shalom Hedaya. Later R' Shalom included the response in his book *Shalom Le'Am*. Over the years, R' Shalom was in correspondence with various other distinguished rabbis of Aram Soba, including R' Yeshayah Dayan (see #203), R' Moshe Cohen (see #164), R' David Kassin (see #322), R' Yaakob Rophe, R' Moshe Harari (see #288), and R' Yaakob Boka'i (see #139).

His Move to Jerusalem

When he was about 28 years of age he visited Jerusalem, staying at the house of R' Yaakob Shaul Elyashar, the *Rishon LeSion* (Chief Rabbi of *Eretz Yisrael*), who was very supportive. And so, he returned to Jerusalem nine years later, this time to stay. He moved from Aram Soba with his entire family, including his father-in-law, R' Yitzhak Labaton. He was quickly integrated into the community of scholars and rabbis of Jerusalem and in 1904, at the age of 32, he was accepted as a *dayan* (judge) in the Sephardic *Bet Din*, where he joined R' Vidal Angel and R' Baruch Alankova. Later, the *Bet Din* was headed by R' Shemuel Nissim Baruch and he was joined by R' Ben-Sion Kouenka, the publisher of the journal *HaMe'asef*. In 1930 he was appointed head of the *Bet Din*, and became *Av Bet Din* for all of the Sephardic congregations in Jerusalem.

He moved from Aram Soba with his entire family, including his father-in-law, R' Yitzhak Labaton. He was quickly integrated into the community of scholars and rabbis of Jerusalem

The Virtues of Ladino. R' Shalom Hedaya's first home in Jerusalem was in the Bukharan neighborhood, where most of the immigrants from Aram Soba lived. This section was blessed with many distinguished scholars and places to study Torah. However, after a few years he moved to the Ohel Moshe section. When asked what drew him to Ohel Moshe, he answered that there he would not understand what people were saying. He explained that the Sephardic Jews of Ohel Moshe spoke Ladino, a language that he did not know well, and so he would be less likely to overhear *lashon hara* (gossip).

His Loss of Sight

During his return to Aram Soba after visiting Jerusalem he developed a serious eye ailment and felt that he was going blind. This forced him to stay home for a long period of time and it seemed to him that his house had become his prison. He wrote about this harrowing experience in his book *Kissei Shelomo* (5662/1902).

During the period of deteriorating vision he continued learning, working largely from memory. The one thing that really bothered him was that he was unable to see at a distance when a scholar entered the

Bet Midrash and so he failed to perform the *mitzvah* of rising in the presence of a sage (*Vayikra* 19:32). However, he specifically asked the congregation to forgive him for not giving the honor that was due them.

As his vision continued to deteriorate, his doctors advised him to travel to Egypt and see an eye specialist in Alexandria. The specialist performed surgery and his eyesight was partially restored. This made it possible for him to work on his major book, *Shalom Le'Am,* consisting of inspirational lectures on charity and acts of kindness. The book was published in Aram Soba when he was only 30 years old.

His Expertise in Kabbalah

He applied himself to the study of Kabbalah in the yeshiva *Bet El* under the guidance of R' Sasson Praseido and then under R' Masoud Alhadad, the author of *Simhat Kohen*. When R' Alhadad passed away in 1927, R' Hedaya was appointed as *Rosh Yeshiva* in his place. This highly respected position entitled him to be called *"HaRav HaHasid"* (The Pious Rabbi). He gave lectures in Kabbalah to the scholars of the yeshiva and when its original building in the Old City was destroyed in an earthquake he continued the lectures in the *Gorjim* synagogue in the Zichron Moshe neighborhood.

From the day that he became the head of the yeshiva he began to attract loyal pupils who were enlightened by his teachings. These included: R' Yehuda Shako, the *Av Bet Din* of the Sephardic congregations in Jerusalem; R' Mori Meshomer, previously *dayan* in the Eden community of Yemen, R' Abraham Pita'el, father-in-law of R' Ovadiah Yosef; R' Nissim Lofez, previously rabbi of the Sephardic community in Rio de Janeiro (see #396); and the renowned Kabbalist, R' Mordechai Sharabi. Besides the scholars from the Sephardic community he also attracted faithful students from the Ashkenaz community, the best known of whom was R' Matityahu Davis of the yeshivat *Etz Haim,* who considered him his primary teacher.

In his later years, R' Hedaya became acquainted with R' Elchanan Wasserman, the sage of Baranovitch, and shared with him his writings in Kabbalah. From that time (1936) forward, the two scholars maintained a regular correspondence on matters of Kabbalah.

In his later years, R' Hedaya became acquainted with R' Elchanan Wasserman, the Sage of Baranovitch, and shared with him his writings in Kabbalah. From that time (1936) forward, the two scholars maintained a regular correspondence on matters of Kabbalah.

This highly respected position entitled him to be called "HaRav HaHasid."

His Piety

One *Motza'e Shabbat* (Saturday night) when his son, R' Obadiah (see #309), was 15 years old, the neighbors came in to hear *Habdalah*. R' Hedaya instructed his son to recite the *Habdalah*, but the boy was nervous and held back. However, R' Hedaya became upset with him and insisted. The son then gave in to his father's wish, but was surprised at the urgency. It was only the following night that he began to understand. That night a Kabbalist scholar came to visit his father and they went into a room and studied Kabbalah together the entire night. Upon further inquiry, Obadiah learned that a 48-hour fast had been set, which was to begin on *Motza'e Shabbat*. The custom in such a case was to stay up learning on the second night. Obadiah then understood that his father did not want to publicize his intention to fast. In fact, when he was offered food in his room, he accepted it, but did not eat it, giving it to poor people instead.

His Bond with R' Yaakob Shaul Elyashar

The bond which he developed with the *Rishon LeSion* during his first visit to Jerusalem remained strong throughout his life. While he was staying at the home of the *Rishon LeSion*, he was treated with unusual warmth and respect. Each night, the *Rishon LeSion* would personally bring the bed linen and make up the bed for his guest. On occasions when the two men would find themselves walking together on the street, R' Hedaya would make a point of walking behind the *Rishon LeSion* out of respect. However, as soon as the *Rishon LeSion* saw who was behind him, he would stop and wait until R' Hedaya caught up with him and they would continue on side by side.

Each night, the Rishon LeSion would personally bring the bed linen and make up the bed for his guest.

His Love for the Malbim

R' Hedaya was fascinated by the *Malbim's* brilliant commentary on *Tanach* and studied it so thoroughly that he could recite extended passages by heart. The *Malbim* (1809-1879) was the Chief Rabbi of Romania and was an outspoken antagonist of the *Maskilim* (Reform Jews). He suffered terribly at the hands of the *Maskilim,* who were instrumental in having him imprisoned on false charges, which led, in turn, to his expulsion from Romania.

In later years, R' Hedaya's son, R' Obadiah, remarked that "a glowing ember of the Malbim's soul was cloaked in the form of my father, R' Shalom."

One day, a scholarly traveler from Europe appeared in R' Hedaya's *shul* in Aram Soba. Many people of the *shul* took the opportunity to ask the visitor for news of European Jewry. R' Shalom was also interested and asked the visitor for his insights into the works of the *Malbim*. Strangely, mention of the *Malbim* aroused a harshly negative reaction from the visitor, who spoke of him in disrespectful terms. When the man left the *shul*, R' Hedaya said to those around him, "That Jew is a heathen." It was not much later that the visitor was, in fact, seen on the street with his head uncovered, smoking a cigar on *Shabbat*. When R' Hedaya was asked how he knew the true nature of this man, he answered, "I felt as though the *Malbim* were standing here and saying to me, 'This man is a heathen.' " In later years, R' Hedaya's son, R' Obadiah, remarked that "a glowing ember of the *Malbim's* soul was cloaked in the form of my father, R' Shalom."

He issued a halachic ruling that in today's conditions a scholar is permitted to demand a stipend from the community.

His Teachings

He was very concerned about the hardships of poverty-stricken scholars and blamed the community for not fulfilling its obligation to them. He pointed out that when scholars are not treated with dignity, qualified young men are discouraged from committing themselves to the scholarly life. This is a tragedy for the Jewish nation, which desperately needs Torah scholars to maintain the continuity of Torah knowledge. In contrast, when scholars are untroubled by financial burdens they present a desirable model of the way life should be lived. The best of the younger generation are then drawn to their example and the nation is enriched.

He urged the Sephardic world to emulate the accomplishments of the Ashkenazim in terms of building large yeshivot for higher learning.

In his major work, *Shalom Le'Am*, he encourages each person who can afford it to take on the complete support of at least one scholar. In that way, the scholar won't be in the awkward situation of being beholden to a number of of individuals.

He encourages each person who can afford it to take on the complete support of at least one scholar.

At the same time he urged the rabbis and teachers of the community to implant the love of learning and the desirability of the scholarly life in the hearts of young men. He encouraged them to make a point of praising the scholars of the community and speaking of them with great respect. He explained that in this way students will be drawn to dedicate all of their energies to the holy pursuit of Torah knowledge and philanthropists will be eager to support them.

He issued a *halachic* ruling that in today's conditions a scholar is permitted to demand a stipend from the community. He stated that each member of the community has a holy obligation to support the community's scholars. He specifically recommended the creation of a special charity fund to be earmarked for the support of promising young scholars (a concept which is now referred to as a *kollel*). He described in glowing terms the benefits of such an arrangement to the donors in terms of the blessing it would bring to their business ventures, the gratification they would find in their personal Torah study, and the joy they would find in their own sons whose scholarly opportunities would be enabled.

In this regard he urged the Sephardic world to emulate the accomplishments of the Ashkenazim in terms of building large *yeshivot* for higher learning, such as the great yeshiva of Pressburg, founded by the renowned *Chatam Sofer*.

He observed that the business community was suffering under an oppressive tax burden. He argued that this was due to the fact that people had not truly accepted the *Ol Torah*, the "yoke of the Torah," and so they were given the "yoke of the government" in its place. To ease the "yoke of the government" they must accept their responsibility for funding holy institutions and for supporting the needy.

He assured the philanthropists who support Torah that they will be fully rewarded in the World to Come. They need not be afraid that since they themselves are not scholars they will be embarrassed by their ignorance. The traditional partnership of Torah supporters and scholars is modeled on the relationship between the tribes of Zebulun and Yissachar, where the merchants of Zebulun provided support for the scholars of Yissachar. When Moshe blessed the tribes he said, "Rejoice, O Zebulun, in your going out." This refers to Zebulun's embarkations on voyages of maritime commerce. R' Hedaya explained that it also refers to the time when Zebulun goes out of this world into the World to Come. Zebulun can rejoice because the partnership with Yissachar will assure Zebulun that he will share in the Torah knowledge that Yissachar studied so hard to acquire.

R' Hedaya put his teachings into practice, personally interceding with young scholars, who were tempted to leave the yeshiva, either to study in secular schools or to get a job. He used every resource at his disposal, including financial assistance, to persuade them to stay with their Torah studies. One of those young scholars who was beset by financial difficulties and who was saved from having to go to work was R' Ezra Attiah, the future *Rosh Yeshiva* of *Porat Yosef* (see #102).

He had a photographic memory, never forgetting anything that he learned. He sometimes spent hours in far-ranging Torah discussions with R' Ezra Attiah. On those occasions his mind would leap from one volume of *Gemara* to another, from one commentator and *halachic* authority to another, all without ever having to open a book.

Through his influence, many young men who had already gone to work were persuaded to return to the yeshiva world. One of the ways he maintained contact with a wide variety of young boys and men was by leading study groups in his house. Among the young men whose life was changed by attending his study groups were the three notable Ades brothers: R' Yaakob (see #41), R' Moshe (see #39), and R' Ezra (see #38).

His Passing

He passed away at the age of 83 on 3 Kislev, 5705 (1945) after a short illness and was buried on the Mount of Olives in Jerusalem. He had a premonition that he would die and told his grandson that he was ready to give up his soul if it was time for him to leave this world. He also said that he could see two departed sages coming to greet him and to welcome him into the Heavenly yeshiva: R' Haim Shaul Dweck (see #228), who was a *Kohen*, and R' Yosef Yedid (see #594), who was a *Levi*.

A year later he appeared in a dream to R' Obadiah, his son. R' Obadiah recalled that in the dream his father's face was shining like the sun. He saw his father studying a sheet of paper containining words which he had written. In his joy at seeing his father, R' Obadiah approached him and said, "I know that you are not allowed to tell me about Heaven, but tell me how you fared in the Heavenly Court." He responded, "I have learned how to walk in the way of life." He added that he was in the company of his humble and pious brother-in-law, R' Yeshuah Attiah. He also said that R' Obadiah's grandfather, R' Haim Mordechai Labaton (see #336), visited them every day and invited them to come to him. He also explained that in Heaven people are not grouped by familial relationship, but by their deeds. People who are alike in their deeds are put together. It is only when all the souls are assembled that they are able to meet souls who are not in their group.

Zebulun can rejoice because the partnership with Yissachar will assure Zebulun that ha will share in the Torah knowledge that Yissachar studied so hard to acquire.

In Heaven people are not grouped by familial relationship, but by their deeds.

His Legacy

Some of the more notable works that he left behind are summarized below:

- *Shalom Le'Am* (Aram Soba 5655/1895). Inspirational lectures on Torah, charity, and acts of kindness. The subject matter was so appropriate to the needs of Aram Soba that weekly classes on the book were given in the synagogues. Many attribute the great respect in Aram Soba for Torah institutions and Torah scholars to the intense study of this book by the community.
- *Seh LeBet Avot* (Jerusalem 5701/1901). Commentary on *Masechet Avot*. The last two chapters were written by his son R' Obadiah.
- *Shalom VaSedek* (Jerusalem 5708/1908). *Hiddushim* (original Torah thoughts) on Kabbalah. Published together with Volume IV of the book *Yaskil Abdi* by his son R' Obadiah. Also included is the

Rabbis of Yeshivat Shaare Orah, Jerusalem
Left to right: First Row: Unknown, Unknown, R' Ezra Husney (see #315), R' Eliyahu Ma'arabi (see #404), R' Shemuel Ezran, R' Yitzhak Hedaya
Second Row: R' Baruch Hedaya, R' Abadur, R' Yaakob Levy, R' Shelomo Peretz, R' Haim Bajio, R' Yitzhak Abu Aziz
Third Row: Unknown, Unknown, R' Abraham Naim, R' Mordechai Meyuchas, R' Beneveneshti, R' Yosef Shayo (see #507), Unknown

eulogy delivered by R' Obadiah on his father.

- *VeDover Shalom* (Jerusalem 5684/1924), responsa on a variety of topics, such as the considerations when a blind person is called up to the *Sefer Torah* in the synagogue.
- *HaHaim VeHaShalom*, Volume I (Jerusalem 5686/1926) and Volume II (Jerusalem 5697/1937), lectures. At the end of both volumes are included some of his son R' Obadiah's *hiddushim* on the *Rambam*. Volume II also includes the manuscripts for two small works, *Sim Shalom* and *Simeni Kahotam*, written by his grandson R' Shalom Yitzhak Mizrahi (see #429).
- *Hiddushim* published in the journal *HaMe'asef* on the books of the *Rishon LeSion* (Chief Rabbi of *Eretz Yisrael*), R' Yaakob Shaul Elyashar, and on the book *Shaare Rahamim* of R' Rahamim Yosef Franco, and others.

R' Moshe Hidary was one of the oldest émigrés from Syria to New York, bringing with him all the traditions of the old country.

In 1902 he edited and prepared for publication the book *Degel Mahane Ephraim* by R' Ephraim Laniado (see #355), the book *Kissei Shelomo* by R' Raphael Shelomo Laniado (see #363), and *Ro'ei Yisrael* by three authors: R' Yehudah Kassin (see #331), R' Raphael Shelomo Laniado (see #363), and his son, R' Ephraim Laniado (see #355).

R' Yitzhak Hedaya

[311] HEDAYA, R' Yitzhak

רבי יצחק הדאיה

(1888 — 1961)

Rabbi, *dayan* (judge), and *darshan* (lecturer) of Aram Soba. He was born in Aram Soba in 1888 to R' Shalom Hedaya (see #310). On his mother's side he was a grandson of R' Yitzhak Labaton, after whom he was named. As a *dayan* (judge), he issued *halachic* (legal) rulings and served on the *Bet Din* of Aram Soba. In 1935 he settled in Jerusalem, where he associated with other rabbis engaged in the study of Torah and Kabbalah. In his later years he endured much pain and suffering, finally passing away on 6 Tishrei, 5722 (1961). He left behind a manuscript of inspirational lectures on the entire Torah. Two of his sons were R' Shalom and R' Moshe. The latter was to serve as Chief Rabbi of Ayelet.

[312] HIDARY, R' Moshe

רבי משה כצ'רי

(— 1945)

Beloved Talmud Torah teacher of Aram Soba and New York. He was one of the earliest émigrés from Syria to New York, bringing with him all the traditions of the old country. His outstanding asset was his patience with children. Any child who had learning difficulties received personal help from the rabbi after school, all done without extra pay. While it was common practice in those days to deal with students with "a carefully placed slap," R' Moshe's students were never dealt with in that way, but were won over by his humor and charm.

After the passing of his first wife, Hanna, R' Moshe married Frieda Haddad. He arrived in New York in the early 1900's with Frieda and his two sons from his first marriage, Jacob (Jack) and Abraham (Al), and his daughter, Bahia. Bahia was refused entry at Ellis Island, due to illness, and was sent to Buenos Aires with an uncle, whom she eventually married. It was not until about 35 years later that her brothers Al and Jack, with Jack's wife Mary, visited her in Bueno Aires. Bahia never had the opportunity to visit the United States again.

Initially, R' Moshe lived on the Lower East Side and started teaching the youngest children in the Shaare Sedek Talmud Torah at 48 Orchard Street. He and Frieda were blessed with additional children, and to make ends meet he was forced to supplement his income by giving haircuts. His talents as a barber brought him a nickel a customer. He never sat down to a meal until all the children had eaten enough. Sometimes he was literally left with the crumbs. He raised his children to be hard workers, never to be idle. If his daughters were just sitting on the couch chatting he would say, "At least tighten the cushion buttons while you are sitting there!"

Among the early Syrian Jewish settlers in Brooklyn, R' Moshe moved his family to the Sea Beach section of Brooklyn, on 65th Street near the *Magen David* Synagogue and Talmud Torah of 67th Street. He would study, tutor, teach, and pray the entire day, only arriving at home late at night. He slept for just a few hours and returned before daybreak.

One of his daughters (Mollie Hidary Beyda) would bring his breakfast in a small bucket early in the morning. One time she accidentally pulled on the light string on *Shabbat* as R' Moshe walked by. The next day he fasted, having been a witness to this desecration. Another time, she was very tempted to wear a new pair of roller skates but he said that it was not allowed on *Shabbat*. While he was in *kneese* (the synagogue), the roller skates were becoming more and more tempting, and she finally succumbed. Next to the stairs leading up to the house was a staircase that led down for coal delivery. As she took her first steps in the roller skates she slipped backwards down the lower stairs. She looked up to see her father, who calmly remarked, "Didn't I tell you that it is not allowed?"

Because of his dire financial straits he was forced to continue giving haircuts. His students would bring the "tuition" often late, to R' Moshe and some would ask for a free haircut to be included with the payment. "Take a seat" was always the reply.

He passed away on 19 Sivan, 5705 (1945) leaving behind three children from his first marriage, Bahia, Jack, and Al, and seven children from his second marriage, Max, Mollie, Rachel, Rose, Ike, Esther, and Joseph. The *Bet Midrash* of the *Mikdash Melech* yeshiva on Brooklyn's Ocean Parkway was named in his memory by his son Max.

R' Moshe Hidary

One time she accidentally pulled on the light string on Shabbat as R' Moshe walked by. The next day he fasted, having been a witness to this desecration.

[313] **HOUSSIN, R' Sadkah**

רבי צדקה חוצין

(1699 — 1773)

Distinguished scholar and *dayan* (judge) of Aram Soba and Baghdad. He is best known for his important work of responsa *Sedakah U'Mishpat* (Jerusalem 5686/1926). An additional volume of this book, with 10 responsa, was published in Tel Aviv (in 5735/1975).

He was born in Aram Soba about 1699. His mother had been experiencing a series of stillbirths and when this baby was born, she put him out of the house, thinking he was dead, as all the others had been. However, when the leader of the community saw the abandoned baby, he saw that he was alive and brought him to R' Shelomo Laniado, the elder (see #368), to be raised. The child was named Sadkah, corresponding to the Hebrew word for charity (צדקה), possibly because of the kindness that had been done in saving him. Although R' Laniado passed away while Sadkeh was still very young, he was taken under the wing of his son, R' Shemuel Laniado (see #372), and so Sadkah grew up as a learned scholar.

In 1743 he was called to serve as a rabbi and *dayan* in Baghdad. A severe epidemic had struck that city in the previous year and the community urgently needed someone to give *halachic* (legal) rulings and judgments. R' Moshe Mordechai, the *Nasi* (community leader) of Baghdad, wrote to Aram Soba, asking the Chief Rabbi, R' Shemuel Laniado (see #372), to send the most suitable person. This was R' Sadkah Houssin and he agreed to go. As a *dayan* in Baghdad, R' Sadkah followed the practice of sitting in judgment alone, rather than as a member of a *Bet Din*. This is a practice which he brought with him from Aram Soba, where it was common for members of the Laniado family to serve as individual "expert" judges in civil cases. He mentions the practice in his book *Sedakah U'Mishpat* (*Hoshen Mishpat*, 1).

עֹשֵׂה צדקה ומשפט נבחר לה׳ מזבח
ספר
צדקה ומשפט
חלק א.
צדקה חוצין
ראובן דוד נאוי
ירושלם
שנת
ISAAC NISSIM RAHAMIM
Rohama, Jerusalem
עטרת תפארת שיבה בדרך צדקה תמצא

Title Page of Sedakah U'Mishpat

In one of R' Sadkah's letters back to R' Laniado, he mentions that he has shipped to him by caravan the manuscript for five books. He asks that they be sent on to Venice to be published, indicating that he would like them to be published in two volumes, one of inspirational lectures and the other responsa. Apparently these books were lost, in addition to many of the other manuscripts that he wrote at various times. However, his book *Orah Sedakah*, containing *hiddushim* (original Torah thoughts) on the *Shulhan Aruch*, was published in Jerusalem in 1984 (5744). Also, his book *Avodat HaSedakah,* consisting of lectures and essays on Kabbalah, was published in Jerusalem in 1987 (5747).

"He is like one of the serafim (fiery angels)."

R' Sadkah was known for his piety. "He is like one of the *serafim* (fiery angels)," wrote R' Raphael Shelomo Laniado (see #363) in his book *Lehem Mishneh* (p. 25). R' Sadkah, himself, writes in one of his responsa (on *Orah Haim,* Section 5): "It was our practice in Aram Soba to fast the entire week and to wait until 72 minutes after sunset on Friday to break our fast, contrary to the Baghdadian community, which would accept *Shabbat* early and break the fast after prayers Friday evening." This was a reference to the custom of fasting during the first week *of Shobabim* [acronym for six weeks from *Perashat Shemot* to *Perashat Mishpatim*]. The fast extended for six days, from Sunday to Friday.

The Spiritual Heights of Aram Soba. R' Abraham Antebi (see #63) makes some fascinating remarks in the end of the first chapter of his book, *Hochmah U'Mussar*, giving us a glimpse at the spiritual heights to which the people of ancient Aram Soba had reached. When he praises the community for all its wonderful customs of Torah learning, he writes, "The custom among some pious people was that during the days of *Shobabim* they would fast an entire week and assemble to say *Selihot* and supplications as on *Yom Kippur*. After prayers they would study Torah the rest of the day and go to the *mikveh* Friday afternoon. Of course, whoever does this has all of his past sins forgiven and he must remain on guard afterward because, as our sages state, the greater the person, the greater is his evil inclination.

"Although this custom is good on its own terms, it is *halachically* forbidden to put oneself at risk of physical danger, especially in this case in which the likelihood of harm is almost certain. I heard that the Chief Rabbi, Hacham Raphael Shelomo Laniado (see #364), protested against it and reprimanded those who practiced it. The proper practice is the one in which many people fast two days and nights and then take a break, after which they fast the remainder of the week (known as *taanit hafsakot*)."

[Editor's note: As unbelievable as it may sound, people actually fasted day and night for a full week and survived. R' Edmond Nahum of the Syrian community in Deal, New Jersey, relates that he knows laymen and even women who practiced this custom in our day. The renowned rabbi, Yisrael Abuchatzeira, also known as the *Baba Sali*, did it from age 13. Concerning the latter custom mentioned, of fasting two days and breaking and fasting the remainder of the week, righteous people in our community practice it to this very day. On the tombsone of Salhah Sutton, wife of Mr. Abraham D. Sutton (see #536) and daughter of R' Shelomo Silvera (see #528), it is noted that she practiced this custom.]

He is believed to have passed away in Baghdad in 1773. R' Yitzhak Nissim, the publisher of *Sedakah U'Mishpat*, writes in the introduction that he saw a collection of lectures from R' Sadkah in manuscript form. Among them was a lecture which the author gave on *Shabbat Shuvah* 1773. A tragic cholera epidemic was ravaging Baghdad that year and R' Sadkah spoke of the loss of three sons to the epidemic: Saadiah, Nissim, and Yaakob. He lamented that his lecture of *Shabbat Shuvah* had turned into a eulogy. Apparently, it was not long before R' Sadkah himself was taken by the same epidemic. He was eulogized by R' Yeshayah Attiah (see #119) as recorded in *Bigdei Yesha* (p. 154). Also eulogizing him was R' Mordechai Galante.

R' Sadkah had another son, R' Moshe Houssin, who was a scholar and a composer of *pizmonim* (hymns). He composed at least 24 *pizmonim*, one of which is still popular among the descendants of the Jews of Baghdad. This is the hymn *"Melech Go'el U'Moshia,"* which is coded with the letters that make up the name "Moshe Houssin."

[314] HUSNEY, R' Eliyahu

רבי אליהו חוצני הלוי

(20th century)

Worthy scholar, *dayan* (judge), and teacher of New York. He served the New York Syrian community for over half a century. R' Eliyahu taught classes in Talmud for advanced students several times a week and helped many individuals with personal problems. However, he refused to take a position with the congregation for fear of losing his religious independence.

He was known for being especially meticulous about adherence to the *halachah* (religious law) as well as all of the *minhagim* (customs and practices) of Aram Soba.

(315) HUSNEY, R' Ezra

רבי עזרא חוצני הלוי

(— 1956)

Eminent rabbi and teacher of *Yeshivat Porat Yosef* in Jerusalem. He was a son of R' Shehidyah (Shaul) Husney and a son-in-law of R' Ezra Harari-Raful (see #304). R' Ezra passed away on Friday, 8 Sivan, 5716 (1956) as he was immersing himself in the *mikveh* for *Shabbat* and was buried the same day.

[316] INDIBO, R' Nissim

רבי נסים הכהן אינדבו

(1857 — 1973)

Distinguished Kabbalist and Chief Rabbi of Damascus. He was born in 1857 and was blessed with a long life. R' Nissim lived for 114 years and his mind was totally clear until his last day.

He lived in the Jewish Quarter of Damascus, next to the *Bet Kneset* (synagogue) *Shevet Ahim*. Growing up in Damascus, he became a student of R' Yitzhak Abulafia (see #35), the Chief Rabbi. He became a *dayan* on the *Bet Din* and after R' Yitzhak passed away in 1910, R' Nissim was appointed to the position. He wrote an approbation to the book *Yaskil Abdi* (Vol. 3) by R' Obadiah Hedaya (see #309).

He was a prolific author of holy books and was widely respected. When the Syrian government sentenced Eli Cohen, the famous Israeli spy, to be hanged, R' Nissim was given permission to visit him and help him say his final prayers and confession.

He passed away on 7 Shevat, 5733 (1973). On the last day of his life he asked his student, R' Yitzhak Assa (see #98), to come to his house. After a while, R' Assa stood up to leave for work but R' Nissim insisted that he stay. R' Nissim, who was a *Kohen*, then instructed R' Assa to ask all of his sons to leave the house. R' Nissim then recited the *Viduy* (Confession) and the *Shema* and silently passed away.

[317] INSER, R' Shemuel

רבי שמואל אינזר

(20th century)

Worthy rabbi and Talmud Torah teacher of New York. He opened up the first synagogue in the Sea Beach/Bensonhurst area of Brooklyn in the early 1900's, a time when few Sephardic Jews lived in the area.

The *Magen David* synagogue was located on 66th Street between 19th and 20th Avenues. Soon the community grew and started receiving large numbers of people from Manhattan and Williamsburg.

R' Inser had a Talmud Torah in his synagogue and he taught many students, a large majority of whom could not pay tuition. His *shamosh* (sexton) was R' Shaul Semah, later the main *shamosh* of the *Magen David Congregation*.

R' Eliyahu Husney

R' Ezra Husney

R' Nissim Indibo

Kassin Lineage. Generations of eminent rabbis and businessmen of the highest moral stature — these made up the famous Kassin family, which played a dominant role in the Jewish community of Aleppo for more than 350 years. The first of these giants of the spirit appeared in Aleppo in the 16th century when Señor Shelomo Kassin (see #328) fled from the clutches of the Spanish Inquisition and sought refuge in Aleppo. His grandson, R' Yomtob Kassin (see #333), became the first of a long line of illustrious rabbis in the Kassin family. The spiritual influence of this saintly family was felt in the city for seven generations, until the ascent of R' Shaul Kassin (see #327) to *Eretz Yisrael* in 1891. In time the religious influence of the Kassin family extended to the New World as well.

[318] **KASSIN, R' Abraham**

רבי אברהם קצין

(1811 — 1896)

Eminent scholar and rabbi of Aram Soba and Jerusalem. He was born in 1811 in Aram Soba, the third son of R' Bekhor Kassin (see #320). R' Abraham was a popular public speaker, and a collection of his inspirational lectures were published as *Likutei Abraham* (Jerusalem 5659/1899). This work was combined with the book *Vaye'esof David* of his brother R' David Kassin (see #322). A new edition of these two books was produced in 1976. He authored additional *hiddushim* (original Torah thoughts), which remained in manuscript form.

He was an active supporter of yeshivot and it was primarily through his personal efforts and support that a new building was put up for the yeshiva Bet El in Jerusalem, under the leadership of R' Obadiah Hedaya.

He frequently traveled to North Africa to raise funds for charitable causes. In about 1890 he moved to Jerusalem, where he devoted himself to intense Torah study. He was blessed with a long life and passed away on 10 Heshvan, 5657 (1896). He was buried in Jerusalem on the Mount of Olives. He left only one son, R' Shaul Kassin (see #327).

Those who prepared the body for reburial reported that his body did not show the ravages of time, a clear indication of his special merit.

[319] **KASSIN, R' Abraham**

רבי אברהם קצין

(1896 — 1965)

Eminent scholar and philanthropist of Jerusalem and Mexico City. He was born in 1896 in Jerusalem to R' Shaul Kassin (see #327). As a boy he studied at the yeshiva *Ohel Moed* until the outbreak of World War I, when his eligibility for the Turkish military draft compelled him to flee to Egypt.

In 1921 he returned to Jerusalem and married Sarah, the worthy daughter of R' Moshe Hedaya (see #308). Soon after the wedding the young couple moved to Mexico City for economic opportunity. In Mexico R' Abraham continued his commitment to Torah study while earning a comfortable living in business. He was an active supporter of *yeshivot* and it was primarily through his personal efforts and support that a new building was put up for the yeshiva *Bet El* in Jerusalem, under the leadership of R' Obadiah Hedaya (see #309). He also saw to it that funds would be provided to support the needy scholars who studied there.

He maintained a cheerful and positive outlook on life despite many personal tragedies and difficulties. He passed away in Mexico City on *Rosh Hodesh* Elul, 5725 (1965) and a year later he was laid to rest on *Har HaMenuhot* in Jerusalem on 2 Av, 5726 (1966). Those who prepared the body for reburial reported that his body did not show the ravages of time, a clear indication of his special merit.

He was blessed with worthy sons, R' Moshe David and R' Shaul, who followed in their father's footsteps and built a beautiful *Bet Midrash* adjacent to the yeshiva *Kol Yaakob* in the Bayit V'Gan section of Jerusalem, under the leadership of R' Yehudah Ades. In conjunction with that initiative they also established the Hesed Le'Abraham Institute, named after their father.

A Bond Through the Generations. When the body of R' Abraham Kassin was sent to *Eretz Yisrael*, Rabanit Esther Ades, the widow of R' Yaakob Ades (see #41), told her sons, R' Yehudah and R' Yosef, to meet the flight at the airport because the deceased was a good friend of their late father. They accompanied the body to its place of burial and were surprised to see that the burial plot was directly opposite that of R' Yaakob, a plot that R' Yehudah had asked to be reserved for himself. He commented to his brother that the *Hevra Kadisha* (Burial Society) must be badly confused. He had expected them to realize that it should be saved for the family. His brother then told him the story that a couple of years ago, R' Abraham came to the home of R' Yaakob and they sat on the sofa talking for about three hours. At the end of the visit, R' Abraham told R' Yaakob that he felt really close to him and didn't want to leave. R' Yosef said he believed that this special connection to their father gave R' Abraham the merit to be buried so close to him. A strong wish expressed in life becomes fulfilled after death.

R' Yehudah told the above story in a eulogy and one of the sons of R' Abraham came up to him afterward and said, "If our parents were so close, I want to be close to you." Eventually, this man became the purchaser of the property where the yeshiva *Kol Yaakob* stands today. When R' Yehudah told his mother the story, she said, "You think the story began with your father? It began with your grandfather. R' Shaul Kassin (see #327) and R' Abraham Ades (see #37) studied Torah together as *havrutot* (learning partners)!"

[320] KASSIN, R' Bekhor

רבי בכור קצין

(1745 — 1855)

Eminent scholar and *darshan* (lecturer) of Aram Soba. He was born in about 1745 in Aram Soba, the older son of R' Yehudah Kassin (see #331). He possessed outstanding character traits, crowned by deep humility. R' Kassin was a popular public speaker and had a great influence on the lives of the many who flocked to his inspirational lectures.

In 1826 he was the first signer on an original bill of sale which is kept in the Ben-Zvi Institute (file no. 302). The second signer was R' Mordechai Dayan (see #186). In 1852 he joined other rabbis of Aram Soba in signing the approbation to the book *Kenisiyah Leshem Shamayim* by R' Menashe Sutton (see #551). (See Document Section, Document No. 31.)

He lived for over a hundred years and passed away in about 5615 (1855). Like his father, he was buried in the "Cave of the Righteous" near the Great Synagogue of Aram Soba. He was blessed with three scholarly sons: R' David (see #322), R' Yitzhak (see #332), and R' Abraham (see #318).

[321] KASSIN, R' David

רבי דוד קצין

(— 1814)

Worthy scholar, *dayan* (judge), and *darshan* (lecturer) of Aram Soba. He was born in Aram Soba, a son of R' Yehudah Kassin (see #331). At the Ben-Zvi Institute [file no. 302] there is an original document dated 8 Adar 2, 5567 (1807) containing the signature of R' David Kassin (second signer) together with that of R' Shelomo Sutton (first signer) and R' Halfon Bekhor Abraham Chasky (see #147), who was the third signer. He passed away in the month of Tevet 5574 (1814).

R' Bekhor Kassin was a popular public speaker and had a great influence on the lives of the many who flocked to his inspirational lectures.

[322] KASSIN, R' David

רבי דוד קצין

(1789 — 1877)

Eminent scholar, *dayan* (judge), and *darshan* (lecturer) of Aram Soba. He was born in Aram Soba, the oldest son of R' Bekhor Kassin (see #320). Like his father before him, R' David was a popular public speaker. He spoke in the synagogue in the evenings on a daily basis, attracting hundreds

ספר

ויאסוף דוד

נדפס

פעה״ק ירושלם תובב״א

Title Page of Vaye'esof David

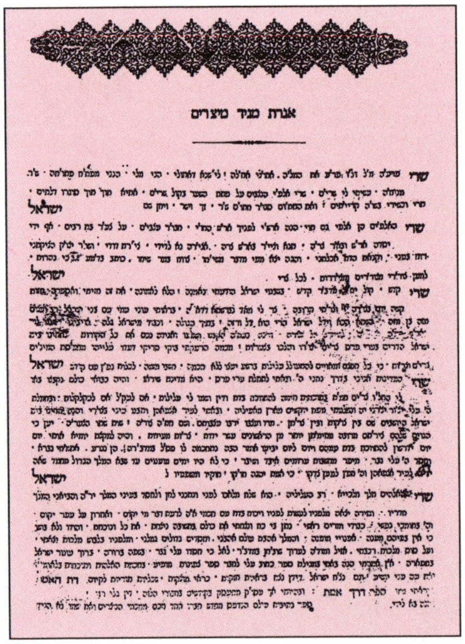

Title Page of *Magid Meitzarim*

of eager listeners. A collection of his inspirational lectures was published as *Vaye'esof David* (Jerusalem 5659/1899). This work was combined with the book *Likutei Abraham* written by his brother R' Abraham Kassin (see #318). A new edition of these two books was produced in 1976. He authored additional *hiddushim* (original Torah thoughts), which remained in manuscript form.

In 1852 he joined other rabbis of Aram Soba in signing the approbation to the book *Kenisiyah Leshem Shamayim* by R' Menashe Sutton (see #551). (See Document Section, Document No. 31.) In the Ben-Zvi Institute (file no. 302) there is an original document which R' David signed together with R' Yaakob Abadi (see #13).

After a long and productive life, R' David passed away in 1877, leaving daughters, but no sons.

[323] KASSIN, R' Eliyahu

רבי אליהו קצין

(1757 — 1830)

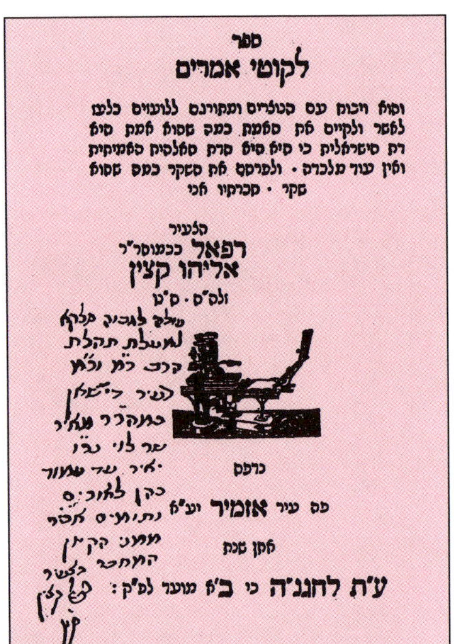

ספר

לקוטי אמרים

הצעיר

רפאל ככמוהר"ר

אליהו קצין

Title Page of *Likutei Amarim*

Eminent scholar and *Av Bet Din* of Aram Soba. He was born in 1757 in Aram Soba, the second son of R' Yehudah Kassin (see #331). A man of considerable wealth, he succeeded his father as head of the Aram Soba *Bet Din*.

In 1822 R' Eliyahu joined other leading rabbis of Aram Soba in signing the approbation for *Yoshev Ohalim* written by R' Abraham Antebi (see #63).

He passed away in about 1830, having authored many *hiddushim* (original Torah thoughts), which were left in manuscript form. His only son, R' Raphael Kassin (see #325), recalled him with unusual love, respect and admiration in the introduction to his book *Derech Haim*.

[324] KASSIN, R' Haim

רבי חיים קצין

(1746 —)

Worthy scholar and rabbi of Aram Soba. He was born in 1746, a son of R' Yehudah Kassin (see #331). Little more is known about him, except for the fact that in the book *Bigdei Yesha*, R' Yeshayah Attiah (see #119) presents a lecture which he delivered on the occasion of the *brit milah* of a son of R' Haim Kassin.

[325] KASSIN, R' Raphael

רבי רפאל קצין

(— 1871)

Distinguished scholar of Aram Soba and Chief Rabbi of Baghdad. He was born in Aram Soba, the only son of R' Eliyahu Kassin (see #323). Thanks to his father's wealth he was able to devote his energies to Torah study. He had an unusual talent for mingling with all manner of people, including royalty. In 1830, the pasha of Iraq, visiting Aram Soba, met R' Kassin and invited him to become the Chief Rabbi of Baghdad, a position which was filled by royal appointment. However, when he arrived in that city, he was opposed by one of the local rabbis, who had aspired to this position. This led to a split in the community, with some supporting R' Kassin and others supporting his opponent. Ultimately, the matter was resolved and R' Kassin occupied the position with much success for many years.

In Baghdad he was frequently called upon to defend the tenets of Judaism in debates with Moslems. However, he was eventually forced to resign from the chief rabbinate and return to Aram Soba. According to tradition, this was due to the machinations of an Arab sheikh who resented R' Kassin's brilliance and his success in confronting other religions. Some said that the sheikh used witchcraft to harm R' Kassin's mental abilities. Apparently, his mind was in a state of confusion upon his return to Aram Soba, where he lived out the remainder of his days, passing away in 5631 (1871). He was eulogized by R' Yaakob Abadi (see #13), as recorded in his manuscript *Kehillat Yaakob*.

He achieved renown for his important book *Derech Haim* (Constantinople 5608/1848). The purpose of the book was to defend the Jewish faith against those seeking to undermine it. It was written in response to the book *Netivot Olam*, which appeared in 1840, authored by a heretical Jew.

In the introduction to his book, R' Kassin referred to other books that he had written, including a four-page letter called *Magid Meitzarim* (Constantinople 5608/1848), which was an appeal to the Jews of Europe to come to the aid of the oppressed Jews of Persia. He also referred to the book *Likutei Amarim* (Izmir 5615/1855), which compared Judaism with Christianity, and was translated into Ladino. The intent was to demonstrate clearly the eternal truths of the Jewish religion for the benefit of both scholars and laymen, with the Hebrew and Ladino versions on facing pages. It received an approbation from R' Haim Palagi, the Chief Rabbi of Izmir (see #449).

He also wrote a book of *hiddushim* (original Torah thoughts), which he called *Lehem HaMa'arechet*. This was an analysis and commentary of the book *Takfo Kohen* by the *Shach* (R' Shabbetai Cohen, the *Siftei Cohen*). R' Kassin's book was published in the 20th century by the yeshiva *Ahavat Shalom* of Jerusalem under the title *Takfo shel Raphael* (Jerusalem 5739/1979). Other books which R' Kassin left in manuscript form include the following:

- *Ma'arechet HaShulhan and Lehem HaMa'arechet. Hiddushim* on the *Shulhan Aruch*, addressing practical issues in *halachah*.
- *Yain HaRoke'ah*. Inspirational lectures on the Torah.

[326] **KASSIN, R' Shaul**

רבי שאול קצין

(19th century)

Worthy scholar and rabbi of Aram Soba. Very little is known about him, other than the fact that in 1852 he joined other rabbis of Aram Soba in signing the approbation to the book *Kenisiyah Leshem Shamayim* by R' Menashe Sutton (see #551). (See Document Section, Document No. 31.)

[327] **KASSIN, R' Shaul**

רבי שאול קצין

(1864 — 1915)

Eminent scholar and rabbi of Aram Soba. He was born in Aram Soba in 1864, a son of R' Abraham Kassin (see #318). R' Shaul excelled in his studies as a youth and rapidly developed into an exceptional Torah scholar of great piety. At age 18 he married Altoon Attiah, the daughter of R' Yaakob Attiah. While in his 20's he wrote many *hiddushim* (original Torah thoughts) on all aspects of Torah, including *Gemara*, *halachah*, and Kabbalah. Before the age of 30 his name became well established for Torah greatness. However, his life in Aram Soba was saddened by the fact that he was not blessed with children who survived infancy.

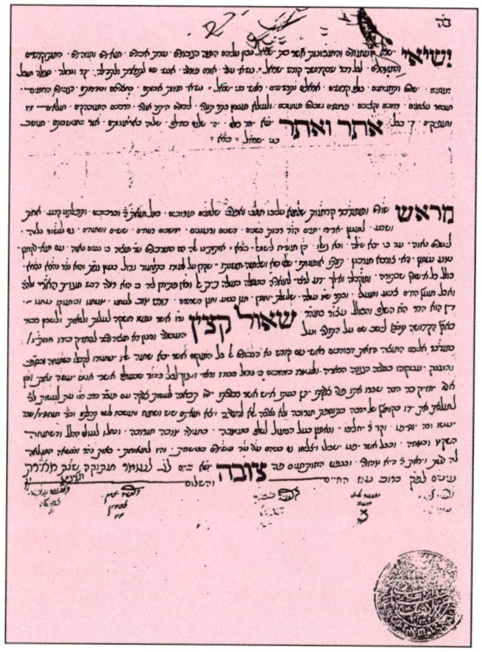

Letter of Rabbis of Syria attesting to greatness of R' Shaul Kassin

The Party Is Over. R' Shaul Kassin's motives for leaving Aram Soba were complex, including, as they did, his love for *Eretz Yisrael* and his hope for the blessing of children in a new land. But what made him finally decide to move was an incident which occurred when one of the respected men of the community, who lived in a nearby courtyard, married off his daughter on a *Motza'e Shabbat* (Saturday night). This man invited non-Jewish musicians to play popular love songs and the celebration was conducted with a distinct lack of modesty.

R' Kassin was deeply angered by the flagrant exhibition and could not restrain himself from admonishing the offenders in very strong terms. He then took his cane and snuffed out all the lanterns. His righteous outburst caused the guests to scatter and the celebration to come to an untimely end. The host was very angry at his neighbor and immediately went to his house to exact his revenge. In his rage, he tore R' Kassin's cloak. This was his very best garment, which he always wore on *Shabbat*. However, despite the fact that

R' Kassin was very poor and the cloak was very expensive, he did not get excited, but simply told the man to calm down.

People of the community, who witnessed this event, encouraged the rabbi to take the man to court on the charge of insulting a Torah scholar and causing him serious financial loss. However, R' Kassin did not listen to them. As tough as he was to defend the principles of holiness, he was soft in defending his personal interest. However, the silence of R' Kassin angered the offender even more. In fact, he proceeded to do everything he could to make R' Kassin's life miserable. In the end the rabbi decided he had no other satisfactory option but to flee, and so he left for *Eretz Yisrael.*

They gathered in the Bet Midrash of the yeshiva Bet El, which was renowned as a center for Kabbalah.

Going to Jerusalem

In 1891 he left for Jerusalem, taking along a letter of introduction from the *Bet Din* of Aram Soba. The letter was signed by R' Abraham Dweck-Khalousi (see #257), R' Eliyahu Hamway (see #271), R' Bechor Mizrahi (see #432), R' Yitzhak Labaton (see #340), and R' Shelomo Safdeyé (see #469). They describe him as a diligent scholar well versed in *Gemara, Rashi,* and *Tosafot*. He is also described as well versed in Kabbalah and the writings of the *Ari'zal*. They urge the rabbis of Israel to help support him in his endeavors.

He was not alone in coming to Jerusalem. A number of other notable young scholars of Kabbalah emigrated from Aram Soba at approximately the same time. These included R' Haim Shaul Dweck (see #228), R' Yomtob Yedid (see #593), R' Yitzhak Shrem (see #519), and R' Abraham Ades (see #37). They gathered in the *Bet Midrash* of the yeshiva *Bet El*, which was renowned as a center for Kabbalah studies. An elderly Kabbalist of the yeshiva was once seen with his eyes full of tears. When asked why he was so heart broken, he answered that he was listening to the deep Torah discussions among the young scholars from Aram Soba, but their ideas were too advanced for him to understand.

Sojourn in Hebron

Before finally settling in Jerusalem he spent three years in Hebron, where he had the opportunity to study with the great Kabbalist, R' Eliyahu Mani, the Chief Rabbi of Hebron. The two scholars formed a close attachment, and when R' Kassin left, R' Mani gave him a handwritten copy of the *siddur* of the *Rashash* (R' Shalom Sharabi), as a parting gesture.

One Is Enough. When R' Shaul Kassin first arrived in Jerusalem he stayed for a few days at the home of one of the notable men of the city, a wealthy individual by the name of Sir Rahamim Mizrahi. This gentleman described his visitor as an extremely self-denying and holy person. At mealtimes he was offered three or four different kinds of foods, but took only one, and that was always the simplest. No amount of entreaties would get him to change his mind. He used to say, "How long is the pleasure of the throat when it swallows food? Just a handbreadth and no more!"

He soon developed into one of the select Kabbalists who focused their prayers according to the concepts of the siddur of the Rashash.

His Home in Jerusalem

He then moved on to Jerusalem, ultimately acquiring an apartment near the yeshiva *Rehovot HaNahar* in the Bukharan neighborhood. This great Kabbalist yeshiva under the leadership of R' Haim Shaul Dweck (see #228) then became his primary Torah-study location. And so he soon developed into one of the select Kabbalists who focused their prayers according to the concepts of the *siddur* of the *Rashash*. It was said that seeing R' Shaul pray with his sweet voice and powerful concentration was like seeing an angel of *Hashem*.

It was his custom to lead the *tefillot* every Friday, because this day is known as the one on which the *kavanot* (meditations) of the entire week are established.

His Weekly Lectures

Following in the footsteps of his forefathers, he developed his oratorical skills and became a popular and influential speaker, delivering moving lectures to the many people who came to hear him. He was a regular *Shabbat* speaker in the great synagogue of the Nahalat Shimon neighborhood, which is adjacent to the tomb of Shimon HaSadik. Despite the long distance from his home and his failing health, he would continue to go there every week because he felt he had to a duty to those who wanted to hear his inspiring words. He was greatly assisted in this by Mr. Abraham Sutton, who was instrumental in making the arrangements for his weekly lectures. (Mr. Sutton eventually moved to Argentina.) Later, during World War I, when many of the residents of Nahalat Shimon were drafted by the Turkish army and others left *Eretz Yisrael* to avoid the draft, he gave his weekly lectures in the *Maskil El Dal* synagogue in the Bukharan neighborhood.

His Generosity

He set aside a sum of money to lend to those in need. Some of the borrowers never paid him back, but he never brought it up to them. When his friends asked him why he didn't take them to court, he said, "Are these people thieves or robbers? I am sure that their circumstances are difficult and they are unable to pay me back. When the time comes and *Hashem* gives them success, they will surely pay. And if it should happen that they don't pay me at all, I forgive them." Sometimes, the same borrowers would return for another loan and he would give them the benefit of the doubt and grant them the loan. He would always follow the ethical principle of, "Judge everyone favorably" (*Abot* 1:6).

His Hatred of Gossip

He was always extremely careful to watch his speech to avoid saying or hearing meaningless chatter, especially *lashon hara* (gossip). On one occasion he was talking with a good friend and the friend began to say something which could be construed as gossip about another person. R' Kassin immediately jumped up and stopped him, saying "How can you speak *lashon hara*? Leave my house! I don't want to hear forbidden talk!" The man left the house, greatly embarrassed. Later, when they met in the street, R' Kassin was very friendly. "Please don't think that I bear any hatred or ill will toward you. It is only because you are my good friend that I was so angry at you. *Lashon hara* is equivalent to the worst sins — idol worship, immorality, and murder. Therefore I stopped you from committing it. But from now on, if you observe good speech practices, we will continue to be good friends."

His Legacy

He edited and published the book *VaYe'esof David* of his uncle R' David Kassin (see #322), adding to it his father's book *Likutei Abraham* (Jerusalem 5664/1904 and 5736/1976).

He left in manuscript form his own commentaries and glosses on various books including *Etz HaHaim* of R' Haim Vital and *Shaar HaKavanot*. The following books have been published:

- *Peri Sadik* (Jerusalem 5698/1938). The *halachot* (laws) of which blessing to say on various foods. Also, *hiddushim* on the *Gemara* and responsa on matters pertaining to *Hoshen Mishpat*. This was bound together with Volume I of *Kerem Shelomo* by his son R' Shelomo Kassin (see #329).
- *Midrash Aseret HaDibrot* (*Eretz Yisrael* 5737/1977). Teachings and interpretations of the *Gemara* pertaining to the Ten Commandnents. This book was published as the third of three books in an anthology called *Hut HaMeshulash*. The first of the three books is *Peri Etz HaGan* by R' Yaakob Kassin (see #330) and the second is *Mitzvat Hashem* by R' Yaakob's son R' Shaul Kassin, current Chief Rabbi of the congregation *Shaare Zion* in Brooklyn. This book consists of teachings on the meanings of various *mitzvot*.

It was his custom to lead the tefillot every Friday, because this day is known as the one on which the kavanot (meditations) of the entire week are established.

"Please don't think that I bear any hatred or ill will toward you. It is only because you are my good friend that I was so angry at you. Lashon hara is equivalent to the worst sins. Therefore I stopped you from committing it."

He set aside a sum of money to lend to those in need. Some of the borrowers never paid him back, but he never brought it up to them.

The outbreak of World War I in 1914 was accompanied by great privation and hardship for the people of Jerusalem, especially for Torah scholars. Many died from disease, including R' Kassin who succumbed to typhus and passed away on 26 Kislev, 5676 (1915). He was eulogized by the great rabbis of Jerusalem.

In Jerusalem he was blessed with three scholarly sons: R' Abraham Kassin (see #319), R' Yaakob Kassin (see #330), and R' Shelomo Kassin (see #329).

[328] **KASSIN, Señor Shelomo**

ס' שלמה קצין

(1540 —)

Patriarch of the Kassin family of Aram Soba. A wealthy merchant, he fled from persecution in Spain and settled in Aram Soba. He became head of the Jewish community of the city and devoted his energies to Torah study and good works.

His two sons, Señor Ephraim Kassin and Señor Menashe Kassin (born about 1590), continued their father's tradition of philanthropy and communal leadership. In the introduction which R' Abraham Laniado (see #345) wrote to the book *Kli Yakar*, he thanks the two brothers for their generous financial assistance.

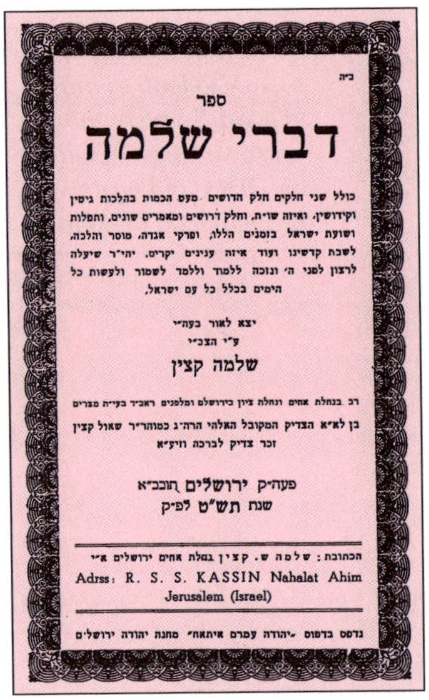
ב״ה

ספר

דברי שלמה

כולל שני חלקים חלק חדושים מעט הכמות בהלכות גיטין וקידושין, ואיזה שו״ת, וחלק דרושים ומאמרים שונים, ותפלות ושועת ישראל בזמנים הללו, ופרקי אגדה, מוסר והלכה, לשכת קדשינו ועוד איזה ענינים יקרים. יהי״ר שיעלה לרצון לפני ה׳ ונזכה ללמוד וללמד לשמור ולעשות כל הימים בכלל כל עם ישראל.

יצא לאור בעה״י

ע״י הצב״י

שלמה קצין

רב בנחלת אחים ונחלת ציון בירושלם ומלפנים ראב״ד בע״ת מצרים

בן לא״א הצדיק המקובל האלהי הרה״ג כמוהר״ר שאול קצין זכר צדיק לברכה וזיע״א

פעה״ק ירושלים תובב״א

שנת תש״ט לפ״ק

הכתובת: שלמה ש. קצין נחלת אחים ירושלים א״י

Adrss: R. S. S. KASSIN Nahalat Ahim Jerusalem (Israel)

נדפס בדפוס ״יהודה עמרם איתאח״ מחנה יהודה ירושלים

Title Page of Dibrei Shelomo

[329] **KASSIN, R' Shelomo**

רבי שלמה קצין

(1909 — 1982)

Distinguished scholar and *dayan* (judge) of Jerusalem and Tel Aviv. He was born to R' Shaul Kassin (see #327) in Jerusalem in 1909 and studied under R' Abraham Ades (see #37) and R' Ezra Attiah (see #102). He served for two years as recording secretary in the Sephardic *Bet Din* of Jerusalem. He subsequently served as *Av Bet Din* (Chief Judge) in Egypt and member of the *Bet Din* of the Rabbinate of *Tel Aviv*. He passed away on 6 Heshvan, 5743 (1982).

His published books are as follows:

- *Nitzotzei Ohr* (Jerusalem 5695/1935). Spiritual guidance for every day of the month, inspirational lectures, and eulogies. This was bound together with *Taharat Bnot Yisrael*.
- *Taharat Bnot Yisrael* (Jerusalem 5695/1935). The *halachot* (laws) of *Niddah* (family purity).
- *Kerem Shelomo* (Jerusalem 5698/1938 and 5702/1942). Two volumes of inspirational lectures, *hiddushim* (original Torah thoughts) on *Gemara*, and responsa. Volume I was bound together with his father's book *Peri Sadik*.
- *Orhot Haim* (Jerusalem 5709/1949). Spiritual guidance on a variety of topics such as praying in times of emergency and Sabbath observance.
- *Dibrei Shelomo* (Jerusalem 5709/1949). Part I consists of *hiddushim* on *halachah*. Part II consists of inspirational lectures and eulogies. Also included are *hiddushim* by the author's brother, R' Yaakob Kassin (see #330).

(330) **KASSIN, R' Yaakob**

רבי יעקב קצין

(1900 — 1994)

Distinguished Kabbalist, *dayan* (judge), and rabbi of Jerusalem and New York. In 1932 he went to New York to raise funds and was invited by the congregation *Shaare Zion* in Brooklyn to serve as their rabbi. He undertook the position the following year and served the congregation faithfully for 62 years until he passed away on 3 Tevet, 5755 (1994).

His Early Years

He was born to R' Shaul Kassin (see #327) in Jerusalem on 23 Nissan, 5660 (1900) and studied in the yeshiva *Ohel Moed*, which was headed by R' Raphael Shelomo Laniado (see #364) and became a forerunner to *Porat Yosef*.

The young boy was unusually mature for his age and so no one questioned the plans for celebrating his *Bar Mitzvah*, even though, due to a mistake in the calculation of dates, he was still only 12 years old. He gave a learned *Bar Mitzvah* discourse and started putting on *tefillin*. Since he was assumed to be 13 years old, his father arranged for him to study the art of becoming a scribe so that he would have a source of income when he grew up. After about six months, the youth had become an expert at writing holy scrolls. But it was then that his father found his birth certificate and realized that he still had half a year to go before he would officially leave his childhood status. No scrolls that he worked on up to that time would be valid and so he returned to the yeshiva *Ohel Moed* for the rest of the year.

With the onset of World War I, the Jews of Jerusalem suffered extreme privation. Owing to the terrible war, communal funds that had previously been sent from abroad were lacking. Famine was everywhere and people had to subsist on such meager fare as chicken feed and orange peels. The scourge of malnutrition became a major source of epidemics, especially typhus. R' Yaakob's father passed away from this dreaded disease in 1917 and his mother passed away two months later. The ravages of hunger, which were hard to bear by the community at large, were especially difficult for orphans like R' Yaakob. The bad food which he ate caused him serious stomach problems which continued for many years. All of this did not discourage him from an intense dedication to Torah study.

In the year 1919, when he was 18 years old, R' Yaakob married Mazal, the daughter of R' Shalom Hedaya (see #310). In 1922, he immersed himself in Kabbalah, studying under R' Haim Shaul Dweck (see #228), R' Abraham Ades (see #37), and R' Yosef Yedid (see #594).

His Years in Porat Yosef

In 1923 he was accepted as a graduate student of the yeshiva *Porat Yosef*, which had just been reestablished and effectively became the successor to *Ohel Moed*. In *Porat Yosef* he studied under R' Raphael Shelomo Laniado, who had been the *Rosh Yeshiva* of *Ohel Moed*.

One of the features of *Porat Yosef* was that a building adjacent to the yeshiva contained 20 beautiful apartments, which were assigned rent-free to 20 senior scholars and lecturers of the yeshiva. The purpose was that they should spend all of their time in the vicinity of the yeshiva and ensure the right Torah environment for the student body. In 1926 R' Yaakob was awarded one of the 20 apartments and for as long as he lived in *Eretz Yisrael*, that is where he resided.

R' Yaakob Kassin as a young man

Besides the regular program of revealed Torah that was studied in *Porat Yosef*, there was a program of Kabbalah studies. These studies were conducted by a special group of selected scholars in a separate annex, which was named *Yeshiva Oz VeHadar*. The Kabbalah scholars devoted night and day to studying the works of the *Ari'zal* and the *siddur* of the *Rashash* (R' Shalom Sharabi). R' Yaakob was one of the first participants in this study circle. He immediately distinguished himself in the depth of knowledge that he acquired. He soon became a lecturer for the group. In later years he often recalled with gratitude the miracle that he, a young man of 25, had been given the opportunity to study in a group of seasoned scholars, many of whose members were 75 years old and more.

R' Kassin as a young man, with his wife Mazal, son Chacham Shaul, and daughter Charlotte

In later years he often recalled with gratitude the miracle that he, a young man of 25, had been given the opportunity to study in a group of seasoned scholars, many of whose members were 75 years old and more.

Halachic Questions from Far and Wide

As R' Yaakob's knowledge of Torah grew, he received an ever-growing number of *halachic* queries. In addition, the great sages of the generation would share with him their responsa, to see if he agreed with their conclusions on intricate legal issues.

The majority of questions which R' Yaakob dealt with during that period were in the highly complex area of divorce and marriage. He had acquired expertise in this field when he had studied it in *Ohel* Moed under the guidance of R' Ezra Attiah (see #102), one of the sharpest minds of the generation.

R' Yaakob Kassin with R' Moshe Feinstein

A highly complicated matter on which his opinion was sought was in reference to a marriage whose validity was in question. It was unclear whether the woman could be released from the marital bond without a *get* (bill of divorce). R' Raphael Ma'arabi (see #405), a great sage from Damascus and later a prominent member of the Jerusalem rabbinate, approached R' Yaakob on this matter.

R' Yaakob Meir, Chief Rabbi

"Fortunate are those who walk in the light of your Torah," concluded the Chief Rabbi. "May many more like you arise in Israel!"

R' Yaakob arranged his responsum, the longest he had written to date, with great care. As the case contained so many ramifications, his answer was comprised of numerous sections and subsections, extending to many pages. Throughout, his complete mastery of the subject is fully evident.

Because he was concerned that his ruling might cause others to stumble, he submitted his response to the Chief Rabbi of *Eretz Yisrael*, R' Yaakob Meir, for approval. In glowing terms, the latter expressed his admiration for R' Yaakob's masterly analysis of all the sources relating to the intricate subject at hand, and for his systematic and logical treatment in the twenty-six sections of his treatise. "Fortunate are those who walk in the light of your Torah," concluded the Chief Rabbi. "May many more like you arise in Israel!"

In light of R' Meir's approbation, R' Yaakob decided to preserve this responsum for future generations. He published it, together with some others of his responsa, in a booklet called *Mishmeret HaKiddushin* (Jerusalem, 5685/1925). Copies were snapped up by Jerusalem's scholarly community as soon as they reached the shops, and before long the entire edition was sold out.

With the publication of this treatise, Rabbi Kassin's encyclopedic knowledge of Torah, his unique ability to analyze a subject, and his lucid and systematic style of presentation became revealed to all. From this point onwards, *halachic* queries began to pour in from all parts of the world.

In 1926, an inquiry arrived from the *Av Beit Din* of Egypt, R' Yehudah Haim Maslaton (see # 413). In introducing his request, the *Av Beit Din* addressed R' Yaakob in exalted terms. After presenting the question, he appealed to his colleague to investigate the matter thoroughly. And yet, he concluded: "I urge His Excellency not to respond at such length or to expand on the subject with such comprehensiveness as he did in the case of his renowned responsum on *Kiddushin*, with its twenty-six sections. Unfortunately, we are unable to swim in such a vast sea. We would value His Excellency's kindness if he would present his interpretation of his ruling as concisely as possible."

His Bond with Rabbi's

R' Yaakob formed a strong attachment to R' Yosef Yedid (see #594), the head of the Sephardic *Bet Din* in Jerusalem. R' Ezra Attiah, the *Rosh Yeshiva* of *Porat Yosef* (see #102), told how when R' Yosef Yedid was looking for a particular ruling among the many books of responsa by the later *halachic* authorities, he would send for R' Yaakob Kassin. R' Yaakob had an encyclopedic knowledge and would immediately identify the book, the chapter, and even the page on which the desired information was located. Many other Torah scholars would turn to R' Yaakob when expert knowledge was needed, but his connection with R' Yedid was unique.

During the period 1924-1925 he also drew inspiration from another great sage, R' Abraham Ades (see #37). From this teacher, he learned *mussar* (spiritual and character development) and a refined sense of the majesty of G-d.

R' Yaakob would bring all doubts or queries to R' Abraham for clarification. In the biography of R' Ades, which R' Yaakob wrote and included in his book *Peri Etz HaGan*, he noted, "During the last two years, 5784 and 5785 (1924-1925), I have benefited from the powerful light of this righteous man. On many occasions, whether day or night, after wrestling with a question of Kabbalah, I would approach him and request his assistance in solving the matter. I was able to recognize something wonderful in his Torah and his expertise. He was a vast storehouse of knowledge, a fountain of understanding and a well of wisdom — accompanied by extreme humility, refinement, piety, and holiness as befits him."

R' Yaakob describes a fascinating anecdote involving R' Ades:

"One day in the year 5684 (1924), I approached my master and asked if he could lend me a certain sum of money. I needed it urgently, but was sure that I would have it back in about two weeks. I had previously lent money to a fellow who had traveled overseas. He had notified me that he was preparing to return to Jerusalem within fifteen days, and I was sure I would be repaid.

"My master shook his head in disbelief, and laughed. 'Why does my master laugh?' I inquired.

"'I will lend you the money,' he replied, 'but know that this man will not come — neither in fifteen days, nor in a month or two.' Surprised, I asked him respectfully how he could make such a statement, when he did not even know who the person was.

"'Just so, I am telling you!' he exclaimed, then continued, 'At any rate, you shall take the money and return it to me after fifteen days, as you state, because I shall need it; but your debtor will not come soon — perhaps he will arrive in six month's time.'

"So it was! Fifteen days went by and then another fifteen days, but there was no sign of the man until exactly six months had passed — just as my master had predicted. I was completely amazed by this."

R' Yaakob did not benefit for long from the wisdom of this righteous man, for R' Ades passed away on the 28th of Av, 5685 (1925).

His First Book on Kabbalah. While only 25 years of age, he wrote his first book in the field of Kabbalah, *Ohr HaLevanah*. During this period he was suffering from a serious and painful stomach ailment. He did not allow this obstacle to prevent him from completing his work which established his reputation among the Kabbalists of Jerusalem. The book, which was published in 1925, received approbations from three of the greatest rabbis of that time: R' Yosef Chaim Sonnenfeld, R' Haim Shaul Dweck (see #228), and R' Aharon Shelomo Maharil.

His Miraculous Recovery from Illness. In his diary, R' Yaakob described an amazing event that took place on the publication of his first book. It is important to recall that during the year of publication, he suffered from the most excruciating pain. The thought entered his mind that the publication of his work might be a merit for him, so that *Hashem* would send him a complete recovery. This hope gave him the strength to continue.

Thus R' Yaakob noted in his diary:

"My dear friend, R' Shelomo Sofioff, told me he dreamt that he was standing in the synagogue of his late father, David Sofioff. During the prayer service, he noticed an old man standing in the northeastern corner, wrapped in his *tallit* and *tefillin* and chanting the prayers with awesome concentration. He was told that this was none other than R' Shalom Sharabi (the *Rashash*)!

"My friend approached him, kissed his hand, and entreated him, 'R' Yaakob Kassin, the son of R' Shaul, is very ill. Please pray for him, that he should be healed; especially since he is a diligent student of the Kabbalah, and recites his prayers with the *siddurim* that you instituted.'

"The *Rashash* replied: 'Yes, for this reason I have come; do not fear, he will recover and all will be well.'

"This is the good news which Mr. Sofioff passed on to me at that time, and indeed it was so. From the year in which I completed and published my book on the *kavanot* (meditations), I began to see relief from my suffering. Part of my illness has already been alleviated, although it has not been uprooted completely."

Thus, in his introduction to his book, R' Yaakob praises *Hashem*, Who enabled him to prevail over his affliction.

"'How shall I repay *Hashem* for all his kindness to me?' (Psalms 116:12). My mouth shall give thanks to *Hashem* and in the midst of the multitude I will extoll him. He has delivered me from all diseases which threatened my soul, and has acquainted me with His Torah — especially with the writings of the Ari and the *siddur* of the *Rashash* — through my master and teacher, R' Shaul Dweck HaKohen." R' Yaakob concludes, "May *Hashem* put an end to our troubles, heal us completely, remove from us all illness and affliction, and fulfill all our heartfelt requests for the good."

The Foundation of Belief

The period at *Porat Yosef* was a very productive one for R' Yaakob. In 1926 he wrote *Yesod Ha'Emunah* (*The Foundation of Belief*). The author's objective was to reinforce faith in the Divine arrangement of the spiritual worlds and to reaffirm the principles of the books of Kabbalah. This book was written at the request of certain individuals of the community of Cairo in Egypt, who saw a need for a polemic against the community of the Dardaim. This group denied the authenticity of the Kabbalah and ridiculed the tradition that the Holy *Zohar* is the work of R' Shimon bar Yochai, claiming instead that it was written by an errant student. [Note: A letter on this issue from R' Kassin's father-in-law, R' Shalom Hedaya (see #310), is provided in the Document Section, Document No. 12. There is also a relevant excerpt from R' Kassin's writings.]

Through this treatise, R' Yaakob dispelled, in no uncertain terms, the confusion which had been created by the corrupt theories of the Dardaim community.

Yesod Ha'Emunah demonstrates R' Yaakob's impressive ability to analyze and clarify the interrelation between the revealed and the hidden aspects of the Torah. It deals in depth with the principle of the Divine transmission of the Kabbalah and with concepts in classical Jewish philosophy and historical research. The treatise was sent to Egypt, and was printed there by the *Keter Torah* Society. Many years later, in 1980, it was published together with several other essays in Brooklyn, New York.

Through this treatise, R' Yaakob dispelled, in no uncertain terms, the confusion which had been created by the corrupt theories of the Dardaim community. These ideas had spread like a plague and caused harm to the dispersed communities of Israel. Jews in the Diaspora, lacking the guidance of an organized rabbinate, had fallen prey to the arguments of these deviants, and had been encouraged to join their ranks. R' Yaakob's dissertation, however, clearly exposed the sect's distorted views, and turned the tide against them. The masses kept far from the heretics and their numbers dwindled so much that they all but disappeared.

The second part of *Yesod Ha'Emunah* is quite distinct from the first, containing a number of essays on different themes. The third part of *Yesod Ha'Emunah* contains a number of responsa by R' Yaakob, as well as a reprint of *Mishmeret HaKiddushin*, a twenty-six-chapter responsum that originally brought him fame.

His Complete Recovery

Even though his suffering from a stomach ailment had been alleviated after the publication of *Ohr HaLevanah in* 1925, the root of the ailment remained, and in due course, the painful condition flared up again. R' Yaakob was forced to ease up on his very intensive study schedule and his creative output declined.

Once again, he consulted the doctors of Jerusalem in the hope of finding a permanent cure for his malady. The opinion of the local physicians was unanimous: An operation was required. Unfortunately, such surgery was beyond their competence. R' Yaakob would have to travel to Europe for the treatment he needed.

But R' Yaakob had absolutely no means of paying for the operation and travel expenses. He delayed fulfilling his physician's orders, in the hope that salvation would come from Heaven. But when his teachers and colleagues at the yeshiva saw his agony — both the physical pain and the mental anguish at having to miss his studies — they took up a collection around Jerusalem, and managed to raise the necessary sum. They gave the money to R' Yaakob, with the suggestion that he travel to Germany, as the doctors had recommended.

In the spring of 1928, R' Yaakob boarded a passenger ship bound for Germany. En route, the vessel anchored for about two weeks in France. By this time, R' Yaakob's entire body was sore. He was not accustomed to sea travel, and his condition had been seriously aggravated. He disembarked from the ship and took a room in a nearby hotel, in order to recover from the rigors of the journey.

News of his arrival soon reached the ears of the chief rabbi of Paris. He paid R' Yaakob a visit, and suggested that he cancel his trip to Germany. It would be better, in his opinion, to have the operation performed at the local Rothschild Hospital by the world-famous surgeon, Dr. Hertz. R' Yaakob accepted this advice and a few days later the operation took place. It was an outstanding success and within a short time, R' Yaakob had returned to perfect health. He quickly returned to Jerusalem, where he lost no time in resuming his study program with renewed strength and enthusiasm.

In later years, R' Yaakob would attribute the success of his operation to the merit of his righteous ancestors, to that of the holy city of Jerusalem, and to his friends, who had prayed on his behalf. About this, he wrote: "*Hashem* came to my rescue. He oversaw the success of the operation and restored me to good health within a short time. I was delivered from the threat of death, and the words of *Tehillim* (118:18): 'You have afflicted me sorely, O G-d, but you have not given me over to death,' were fulfilled in me. Praised be *Hashem* who has not only sent me a complete recovery, but has restored my original vigor and has saved me from all kinds of sorrows."

In later years, R' Yaakob would attribute the success of his operation to the merit of his righteous ancestors, to that of the holy city of Jerusalem, and to his friends, who had prayed on his behalf.

Founding the Yeshiva Gan HaLevanon

One of R' Yaakob's greatest achievements of those days was the founding of *Yeshivat Gan HaLevanon*. This yeshiva attracted the finest scholars, who flocked to hear the daily lectures in Torah and Kabbalah delivered by Yaakob. In R' Yaakob's diary, he discloses his motive in setting up this new institution:

"When I was suffering from the terrible disease, with my very life in danger, I made a promise to *Hashem* that should I fully recover, I would make every effort to inaugurate an institution which would promote the honor of Heaven. Within its framework, I would dedicate my strength and talents to further the glory of the Torah.

"With the help of my revered rabbis and the honored community leaders, I was able to fulfill my vow. This year, 5687 (1927), we established the yeshiva *Gan HaLevanon*; for it is a garden of Torah in Jerusalem, the land of the Levanon. Praised be *Hashem*, Who has granted me the merit to make my dream a reality. Within these walls, scholars and rabbis toil day and night in both the mystical and revealed branches of the Torah. They are being supported with funds raised by our generous brethren within the country and abroad."

"With the help of my revered rabbis and the honored community leaders, I was able to fulfill my vow. This year, 5687 (1927), we established the yeshiva Gan HaLevanon; for it is a garden of Torah in Jerusalem."

Many of the scholars who came to *Gan HaLevanon* were sages advanced in years, who had spent most of their lives in the study halls of Torah. Nevertheless, they eagerly gathered to hear R' Yaakob speak. For, despite his youth, he was recognized as an authority in the revealed Torah and in the field of Kabbalah.

The members of the yeshiva's board of directors were all associates of R' Yaakob from *Porat Yosef*. The president was R' Nissim Eliashar, former president of *Porat Yosef*, and president of the board of the Sephardic community. The members of the board comprised: R' Shalom Mordechai Azulai, a member of the *Bet Din* of the *Adat HaMa'aravim*; R' Moshe Ades (see #39), a member of the Sephardic *Bet Din*; R' Yosef Shloush, leader of the *Adat HaMa'aravim*; and communal activist; and R' Eliyahu Yosef Shamah (see #500), one of the founders of *Yeshivat Porat Yosef*.

When the rabbinical leaders of the city saw the great influence the new yeshiva was having on religious life in Jerusalem, they convinced local philanthropists to contribute generously to its upkeep. In 1931, R' Yaakob himself made an appeal for donations throughout the land and abroad. He emphasized that *Yeshivat Gan HaLevanon* was a nonpartisan institution, which represented all the different communities and which was completely endorsed by the rabbinic leadership of Jerusalem.

His Humility

In 1928, the Kabbalist, R' Rahamim Shrem (see #514), was preparing to publish Part II of his major work on the Kabbalah, *Shaare Rahamim*. The author sought an experienced scholar to critically review the work, and verify the accuracy of its statements.

R' Shrem was elated to discover R' Yaakob Kassin, who eminently qualified for the assignment. Not only his comprehensive knowledge of all areas of Torah, but his gift for writing in an elegant literary style made him the perfect choice.

When R' Shrem requested his assistance, R' Yaakob readily accepted the assignment — but only on condition that his role as editor remain a secret. He imposed this condition, it seems, due to his extreme humility.

When R' Shrem requested his assistance, R' Yaakob readily accepted the assignment — but only on condition that his role as editor remain a secret. He imposed this condition, it seems, due to his extreme humility; he could not visualize himself as being chosen for a task above all the great sages in the city!

R' Yaakob reviewed the entire manuscript, made corrections, and added many comments of his own prefaced by the words: "The editor says ...." The end result was a text that was substantially improved.

When the book finally reached publication, the leading Kabbalists of the day were as excited by the editor's comments as they were by the text itself. They were amazed that he had chosen to hide his identity, when the genius of his entries could have won him much glory. But in doing so, R' Yaakob was giving heed to the counsel of our Sages, who taught that a scholar should compose one book anonymously, as indeed had been the practice of great men in every generation.

R' Rahamim Shrem himself acknowledged that the second part of his book, which had been edited by R' Yaakob, was superior to the rest. In a latter part of the book, R' Shrem writes that Part II, "was arranged by a very great scholar in the revealed and mystical branches of Torah, who added many precious and delightful *hiddushim* (original Torah thoughts)." Indeed, it has been accepted by students of Kabbalah that this second part is the most important one in the book, and it alone is sufficiently trustworthy to rely on for practical decisions in matters of Kabbalah.

After R' Yaakob read the entire book and realized its merit, he wrote a letter of recommendation. Thus, we find his approbation appearing alongside those of the other leading rabbis of Jerusalem in that period: R' Yosef Haim Sonnenfeld, R' Yosef Yedid (see #594), R' Haim Shaul Dweck (see #228), R' Shelomo *Maharil*, R' Yaakob Haim Sofer (the *Kaf HaHaim*, (see #532); R' Hizkiah Shabbetai (see #495), and R' Shalom Hedaya (see #310), who was R' Yaakob's father-in-law.

On the surface, it may seem incredible that such a young man—a mere 28 years of age—could have presented his approbation together with the elders of the city.

On the surface, it may seem incredible that such a young man — a mere 28 years old — could have presented his approbation together with the elders of the city. Only the fact that his greatness was already recognized in those days made this possible, and thus R' Yaakob's recommendation had great value.

The depth of scholarship, which earned R' Yaakob a place among Jerusalem's leading scholars, was noted by his father-in-law in his own approbation to *Shaare Rahamim*. About the editor, he wrote as follows:

"The author of this work ... moved by his characteristic fear of Heaven, was concerned that mistakes might have crept into his book, or that he may have writen something incorrect. In order to prevent this, he handed over his labor to an adept sage, a holy man of Israel, an authority in the Torah, master of deep secrets, who worked on it, improved it, and arranged everything correctly. He added comments of his own and supplied additional insights and perspectives."

Another of R' Yaakob's original compositions to be included in *Shaare Rahamim* was the small treatise: *"A Concise Treatment of the Laws of Terumot and Maaserot, and the Matanot Kehunah."* This is a lucid and systematic presentation of the laws pertaining to these subjects, relevant customs observed in Jerusalem, and rulings and insights of the classical masters of the Kabbalah. R' Yaakob also included the formula to be recited when separating the priestly tithes. The formula used was an accurate and authentic version, which was widely accepted among the inhabitants of Jerusalem. Owing to the great importance of the laws covered in this treatise, R' Yaakob's brother, R' Shelomo (see #329), reprinted the work ten years later, as part of R' Shaul Kassin's work *Peri Sadik* (Jerusalem, 5698/1938) (see #327).

His Appointment as Dayan

In 1928 R' Yaakob was appointed to sit on the Sephardic *Bet Din* together with R' Hizkiah Shabbetai (see #495), R' Ben-Sion Kouenka, and R' Abraham Philosoph. News of his admission to the *Bet Din* spread quickly. Questions addressed to R' Yaakob streamed in from all corners of the world and he was called upon to solve many complex *halachic* problems. These included inquiries of a private nature, relating to such matters as marriage, divorce, personal status, and questions touching upon communal and national issues, relevant to the time and the generation.

His Encyclopedic Work

In 1931, R' Yaakob published his famous book, *Peri Etz HaGan* (*The Fruit of the Tree of the Garden*). Encyclopedic in scope, the work is a treasurehouse of Torah. R' Yaakob arranged the material in three parts.

The first part contains biographies of prominent sages and discussions about their ethical teachings. Among those presented are the *Rashash* (R' Shalom Sharabi) and his sons, R' Gedalyah Hivan, and R' Yaakob's father, R' Shaul Kassin. It continues with accounts of the lives of R' Yaakob's master and teacher, the Kabbalist R' Abraham Ades, the communal leader Nissim Nahum (see #437), and others. In addition, it includes an overview of the author's own life.

News of his admission to the Bet Din spread quickly. Questions addressed to R' Yaakob streamed in from all corners of the world and he was called upon to solve many complex halachic problems.

The second part of his book comprises solutions to problems raised by R' Yosef Haim of Baghdad (the *Ben Ish Hai*) in his work *Imrei Binah*. In the last part, R' Yaakob presents the order of the *kavanot* (meditations) for the prayers and the sounding of the *shofar* on Rosh Hashanah, together with appropiate explanations for the beginner, and concludes his book with a number of discourses and liturgical poems.

The book won the stamp of approval of the leading rabbis and leaders of his day: R' Yosef Haim Sonnenfeld, R' Hizkiah Shabbetai (see #495), and R' Shalom Hedaya (see #310).

These distinguished rabbis wrote approbations which, in addition to their high praise of the book and its author, also included endorsements of *Yeshivat Gan HaLevanon*. They also appealed to the public to assist and support the efforts of the author in his many activities for the advancement of Torah and for the communal welfare.

In his remarks, R Yosef Haim Sonnenfeld stressed that "the fear of G-d pervades every page of this book, whatever the topic happens to be. Fortunate indeed will be those who will take its teachings to heart."

In his remarks, R Yosef Haim Sonnenfeld stressed that "the fear of G-d pervades every page of this book, whatever the topic happens to be. Fortunate indeed will be those who will take its teachings to heart."

His Dedication to Torah Study

The astounding dedication with which R' Yaakob committed himself to Torah study is suggested in the following lines from the book *Kerem Shelomo* by his younger brother, R' Shelomo Kassin (see #329):

"I have been privileged to observe the splendor of my elder brother, long may he live, our master and teacher, the *Gaon* R'

Yaakob Kassin. From his earliest years, he has been relentless in his single-minded devotion to his studies, his spirit of self-sacrifice, and his burning desire to toil unceasingly in the Torah — until he merited to master even the wisdom of the *Ari'zal*.

"With my own eyes, I have seen my brother fight against sleep while grappling with a difficult text, or composing the hiddushim."

"With my own eyes, I have seen my brother fight against sleep while grappling with a difficult text, or composing the *hiddushim* in which G-d and men rejoiced. Words would flow from him as if from a spring. It was as though his pen would magically write on its own, as they say about the *Hida*. Even when he was in agony from severe heart pains (thank G-d, he has now recovered), the suffering did not deter him from writing his *hiddushim*. Happy is she who bore him, and may there be many more like him! May he merit to fulfill the words of the *Tanna* R' Yohanan: 'Whoever observes the Torah in poverty will ultimately observe it in wealth.'

In 1932, R' Yaakob was selected to travel to the United States on behalf of the Sephardic orphanages of Jerusalem.

"He has already written several holy texts, such as his books *Ohr HaLevanah* and *Peri Etz HaGan*. His treatise *Tochahat Meguleh* has been reprinted in the book *Sama d'Hai*. There is also the collection *Mishmeret Kiddushin* and various other writings. During his present holy mission as spiritual leader of holy communities in Brooklyn, New York, he is enacting decrees and establishing preventative measures to strengthen Torah study and observance. With an abundance of love and compassion, he is devoting himself to bringing the light of Torah to his congregants, to whose welfare he is totally dedicated. He has endeared himself to all to such an extent that he is regarded almost as an angel of G-d. Nothing I write can do him justice."

"He has endeared himself to all to such an extent that he is regarded almost as an angel of G-d. Nothing I write can do him justice."

This eloquent testimony — by the brother closest to him while he was in Jerusalem — makes it a little easier to understand how R' Yaakob could have accomplished so much by the age of 31. From the writing of responsa and numerous compositions in all areas of the Torah, to founding a yeshiva and disseminating knowledge among the students, to serving as a *dayan* on a *Bet Din*, to the acquisition of various other skills which were of great benefit to many people — all this was only possible on account of his extraordinary dedication and diligence.

Emissary of the Rabbis

In 1932, R' Yaakob was selected by the *Rishon LeSion* (Chief Rabbi of *Eretz Yisrael*) R' Yaakob Meir and R' Ezra Harari-Raful (see #304) to travel on a fund-raising mission to the United States on behalf of the Sephardic orphanages of Jerusalem. R' Yaakob wanted to decline this mission, on account of his full agenda and the burden of his duties in Jerusalem. His wife and four children also depended on his continued presence. However, he finally submitted to the pressure of the rabbis, who believed him to be the ideal emissary, a person who could successfully carry out the mission with dignity and honor. And so he agreed to go abroad for two months.

On his arrival in New York, he was welcomed by the rabbis and lay leaders of the Syrian community. He quickly made friends with a group of local scholars, who were anxious to learn Kabbalah from him, for R' Yaakob's fame in this area had long preceded his arrival. Regular study sessions conducted by R' Yaakob continued throughout the duration of his sojourn in New York.

The two months that R' Yaakob originally intended to spend in America eventually stretched out to six. This was in response to the pleas of the community, who repeatedly begged him to extend his stay in order to benefit from his knowledge a little longer. The results of his fund-raising campaign also exceeded his expectations, thanks to the assistance of prominent members of the community, who collected large sums on his behalf.

The Syrian community of New York at that time was lacking a rabbi. The elders and officers of the community were very impressed with R' Yaakob, and entreated him to remain in their midst and to accept the position of Chief Rabbi. R' Yaakob declined this proposal, and emphatically rejected any suggestion that he relocate to New York, for he believed his place to be in Jerusalem and not in the Diaspora.

After relentless pleading on the part of the rabbis, and especially on the part of the distinguished community leaders Mr. Isaac Shalom (see #497) and Mr. Shelomo (Selim) Grazi, a compromise was reached. R' Yaakob signed a contract that should it enter his mind, at some future time, to leave the Holy Land to serve as rabbi in a Diaspora city, the Syrian community of New York would have first entitlement to his services for the period of one year.

This was not the only offer of a rabbinical position which R' Yaakob received during this period. Before he returned home, he traveled to Mexico to visit his older brother, R' Abraham Kassin (see #319), and stayed in his home for a few days.

There, he made the acquaintance of the leaders of the community, who were quick to recognize R' Yaakob's greatness and special personality. They also urged him to remain with them and assume the mantle of leadership. His brother made a valiant attempt to persuade R' Yaakob to accept the position. He told him about the quality of life in Mexico, about the house that would be allocated to him along with several servants to attend to his needs, and also about the handsome salary he would be receiving, two or three times larger than that which had been promised to him in New York.

But R' Yaakob categorically refused, explaining that he had already signed an agreement with the congregation in Brooklyn, giving them first option on his services should he decide to enter the rabbinate, and he would not go back on his word. Besides, he did not have the slightest intention of leaving Jerusalem.

A full six months after his arrival in the United States, R' Yaakob returned to Jerusalem, to his family and his colleagues. He was welcomed with royal honor. Everyone was delighted with the results of his mission, which had rescued several institutions from their financial difficulties.

When the rabbinical leaders of Jerusalem saw how successful R' Yaakob had been in collecting funds in New York, they prevailed upon him to travel to Egypt on a similar assignment. In Egypt, too, his mission was crowned with success, and there, too, he was offered a position — that of a *dayan* on the *Bet Din*. This office carried an excellent salary, since in those days the Jewish community in Egypt was among the most affluent in the world.

After his return to Jerusalem, he also received a letter of seven pages from the head of the Jewish community in Argentina, urgently requesting him to accept a position as rabbi, and offering very favorable conditions. Needless to add, R' Yaakob did not consider any of these propositions, for he remained firm to his commitment to the Syrian community of Brooklyn, that it would be the first congregation he would lead, should he decide at any time to officiate as rabbi.

In the twelve months that followed his return from New York, no less than ten letters were dispatched to R' Yaakob by the leaders of the Syrian community of Brooklyn, urging him, with all the eloquence at their command, to return to the community as its Chief Rabbi. They informed him of their deep affection for him, and pointed out that they found separation from him very difficult.

The rabbis of Jerusalem of that time, with whom he consulted on this topic, recommended that he accede to their request. In doing so, they pointed out, not only would he be widening his horizons — for he had already achieved so much that there was little further scope for accomplishment in Jerusalem — but would also gain valuable experience in the field of the communal rabbinate. His revered father-in-law, R' Shalom Hedaya, also advised him to accept the post.

R' Yaakob saw the hand of Providence in his life, and without further ado, replied that he would officiate as their rabbi for the suggested period of one year. Ultimately, the year stretched out to a period of sixty-two consecutive years as leader of the Syrian community in New York!

When he wrote to the leaders of the Brooklyn community informing them of his decision, R' Yaakob attached the draft of a proclamation declaring the community's acceptance of his rabbinical authority. The

R' Yaakob signed a contract that should it enter his mind, at some future time, to leave the Holy Land to serve as rabbi in a Diaspora city, the Syrian community of New York would have first entitlement to his services for the period of one year.

In the twelve months that followed his return from New York, no less than ten letters were dispatched to R' Yaakob by the leaders of the Syrian community of Brooklyn, urging him, with all the eloquence at their command, to return to the community as its Chief Rabbi.

In Egypt, too, his mission was crowned with success, and there, too, he was offered a position — that of a dayan.

Thus it was that in the middle of Tammuz in the year 5693 (1933), R' Kassin and his family boarded a ship for the three-week voyage to America.

community leaders were to sign it, as was the custom in all congregations of integrity. The document was couched in exceptionally humble language, omitting all titles of honor. From here we can see signs of R' Yaakob's special approach to leadership, one which became more and more apparent throughout the years of his service.

The text of the proclamation follows:

"We, the managers and officials of the community of Syrian Jews in the city of glory, New York, whose signatures appear below, hereby declare and confirm in the name of our association, *Magen David*, and its auxiliary bodies, that it is the desire of us all to receive R' Yaakob S. Kassin of Jerusalem into our holy camp, as the one authorized to manage, control, and direct all the affairs of the community, both material and spiritual. He is empowered to enact decrees, initiate improvements, and exercise his leadership in any way which he considers to be for the public benefit (in consultation with the rabbis or with the council of the congregation). We willingly accept all this upon ourselves without any opposition. In true and just confirmation of the above, we affix our signatures hereto in the month of Adar, 5693, and all our words remain firm ...".

When the elders of the community received this document, they immediately signed it and returned it to R' Yaakob. Attached was a special letter of the rabbis, bestowing their blessings and confirming his appointment by the lay leadership. The rabbis endorsed wholeheartedly the conferring of the power on R' Yaakob to direct all the affairs of the community.

R' Yaakob Kassin in his later years

Thus it was that in the middle of Tammuz in the year 5693 (1933), R' Kassin and his family boarded a ship for the three-week voyage to America. The Jewish community of New York made extensive preparations to welcome the distinguished newcomer. As it happens, however, the ship dropped anchor in New York a day earlier than anticipated. Nobody knew about this except for two individuals, who learned of the early arrival from the shipping company. These two were the only ones on hand to welcome the rabbi and to assist him with his belongings and with the immigration formalities.

R' Hedaya therefore hastened to dispatch a letter to the benefactor Mr. Isaac Shalom, informing him that the community's new rabbi and his family were on their way.

R' Yaakob's father-in-law, R' Shalom Hedaya, knew how difficult it was for his son-in-law to leave his native Jerusalem. R' Hedaya therefore hastened to dispatch a letter to the benefactor Mr. Isaac Shalom, informing him that the community's new rabbi and his family were on their way, and urging him to help them with all the resources at his disposal. He wrote, "A wise man will appreciate that their transition toward a happy life in your holy domain is as traumatic for them as the separation of the soul from the body. I therefore ask, after begging [your] pardon, that [you] stand at the right hand of the eminent Rabbi and *Gaon*, Yaakob S. Kassin, my son-in-law and the light of my eyes. I beseech you to extend your help to him at all levels, to satisfy all his needs, and to ensure that he be blessed with peace and tranquility under the wings of Divine Providence. As a reward for your help, may merit descend upon you and those like you. Happy are the mothers that bore you! May many more like you rise up in the land! May you enjoy many successes in the midst of wealth, honor, and good health."

Eventually, R' Yaakob and his family were received with great rejoicing. Thanks to the support and encouragement of the heads of the community and its members, the new arrivals were able to settle quickly into their new home. As the Kassin family had not yet mastered English, they were forced to remain at home for days on end, and would have been unable to make even the most routine arrangements, were it not for the help of their new friends in the city.

His Work in the Community

In 1933 when R' Yaakob took up his position, the community of Aram Soba Jews in New York comprised about 600 families. The majority were united under the umbrella organization *Magen David* in Bensonhurst, Brooklyn. The Aram Soba community also had other synagogues, and there was, in addition, the *Ahi Ezer* synagogue of Jews from Damascus. Besides the main Talmud Torah called *Magen David*, in which about four hundred boys studied, there were also other local *Talmudei Torah*.

Also affiliated to the local community was the *Rodfei Sedek* Burial Society, and the *Maoz L'Ebyon* institution which assisted the poor and the indigent throughout the year, and especially before the Festivals. This latter organization was especially busy, for during those years the community was far from affluent, and the entire country, moreover, was in a state of economic depression.

The community was fortunate to have among its members scholars and teachers of repute, and men of special virtue, who would frequent the synagogues and study halls morning and evening.

From the moment that R' Yaakob arrived, he began to organize and strengthen the community's institutions. He suggested — and subsequently implemented — methods of improving the education of the youth. This was to receive the highest priority among the activities of the community, for only the youth could ensure its future.

He worked nonstop in this holy activity, until he had virtually no spare time for himself or his family. During those first years, he would remain in the Talmud Torah to learn with and to test the boys until late at night. In addition, he would perform *brit milah* (circumcision) on all the infants born in the community, although eventually, due to the rapid growth of his communal responsibilities, he was forced to pass on this function to another person.

The financial situation of the Talmud Torah and the synagogue was very precarious in those days, and for many years R' Yaakob would devote much of his time to the arduous task of fund-raising.

During his many years of service to his community, he helped to solve problems in numerous households and restored peace between man and his fellow and between husband and wife. Wherever he was and on every occasion he would seek solutions to difficulties, and his enterprise extended to all the needs of the community, both spiritual and material.

In addition to all this, he would teach Talmud and its commentaries to young men, and to a few select individuals he would impart a little of his knowledge of the Kabbalah. He even trained a few young men in the laws and practice of *shehitah* (kosher slaughter).

R' Yaakob also founded a *Bet Din* to deal with monetary disputes and matters of marital status. He officiated as head of the *Bet Din*, and with him on the bench sat R' Matloub Abadi (see #9) and R' Eliyahu Husney (see #314). His son R' Shaul Kassin was secretary to the *Bet Din*.

In the United States, R' Yaakob continued to produce an ongoing stream of *halachic* rulings. These dealt with all kinds of complex situations, in all areas of daily life, including an edict against accepting converts. (See Document Section, Document No. 3.) Questions arrived not only from cities across the United States, but also from distant countries and even from *Eretz Yisrael*. Many were addressed to him by prominent members of the rabbinate. R' Yaakob attended promptly to all these inquiries in his usual thorough, expert, and compassionate manner, despite the many pressures of his office and his many other activities for the public welfare.

From the moment that R' Yaakob arrived, he began to organize and strengthen the community's institutions.

Title Page of Peri Etz HaGan

His Legacy

After serving the Syrian community in New York faithfully for 62 years he passed away on 3 Tevet, 5755 (1994). He was succeeded by his son R' Shaul Kassin and his son-in-law R' Baruch Ben-Haim, married to his daughter Charlotte.

His impact on the Syrian community in New York deserves a book in itself. To further appreciate his greatness, the reader is referred to the book *Princely Wisdom* (see below).

He was blessed with six worthy sons: Hacham Shaul, Abraham, Yitzhak, Meir, Yehudah, and Moshe. As noted above he was a prolific editor and author of holy books. His major works are summarized below.

- *Ohr HaLevanah* (Jerusalem 5685/1925). An anthology of the meditations appropriate to various *mitzvot* such as the Blessing on the Moon and the prayers for *Rosh Hodesh*, from the writings of the *Rashash* (R' Shalom Sharabi) and other Kabbalist authors.
- *Tochahat Meguleh* (Jerusalem 5684/1924). Moral guidance on issues such as feminine modesty, mixed dancing, women's hair covering, and jealousy among women.
- *Mishmeret HaKiddushin* (Jerusalem 5685/1925). Responsa on issues related to marriage and divorce.
- *Imrei Binah* (Jerusalem 5691/1931). Two volumes containing *hiddushim* on a variety of topics. At the end of the book he provides a history of the Kassin family. Volume I is bound together with *Peri Etz HaGan*.
- *Peri Etz HaGan* (Jerusalem 5691/1931). Part I is mostly historical. It contains biographies of various rabbis who came from Aram Soba, such as R' Shaul Kassin (see #327) and R' Abraham Ades (see #36), as well as biographies of various Kabbalists of Jerusalem and other places, such as R' Shalom Sharabi, R' Gedaliah Hevan, and R' Nissim Nahum (see #437). Part II presents the meditations and poetic *pizmonim* (hymns) appropriate to various *mitzvot* such as the prayers of *Rosh Hashanah, Yom Kippur*, and *Sukkot*. The book was reissued in 1977 as part of an anthology called *Hut HaMeshulash* (*Eretz Yisrael* 5737/1977).

ספר

מחנה יהודה

NELLA STAMPERIA DI GIO. VINC. FALORNI

Con Approvazione.

Title Page of Mahane Yehudah

- *Yesod Ha'Emunah* (Brooklyn 5741/1981). Seven parts, beginning with essays on the basis of faith and continuing with related topics from a Kabbalistic point of view. The book also contains inspirational lectures and responsa.
- *Kassinei Aretz* (Jerusalem 5755/1995). The book was published after the death of the author by the yeshiva *Ahavat Shalom* of Jerusalem, headed by R' Yaakob Moshe Hillel. It begins with the eulogy that R' Hillel delivered for R' Yaakob. This is followed by biographical and historical information about R' Yaakob and the Kassin family. The main body of the book contains responsa on a variety of topics such as men going bareheaded and determination of the *Yobel* (Jubilee) year. In addition there are *hiddushim* on the *Gemara*, lectures, and eulogies.
- *Princely Wisdom* (Jerusalem 5756/1996). This English-language book on the life and teachings of R' Yaakob was adapted from *Kassinei Aretz* by the yeshiva *Ahavat Shalom* of Jerusalem.

[331] **KASSIN, R' Yehudah**

רבי יהודה קצין

(1708 — 1783)

Distinguished scholar and *Av Bet Din* (Chief Judge) of Aram Soba. He was born in Aram Soba in 1708, a son of R' Yomtob Kassin (see #333). He is known for his important book *Mahane Yehudah* (Livorno 5563/1803). Volume I of this book is essentially an extended *halachic* (legal) ruling in which R' Yehudah displays an enormous amount of Torah knowledge and learned analysis. The issue in question, which arose in the 1760's, concerned the status of the Francos. They were European Jews from France and Italy who had settled in Aram Soba for business reasons. They maintained their citizenship status and enjoyed the protection of the consuls of the European powers. The Francos liberally supported communal institutions in Aram Soba, but refused to pay the regular taxes and did not accept the authority of the community, claiming that they were not permanent residents.

R' Kassin essentially agreed with the Francos and defended them against R' Raphael Shelomo Laniado (see #363), the Chief Rabbi of Aram Soba, who insisted that the Francos must accept local authority. R' Laniado's arguments were presented at great length in his book *Bet Dino shel Shelomo*.

However, R' Kassin argued that the importance of maintaining peace in the city was paramount. His view was endorsed by 10 other rabbis of the city, including two of the sons of R' Raphael Shelomo Laniado (see #363): R' David Laniado (see #351) and R' Eliyahu Laniado (see #353). R' Kassin also received an endorsement from the Chief Rabbi of Damascus, R' Moshe Galante, and from the following distinguished rabbis of Jerusalem: R' Yomtob Algazi, R' Yosef Meyouhas, and R' Mansour Marzouk.

Despite their strong difference of opinion in this matter. R' Laniado and R' Kassin treated each other with great respect, each recognizing that the motives of his opponent were pure. R' Kassin was especially considerate of the dignity and respect of R' Laniado, whom he greatly admired. This controversy continued over several years, and came to an end only after the number of Francos dwindled.

In 1775 another controversy arose in which R' Laniado and R' Kassin took opposing sides. The issue pertained to a practice which was common in those days of going to the grave marker of Ezra HaSofer in Tedef (a small town near Aram Soba) to pray. Because of the remote location of this site, the practice incurred the risk of desecrating *Shabbat* or *Yom Tob* by violating the *tehum* (bounds of permissible movement). And so R' Laniado issued a ruling against continuing in the practice. That year there was an unusual amount of sickness in Aram Soba and many people felt that it was because people were no longer going to Tedef to pray. Accordingly, R' Kassin, who was older than R' Laniado and had seniority in the position of rabbi, issued an opposing ruling, directing that the practice should be resumed. The issues involved in this controversy are described in the book *Ohel Yesharim* of R' Abraham Antebi (section *Shaar HaGeulah*, page 104, Jerusalem issue).

R' Kassin left many other *hiddushim* in manuscript form. Some of them were subsequently published by R' Shalom Hedaya (see #310) in the book *Ro'ei Yisrael* (Jerusalem 5664/1904) and in Volume II of *Mahane Yehudah* (Jerusalem 5719/1959), which is an analytical commentary on the *Rambam*. Another of his books, called *VeZot LiYehudah*, containing inspirational lectures on *Shemot*, remained in manuscript form until 1985 (5745) when it was published in Jerusalem by the yeshiva *Ahavat Shalom*. In R' Laniado's book *Bet Dino shel Shelomo* (*Hoshen Mishpat* 18), he mentions a particularly difficult question for which he turned to R' Kassin for help. Other *hiddushim* were included in the anthology *Otzrot Hachmei Aram Soba al HaRambam* (Jerusalem 5749/1989) that was published by the Aram Soba Foundation.

The Francos liberally supported communal institutions in Aram Soba, but refused to pay the regular taxes and did not accept the authority of the community, claiming that they were not permanent residents. R' Kassin argued that the importance of maintaining peace in the city was paramount.

In 1738 R' Kassin visited *Eretz Yisrael* and spent five years there in study and prayer. Though in frail health he lived to a ripe old age. He passed away on 19 Heshvan, 5544 (1783) and was buried in the "Cave of the Righteous" near Aram Soba's Great Synagogue.

He was buried in the "Cave of the Righteous" near Aram Soba's Great Synagogue.

He was blessed with four scholarly sons: R' Haim (see #324), R' David (see #321), R' Eliyahu (see #323), and R' Yosef. He also had two daughters; one became the wife of R' Haim Attiah and the other became the wife of R' Menashe Kassin.

He was eulogized by the great rabbis of his generation, among whom were R' Yeshayah Attiah (see #119), as recorded in his book *Bigdei Yesha*, R' Yitzhak Attiah (see #120), as recorded in his book *Yikra DeHa'ye*, and R' Abraham Sutton (see #535), as recorded in his book *Malel Le'Abraham*.

[332] KASSIN, R' Yitzhak

רבי יצחק קצין

(1809 — 1897)

Worthy scholar and rabbi of Aram Soba. He was born in Aram Soba in 1807, the second son of R' Bekhor Kassin (see #320). He was a man of many fine personal attributes and was especially known for his humility. He passed away after a long and meritorious life in the month of Av 5657 (1897).

ספר
נכח השלחן

Title Page of
Nochah HaShulhan

At age 70, R' Haim Mordechai was disturbed that he did not have a daughter. He decided to marry a younger woman, who could bear him daughters.

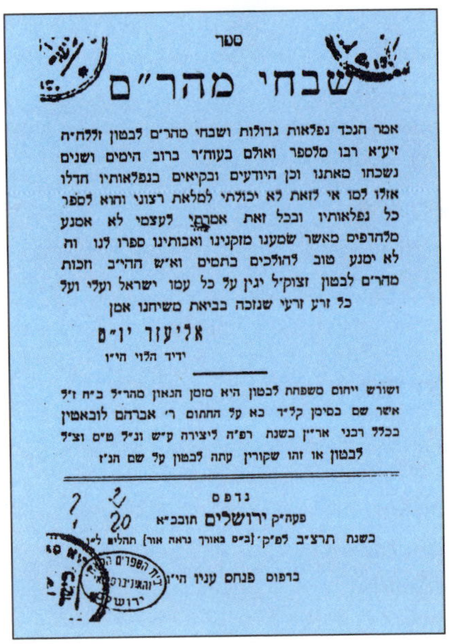

ספר
שבחי מהר"ם

Title Page of
Shivhei Maharam

[333] **KASSIN, R' Yomtob**

רבי יום טוב קצין

(16th century)

Eminent scholar and *Av Bet Din* (Chief Judge) of Aram Soba. He was a grandson of Señor Shelomo Kassin (see #328) and began the rabbinic tradition in the Kassin family, serving as head of the Aram Soba *Bet Din*. He was the father of R' Yehudah Kassin (see #331).

[334] **LABATON, R' Abraham**

רבי אברהם לבטון

(— 1905)

Worthy scholar of Aram Soba. He was the son of R' Halfon Labaton (see #337) and the grandson of R' Haim Mordechai Labaton (see #336). His grandfather mentions him in the introduction to his book *Nochah HaShulhan*. He passed away on 8 Nissan, 5665 (1905).

[335] **LABATON, R' Eliezer**

רבי אליעזר לבטון

(— 1888)

Worthy scholar and rabbi of Aram Soba. He was the second son of R' Haim Mordechai Labaton (see #336). His father mentions him in the introduction to his book *Nochah HaShulhan* together with his brothers, R' Halfon and R' Yosef Labaton. He passed away on 10 Elul, 5648 (1888).

[336] **LABATON, R' Haim Mordechai**

רבי חיים מרדכי לבטון

(1780 — 1869)

Distinguished scholar and *Av Bet Din* (Chief Judge) of Aram Soba. He was born in 1780 to R' Halfon Labaton and his wife Luna. Many stories are told about his birth and childhood. Some of these were described by R' Eliezer Yedid (see #590) in the book *Shivhei Maharam*.

He was a member of a pact that was formed by a number of Aram Soba scholars to strengthen their mutual resolve and commitment to Torah study. The document of commitment was signed in 1829.

He is known for his greatness in Torah and his valuable book *Nochah HaShulhan* (Izmir 5628/1868), consisting of responsa on a variety of topics, such as the role of Jewish ministers in the Ottoman government and the differences in the form of the *ketubah* (marriage contract) between the Sephardim (Spanish community) and the *Mustarabim* (Aram Soba native community). The introduction to the book was written by a number of rabbis in 1865 and contains glowing praises of the author. The book was published through the efforts of his grandson R' Yitzhak Labaton (see #340). To earn his livelihood he engaged in the soap trade in Aram Soba.

R' Haim Mordechai also wrote the manuscript for *Ben Yair*, a book of inspirational lectures oriented to *halachah*. It was published in 1925 (Jerusalem 5685) by his great-grandson, R' Obadiah Hedaya (see #309).

There are three original documents at the Ben-Zvi Institute with his signature on the first line, indicating his considerable stature and position in the community. These are dated 1826, 1840, 1852.

He married Morhava and had three scholarly sons: R' Halfon (see #337), R' Eliezer (see #335), and R' Yosef (see #341). In addition, he raised his niece, who was orphaned, as one of his own until she married. His oldest son R' Halfon died before his father, leaving three young sons and a daughter, who were raised by R' Haim Mordechai.

At age 70, he was disturbed that he did not have a daughter, because he felt that he had not fulfilled the *mitzv*ah of procreation, which requires at least one son and one daughter. After much discussion, he decided to marry a younger woman, who could bear him daughters. The woman worried about whether he could raise daughters because of his age, but he promised he would be there to marry them off. Sure enough, his wife bore him a daughter, Luna, who was wed to R' Ezra Swed (see #572).

R' Haim Mordechai passed away on 20 Sivan, 5629 (1869), just after the end of the Sabbath.News of his death spread far and wide, including Jerusalem. The Chief Rabbi, R' Shemuel Laniado (see #372), spoke of him in his approbation to the book *Ha'ach Nafsheinu* of R' Abraham Hamway (see #269).

[337] **LABATON, R' Halfon**

רבי חלפון לבטון

(— 1847)

Worthy scholar and Kabbalist of Aram Soba. He was the elder son of R' Haim Mordechai Labaton (see #336). He was an intense and pious Torah scholar, never wasting a moment. The story is told that late one night he was engrossed in learning by the light of a small kerosene lamp. His mother was concerned that the light might go out and he would be unable to find his way in the dark, and so she urged her husband to tell him to go to sleep. He replied, "Don't be afraid, as long as Halfon is sitting and learning, the light will not go out." And so it was.

He died in 5607 (1847) at a relatively young age, during the life of his father. He left three scholarly sons; R' Mordechai (see #339), R' Abraham, and R' Yitzhak Labaton (see #340). He also left behind a number of manuscripts, which appear to have been lost over the passage of time. However, one of his *hiddushim* (original Torah thoughts) was quoted by his father in the book *Nochah HaShulhan*.

[338] **LABATON, R' Halfon**

רבי חלפון לבטון

(1870 — 1923)

Worthy scholar of Aram Soba. He was born in 1870 and appears to have been the son of R' Abraham Labaton (see #334) and a grandson of the earlier R' Halfon Labaton (see #337). He passed away on 8 Kislev, 5684 (1923).

[339] **LABATON, R' Mordechai**

רבי מרדכי לבטון

(— 1903)

Worthy scholar and rabbi of Aram Soba. He was the first son of R' Halfon Labaton (see #337). In 1865 he joined other rabbis of Aram Soba in signing the approbation for the first book-printing initiative of the city,(see Document Section, Document No. 25), which was introduced by R' Abraham Sasson and his sons (see #475). He passed away on 7 Heshvan, 5663 (1903).

[340] **LABATON, R' Yitzhak**

רבי יצחק לבטון

(— 1911)

Eminent scholar and *dayan* (judge) of Aram Soba and Jerusalem. He was the third son of R' Halfon Labaton (see #337) and a grandson of R' Haim Mordechai Labaton (see #336). He was an expert in the entire *Shulhan Aruch,* which he knew by heart. He was also an expert in the preparation of business contracts, partnerships, and leases.

"Don't be afraid, as long as Halfon is sitting and learning, the light will not go out."

In 1857 he married Rachel, the daughter of R' Yosef Alfia. For many years he served as a *dayan* in Aram Soba and in 1899 he moved to Jerusalem together with his son-in-law R' Shalom Hedaya (see #310). In Jerusalem he was appointed as *dayan* to the Sephardic *Bet Din* (high court).

For many years he served as a dayan in Aram Soba and in 1899 he moved to Jerusalem together with his son-in-law R' Shalom Hedaya.

Life had been good in Aram Soba but conditions in Jerusalem were difficult. However, R' Labaton bore them in good spirits, happy as he was to be in the Holy City. He had focused on the study of *halachah* through most of his life, but in his old age he began to learn Kabbalah.

He passed away on *Rosh Hodesh* Kislev, 5672 (1911) and was eulogized by R' Yitzhak Laniado (see #382) and his son-in-law R' Shalom Hedaya, among others, as recorded in the book *Vayizra Yitzhak*. It was reported that after his death he appeared in a dream to his son-in-law, R' Shalom Hedaya (see #310). In the dream R' Labaton said that all the Torah which he had learned throughout his life did not help in the Heavenly *Bet Din* as much as the Kabbalah which he learned toward the end of his days.

He wrote a number of responsa while still in Aram Soba and maintained an active correspondence with many of the rabbis of Jerusalem. Some of his *hiddushim* (original Torah thoughts) were included in the journal *HaMe'asef*, published by R' Ben-Sion Kouenka and in the following books:

- *Kapei Aharon* of R' Aharon Ezriel.
- *Yisa Berachah* and *Simhah Le'Ish* of the *Rishon LeSion* (Chief Rabbi of *Eretz Yisrael*), R' Yaakob Shaul Elyashar.
- *Dibrei Shalom* of his son-in-law R' Shalom Hedaya.
- *Shaare Rahamim* of R' Rahamim Yosef Franco (*Yoreh Deah* 14).

In the book *Simhah Le'Ish*, the *Rishon LeSion* talks about receiving a letter containing a *halachic* (legal) opinion by R' Yitzhak Labaton, which is based on a question that had been asked of him in Aram Soba. He also mentions favorably R' Yitzhak's son-in-law R' Shalom Hedaya, who was later to become the *Av Bet Din* (Chief Judge) in Jerusalem.

Some of R' Yitzhak's responsa were arranged in a publication entitled *Oseh Hayil*, which was appended to the book *Ben Yair* of his grandfather R' Haim Mordechai Labaton (see #336) (Jerusalem 5685/1925). It was published by his grandson, R' Obadiah Hedaya (see #309), who also appended it to Volume I of his own work *Vayikach Obadiahu*. The introduction, which was written by R' Shalom Hedaya, praises R' Yitzhak profusely.

[341] **LABATON, R' Yosef**

רבי יוסף לבטון

(— 1899)

Worthy scholar and Kabbalist of Aram Soba and Jerusalem. He was the third son of R' Haim Mordechai Labaton (see #336). His father mentions him in the introduction to his book *Nochah HaShulhan* together with his brothers, R' Halfon and R' Eliezer Labaton. In 1852 he joined other rabbis of Aram Soba in signing the approbation to the book *Kenisiyah Leshem Shamayim* (see Document Section, Document No. 31) by R' Menashe Sutton (see #551).

In his later years he moved to Jerusalem and joined the Kabbalist yeshiva Bet El.

In his later years he moved to Jerusalem and joined the Kabbalist yeshiva *Bet El*. It appears that the move to Jerusalem occurred in 1890 and that he was accompanied by his son-in-law, R' Yomtob Yedid (see #593). He passed away on 12 Av, 5659 (1899).

[342] **LAHMI, R' Ezra**

רבי עזרא לחמי

(19th century)

Worthy scholar and rabbi of Aram Soba. A son of R' Shalom Lahmi (see #343), he was a teacher in the Talmud Torah and an author of holy books. His book of responsa entitled *Shaare Ezra* and a book of *hiddushim* (original Torah thoughts) entitled *Zechor Davar Le'Avdecha* were both left in manuscript form. However, in 1982 R' Saadiah Menir arranged for *Zechor Davar Le'Avdecha* to be published together with *Shalom Le'Am* of R' Shalom Chasky (see #149) (Jerusalem 5742/1982).

[343] **LAHMI, R' Shalom**

רבי שלום לחמי

(19th century)

Worthy scholar and rabbi of Aram Soba. His son, R' Ezra (see #342), writes that on a number of occasions R' Shalom was invited to serve as a *dayan* (judge) on the *Bet Din* of Aram Soba, but refused. In 1865 he joined other rabbis of Aram Soba in signing the approbation for the first book-printing initiative of the city (see Document Section, Document No. 25), which was introduced by R' Abraham Sasson and his sons (see #475).

Laniado Lineage. The illustrious Laniado family originated in Spain and came to be associated with Aram Soba after the expulsion of 1492. The first member of the family to arrive in Aram Soba was R' Shemuel Laniado, who came to Aram Soba via Adrianople, Turkey. The special prominence of the family in Aram Soba began in the third generation, when R' Shemuel's grandson (commonly known as the *Baal HaKeilim*) was appointed Chief Rabbi, at the personal recommendation of R' Yosef Karo, the *Bet Yosef*.

From that origin, the family has expanded and grown many branches, with most of its children serving as rabbis in Aram Soba, Egypt, Mesopotamia, and elsewhere. Variations on the family name, such as Laniado-Malki Shuba Laniado-Somech, and Laniado-Sojir were adopted to distinguish between members of the family with the same name. A partial listing of the rabbis of this family was prepared by R' Meir Abraham Laniado (see #358) and published in the book *Ro'ei Yisrael VeDegel Mahane Ephraim*. This listing covers ten generations from the generation of the first R' Shemuel Laniado to the generation of the writer.

After eleven generations of consecutive chief rabbis from the same family, the distinctive Laniado role ended only when one rabbi died young and there wasn't a son old enough to take over. There have been a number of chief rabbis in the recent era from other families, notably Sutton, Dweck, and Antebi, but no family held the crown of piety and leadership of the community for longer than the Laniados.

[344] LANIADO, R' Abraham

רבי אברהם לנייאדו

(— 1585)

Eminent scholar and rabbi of Aram Soba in the 16th century. He was the father of R' Shemuel Laniado, the *Baal HaKeilim* (see #376). R' Shemuel quotes some of his father's Torah thoughts in his own writings. R' Yitzhak Badhab in his book *Ki BeYitzhak* (Jerusalem 5688/1928) (p. 21) provides a copy of a document "A Commitment to Migrate to *Eretz Yisrael*," which was signed by R' Abraham Laniado, among others. (See Document Section, Document No. 36.) The document is dated 4 Sivan, 5297 (1537). R' Abraham passed away in 1585.

[345] LANIADO, R' Abraham

רבי אברהם לנייאדו

(early 17th century)

Eminent scholar and rabbi of Aram Soba. His father, R' Yitzhak (see #383), sent him as a youth to Safed to study in the yeshiva of R' Yosef Karo. After undergoing many hardships in that city he returned to Aram Soba where he married the daughter of R' Shemuel Laniado, the *Baal HaKeilim* (see #376), who was apparently his uncle, and who provided for his support.

R' Laniado was in Venice in 1603 (5363) and in that year saw to the publication of his father-in-law's work *Kli Yekar*, a commentary on the major prophets, and of his own work *Magen Abraham*, consisting of inspirational lectures. He also wrote *Nekuddot HaKesef* (Venice 5379/1619), a commentary to *Shir HaShirim* which was published with the text, the Aramaic *Targum* (translation), and a Ladino translation by his son-in-law, R' Moshe Laniado (see #360). In the introduction to this work, R' Abraham states that he also wrote a commentary to the Torah entitled *Torat Hesed*, and to the five *Megillot*, the *Haftarot*, *Tehillim*, *Mishlei*, *Iyob*, and *Daniel*.

The author of *Otsar Yisrael* (Vol. 5, page 310) writes that he has in his possession in Vienna some responsa by R' Abraham. These were subsequently published, together with glosses, by Friedland (Vienna 1860). Other responsa were published under the title *Degel Mahane Ephraim* (Jerusalem 5662/1902).

Title Page of Magen Abraham

[346] LANIADO, R' Abraham

רבי אברהם לנייאדו

(early 17th century)

Chief Rabbi of Aram Soba in the 17th century. He was a son of R' Shemuel Laniado, the *Baal HaKeilim* (see #376). After the death of his father in 1605 he assumed the role of Chief Rabbi of the city. He was respected thoughout

He exerted his influence forcefully to maintain the high moral tone of the community and to discourage laxity in observance of the mitzvot.

the city for his Torah knowledge and the dignity with which he conducted his office. He was a wealthy man who did not feel the need to show favor to anyone. He exerted his influence forcefully to maintain the high moral tone of the community and to discourage laxity in observance of the *mitzvot.*

However, the responsibilities of his office were very demanding and he was unable to devote as much time as he would have liked for the work of preparing his father's manuscripts for publication, or even for completing the writing of his own *hiddushim* (original Torah thoughts). These tasks were left to his own six sons. The oldest son, R' Shelomo, was referred to by the people of his generation as "the elder" (see #368). When he prepared his grandfather's book *Kli Paz* for publication, he explained in the introduction how his father was overburdened with rabbinical duties. Two other sons, R' Yitzhak (see #384) and R' Levi (see #357), also worked on that project.

In about 1623 R' Abraham left Aram Soba and settled in Jerusalem. That was also the year in which he signed the approbation to the book *Zoharei Hamah* by R' Abraham Azulai.

[347] **LANIADO, R' Abraham**

רבי אברהם לנייאדו

(— 1746)

Eminent scholar and rabbi of Aram Soba. He was a son of R' Shemuel Laniado (see #372) and a brother of R' Raphael Shelomo Laniado (see #363). Two of his responsa were published in his brother's book *Bet Dino shel Shelomo.* His father-in-law was R' Michael Harari (see #284). R' Abraham passed away at a relatively young age in 1746. He was eulogized by R' Obadiah HaLevy (see #392), as recorded in the book *Hazon Obadiah.*

[348] **LANIADO, R' Abraham**

רבי אברהם לנייאדו

(— 1872)

Worthy scholar and rabbi of Aram Soba. In 1865 he joined other rabbis of Aram Soba in signing the approbation for the first book-printing initiative of the city (see Document Section, Document No. 25), which was introduced by R' Abraham Sasson and his sons (see #475). In 1868 he signed the approbation to *Hadar Ezer* of R' Yitzhak Shrem (see #517). He passed away on the first day of Pesah 5632 (1872) and was buried in the "Cave of the Righteous" near Aram Soba's Great Synagogue.

[349] **LANIADO, R' Abraham**

רבי אברהם לנייאדו

(— 1882)

Worthy scholar and Kabbalist of Aram Soba in the 19th century. He was born in Aram Soba, the son of R' Obadiah Laniado (see #362). At some point he left Aram Soba and moved to Jerusalem, becoming one of the Kabbalist scholars of the yeshiva *Bet El.* He passed away on 7 Adar, 5642 (1882). His son was R' Meir Laniado (see #358).

[350] **LANIADO, R' Bekhor Raphael**

רבי בכור רפאל לנייאדו

(— 1865)

Worthy scholar and rabbi of Aram Soba. He passed away on 11 Iyar, 5625 (1865).

[351] **LANIADO, R' David**

רבי דוד לנייאדו

(— 1799)

Eminent scholar and *dayan* (judge) of Aram Soba. He was a son of R' Shemuel Laniado (see #372). R' David signed along with other rabbis of Aram Soba the approbation for the work *Mahane Yehudah* of R' Yehudah Kassin (see #331). He passed away on 21 Kislev, 5560 (1799) and was eulogized by R' Abraham Sutton (see #535), as recorded in his book *Malel Le'Abraham* (Sect. 8).

[352] **LANIADO (MALKI SHUBAH), R' David-Sion**

רבי דוד־ציון לנייאדו (מלכי שובה)

(1899 — 1969)

Eminent scholar and biographer of Aram Soba. R' Laniado devoted a good part of his life to collecting biographical details about the Torah scholars and rabbis of Aram Soba, and publishing his findings in a monumental book, *LiKedoshim Asher Ba'Aretz.* That effort has served as the primary resource for the book you are now reading. It is clear that a driving force behind his labors was the deep love which he felt for pious and learned men who had preserved the unbroken tradition of Torah in Aram Soba over the years.

He published his findings in a monumental book, LiKedoshim Asher Ba'Aretz. That effort has served as the primary resource for the book you are now reading.

R' David-Sion Laniado

Many members of the Laniado family were also referred to by the name Malki Shubah after a famous hymn that was apparently written by R' Shelomo Laniado, a great grandfather of R' David-Sion.

R' David-Sion lived most of his life in Jerusalem, where most people knew him as "Hacham David."

His Early Years

He was born in Aram Soba on 26 Kislev, 5660 (1899) to R' Shelomo Laniado (see #367). He studied in the Talmud Torah there and later recalled one of his most memorable teachers, R' Haim Cohen (Tourgeman), who implanted a sense of piety in his students. Subsequently he studied in the yeshiva of Aram Soba under R' Shelomo Zafrani (see #598). When he reached the age of 18 he experienced a powerful desire to be in *Eretz Yisrael*. This desire did not diminish and so in Sivan 1919 he left his parents and family and came to Jerusalem.

In 1925 he married Mazal Zebede, who became his faithful companion and mother of his children. They lived in one of the small apartments maintained by the philanthropist Señor Aharon Silvera (see #522) for poor scholars in the Mahane Yehudah section.

His Terrifying Sojourn in Hebron

A few months before the Arab pogroms of 1929, he took his wife and two young children to live in Hebron so that he could pray at the *Maarat HaMachpelah* (Cave of the Patriarchs), where the Patriarchs are buried. While there he studied under the guidance of the senior Torah scholars of the city. Among these were R' Hanoch Hasson, the *Av Bet Din* (Chief Judge) of the Sephardic *Bet Din*, who was later killed in the pogroms, and R' Yaakob Yosef Slonim, the *Av Bet Din* of the Ashkenazic *Bet Din*. He also studied with R' Meir Shemuel Castille, who was a *dayan* (judge) of the Sephardic *Bet Din*, and with R' Meir Franco. He prayed daily at the *Maarat HaMachpelah* and he later spoke about the mystical powers which he sensed there. There were times when one of his two children was sick and he brought the child with him to that sacred place to seek healing from *Hashem*. On such occasions he was amazed and gratified to see almost instantaneous recovery.

גדולים מעשה צדיקים יותר ממעשה שמים וארץ

זה השער לה׳ צדיקים יבואו בו

בהג״ר עמ״י ספר עש״ו ובס״ד

לקדושים אשר באר״ץ

זאת המחברת כוללת מקצת נוסחי מצבות קודש של מרנן ורבנן קדישי עליון חכמי ספרד בארץ ובבולה מחו״ר אר״ץ ושמות ספריהם שבכתב יד ושנדפסו וקצת שמות רבני גולת בבל יע״א וקצת נוסחי מצבות מחו״ר דמשק וסלוניק ואזמיר יע״א זיע״א.

ואודה לאל אשר עזרני להוציא לאור מחשבתי הטובה לפועל לפרסם שמותם הקדושים ולעורר זכותם בעולם נפשם בתוזי״א וצוקללה״ה ותנצב״ה ניע״א.

יהי״ר שזכותם וזכות תורתם וקדושתם יגן עלינו ועל זרעינו וזרע זרענו עד סוכ״ה להיות תמיד חלקנו בחיים טובים ארוכים ומתוקנים על התורה ועל העבודה ועל גמילות חסדים ויהיו כל מעשינו לשם שמים ולראות כל ימי חיינו בטוב ירושלים אכי״ר.

כה עתרת זה יכתוב ידו המקוה רחמי הצור לבדו ומצפה תמיד לישועת ה׳ וחסדו

ע״ה דוד ציון לאניאדו הי״ו בכמהרש״ל זללה״ה

נדפס פעיה״ק ירושלים תוב״ב אכי״ר
שנת ש׳ב׳ת׳י׳ בבית ה׳ כל ימי חיי וגו׳

בדפוס י. ע. איתאח טל. 61292

צדיקים במיתתם קרויים חיים זיע״א

Title Page of LiKedoshim Asher Ba'Aretz

One day as he went to the tomb he was beset by a gang of hoodlums. As it happened, an important sheikh was standing nearby and R' Laniado desperately called out for help. The sheikh rebuked the hooligans, telling them that they should have respect for a scholar. Fortunately, his remarks shamed them and they abandoned their quarry. R' Laniado quickly ran home, but on the way he encountered other gangs of thugs brandishing their knives and saying, "We will get you!" When he arrived home, his Arab neighbor urged him to get his wife and children out of the city. Although the family was terrified, they managed to flee from Hebron, passing the corpses of slaughtered Jews on the way.

One day as he went to the tomb he was beset by a gang of hoodlums.

They came upon a cave and decided to seek shelter there, but it was not long before the rioters arrived and began to seal the mouth of the cave, saying, "If you Jews are here you won't get away alive! We will come back and finish you off." With his young children screaming in fear, R' Laniado prayed desperately to *Hashem*, begging for His mercy in the merit of the ancestors buried in this holy city. It was not long before his prayers were answered; a passing troop of British soldiers heard the cries and brought the family to Jerusalem.

He did not forget the miracle of his redemption and upon his return to Jerusalem he took upon himself daily and weekly devotions.

He did not forget the miracle of his redemption and upon his return to Jerusalem he took upon himself daily and weekly devotions. He made up with his colleague R' Yitzhak Alfia (see #46) to recite the entire book of *Tehillim* three times each day, without interruption. (This practice is highly regarded by Kabbalists, considering it equal to 65,000 fast days.) In addition, he would get up early every *Shabbat* morning in summer and winter to take his children (and later his grandchildren) and their friends to the Nahalot section of Jerusalem, where they would chant the traditional *bakashot* (supplications). He allowed nothing to dissuade him from these holy commitments.

The story of his Hebron experience didn't end there. After the victims of the massacre had been buried he went back to retrieve one of the Torah scrolls that had been abandoned. While riding in a truck to Jerusalem he briefly allowed himself the luxury of questioning *Hashem*'s ways, thinking, *Is this the reward for Torah?* Immediately, the truck went out of control, crashing by the side of the road. That caused one of the handles of the Torah that he was holding to strike his lip and gash it, which required medical attention. He took the lesson to heart. In later years, after his children had grown up, he would recount this experience to them. The moral was clear, "Never question the ways of *Hashem*, even for a brief moment."

Return to Jerusalem

Upon his return to Jerusalem, Hacham David took a position as *shamosh* (sexton) of the Silvera *Bet Midrash* in the apartment complex where he had previously lived. The *Bet Midrash*, officially named *Zechut Aharon* after its founder Señor Aharon Silvera, was a popular destination for Torah scholars because of its huge library of holy books.

Over the years Hacham Laniado arranged for various *yeshivot* to make use of the Silvera *Bet Midrash* as a primary study location (see Part I). These included *Porat Yosef* and various Ashkenaz *yeshivot*, which were grateful for Hacham David's warm hospitality.

His Apartment

Hacham David, his wife, and children lived in a tiny, cramped apartment next to the *Bet Midrash*. On days when the number of scholars in the *Bet Midrash* was greater than usual, the study desks overflowed into the Laniado apartment, but with no objection from Hacham David who was happy to see more people learning Torah. On one occasion, when the children of R' Yaakob Ades (see #41) complained about the lack of space in their apartment, he brought them to the Laniado apartment to show them that they didn't have it so bad after all.

Over the years, his valiant wife Mazal raised 14 children in the same tiny apartment. Hacham David often had the opportunity to move to larger quarters. However, he always declined, saying, "I have lived here in Silvera, in *Hashem*'s house, all the days of my life."

His Great Work

He would go to the old Aleppo cemetery, and record the inscriptions on each tombstone of the hundreds of Sephardic rabbis buried there.

From time to time Hacham David would return to Syria to visit his parents in Aram Soba. He would make use of the opportunity to reestablish contact with the great scholars of the city. Also on those occasions, he would go to the old Aleppo cemetery, and record the inscriptions on each tombstone of the hundreds of Sephardic rabbis buried there. He would spend a lot of his time cleaning off old tombstones and reading the epitaphs. After a long hard day he would come home all muddy and dirty. His wife would ask him where he had been and what he had been doing. He just excused the dirt as a minor incident, not revealing his activities.

He did not allow the risk or the physical exertion to keep him from his holy mission. "If everyone leaves Syria," Hacham David reasoned, "who will remember these great people? Great-grandchildren won't know their great ancestors." He sensed that he had a duty "to publicize the names of these great people, because if you talk about them you invoke their *zechuyot* (the merits of their good deeds), and so their souls will rest in peace and their children will inherit their place in the world."

He used to say *Kaddish* at all prayers, even when he didn't have a *yahrtzeit*. Hacham Yosef Harari-Raful, the *Rosh Yeshiva* of *Ateret Torah,* once asked him why he was always saying *Kaddish*. He answered, "There are souls that have been abandoned from days of old with no one to say *Kaddish* for them. I say *Kaddish* for them."

He painstakingly assembled biographical details on hundreds of the rabbis and scholars who had lived in Aram Soba over the years. Besides the inscriptions on tombstones he researched the many old manuscripts of holy books that were kept in synagogues and private collections. He put all of this material into a book, which he named *LiKedoshim Asher Ba'Aretz* after the verse in *Tehillim* (16:3), לקדושים אשר בארץ, "For the sake of the holy ones who are [interred] in the earth." (The word אר"ץ, *Aretz*, is a common abbreviation for "Aram Soba.")

The original volume appeared in 1932. Over the next two decades he managed to publish two additional volumes: one covering the scholars who had moved to Jerusalem and were buried there, and another, covering scholars buried in other cemeteries in Damascus, Izmir, and Salonika. Finally, in 1952 he was able to combine all of his previous work into a single volume.

In 1965, in honor of the holiday of *Sukkot,* he published a collection of over 40 pictures of Aram Soba scholars, which he had painstakingly gathered from a variety of sources in Aram Soba and elsewhere.

After his death, others took up the holy work, including R' David Sharikaz, R' Eliyahu Attiah (see #109), and R' Ephraim Levi. Together with Hacham David's sons they published a complete revision in 1980, which incorporated the pictures that Hacham David had assembled. Three years earlier his sons had arranged for the printing of *Likutei David* (Jerusalem 5737/1977), based on other manuscripts left by their father. This material included biographies of various great Torah scholars and anecdotes of Jerusalem.

Tombstones of Aleppo

His Bonds with Torah Scholars

Hacham David loved all Torah scholars, but developed a special bond with the *Saba Kadisha*, R' Shelomo Eliezer Alfandri (see #44). Although the *Saba Kadisha* referred to other rabbis and scholars by their formal names, he made a point of referring to R' David-Sion as "Hacham David." One of Hacham David's sons had the special merit of being held by the *Saba Kadisha* at his *brit milah*. At the time, the *Saba Kadisha* was an old man and couldn't leave his house. Out of respect for his student, the *Saba Kadisha* allowed the *Brit Milah* to be held in his own home so that he might serve as *sandak* without endangering his health.

Out of respect for his student, the Saba Kadisha allowed the Brit Milah to be held in his own home so that he might serve as sandak without endangering his health.

When the *Saba Kadisha* was on his deathbed and was being attended by many worthy scholars and rabbis, when he wanted some water to drink, the one he requested to bring it to him was Hacham David.

Before *Pesah* in the last year of the *Saba Kadisha's* life he asked that Hacham David's wife, Mazal, should be the one to check his *maror* for the *Seder*, saying that he trusted no one else to perform this exacting task.

Hacham David was also very close to R' Yitzhak Alfia (see #46), who joined him in organizing projects to spread Torah among the Jews of the city.

In 1965, in honor of the holiday of Sukkot, he published a collection of over 40 pictures of Aram Soba scholars.

His Benevolence

People often came to him to ask for help and advice, which he gave with a friendly smile. No one was ever turned away empty-handed. He was known to show up at a sickbed at any time of day or night, in all kinds of weather, whether near or far, to comfort the sick and dying and offer solace to the bereaved.

He loved books and his library, with its fine leather bindings, impressed everyone who saw it. However, aside from his library, he remained a poor man throughout his life.

He sometimes went on fund-raising missions to the U.S. and Europe and in his later years he served as a rabbi in the town of Kfar Shalem near Tel Aviv. He loved books and his library, with its fine leather bindings, impressed everyone who saw it. However, aside from his library, he remained a poor man throughout his life, because his first priority was always to help those in need.

R' Mordechai Sharabi

His Passing

He passed away on 9 Heshvan, 5730 (1969). He never wanted to trouble anybody about his old age and death. Not only had he prepared his grave and tombstone, he bought his shrouds as well. One day one of his sons saw his mother hanging out long white pieces of cloth that didn't look like normal sheets. He asked her what they were and she answered nonchalantly, "It's your father's shrouds. I wash them and hang them up occasionally to save them from moths." This is how the generations of old lived the *Gemara* that states, "Let him remind himself of the day of death" (*Berachot* 5a).

The family asked to compensate for the cost of the tikkun. R' Sharabi said, "Don't worry about it. Hacham David paid for it in his lifetime."

After he passed away the great Kabbalist, R' Mordechai Sharabi, came to the mourners' home with ten Kabbalists to pray and thereby make a *tikkun* (spiritual repair) for the soul of the deceased. After the *tikkun*, money is generally set aside and given to charity. The family asked to compensate for the cost of the *tikkun*. R' Sharabi said, "Don't worry about it. Hacham David paid for it in his lifetime."

His Legacy

Today, the *Kollel Darchei David* under the leadership of R' Shemuel Pinhasi is named for him; Torah scholars are learning in his merit, and many children and grandchildren continue in his ways.

His other books are:

- *Likutim MiSefer Kli Hemdah* (Jerusalem 5691/1931). Selected commentaries from the book *Kli Hemdah* of R' Shemuel Laniado (see #376).
- *Melitz Tov* (Jerusalem 5686/1926). Selected prayers for special purposes, such as a *tefillah* for a husband to pray when his wife enters her seventh month and *tefillot* against the evil eye.

[353] LANIADO, R' Eliyahu

רבי אליהו לנייאדו

(— 1786)

Eminent Kabbalist and *dayan* (judge) of Aram Soba and Damascus. He was a son of R' Shemuel Laniado (see #372) and a brother of R' Raphael Shelomo Laniado (see #363). He was blessed with two scholarly sons: R' Yaakob Laniado (see #378) and R' Shemuel Laniado (see #374).

In 1822 there was a major earthquake in Aram Soba, which induced many families to leave for Damascus. R' Laniado was among them.

He was one of those who signed the introduction to his brother's books *Bet Dino shel Shelomo* and *HaMaalot LeShelomo*. He also signed the introduction to *Mahane Yehudah* of R' Yehudah Kassin (see #331). He passed away on 5 Elul, 5546 (1786) and was eulogized by R' Abraham Sutton (see #535), as recorded in *Malel Le'Abraham* (16). He was also eulogized by R' Yeshayah Attiah (see #119), as recorded in *Bigdei Yesha* (p. 104).

[354] LANIADO, R' Eliyahu

רבי אליהו לנייאדו

(1838 — 1868)

Worthy scholar and rabbi of Aram Soba. He was a son of R' Shelomo Laniado (see #365) and the grandfather of R' David-Sion Laniado, author of *LiKedoshim Asher Ba'Aretz* (see #352). He was blessed with two scholarly sons, R' Shelomo Laniado (see #367) and R' Yitzhak Laniado (see #382), in addition to two worthy daughters. Tragically, R' Eliyahu passed away at the age of 30 in 1868.

Note: There was an additional 19th-century scholar of Aram Soba with the name R' Eliyahu Laniado. Not much is known about him other than his date of passing: 13 Heshvan, 5645 (1884).

In addition, there were three 19th-century scholars of Damascus with the name R' Eliyahu Laniado. Not much is known about them other than their dates of passing: 4 Elul, 5629 (1869), *Rosh Hodesh* Heshvan, 5649 (1888), 8 Elul, 5688 (1928).

[355] **LANIADO, R' Ephraim**

רבי אפרים לנייאדו

(— 1805)

Distinguished Chief Rabbi and *Av Bet Din* (Chief Judge) of Aram Soba from 1787 to 1805. His father was R' Raphael Shelomo Laniado (see #363), the previous Chief Rabbi and *Av Bet Din*. When his father grew old, he bequeathed the position and its responsibilities to his son.

The position had become somewhat controversial as it involved judging financial disputes by one person, exclusively. However, R' Raphael Shelomo insisted that since he had served in that role for close to 40 years and his son was now fully qualified to assume its responsibilities, no one had the right to prevent him from doing so. He argued this case in a lengthy halachic (legal) ruling, which was subsequently included in his book *Kiss'e Shelomo* (sect. 1). In this ruling, R' Raphael lists the genealogy of the Laniado family in Aram Soba back to its patriarch, R' Shemuel Laniado. He argues that those who were protesting his son's acendancy to the position were not really against his son but against himself. He speaks of his son's abilities, as demonstrated by his many scholarly writings, including 27 responsa, 24 halachic rulings, and over 50 inspirational lectures. He now claims the right to pass his rights on to his son and states unequivocally that no one has the right to diminish his son's authority by forcing him to share it. It is also discussed in *Sedakah U'Mishpat* by R' Sadkah Houssin (see #313).

R' Ephraim did not leave male children and passed away 11 years after his father. He served in his father's position for 18 years from 1787 until his death on 28 Shevat, 5565 (1805). He was eulogized by R' Abraham Sutton (see #535), as recorded in *Malel Le'Abraham* (sect. 18).

Many of the *hiddushim* (original Torah thoughts) of R' Ephraim were published in his books *Degel Mahane Ephraim* (Jerusalem 5662/1902) and *Ro'ei Yisrael* (5664/1904), through the efforts of R' Shalom Hedaya (see #310). Among the many responsa in these books, he dealt with the issue of wearing wigs, the pearl trade with Livorno, and the case of a wealthy man who had been excused from taxes by the king. The book *Ro'ei Yisrael* also contains responsa by his father, R' Raphael Shelomo Laniado, and by R' Yehudah Kassin (see #331). Two other books of responsa by R' Ephraim were never published.

R' Ephraim also wrote introductions to his father's works *Yad shel Shelomo* and *Maalot LeShelomo*, and he has a long responsum in the book *Beirach Moshe* of R' Moshe Galante, the Chief Rabbi of Damascus (sect. 14).

R' Raphael lists the genealogy of the Laniado family in Aram Soba back to its patriarch, R' Shemuel Laniado.

[356] **LANIADO, Señor Haim Moshe**

סי' חיים משה לנייאדו

Wealthy philanthropist of Aram Soba. He was a son-in-law of R' Yitzhak Moshe Abulafia, author of the book *Lev Nishbar*, and sponsored the publishing of his father-in-law's book.

He argues that those who were protesting his son's acendancy to the position were not really against his son but against himself.

[357] **LANIADO, R' Levi**

רבי לוי לנייאדו

Chief Rabbi of No-Amon, Egypt. He was the second son of R' Abraham Laniado (see #346) and a brother of R' Yitzhak Laniado (see #384). R' Levi and his brother R' Yitzhak worked on the printing of their grandfather's book, *Kli Paz*, and they are highly praised in the introduction written by R' Moshe Zechut. Their older brother, R' Shelomo, the elder (see #368), also mentions them favorably in the introduction which he wrote to the same book.

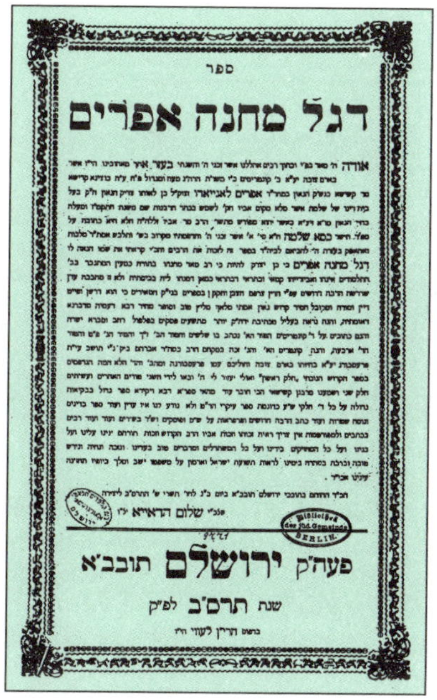
ספר
דגל מחנה אפרים
פעה"ק ירושלם תובב"א
שנת תרס"ב לפ"ק

Title Page of Degel Mahane Ephraim

[358] **LANIADO, R' Meir**

רבי מאיר לנייאדו

(— 1911)

Eminent scholar and genealogist of the Laniado family. He was born in Aram Soba and settled in Jerusalem, where he became the administrator of a charity fund for the poor. He worked devotedly to meet the needs of the many impoverished families of Jerusalem, especially at holidays such as *Purim* and *Pesah*.

R' Meir researched the genealogy of the Laniado family and recorded its illustrious lineage through ten generations.

R' Meir researched the genealogy of the Laniado family and recorded its illustrious lineage through ten generations from the time of R' Shemuel Laniado, the *Baal HaKeilim*. The genealogy is included at the beginning of the combined book *Ro'ei Yisrael* and *Degel Mahane Ephraim* (Jerusalem 5664/1904).

He was a son of R' Abraham Laniado (see #349). In 1826 he married Rina, the daughter of R' Shelomo Harari-Raful. His four scholarly sons, representing the 11th generation of the Laniado family, were R' Abraham, R' Raphael Shelomo (first *Rosh Yeshiva* of *Porat Yosef*, see #364, named after his grandfather, R' Shelomo Harari-Raful), R' Obadiah, and R' David. At his passing he was eulogized by R' Yitzhak Laniado (see #382) in his book *Vayizra Yitzhak* (lecture no. 1). He passed away on 17 Nissan, 5671 (1911).

[359] LANIADO, R' Moshe (Dib)

רבי משה (דיב) לנייאדו

(1892 — 1968)

Eminent blind scholar of Aram Soba. At the young age of 5, he lost his eyesight due to illness.

Eminent blind scholar of Aram Soba. He was born in Aram Soba in 1892 to R' Shaul (Dib) Laniado. On his mother's side he was a grandson of R' Moshe Harari (see #291). At the young age of 5, he lost his eyesight due to illness. Despite that handicap he attended the Talmud Torah and kept up with the children of his age level. He learned Gemara under R' Ezra Shayo (see #505) and became an outstanding scholar, devoting himself to his studies from early in the morning until late at night. Usually a friend would read to him from the holy books. With his mind's eye, he had total clarity of vision and many people came to him to consult with him on their business affairs and other matters. He served as an adviser to litigants before the Bet Din and skillfully represented their interests.

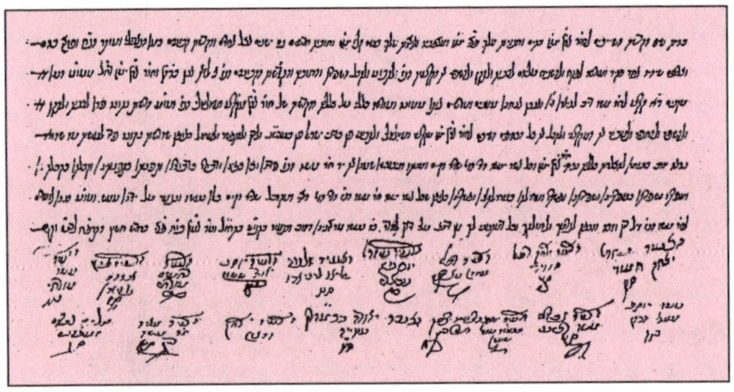

Appointment of R' Laniado as administrator of properties invested for the rabbis of Aram Soba

In 1927 he was appointed by the *Bet Din* to manage the assets of the Aram Soba congregation and the *Bet Nasi* synagogue, including the properties which provided support for the scholars and rabbis of the community. (See Document Section, Document No. 1.) In 1948 when an Arab mob set fire to the synagogue he organized the effort of rebuilding it.

He had an excellent voice and was able to sing from a repertoire of over one thousand songs and poems, which he had committed to memory. In 1962 he moved to *Eretz Yisrael* and took up residence in Tel Aviv. There he would go every day to the *Bet Midrash* called *Hen Mordechai* to hear Torah from R' Moshe Tawil (see #586). He became ill in 1967 and endured about a year and half of painful sickness, before passing away on 28 Tishrei, 5729 (1968). He is buried in the cemetery of Holon.

[360] LANIADO, R' Moshe

רבי משה לנייאדו

Worthy scholar of Aram Soba. He was a son of R' Shemuel Laniado, the *Baal HaKeilim* (see #376). He married his niece, the daughter of his sister and her husband R' Abraham Laniado (see #345), a cousin. He is mentioned in glowing terms in the introduction to his father's book *Nekudot HaKesef*.

[361] LANIADO, R' Obadiah

רבי עובדיה לנייאדו

(— 1817)

Worthy scholar and rabbi of Aram Soba. He was a son of R' Shemuel Laniado (see #374), and a grandson of R' Eliyahu Laniado (see #353). He was a pious and humble man, who was praised by R' Moshe Sutton in his manuscript *Sefer HaZichronot*. He passed away on 2 Heshvan, 5578 (1817).

[362] LANIADO, R' Obadiah

רבי עובדיה לנייאדו

(— 1909)

Worthy scholar and rabbi of Aram Soba. He was a brother of R' Shelomo Laniado (see #366). R' Obadiah passed away on 24 Shevat, 5669 (1909).

[363] LANIADO, R' Raphael Shelomo

רבי רפאל שלמה לנייאדו

(— 1793)

Chief Rabbi and *Av Bet Din* (Chief Judge) of Aram Soba. He was referred to as the

"Marshal" (which is an acronym of his name) and as "Señor Hacham." He was the firstborn son of R' Shemuel Laniado (see #372) and held the senior rabbinic position in Aram Soba from 1740 until 1787, when he bequeathed the position to his son R' Ephraim Laniado (see #355). He was noted for his firmness which left no place for compromise. He did not refrain from using the power of excommunication *(herem)* to enforce his righteous judgments. However, he was careful to avoid controversy for its own sake.

In the 1760's he sought to impose the authority of the rabbis and the local community customs on the Francos. They were European Jews from France and Italy who had settled in Aram Soba for business reasons and enjoyed the protection of the consuls of the European powers. The Francos liberally supported communal institutions, but refused to pay the regular taxes and did not accept the authority of the community, arguing that they were not permanent residents. Led by R' Yehudah Kassin (see #331), many other rabbis of the town opposed him, arguing that there were valid grounds for the position of the Francos and that it should be accepted in the interest of peace. This controversy continued over several years, and came to an end only after the number of Francos dwindled.

He also became embroiled in a dispute over the succession to his position of his son R' Ephraim Laniado (see #355). The position had become somewhat controversial as it involved judging financial disputes by one person, exclusively. R' Raphael Shelomo insisted that since he had served in that role for close to 40 years and his son was now fully qualified to assume its responsibilities, no one had the right to prevent him from doing so. He argued this case in a lengthy *halachic* (legal) ruling, which was subsequently included in his book *Kiss'e Shelomo* (sect. 1). It is also discussed in *Sedakah U'Mishpat* by R' Sadkah Houssin (see #313) (on *Hoshen Mishpat*).

His published works include:

- *Bet Dino shel Shelomo* (Constantinople 5535/1775), responsa.
- *Lehem Shelomo* (Constantinople 5535/1775), elucidations in *halachah.*
- *HaMa'alot LeShelomo* (Constantinople 5535/1775), inspirational lectures.
- *Kiss'e Shelomo* (Jerusalem 5661/1901), responsa; published through the efforts of R' Shalom Hedaya (see #310).

ספר

בית דינו של שלמה

נדפס

בקושטאנדינה

Title Page of Bet Dino shel Shelomo

Some of his responsa were also published by R' Shalom Hedaya (see #310) in *Ro'ei Yisrael* (Jerusalem 5664/1904) together with responsa of his son R' Ephraim (see #355). Others were included in the anthology *Otzarot Hachmei Aram Soba al HaRambam* (Jerusalem 5749/1989) that was published by the Aram Soba Foundation.

He passed away on 7 Tevet, 5554 (1793).

R' Laniado's name is mentioned in many books written by rabbis of our generation. Hacham Ovadiah Yosef, in his book *Yabia Omer* (Vol. II, *Orah Haim*, 21), discussing the opinion that the proper amount of time to wait before ending *Shabbat* is 72 minutes after sunset, quotes R' Shelomo Laniado's reaction to this ruling: "I got up in *shul* and announced this, and warned people that it was sinful to wait any less. Everyone accepted upon themselves to wait 72 minutes. I commanded in the largest *shul* in Aleppo, that *Arbit* shouldn't be said until an hour and fifteen minutes after sunset. No candles should be lit, and no work should be done." He continues, "We even made a *herem* (religious edict) on this, and the *Hachamim* got together and agreed, and accepted it on the future generations." (See Document Section, Document No. 26.)

[364] LANIADO, R' Raphael Shelomo
רבי רפאל שלמה לנייאדו
(1876 — 1925)

R' Raphael Shelomo Laniado

Distinguished scholar, *dayan*, and educator of Jerusalem. He was appointed *Rosh Yeshiva* when *Ohel Moed* was founded and later assumed that position in *Porat Yosef.*

He was born in Aram Soba in 1876 to R' Meir Laniado (see #358) and as a young man he studied under R' Yosef Yedid (see #594) and R' Ezra Hamway (see #272). He also studied Kabbalah under R' Abraham Ades (see #37).

His Early Years in Aram Soba

It was a marvelous and inspiring sight to see three generations of Jewish heritage sitting together to resolve halachic issues.

Together with R' Eliyahu Shamah (see #500) he was a co-founder of the *Sedakah U'Marpeh* organization in Aram Soba, which opened a medical clinic to treat the needy of the town.

In later years his teacher R' Yedid recalled young Raphael Shelomo's unusual diligence and dedication to Torah studies. He noted that at the age of 14, the boy often stayed up the entire night immersed in his studies, together with his worthy study partner R' Aslan Esses (see #260) and they did not use the days following such nights to catch up on their sleep.

At the age of 14, the boy often stayed up the entire night immersed in his studies.

His Life in Jerusalem

In 1900 he moved to Jerusalem and was accepted as a teacher in the Talmud Torah of the Bukharan congregation. In 1907 the yeshiva *Ohel Moed* was founded in Jerusalem through the efforts of R' Laniado and R' Ezra Harari-Raful (see #304). R' Laniado served as *Rosh Yeshiva* in the new institution until the outbreak of World War I. The yeshiva was established primarily to meet the needs of scholars from Aram Soba. Among its first scholars were R' Ezra Attiah (see #102), R' Yaakob Ades (see #41), R' Moshe Ades (see #39), R' Nissim Lofez (see #396), and R' Abraham Harari-Raful (see #302), all of whom were students of R' Raphael Shelomo and were to became important scholars and rabbinical authorities in their own right.

R' Laniado served as Rosh Yeshiva in the new institution until the outbreak of World War I.

During these years he also gave *Gemara* classes in the *Bet Midrash Doresh Sion* and his *hiddushim* (original Torah thoughts) on the tractate *Baba Kama* were developed there.

At the outbreak of World War I the threat of being drafted into the Turkish army became a severe problem for him. Fortunately, after a great deal of effort on the part of the leading rabbis of that time, he managed to get excused.

With the founding of the yeshiva *Porat Yosef* in 1923 he was called to be the first *Rosh Yeshiva*, a position which he held until his death in 1925. R' Ezra Attiah, his trusted student from *Ohel Moed*, was at his right hand in the running of the yeshiva and ultimately became his successor.

During this period he sat on the *Bet Din* of the Syrian community in Jerusalem together with his teacher R' Yosef Yedid and R' Yedid's own teacher R' Abraham Ades. It was a marvelous and inspiring sight to see three generations of Jewish heritage sitting together to resolve *halachic* issues.

His Approach to Education

R' Laniado believed in frequent testing to ensure that the students grasped the subject matter of their studies. He showed warmth and caring to each student, as well as great humility. He greeted each student with a smile and made a point of treating him as an individual.

His Passing

He passed away on 15 Shevat, 5685 (1925) at the young age of 49. His death was made more heartbreaking by its suddenness. On Thursday he was teaching his students and on *Shabbat* the doctors gave up all hope. The great Kabbalist R' Abraham Ades, while asleep, spoke some words. When he awoke, he was asked if he knew what he said. He answered, "In my dream my lips uttered the expression, 'R' Shelomo Laniado is ill,' but I surely hope it was meaningless."

"In my dream my lips uttered the expression, 'R' Shelomo Laniado is ill,' but I surely hope it was meaningless."

Word of R' Laniado's illness had not been publicized in Jerusalem, but the next day (Sunday), R' Yosef Tawil came to R' Ades to ask him to pray for his wife who was very ill. R' Ades replied, "Your wife will recover, but as for R' Shelomo Laniado, I fear for his life." After the truth became known, R' Ades was asked whether he had prophetic powers. He replied, "I am not a prophet but I sensed the situation during my prayers. Whenever I tried to pray for him, I forgot his name. And as much as I tried, it didn't come to me. This made me very worried."

"I am not a prophet but I sensed the situation during my prayers. Whenever I tried to pray for him, I forgot his name. And as much as I tried, it didn't come to me."

The day of R' Laniado's passing was Monday, the 15th of Shevat. In the late afternoon R'

Ades was sitting and learning by the light of a candle, as was his usual practice. Suddenly, a darkness passed before his eyes and the light of the candle seemed to go out. He looked up and asked his sister who was in the house with him, "Why have you put out the light?" She replied, "I haven't touched the light at all, and look, it is still burning nicely." He thought for a moment and said, "A darkness came over my eyes. This is a sign that R' Raphael Shelomo Laniado has been taken from us. But tell no one of this." An hour later the news arrived from the Old City that R' Laniado had passed away, and it was at the very moment that R' Ades had sensed the passing darkness.

Among those who spoke at his funeral was his teacher, R' Yosef Yedid (see #594), whose words are printed in the book *Yemei Yosef* (Vol. II, p. 478) (Brooklyn 5734/1974).

His Legacy

He left two worthy sons: R' Meir (who became a renowned lawyer in Jerusalem) and R' Abraham.

A portion of his *hiddushim* under the name *Hayei Shelomo* are printed at the end of the anthology *MeHalab Ha'Aretz* (Jerusalem 5726/1966), published by R' Yosef Shayo (see #507).

One of his *halachic* (legal) rulings was published in the booklet *Din U'Mishpat* (Jerusalem 5670/1910). This document was countersigned by R' Yosef Yedid (see #594) and R' Yitzhak Labaton (see #340).

Additional *hiddushim* were printed recently by R' David Zafrani of Lakewood, under the title *Ateret Shelomo*.

[365] LANIADO, R' Shelomo
רבי שלמה לנייאדו
(— 1867)

Worthy scholar and rabbi of Aram Soba. He was a son of R' Shemuel Laniado (see #373), author of *Shulhan HaMelech*, and the father of R' Eliyahu Laniado (see #354). He passed away on *Rosh Hodesh* Adar 2, 5627 (1867).

[366] LANIADO, R' Shelomo
רבי שלמה לנייאדו
(— 1918)

Worthy scholar and rabbi of Aram Soba. He was a brother of R' Obadiah Laniado (see #362). He passed away on 20 Tishrei, the fourth day of *Hol HaMoed Sukkot* 5679 (1918).

[367] LANIADO, R' Shelomo
רבי שלמה לנייאדו
(— 1932)

Worthy scholar and rabbi of Aram Soba. He was a son of R' Eliyahu Laniado (see #354) and the father of R' David-Sion Laniado, author of *LiKedoshim Asher Ba'Aretz* (see #352). He was the first signer of the approbation to the book *Minhat Yehudah* of R' Yehudah Attiah (see #118). The other signers were R' Yosef Yedid (see #594), R' Ben-Sion Kouenka, and R' Shalom Hedaya (see #310).

R' Shelomo Laniado

In 1901 his name appeared in the list of Aram Soba scholars receiving a weekly stipend from the special fund that had been set up for the support of worthy individuals who dedicate their lives to Torah study. (See Document No. 30.) In 1906, together with other scholars and rabbis of Aram Soba, he signed a *halachic* ruling directed against those who desecrate *Shabbat* (see page 4-1). He passed away in Aram Soba on 7 Shevat, 5692 (1932).

[368] LANIADO, R' Shelomo [the Elder]
רבי שלמה לנייאדו [הזקן]
(— 1700)

Chief Rabbi and *dayan* of Aram Soba from 1650 to 1700. He inherited his official position from his father, R' Abraham Laniado (see #346), who was the son of R' Shemuel Laniado, the *Baal HaKeilim*. He sat on the Aram Soba *Bet Din* together with R' Yosef Dayan (see #209). They both signed the approbation to the book *Hevel Bnai Yehudah* of R' Yehuda Habilio in 1695.

Chief Rabbi and dayan of Aram Soba from 1650 to 1700.

In the long-running dispute between R' Raphael Shelomo Laniado (see #363) and R' Yehudah Kassin (see #331) on whether the Francos were required to pay the regular taxes, his published opinion was that the Francos should be free of those obligations. However, R' Raphael Shelomo relied on the views expressed by his own father, R' Shemuel (see #372), saying they outweighed those of R' Shelomo, the elder. (Refer to *Bet Dino shel Shelomo*, page 24.) In contrast, R' Kassin (writing in *Minhat Yehudah*, second appendix, page 11) argued that the views of R' Shelomo, the elder, outranked those of R' Shemuel. R' Kassin was effusive in his praise of R' Shelomo. He suggested that R' Shelomo was so saintly that the *Shechinah* (Divine Presence) would already have descended upon him, except that the people of the generation did not merit having such a revelation in their time. He cited praises of R' Shelomo by other great *halachic* (legal) authorities of the day: Maharam ben Habib, R' Eliezer Alush, and R' Eliezer Arha.

He suggested that R' Shelomo was so saintly that the Shechinah (Divine Presence) would already have descended upon him, except that the people of the generation did not merit having such a revelation in their time.

He was blessed with a long life and held his position for about 50 years from 1650 to 1700. The *hiddushim* (original Torah thoughts) of R' Shelomo, including the book *Midrash Shelomo*, were tragically lost, as were those of so many other scholars. However, he saw to the publishing of his grandfather's work, *Kli Paz*. One of his responsa was published in *Korban Isheh* of R' Eliyahu Shamah (see #499) (on *Hoshen Mishpat*, 34).

It is unclear how the Chief Rabbinate passed from R' Shelomo, the elder, to R' Shemuel Laniado (see #372), the father of the *Marshal* (see #363). It appears that R' Shelomo had no sons, or at least none that were suitable for the Chief Rabbi position and so the senior rabbis of the city chose R' Shemuel in his place, as described in *Kiss'e Shelomo* (sect. 1).

R" Shemuel Laniado (#371) was the first of the line of Laniado rabbis.

Another reference to the views of the *Marshal* may be found in the book of responsa *Haim Sha'al* of the *Hida* (R' Haim Yosef David Azulai) (Vol. II, 18).

[369] LANIADO, R' Shelomo Moshe

רבי שלמה משה לנייאדו

(1868 — 1938)

Eminent scholar and rabbi of Baghdad. He was born in Baghdad in 1868, a son of R' Shech Shaul Laniado and a descendant of the illustrious Laniado family of Aram Soba. On his mother's side he was a grandson of the distinguished Kabbalist, R' Sasson Mordechai Moshe, author of *Davar Be'Ito*, *Mizmor Le'Asaf*, *Kol Sasson*, *Imrei Sasson*, and *Tehillah LeDavid*. R' Shelomo Moshe studied in the yeshiva of his grandfather and in 1914 he was appointed to be its head.

In 1925 he was the first of the scholars and rabbis of *Midrash Meir Eliyahu* in Baghdad to sign the approbation on a *halachic* (legal) ruling as to whether it is permitted to destroy a a number of small synagogues in order to build a larger one on the same foundation. In 1926 he wrote the introduction to *Sedakah U'Mishpat*, a work of responsa by R' Sadkah Houssin (see #313). He passed away on 7 Av, 5698 (1938).

[370] LANIADO, R' Shelomo Raphael Shimon

רבי שלמה רפאל שמעון לנייאדו

(1929 — 1947)

Young scholar of Tel Aviv. He passed away at the age of 18 on the day before *Rosh Hodesh* Av, 5707 (1947).

[371] LANIADO, R' Shemuel [First of the Line]

רבי שמואל לנייאדו

(— 1532)

First of the line of Laniado rabbis. He apparently settled in Adrianople (Turkey) after the expulsion from Spain in 1492 and subsequently moved to Aram Soba. From that point on, the name Laniado became closely identified with Aram Soba. His son was R' Abraham Laniado (see #344) and his grandson was R' Shemuel Laniado, the *Baal HaKeilim* (see #376). The first contemporary mention of the original R' Shemuel is in the responsa of *HaRe'em*, R' Eliyahu Mizrahi (Vol. I, sect. 52). R' Raphael Shelomo Laniado (see #363), in his book, *Kiss'e Shelomo* (sect. 1), writes: "We know from our family tradition that the family originated in an expulsion, but we don't know from where or who was involved, but we assume that the R' Shemuel Laniado mentioned by R' Eliyahu Mizrahi was the first."

[372] LANIADO, R' Shemuel

רבי שמואל לנייאדו

(— 1750)

Distinguished Chief Rabbi of Aram Soba for 40 years. It is believed that his father was a scholar named R' Shelomo Laniado. However, little else is known about him. R' Shemuel married the daughter of R' Haim Dweck (see #227). His son was R' Raphael Shelomo Laniado (see #363), the author of *Bet Dino shel Shelomo* and a student of R' Shemuel Laniado, the elder (see #368). In the Laniado lineage recorded by R' Meir Laniado (see #358), he is listed as the fifth generation after the *Baal HaKeilim*. He passed away on 28 Adar, 5510 (1750).

He took issue with the Francos and forcefully demanded that they accept the same obligations as the other Jews of Aram Soba. They were European Jews from France and Italy who had settled in Aram Soba for business reasons and enjoyed the protection of the consuls of the European powers. The Francos liberally supported communal institutions, but refused to pay the regular taxes and did not accept the authority of the community, arguing that they were not permanent residents. This issue continued to be a problem in the later half of the century when R' Raphael Shelomo Laniado (see #363) was Chief Rabbi.

He was a colleague of R' Shemuel Dweck (see #242), R' Moshe Harari (see #288), R' Shemuel Pinto (see #462), and R' Yosef Nawy (see #439), and he joined them in signing a *halachic* (legal) ruling against eating grape leaves because of worm infestation, as recorded in the book *Hanan Elokim* by R' Haim Abulafia. (See Document Section, Document No. 13.) In 1715 he joined the same rabbis in signing a *halachic* ruling concerning the validity of Kabbalah and the writings of the *Ari'zal*. (See Document Section, Document No. 10.)

His colleague R' Sadkah Houssin (see #313) mentions him with great admiration in his book *Sedakah U'Mishpat* (*Orah Haim*, 5). He is also spoken of with great admiration in the book *Bet Dino shel Shelomo* by his son R' Raphael Shelomo Laniado (see #363).

[373] LANIADO, R' Shemuel

רבי שמואל לנייאדו

(18th century)

Distinguished scholar and rabbi of Aram Soba. His father's name was R' Shelomo Laniado, as was the name of his son. He married the daughter of R' Raphael Shelomo Laniado (see #363), author of the book *Bet Dino shel Shelomo*.

His son R' Shelomo Laniado (see #365) was the grandfather of R' Shelomo Laniado (see #367). He lived in the time of R' Raphael Shelomo Laniado (see #363) and was known for his important work, *Shulhan HaMelech* (Aram Soba 5683/1923). This is a collection of *halachot* (laws) which are applicable to the present times. This work was published through the efforts of R' Ezra Lofez (see #395). The introduction was written by the author in 1804.

When he passed away he was eulogized by R' Abraham Sutton (see #535), as recorded in his book *Malel Le'Abraham* (sect. 19).

R' Shemuel Laniado (#372) was the distinguished Chief Rabbi of Aram Soba for 40 years.

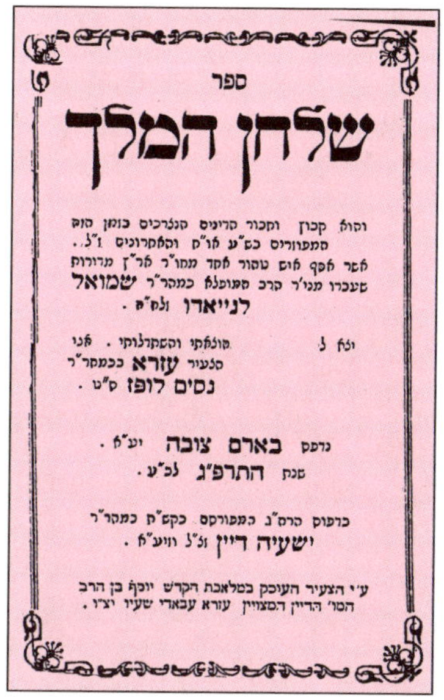
ספר
שלחן המלך
והוא קבוץ וקצור הדינים הנצרכים בזמן הזה המפורשים בש"ע או"ח והאחרונים ז"ל.
אשר אסף איש טהור אחד מחו"ר אר"ץ מדורות שעברו מגי'ר הרב המופלא כמהר"ר שמואל לנייאדו זלה"ה.
ויצא ל[illegible] הוצאתי והשתדלותי. אני הצעיר עזרא כמהר"ר נסים לופז ס"ט.
נדפס בארם צובה יע"א. שנת התרפ"ג לפ"ע.
בדפוס הרה"ג המפורסם כקש"ת כמהר"ר ישעיה דיין זצ"ל וזיע"א.
ע"י הצעיר העוסק במלאכת הקדש יוסף בן הרב המו' הדיין המצויין עזרא עבאדי שעיו יצ"ו.

Title Page of Shulhan HaMelech

[374] LANIADO, R' Shemuel

רבי שמואל לנייאדו

(18th – 19th century)

Eminent Chief Rabbi of Aram Soba. He was a son of R' Eliyahu Laniado (see #353) and the father of R' Obadiah Laniado (see #361). In the Laniado lineage recorded by R' Meir Laniado (see #358), he is listed as the seventh generation after the *Baal HaKeilim*.

He served as the Chief Rabbi of Aram Soba in the period between R' Ephraim Laniado (see #355) and R' Eliyahu Shamah (see #499). When he passed away he was eulogized by R' Abraham Sutton (see #535), as recorded in his book *Malel Le'Abraham* (sect. 19).

[375] LANIADO, R' Shemuel

רבי שמואל לנייאדו

(17th century)

Chief Rabbi of No-Amon and Alexandria, Egypt. He was a son of R' Levi Laniado (see #357). In the Laniado lineage recorded by R' Meir Laniado (see #358), he is listed as the fourth generation after the *Baal HaKeilim*. After his father passed away, he was appoint-

Title Page of Kli Yakar

Title Page of Kli Paz

ed to his father's position as Chief Rabbi of No-Amon. He subsequently moved to Alexandria, where he held the same position. When he passed away, he was eulogized by R' Shemuel Laniado (see #372), the father of R' Raphael Shelomo Laniado (see #363), the author of *Bet Dino shel Shelomo*.

[376] LANIADO, R' Shemuel [Baal HaKeilim]
רבי שמואל לנייאדו [בעל הכלים]

(— 1605)

Distinguished Biblical commentator and Chief Rabbi of Aram Soba. He was known from the title of most of his works as the *Baal HaKeilim*. He was born in Aram Soba in the early 1500's to R' Abraham Laniado (see #344) and went to Safed to study under R' Yosef Karo, the *Bet Yosef*. When the *Bet Yosef* received a letter from the Jewish community of Aram Soba asking him to help them find a chief rabbi, he chose his student R' Shemuel. As a descendant of Spanish Jews, R' Shemuel was particularly well suited to serve the needs of the many who had arrived in Syria after the expulsion from Spain in 1492. And as a brilliant scholar, he was sure to earn the respect of the indigenous community which had lived in Syria from ancient times. The *Bet Yosef* responded, "I am sending you someone who is equal to me."

The *Baal HaKeilim* occupied his position for almost 40 years, leaving one son, R' Abraham (see #346), and two scholarly sons-in-law. One was R' Abraham, the son of his brother R' Yitzhak (see #345), and the other was R' Mordechai Cohen (see #163). He passed away in 5365 (1605).

His primary published works are:

- *Kli Hemdah* (Venice 5356/1596, Prague 5370/1610), commentary on the Torah.
- *Kli Yakar* (Venice 5363/1603), commentary on the early prophets.
- *Kli Paz* (Venice 5417/1657), commentary on *Yeshayahu*.

The Value of Salted Fish. The *Baal HaKeilim* named his books after valuable objects to remind himself of the miracle *Hashem* performed for him during his journey to Syria. While on the boat, he befriended a man who was in the possession of many barrels of salted fish. The man died on the boat, and as the captain did not have any desire to keep the fish, he offered to sell the barrels to R' Shemuel. He purchased them, but when he arrived at the home that the Syrian community had prepared for him, he was surprised upon opening these barrels. There wasn't any fish — there were diamonds, pearls, and jewels! Rather than needing the support of the community, R Shemuel arrived with the ability to support others both spiritually and financially. This eased his transition into the new position and enabled him to gain respect with greater facility.

R' Sion Yitzhak Laniado

Many of his works have remained in manuscript, including *Kelim MiKelim Shonim* on the later prophets (with the exception of *Hoshea* and *Yoel*), *Kli Golah* on *Eichah*, and *Mevakesh Hashem*, a commentary on the Torah which he mentions in *Kli Hemdah*. He also wrote a commentary entitled *Sechel Tov* on the *Midrash Shoher Tov* which was in the possession of the *Hida* (R' Haim Yosef David Azulai).

In 1863 (5623) R' Yoel Bloch published a commentary on *Tehillim*, consisting of Torah thoughts assembled from *Kli Hemdah*. This book, called *Teru'at HaMelech*, was reprinted by R' David-Sion Laniado in 1931, but all the copies mysteriously vanished and it was reissued by his son Shelomo Laniado in 1978.

[377] LANIADO, R' Sion Yitzhak
רבי ציון יצחק לנייאדו

(— 1947)

Eminent scholar and rabbi of Aram Soba. He was active in the community and in teaching students. He was known as one of the deeply analytical thinkers of Aram Soba. Many of his *hiddushim* (original Torah thoughts) appeared in the journal *HaMe'asef* published in Jerusalem by R' Ben-Sion Kouenka.

He apparently left inspirational lectures in manuscript form, one of which is quoted in the book *She'erit Yaakob* (lecture no. 2 for *Shabbat Zachor*) by R' Yaakob Shaul Dweck (see #248). He also served the community as a secretary of the *Bet Din ("Safra Dedayna")* and as a *shohet* (ritual slaughterer).

He had such a beautiful voice that Arab residents of the city would often come to hear him sing in the synagogue on *Motza'e Shabbat*. He may have been the author of the well-known hymn *"Ana Kiviti."*

He was a son of R' Abraham Laniado and a cousin of R' Shaul Laniado. He passed away in the month of Heshvan, 5708 (1947).

[378] LANIADO, R' Yaakob

רבי יעקב לנייאדו

(— 1889)

Worthy scholar and rabbi of Damascus. He is believed to have been a son of R' Eliyahu Laniado (see #353). He passed away on 15 Adar, 5649 (1889).

[379] LANIADO (MALKI SHUBAH), R' Yehudah

רבי יהודה לנייאדו (מלכי שובה)

(— 1902)

Worthy *darshan* (lecturer) and *shohet* (ritual slaughterer) of Aram Soba. His excellent inspirational lectures on *Tanach* remained in manuscript form. He was a son of R' Yitzhak Laniado and he, in turn, was blessed with a son who was named Yitzhak (see #381). He passed away on 19 Adar, 5662 (1902).

[380] LANIADO, R' Yeshayah

רבי ישעיה לנייאדו

(— 1722)

Worthy scholar of Aram Soba. He passed away on 3 Tamuz, 5482 (1722)

[381] LANIADO (MALKI SHUBAH), R' Yitzhak

רבי יצחק לנייאדו (מלכי שובה)

(1872 — 1916)

Worthy scholar and teacher of Aram Soba. He was born in 1872, the son of R' Yehudah Laniado (see #379). R' Yitzhak taught *Gemara* in the general Talmud Torah of Aram Soba and in the Talmud Torah for orphans that was under the management of the Silvera family of Aram Soba. He passed away at a relatively young age on 15 Shevat, 5676 (1916) and left no sons.

[382] LANIADO, R' Yitzhak

רבי יצחק לנייאדו

(— 1917)

He had such a beautiful voice that Arab residents of the city would often come to hear him sing in the synagogue.

Eminent scholar and Kabbalist of Jerusalem. He was born in Aram Soba, a son of R' Eliyahu Laniado (see #354) and a brother of R' Shelomo Laniado (see #367). As a young man he moved to Jerusalem and became a student of R' Meir Laniado (see #358). At the outbreak of World War I he was forced to go to New York. Circumstances prevented him from returning to Jerusalem and so he went on to Buenos Aires, where he continued on his lifelong path of strengthening Torah among the Jewish people. In that city he introduced many improvements in religious practice.

וזה ספר

ויזרע יצחק

מיוסד על אדני פז ברזי דאוריתא על פי הקדמות, שרשיות מזוהרא דרשב"י זיע"א והתקונים ומדברי רבינו האר"י זצ"ל, ויחובר אליו דרושים לבר מצוה ודרושים לזקרא דחיי חברו הרב המקובל הסיד, ועניו כמוהר"ר יצחק אליאו לאניאדו ז"ל. הנה וסודרו אותיותיו על יד בנו המשתדל

נדפס פה ארם־צובה יע"א

בשנת לדיק כת'מר יפ'ר'ח' לפ"ק

בדפוס הר' עזרא חיים מדמשק יל"ו

IMPRIMERIE AL-KAMAL ALEP

Title Page of Vayizra Yitzhak

He was a man of great humility. In the eulogy, which he delivered on the depth of his teacher, R' Meir Laniado, he spoke of himself as knowing far less than any of his friends and acquaintances. The eulogy is recorded in his book of inspirational lectures *Vayizra Yitzhak* (6), which is printed at the end of the anthology *MeHalab Ha'Aretz* (Jerusalem 5726/1966), published by R' Yosef Shayo (see #507). On the first printing of his book in Aram Soba in 1928 (11 years after his death), it received a signed approbation by 10 scholars of Aram Soba, residing in Jerusalem.

In the will which he wrote before his death he asked not to be eulogized and and he specified a very simplistic wording for his gravestone.

He passed away on 17 Tishrei, 5678 (1917), a great zealot for the Torah, for his people, and his land. In the will which he wrote before his death he asked not to be eulogized and he specified a very simplistic wording for his gravestone. Despite his request, he was eulogized in each of the cities where he had left his mark: Buenos Aires, New York, and Jerusalem. In Buenos Aires, his intense devotion to *mitzvot* was remembered by R' Shaul Sutton, the Chief Rabbi of the city. In New York he was praised by the local rabbis, who had become impressed by his greatness in Torah.

In Jerusalem he was eulogized by R' Raphael Shelomo Laniado (see #364), the first head of *Porat Yosef*, who explained that R' Yitzhak had traveled abroad because of the need to marry off his daughter, which is a great *mitzvah*. He had been prevented from returning to *Eretz Yisrael* because of travel restrictions and so he helped Jews in the place where he was. R' Shelomo pointed out that surely R' Yitzhak did not lose his reward and it was as though he was buried in *Eretz Yisrael*, especially since he had purchased land and built a house there. The *Ibn Ezra* says that anyone who owns a piece of *Eretz Yisrael* is as though he has a portion of the World to Come.

[383] **LANIADO, R' Yitzhak**

רבי יצחק לנייאדו

Eminent scholar and rabbi of Aram Soba. He was the son of R' Abraham Laniado (see #344) and the brother of R' Shemuel Laniado, the *Baal HaKeilim*. His son, R' Abraham Laniado (see #345), speaks of him as a great scholar in the introduction to his book *Magen Abraham*. It appears that R' Yitzhak had no other sons.

[384] **LANIADO, R' Yitzhak**

רבי יצחק לנייאדו

Worthy scholar and rabbi of Aram Soba. He was a son of R' Abraham Laniado (see #346) and a grandson of R' Shemuel Laniado, the *Baal HaKeilim*. R' Yitzhak and his brother R' Levi worked on the printing of their grandfather's book, *Kli Paz*, and they are highly praised in the introduction written by R' Moshe Zechut. Their older brother, R' Shelomo, the elder (see #368), also mentions them favorably in the introduction which he wrote to the same book.

[385] **LANIADO, R' Yitzhak**

רבי יצחק לנייאדו

Worthy scholar and dayan (judge) of Basra (Iraq). He was a son of R' Shemuel Laniado (see #372). One of his responsa was found among the papers of R' Sadkah Houssin (see #313), who corresponded with him.

[386] **LANIADO, R' Yosef David**

רבי יוסף דוד לנייאדו

(— 1840)

Martyred scholar of Aram Soba. He was killed in the riots associated with the notorious Damascus blood libel, which occurred in 1840. At the Ben-Zvi Institute there is an original document dated 5 Heshvan, 5552 (1791) on which may be found the signatures of R' Yosef David Laniado, R' Eliyahu Abadi (see #4), and R' Ezra Sayagh (see #492) (file no. 302).

[387] **LANIADO, R' Yosef**

רבי יוסף לנייאדו

(— 1854)

Worthy scholar of Damascus. He left Damascus and settled in *Eretz Yisrael*, where he passed away on 26 Kislev, 5615 (1854). He was buried on the Mount of Olives, Jerusalem.

[388] **LANIADO AL-SAGIR, R' Ezra**

רבי עזרא לנייאדו אל־זגיר

(— 1869)

Worthy scholar and rabbi of Aram Soba. His name appears in a memorial listing of scholars on a manuscript (p. 12) of R' Yaakob Abadi (see #13). This listing indicates that a eulogy for R' Ezra was delivered on 23 Heshvan, 5629 (1869).

[389] **LEVY, R' Haim**

רבי חיים הלוי

(— 1905)

Worthy scholar of Aram Soba. He passed away on *Rosh Hodesh* Av, 5665 (1905).

[390] LEVY, R' Shimon Yisrael

רבי שמעון ישראל הלוי

(— 1937)

Worthy scholar of Aram Soba. He passed away on 2 Av, 5697 (1937). During the course of a eulogy delivered by R' Eliyahu Lofez (see #394), he was described as having fulfilled the teaching of our sages, "I grew up among scholars all of my days and never found anything as good for a person as silence" (*Pirkei Abot* 1:17). This eulogy is recorded in R' Eliyahu's book *Ben Abihayil*.

[391] LEVY (CHABOT), Mr. Morris

מר משה ישעיה (שבות) הלוי

(— 1971)

Worthy philanthropist of Aram Soba and America. He expressed his love for Torah by supporting Torah institutions in Aram Soba, Jerusalem, and New York. After immigrating to the U.S. he continued with his charitable work with renewed dedication.

He understood the necessity of capturing the interest of the community's youth and teaching them an appreciation of their heritage through coordinated social, educational, and religious services and programs. He was one of the planners of the *Shaare Zion* Congregation in Brooklyn and became its first President.

He founded the *Magen David* Community Center in Brooklyn, which became the *Magen David* Yeshiva and which has the cornerstone in his name. In addition, he directly assisted R' Abraham Kalmanowitz to raise funds for the *Mirrer Yeshiva* in Brooklyn.

He passed away in the U.S. on 9 Elul, 5731 (1971) and was brought to rest on the Mount of Olives, Jerusalem, next to his brother-in-law Mr. Isaac Shalom (see #497), whom he worked with in his lifetime. He was remembered as a major supporter of *Yeshivat Porat Yosef* and *Yeshivat Ohr HaHaim*.

[392] LEVY (MIZRAHI), R' Obadiah

רבי עובדיה הלוי (מזרחי)

(1707 — 1787)

Eminent scholar of Aram Soba. He is known for his important book *Hazon Obadiah* (Livorno 5547/1787), containing inspirational lectures based on the Torah as well as responsa. The book also contains a lengthy and revealing introduction. Published in the same binding was his book *Hazon LeMoed*, containing responsa on various topics. He included a responsum that he had found in a rubbish bin and that he identified as having been authored by R' Shemuel Pinto (see #462)), a grandson of the *Rif* (R' Yoshiyahu Pinto) (see #463).

ספר חזון למועד

נדפס פה ליוורנו יע"א

שנת וישראל

IN LIVORNO 1787.

Nella Stamperia di Gio. Vincenzo Falorni

Con Approvazione.

Title Page of Hazon LeMoed

He was born in 1707 to R' Abraham Levy and devoted his life to learning Torah. He passed away in Adar of 5547, the year in which his book was published. Among those who eulogized him was R' Yeshayah Attiah (see #119), as recorded in *Bigdei Yesha* (p. 100).

It appears that he had only one daughter, Lunah, whom he dearly loved. She had four children, two of whom died in their first week. The other two, a boy and a girl (Yosef and Veda Sasson), survived, but their mother died while they were still young. The boy Yosef Sasson was then about eight years of age.

Mr. Morris Levy (Chabot)

In the introduction to *Hazon Obadiah* he writes that his father R' Abraham Levy once happened to be in the *Bet Midrash* and saw the scholars engaged in lively discussion. This sight fascinated him so much that he resolved to sustain his own little boy in learning as long as he would live. From that day forward he personally accompanied the child to school and sat with him in the classroom from morning to night, sacrificing all other interests. "And so," writes R' Obadiah, "although I haved lived sixty years I have not paid any attention to material matters but have totally devoted myself to learning Torah." After his father passed away he continued to devote himself to Torah, but he was no longer insulated from worldly cares and had to contend with financial worries.

"Although I haved lived sixty years I have not paid any attention to material matters but have totally devoted myself to learning Torah."

During his last years he was occupied with the difficulties of preparing his book for publication. He got some help from various benefactors to pay for the printing costs, especially "Los Señores Francos," but it was not enough, partly because of the burdensome taxes involved. He ended up having to sell his entire personal library of holy books and to mortgage his house.

He also talks about the tragic loss that can befall holy writings which are not properly preserved.

He also talks about the tragic loss that can befall holy writings which are not properly preserved. He describes the occasion on which he came upon a receptacle filled with garbage, from which a paper was sticking out. This led him to dig in the dirt and discover a hand-written manuscripts of R' Shemuel Pinto (see #462) and so he included them in his book *Hazon LeMoed* as mentioned above.

[393] LOFEZ, R' Abraham

רבי אברהם לופס

(1906 —)

Worthy scholar and teacher of Jerusalem. He was the fourth son of R' Yaakob Lofez (see #400). He was born in Aram Soba in 1906 and moved to Jerusalem as a child with his parents. He studied Torah in the *yeshivot* of Jerusalem and became a teacher in the yeshiva *Porat Yosef.*

[394] LOFEZ, R' Eliyahu

רבי אליהו לופס

(1890 — 1938)

R' Eliyahu Lofez

Eminent scholar, educator, and *dayan* (judge) of Jerusalem. He was one of the outstanding scholars of the yeshiva *Porat Yosef* in the Old City for a period of about 15 years. In his later years he was a member of the Sephardic *Bet Din* of Jerusalem as well. He helped found the neighborhood of Bayit V'Gan and became its rabbi. This was a daring move as in the 1920's and 1930's Bayit V'Gan was considered very far from the city center.

His Early Years

He was the second son of R' Yaakob Lofez (see #400) and was born in Aram Soba on 10 Tevet, 5650 (1890). He became a student of R' Ezra Shayo (see #505) and was such an excellent student that in 1905 when he was only 15 years old, he was asked to teach *Gemara* to other students.

In 1911 war conditions threatened the Turkish empire because of a conflict between Turkey and Italy for the possession of Tripoli, so he moved to Egypt with his parents and brothers. There he engaged in business to help out his family in difficult times. With the end of the Italo-Turkish war in 1913, the family moved to Jerusalem. There he studied at the yeshiva *Ohel Moed*, which had just been established by R' Ezra Harari-Raful (see #304) and by R' Raphael Shelomo Laniado (see #364), who was the *Rosh Yeshiva*.

Unfortunately, World War I broke out a year later and the Turkish authorities were seeking to draft Jewish men into the army. This was a great challenge for the *Rosh Yeshiva*, R' Raphael Shelomo Laniado, who did what he could to hide his students from the attention of the authorities.

Fortunately, the Lofez family, who had Italian nationality, were exempt. However, the Turkish authorities expelled all foreign nationals from *Eretz Yisrael*. Thus, the Lofez family was forced to leave the country and travel to Anatolia (Turkey). However, R' Eliyahu managed to help a number of other Torah scholars flee from military conscription. During the next few years they moved around a lot, during which time R' Eliyahu was the informal leader of dozens of Jewish families. When the refugees arrived in a new place, they sought out the local Jewish community and it was generally R' Eliyahu who worked to obtain help for the people who depended on him.

When they arrived in the city of Ankara they received a very warm reception from the local Jewish townspeople.

Life in Turkey

When they arrived in the city of Ankara they received a very warm reception from the local Jewish townspeople, who wanted to establish a permanent fund for their support out of respect for their Torah learning. Despite their generosity, R' Eliyahu did not wish to be dependent on them, asking only for some guidance in the local ways of business. He quickly learned what he needed to know, including the Turkish language, and succeeded in earning his living.

Unfortunately, it was not long before the Turkish authorities issued a ruling that the newcomers must be dispersed through a number of towns, three or four families per town. Despite their pleas for mercy, the Lofez family was sent away to a Christian town called Bai Bazaar. As it happened, the town and the surrounding countryside were beautiful, but the townspeople were unfriendly toward Jews and refused to rent them a place to live. Finally, after much effort they managed to rent what was described as a dump of a place at the edge of the town. However, when they arrived they found palatial quarters which had once been a school. The townspeople were amazed at the good fortune of these Jews and began to show them respect. The local ruler gave them permission to engage in business and it was not long before they were admired and respected for their integrity and the dignity with which they conducted themselves.

Returning to Jerusalem

With the end of the war in 1919 the family was finally able to return to Jerusalem. They traveled by way of Constantinople, where R' Eliyahu spent time in the yeshiva, engaged in Torah discussions with R' Raphael Saban and his colleagues. The scholars of Constantinople were impressed by the erudition of the Lofez visitors and tried to get them to stay, but they were intent upon returning to Jerusalem.

From Constantinople they boarded a ship bound for Jaffa. In the hold of the ship were a number of Jewish soldiers who had been in the Turkish army and were now returning home. Most of them were seriously ill with possibly contagious diseases. R' Eliyahu saw it as his duty to go down repeatedly and do what he could for them, bringing food and water. He gave no concern for his own health, trusting in *Hashem*. Through his nursing care, many survived who would otherwise have died on that difficult voyage.

Through his nursing care, many survived who would otherwise have died on that difficult voyage.

Upon his return to Jerusalem in 1919 R' Eliyahu resumed his studies in the yeshiva *Ohel Moed*. However, after two years the financial condition of the yeshiva had deteriorated to the point where he was forced to leave and attend the respected Ashkenaz yeshiva *Torat Haim* in the Old City. He was one of the very few Sephardic scholars accepted by this venerable yeshiva.

In 1923, when the yeshiva *Porat Yosef* was opened in the Old City through the initiative of the philanthropist Yosef Abraham Shalom, he learned in that yeshiva and a few months later was hired as a lecturer in *Gemara*. He continued in this capacity for 15 years until his death.

His Torah Learning

He was intensely committed to the study of Torah throughout his life. Despite their difficult economic conditions, his parents did not push him back into the world of business, but allowed him to devote himself to learning. In his later years he refused to sleep in a bed, but napped for a few minutes at a time in a chair at his desk in the yeshiva. He would do the same while studying Kabbalah, alone in his house.

His short naps did not prevent him from dreaming, but his dreams were an expression of his deep longing for the redemption of the Jewish people. He writes that on Friday night, 8 Nissan, 5697 (1937), he had a dream in which he was shown an interpretation to the verse, *"But as for you, do not fear, My servant Yaakob, says Hashem; and do not be afraid, Yisrael; for, behold, I will save you from afar, and your descendants from the land of their captivity; and Yaakob will return, and will be at peace and tranquil, and none will make him afraid." (Yirmiyahu* 30:10). In this verse there seems to be an unnecessary duplication in the phrases, *"I will save you from afar, and your descendants from the land of their captivity."* The explanation that R' Lofez was given in the dream is that although the possibility of a good outcome may seem to you remote — that is, "מרחוק, *from afar* [not physically, but conceptually far]" — because of the many who rise up against you and prevent you from living in your land (such as the Arabs and their apologists of our day), do not think so because I will save your children from that which seems distant and will bring them from the land of their captivity.

His dreams were an expression of his deep longing for the redemption of the Jewish people.

He was following a family tradition pioneered by R' Nissim Lofez (see #396), who taught Hok LeYisrael to the community every day.

His Classes for Laymen

Each day after the morning prayers he would conduct a two-hour class for laymen in *Hok LeYisrael*, a multivolume work that provides study material in both the Written and Oral Torah for every day of the year. In this he was following a family tradition pioneered by R' Nissim Lofez (see #396), who taught *Hok LeYisrael* to the community every day.

His Public Activism

In 1920, shortly after his return to Jerusalem, Arabs rioted in the Galilee and in Jerusalem, killing a number of Jews. R' Eliyahu was concerned that a factor contributing to these tragic events might have been Jewish negligence in performing *mitzvot*. He organized a team of *sofrim* (scribes) who went from door to door checking for defects in *mezuzot* and repairing them where necessary. The *sofrim* also went into the synagogues and checked the *tefillin* of the worshippers. He set up a fund to help poor people pay for quality *tefillin*. Service for the Bukharan neighborhood began in 1921 and for the *Nahalat Sion* neighborhood in 1930.

He also recognized the need to provide a *Gemilat Hesed* loan fund for Torah scholars. He combined this with a general fund for *tefillin* and *mezuzot*, calling the combined fund *Tov VaHesed*.

His abiding faith in Hashem's help was vindicated; after that day of communal prayers in Jerusalem, many months went by without further depredations or tragedies.

When Arab riots blazed across the country in 1936, R' Eliyahu agonized over the loss of Jewish life. He was active with the rabbis of Jerusalem in organizing a public fast day. His abiding faith in *Hashem*'s help was vindicated; after that day of communal prayers in Jerusalem, many months went by without further depredations or tragedies.

In his later years he joined the Sephardic *Bet Din* of Jerusalem and used all his powers to promote peace and to resolve conflicts between individuals, especially between husbands and wives. He was also active in community affairs, presiding as chairman of the town council of the Bayit V'Gan neighborhood, in the west of Jerusalem.

His Bond with His Students

He was very close to his students in *Porat Yosef* and had a strong influence in keeping them at their Torah studies despite the academic temptations of the secular schools which were open to them. He encouraged his students to develop and publish their own *hiddushim* (original Torah thoughts). He took pride in their accomplishments and did not hesitate to show it.

His students sensed that he cared about them as a father cares for his children. As a result, his words of guidance and advice were able to penetrate to the core of their being. He chose his words carefully and it was obvious to his listeners that he had thought them through and that he spoke only when he had something really important to say.

On one occasion he told his student, R' Yehudah Sadkah (see #468), "I am happy because I have become a 'grandfather' through you. You have been my dear student and now you have become a teacher of students, giving them the same spirit that you absorbed from me."

He believed strongly in doing personal kindnesses for a fellow Jew and sought to inculcate this practice into his students. On one occasion he took a few of his students to visit an elderly man who was very ill. While they were there, he personally attended to the man's needs in order to give the students an indelible image of the right way to behave.

His Legacy

He was known to have written two books of inspirational lectures, which were published together after his death (Jerusalem 5726/1966): *Imrei Fi* and *Ben Abihayil.*

He suffered from painful illnesses throughout his life and finally passed away on 4 Tamuz, 5698 (1938) at the age of 48. A year after his death a memorial book of recollections and biographical notes titled *Mi'Yekirei Yerushalayim* (Jerusalem 5699/1939) was published by his son R' Yaakob Lofez. R' Yaakob lost his life in the battle for Jerusalem during the War of Independence on 11 Tamuz, 5708 (1948).

[395] LOFEZ, R' Ezra

רבי עזרא לופס

(1854 — 1924)

R' Ezra Lofez

Eminent scholar and rabbi of Aram Soba. He was the elder son of R' Nissim Lofez (see

#396) and was born in Aram Soba in 1854. He taught in the Talmud Torah and was engaged in printing books from original manuscripts of the scholars of Aram Soba. He was a partner with R' Yeshayah Dayan (see #203) in the management of his printing firm.

He briefly settled in Jerusalem during the period of 1913-1914, but owing to the difficult conditions at the time he was forced to return to Aram Soba. He then became involved in managing the *mikvaot* (ritual baths) of the city and supervising their *kashrut*. On his own initiative he would go around every Friday to encourage merchants and craftsmen to close their shops for *Shabbat* at an early hour.

He published the book *Sava'ah Yikarah* (Aram Soba 5665/1905) by R' Aleksander Ziskind, the author of the book *Yesod VeShoresh Ha'Avodah*. He used this opportunity to include some of the *hiddushim* (original Torah thoughts) of his father, R' Nissim, and a lecture of his own.

He also edited and prepared for publication the manuscript of the book *Shulhan HaMelech* (Aram Soba 5683/1923) by R' Shemuel Laniado (see #373).

In addition, he authored his own book of inspirational lectures entitled *Magen Ezra*. In his last years he was busy getting it published but he was unable to do so, except for an incomplete edition which was produced in Jerusalem in 5674 (1914). He passed away on 25 Iyar, 5684 (1924).

[396] **LOFEZ, R' Nissim**

רבי ניסים לופס

(1833 — 1894)

Distinguished scholar and rabbi of Aram Soba. He was born in 1833 to R' Ezra and became one of the greatest scholars of his time. When he was only 26 years of age he lost his eyesight, but did not let that stop him from continuing to study Torah with love and intensity. Because of his great piety and his understanding of human nature, he was given the task of interviewing emissaries who came to Aram Soba from *Eretz Yisrael*. Despite his lack of physical vision, it was felt that he could quickly gain insight into their true needs.

He wrote a commentary on the *Rambam*, but it has unfortunately been lost. Some of his *hiddushim* (original Torah thoughts) were published in the book *Sava'ah Yakirah* by R' Aleksander Ziskind, which was edited by his son R' Ezra Lofez (Aram Soba 5665/1905).

He passed away on 17 Iyar, 5654 (1894) and was eulogized by R' Yaakob Shaul Dweck (see #248), who described him as a complete scholar in all aspects of Torah, both the revealed and the mystical. Part of the eulogy is printed at the end of the book *Shulhan HaMelech* by R' Sadkah Houssin (see #313). He was blessed with two sons: R' Ezra and R' Yaakob Lofez (see #395 and #400).

ספר
צוואה יקרה
אשר צוה לבניו הרב המפורסם צדיק
קדוש וטהור, כמהר"ר אלכסנדר
זיסקינד זצוק"ל בעה"מ
ס' הקדוש יסוד ושורש העבודה.
ונספח אליו
דרוש יקר מדרושי א"א מו"ר הרה"ג
צדיק וחסיד פרוש וטהור כמהר"ר נסים
לופס זצ"ל. ונוסף בו איזה
חדושים משלי. ועוד דרוש אחד
ממני אני הפעוט עבדא דרבנן ותלמיד'
חשוב כאין וכאפס. והוא הצעיר עזרא
בכמהר"ן לופס ס"ט.
פה ארם צובה יע"א.
סתר"ה לפ"ק.

Title Page of Sava'ah Yikarah

[397] **LOFEZ, R' Nissim**

רבי ניסים לופס

(1884 — 1950)

Eminent scholar and rabbi of Aram Soba, Brazil, and Jerusalem. He was the eldest son of R' Yaakob Lofez (see #400) and a grandson of R' Nissim Lofez (see #396).

He was born in Aram Soba on 17 Kislev, 5645 (1884), and in 1913 at the age of 29 he moved to Jerusalem with his parents. There he briefly studied Torah under R' Raphael Shelomo Laniado (see #364) and R' Ezra Harari-Raful (see #304), becoming one of the first scholars of *Yeshivat Ohel Moed*.

R' Nissim Lofez

However, because of the difficult conditions in Jerusalem he was forced to return to Aram Soba, where he learned the arts of *shehitah* (ritual slaughtering) and *brit milah* (circumcision). He then went to South America and settled in Brazil. While there he designed and published a Jewish calendar containing the laws and customs pertaining to the Jewish holidays. He then became the rabbi of the Sephardic community in Rio de Janeiro. In this position he was engaged with providing for all the spiritual needs of the community including a *mikveh* (ritual bath), a synagogue, and a Talmud Torah.

In 1935 he returned to Jerusalem and became a Kabbalist scholar of the community. Among other things, he administered the af-

R' Shalom Lofez

fairs of the Aram Soba community in Jerusalem. He was very concerned with the poverty-stricken members of the community and regularly gave them everything he had, while maintaining a cheerful disposition. He passed away on 25 Tevet, 5710 (1950). One of his sons was R' Saadiah Lofez (#398).

[398] LOFEZ, R' Saadiah

רבי סעדיה לופס

(1925 — 1973)

Worthy scholar and public servant of Jerusalem. He was born in Brazil in 1925, the third son of R' Nissim Lofez (see #397). The family moved to Jerusalem when he was 10 years old and he immediately enrolled in

R' Saadiah Lofez standing with Mr. I. Shalom sitting below. Extreme right: R' Ezra Attiah

He leveraged his government influence to expand the support for existing yeshivot.

the yeshiva *Porat Yosef*. He was a naturally gifted person and upon completing his course of study at the yeshiva, he turned to community service in order to use his talents for the benefit of Torah.

He started by joining the staff of the Chief Rabbi of Tel Aviv-Jaffa, Rabbi Y.M. Toledano. This led to a position as a deputy general director in the Ministry of Religion. He leveraged his government influence to expand the support for existing *yeshivot* and to promote the formation of new *yeshivot*. He also worked to raise the dignity of rabbis and increase their salaries. In this way he was able to assist many poverty-stricken scholars. He also promoted the publishing of holy books and assisted authors in publishing their work.

Tragically, the good days did not last and he suffered for four years from a painful illness, finally passing away on 24 Heshvan, 5733 (1973). He left behind a young widow, the daughter of R' David Laniado (see #352), and small children.

[399] LOFEZ, R' Shalom

רבי שלום לופס

(1904 — 1994)

Activist scholar of Jerusalem and rabbi of Acre (*Acco*). He was born in 1904 in Aram Soba, the youngest son of R' Yaakob Lofez (see #400). His family moved to Jerusalem in the winter of 1908.

Memories of Jerusalem

R' Shalom had many memories from his youth in Jerusalem of old. He remembered at age 4½ being awakened early one morning to go to the funeral of R' Shmuel Salant, Chief Rabbi of Jerusalem, who passed away at the age of 93. He remembered the weeping crowds of people and it had a lasting impression on him.

He remembered walking in the streets of Meah Shearim and going into a synagogue in the middle of a *brit milah* (circumcision), and the *mohel* was none other than the saintly R' Yosef Chaim Sonnenfeld. He would tell his grandchildren years later the great impact that the sight of the *gadol hador* (leading scholar of the generation) performing a *milah* with alacrity and precision had on him.

His father once sent him to *Yeshivat Bet El* on a mission and he saw the angelic Kabbalists of old. He saw an elderly scholar standing in the corner saying *"Asher Yasar"* from a *siddur* with the *kavanot* (focused thoughts) of the *Ari'zal*, with a furrowed brow and full concentration for twenty minutes. That sight remained etched in his heart for ever.

A Developing Scholar

He was admitted to the *Yeshivat Porat Yosef* in the old city and studied under R' Raphael Shelomo Laniado (see #363). By age 19 he had mastered the entire Talmud (*Gemara*), *Shas,* and *Poskim (halachic* commentaries). He received his *semichah* (rabbinical ordination) in 1931 at the age of 26.

In 1936 he joined R' Yehudah Sadkah (see #468) in starting a youth group called "*Mekabsiel*" to strengthen religious practices among young people. They began with Torah classes at night and ultimately developed it into a full-day program. Many children were saved through their efforts.

A Developing Innnovator

He was involved in many community issues. In 1938, after finding a lot of corruption in the *Sefer Torah*, *tefillin*, and *mezuzot* trade due to unscrupulous scribes, he spearheaded the first official supervising system called *Mishmeret Stam*.

He joined the staff of *Porat Yosef* and taught in the Katamon branch. He wasn't complacent and he always looked for opportunities to help the youth that were drifting. He started an elementary school in Mosrara and was active helping the new *olim* (immigrants) from Sephardic lands.

He was one of the founders of the *Mazhirai Shabbat* organization that went around Friday afternoons to storekeepers to remind them that *Shabbat* was coming and to close their stores. He got the idea from what his father told him they had done in Aram Soba.

His Mission to Acre

In 1940 he was offered a position as rabbi of Acre (*Acco*) by R' Ben-Sion Ouziel, Chief Rabbi of Eretz Yisrael. Hacham Ezra Attiah (see #102) also suggested him for the position. At first he was undecided; it wasn't easy to leave Jerusalem. However, one night his father came to him in a dream and told him that the Hebrew word Acco (**עכו**) is the acronym for a Hebrew phrase (**עמוד כגבר והתגבר**), which means "Stand up like a man and overcome." He then realized it was his duty to take on the assignment.

To his surprise there were no daily minyanim (prayer services) in a city of a few thousand Jews, made up of new *olim* of Sephardic background. He would gather people for prayers in the morning and then go through the market in the afternoon for *Minhah* and *Arbit* services. He pressured them and charmed them and his work paid off. After a short while he built a large new synagogue and rallied the people around him. He named it *Avodat Yisrael*, "the work of the Jew," a name which he explained at the opening day: Everyone is involved with their work but they have to know that the work of the Jew is his prayer and religion.

He didn't stop there. He opened the first religious elementary school in Acre. Not long afterwards he opened a *Bet Yaakob* school for the girls. He fought for proper *kashrut* and modesty as well. His impact is felt in Acre and the entire region to this day.

Towards the end of his life he opened the yeshiva *Emet LeYaakob* in the name of his father, R' Yaakob, who had passed away in 1937 at age 69.

He passed away on 26 Heshvan, 5755 (1994).

[Editor's note: Further information on his life may be found in a biography titled, *Eved Ne'eman* (Feldheim — Jerusalem 2003), with an introduction by his son-in-law, the former Chief Rabbi of Israel, Rabbi Eliyahu Bakshi-Doron. The book also includes a lengthy introduction on the many rabbis of the Lofez family over the generations.]

R' Yaakob Lofez

[400] LOFEZ, R' Yaakob
רבי יעקב לופס
(1867 — 1937)

Eminent scholar and Kabbalist of Aram Soba and Jerusalem. In Aram Soba he was the president and director of the *Malbish Arumim* charity organization, traveling to distant places to raise funds for the organization. In addition to his other talents, he was an effective and persuasive speaker.

His Early Years in Aram Soba

He was the second son of R' Nissim Lofez (see #396) and was born in Aram Soba on *Rosh Hodesh Heshvan*, 5628 (1867). Even in his youth he was extremely pious, avoiding any worldly pleasure. The hour of midnight would never find him asleep. On one of his trips abroad he stayed with R' Moshe Franco, the Chief Rabbi of Constantinople. R' Franco was so impressed by his visitor that he said of him,

He stayed with R' Moshe Franco, the Chief Rabbi of Constantinople. R' Franco was so impressed by his visitor that he said of him, "Surely, he is one of the 36 righteous men of our generation."

"Surely, he is one of the 36 righteous men of our generation."

He was very concerned about the spiritual health of his community. He would use every opportunity to encourage the people to better themselves. Among other things, he spoke out strongly against the practice of shaving one's beard with a razor. His heartfelt and sincere words were so persuasive that he caused many to change their ways.

On Friday afternoons he would walk through the streets of Aram Soba reminding tradespeople to shut their shops early, in time for *Shabbat*.

Egypt, Eretz Yisrael, and Turkey

In 1911 conditions in Aram Soba became unsettled because of the Italo-Turkish war over the possession of Tripoli. R' Yaakob took his family to Egypt where they stayed for 2 years, before moving to Jerusalem.

In Elul 1913, at the age of 46, he moved to Jerusalem with his family and joined the Kabbalist scholars of the *Yeshivat Rehovot HaNahar.* Later, with the opening of *Yeshivat Porat Yosef* in Jerusalem, he became one of its first scholars.Unfortunately, World War I broke out a year later and the Turkish authorities expelled all foreign nationals from *Eretz Yisrael*. Thus, the Lofez family, who had Italian nationality, was forced to leave the country and travel to Anatolia (Turkey) together with a number of other refugee families.

A Silk Coat for the Jerusalem Rabbi. When R' Yaakob Lofez and the refugee families arrived in the city of Ankara they received a very warm reception from the local Jewish townspeople, who were especially respectful to R' Lofez, treating him as the representative of the Jews of Jerusalem. On one occasion he sought to buy a silk coat, suitable for a rabbi, from a certain widow. However, she asked a very high price, which he could not afford. That night her husband appeared to her in a dream and directed her to give the coat to the "Jerusalem Rabbi." She ignored the dream and so he appeared to her again the following night, threatening her with a terrible end if she did not give up the coat. This shook her up. The next morning she woke up early and sought out R' Yaakob, giving the coat to him as a gift and asking his forgiveness. This story quickly spread throughout the town, so that soon everyone in Ankara recognized the greatness of the "Jerusalem Rabbi."

In 1923 he was appointed as a senior lecturer at Porat Yosef.

With the end of the war in 1919 he finally returned to Jerusalem and in 1923 he was appointed as a senior lecturer at *Porat Yosef*.

His Joy in Mitzvot

Each morning when he recited the *Shirat HaYam* (Song of the Sea) he would be filled with the joy of the great salvation experienced by the Jewish people when they were freed from Egyptian slavery. He often could not contain himself and would go out to the veranda of the synagogue, walking back and forth so that he could better visualize himself walking on the dry land in the midst of the waters of the sea.

Each morning when he recited the Shirat HaYam (Song of the Sea) he would be filled with the joy of the great salvation experienced by the Jewish people when they were freed from Egyptian slavery.

On *Shabbat* he was thrilled to be in the presence of *Shabbat Malketa* (Queen *Shabbat*). His joy was evident in his exuberant singing of praises to *Hashem* in the *Shabbat* prayers.

He also experienced great joy each morning when he put on *tefillin*, managing to perform this defining *mitzvah* up to his dying day. He was able to demonstrate his love for the *mitzvah* during his final illness by helping a patient in the next bed put on *tefillin*.

His Legacy

He passed away on 17 Kislev, 5697 (1937), leaving four scholarly sons: R' Nissim, R' Eliyahu (see #394), R' Abraham, and R' Shalom, who was the rabbi of Acre (*Acco*). Even in his final moments his mind was still totally clear and he asked members of his family to immerse him in a *mikveh*.

[401] **LOFEZ, R' Yitzhak**

רבי יצחק לופס

(17th century)

Eminent scholar and rabbi of Aram Soba. He wrote a book dealing with the theological arguments posed by Christian missionaries. This book, entitled *Kur Mesaref Ha'Emunot U'Mareh Ha'Emet*, remained in manuscript form for about 150 years. In 1847, when it was in the possession of R' Yitzhak Altaras and his father-in-law R' Aharon Altaras, it was finally published in Metz by the latter.

R' Yitzhak had a son named Aharon, who had a son named Ezra. R' Ezra had many children, but all died in infancy. One day, when the wife of R' Ezra was pregnant she went to the town of Tedef to prostrate herself at the grave of Ezra HaSofer and pray for a healthy child. She stayed there for the remainder of her pregnancy. The merit of that righteous man helped, as she gave birth to a viable child, who was named Nissim (see #396).

[402] **MALEH, R' Yaakob (Jacob)**

רבי יעקב א'למאליח

(1882 — 1961)

Worthy scholar of Aram Soba and New York. He authored the book *Vayisa Yaakob* in which he included some of the *hiddushim* (original Torah thoughts) of his father-in-law, R' Ezra Hamway (see #272).

He was born in Aram Soba in 1882 to R' Shemuel Maleh. R' Yaakob later described his father as "a pursuer of *mitzvot*, who excelled particularly in his kindness to others." His mother Mazal was an unusual woman who fasted every Monday and Thursday and never missed a Thursday-evening session in the synagogue, spending the entire night praying. She would provide the Torah scholars with food and delicacies, entreating *Hashem* that her own children should grow up to be His true servants and Torah scholars.

When he reached the age of 17 his mother was instrumental in arranging for his marriage to the daughter of R' Ezra Hamway. He remained forever grateful to her for setting him on the path of Torah.

He studied Torah and the laws of *shehitah* (ritual slaughter) under his distinguished father-in-law, R' Ezra Hamway. While still in Aram Soba, he began work on the book *Vayisa Yaakob* (Jerusalem 5716/1956) consisting of an anthology of *hiddushim*, sermons, and lectures. It also includes some of the *hiddushim* of his father-in-law. In addition, the book contains two of the eulogies that were delivered after R' Hamway's death. One is by R' Yaakob Kassin (see #330), the rabbi of the congregation *Magen David* in Brooklyn. The other is by R' Yaakob Maleh.

ספר
כור מצרף האמונות ומראה
האמת
...
ולדעת מה שתשיב
לאפיקורס.
METZ,
IMPRIMERIE DE J. MAYER SAMUEL, QUAI SAINT-PIERRE, 15.

Title Page of Kur Mesaref Ha'Emunot U'Mareh Ha'Emet

An English translation of *Vayisa Yaakob* was published by *OROT* Institute of Lakewood, New Jersey, in 2004 through the efforts of his children and grandchildren.

R' Yaakob Maleh (also known as Mr. Jacob Maleh) moved to the United States, where he completed work on *Vayisa Yaakob*. In America his wife gave birth to a son who subsequently passed away, and to a daughter Sadie (who later married her uncle, Jack Hamway, son of Hacham Ezra). When Jacob's wife Senyar also passed away at a young age, R' Hamway sent his next daughter, Jamile, to America to marry him.

Mr. Jacob Maleh

Mr. Jacob Maleh passed away in New York on 14 Elul, 5721 (1961). He and his wife Jamile were blessed with two worthy sons: Yitzhak Mordechai (Mr. Irving Maleh) and Moshe (Mr. Moe Maleh).

[403] **MANSOUR, R' Yosef**

רבי יוסף מנצור

(— 1943)

Worthy scholar and merchant of Aram Soba and Brooklyn. In his later years he moved to the United States where he was known for his unusual and beautiful Torah reading. When he officiated at the *tebah (bimah)*, there was no one equal to his intensity, his clarity, and his inspiration. He made a living by selling religious articles. R' Yosef passed away on 12 Tamuz, 5703 (1943).

He left four sons — Mourad, Michelle, Isaac, and Eli — and a daughter, Mary, and many prominent granchildren following in his

R' Eliyahu Ma'arabi

Under the guidance of R' Dweck he soon became one of the select few who prayed with the special kavanot (meditations) of the Rashash.

He was active in good works and became the head of Sedakah U'Marpeh committee, which provided medical assistance to the needy of Aram Soba.

ways. Two grandsons were given his name: Joseph M. Mansour and Joseph E. (father of R' Eli Mansour.)

[404] **MA'ARABI, R' Eliyahu**

רבי אליהו מערבי

(1873 —)

Worthy scholar and Kabbalist of Aram Soba. He was born in Damascus in 1873 to R' Moshe Ma'arabi. He would have liked to spend all his time learning Torah, but was forced to earn his living as a tailor. Although he tried leaving for Jerusalem on a number of occasions, circumstances always prevented him from doing so. One day he simply decided to begin a fast, which would not end until he left Damascus for Jerusalem. And so he fasted for 40 days until he finally achieved his objective, which happend to be just before the outbreak of World War I.

In Jerusalem he continued to work at his chosen profession until one day when he was sitting in the *Bet Midrash* and got into a conversation with R' Haim Shaul Dweck (see #228). R' Dweck persuaded him to leave his occupation and devote himself to learning Torah and Kabbalah. He advanced very quickly in these studies under the guidance of R' Dweck and soon became one of the select few who prayed with the special *kavanot* (meditations) of the *Rashash* (R' Shalom Sharabi).

In 1924 he prepared the book *Sama D'Hayi* by R' Raphael Manirsi for publication and added an appendix of his own on observance of *shemirat habrit* (guarding oneself from immorality). He dedicated the book to the memory of his son R' Moshe Ma'arabi, who had passed away at a young age on 22 Av, 5682 (1922).

(405) **MA'ARABI, R' Raphael Menahem**

רבי רפאל מנחם מערבי

(1863 — 1933)

Eminent scholar and Kabbalist of Damascus and Jerusalem. He was born in Damascus in 1863 and became one of the prominent scholars of the city. In about 1923 he moved to Jerusalem, where he was counted among the most renowned Torah scholars in both the mystic and revealed aspects of Torah. He passed away on 23 Tevet, 5693 (1933) and was buried on the Mount of Olives in Jerusalem.

[406] **MARCUS, R' Natan**

רבי נתן מרקוס

(— 1920)

Worthy scholar and rabbi of Aram Soba. One of his responsa was published in the book *Peh Eliyahu* of R' Eliyahu Hamway (see #271). He also contributed a responsum to the journal *HaMe'asef* by R' Ben-Sion Kouenka (2nd year, no. 73). The responsum was sent from Aram Soba on 6 Tevet, 5657 (1897) and was signed R' Natan Ezra Marcus, among others.

He was active in good works and became the head of *Sedakah U'Marpeh* committee, which provided medical assistance to the needy of Aram Soba. He passed away on 23 Tamuz, 5680 (1920).

[407] **MARCUS, R' Shelomo**

רבי שלמה מרקוס

(— 1905)

Worthy scholar of Aram Soba. He was characterized by his in-depth Torah knowledge, his ability to sing sweet *pizmonim* (hymns), and his activities in support of the soup kitchen for the poor. He passed away on 23 Tamuz, 5665 (1905).

[408] **MARINI, R' Yosef**

רבי יוסף מאריני

(— 1825)

Worthy scholar and rabbi of Aram Soba. He was the son of Señor Abraham Hai Marini, a wealthy and scholarly man. His father-in-law was R' Yosef Shamah (see #502). He also had a scholarly brother named R' David Marini. He passed away early in the month of Adar, 5585 (1825) and was was eulogized by R' Yitzhak Attiah (see #120), as recorded in his book *Vayikra Yitzhak* (Lectures, page 105b).

[409] **MASLATON (TARAB), R' (Ben-) Sion**

רבי בן ציון טראב־מסלתון הכהן

(1915 — 1999)

Eminent rabbi and spiritual leader of the *Ahi Ezer* Congregation in Brooklyn for 40 years.

He was born in 1915 in Damascus to R' Mordechai and Sarah Maslaton (see #409). He was preceded by three boys, all of whom died at a young age, so that when Hacham Ben-Sion was born he was held 24 hours a day, until his *brit milah* (circumcision). At his *brit milah*, his father named him Ben-Sion, the son of Zion, to suggest that this child belongs to *Hashem*. After he grew up, people generally referred to him as "Hacham Sion."

When he was 5 years old, his parents immigrated to the United States and he grew up in New York.

As a young boy, he was taught by his father how to be a scribe, that is, how to write Torah scrolls, *tefillin* and *mezuzot*. He learned *shehitah* (kosher slaughtering) from his brother-in-law, Mr. Morris Bibi, and from the Chief Rabbi, R' Yaakob Kassin (see #330).

When asked to recall what stood out about him in her mind, his wife said, "From the day we got married he was always with a *sefer* (holy book). He left with a *sefer* to work and came back with a *sefer* from work. When he was home he continued learning."

In 1959 his father, who had been the spiritual leader of the *Ahi Ezer* congregation in Brooklyn for over 50 years, passed away and Hacham Sion was asked to take his place. This required a major change in lifestyle as he was not comfortable with the respect and honors associated with a rabbinical position.

Throughout his life he was a loving person, who cared for the needs of other human beings. When a person who spoke only English came to his *Gemara* class, which was given in Arabic, he would make a point of repeating the text and explaining it in English.

Shortly before *Purim*, one of his congregants was mugged and beaten up. This affected the man's ability to concentrate so that when the *Megillah* was read in the synagogue on *Purim*, he told a friend that he was not sure if he had heard all the words. Hacham Sion overheard this remark and immediately took him to another room, where he read the entire *Megillah* for him.

He passed away on 17 Tishrei, 5759 (1999). Before he died, his son R' Mordechai started a congregation and *kollel* in his name, *Keter Sion*, to continue his teachings and preserve his memory.

Hacham Ben-Sion Maslaton (Tarab) with R' Yitzchak Kaduri.

[410] MASLATON (TARAB), R' Ezra

רבי עזרא טראב־מסלתון הכהן

(20th century)

Eminent scholar and *Av Bet Din* (Chief Judge) of Damascus. He was the son of R' Eliyahu Maslaton and the father of R' Yehudah Haim Maslaton, the *Av Bet Din* (Chief Judge) of Egypt (see #413). He authored two books of inspirational lectures: *Sefer Ezra* (Jerusalem 5673/1913) and *Vayomer Ezra* (Jerusalem 5674/1914). He also authored two books of responsa: *Shaare Ezra* and *Mili D'Ezra*. He was a colleague of R' Yitzchak Abulafia (see # 35) and corresponded with R' Yaakob Shaul Elyashar.

R' Eliyahu Maslaton

[411] MASLATON (TARAB), R' Mordechai

רבי מרדכי טראב־מסלתון הכהן

(1876 — 1959)

Eminent rabbi and spiritual leader of the *Ahi Ezer* Congregation in Brooklyn for over 50 years.

He was born in 1876 in Damascus to R' Yosef and Rivkah Maslaton. He became a *hazzan* (cantor) and *ba'al koreh* (reader of the Torah) in the *Ahi Ezer* synagogue of Damascus. He studied under R' Yosef Antebi (see #85).

His life was one of extreme poverty. There were even times when his wife left empty pots on the stove to make it seem as though they had food in the house and thereby avoid the embarrassment of total destitution.

In 1920 he immigrated to New York to become a rabbi in the synagogue that his brother-in-law, Basil Cohen, was instrumental in founding. They called the synagogue, *Ahi Ezer Damasek*, which later became just *Ahi Ezer*. R' Mordechai's spiritual duties kept him fully occupied around the clock, studying Torah, providing guidance to his flock, and teaching classes of all ages at the Talmud Torah and the congregation. On many days his wife or children would have to bring him supper.

R' Mordechai Maslaton

R' Mordechai Maslaton (left), R' Yaakob Kassin (right), Morris Bibi (center)

Toward the end of his life, a man came to him with his son David and said, "Rabbi, give me a blessing so that he will stop stuttering." R' Mordechai gave his blessing and the very next day the boy stopped stuttering. That boy grew up to become the famous Rabbi David Ozeri.

He was a close friend of R' Yaakob Kassin (see #330), the rabbi of the *Shaare Zion* congregation. The two friends worked together over a period of 25 years to prepare the book *Bet Yaakob* of his brother R' Yaakob Maslaton (see #412) for printing. R' Mordechai did not live to see the completion of their efforts, passing away on 21 Adar, 5719 (1959). Finally, his son Hacham Sion (see #409), who took over his father's rabbinical position with *Ahi Ezer*, completed the task and the first volume was published in 1964. He helped publish his brother's book, *She'erit Yaakob,* as well.

R' Mordechai's spiritual duties kept him fully occupied around the clock. On many days his wife or children would have to bring him supper.

"Just as throughout his life he thanked people, so it was at the end of his life. After the tevilah was finished, he lifted his hand in gratitude."

Toward the end of R' Sion's life he worked on publishing a large portion of his father's writings and called the book, *Doresh Tob*. However, he passed away before it appeared in print.

At the end of his life, R' Mordechai went to Florida for a vacation, with the intention of returning to New York in time for a dinner which the synagogue had planned in his honor, to thank him for all the years of service. Tragically, he died the day before the dinner. This was consistent with his lifelong habit of running away from honors.

While he was in Florida, a man came crying to him, "Rabbi, my tree stopped giving fruit. Please give it a blessing so that it should start giving fruit again." He gave his blessing and after that the tree always gave an abundance of fruit.

When R' Mordechai died, R' Kassin did the *tevilah* (ritual purification) on his body and said afterwards, "Just as throughout his life he thanked people, so it was at the end of his life. After the *tevilah* was finished, he lifted his hand in gratitude."

R' Yaakob Maslaton

His sons were Joe (father of R' Murray Maslaton of *Emek HaTorah*), Hacham Sion (see #409), and Jack. His daughters were Rachel married to Ezra Tawil, Bahia married to Phil Kubie, Rebecca married to Morris Bibi, and Esther married to Nouri Dayan. His many grandchildren and great-grandchildren continue to follow his example of devotion to Torah and *mitzvot*.

[412] MASLATON (TARAB), R' Yaakob

רבי יעקב טראב־מסלתון הכהן

(1862 — 1923)

Distinguished scholar and *Av Bet Din* (Chief Judge) of Beirut. Because of his high position, wherever he walked, R' Yaakob was guarded by two men with guns. In addition to his published works (described below), he actively corresponded with rabbis in other cities on *halachic* (legal) issues, especially the *Rishon LeSion* (Chief Rabbi of *Eretz Yisrael*), R' Yaakob Shaul Elyashar.

He passed away 22 Tevet, 5683 (1923) and was eulogized by R' David Sutton (see #538), as recorded in *Ya'aleh HaDas* (p. 147). At his funeral, his body was never put down on ground. It was carried all the way to the cemetery. He was blessed with two sons: R' David and R' Yechezkel.

He authored a number of scholarly works, among which were two books of inspirational lectures that were published in Jerusalem seven years after his death: *Debar Tob* and Volume I of *She'erit Yaakob*. Volume II of *She'erit Yaakob*, consisting of responsa, commentary on the *Rambam*, and laws of divorce, was published in Jerusalem two years later.

His brother was R' Mordechai Tarab-Maslatan (see #411), rabbi of the *Ahi Ezer* congregation in Brooklyn. R' Mordechai worked with R' Yaakob Kassin (see #330) over a period of 25 years to prepare another book by R' Yaakob Maslaton, *Bet Yaakob*, for publication. After R' Mordechai's death, his son, R' Sion, continued the holy work and in 1964 with the help of good-willed people of the community published the first volume, containing inspirational lectures on the Torah. The second volume, including an introduction by R' Ovadiah Yosef, Chief Rabbi of Israel, was published eight years later. Both volumes were printed in Jerusalem.

[413] MASLATON (TARAB), R' Yehudah Haim

רבי יהודה חיים טראב־מסלתון הכהן

(— 1945)

Eminent scholar and *Av Bet Din* (Chief Judge) of Egypt. He was the son of R' Ezra Maslaton, the *Av Bet Din* of Damascus (see #410).

His published works are as follows:

- *She'erit Yehudah* (Cairo 5698/1938), responsa, supplemented with *Vaya'al Eliyahu*, a book of inspirational lectures by his grandfather R' Eliyahu Yaakob Tarab-Maslaton.
- *Vezot LeYehudah* (Cairo 5697/1937), responsa on the four parts of the *Shulhan Aruch*, supplemented with *Vayomer Yehudah*, a book of inspirational lectures. He received an approbation from R' Haim Nahum, the Chief Rabbi of Egypt.

[414] MATALON, R' Ezra

רבי עזרא מטלון

(— 1888)

Martyred young scholar of Aram Soba. He and his brother R' Yehezkel were lynched by a riotous mob in the dead of night on 24 Iyar, 5648 (1888).

[415] MEHANAH, R' Moshe

רבי יוסף מחנה

(— 1939)

Worthy scholar and Kabbalist of Aram Soba. During World War I he traveled to Mexico, where he was a teacher. He passed away on 29 Adar, 5699 (1939).

[416] MENAGED, R' Shelomo

רבי שלמה מנג'ד

(19th century)

Worthy scholar and teacher of Aram Soba. He was originally a rabbi in Damascus and came to Aram Soba to be a teacher in the Talmud Torah. He was later joined by his son, R' Yosef Menaged (see #417). He had a reputation for devoting himself to the welfare of his students and teaching each boy according to his merit, without regard to family wealth or connection.

He composed the hymn *"Ohr Sah U'Mesuhesah,"* which is part of the special prayers *(bakashot)* of Aram Soba. At his death he was eulogized by R' Yaakob Abadi (see #13) and R' David Kassin (see #322). He was blessed with four sons: R' Nissim, R' Yosef (see #417), R' Moshe, and R' Ezra.

[417] MENAGED, R' Yosef

רבי יוסף מנג'ד

(— 1917)

Worthy scholar and teacher of Aram Soba. Both he and his father, R' Shelomo Menaged (see #416), taught in the Aram Soba Talmud Torah. He passed away in Jerusalem on 24 Iyar, 5677 (1917).

[418] MISHAN, R' Eliyahu

רבי אליהו משען

(— 1882)

Distinguished Kabbalist of Aram Soba and performer of miracles. He was born to R' Abraham Mishan, a pious and righteous man. Despite his brilliance in Kabbalah, he earned his livelihood by teaching young children. He earned renown for his book on Kabbalah, *Sefat Emet* (Jerusalem 5664/1904), which was published through the efforts of R' Shaul Kassin (see #327) and R' Ezra Harari-Raful (see #304). An introduction, full of praises for the author, was written by a number of scholars and rabbis of Aram Soba who were residing in Jerusalem at the time the book was published.

Among those who turned to him with questions on the mystical aspects of Torah were the Kabbalists R' Yedidyah Raphael Abulafia of Jerusalem and R' Moshe Galante, the Chief Rabbi of Damascus. He was a colleague of the Kabbalist R' Nissim Harari-Raful (see #305), author of the book *Alei Nahar*. R' Haim Shaul Dweck (see #228) considered

R' Yehuda Haim Maslaton

R' Shelomo Menaged had a reputation for devoting himself to the welfare of his students and teaching each boy according to his merit, without regard to family wealth or connection.

R' Mordechai worked with R' Yaakob Kassin (see #330) over a period of 25 years to prepare another book by R' Yaakob Maslaton, Bet Yaakob, for publication.

Title Page of Sefat Emet

ספר

שפת אמת

אשר חברתי אני הצעיר אליהו משען המכונה זגיר

הרושים מני אנא דארעא קטינא. נלעה לשון אין בינה-לא דעת ולא תבונה. בריה קלה כתיתי מכתת שיעוריה. גברא דלא גמיר ולא סביר קטן הכמות וקטן האיכות זעירא ולאו מן תלמידייא על ה' אלהיו מובטח ומשען

אליהו משען

בן בכר אברהם משען זגיר

נדפס

פעה"ק ירושלם תובב"א

שנת תרס"ד לפ"ק

R' Haim Shaul Dweck (see #228) considered him his teacher in Kabbalah.

him his teacher in Kabbalah. The prayer in the handwritten *siddur* that is illustrated here was written by R' Mishan. He passed away on 20 Adar 2, 5642 (1882).

Siddur in original handwriting of R' Eliyahu Mishan

Some of his *hiddushim* (original Torah thoughts) were published in the book *Me-Halab Ha'Aretz* (Jerusalem 5726/1966) of R' Yeshayah Dayan (see #203). His other published works are:

Darkei Emet (Jerusalem 5749/1989). *Hiddushim* on Torah, *Tanach*, and *Gemara* following both the revealed and mystical approaches. Also included are eulogies. This was bound together with an updated edition of *Sefat Emet*.

Yad Eliyahu (Jerusalem 5749/1989). Responsa and *hiddushim* on the *Gemara*, *Rambam*, and *Shulhan Aruch*. This was bound with the book *Sedek VeShalom* containing responsa on the teachings of the *Ari'zal* (R' Yitzhak Luria) and the *Rashash* (R' Shalom Sharabi).

[419] MISHAN, R' Michael

רבי מיכאל משען

(— 1913)

Eminent rabbi and Kabbalist of Aram Soba. He passed away on 8 Av, 5673 (1913).

[420] MISHAN, R' Mordechai Haim

רבי מרדכי חיים משען

(— 1925)

Worthy rabbi and *darshan* (lecturer) of Damascus. He passed away on 28 Iyar, 5685 (1925), apparently childless.

[421] MISHANIEH, R' Ezra

רבי עזרא משענייה

(1903 — 1985)

Hacham Ezra Mishanieh, 1963

Worthy Talmud Torah teacher of New York. He was born in Aram Soba in 1903 to Yitzhak and Sarah Mishanieh. Orphaned at a young age, he attributed his education to his grandmother who worked as a cook at the *Kitab* (Talmud Torah) of R' Yitzhak Aboud (see #33). Each day she took him with her to the *Kitab* and in time he became a prize student. However, he was very poor and learning was his life.

He emigrated alone to America in 1921. Upon his arrival in New York he immediately began tutoring young boys and started his life of teaching. He taught three generations of the Syrian community at the *Magen David* Talmud Torah, which was like home to him.

In the early 1900's there was no Jewish day school for Sephardic children. Young boys attended Talmud Torah classes in the late afternoon after a full day at the local public school. Teachers like R' Ezra were poorly paid and yet, despite great obstacles, they succeeded in imparting the basic skills of Torah learning to their students.

Operating on a shoestring, he managed to turn simple items into prizes and use them as motivational tools. For example, he would take pencils and crack them into pieces and sharpen them. He would take books from the *genizah* (container for old and discarded *sefarim*) and rebind them. At the same time he was known for maintaining a disciplined learning environment. Boys were not allowed to go home until they knew the material.

R' Ezra always received the difficult class. Although some of his students at the time didn't appreciate his teaching, years later they would comment, "If not for him I wouldn't know how to read."

During his off-hours from teaching he served the community in many other ways, generally without remuneration. He ran the youth *minyan* (prayer group) at the *Shaare Zion* synagogue, visited the sick, and comforted the mourners. Some people of the community tried to persuade him to get a license to officiate at weddings. However, he refused, saying, "Our community has rabbis; I don't want to take away their livelihood." He also served as the *hazzan* (cantor) for the high holidays in the *Bnai Yosef shul* on Avenue P and blew the *shofar* there.

In 1931 he married Bahia, the daughter of Aslan Esses. They were blessed with two daughters: Sally Ashkenazi and Renee Enker. R' Ezra passed away on 22 Heshvan, 5746 (1985).

[422] MISSRY, R' Ezra

רבי עזרא מצרי

(19th century)

Worthy scholar of Tiberias. He was born in Aram Soba and moved to Tiberias. However, because of his difficult economic circumstances he was forced to seek help. Therefore in 1830 the rabbis of Tiberias wrote to R' Haim Mordechai Labaton (see #336), asking him to approach the philanthropists of Aram Soba for help.

[423] MIZRAHI, R' Moshe

רבי משה מזרחי

(20th century)

Worthy Talmud Torah teacher of New York. In addition to being a modest and conscientious teacher, he served as *hazzan* (cantor) in the Orchard Street synagogue on the Lower East Side, whenever needed.

His children were activists in the community. One son organized a *Tehillim* class in the *Shaare Zion* Congregation, which met every *Shabbat* for almost 40 years. The attendance reached over 100 people weekly. Another son followed in his father's footsteps as a *hazzan*. A third son (Yitzhak) became known for his benevolence to people in need.

[424] MIZRAHI, R' Moshe Ezra

רבי משה עזרא מזרחי

(1863 — 1955)

Chief Rabbi and *Av Bet Din* (Chief Judge) of Aram Soba. R' Moshe became the last of the rabbis of Aram Soba to remain in Syria after the emigration of most of the community following the declaration of the State of Israel.

He served on the *Bet Din* together with R' Shaul Dweck (see #239), R' Eliyahu Hamway (see #271), who was the *Av Bet Din* until 1916, and R' Ezra Hamway (see #272), who was the *Av Bet Din* until 1935. After R' Ezra Hamway left for *Eretz Yisrael*, R' Moshe assumed the *Av Bet Din* position, serving with R' Ezra Shayo (see #505).

His Younger Years

He was born in Aram Soba in 1863, a son of R' Ezra Mizrahi. His father passed away before he was born and he was therefore named after him. He was educated in the Torah institutions of the city. His teachers were R' Haim Cohen, R' Yitzhak Bekhor Mizrahi (see #432), and R' Moshe Swed (see #573). He was a colleague of R' Shaul Kassin (see #327) and of R' Shalom Hedaya (see #310), who became his father-in-law. He began his studies of Kabbalah with R' Abraham Antebi (see #64), but after a short while R' Abraham said to him, "You no longer need me. You have already exceeded me."

In 1944 the Admor (Grand Rabbi) of Belz, R'Aharon Rokeach, was an honored guest in R' Moshe's home.

As a young man of 27 he was already worthy enough for his signature to appear on a document together with that of R' Abraham Ades (see #37) and R' Meir Laniado (see #358).

After the death of his first wife, he married the daughter of R' Shalom Hedaya (see #310), who gave birth to a son and a daughter. However, it was not long before this wife also died. The son born to his second marriage, R' Shalom Yitzhak Mizhrahi (see #429), was brought up in the house of R' Hedaya and became a *dayan* (judge) in the Appeals Court in Jerusalem.

His selfless act of sanctifying the Name of Hashem soon became known among the entire population of Aram Soba, both Jew and gentile.

Worthy Visitors

R' Moshe spent all of his time in the *Bet Midrash*, studying and teaching, from midnight until after *Tefillat Arbit*. His eminent son, R' Shalom Yitzhak, once came to visit him in Aram Soba. R' Moshe happened to be teaching a *shiur* (Torah class) when his son arrived. Although R' Moshe had not seen his son for many years, he did not interrupt the class, but got up to see him after the *shiur* was over. They subsequently spent many months learning together. R' Moshe had such respect for his son that he would stand up whenever his son came into the room.

In 1944 the *Admor* (Grand Rabbi) of Belz, R' Aharon Rokeach, escaped from Europe and came to Aram Soba on his way to *Eretz Yisrael*. While in Aram Soba he was an honored guest in R' Moshe's home.

His Heroism

In 1948, Arab mobs were rampaging throughout Aram Soba, burning and looting synagogues and Jewish property. R' Moshe was in the Great Synagogue of Aram Soba learning To-

R' Moshe Ezra Mizrahi

rah at the time, but did not allow himself to be disturbed by what was happening. As the noise of the approaching mob grew louder, all of the other scholars who were there ran out in fear. However, R' Moshe ignored the sounds and continued studying until the mob broke in with cries of "Kill the Jew!"

R' Rahamim Mizrahi

Up until that point the Arabs had always treated R' Moshe with respect because he had a reputation for integrity and wisdom. However, seeing him there now, they yelled at him to get out and they made their preparations to burn the building and the holy Torah scrolls. R' Moshe refused to budge and said firmly that he would not move from the spot even if they burned the building around him. Ultimately, they did succeed in their destruction, but they did not harm him in any way. His selfless act of sanctifying the Name of *Hashem* soon became known among the entire population of Aram Soba, both Jew and gentile. His courage became an inspiration to all of his people.

His Later Years

In his later years R' Moshe was accompanied to and from the *Bet Midrash* by R' David Boka'i. However, as R' Moshe became increasingly frail, R' David began to fear that one day R' Moshe would trip and fall. And so R' David decided to stop accompanying him; he did not want to be responsible for a tragedy. That night he had a dream in which the following verse was shown to him: "The Torah of his G-d is in his heart; his footsteps will not falter" (*Tehillim 37*:31). This experience restored R' David's confidence and he resumed accompanying R' Moshe as before, trusting that *Hashem* would protect him.

His Legacy

R' Moshe passed away on 6 Av, 5715 (1955). On the day of his funeral all work in Aram Soba stopped and he was mourned by every Jew of the city.

A number of his *hiddushim* (original Torah thoughts) appeared in the journal *HaMe'asef* published in Jerusalem by R' Ben-Sion Kouenka. However, he left many other *hiddushim* which were not published in his lifetime. The author of the book *Ohalei Shem* mentioned the fact that R' Moshe had a treasure-house of works that could benefit the world but he could not afford to publish them.

In 2002 R' Rahamim Moshe Shayo published a book containing many of the *hiddushim* of R' Moshe. Among other things it deals with questions of partnerships with non-Jews and whether it is permitted to wear glasses when one goes out on *Shabbat*. The book was named *Dibrei Moshe* to correspond with the book *Dibrei Shalom*, written by his eminent son, R' Shalom Yitzhak Mizrahi.

[425] MIZRAHI, R' Nissim

רבי נסים מזרחי

(— 1665)

Holy rabbi and miracle worker of Aram Soba. Because of his reputation for performing miracles, many people came to pray at his grave. A tradition developed that all those who prayed at his grave for relief of pain and suffering would be immediately answered. He passed away on 18 Av, 5425 (1665).

One of R' Nissim' *hiddushim* (original Torah thoughts) is quoted in the book *Hebel Bnei Yehudah* (p. 42a) by R' Yehudah Habilo, who lived for a time in Aram Soba. That book received approbations from Aram Soba scholars R' Shelomo Laniado, the elder (see #368) and R' Yosef Dayan (see #209).

[426] MIZRAHI, R' Rahamim

רבי רחמים מזרחי

(20th century)

Worthy scholar and public servant of Aram Soba. Among his other positions he served as the manager of the Orphanage Home of Aram Soba. He was mentioned in the writings of R' Hizkiah Shabbetai, the Chief Rabbi of Aram Soba (see #495).

[427] MIZRAHI, R' Shabbetai

רבי שבתי מזרחי

(— 1924)

Saintly scholar of Aram Soba. He had a reputation for being the first person in the *Bet Midrash* each morning. He passed away on 7 Kislev, 5684 (1924).

[428] MIZRAHI, R' Shalom

רבי שלום מזרחי

(19th century)

Worthy scholar and rabbi of Aram Soba. In 1865 he joined other rabbis of Aram Soba in signing the approbation for the first book-printing initiative of the city (see Document Section, Document No. 25), which was introduced by R' Abraham Sasson and his sons (see #476). He was the father of R' Yitzhak Bekhor Mizrahi (see #432).

[429] MIZRAHI, R' Shalom Yitzhak

רבי שלום יצחק מזרחי

(1920 — 1995)

Eminent scholar and rabbi of Jerusalem. He was born in Aram Soba in 1920, the only son of R' Moshe Ezra Mizrahi, the last Chief Rabbi and *Av Bet Din* (Chief Judge) of the city (see #424). His mother was Rina, daughter of R' Shalom Hedaya (see #310). He was named after his grandfather R' Shalom and after his great-grandfather, R' Yitzhak Labaton (see #340).

His Younger Years

When he was still a baby his mother became very ill and it became necessary for her to go to *Eretz Yisrael* for medical treatment. However, the treatment was unsuccessful and she succumbed to her illness, passing away at the young age of 28, when he was only 2 years old. His grandfather R' Shalom Hedaya, who lived in Jerusalem, had formed a close friendship with his father R Moshe Ezra and that is how it came about that R' Moshe Ezra married R' Shalom's daughter. After she died the two friends engaged in urgent discussions about the child's future. Both R' Shalom and his wife Sarah argued that it would be best for the child to be raised in the elevated spiritual environment of Jerusalem. They persuaded R' Moshe Ezra to entrust the child to their faithful hands and so they brought him up as though he were their own.

Growing up in the home of R' Shalom Hedaya, who was an intensely pious Kabbalist and a *dayan* (judge) in the Sephardic *Bet Din* of Jerusalem, was an inspirational experience for the young boy. The influence of his grandfather and mentor was readily noticeable and it was not long before his friends called him *"Shalom HaHasid,"* Shalom the Pious. It was apparent that a promising future as a great scholar lay ahead of him. The child became greatly attached to R' Shalom, and they were frequently seen walking together. The bonding of age and youth was an inspiring sight for the people of the neighborhood.

R' Shalom Yitzhak Mizrahi

His Teachers

In 1938 at the age of 18 he was admitted to the illustrious yeshiva *Porat Yosef* in the Old City of Jerusalem. There he studied under the *Rosh Yeshiva*, R' Ezra Attiah (see #102), and under the scholars R' Yaakob Ades (see #41) and R' Eliyahu Lofez (see #394). In the same year he married Matilda, the daughter of R' Ezra Abadi Shayo (see #505). After his marriage he became a lecturer in *Porat Yosef* and in the yeshiva *Shaare Sion*, established by the great R' Ben-Sion Azulai. His lectures were famous for their thoroughness and depth, and the conceptual approach that he imparted to his students.

Besides his formal studies, he had the benefit of living in an area of Jerusalem which was home to many of the great scholars of the day. Even as a young boy he sought them out for guidance. Among these were R' David Jungreis, R' David Levin, R' Aryeh Levin, and R' Pinchas Epstein (Head of the Jerusalem *Bet Din*). R' Epstein was impressed by the evident earnestness of the young boy, especially the intensity of his prayers. He asked the boy to show him the *hiddushim* (Torah thoughts) he had written in his notebook and liked what he saw. He encouraged the boy to keep it up and to record every new thought that he developed.

R' Shalom was also in close contact with R' Tzvi Pesach Frank, the Chief Rabbi of Jerusalem, who was one of the great *halachic* authorities of the time. He would turn to R' Frank whenever he had a *halachic* question that needed resolution.

Seeing His Father Again

When his grandfather passed away in 1945, he traveled to Aram Soba to see his father for the first time after a separation of 24 years. R' Shalom was then only a young man of 25, but he already had the reputation of being a brilliant scholar. His father, who was

The influence of his grandfather and mentor was readily noticeable and it was not long before his friends called him "Shalom HaHasid," Shalom the Pious.

Father and son spent three happy months in each other's company, learning Torah together.

then about 82 years old and the Chief Rabbi of Aram Soba, would stand up out of respect for R' Shalom's Torah knowledge whenever his son entered the synagogue. Father and son spent three happy months in each other's company, learning Torah together.

His Prayers

R' Shalom's prayers were marked by great intensity of feeling. He would choose a quiet corner of the synagogue so that he could give the prayers his complete concentration. Many who saw him at his prayers received an impression that stayed with them for a lifetime. When R' Shalom prayed it seemed almost as though he had never said that prayer before.

R' Eliyahu Lofez (see #394) would refer to his way of praying as a model of what everyone should try to achieve.

During the period when he was studying in *Porat Yosef*, his teacher, R' Eliyahu Lofez (see #394), would refer to his way of praying as a model of what everyone should try to achieve. R' Lofez told the students that some people prayed as though they were sending a letter to *Hashem*, while others prayed as though they were reading a letter in *Hashem's* presence — that was R' Shalom.

In his later years he would say *Birkat HaMazon* (Grace after Meals) from a *Rosh Hashanah mahzor* (prayerbook). In this way he felt that the Day of Judgment would never be far from his mind.

His Humility

He distanced himself from any semblance of pride or self-promotion. Despite his erudition he always tried to behave like the most ordinary of people. When he attended a session of the *Bet Din*, he would put on a long coat appropriate for the respect of the institution. However, immedidiately upon his return home he would hang up the rabbinical cloak and put on a short jacket so that people would not treat him as someone special. It was only after many years and much persuasion by his family that he consented to wear his long coat outside of the *Bet Din*.

In privacy he would continue his prayers wearing both sets of tefillin *at the same time to fulfill the opinion of the Kabbalah as well.*

His Piety

He took great pains to perform each *mitzvah* in the most correct way possible. Thus, he took upon himself any practice which could raise the level of his observance, but he did so quietly and in secret so others would be unaware. He started his prayers with *tefillin* made according to the *halachic* interpretation of *Rashi* and then put on another set of *tefillin* made according to *Rabbeinu Tam*; finally, in privacy he would continue his prayers wearing both sets of *tefillin* at the same time to fulfill the opinion of the Kabbalah as well.

His Legacy

From his earliest years R' Shalom wrote out his *hiddushim*. When he was 18, the manuscripts for two small works, *Sim Shalom* and *Simeni Kahotam*, were published in his grandfather's book *HaHaim VeHaShalom*, Volume II (Jerusalem 5697/1937). He continued to write *hiddushim* but because of his deep humility he refused to allow them to be published. Finally, in his last years his family persuaded him to release a two-volume book of *hiddushim* on *halachah* named *Dibrei Shalom* (Jerusalem 5753/1993 and 5754/1994). The book also includes notes by his son, R' Yaakob Mizrahi. He passed away on 26 Tevet, 5755 (1995).

[430] **MIZRAHI, R' Shimon**

רבי שמעון מזרחי

(19th century)

Worthy scholar and rabbi of Aram Soba. His father was R' Moshe Mizrahi. In 1865 he joined other rabbis of Aram Soba in signing the approbation for the first book-printing initiative of the city (see Document Section, Document No. 25), which was introduced by R' Abraham Sasson and his sons (see #475).

[431] **MIZRAHI, R' Yitzhak**

רבי יצחק מזרחי

(19th century)

Worthy scholar and rabbi of Aram Soba. He was the father of R' Shalom Mizrahi (see #415) and the grandfather of R' Yitzhak Bekhor Mizrahi (see #94). In 1828 he joined R' Haim Ashkenazi (see #336) and R' Shalom Chasky (see #149) in signing a document of the *Bet Din*.

[432] **MIZRAHI, R' Yitzhak Bekhor**

רבי יצחק בכור מזרחי

(— 1905)

Dayan and *Av Bet Din* (Chief Judge) of Aram Soba. He authored a book of responsa on the four parts of the *Shulhan Aruch*, which remained in manuscript form. One of his responsa is included in the book *Et Sofer* (*Hoshen Mishpat*, 17) by R' Ezra Tawil (see #582). When he passed away on 3 Shevat, 5665 (1905) he was eulogized by R' Eliyahu Hamway (see #271), one of his colleagues on the *Bet Din*.

[433] **MORSAYA (BOBO), R' Shemuel**

רבי שמואל מורסייא (בובו)

(19th century)

Worthy scholar and rabbi of Aram Soba. He was a son of R' David Morsaya and the grandfather of the later R' Shemuel Morsaya (see #434). He composed the hymn *"Shir Hadash"* which is part of the special prayers for *Shabbat* that were published in the book *Mikra Kodesh* (Livorno 5644/1884).

He is mentioned in the preface to *Zichron Tob* of R' Moshe Rosa (#467) (Livorno 5595/1835). He also wrote an approbation to the book.

[434] **MORSAYA (BOBO), R' Shemuel**

רבי שמואל מורסייא (בובו)

(— 1904)

Worthy scholar and rabbi of Aram Soba. He was a son of R' David Morsaya and a grandson of the earlier R' Shemuel Morsaya (see #433). He studied Kabbalah with R' Ezra Tawil (see #582) and R' Shelomo Safdeyé (see #469). The outcome of this collaboration was the book *Emet Me'Aretz* (Jerusalem 5748/1988), published by the yeshiva *Ahabat Shalom*. He passed away in 5664 (1904).

[435] **MOUNSA, R' Yaakob**

רבי יעקב מונסא

(1874 — 1949)

Eminent Kabbalist and educator of Damascus and Jerusalem. He was born in Damascus in 1839 to R' Yosef Mounsa and managed the Talmud Torah of the city. In 1919 he moved to Jerusalem, where he lived for the remainder of his days. In time, he became one of the senior Kabbalists of Jerusalem who prayed with the special *kavanot* (meditations) of the *Rashash* (R' Shalom Sharabi). In fact he sought to do every waking act with the special considerations of the *Rashash* (eating, drinking, washing, etc.).

R' Yaakob Mounsa

He had kept his plans for moving out of Damascus a secret to everyone, even his wife. One day, he walked out of the synagogue carrying only his *tallit* and *tefillin* and headed to the railway station. He simply got on a train and was on his way to *Eretz Yisrael*. Fortunately, he met one of his acquaintances at the station and, through him, informed his wife and family that he had gone to Jerusalem. Once he arrived, he sent for his family to join him. He then explained why he had behaved in such a strange way. He said that if he had attempted to go in a normal manner, the people of the community would never have allowed him to depart.

In Jerusalem he formed an association with other immigrants from Damascus and together they founded the yeshiva *Yagdil Torah*. In this yeshiva, the mystical works of the *Ari'zal* were studied from midnight until dawn. Then, during the day the plain meaning of the texts would be studied. It was customary for the students and staff to pray *Minhah* each Friday afternoon at the *Kotel*.

Later, he began learning at *Yeshivat Rehovot HaNahar*, where Hacham Haim Shaul Dweck (see #228) was the *Rosh Yeshiva*. R' Haim Shaul once said, "If my only purpose in coming here was to teach R' Yaakob the mystical Torah of the Kabbalah and the deeper meaning of the *tefillot*, it would have been sufficient."

At a later point he founded on his own a yeshiva for the study of Kabbalah, which he called *Emet VeShalom*. One of his students in Kabbalah was R' Sulaman Moussafi.

In the last year of his life, after he had led the prayers on *Yom Kippur*, he told his family that he saw a difficult winter ahead. Then, after a short time he became ill and a few months later he passed away on 3 Adar, 5709 (1949).

[436] MOUNSA, R' Yosef

רבי יוסף מונסא

(1879 — 1977)

R' Mordechai Meyuhas

Chief *Shohet* of Jerusalem. He was born in Damascus in 1879 to R' Yaakob Mounsa (see #435). When he was 10 the family moved to Jerusalem and once he became of age he was enrolled in the yeshiva *Porat Yosef*. Among the courses of study at the yeshiva he learned the art of *shehitah* and so was able to combine the learning of Torah with a holy occupation. After the passing of R' Mordechai Meyuhas, the Chief *Shohet* of Jerusalem, he was appointed to that position.

He refused to participate in the labor strikes which broke out from time to time among the *shohatim* of Jerusalem, arguing that he could not bear the thought that such an action might lead to someone eating meat that was not kosher. His knowledge of *shehitah* was vast and his rulings on *shehitah* practices were accepted without objection. He taught the art of *shehitah* to many apprentice *shohatim* without expectation of reward.

R' Yosef Mounsa

He was able to continue in his holy work almost until his last days. In eulogizing him, R' Yehudah Sadkah, the *Rosh Yeshiva* of *Porat Yosef* (see #468), said that he fulfilled the three expectations that *Hashem* seeks from every man: (1) to do *mishpat* (act in accordance with the *halachah*); (2) to love and help others; (3) to behave humbly and graciously at all times. He passed away on 13 Adar, 5737 (1977).

[437] NAHUM, R' Nissim

רבי נסים נחום

(1867 — 1927)

Distinguished philanthropist and Kabbalist of Jerusalem and Egypt.

Distinguished philanthropist and Kabbalist of Jerusalem and Egypt. Although not a Syrian rabbi, he played a critical role in establishing the framework for the study of Kabbalah by the Syrian rabbis in Jerusalem. One of the major Kabbalah institutions was the great yeshiva *Rehovot HaNahar*, which he founded together with R' Haim Shaul Dweck (see #228). He personally funded a number of other important initiatives, many anonymously. For example, he funded the publishing of many holy books, a task which was far beyond the means of the poverty-stricken Torah scholars of Jerusalem.

He was born into a wealthy home in Tripoli in 1867, the youngest of seven sons. His parents, Khalafalah and Rivkah Nahum, respected Torah and regularly hosted visiting rabbis who came to Tripoli seeking help. However, the Nahum sons were given a secular education to prepare them for the business world. So, after graduating, the young Nissim joined his brothers in the family business.

One day when he was about 20 years old a visiting rabbi from Jerusalem gave him an amulet, consisting of a holy text in a silver case. Somehow this amulet had a tremendous effect upon him; it created in him a spiritual awakening which changed his entire life. From that point on he separated himself from his business activities and from worldly pleasures. He devoted himself to the study of Torah and practiced physical self-denial such as fasting and sleeping on a thin mat to atone for the sins of his youth. In the course of time he opened a *Bet Midrash* where working people could come to study Torah before dawn. His *Bet Midrash* also fostered the study of Torah by young people, to counter the pervasiveness of secular education in Tripoli.

The family business continued to provide him with a comfortable income, which he generously shared with Torah causes and needy people. About 10 years after his spiritual awakening, his father passed away and his mother said she would very much like to go to *Eretz Yisrael* then. Being tied to a successful business, none of the sons wanted to accompany her — except her youngest, R' Nissim. Upon his arrival in Jerusalem, he walked into a *Bet Midrash*. He was dressed in plain clothing, hiding evidence of his wealth. He randomly asked the men learning there, "Will you learn with me?"

The response was disappointing. It seemed that he was unable to grab anyone's attention — until he came upon the renowned Kabbalist, R' Haim Shaul Dweck.

The pair learned together for months and grew closer. R' Nahum was so impressed by R' Dweck that they founded *Yeshivat Rehovot HaNahar* together. R' Dweck was the *Rosh Yeshiva*; R' Nahum provided the funding. The men who learned in this yeshiva were mostly scholars from the Syrian community. In effect, R' Nahum was the first person to start a yeshiva for *Mekubalim* (Kabbalists). Kabbalah in Jerusalem today owes its strength to this yeshiva. R' Nahum also started a sister yeshiva for Ashkenazim called *Shaar HaShamayim*.

R' Nissim became one of the steady students of the yeshiva and, in time, he became one of the senior Kabbalists of Jerusalem who prayed with the special *kavanot* (intentions and thoughts) of the *Rashash* (R' Shalom Sharabi).

In 1916, at the time of World War I, the military situation forced R' Nahum to leave Jerusalem and so he moved his family to No-Amon in Egypt. There he continued with worthy initiatives, such as the chain of Torah centers called *Hevrat Keter Torah*. The first of these centers was established in Cairo, followed by those in Alexandria, Aleppo, Damascus, Beirut, Jerusalem, Tripoli, and elsewhere. Chief Rabbi Yaakob Kassin (see #330), in his book *Peri Etz Hagan*, quotes a 1918 newspaper article from the religious publication, "Egypt Jerusalem," which tells of a tremendous *Bet Midrash* that was opened for all the great rabbinical refugees who were leaving Jerusalem because of the world war, crediting R' Nahum with its foundation. The article said, "We haven't had, in hundreds of years, such an upsurge of Torah in Egypt." In 1916, there were 300 members of this Torah center in Cairo alone.

After the war, R' Nissim returned to Jerusalem and renewed his work for the benefit of the study of Kabbalah . He was blessed with worthy sons and sons-in-law who became great rabbis. His sons were: R' Klafo, R' Reuben, and R' Emanuel. His first son-in-law was R' Abraham Sutton (see #535) and his second was R' Matloub Abadi (see #9). In his later years he suffered from a stomach ailment, a sickness which is said to be characteristic of the righteous and he died of it on 16 Shevat, 5687 (1927).

R' Nissim Nahum with his family. He is holding his daughter Esther future wife of R' Matloub Abadi (see #9)

"We haven't had, in hundreds of years, such an upsurge of Torah in Egypt."

[438] NAWI, R' Elisha

רבי אלישע נאווי

(late 17th century)

Eminent scholar of Aram Soba. He is mentioned by R' Yosef Almoshnino in his book *Edot BiYehosef* (Constantinople 5480/1720). In responsum no. 33 R' Yosef wrote that he wasn't really satisfied with his effort and was thinking of adding more detail, but since the eminent R' Elisha Nawi had already signed on it, and had commented on some aspects, he had decided to leave it as it was.

[439] NAWI, R' Yosef

רבי יוסף נאווי

(early 18th century)

Eminent scholar of Aram Soba. He was the son of R' Elisha Nawi (see (#438) and the father-in-law of R' Shimon Dweck (see #246), author of the book *Rei'ah HaSadeh*. His son-in-law mentions him a few times in his book in highly laudatory terms. In 1715 he signed a *halachic* (legal) ruling together with other rabbis of Aram Soba concerning the validity of Kabbalah and the writings of the *Ari'zal*. (See Document Section, Document No. 10.)

[440] NEHMAD, R' Abraham

רבי אברהם נחמד

(— 1874)

Worthy scholar and rabbi of Aram Soba, who was known for his kindnesses to the poor. He passed away on 2 Tishrei, 5635 (1874).

[441] NEHMAD, R' Aharon

רבי אהרן נחמד

(19th century)

Eminent scholar and rabbi of Aram Soba. He joined with other rabbis of Aram Soba

R' Nissim's first son-in-law was R' Abraham Sutton and his second was R' Matloub Abadi.

in 1852 in signing the approbation on *Kenesiyah Leshem Shamayim* (see Document Section, Document No. 31) of R' Menashe Sutton (see #551). R' Nehmad was invited by the community of Baghdad to serve as their *Av Bet Din* (Chief Judge), but tragically died on the way and was buried in the town of Urfa. He was the grandson of R' Aharon Nehmad (see #442) and a son of R' Shelomo Nehmad (see #447).

[442] **NEHMAD, R' Aharon**

רבי אהרן נחמד

Worthy scholar of Aram Soba, known for his piety and modesty. He married the daughter of R' Haim Cohen (see #162) and was blessed with a son, R' Shelomo Nehmad (see #447).

[443] **NEHMAD, R' Binyamin**

רבי בנימין נחמד

(19th century)

Worthy rabbi and scholar of Tiberias, known for his fund-raising missions throughout the Middle East. He was born in Aram Soba and settled in Tiberias, where he became an emissary of the community. In 1857 he was sent to Morocco and while he was there, he signed the approbation to *Maaseh Rokeach* of R' Masoud Hai Rokeach. In 1863 he went to Tripoli and in 1865 he was sent to Kurdistan, Baghdad, and Yemen, among others. While in Kurdistan he was witness to the sad plight of the Jewish community. The Kurdish Jews were subject to harsh ill-treatment by their neighbors and many were killed. He resolved to awaken the world to the situation and wrote letters to nearby communities, such as Baghdad, to come to the aid of their brethren.

R' Meir was drawn to community service and became one of the founders of the Bikur Holim organization of Aram Soba.

R' Meir Rahamim Nehmad

[444] **NEHMAD, R' Haim**

רבי חיים נחמד

(1840 — 1916)

Worthy rabbi and teacher of Aram Soba. He was born in Aram Soba in approximately 1840 to R' Shelomo Nehmad (see #447). He studied Torah under his father's tutelage and was ordained for the rabbinate. He served as a teacher in the Talmud Torah of Aram Soba for over 40 years. In 1906, together with other scholars and rabbis of Aram Soba, he signed a *halachic* (legal) ruling directed against those who desecrate *Shabbat* (see Document Section, Document No. 27). He passed away on 29 Iyar, 5676 (1916).

[445] **NEHMAD, R' Haim Yosef**

רבי חיים יוסף נחמד

(— 1787)

Rabbi and community emissary of Tiberias. He was born in Aram Soba and settled in Tiberias, where he became an emissary of the community. In 1774 he was sent to Tripoli. His signature appears on a letter of introduction to R' Abraham Aryeh in 1785. R' Nehmad is believed to have passed away in 1787, while still a relatively young man.

[446] **NEHMAD, R' Meir Rahamim**

רבי מאיר רחמים נחמד

(1876 — 1943)

Worthy rabbi and community leader of Aram Soba. He was born on 6 Heshvan, 5636 (1876) to R' Haim Nehmad (see #444). He studied Torah under R' Ezra Hamway (see #272) and was ordained as a rabbi at a fairly young age. R' Meir was drawn to community service and became one of the founders of the *Bikur Holim* organization of Aram Soba. This organization was primarily concerned with providing for the medical needs of poor people. Later, he joined R' Raphael Shelomo Laniado (see #364), R' Natan Marcus (see #406), and R' Eliyahu Yosef Shamah (see #500) in founding the *Sedakah U'Marpeh* organization, which opened a medical clinic in Aram Soba. To obtain funds for the new venture, R' Eliyahu Shamah went on a mission to Egypt while R' Nehmad met with various wealthy people of Aram Soba. The clinic survived until 1934 when R' Nehmad moved to Tel Aviv.

Throughout the years R' Nehmad was active in helping people from Aram Soba immigrate to *Eretz Yisrael*. He was the chairman of the Aram Soba emigration organization.

His book, *Keter Aram Soba* (Jerusalem 5693/1933), was a historical analysis of one of the four "crowns" (ancient Torah scrolls) in the old synagogue of Aram Soba.

His *hiddushim* (original Torah thoughts) appeared in various places, including the journal *HaMe'asef* published in Jerusalem by R' Ben-Sion Kouenka.

R' Nehmad passed away on 24 Iyar, 5703 (1943) in Tel Aviv, leaving three sons. The oldest, R' Haim, passed away in 1976 in New York. The second, R' Moshe, went to Argentina. The youngest son, R' Ezra, settled in Petah Tikvah and married the daughter of R' Obadiah Hedaya (see #309). He followed his father's footsteps in public service, becoming one of the founders of the rabbinical *Bet Midrash* in Petah Tikvah, called *Be'er Moshe*.

[447] **NEHMAD, R' Shelomo**

רבי שלמה נחמד

(1796 — 1869)

Distinguished rabbi and *Av Bet Din* (Chief Judge) of Aram Soba. He was born in 1796 to R' Aharon Nehmad (see #442). From the family history written by his grandson, R' Meir Rahamim Nehmad (see #446), we know that he excelled in his studies as a boy. In fact, he already had the reputation of being a Torah scholar at the age of 17 and was considered a very desirable match. R' Yeshayah Harari-Raful (see #306), one of the wealthiest men of Aram Soba, chose him to marry his daughter, Esther, and gave the young couple a fine dowry.

After marriage, R' Shelomo continued his devotion to learning, but also engaged in business on the side. Accordingly, by the time he was 40 he had developed a reputation as a great scholar, as well as a person knowledgeable in the ways of the world. His reputation reached Baghdad, where the community invited him to be its Chief Rabbi. He went to Baghdad, but at the end of a six-month trial period, he decided not to accept the offer. He found that he could not bear the separation from his native city and from his fellow rabbis.

In 1858 when the senior rabbi and *Av Bet Din* (Chief Judge) of Aram Soba, R' Abraham Antebi, passed away, R' Haim Mordechai Labaton (see #336) was appointed in his place. At the same time, R' Nehmad was appointed a member of the *Bet Din*, together with R' Shalom Chasky (see #149). When R' Labaton was appointed Chief Rabbi *(Hacham Bashi)* by the Turkish authorities, R' Nehmad was designated his second-in-command. He was especially active in dealing with community affairs affecting the governmental authorities. Sitting on the *Bet Din,* he impressed his colleagues, not only with his expertise in *Gemara* and *halachic* (legal) rulings, but with his ability to delve into issues and get to the bottom of the matter under consideration. In later years when R' Labaton became too weak to leave the house, R' Nehmad was appointed to be the *Av Bet Din* (Chief Judge) and the entire adminstration of the community was turned over to him.

In 1859 he traveled to Egypt to visit his rich nephew Eliyahu Nehmad who was childless. R' Shelomo persuaded him to donate a large sum of money to build a yeshiva in Aram Soba in his name. With this money, R' Nehmad built a yeshiva on the roof of the synagogue *Bet Nasi*. It included a large airy study hall with beautiful furniture and a rich library. He also established a fund to support five full-time Torah scholars. In 1869 the community of Aram Soba asked the Turkish Sultan in Istanbul to give an official Hacham Bashi appointment to R' Nehmad. Tragically, on 27 Elul, 5629 (1869), the very day the formal notification arrived in Aram Soba, R' Nehmad died.

He wrote many *hiddushim* (original Torah thoughts) on the *Bet Yosef*, as well as many *halachic* rulings and inspirational lectures, but all were sadly lost due to the moisture in the chest in which they were kept.

His reputation reached Baghdad, where the community invited him to be its Chief Rabbi. However, he found that he could not bear the separation from his native city and from his fellow rabbis.

He was appointed to be the Av Bet Din (Chief Judge) and the entire adminstration of the community was turned over to him.

He built a yeshiva on the roof of the synagogue Bet Nasi. It included a large airy study hall with beautiful furniture and a rich library.

[448] **NEHMAD, R' Yehudah**

רבי יהודה נחמד

(1761 — 1847)

Eminent rabbi of Tiberias. He was born in Tiberias in 1761 and is believed to have been the son of R' Haim Yosef Nehmad (see #445). In 1805, together with other rabbis of Tiberias, he signed a letter of authorization to R' Haim Yisrael Raphael Sagri to serve as an emissary of the community. He himself went as an emissary a number of times too.

> *The number of scholars in the Ehad yeshiva was 13, corresponding to the gematria of the Hebrew word אחד.*

In 1831 he was sent to Aram Soba. However, when he arrived in Damascus, the people of the city did not allow him to complete his trip in consideration of his age and the severe cold weather at that time in Aram Soba. So instead of going to Aram Soba himself, he sent a letter addressed to the Chief Rabbi of Aram Soba, R' Abraham Antebi (see #63), as well as to R' Matloub Menashe Sutton (see #548), and to R' Yitzhak Shalom, who was one of the well-to-do men of the city. In his letter, he asked them to act for him and send a suitable donation to Tiberias. He also included a letter of endorsement from R' Haim Nissim Abulafia, in which he speaks highly of R' Yehudah. R' Yehudah is also praised in the introduction written by R' Yaakob Shaltiel to his book *Emet LeYaakob* (Livorno 5603/1843). R' Nehmad passed away in Tiberias in 1847, leaving no sons.

[449] **PALAGI, R' Haim**

רבי חיים פלאג'י

(— 1868)

Distinguished Chief Rabbi of Izmir. He was considered by many to be the greatest rabbi of his generation. He wrote many books, one of the most noteworthy being *Lev Haim*. He passed away on 17 Shevat, 5628 (1868). [Although not of Syrian descent his name is recorded in *LiKedoshim Asher Ba'Aretz*, obviously due to his strong connection to the Syrian community. His life deserves an entire chapter, but he is only mentioned here briefly in passing, trusting that other publications will do justice to his great achievements.]

R' Ben-Sion Paredes

[450] **PAREDES, R' Ben-Sion**

רבי בן־ציון פאראדיס

(1862 — 1943)

Eminent Kabbalist, *darshan* (lecturer), and teacher of Jerusalem. He was born in Jerusalem on 27 Kislev, 5622 (1862) to the Kabbalist Eliyahu Paredes (see #452) of Aram Soba. In his youth he taught in the Sephardic Talmud Torah of Jerusalem and in the Bukharan Talmud Torah. He was counted among the illustrious scholars of the *Bet El* yeshiva and the *Ehad* yeshiva. (The number of scholars in the *Ehad* yeshiva was 13, corresponding to the *gematria* of the Hebrew word אחד.) In addition, he was known as a popular *darshan* (lecturer).

He passed away on 1 *Rosh Hodesh* Adar, 5703 (1943), leaving many *hiddushim* (original Torah thoughts) in manuscript form. Some were published in the journal *Ohr Torah* by his son R' Eliyahu Paredes (see #451).

[451] **PAREDES, R' Eliyahu**

רבי אליהו פאראדיס

(1893 — 1972)

R' Eliyahu Paredes

Distinguished Chief Rabbi of Jerusalem. He was born in Jerusalem on 17 Tamuz, 5653 (1893), a son of R' Ben-Sion Paredes (see #450) and a grandson of the earlier R' Eliyahu Paredes (see #452) of Aram Soba. He was an excellent student and was ordained as a rabbi by the following notable rabbis of the time: the *Rishon LeSion* (Chief Rabbi of *Eretz Yisrael*) R' Ben-Sion Meir Hai Ouziel, the *Av Bet Din* (Chief Judge), R' Hizkiah Shabbetai (see #495), and the *Av Bet Din* R' Yosef M. HaLevi.

Originally, he resisted offers of a rabbinical position, preferring to earn his own livelihood by teaching. Thus, over a period of 40 years he taught students in the Talmud Torah of the Old City, nurturing tens of thousands of young boys and men. He was a tall distinguished-looking man, who made a lasting impression on people. He taught his students the love of Torah and *mitzvot*, the love of the Jewish people, and the love of *Eretz Yisrael*. At the same time he took an active part in community affairs.

In 1953 he accepted a position as Chief Rabbi of Ramat Gan, which he occupied until 1961 when was chosen to be the Chief Rabbi of Jerusalem.

His *hiddushim* (original Torah thoughts) were published in the Torah journals *Ohr Torah, Kol Sinai, Noam, Zichron Meir, Ohr HaMeir,* and *Kol Torah*, and in a journal put out in his memory (Jerusalem 1974).

He was an impressive public speaker and was often called upon to go to other countries as an emissary of the charitable institutions and *yeshivot* of Jerusalem. He was a charismatic person who exerted a positive influence on all the people with whom he came into contact.

He was blessed with a long life and did not show the effects of aging. In fact, he was able to continue in his position as Chief Rabbi until the last day of his life, 11 Nissan, 5732 (1972).

[452] **PAREDES (PARDES), R' Eliyahu**

רבי אליהו פאראדיס (פרדס)

(1834 — 1874)

Pious scholar and Kabbalist of Aram Soba and Jerusalem. He was born in Aram Soba in 1834 and became orphaned at a very young age. At the age of 15 he managed to go to Jerusalem where he studied under the Kabbalist R' Vidal Kouenka. R' Eliyahu's brilliant mind and phenomenal memory helped him advance in his studies. It was not long before his teacher came to realize his great ability and potential, so he brought him to his home to teach him Kabbalah. He also gave him his daughter Mercada as a wife.

After the wedding he devoted himself to his studies at the yeshiva *Hesed El* and at the yeshiva *Bet El*. His habit was to leave home on *Motza'e Shabbat* (Saturday night), not returning until Friday night after the *Arbit* prayers. During the week he subsisted on a bare minimum of food and fasted frequently. It was said about him that he never looked at a woman.

R' Eliyahu did not limit his Torah studies to his own learning, but made a practice of teaching working people in the early hours before dawn and in the late afternoon.

R' Eliyahu did not limit his Torah studies to his own learning, but made a practice of teaching working people in the early hours before dawn and in the late afternoon. He loved *mitzvot* and enjoyed making *tzitzit* for friends and acquaintances. He also faithfully checked the *mezuzot* of people throughout Jerusalem. After *Yom Kippur* he would go around the neighborhood offering to check the *kashrut* of people's *sukkot*.

He passed away at the age of 40 on 2 Elul, 5634 (1874). His grieving widow and two children (a son and a daughter) were left destitute and an international appeal was made to provide them with support. His son, R' Ben-Sion Paredes (see #450), a scholar in his own right, was to become the father of the next great R' Eliyahu Paredes (see #451).

Picciotto Lineage. The story of the illustrious Picciotto family in Aram Soba originated with the eminent scholar and philanthropist, Señor Hillel Haim Picciotto of Livorno, who settled in Aram Soba in 1771. His sons and grandsons served as consuls of various European powers, including Austria, France, Italy, and Prussia. Altogether five generations of the family served as consuls in Aram Soba, defending the interests and needs of the Jewish people in every way they could. They had a well-deserved reputation for their material assistance to *yeshivot* and charities. At the same time they were all learned men and were deeply involved in the study of Torah. Travelers from Lithuania and Russia who passed through Aram Soba on their way to Jerusalem wrote in letters home about the "angels of mercy and love" who helped them in Aram Soba. Those angels were the Picciottos. In 1828 the poet R' Adam Levenson wrote a poem called *"Shir Tehilat Yesharim"* in honor of the Picciotto family. The poem may be found in the book *Yehudei HaMizrach Be'Eretz Yisrael.*

R' Aharon Tawil (see #580) in his book *Yisaschar U'Zevulun* cites the Picciotto family as a wonderful example of the reward for supporting and helping Torah scholars. The wealth and stature of the Picciotto family were preserved through five generations because of their righteous behavior and their good works, which were continued in each generation.

ספר
ויחל משה
כולל
דרשות ודברי מוסר
על
ספר בראשית
מהצעיר
חי משה פיג'וטו ס"ט
שנת תקעד לפ"ק
ביינה

Title Page of Vayehal Moshe

[453] PICCIOTTO, Señor Eliyahu

סי' אליהו די פיג'וטו

(— 1890)

Worthy scholar and notable philanthropist of Aram Soba and Jerusalem. In Jerusalem he founded the yeshiva which was named after him, *Kisei Eliyahu,* headed by the *Rishon LeSion* (Chief Rabbi of *Eretz Yisrael*), R' Yaakob Shaul Elyashar. The yeshiva continued to serve the community until 1896. Señor Picciotto passed away 6 years earlier in 1890. R' Abraham Antebi (see #63) spoke of him and his sons with high praise in his book *Mor Ve'Ahalot* and in the introduction to *Hochmah U'Mussar*. He was seen as a man whose mission was to shield and protect the community.

[454] PICCIOTTO, Señor Hai Moshe

סי' חי משה די פיג'וטו

(— 1816)

Eminent scholar and philanthropist of Aram Soba. He was a son of R' Hillel Haim Picciotto (see #457). He was the author of a book of inspirational lectures on the Torah (*Bereshit* and *Shemot*), called *Vayehal Moshe* (Vienna 5574/1814). In the introduction he expresses deep gratitude to his worthy father for raising him in an environment where he was exposed to scholars and rabbis. He admits to having spent some time as a merchant, beginning when he was 18 years of age, but it seems that he overcame the temptation to engage in a life of business. He then talks about having prayed to *Hashem* for worthy sons and was answered with two scholarly sons: Señor Hillel (Haim-Hillel) (see #456) and Señor Raphael.

He had total trust in the power of Torah to protect the community and he applied that trust directly into his business affairs.

Reliable Insurance. R' Hai Moshe Picciotto had total trust in the power of Torah to protect the community and he applied that trust directly into his business affairs. As an importer of goods from France he had the practice of taking out insurance on each shipment. However, he decided that instead of paying the premium to an insurance company, he would pay it to Torah scholars whose dedicated learning would protect his property even better than any insurance company would do. This approach worked well and he never suffered a loss. On one occasion, the ship was late and he became concerned that it might have been lost at sea, possibly because the Torah scholars were not learning properly. However, after a few days the shipment arrived, with nothing missing. He realized that he had unfairly indicted the scholars in his heart and went to the *Bet Midrash* (the *Bet Señor Moshe)* where the scholars were learning, and begged their forgiveness.

One of the responsa of R' Hai Moshe appears in the book *Gedulat Mordechai* by R' Mordechai Galante. He wrote additional *hiddushim* (original Torah thoughts) which remained in manuscript form.

Señor Hillel married the daughter of R' Moshe Galante, the Chief Rabbi of Damascus. In the introduction to his book *Beirach Moshe*, R' Galante praises R' Hai Moshe and his two sons in glowing terms. He passed away on 26 Tevet, 5576 (1816).

[455] PICCIOTTO, Señor Hillel

סי׳ הלל די פיג׳וטו

(— 1884)

Worthy scholar and notable philanthropist of Aram Soba. He was apparently a son of the philanthropist Señor Eliyahu Picciotto (see #453). He passed away on 12 Tamuz, 5644 (1884), seemingly while his father was still alive.

[456] PICCIOTTO, Señor Hillel (Haim-Hillel)

סי׳ הלל (חיים־הלל) די פיג׳וטו

(19th century)

Worthy scholar of Aram Soba. He was a son of R' Hai Moshe Picciotto (see #454) and a son-in-law of R' Moshe Galante, the Chief Rabbi. He is mentioned with great respect by R' Yitzhak Harari (see #295) in his book *Zechor LeYitzhak* (sect. 2, sect. 54).

[457] PICCIOTTO, Señor Hillel Haim

סי׳ הלל חיים די פיג׳וטו

(— 1773)

Eminent scholar and philanthropist of Livorno and Aram Soba. He was born in Livorno, a son of R' Shemuel Picciotto and a son-in-law of R' Moshe Ben Habib. In fact, he was the first member of the illustrious family Picciotto to arrive in Aram Soba from Livorno. His initial visit to Aram Soba on a business trip was in 1732. However, he then returned to Livorno and continued to go back and forth on business until 1771 when he settled permanently in Aram Soba. As a wealthy merchant he was very concerned about supporting worthy institutions. He was especially generous in helping the poor people of Jerusalem.

He passed away on 16 Nissan, 5533 (1773), two years after settling permanently in Aram Soba. He was survived by his worthy sons: Señor Hai Moshe Picciotto (see #454) and Señor Raphael Picciotto (see #459). One of those who eulogized him was R' Yeshayah Attiah (see #119), as recorded in his book *Bigdei Yesha* (p. 94a).

He was especially generous in helping the poor people of Jerusalem.

[458] PICCIOTTO, Señor Moshe

סי׳ משה די פיג׳וטו

(— 1894)

Worthy scholar and philanthropist of Aram Soba. He was a son of Señor Eliyahu Picciotto (see #453). Like his father and brothers he committed himself to supporting worthy causes in Aram Soba and Jerusalem. He passed away on *Rosh Hodesh* Adar 2, 5654 (1894).

He had a son R' Daniel Picciotto, who passed away at a relatively young age, while his father was still alive. R' Daniel left a 9-year-old boy named Moshe, who was brought up in his grandfather's house. The young boy studied in the yeshiva which was funded by the members of his family. When he grew up he went into the textile business. In 1899 he moved to Manchester, where he occupied himself with serving the needs of the community. He especially helped those who wished to settle in *Eretz Yisrael*, providing them with the means to earn a living.

[459] PICCIOTTO, Señor Raphael

סי׳ רפאל די פיג׳וטו

(— 1827)

Eminent scholar and philanthropist of Aram Soba and Tiberias. Señor Raphael served as the consul for Austria and Prussia. He was born in Aram Soba and in 1817 moved to Tiberias. There he purchased a property, which became known as *Bet Picciotto,* on which he built a yeshiva for use by scholars. He lived in Tiberias for 10 years before passing away on 3 Shevat, 5587 (1827). When word of his passing reached Aram Soba he was eulogized by R' Yosef Raphael Sasson. Some of the events of his life are reviewed in the book *Tov Re'i* of R' Yosef Haim Yaluz (Jerusalem 5694/1934).

In Tiberias he purchased a property, which became known as "Bet Picciotto," on which he built a yeshiva for use by scholars.

Señor Raphael was a son of Señor Hillel Haim Picciotto (see #457) and a brother of Señor Hai Moshe Picciotto (see #454). He was blessed with four sons: Ezra Haim, Eliyahu, Moshe, and Daniel. The oldest, Ezra Haim, passed away on *Rosh Hodesh* Av, 5582 (1822) while his father was still alive. He left six sons.

In memory of Señor Ezra Haim, a eulogy was delivered by R' Yitzhak Attiah (see

#120), which is recorded in his book *Vayikra Yitzhak*. R' Yitzhak happened to be in Livorno at the time, seeing to the printing of his books, and so he did not get word of the death of Señor Ezra Haim until the following year, which is when he delivered the eulogy. In the course of the eulogy he mentioned two of the six sons of the deceased: Señor Raphael and Señor Hillel. He noted that Señor Raphael had established himself in Marseilles and he wished him well. He also mentioned Señor Eliyahu, the brother of the deceased, who was also a well-to-do philanthropist.

A Beloved Horse. Señor Raphael Picciotto (see #459) had a beautiful white horse, which he enjoyed riding on trips out of the city. However, it happened that the horse fell ill and died. Señor Raphael was very upset about this and felt as though he had lost a loved one. Various rabbis tried to calm him down but to no avail. Finally, R' Mordechai Attiah found words of comfort in a verse in *Tehillim* (50:9), "I take not from your household any bull, [nor] from your stables any he-goats." The Hebrew word for "bull" in this verse is *"par"* (פר), whose letters form an acronym for "Picciotto Rivkah," the wife of Señor Raphael. The hidden meaning of the verse becomes apparent when one reads it as, "I take not from your household Picciotto Rivkah, [but instead as a *kapparah*, I take] from your stables, he-goats [a horse]. When he heard these thoughtful words, Señor Raphael was immediately comforted. (Note: *Kapparah* is the term used for the sacrifice of an animal to redeem the sins of a person.)

[460] **PICCIOTTO, Señor Raphael**

סי' רפאל די פיג'וטו

(— 1859)

Eminent scholar and philanthropist of Aram Soba. He was born in Aram Soba to R' Hai Moshe Picciotto (see #454). He was a nephew to the earlier Señor Raphael Piciotto (see #459). Señor Raphael assumed the position of consul for Russia and Prussia, in place of his father. In 1854 he moved to Tiberias to live out his remaining years in *Eretz Yisrael*. He passed away in approximately 1859.

[461] **PINTO, R' Daniel**

רבי דניאל פינטו

(— 1681)

Worthy scholar and rabbi of Damascus and Aram Soba. He was born in Damascus to R' Yoshiyahu Pinto (see #463). After the death of his father in 1648 he moved with his family to Aram Soba. R' Daniel wrote a book of inspirational lectures called *Lehem Hamudot*, which remained in manuscript form. He passed away on 17 Av, 5441 (1681).

[462] **PINTO, R' Shemuel**

רבי שמואל פינטו

(— 1715)

Eminent scholar and rabbi of Aram Soba. He was a son of R' Daniel Pinto (see #461) and a grandson of the great rabbi, the *Rif* (R' Yoshiyahu Pinto) (see #463).

R' Obadiah HaLevy (see #392) in his book *Hazon Obadiah* writes that in a trash pile he discovered the manuscript of a *halachic* (legal) ruling in the case of an *agunah* (deserted woman). After carefully studying it, he concluded that it must have been issued by R' Shemuel Pinto, the grandson of the *Rif*. This appears to have been one of the many responsa in a book which was written by R' Pinto, but never published.

He passed away on 6 Kislev, 5476 (1715). In that year he signed a *halachic* ruling together with other rabbis of Aram Soba concerning the validity of Kabbalah and the writings of the *Ari'zal*. (See Document Section, Document No. 10.)

[463] PINTO, R' Yoshiyahu [Rif]

רבי יאשיהו פינטו

(1565 — 1648)

Distinguished scholar and rabbi of Damascus. He was also known by the name *Rif*, which is an abbreviation of the first letters in "R' Yoshiyahu Pinto." He was born in Damascus in approximately 1565 to R' Yosef Pinto and studied Torah there under R' Yaakob Abulafia. He quickly became known for his intense dedication to learning and was ordained as a rabbi.

R' Pinto wrote a number of scholarly books, most of which include the word *"kesef"* (silver) in the title. He explains in the introduction to his book *Kesef Sarouf*, that he always felt inadequate in his ability to serve *Hashem* as he should, but that the idea of silver comforted him and gave him hope. Just as silver can be made purer through smelting, so can a person be continually refined and purified. He passed away in the month of Adar, 5408 (1648). A year later he was eulogized by his son-in-law R' Shemuel Vital, the son of R' Haim Vital. The eulogy was recorded in R' Shemuel's book *Mekor Haim* (lecture 31).

The books authored by R' Yoshiyahu Pinto are as follows:

- *Kesef Nivhar* (Venice 5381/1621). Inspirational lectures on the Torah. He began to prepare the book for printing in Damascus in 1605 and loaned a sum of money to the printer to pay for the printing equipment that he would need. However, the quality of the printed result was unacceptable and he had to send the book to Venice to be printed. R' Yaakob Abulafia provided an approbation, praising the author highly for his knowledge of Torah.
- *Kesef Mezukak* (Venice 5385/1625). Inspirational lectures on the Torah (125 lectures).
- *Me'or Einaim* (Vol. I, Venice 5385/1625, Vol. II, Mantua 5500/1740). Commentary on *Ein Yaakob* (narratives of the *Gemara*). Each volume was initially published by itself and was subsequently published together with the text of *Ein Yaakob*. The commentary of the *Maharsha* was also added to Volume I.
- *Kesef Sarouf* (Amsterdam 5489/1729). Commentary on *Mishlei*. Publishing was arranged by R' Yitzhak Moshe Lofez, who received the manuscript from a grandchild of the author.
- *Nivhar MiKesef* (Aram Soba 5629/1869, Sasson Press). Responsa on the four parts of the *Shulhan Aruch*. This was the first original work to be printed by the new Aram Soba press of R' Abraham Sasson (see #475).
- *Kesef Nimas*. Commentary on *Eichah*. Never published, although it was mentioned by the *Hida* (R' Haim Yosef David Azulai) in his index of books.
- *Kevusat Kesef*. Selected *halachot*. Never published. This book was originally intended for use by students as a review book. However, the depth of insight that it revealed was highly praised by R' Abraham Sasson, who edited *Nivhar MiKesef* for printing. R' Eliyahu Hai Sasson (see #476), the son of R'Abraham, writes in *Toldot HaRif*, a biography of Señor Pinto which is an appendix to *Nivhar MiKesef*, that the manuscript for *Kevusat Kesef* is stored in the *Bet Midrash* of R' Hai Moshe Picciotto (see #454) in the care of Señor Raphael Picciotto (see #460), consul of Russia and Prussia.

He wrote a number of scholarly books, most of which include the word "kesef" (silver) in the title. Just as silver can be made purer through smelting, so can a person be continually refined and purified.

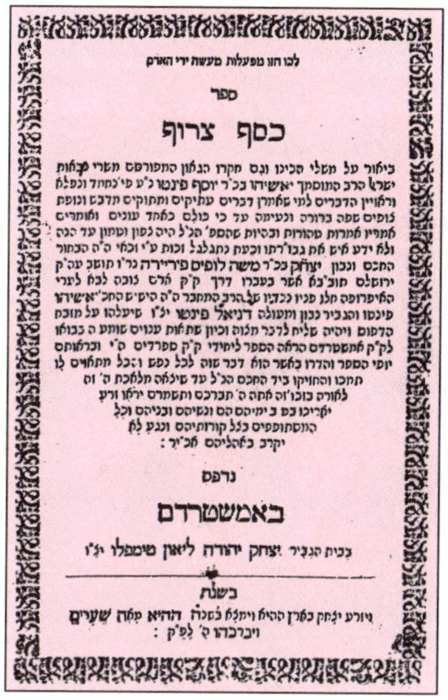
ספר
כסף צרוף
באמשטרדם

Title page of Kesef Sarouf

Nivhar MiKesef was the first original work to be printed by the new Aram Soba press of R' Abraham Sasson (see #475).

[464] PINYERO, Señor Abraham

סי' אברהם פינירו

(— 1764)

Eminent philanthropist of Aram Soba. He was one of the major supporters of the scholars of the city. He passed away on 17 Sivan, 5524 (1764) and was eulogized by the Chief Rabbi of Aram Soba, R' Raphael Shelomo Laniado (see #363). He was survived by a young son Yaakob and a young daughter Deborah.

ספר
כסף מזוקק
IN VENETIA

Title page of Kesef Mezukak

[465] RABIA (SUTTON), R' Abraham

רבי אברהם רביע (סתהון)

(1890 — 1972)

Eminent scholar and rabbi of Aram Soba and Tel Aviv. He was born in Aram Soba in 1890 to R' Moshe Rabia, but became orphaned at a young age and grew up in the general orphans' home of the city. He studied Torah under R' Ezra Shayo (see #505) and R' Abraham Antebi (see #64).

For many years he taught *Gemara* at the orphans' home and in 1945 he decided to settle in *Eretz Yisrael*. As he attempted to cross the border, he was picked up by British troops and held in a stockade. However, it wasn't long before the Haganah attacked the camp and freed its inmates. He was then able to resume his journey and settled in Tel Aviv where he became rabbi of the congregation of Aram Soba immigrants. In his later years he suffered from severe illness, finally passing away on 7 Tevet, 5733 (1972). He was survived by worthy children who followed in his footsteps. One of his sons-in-law was R' Shalom Hedaya.

R' Yehudah Sadkah as a young man

[466] ROSA, R' Haim

רבי חיים רוזה

(— 1771)

Worthy scholar and rabbi of Aram Soba. When he passed away he was eulogized by R' Obadiah Levy (Mizrahi) (see #392), as recorded in his book *Hazon Obadiah* (p. 115). He passed away in 5532 (1771).

[467] ROSA, R' Moshe

רבי משה רוזה

(19th century)

Eminent scholar and rabbi of Aram Soba. His father's name was R' Reuben Rosa. He is known for having written a book of spiritual guidance called *Zichron Tob* (Livorno 5595/1835). In it he mentions a number of books that he has written and hopes to see published:

- *Vayivhar Moshe*. Commentary on the Torah.
- *Ohel Moshe*. Two volumes, clarifying difficult passages in the introductions to a number of books.
- *Gan Hashem*. Lectures on the mystical approach to Torah.
- *Ohr Nogah*. Principles of Kabbalah.
- *Anfei Zutrei*. Meaning of the *halachot* (laws).
- *Sefer HaDrushim*. Inspirational lectures.

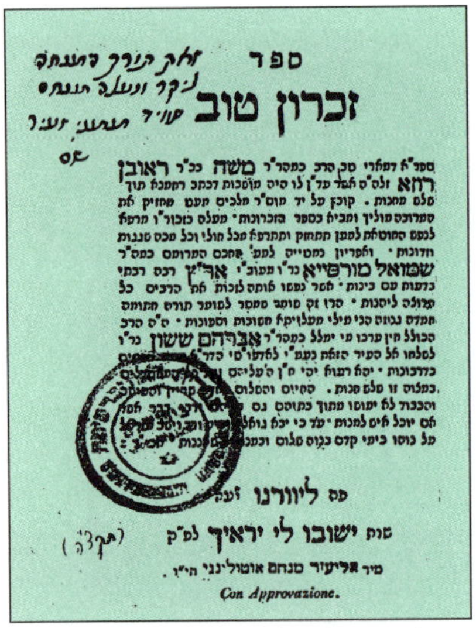

ספר

זכרון טוב

משה ... ראובן רוזא

שמואל מורפייא

אברהם ששון

פה ליוורנו

שנת ישובו לי יראיך לפ"ק

Con Approvazione.

Title Page of Zichron Tob

[468] SADKAH, R' Yehudah

רבי יהודה צדקה

(1909 — 1992)

Distinguished *Rosh Yeshiva* of *Porat Yosef* in Jerusalem. He was also the first teacher of many of our rabbis. At the age of 21 he taught a group of 11-year-olds the entire tractate *Eruvin* during their first year of yeshiva. Hacham Ben-Sion Abba Shaul (see #24), Hacham Sion Levi, Hacham Ovadiah Yosef, and Hacham Baruch Ben-Haim were all part of R' Sadkah's "wonder class" and eventually grew to be his equals.

In the middle of the school day, during an hour when they would normally be on a break, R' Sadkah would take his students to an empty *Bet Midrash* and continue to teach them Torah. He wanted them to be accustomed to learning in private, with modesty, and without all the accolades that may come with Torah scholarship.

R' Sadkah taught that just as it was required to put on *tefillin* of the hand (representing the workingman) and *tefillin* of the head (representing those learning) without any interruption in between, so too, the rabbi and the workingman are inexorably connected. He encouraged laymen to learn and demanded diligence from them. He would quote the book *Hochmah U'Mussar* by R' Abraham Antebi (see #63), attributing the success of the Syrian community to the workingmen who would rise early and then stay up late to learn Torah both morning and night.

R' Sadkah would quote the beginning of the second *perashah* of the Torah to describe his formula for learning. *"Eileh toldot Noah, Noah ish sadik"* ("This is the history of Noah, Noah was a righteous man") — this is how one becomes a *sadik* (righteous man). The letters in "Noah" (נח) are also the initials for *"nekudat hazot"* (נקודת חצות) (the exact moment of midnight) and *"netz hamah"* (נץ חמה) (first light of sunrise). R' Sadkah recommended that men stay up learning until *hazot* (midnight), and then wake up for morning prayers at *netz* (sunrise). By refraining from material desires, R' Sadkah showed that it can be feasible to carry on naturally with a minimal amount of sleep. This seemingly unsustainable regimen is said to have the power to elevate men to the status of angels.

R' Sadkah was a sixth-generation descendant of R' Sadkah Houssin (see #313) and so preserved the name of his forebear, which means "charity."

R' Sadkah credited his mother, the niece of the *Ben Ish Hai* (Chief Rabbi of Baghdad), for guiding him properly in Torah. When he was young, his mother was bold enough to pull him out of a yeshiva when she had misgivings about the *Yirat Shamayim* (fear of G-d) of the teachers. She was keenly aware and interested in her son's education and always offered him sage advice.

His entire life, R' Sadkah maintained a *Taanit Ra'avad* — whenever he ate something he liked, he would leave over the last bites as an act of self-control. Also, to mourn the destruction of the *Bet HaMikdash,* he would not eat meat or drink wine on Mondays and Thursdays. The *Shulhan Aruch* cites a custom of fasting on these days and the *Kaf HaHaim* advises to refrain from meat and wine for those who wish to follow this custom but are unable to fast twice a week.

His legacy lives on with his many students. His son R' Moshe took over the position of *Rosh Yeshiva* of *Porat Yosef*'s Geulah branch and many of his deep insights were printed in his book *Kol Yehudah.*

R' Yehudah Sadkah in his later years

[469] **SAFDEYÉ (BAWABE), R' Shelomo**

(— 1904)

רבי שלמה צפצ'ייה

Distinguished scholar and Chief Rabbi of Aram Soba at the end of the 19th century. He assumed the position of Chief Rabbi after the retirement of R' Abraham Dweck-Khalousi (see #257) in 1895.

He was a descendant of R' Yosef Safdeyé, an eminent 18th-century scholar and rabbi of Aram Soba, who passed away in the month of Shevat 5496 (1736). R' Yosef was a contemporary of R' Shemuel Laniado (see #372), R' Sadkah Houssin (see #313), and R' Yehudah Kassin (see #331). He had two brothers, R' Yeshuah and R' Abraham, and a son named R' Shelomo, who was apparently a great-grandfather of R' Shelomo Safdeyé (Bawabe), the Chief Rabbi.

R' Shelomo Safdeyé (Bawabe) was an extremely pious man, who lived a very long life. He had no sons, only daughters. He passed away on 29 Av, 5664 (1904) in the town of Tedef, which is near Aram Soba, and that is where he was buried, next to the grave of R' Michael Ashkenazi (see #95).

He studied Kabbalah with R' Ezra Tawil (see #582) and R' Shemuel Morsaya (see #434). Their collaboration resulted in a book of *hiddushim* (original Torah thoughts) on Kabbalah, *Emet Me'Aretz* (Jerusalem 5748/1988), published by the yeshiva *Ahabat Shalom*.

When word of his passing reached Jerusalem, he was eulogized by R' Meir Laniado (see #358) in a large gathering, as recorded in the book *MeHalab Ha'Aretz* (section *Ha'ye Shelomo*, page 105-106) of R' Yosef Shayo (see #507).

The local Arabs wanted to take the body to their own cemetery, but this was resisted by the Jewish community and so he was buried properly. His burial place became a destination for all people, even Arabs, who had particular needs or problems that they hoped to be resolved through prayers at his graveside.

His burial place became a destination for all people, even Arabs, who had particular needs or problems that they hoped to be resolved through prayers at his graveside.

He was the author of a manuscript book of responsa on practical *halachic* issues, which also included *hiddushim* (original Torah thoughts) on Kabbalah. One of his responsa was published in the book *Maaseh Ish* of R' Yaakob Shaul Elyashar, the *Rishon LeSion* (Chief Rabbi of *Eretz Yisrael*) (*Even HaEzer* 8). In introducing this material, the

His father was the scion of a highly respected Aleppo family, whose roots in the banking business began during the age of the Ottoman Empire.

Rishon LeSion speaks of R' Safdeyé with the immense admiration and the highest praise. He is also spoken of admiringly by R' Shalom Hedaya (see #310) in his book *Shalom Le'Am*, who attributes his own success in part to R' Safdeyé's financial aid and moral support when he was a young orphan, as he otherwise would have had to go to work.

Mr. Edmond J. Safra

[470] **SAFRA, Mr. Edmond J.**

מר אדמון צפרא

(1931 — 1999)

Eminent philanthropist and international banker of Beirut and Sao Paulo. A deeply religious man, he dedicated himself and his great wealth to the preservation of our Jewish heritage. He financed the restoration, construction, and maintenance of synagogues, schools, and *yeshivot* in more than twenty countries around the world.

His Roots

He was born to Mr. Jacob Safra in the summer of 1931 in the resort town of Aley, near Beirut. His father was the scion of a highly respected Aleppo family, whose roots in the banking business began during the age of the Ottoman Empire. The family bank in Aleppo was headed by Mr. Yosef Safra, who actively supported all the major institutions of the city. Yosef's daughter Esther married Jacob Safra, who was the son of Eliyahu Safra, Yosef's first cousin. Their union was blessed with four talented sons to carry on the family tradition for banking and philanthropy. The second son was Edmond Safra. The other three were Elie, Moise, and Joseph.

Jacob Safra moved to Beirut in 1921 at a time when business conditions in Aleppo were becoming especially difficult because of the success of the Suez Canal, which had replaced the overland trade route through Aleppo. Six Aleppo families immigrated to Lebanon at the same time, giving Jacob Safra the push he needed to start his own branch of the Safra bank in Beirut.

The Beirut Jewish community actually began in the late 1860's. Until then, Lebanese Jewry was focused in Sidon and the mountains of the south. The first synagogue of Beirut was built by Sir Moses Sassoon of India and named *Magen Abraham* to memorialize his father Abraham Sassoon. It was one of the most beautiful synagogues in the Middle East. Jacob Safra insisted on having a part in it and in the late 1920's he added a *Bet Midrash*, naming it *Midrash Eliyahu* in memory of his own father.

The Magen Abraham Synagogue of Beirut

The Lebanese community in those years numbered between 3,000 and 4,000 families until the influx of Syrian Jews after the riots of the late 40's, when it grew to 12,000. Jacob Safra almost single-handedly supported the major Jewish institutions of Lebanon, among them: *Bikur Holim* (aid to the sick), *Mohar Betuloth* (for poor brides), *Matan B'Seter* (for the poor), *Tipat Halab* (for newborns and their mothers), and the Jewish clinic for the poor.

The Lebanese Jews would spend the summer months in the resort town of Aley, where Edmond was born in 1931. On occasion the families staying in Aley for the summer would spend the High holy Days there, but the small local synagogue could not accommodate the large crowd. Jacob Safra would open his house to the overflow *minyan* of over a hundred people. This lasted for a period of over 30 years. Every year on the eve of *Shabuot* over a hundred men would gather in his house for the all-night reading of the *Tikkun*. All of his sons kept this custom strongly and always made sure to spend *Shabuot* night in a synagogue that would reflect their family tradition. Interesting to note, Mr. Jacob Safra passed away on *Ereb Shabuot* (1963).

During the years when Edmond grew up there was no yeshiva in Beirut so his father hired private tutors to give him a Torah education, among them Hacham Nissim Tabbakh, Hacham Moussa Jajati, and Hacham Alfia.

Edmond Safra lost his mother when he was only 12 years old. He later confided to his assistant, Marcos Zalta, that this loss was a tremendous blow to him. In fact, his memory of her became a great inspiration for his charitable deeds. He always remembered how she would go around Beirut, sending poor Jewish families to her home to ask her husband Jacob for help.

Building a Business

Working alongside his father, the young Edmond was destined to extend his family's reputation for trust throughout the world. The boy was just 16 when he went to Milan to work on behalf of his family's banking business. Following Edmond's recommendation, the Safra family moved to Brazil, where father and son founded Banco Safra S.A., today one of Latin America's most highly respected banking institutions. Later, Edmond Safra was to become founder and honorary chairman of the Republic National Bank of New York, among various other banking institutions.

Edmond Safra greeting Hacham Ovadiah Yosef and Hacham Ben-Sion Abba Shaul in Yeshivat Porat Yosef

His Love for Synagogues

He inherited his father's love for synagogues and on business trips, when seeing an old synagogue in ruins, he would pay for its refurbishment. When still in his 20's he refurbished a synagogue in Rhodes, Greece, and later the ancient Spanish synagogues of Madrid and Toledo. Throughout his life he continued to repair the small ancient synagogues that the Jews of Spain had built while fleeing the Inquisition, some of them as far as the Dutch Caribbean.

> *He inherited his father's love for synagogues and on business trips, when seeing an old synagogue in ruins, he would pay for its refurbishment.*

Left to right: Mr. Elie Safra Rabbi Yaakob Attiah, R' Yehudah Ades, Mr. Edmond Safra, and R' Harel

He built the Bet Yaakob synagogue of Sao Paolo, named in memory of his father. The synagogue was under the leadership of Hacham Shahud Shrem (see #515), originally from Aleppo and Beirut. Later the position was filled by R' Ephraim Laniado, son of Hacham David-Sion (see #352). In

Edmond speaking at the dedication of the Bet Yaacob complex at Bat Yam

the United States he gave generously to the new building of the congregation *Shaare Zion* and his family name is on the building. He dedicated the *hechal* (Torah ark) in the Sephardic synagogue of Deal, New Jersey. The synagogue of Turnberry, Florida is known as the Edmond J. Safra synagogue.

For a long time, he yearned to build a new synagogue for Manhattan's Jewish community. After a lengthy search, he eventually bought two townhouses near the corner of Fifth Avenue and East 63rd Street. He contacted a lawyer to check on the zoning. It turned out that those were the only two on the block that were not zoned as landmark buildings and so construction of the synagogue was possible. The existing buildings were made available for prayer and study almost immediately. However, Mr. Safra passed away before the construction of the synagogue could begin. Under the close supervision of his wife, Lily Safra, the new building was completed in 2002, three years after his passing. The Edmond J. Safra synagogue of New York, which was dedicated in the presence of the Chief Rabbi of Israel and the mayors of New York City and Jerusalem, became part of his eternal legacy.

R' Attiah, who originated from Aleppo became Edmond Safra's rabbi, confidant, teacher and mentor. In fact Mr. Safra honored R' Attiah over all men, next to his own father.

His Commitment to Torah Learning

Mr. Safra donated many Torah scrolls and sacred books to *yeshivot* and synagogues. In Israel, Mr. Safra had a special concern for *Yeshivat Porat Yosef* and its scholars. When the yeshiva's building overlooking the *Kotel Maarabi* (Western Wall) was rebuilt after the Six Day War, he dedicated the *Bet Midrash* in the name of his father. He preferred the *Bet Midrash* over the synagogue because the *Bet Midrash* is used for learning all week and the synagogue is primarily for *Shabbat*.

Edmond with R' Shraga Moshe Kalmanowitz

He also restored the graves of Rabbi Meir Baal Haness in Tiberias and Rabbi Shimon bar Yochai in Miron and ensured that Torah would always be studied there by opening *yeshivot* and Talmud Torah schools at the sacred sites. Mr. Mourad Kattan related that Mr. Safra shipped gold with no insurance. He gave the equivalent money to the charity of Rabbi Meir Baal Haness instead.

When R' Yaakob Ades (see #42) passed away in 1962, Mr. Safra helped his son, R' Yehudah Ades, establish the *Yeshivat Kol Yaakob* in R' Yaakob's memory.

He had a close connection to R' Eliyahu Shrem (see #509) of *Yeshivat Torah V'Horaah* of Tel Aviv. R' Shrem was also involved in maintaining the tomb of Rav Shimon bar Yohai and Mr. Safra became actively involved in the rebuilding and expansion of that holy site.

He established the *Bet Yaakob* education complex in Bat Yam under the leadership of R' Yaakob Attiah, the rabbi of the Lebanese congregation in that city. R' Attiah, who originated from Aleppo became Edmond Safra's rabbi, confidant, teacher and mentor. In fact Mr. Safra honored R' Attiah over all men, next to his own father. The educational complex houses a *Bet Midrash* and a *kollel* of 30 *avreichim* (young scholars) who come from Bnei Brak every day. It also contains a synagogue and *mikvaot* (ritual baths) for men and women.

With R' Yaakob Attiah's help, Mr. Safra also provided the funding to publish the book *Minhat Yeh*udah of R' Yehudah Attiah (see #118). The book was prepared for publication by R' Ephraim Attiah, the youngest son of the author, and was dedicated in memory of Mr. Safra's parents.

He participated with Mr. Isaac Shalom (see #497) in supporting the *Ozar HaTorah* organization and helping R' Pardo's education complex in Israel for girls known as *Ohr HaChaim*.

In America he gave generously to many *yeshivot,* among them *Yeshivat Magen David* where he dedicated the third floor and the dining room.

On a visit to America in the 80's he dedicated two Torah scrolls to the *Shaare Zion* congregation. He was approached by R' Shraga Moshe Kalmanowitz and invited to visit the Mirrer Yeshiva, which was only a few blocks from *Shaare Zion*. He accepted the offer and visited the *Bet Midrash* on a Sunday afternoon. He walked straight to the *hechal*, bowed his head, kissed the *parochet* (curtain), and recited a short prayer. He then turned around and saw the hundreds of young men learning with such excitement in very cramped quarters. He was so moved that he began to cry; it hurt him to see them learning in such cramped accommodations. He turned to one of his American confidants and said, "We must help expand this *Midrash*." On the spot he pledged $100,000 to the Mirrer Yeshiva.

He had a warm relationship with Hacham Ovadiah Yosef, who would call him to chat on occasion. He was on friendly terms with the Chief Rabbi of Switzerland, R' Safran, and the Chief Rabbi of France, R' Sitruk.

Rabbi Abraham Abadie (see #3) had a long-standing relationship with Mr. Safra dating back to a time when they were both living in Lebanon. During one of the last meetings that took place between the Rabbi and Mr. Safra, Elie Abadie, youngest son in the Abadie family, accompanied his father to Republic National Bank. Rabbi Abadie proudly introduced his son to Mr. Safra, and explained that he was studying to become a rabbi. Mr. Safra's comment echoes an ironic foreshadowing of things to come. He looked at the young Rabbinical student, and mentioned the need for young Sephardic rabbis in the community. He told Rabbi Abraham Abadie, "I am sure your son Elie will provide a tremendous service to the community." Twenty-two years later Rabbi Elie Abadie serves as the spiritual leader of the Edmond J. Safra Synagogue on Manhattan's Upper East Side.

His Other Charitable Works

Mr. Safra also donated to numerous other causes, such as hospitals, cultural institutions, and humanitarian associations throughout Israel and around the world.

He had great empathy for the poor and needy. A few hundred families in Israel, South America, and Iran received monthly checks from his foundation. His assistant, Marcos Zalta, recalled how one year, just before *Pesah*, Mr. Safra woke him up at 1 o'clock in the morning in a panic. Apparently, unable to sleep, he had stepped into an office that Mr. Zalta kept in Mr. Safra's home and found a letter from someone on his fax machine. "Come here, it's urgent," he insisted. It was a letter from a woman who was raising money for a number of very poor families, each of which was described in the letter. He wouldn't sleep until Mr. Zalta called later and assured him that all of the families would be taken care of and that they would have enough food for *Pesah*.

At the dedication of the Sephardic Mikveh
Left to right: Sonny Laniado, Mayor Beame, R' Hecht, Edmond Safra, Ike Hidary, Manny Haber, R' Elnadav, and Mr. Nouri Dayan

When one of his many housekeepers fell ill and needed emergency heart surgery, he accompanied her to the hospital and spent the entire day there so he could see her when she awoke, because her family was far away in Brazil. She told Mr. Zalta afterwards that seeing Mr. Safra with his famously warm and beautiful smile was the only thing that gave her the strength to survive the ordeal.

When he was approached by beggars on the street, he insisted on always giving something. He explained to Mr. Zalta that it didn't matter that these people might be drug addicts or alcoholics. He felt that one must have compassion for whatever may have been the circumstances that led them to beg on the street.

He noticed that many Jewish college students were in Geneva with no kosher restaurant, so he funded a kosher restaurant. Even though it ran at a loss, he kept it going and made sure the owner had a profit.

Praying at the groundbreaking ceremony of the Republic National Bank World Headquarters located in New York
Left to right: Miro Sutton, Edmond Safra, and Rabbi Yaakob Kassin (#330)

When it came time to allocate the estate of Halfon and Jacob Laniado, he was instrumental, together with Mr. Yehezkel Chouela of Montreal, Mr. Isaac Shalom (see #495), and the Klausenberg Rebbe, in directing the building and funding of the Laniado Hospital, operated under the guidelines of *halachah*.

Edmond Safra lighting a candle in honor of Eliyahu HaNabi at a Brit Milah. Mickey Kairey to his right

"No one remains here forever. When you leave, two angels will accompany you, due to the merit of bringing purity and holiness to the community with your involvement in this special project."

He won't enter the building at all until the Hanukat HaBayit is done and all the mezuzot are up." From the day the bank opened, he hired ten rabbis to come daily to recite the entire Tehillim. When he sold the bank, they moved to his synagogue in Manhattan.

He was involved in building the Sephardic *mikveh* (ritual bath) of the Brooklyn community on Avenue S. Mr. Ike Hidary, the treasurer of that project, related the following story: At the grand opening ceremony, Rabbi Shraga Moshe Kalmanowitz addressed the crowd. He turned to Edmond and said, "No one remains here forever. When you leave, two angels will accompany you, due to the merit of bringing purity and holiness to the community with your involvement in this special project."

His Faith

With all his wealth and fame he kept the *emunah peshutah* (simple, sincere faith) instilled in him by his parents and teachers as a young boy. When talking with a close confidant about his business goals and aspirations, and complaining a little about not seeing enough gains, his assistant reminded him, "The *Gemara* says that someone who has food for today but worries about tomorrow is called one of the *ketanei emunah* (those with limited faith)." Edmond immediately took this rebuke to heart, saying earnestly, "*Hatati, aviti, pashati*" (I have sinned greatly). In contrition, he beat his fist on his heart and said, "You will never hear me complain again."

People with simple faith pay close attention to the reading of the Torah portion when they are called up for their *aliyah* (blessing on the Torah). He once received an *aliyah* during which the reading was, "*Hashem imcha b'chol asher telech*" (G-d is with you wherever you may go). He pointed his finger to the heavens and remarked to the man next to him, "Did you hear what He is telling me?"

Mr. Safra once told Rabbi Isaac Dwek that he sees a miracle once a month.

In the Republic National Bank world headquarters at 5th Avenue. and 40th Street in Manhattan, when he opened the bank he invited 10 community rabbis to read the entire *Tehillim* before the *Hanukat HaBayit* (inauguration) reception. One of the rabbis asked a bank officer, "Where is Mr. Safra?" The answer was, "He's not here; he's never been here. He won't enter the building at all until the *Hanukat HaBayit* is done and all the *mezuzot* are up." From the day the bank opened, he hired ten rabbis to come daily to recite the entire *Tehillim*. When he sold the bank, they moved to his synagogue in Manhattan.

His Humility

He remained humble throughout his life, as illustrated by the following story. A high-ranking officer in the bank, who was a relative of Mr. Safra, was once complaining to him in a rude fashion to the effect that Mr. Safra was interfering in his plans for growth. Mr. Safra gave him a shocked look and said, "Shame on you, after all I have done for you." This man knew very well what Mr. Safra was referring to. After all, Edmond Safra had given him the opportunity to succeed in business and had helped him during difficult times in his personal life. Nevertheless, the man responded, "What have you done for me? You were just a messenger of G-d. I gave you the opportunity to do a kindness." Mr. Safra's response was, "I am sorry. Forgive me."

His assistant, Marcos Zalta, recalled how Mr. Safra never seemed to accept that he was more important than anyone else. Once, they had traveled to Frankfurt to meet with the chairman of Deutschebank, then the largest bank in the world. "Mr. Safra kept reminding me how important this man was and I kept reminding Mr. Safra how important Mr. Safra was. When we walked into the meeting, the chairman was surrounded by Deutschebank's top executives and they all fell over themselves telling Mr. Safra how much they admired him, how they followed his every move, and thought he was the greatest banker in history. Mr. Safra accepted the compliments with his characteristic grace, but afterwards said, 'They didn't mean it, they were just trying to flatter me'"

His Legacy

Edmond J. Safra followed the teachings of traditional Judaism throughout his life and was a champion of Jewish communities the world over. Shortly before he died in 1999, he established and endowed the Edmond J. Safra Philanthropic Foundation, ensuring that needy individuals and organizations would continue to receive assistance and encouragement for many years to come. His wife Lily is the president of the foundation and continues his philanthropic work in his memory.

He never forgot his younger years among the French-speaking Jews of Beirut and so he had a special interest in helping the Jews of France. In fact, he dedicated an entire yeshiva building there.

During the last years of his life, Mr. Safra lived in the French-speaking city of Geneva, Switzerland. That is where he breathed his last, and it was there that he was buried. His good friend, R' Sitruk, the Chief Rabbi of France, spoke at the funeral.

To carry on his self-defined mission of spreading Torah learning, the philanthropic foundation that carries his name has funded a 73-volume of translation of the Talmud to make the sacred text more accessible to French-speaking people around the world. Some six volumes will be produced by the Artscroll organization each year, with the entire project expected to take well over a decade to complete.

The above is only one of scores of important projects that the foundation is funding throughout the world in fulfillment of Mr. Safra's wishes. Among these are seven projects in Argentina, including the *Yesod HaDath* School *and the Sucath David* Community Center. In Austria the foundation provides funding to the Jewish Cemetery of Hohenems.

France is the beneficiary of 23 projects aided by the foundation, including the network of *Ozar HaTorah yeshivot* and the *Yeshiva Ketanah* of Marseilles. There are 49 projects in Israel where foundation funding is generously given. Among these are the Aleppo Heritage Center, construction of 15 synagogues throughout Israel, the *Kol Yaakob* yeshiva of Jerusalem, Rav Meir Baal Haness of Tiberias, *Merkaz Torani* of Raananah, *Ohr HaChaim* of Jerusalem, *Porat Yosef* yeshiva of Jerusalem and the *Shuvi Nafshi* Foundation.

In the Netherlands, the Safra foundation supports the Sephardic Synagogue of Amsterdam. There are no less than 87 projects and institutions in the United States that receive needed funding from the foundation. Among the most notable of these are the following Brooklyn congregations: *Ahiezer, Ohel David and Shlomo*, and *Shaare Zion*. Other important congregations receiving foundation assistance include the Congregation *Beit Yaakov* of Baltimore and congregations carrying the Edmond J. Safra name in Deal,New Jersey New York, and Turnberry.

Among the many other countries where significant foundation support is directed, it is important to mention Italy, Russia, Switzerland, and the United Kingdom.

Mr. Safra was eulogized in the *Shaare Zion* synagogue of Brooklyn, New York. His cousin and associate, Mr. Miro Sutton, referred to the Safra family as royalty and to Edmond as its crown prince. He made the following analogy: The British look to the house of Windsor, the Dutch look to the house of Orange-Nassau. Our Sephardic community looked up to the house of Safra. Mr. Zalta spoke of his personal memories, working alongside Mr. Safra for over five years. He recalled that Mr. Safra never lost patience with anyone and that when he, Mr. Zalta, lost patience, Mr. Safra would remind him, "If you want to be a big cup, you had better learn how to be big and strong enough to carry all of the little cups around you."

He noted that Mr. Safra had so much respect for others that he never told Mr. Zolta that he was wrong about anything. What he would do instead was to ask him, "Are you sure of your answer?"

The philanthropic foundation that carries his name has funded a 73-volume of translation of the Talmud to make the sacred text more accessible to French-speaking people around the world. Some six volumes will be produced by the Artscroll organization each year, with the entire project expected to take well over a decade to complete.

The Safra French Edition

R' Abraham Salem

Besides the material and financial assistance, he treated each young man with courtesy and kindness to help him face up to the challenges of married life.

Mr. Safra honored his father and mother to an extraordinary degree and was constantly dedicating new synagogues in their honor. He had a large portrait of his father next to his desk in every office around the world. The driving force behind his success in banking was to glorify the Safra name and make his father proud of him.

[471] SALEM, R' Abraham

רבי אברהם סאלם

(— 1938)

Eminent Kabbalist and teacher of Aram Soba. He nurtured many students in Aram Soba and Jerusalem. When he came to Jerusalem his scholarly depth was quickly recognized and he was accepted as a worthy colleague. Some of his *hiddushim* were published under the name *Ha'ye Abraham* by R' Yosef Shayo (see #507) at the end of the anthology *MeHalab Ha'Aretz*. He was blessed with scholarly sons: R' Natan Salem (see #472) and R' Shelomo Salem (see #473). His daughter Bolisa married Hacham Ezra Attiah (see #102), who was later to become *Rosh Yeshiva* of *Porat Yosef*.

He passed away on 24 Nissan, 5698 (1938).

Salem family picture,
Second row: R' Abraham Salem
Above him to right: his son R' Natan
Second row, second to right: his son-in-law R' Ezra Attiah

[472] SALEM, R' Natan

רבי נתן סאלם

(1896 — 1975)

Eminent scholar, Kabbalist, and activist of Aram Soba and Jerusalem. He was born in Aram Soba in 1896, to R' Abraham Salem (see #471). His mother Sarah was a daughter of the illustrious house of Harari-Raful.

His Early Years in Aram Soba

From his youngest years he grew up among scholars and he modeled himself on them. His father arranged for him to study under R' Yosef Haim Cohen, the *Rosh Bet Din* of the congregation of *Mustarabim*.

One of his first major initiatives was the *Hachnasat Kallah* fund, which he established and managed. With the proceeds of the fund he was able to provide respectable amounts to help young scholars start their new homes. Besides the material and financial assistance, he treated each young man with courtesy and kindness to help him face up to the challenges of married life.

He was a member of a group of scholars who met in a room near the Great Synagogue of Aram Soba to immerse themselves in the study of Kabbalah around the clock. Subsequently, the entire group moved to Jerusalem.

A Scholar in Jerusalem

In Jerusalem he studied under R' Haim Shaul Dweck (see #228), R' Yosef Yedid (see #594), and R' Ezra Attiah (see #102).

He was a pillar of strength among the scholars of Aram Soba in Jerusalem, helping them organize their social services and other institutions. One of his neighbors in Jerusalem was R' Hizkiah Shabbetai (see #495), Chief Rabbi of Aram Soba. R' Shabbetai approached R' Salem, saying that he felt his days were coming to an end and he had not studied every part of the Torah that he felt he should. They arranged to study together the *Rambam's* treatment of the *halachot* of sanctifying the New Moon (*Kiddush HaHodesh*). For this purpose they met in the yeshiva *Shaarei Orah* in the synagogue *Yagel Yaakob* in Jerusalem.

Shortly before R' Shabbetai passed away he requested that at his funeral, two specific rabbis should recite the *piyut*(hymn), *"Lecha Eli Teshukati"* (My G-d, I Yearn for You), that opens the *Yom Kippur* service. He named the two rabbis: R' Yitzhak Nissim, who was the *Rishon LeSion* (Chief Rabbi of *Eretz Yis-*

rael), and R' Salem. As his body was being carried from his house to the cemetery, the two rabbis recited the *piyut.*

R' Salem earned his livelihood in Jerusalem as a teacher of *Gemara*. Initially he taught in the Talmud Torah *Benei Sion* and subsequently in the Talmud Torah *Doresh Sion*. However, when the latter Talmud Torah was placed under the auspices of the Jewish National Fund, he immediately resigned. He then went to the Talmud Torah *Magen David*, which had been established by R' Ezra Harari-Raful (see #304) and his son R' Aharon Harari-Raful (see #303). He stayed in *Magen David* a number of years and ultimately became its principal.

A Life of Teaching

He stayed in Magen David a number of years and ultimately became its principal.

Early-Morning Robbers. One early morning when both he and his wife were out of the house to attend *Selihot* services, their house was robbed. All objects of value were taken, including money and other property that he was holding for a charity fund. When they returned home and found the entire house in disarray, he showed no concern over the loss of his own property, just about the loss of that which belonged to the charity. He consoled his wife, saying that she should not feel too much anguish over the loss; perhaps the robbers would do *teshuvah* (penance) and they would return what they took. The verse says, "Sins will cease from the earth" (*Tehillim* 104:35) — that is sins, but not sinners. In other words, we hope for the destruction of sin, but not the destruction of the sinner, for we pray that he will repent.

He then presented the situation to the *Bet Din*, which at that time was headed by R' Ben-Sion Abba Shaul (see #24) to see if R' Salem was liable for the loss to the charity fund. The ruling was that he was not responsible because he had done everything that could reasonably be expected to safeguard the property of the fund. Furthermore, this was public money and no one could make a claim against him. However, the *Bet Din* advised him that in the future, whenever he gave money to charity he should do it with a condition that if he does have any outstanding liability to charity, this new donation should be counted against it. Still, despite being cleared by the *Bet Din*, his conscience continued to bother him. Could he not have taken additional steps to protect the property of the charity fund? He was never able to give himself a satisfactory answer and so he finally sold a piece of land that had come to him as an inheritance, and used the proceeds to provide compensation to the charity fund for everything that had been taken. It was only then that his mind was at peace. (The topic is discussd in *Ohr LeSion, Hoshen Mishpat* Vol. I sec. 7.)

His Legacy

He was blessed with a scholarly son, R' Abraham Salem, who became the head of the *Kollel Porat Yosef* and subsequently *Rosh Yeshiva* of *Meor HaTorah* in Jerusalem. R' Natan Salem passed away on Thursday night, 9 Kislev, 5736 (1975). The funeral took place the same day and he was buried on *Har HaMenuhot*.

He left behind wonderful memories of a beloved teacher, who had influenced his young students during a critical time of their lives.

In later years one of his students recalled that when he was a youngster of 8 or 9, they were told by boys of another Talmud Torah that a show for children was scheduled to take place that afternoon in the hall adjacent to the Talmud Torah. All the youngsters were excited about the prospect of going to it. However, Hacham Natan Salem gathered his students together and gravely announced that there was no absolute prohibition against going to the show, but that anyone who did so should be aware that he would be giving up his chance at receiving a piece of the tongue of the Leviatan, which would be provided at the banquet of the righteous when the Messiah comes. These words had their desired effect.

R' Natan Salem

He then called him over and whispered something in his ear.

He recalled that on another occasion all the students of the Talmud Torah went on an outing with their teachers to the Dead Sea area and on the way their bus got stuck in the sand for no apparent reason. The driver tried everything he could, but was unable to get the bus moving again. Finally, Hacham Natan asked the boys to get off the bus and to help push, while repeating three times the verse *V'yhi Noam* (*Tehillim* 90:17), which ends: "May He establish our handiwork for us; our handiwork may He establish." With this the bus immediately jumped out of its rut and began to move. In addition to their amazement at this wonder, they all received a lesson for life that anything may be accomplished through the power of prayer.

The same man recalled with fondness the day that Hacham Salem took his class on their annual outing to Bnei Brak to visit the *Hazon Ish* in his residence. This experience made a tremendous impression on each boy — to see this plain, humble Jew, bending over his wooden table, with a house full of holy books, engaged in the study of Torah. They were grateful to *Hashem* that they were given the opportunity of receiving a blessing from him.

An elderly woman visited a daughter-in-law of Hacham Natan and told her a fascinating story, which illustrates his way with children. In her younger years, this woman had been a nurse in an infant-welfare clinic. Her duty was to go around to all the schools to administer injections to immunize the children against sickness. When she came to the Talmud Torah *Magen David*, there was one child who wept bitterly and adamantly refused to receive his shot. After returning home that night, he refused to return to school altogether, and stayed away for an entire week, all for fear of the injection. When Hacham Salem heard about it, he persuaded the boy to return to school. He then called him over and whispered something in his ear. Immediately, the child agreed to take the injection with no further resistance. The nurse was amazed and asked the child what the rabbi had said to him. He answered that the rabbi had promised him that if he recited the entire verse *"Shema Yisrael"* he would have fear of no one other than *Hashem*, and so nothing would hurt him. This is exactly what he did, and it worked. After that, whenever a child resisted the injection, the nurse would tell him to say *"Shema Yisrael,"* and that would take away all fear and pain. She found this to be very effective.

R' Shelomo Salem

His Humility

A story illustrating his humility was told by R' David Attiah, *Rosh Kollel* of *Hechal Ezra* (son of R' Ezra Attiah; see #102). When R' Salem became old and found it difficult to walk, he was concerned about becoming a burden on his family. He told R' David, "If I get to the point where I am unable to take care of myself, please put me in a nursing home; I don't want to be a burden on my wife and son, causing him to lose time from Torah study." It was awesome to hear words like these spoken by someone who worked all his life to help keep people out of having to resort to places like that.

[473] SALEM, R' Shelomo

רבי שלמה סאלם

(1898 — 1978)

Worthy scholar and teacher of Aram Soba and Jerusalem. He was born in Aram Soba in about 1898, a son of R' Abraham Salem (see #471). He earned his livelihood as a teacher of *Gemara* and in his later years he was the principal of the *Magen David* Talmud Torah in Jerusalem. He was blessed with a beautiful singing voice with which he pleased *Hashem* and his fellow man. He passed away on *Rosh Hodesh* Nissan, 5738 (1978).

[474] SARDAR, R' Yaakob

רבי יעקב סרדאר הלוי

(— 1964)

Worthy scribe and Kabbalist of Aram Soba. He was totally dedicated to the quality of his craft and to the elevated thoughts with which he accompanied his work. He passed away on 9 Shevat, 5724 (1964).

[475] SASSON, R' Abraham

רבי אברהם ששון

(— 1869)

Distinguished printer of Aram Soba. A son of R' Yeshuah Sasson (see #482) and a grandson of R' Yisrael Sasson (see #483), he started the first Hebrew printing press in Aram Soba. This was a bold thing to do in that time, involving great danger, the risk of substantial loss, fear of competition, etc. The introduction of a Hebrew press was a great boon to the community and R' Abraham received much encouragement from the rabbis of Aram Soba. In 1865, to help him protect his investment they issued an official endorsement of the new venture, prohibiting anyone from starting a competing press over a period of 20 years. (See Document Section, Document No. 25.)

Prior to the introduction of the press, R' Sasson would manage the printing of books by painstakingly copying the manuscripts and bringing them to distant places where printing establishments were located. Among the many works which he published in this way was his grandfather R' Yisrael Sasson's book *Keneset Yisrael* and his father R' Yeshuah Sasson's book *Yeshuat Yisrael* (Livorno 5617/1857), both of which were bound in one volume. He also edited the book *Mikra Kodesh* (Livorno 5624/1864), containing prayers and *pizmonim* (hymns) for special occasions, supplemented by commentary and spiritual guidance.

Traveling to distant places to get books printed was very dangerous and time consuming, so R' Abraham began to consider the possibility of opening a printing shop in Aram Soba. He was also motivated by the fact that the 1850's and 1860's were a time of intellectual ferment in Syria, with many Arabic and Christian printing establishments being started. He sent his son R' Eliyahu Hai (see #477) to Livorno to learn the printing trade firsthand.

Once the printing press was established in Aram Soba, R' Abraham inaugurated it by producing reprints of well-established books of spiritual guidance, such as R' Haim Vital's book *Shaare Kedushah* (5626/1866) and *Alim LeTerufah* of the *Ramban* together with *Iggeret Mussar* of the *Vilna Gaon* (5626/1866). Books like these were always in demand and there was less risk in finding a market. It was only in 1869 that the first new work was produced. This was *Nivhar MiKesef*, a book of responsa written by R' Yoshiyahu Pinto (see #463), for which R' Abraham did the final editing before typesetting.

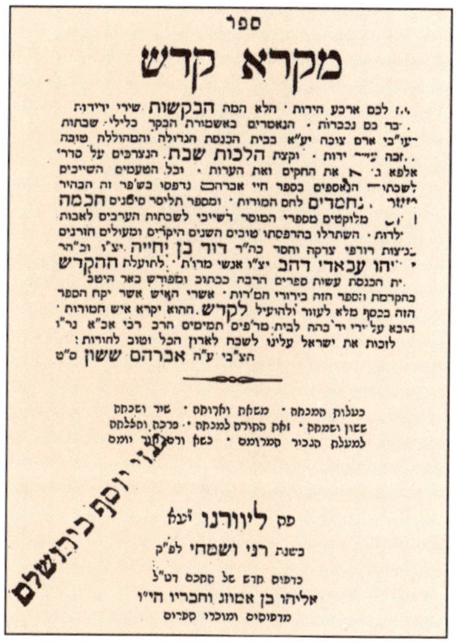

Title Page of Mikra Kodesh

The Sasson press remained in operation for seven years and was closed with the departure of R' Eliyahu Hai to Jerusalem, where he continued his activities in the printing field. The reason for the discontinuance of the Sasson press is not known, although it is likely that the difficult economic conditions in Aram Soba were a factor. Altogether 14 books were produced over the eight-year period, of which nine were books of spiritual guidance, three were books of responsa, and two were books of *pizmonim* (poetic hymns). Of the 14 books only seven were the product of Aram Soba scholars.

ספר

עלים לתרופה

והוא אגר' מוסר מהמאור הגדול

הגאון רבינו הרמב"ן זצ"ל ששלח

לבנו · ועוד אגרת מוסר ששלח

לבני ביתו הגאון רבינו אליאו

מווילנא זצ"ל זיע"א :

נדפס בארם צובה יע"א

Title Page of Alim LeTerufah, One of the first books printed in the Sasson press

R' Yeshayah Dayan (see #203) waited until the 20-year ban was up before opening his own press, even though the Sasson press had closed.

R' Abraham was blessed with three sons: R' Yeshuah Hai, R' Eliyahu Hai, and R' Moshe Hai. The two youngest sons worked in the printing business with their father. He passed away on 25 Kislev, 5630 (1869).

The Sasson family was known for their musical talent. The ability to sing was passed down from generation to generation. R' Abraham, his father R' Yeshuah, his grandfather R' Yisrael, and great-grandfather R' Yosef were all known as great singers.

[476] SASSON, R' Eliyahu

רבי אליהו ששון

(— 1848)

Eminent scholar and rabbi of Aram Soba. He was a son of R' Yisrael Sasson (see #483), and was the author of two or

R' Abraham inaugurated it by producing reprints of well-established books of spiritual guidance.

more manuscripts. One was an elucidation of R' Eliyahu Mizrahi's commentary on the Torah. The other was a book of responsa. He passed away in 5608 (1848) leaving two scholarly sons: R' Yisrael and R' Shaul.

[477] **SASSON, R' Eliyahu Hai**

רבי אליהו חי ששון

(19th century)

Distinguished printer of Aram Soba. A son of R' Abraham Sasson (see #476), he was the driving force behind the city's first Hebrew printing press, which his father introduced. When R' Eliyahu Hai moved to Jerusalem in 1873, the printing press was closed.

He and his brother R' Moshe Hai are highly praised in the introduction, written by their father R' Abraham, to the book *Nivhar MiKesef* of R' Yoshiyahu Pinto. R' Eliyahu Hai wrote a biography of the author, which he appended to the book.

[478] **SASSON, R' Faradj**

רבי פראג' ששון

(— 1910)

Worthy scholar and rabbi of Aram Soba. He passed away on 28 Adar 2, 5670 (1910).

[479] **SASSON, R' Meir**

רבי מאיר ששון

(— 1865)

Worthy scholar and rabbi of Aram Soba. He passed away on 4 Sivan, 5625 (1865) and was eulagized by R' Yaakob Abadi (see #13).

[480] **SASSON, R' (Raphael) Moshe**

רבי (רפאל) משה ששון

(— 1885)

Eminent scholar and chief scribe of Aram Soba. He also authored a work containing responsa on the *halachot* of preparing Torah scrolls, *tefillin*, and *mezuzot*. He is believed to have signed the approbation to the book *Yashir Moshe* of R' Moshe Dayan (see #192) using the name Raphael Moshe Sasson.

He joined R' Aharon Choueka (see #153) and R' David Kassin (see #322) in signing a *halachic* (legal) ruling, which was subsequently published in the book *Imrei Noam* (Aram Soba 5658/1898) by R' Yeshayah Dayan (see #203).

He was a brother of R' Yisrael Sasson (see #484). In 1844 he joined R' Moshe Cohen (see #164) and R' Nissim Yeshayah Harari in a pact of friendship, a conscious observance of the *mitzvah*, ואהבת לרעך כמוך, "you shall love your neighbor as yourself" (*Vayikra* 19:18). They solemnized the pact with a contract of friendship which all three signed.

In the same year his name appeared on a contract dealing with inheritance, which he signed together with R' Shelomo Nehmad (see #447) and R' Moshe Cohen.

He passed away on *Rosh Hodesh* Av, 5645 (1885).

[481] **SASSON, R' Shelomo**

רבי שלמה ששון

(— 1865)

Worthy scholar and rabbi of Aram Soba. He was a son-in-law of R' Yeshayah ben Elazar Hai Dayan (see #202).

[482] **SASSON, R' Yeshuah**

רבי ישועה ששון

(— 1828)

Eminent scholar and rabbi of Aram Soba. He was a son of R' Yisrael Sasson (see #483) and was known for his important book of inspirational lectures on the Torah, *Yeshuat Yisrael*. This book was published by his son R' Abraham Sasson (see #476) together with R' Yisrael Sasson's book *Kenesset Yisrael* (Livorno 5617/1857). He received approbations from leading rabbis of Jerusalem and Livorno, among others. He also joined the rabbis of Aram Soba in signing the introduction to the book *Yoshev Ohalim* by R' Abraham Antebi (see #63).

R' Yeshuah had a difficult and tragic life. In the introduction to his book he speaks of his first wife who suffered eight miscarriages, before passing away. When his second wife, Rachel, gave birth to a boy he was overjoyed and made a great celebration "with wine and beer." However, his wife was unable to nurse the baby properly and after eight months of suffering it died.

R' Yeshuah himself did not live a long life and passed away in 1828 before finishing his introduction. It was completed for him by the publisher, who appears to have been his grandson. He writes that Rachel ultimately gave birth to two surviving sons: R' Abraham and R' Yosef. When she also passed away he married a third wife, Sarah. With Sarah, R' Yeshuah had two daughters and one son. He named one of the girls Sabtiah after his mother and he named the other Hanolah. He named the boy Raphael. With the passing of R' Yeshuah, the responsibility of raising the children fell to his oldest son R' Abraham.

[483] **SASSON, R' Yisrael**

רבי ישראל ששון

(— 1810)

Eminent scholar and rabbi of Aram Soba. He was a son of R' Yosef Sasson (see #488) and was known for his important book of responsa, *Kenesset Yisrael*. This book was published by his grandson, R' Abraham Sasson (see #476), together with his son's book *Yeshuat Yisrael* (Livorno 5617/1857). He received approbations from leading rabbis of Jerusalem and Livorno, among others.

He also wrote a commentary on *Orah Haim*, named *Bet Yisrael*, which remained in manuscript form. His grandson, who saw to the publishing of *Kenesset Yisrael*, included a section of *Bet Yisrael* in it, with the expressed hope that an opportunity would arise to publish the entire book.

R' Sasson was a colleague of R' Eliyahu Shamah (see #499), who makes frequent references to him in his book *Korban Isheh*. A number of responsa written by R' Sasson were included in the book. R' Sasson joined R' Shamah in signing the introduction to the book *Zechor LeYitzhak* by R' Yitzhak Harari (see #295). In addition, all three joined in signing the introduction to *Beirach Moshe* by R' Moshe Galante, the Chief Rabbi of Damascus. In addition, he signed an approbation to *Zera Yitzhak* by R' Yitzhak Attiah (see #120).

R' Sasson passed away on 27 Sivan, 5570 (1810). He was blessed with five scholarly sons: R' Yeshuah, R' Yitzhak, R' Yosef, R' Eliyahu, and R' Ezra.

[484] **SASSON, R' Yisrael**

רבי ישראל ששון

(— 1889)

Worthy scholar of Aram Soba. His father is not known, but he was a grandson of the earlier R' Yisrael Sasson, the author of Kenesset Yisrael (see #483). He was the father of R' Yomtob Sasson (see #486) and passed away in Jerusalem on 6 Adar, 5649 (1889).

Note: An additional scholar by the name of R' Yisrael Sasson lived in Damascus. He passed away there on 17 Nissan Adar, 5634 (1874). However, not much else is known about him.

זה
ספר הבהיר
כנסת ישראל
חלק ראשון
שאלות ותשובות על ארבעה טורים
פה ליוורנו יע"א
ברפוס המשובח
של שלמה בילפורטי וחברו ס"ט

Title Page of *Kenesset Yisrael*

[485] **SASSON, R' Yisrael**

רבי ישראל ששון

(19th century)

Worthy scholar and *dayan* (judge) of Aram Soba. He was one of the rabbis who signed the approbation for the printing initiative (see Document Section, Document No. 25) of R' Abraham Sasson (see #475). He passed away on 25 Tevet, but the year of his death is unknown.

R' Yisrael Sasson (# 483) was an eminent scholar and rabbi of Aram Soba. He was a son of R' Yosef Sasson (see # 488) and was known for his important book of responsa.

[486] **SASSON, R' Yomtob**

רבי יום טוב ששון

(— 1861)

Eminent Kabbalist and rabbi of Jerusalem. He was a son of R' Yisrael Sasson (see #484) and came to Jerusalem as a young boy. In Jerusalem he applied himself to Torah study, excelling in both the revealed and the mystical approach. Because of his piety and dedication he was appointed to head the Kabbalist yeshiva *Bet El*. He passed away on 25 Av, 5681 (1921) and was eulogized by R' Yosef Yedid (see #594).

R' Yomtob Sasson

[487] **SASSON, R' Yosef**

רבי יוסף ששון

(— 1843)

Worthy scholar and rabbi of *Porat Yosef*. He was born in Aram Soba, a son of R' Yehudah Sasson and moved to Jerusalem, where he became a lecturer and teacher at the yeshiva *Porat Yosef*. He was known as a man of great humility and gentleness, who had a remarkable impact on his many students. He passed away on 7 Iyar, 5703 (1943).

Worthy scholar and rabbi of Porat Yosef.

R' Yosef Sasson (#487)

[488] SASSON, R' Yosef

רבי יוסף ששון

(19th century)

Worthy scholar and rabbi of Aram Soba. He was the brother of R' Moshe Sasson and R' Eliyahu Sasson. R' Yosef was blessed with two scholarly sons: R' Yisrael Sasson (see #483), who praised him in his book *Kenesset Yisrael*, and R' Raphael Moshe Sasson (see #480).

[489] SASSON, R' Yosef (Raphael)

רבי יוסף (רפאל) ששון

(— 1832)

Eminent scholar and rabbi of Aram Soba. In 1827 he delivered a eulogy for Señor Raphael Picciotto (see #459), as described by R' Yosef Haim Yaluz in the book *Tov Re'i* (Jerusalem 5694/1934). In the following year his name appeared on a document signed by the rabbis of Aram Soba to guarantee a pledge for support of the scholars of the city.

In 1831 he joined R' Abraham Antebi (see #63) in signing a document of arbitration in a claim by the widow of Señor Raphael Picciotto against the heirs of her deceased husband. In the same year seven leading rabbis of Tiberias sent a letter to him asking for his help and introducing their emissary R' Yehudah Nehmad (see #448). The letter showed much respect for R' Sasson and praised him as a great Torah scholar.

He passed away on 25 Tamuz, 5592 (1832).

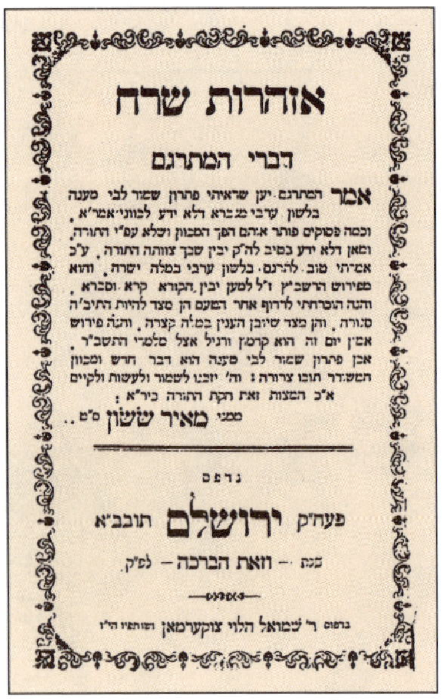

אזהרות שרח

דברי המתרגם

ממני מאיר ששון ס"ט..

נדפס

פעה"ק ירושלם תובב"א

בשנת — וזאת הברכה — לפ"ק

בדפוס ר' שמואל הלוי צוקערמאן ושותפיו הי"ו

Title Page of Azharot Shareh

[490] SASSON (ADJMI), R' Eliyahu Hai

רבי אליהו חי ששון עג'מי

(— 1861)

Worthy scholar and rabbi of Aram Soba. According to his grave marker he passed away on 28 Heshvan, 5622 (1861). However, little else is known about him.

[491] SASSON (ADJMI), R' Meir

רבי מאיר ששון עג'מי

(— 1911)

Eminent scholar and scribe of Aram Soba. He was an expert in preparing Torah scrolls, *tefillin*, and *mezuzot*. He also authored a number of scholarly works, most of which involved Arabic-Hebrew translations as indicated by the Arabic word *Shareh* in the title:

- *Mishlei Shareh* (Jerusalem 5644/1884). Arabic translation of the book of *Mishlei*.
- *Tehillim* (Jerusalem 5645/1885). Hebrew text and Arabic commentary on the Book of *Tehillim* with elucidation based on the earlier commentators.
- *Kohelet Shareh* (Jerusalem 5645/1885). Arabic translation of the Book of *Kohelet*.
- *Iggeret Mi Kamocha* (Jerusalem 5645/1885). Commentary on the poetic hymn *"Mi Kamocha"* by R' Yehudah HaLevi. The hymn recounts the story of *Purim* and is customarily recited on the *Shabbat* before *Purim (Parashat Zachor)* in Aram Soba.
- *Azharot Shareh* (Vol. I Jerusalem 5646/1886, Vol. II Aram Soba 5648/1888). Arabic translation of the 613 *mitzvot* broken into two parts, positive and negative commandments, as defined by R' Shelomo Ibn Gabirol. This is read on the holiday of *Shabuot*.
- *Eichah Shareh* (Aram Soba 5648/1888). Arabic translation of the book of *Eichah*.
- *Iyob* and *Kohelet Shareh* (Aram Soba 5649/1889). Arabic translation of the Books of *Iyob* and *Kohelet*.

His books received approbations from the leading rabbis of Aram Soba.

In 1901 his name appeared in the list of Aram Soba scholars receiving a weekly stipend from the special fund that had been set up for the support of worthy individuals who dedicate their lives to Torah study (see #267 and Document Section, Document #30). His name was the first on the list, indicating the high esteem in which he was held. He passed away on 9 Tevet, 5672 (1911).

[492] SAYAGH, R' Ezra

רבי עזרא צייג

(— 1807)

Eminent scholar and rabbi of Aram Soba. He joined other rabbis of Aram Soba in signing the introduction to the book *Mahane Yehudah* of R' Yehudah Kassin (see #331). He himself was the author of the manuscript *Pri Etz Hadar*, consisting of inspirational lectures on the Torah and the five *Megillot*. At the Ben-Zvi Institute (file no. 302) there is an original bill of sale dated 1792. R' Sayagh's name appears there as the third signer after R' Yosef David Laniado (see #386) and R' Eliyahu Abadi (see #4).

He passed away on 14 Shevat, 5567 (1807), leaving three scholarly sons: R' Shabbetai, R' Moshe (a worthy *shohet* [ritual slaughterer]), and R' Yosef. He was eulogized by his son-in-law R' Moshe Swed (see #573), as recorded in the book *Masveh Moshe*, and by R' Abraham Sutton (see #535), as recorded in the book *Malel Le'Abraham*.

[493] SAYAGH, R' Ezra

רבי עזרא צייג

(— 1906)

Worthy scholar and teacher of Aram Soba. He was a teacher of young boys and appears to have been a descendant of the earlier R' Ezra Sayagh (see #492). He passed away on 25 Iyar, 5666 (1906).

SCHWEKY, see CHOUEKA

[494] SHABBETAI, R' Abraham

רבי אברהם שבתי

(— 1889)

Eminent scholar and rabbi of Aram Soba and Jerusalem. In 1876, together with other scholars and rabbis of Aram Soba, he signed a letter of excommunication against the makers of cheese who were desecrating *Shabbat* by working a seven-day week. (See Document Section, Document No. 28.) The letter was countersigned by a number of faithful cheesemakers who committed themselves to abide by the restrictions. Later in life he moved to Jerusalem, where he was respected for his Torah knowledge, both revealed and mystical. He wrote a manuscript of moral guidance and inspirational lectures for the High Holy Days.

He was a learning partner of R' Nissim Harari-Raful (see #305). They would fast the entire week during *Shobabim* [acronym for six weeks from *Perashat Shemot* to *Perashat Mishpatim*]. The fast extended for six days, from Sunday to Friday. (See #313 for a lengthy discussion on these weeklong fasts.)

He passed away on 21 Iyar, 5649 (1889).

Title Page of Iyob and Kohelet Shareh

[495] SHABBETAI, R' Hizkiah

רבי חזקיה שבתי

(1862 — 1955)

Distinguished Chief Rabbi of Aram Soba, Jaffa, Tripoli and Chief *Av Bet Din* (Chief Judge) of Jerusalem. He was born in Salonika in 1862 to R' Gabriel Yehoshua Shabbetai. His family moved to Jerusalem while he was still a boy. He studied there in the *Bet Midrash Doresh Sion* and in the yeshiva *Hesed El*. He was sent a number of times to other countries as an emissary of the Torah institutions of Jerusalem and Hebron.

R' Hizkiah Shabbetai

In the year 1900 he was appointed as Chief Rabbi of Jaffa, a position which he held until 1904. He then served as Chief Rabbi of Tripoli (Libya) until 1908. In that year R' Hizkiah was then called to Aram Soba where he served as Chief Rabbi until 1924. His official position in Aram Soba gave him the status of a government dignitary. As part of the honors due his office, his carriage was always preceded by two mounted Jewish guardsmen. All police officers of the city were required to stand up and salute when he passed by. On his chest he wore a medallion that had been sent to him by the Turkish sultan in Istanbul.

He used his position for the honor of Heaven and did not hesitate to rebuke those who publicly violated rabbinical authority. Individuals who steadfastly refused to comply were subject to excommunication, and their names were posted in every synagogue of the city. There was a case of a man whose wife committed adultery but he refused to divorce her as directed by the *Bet Din*. After consulting with the rabbis of

All police officers of the city were required to stand up and salute when he passed by. He used his position for the honor of Heaven and did not hesitate to rebuke those who publicly violated rabbinical authority.

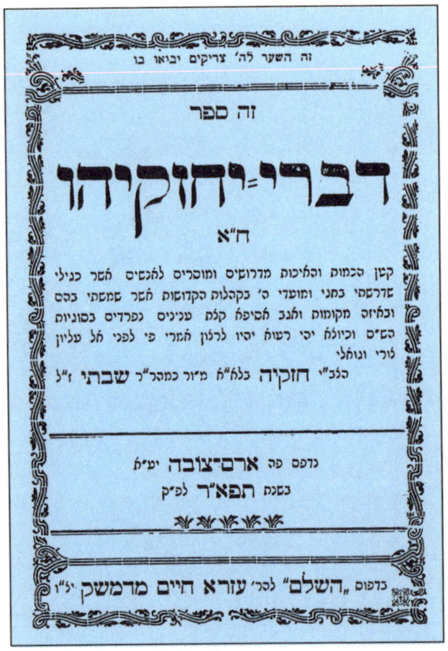

זה השער לה׳ צדיקים יבאו בו

זה ספר

דברי־יחזקיהו

ח״א

קטן הכמות והאיכות מדרושים ומוסרים לאנשים אשר כגילי שדרשתי בחגי ומועדי ה׳ בקהלות הקדושות אשר שמשתי בהם ובאיזה מקומות ואגב אסיפה קלת ענינים נפרדים בסוגיות הש״ס וכיוצא יהי רצון יהיו לרצון אמרי פי לפני אל עליון צורי וגואלי

הצב״י חזקיה בלא״א מ״ור כמהר״ר שבתי ז״ל

נדפס פה ארם־צובה יע״א

בשנת תפא״ר לפ״ק

בדפוס „השלם" לכר׳ עזרא חיים מדמשק יצ״ו

Title Page of Dibrei Yehezkiyahu

the city, R' Shabbetai excommunicated the individual. Each year when the *Hatarah* (public release of vows and excommunications) was made before *Rosh Hashanah*, R' Shabbetai would personally announce, "We release all vows and excommunications, except those of [the man in question]."

During World War I, he devoted his energies to helping scholars avoid being drafted into the Turkish army and to getting support for the many children who were orphaned during the war. In 1926 he returned to Jerusalem, where he served his remaining days as *Av Bet Din* (Chief Judge), as well as a member of the Chief Rabbinate of Israel. He passed away in Jerusalem at an advanced age on 23 Av, 5715 (1955).

One of his neighbors in Jerusalem was R' Natan Salem (see #472). One day R' Shabbetai approached R' Salem, saying that he felt his days were coming to an end and he had not studied every part of the Torah that he felt he should. They arranged to study together the *Rambam's* treatment of the *halachot* of sanctifying the New Moon (*Kiddush HaHodesh*). For this purpose they met in the yeshiva *Shaarei Orah* in the synagogue *Yagel Yaakob* in Jerusalem.

Left to right: R' Abraham Shrem, R' Ezra Attiah (#102), Mr. Isaac Shalom, R' Yaakob Ades (#41), R' Yehudah Sadkah (#468)

Shortly before he passed away he requested that a specific *piyut* (hymn) traditionally said on the eve of *Yom Kippur* be recited at his funeral by R' Yitzchak Nissim, who was the *Rishon LeSion* (Chief Rabbi of *Eretz Yisrael*), and R' Salem. As his body was being carried from his house to the cemetery, the two rabbis recited the *piyut "Lecha Keli Teshukati"* (My G-d, I Yearn for You).

He authored a number of books during the course of his active life.

- *Dibrei Yehezkiyahu* (Aram Soba 5681/1921). Inspirational lectures which the author delivered in various cities on a variety of occasions.
- *Dibrei Hizkiyahu* (Vol. I Jerusalem 5695/1935, Vol. II Jerusalem 5712/1952). Responsa and *hiddushim* (original Torah thoughts) on *Gemara*. *Dibrei Yehezkiyahu* was also included at the end of Volume I of this book.
- *Megillat Sefer (Jerusalem 5654/1894)*. Booklet containing a lecture which he delivered on the occasion of the completion of a new Torah scroll in 1894.

Some of his *hiddushim* were incorporated into *Shaare Rahamim* of R' Rahamim Yosef Franco.

Other *hiddushim* appeared in the journal *HaMe'asef* published by R' Ben-Sion Kouenka.

[496] SHABBETAI, R' Moshe

רבי משה שבתי

(— 1869)

Worthy scholar and administrator of charitable institutions in Aram Soba. He passed away on 26 Tevet, 5630 (1869).

SHABOT, see CHABOT

[497] SHALOM, Mr. Isaac

מר יצחק שלום

(1885 — 1968)

Distinguished philanthropist and civic leader. He was a unique individual who became renowned for his efforts on behalf of the American Syrian Jewish community, and as founder of the Ozar HaTorah schools for the Sephardic children of Israel, North Africa, and Europe.

Humble Beginnings

He was born in 1885 in Aram Soba to Josef and Nizha Shalom, G-d-fearing people of modest means. As a teenager, Isaac became a textile salesman working for a local merchant in Aram Soba. An attempt at starting his own business was not financially rewarding, but served as a good learning experience.

In 1910, at the age of 25 Isaac Shalom joined the great wave of immigrants making their way to the United States. Like many of his countrymen he became a door-to-door linen peddler on the teeming streets of Manhattan's Lower East Side. Like many of the other peddlers from Syria he spoke no English and had to wear his name and address pinned to the front of his coat for identification. However, Isaac distinguished himself as an outstanding salesman. He soon became one of the "Oriental" jobbers, a group of ten Syrian merchants headquartered on Allen Street. With the improvement in his situation, Isaac sent for his family and in 1917 he married Alice Chabot, sister of Morris (Chabot) Levy (see #391) and Mr. Bert Chabot (Levy), who is remembered in her own right for her work in the community.

Growth of a Leader

In 1919 he established the handkerchief firm of I. Shalom & Co., which developed into one of the leading manufacturers of men's and ladies' accessories in the U.S. However, for Isaac Shalom, material success meant very little. It was just a means by which he could advance his spiritual goals.

As a lifelong supporter of worthy causes, he became a central figure in the growing community which had begun to cross the river, leaving the crowded tenements of the Lower East Side for the tree-lined avenues of Brooklyn. He organized and led the congregation *Shaare Zion*, which was the first American congregation devoted to preserving the traditions and heritage of Aram Soba. He worked to help the thousands of arrivals from Syria and Egypt adjust to their new life in America. Besides providing assistance in finding a place to live and a way to make a living, he looked after the newcomer's spiritual welfare, arranging for rabbis and teachers to ensure that the link with the Aram Soba heritage was preserved.

He was a man of honor, well liked and well trusted, often called upon to arbitrate disputes. His last name, meaning "peace," was certainly no misnomer.

Mr. Isaac Shalom discussing the Gemara with R' Yehudah Sadkah (#468) and R' Ezra Attiah (#102), with R' Abraham Shrem in background

International Benefactor

In 1934 Isaac and his wife traveled to the Europe and the Middle East at the behest of Mr. Joseph Shamah (see #500), who was a devoted activist for Jewish education. What they found was one million Jews of Sephardic descent, mired in poverty and oppression. He realized that without schooling and the Western tools of

Mr. Isaac Shalom addressing a gathering of rabbis —on his right: R' Porush; On his left, R' Yaakob Ades (#41), R' Yitzhak Dayan (#205), and R' Ezra Attiah (#102)

progress the children of these communities would soon be lost entirely to their heritage. Nor could he ignore the threat which the Nazis posed to the Jews of Europe. He worked closely with R' Abraham Kalmanowitz, who led the entire Mirrer Yeshiva to safety through Siberia to Shanghai, and with R' Aharon Kotler, who took the same route with some of his students, emerging to found the Lakewood

R' Abraham Kalmanowitz and Mr. Isaac Shalom

Rabbis of Porat Yosef gather to greet Mr. Isaac Shalom
Left to right: R' Ezra Ades (#38), two unknown, R' Elchonon Sorotzkin, R' Yehudah Sadkah (#468), R' David Shaharbani, R' Ezra Shrem (#510), R' Yaakob Ades (#41), philanthropist Solomon Sasson, R' Ezra Attiah (#102), Mr. I. Shalom, R' Obadiah Hedaya (#309)

Yeshiva and the *Vaad Hatzolah* (committee for Jewish rescue in the United States). He worked with R' Eliezer Silver, Mr. Irving Bunim, and many other leaders of the *Vaad Hatzolah,* traveling to Washington to meet with President Roosevelt and other senior government people in numerous attempts to ransom individuals from Europe.

Mr. Isaac Shalom touring the Middle East, 1945

While the Holocaust laid waste to Eastern Europe, the heritage of the Bet Yosef in the Middle East, especially in North Africa, was under siege from the threat of assimilation, fueled by hardship and despair. In 1940, together with Joseph Shamah he established the committee to save Sephardic Jewry.

After the war, he remembered the determination of R' Abraham Kalmanowitz in saving the Mirrer Yeshiva and enrolled him in the massive challenge of saving Moroccan Jewry. He promised to stand at his side and persuaded him to make a momentous trip to North Africa in 1947. In a letter home, R' Kalmanowitz wrote: "Throughout Morocco, Algeria, and Tunisia, I found approximately 60,000 Jewish children, over 10,000 of whom have been swallowed up by the Alliance schools, which are completely devoid of Torah. Of the approximately 40,000 remaining children ... most study in *chedarim* or *Talmudei Torah,* while a completely neglected minority have no formal education at all.

"Unfortunately, the *chedarim* (elementary schools) and *Talmudei Torah* are in a very sorry state, with no *sefarim* (books), no qualified teachers, and no capacity for absorbing the students already learning in them. Their site and location makes it impossible to serve the needs of the *talmidim* even if we were to try to renovate them. I found 120 children crowded together on the floor in one dingy, filthy, poorly lit small room, with just two *Chumashim* and one teacher for all of them. In the communal Talmud Torah too, there were a hundred children in one class, with a single *melamed* (teacher)."

Through their joint efforts they founded *Ozar HaTorah*, an organization that provided Hebrew education for tens of thousands of Jewish children in France and in the Arab countries of North Africa and the Middle East. Graduates of the *Ozar HaTorah yeshivot* went on to become leaders and rabbis of Jewish communities throughout the world.

Even after *Ozar HaTorah* was established, children still had to be plucked from hundreds of cities, towns, and villages across the length and breadth of Morocco, Algeria, and Tunisia. This involved tremendous efforts on the part of the leaders of *Ozar HaTorah* in Morocco, and R' Kalmanowitz, with Isaac Shalom, never ceased pushing them to their limits, giving them *chizuk* to persevere and praising them for their efforts.

By 1948, just one year after his initial trip to Morocco, R' Kalmanowitz wrote a letter to his friend and European contact, R' Yitzchak Sternbuch, saying that thus far they had already opened "twenty-eight *yeshivos ketanos* and twenty Talmud Torahs." This was an amazing achievement for R' Kalmanowitz and Mr. Shalom. It was in effect a revolution of major proportions. Without a doubt, the unusual *Siyata Dishmaya* (help from Heaven) they merited was in keeping with their faith that if one throws himself into the work of *Hashem* without ulterior motives, one is rewarded by *Siyata Dishmaya* that transcends nature.

Surprise for the Joint. The story is told that Isaac Shalom approached the Joint Distribution Committee (JDC) and offered to construct the edifices which would serve *Ozar HaTorah's* schoolchildren, if the Joint would agree to provide the financial support for the overhead, i.e. teacher's salaries, maintenance, food, etc. Thinking that he would probably not construct more than one or two schools, the JDC accepted. We can well imagine their shock when in the short period of five years, the student population reached 10,000, with schools throughout North Africa! After a while, enrollment increased to 20,000 students. Today, many of their alumni reside in *Eretz Yisrael.*

Charity was a top priority and a natural part of his daily routine. His *Neveh Shalom* foundation dispensed funds the world over and always employed one or two people at his office, I. Shalom and Co.

Mr. Shalom's support of *Eretz Yisrael* was inspirational. He invested in Amcor Ltd., which developed into one of Israel's major companies. The profits realized from this initiative were used to further his commitments to the land and its people. Sensitive to the spiritual void at the time, he was instrumental in building and sustaining a number of *yeshivot*, including *Porat Yosef*, the Yeshiva High School in Herzliyah, *Yeshiva Neveh Eretz of* R' Eliyahu Raful, and many others. He also made sure that the teachers of the *yeshivot* were paid well, so that they could dedicate their efforts toward developing the next Torah generation.

The Beginnings of Ohr HaChaim and the Laniado Hospital of Netanyah. It all started when R' Yehoshua Heller of the *Ponevezh Yeshiva* made his annual visit to the office of Mr. Isaac Shalom. Mr. Shalom listened intently as R' Heller described the situation of Sephardic Jewry in Israel and abroad, and his eyes lit up when he heard about the success of *Ozar HaTorah* and the devotion of its staff. R' Heller then told how the *Ponevezher Rav*, R' Yosef Kahaneman, had started a new girls' school. He then explained that the *Ponevezher Rav* assigned him to the new institution to help them build a new building. The girls were coming in droves and there was nowhere to place them.

Mr. Shalom asked, "Are you referring to R' Pardo's new institution (*Ohr HaChaim*)?"

The Klausenberger Rebbe

"Yes," answered R' Heller. "Do you know him?"

Mr. Shalom said, "He came to my office last week and showed me pictures and documents. I would have investigated more if I thought I could help him. What can I do? My abilities to give aid abroad are limited. I told him I would give him a token donation and he burst into tears."

The fact that R' Pardo burst into tears touched R' Heller to the point that he too began to cry. Mr. Shalom didn't understand. "What's wrong, R' Heller?" he asked.

R' Heller answered, "I'm not crying and R' Pardo isn't crying. It's the tears of the hundreds of girls living in crowded conditions and the tears of the thousands would-be students." Then R' Heller had an idea.

"Whatever happened with the estate of the philanthropists Jacob and Halfon Laniado?" he asked. The Laniado's had left a large sum of money for which Mr. Shalom was the executor. The condition of the legacy was that the bulk of the money would go toward building a hospital. Mr. Shalom had consulted with the *Ponevezher Rav*, who said that under no circumstances could he open a hospital that wasn't run by religious people and under the guidelines of *halachah*. In a hospital run by irreligious people there would be abortions and removal of organs in improper ways, nonkosher food would be served, and *Shabbat* would be desecrated. However, Mr. Shalom was concerned about the money lying idle. He said that if they build a hospital now, the leftover money could go for a yeshiva. The *Ponevezher Rav* answered, "Have patience. The time will come and a hospital will be built according to *halachah*."

Mr. Shalom answered R' Heller, "I am waiting for the right opportunity."

"Did you ever hear of the *Admor* (Grand Rabbi) of Klausenberg?"

"No," answered Mr. Shalom.

Rabbi Moshe Pardo

"He is a Holocaust survivor, who lost his whole family during the war. He is rebuilding his community in Israel. During his torturous stay in the concentration camps, seeing all the death and destruction, he vowed that if he survived he would open a hospital to save Jewish lives. The *Klausenberger Rebbe* is now in New York looking for a donor." Mr. Shalom started to dance with joy and clap his hands. "Set up a meeting with the Rebbe. We will build the Laniado hospital [which is in Netanyah] and the surplus will build a dormitory for *Ohr HaChaim*."

R' Heller wasn't finished. "R' Pardo needs to be compensated for his tears."

Mr. Shalom took out his checkbook and wrote a check on the spot for $50,000. He then spoke to his friend David Mishan who sat behind him in *shul* and asked him to help. Mr. Mishan donated an entire building that stands in his name. He also asked his friend, Mr. Joe Ades, and he donated a building as well. This is one story of many that illustrates Isaac Shalom's benevolence, ingenuity, and concern for Torah education, and above all his practice of always consulting with rabbis on matters of community service.

Isaac Shalom founded Magen David, first as a Talmud Torah, and then in 1946 as a fullfledged yeshiva.

Torah Education in Brooklyn

Back in Brookyn, Isaac Shalom founded *Magen David*, first as a Talmud Torah, and then in 1946 as a fullfledged yeshiva. He encouraged friends and associates to remove their children from the public schools and enroll them in *Magen David*. At first, people were reluctant, but his charisma coupled with the deep reverence the community had for him won them over. Today, *Magen David* is a major yeshiva serving the religious needs of the greater Syrian Jewish community.

He encouraged young men to continue with higher Torah education. R' Yitzhak Dwek of Deal, New Jersey, relates that it was Mr. Isaac Shalom who encouraged him to continue learning in the Baltimore yeshiva, *Ner Yisrael*.

The Beginnings of Magen David. Mr. Isaac Shalom's courageous role in the building of *Magen David* was graphically described by Mr. Ralph Tawil, the first president of the yeshiva. These are essentially his words, as spoken during the course of an interview:

Isaac Shalom signing the mortgage for the yeshiva building

It was 1945. That was the year in which the first Sephardic Community Center was built. The community was in favor of building a social center, but very few people wanted a yeshiva. You have to understand, a yeshiva was something that was [seen as] un-American. It was the "isolationists" who wanted the yeshiva; the "people" wanted their children to mix with the rest of the American children [in public schools]. So we made a deal with them. We would take one floor, and they would take two floors. They took the basement and first floor, and we took the second floor.

We had a very difficult time convincing parents and children to attend the yeshiva. But luckily for us, there were a lot of problems in the public school system, so for the safety of the children, people started to send them to our school.

The first 17 or 18 years of *Magen David* yeshiva were a struggle, an unbelievable struggle, there was absolutely no money, no backing. We kept it going with Scotch tape, day by day; teachers didn't get paid for months and months. Most of the time we had no heat in the building. Lunches were served because we got grants from the government and were able to feed the children. But the money situation was really a disaster; there was just nobody who was interested in supporting us. But we persevered, we stayed with it, and eventually it became what it is today, perhaps one of the greatest Sephardic institutions in America.

The yeshiva he built

After a very short time, we didn't have enough classrooms. We started with 70 children; before we turned around, we had 100 children. I was the president at the time and Mr. Shalom had called me and said, "Ralph, get the carpenters and build a classroom in the first-floor hallway." I said, "Mr. Shalom, the first floor?"

He answered, "Who will know? No one comes anyway. They have plenty of hallways and rooms that they don't use. Did you ever see anyone in the building? Nobody comes. And when they do come, they go straight to the basement."

So we went ahead and constructed one classroom [on the first floor]. When the board of directors found out about it eight months later, they called a special meeting. At that meeting there were 32 members of the board of the center, and five or six members of the yeshiva. It was wild. They yelled, "How could you take something that doesn't belong to you?"

Mr. Shalom apologized, "We're sorry, but there were too many children. We couldn't help it."

They shouted, "This can't continue, we don't care what you do but you can't take any more classrooms." We agreed, and unanimously signed an agreement. Everyone agreed that there would be no more classrooms on the first floor.

As soon as I returned home, I received a telephone call from Mr. Shalom, "Tomorrow morning, get a carpenter, build two more classrooms."

So I said, "Mr. Shalom, we just signed ..."

"What signed? In another two to three weeks we will have another 40, 50 children. Where will we put them? They have nothing there; just do it. No one will know the difference; it will take them two years to find out."

"We went ahead and constructed two more classrooms and indeed it took them close to a year to find out, and when they found out, the telegrams started to fly: "Emergency Meeting! Emergency Meeting!"

All 32 members of the board of directors appeared and once again, they were yelling to high heaven. The chairman asked the secretary, "Will you please read the minutes?" And the secretary, very eloquently and very slowly, read the minutes: "Under no circumstances is anyone allowed to change the character of the building and create any more classrooms, signed by Mr. Isaac Shalom, Mr. Ralph Tawil, and all 32 members of the center's board."

"What happened?"

"We made a mistake."

"What do you mean, you made a mistake?"

"We made a mistake; didn't you ever make a mistake? Anyway, now we have two classrooms full of children and we can't send them home."

They started to loudly complain and make a commotion, and Mr. Shalom said.

"I told you it was a mistake — finished; what else do you want to talk about?"

They looked at him, "What do you mean what else? We want to talk about these classrooms."

Groundbreaking for new yeshiva building
Left to right: Philanthropist Mr. Edmond Safra (#470), R' Yaakob Kassin (#330), R' Shaul Kassin, R' Baruch Ben-Haim

"I thought we finished talking about them. I told you it was a mistake. Next subject. Let's talk about something else! So that's the status quo, talk about something else now."

The children were coming from all over and within a year or two, the entire first floor was converted into classrooms. During that time, Mr. Shalom called me one day and said, "Let's go down to the basement." We went to the basement, where there were bowling lanes. There wasn't a single soul in the place. Mr. Shalom looked at me and said, "Do you see anyone here? When do the people come? I don't know. I don't think anyone comes here. Ralph, we are going to convert this basement into a lunchroom. It will take them two years to find out about it, perhaps more. Tomorrow morning, let's start working."

The next day, we started to work and converted that space into a lunchroom. They never found out about it. It was meant to be. That building was meant to be a yeshiva; and the credit goes to the entire community. If it weren't for the fact that people wanted a community center, it wouldn't have all happened. They raised the money, even though it was for building a center, and each and every one of those people deserves credit for building a yeshiva in our community!

This is how we began, with four children on 66th street — four children we had, girls no less. We couldn't take a chance and put boys in the yeshiva because we didn't think we would succeed. With the girls, it didn't matter, they would get married anyway. So then we got the boys' classes, and it went on; and today, thank G-d, we have thousands of students.

Memories from Hacham Matloub. The following is a translation of a letter written by R' Shaul Matloub Abadi (see #9) to Leo and Joe Esses, entitled, *"The Memory of the Righteous Should Be Blessed."* It is an appreciation of Mr. Isaac Shalom.

To my dear and precious students, the blessed brothers, Mr. Leo Esses, president of *Yeshivat Magen David,* and Mr. Joe Esses, head of the current Journal Committee.

The *sadik* [righteous person] who we have highlighted is your uncle, the late Isaac Shalom, the founder of our dear yeshiva that is named after him.

I visualize him still alive in front of us, as he was when he came to the yeshiva early Sunday mornings and any day off. He would go from class to class to check on the [boys'] conduct and their achievements. His very presence brought radiance to our institution. He brought with him G-d's Divine Presence. There was great benefit to the teachers and the students when they knew there was an eye watching over them and supervising their actions. His involvement in giving out awards always strengthened the weaker ones and caused great satisfaction to the dedicated teacher looking for approval and encouragement from the founder of the institution. It goes without saying that the tests he gave the students added increased enthusiasm to their learning. In this area we truly have no replacement for him.

He should be remembered as well for his special concern with proper pronunciation in the *siddur* and *Humash* which is not less important then proper understanding.

He constantly demanded proper reading from the students with the correct Sephardic pronunciation in accordance with the tradition for which we've always been known. We have a source for this in the *Hazal* (our Sages of the Talmud*)*. The *Gemara* (*Baba Batra* 21) explains that the reason Yoab didn't destroy the females of Amalek [as he was instructed] was because his teacher mispronounced the word "*zecher*" which means "remembrance" and pronounced it "*zachar*" which means "male." And for this mistake Yoab cursed him. Therefore, the *Shulhan Aruch* (*Yoreh Deah,* 245) states, "One should only appoint a teacher who reads with proper pronunciation."

The loss of a *sadik* makes its impression on his surroundings. We all have to strengthen ourselves to make sure that the glory of the yeshiva doesn't leave with him.

When Isaac Shalom's close friend, R' Moshe Pardo, heard that he was sick, he flew to America to visit him on his deathbed. When R" Pardo came into the room, Mr. Shalom began to cry. R' Pardo tried to calm him down and said, "You have nothing to fear; all your merits will acompany you." Mr. Shalom replied, "I am not crying because I fear death. I am crying because I realize that I will not be able to help a fellow Jew again."

His Passing

He passed away in New York *Ereb Rosh Hodesh* Av, 1968 and was buried in Jerusalem. He is survived by his sons Joseph, Steven, and Henry, and daughters, Norma Hedaya and Muriel Attie.

[498] **SHAMAH, R' David**

רבי דוד שמאע הלוי

(1900 — 1976)

Worthy scholar and Talmud Torah teacher of New York. He was born in Aram Soba in approximately 1900 to R' Raphael and Rachel Shamah. R' Matloub Abadi (see #9) described him as the best of all his students.

Settling in America

After immigrating to the United States in 1920, he earned his living as a peddler. He married Bahia (Becky) Mugrabi in 1926. On one occasion the buyer of a major department store gave him an order for linen tablecloths. After leaving the store, he returned to tell the buyer that the cloths were not linen. Needless to say, she was very impressed by his honesty and promised him a reorder.

A Presence in the Community

He was a very modest and pious man whose entire life was devoted to Torah and good deeds. Whenever he heard of any two people in conflict, he did his best to make peace between them.

He was a very modest and pious man whose entire life was devoted to Torah and good deeds.

When a death occurred in the community, he would spend the week of the *shivah* (mourning period) in the mourners' home reading *Tehillim* and conducting the services. Through this he became close to the family of the deceased and brought many people closer to religion.

Hacham David officiated as rabbi in the "upstairs *minyan*" on 67th Street. However, he wasn't a great orator and the *shul* brought in a young Ashkenazic rabbi to give speeches, in a sense replacing Hacham David. Not only didn't he pro-

R' David Shamah

test, but when he saw that the young rabbi was nervous, he prepared the first speech for him. The theme was, "All Jews are brothers," so that he would feel comfortable as an Ashkenazic man among Sephardim.

He would celebrate *Purim* in the traditional way, drinking until he reached a level of mild intoxication. He celebrated this experience by sitting with his friend Hacham Eliyahu Menaged, the *hazzan* of *K'nees Sithon* (The Sutton Shul), and together they would sing *pizmonim* (hymns).

A Teacher of His People

When the Jews were expelled from Egypt in the 1950's, some came to the United States very poor financially. Their children could not get into a Hebrew school for lack of funds. Hacham David, as he was called by everyone, gathered all these children from the streets and taught them Torah basics.

He was once seen waiting outside Public School 205 for a child, who couldn't afford to go to Talmud Torah, to give him reading lessons free of charge. The boy was so moved when he saw the rabbi waiting for him he couldn't refuse. Continuously in poor health with many physical handicaps, he worked under a tremendous strain. He gathered these children into the Talmud Torah building on 67th Street in Brooklyn and spent as much time as possible with them.

He even taught children who were mentally impaired in a generation when special children were neglected.

He even taught children who were mentally impaired in a generation when special children were neglected. When his family saw him teaching such a child they said, "He's not obligated to learn. Why are you teaching him?" In response he gave the boy a candy and the boy made the *berachah* (blessing) *"shehakol"* loud and clear. Hacham David turned to his family and said, "Now what do you say ?"

His son Jack once overheard two boys talking to each other in the schoolyard. One said, "I can't afford *Bar Mitzvah* lessons. What should I do ?" The other boy answered, "I know a rabbi, Hacham David Shamah, who gives lessons for free." When Jack proudly described the incident to his father, Hacham David asked, "How many boys were there?" Jack answered, "One or two." Hacham David said, "Bring me ten boys like that."

He taught in all weather, rain or shine, even going out to tutor his students in the bitter cold and fierce snowstorms. At times he would go to give free *Bar Mitzvah* lessons only to find out that the father couldn't read and he would end up teaching the entire family.

His son once asked in jest, "How do I know if the Jewish religion is true? Maybe I will join the Christians or Moslems." His father answered, "No problem. Join any religion you want. But only on the following condition. Go to any of our synagogues; when the *hazzan* [cantor] makes a mistake and says "Ah" instead of "Eh" and no one corrects him, then you can join another religion. That scenario will never happen because we have a tradition going back to Moshe Rabbeinu at Mount Sinai. If someone makes a mistake it is immediately corrected. Our religion hasn't changed and can't be changed."

A Righteous Man in Sickness and in Health

He was once getting on a bus and the driver unintentionally closed the door on his hand. Two fingers were severed. He had a foolproof case against the driver and the city. However, when he learned that the driver was Jewish, he immediately dropped the case.

At the end of his life he was on life-support systems in the hospital and was not able to talk. The nurse was trying to feed him and he wouldn't eat. A visitor noticed that his *kipah* had fallen off and placed the *kipah* back on his head. Immediately, Hacham David resumed eating.

His son once asked him, "Dad, you're killing yourself, teaching and helping the community without pay or recognition. Would you do it all again?" He said, "I came to this world to serve our community. I would do it again with ten times the effort."

He passed away on 9 Adar, 1976. The entire *Yeshivat Magen David* attended the funeral. He was survived by his sons Ralph, Herb, Jack, Joe, and his daughter Shirley who married Max Hidary.

[499] **SHAMAH, R' Eliyahu**

רבי אליהו שמאע הלוי

(— 1814)

Distinguished scholar and *dayan* (judge) of Aram Soba. He was born in Aram Soba to R' Yosef Shamah. R' Eliyahu served as senior *dayan* in the *Bet Din* of Aram Soba together with R' Moshe Dweck (see #233) and R' David Shelomo Sutton. At the Ben-Zvi Institute there is an original *halachic* (legal) ruling (file no. 302) with all three signatures, dated 1807.

He is especially known for his important book *Korban Isheh* (Livorno 5581/1821), consisting of responsa, *hiddushim* (original Torah thoughts), and inspirational lectures. It received a glowing approbation from the rabbis of Livorno. Note that the word *Isheh* (אש"ה) in the name of the book is an acronym for R' Shamah's name **אליהו שמאע הלוי**. He also wrote the book *Machshirei Milah* (Livorno 5553/1794) on the *halachot* of *brit milah*.

In 1804 he joined other rabbis of Aram Soba in signing the approbation to the book *Beirach Moshe* of R' Moshe Galante, the Chief Rabbi of Damascus . He also contributed a responsum to that book (sect. 35) together with his colleague R' Yitzhak Harari (see #295). He also joined his colleague R' Yosef Sasson (see #489) in signing the introduction to the book *Zechor LeYitzhak* by R' Yitzhak Harari (see #295).

He passed away on 11 Iyar, 5574 (1814) in one of the epidemics that periodically struck Aram Soba. Among those who eulogized him were R' Abraham Sutton (see #535), as recorded in the book *Malel Le'Abraham* (eulogy no. 28) and R' Moshe Swed (see #573), as recorded in the book *Masveh Moshe* (p. 139).

R' Eliyahu had always been ready to sacrifice himself for the community. It was reported that he prayed tirelessly to *Hashem* to rescue Aram Soba from the epidemic of 1814. His prayers for the city were answered, but he himself succumbed. Earlier he had been active in saving the community from depredation at the hands of anti-Semites who were instigating a blood libel.

R' Eliyahu's son was R' Yosef, who had a son named Eliyahu after his grandfather. That R' Eliyahu also had a son Yosef, whose son R' Eliyahu was to become a distinguished philanthropist and civic leader of the Aram Soba community in *Eretz Yisrael* (see #500).

ספר

קרבן אשה

נדפס

ליוורנו

בשנת

NELLA STAMPERIA DI PIETRO MEUCCI.

Con Approvazione.

Title Page of Korban Isheh

[500] **SHAMAH, R' Eliyahu**

רבי אליהו שמאע הלוי

(1881 — 1934)

Distinguished philanthropist and community leader of the Aram Soba community in *Eretz Yisrael*. He was a grandson of the earlier R' Eliyahu Shamah (see #499) and was born in Aram Soba in 1881 to R' Yosef Shamah. However, his father passed away when young Eliyahu was only 12 years old.

As a youth he took an active role in the charitable and Torah organizations of the city. He was deeply involved in the ongoing problem of getting proper medical treatment for the sick people of Aram Soba. This led to his role as one of the founding leaders of the *Sedakah U'Marpeh* organization, which opened a clinic in Aram Soba.

R' Eliyahu Shamah (# 500)

He left Aram Soba shortly before the outbreak of World War I and lived in various countries doing business as opportunities arose. R' Eliyahu's love for *Eretz Yisrael* inspired him to leave a successful and respectable life in North America and move his family to Jerusalem, in the mid-1920's. There, he dedicated himself to the development of education for the Jewish community in *Eretz Yisrael* and around the world.

He played management and leadership roles in the yeshiva *Porat Yosef*, the Jerusalem City Government, the *Agudat Yisrael* organization, and the World Sephardic Congress. He also became president of the Aram Soba congregation in Jerusalem.

R' Eliyahu (# 499) had always been ready to sacrifice himself for the community. It was reported that he prayed tirelessly to Hashem to rescue Aram Soba from the epidemic of 1814. His prayers for the city were answered, but he himself succumbed.

His role in the establishment of Porat Yosef was especially critical. There came a point where all of the original supporters abandoned the project because of a serious problem that had arisen.

His role in the establishment of *Porat Yosef* was especially critical. There came a point where all of the original supporters abandoned the project because of a serious problem that had arisen. It was R' Eliyahu who came to the rescue and took upon himself the responsibility for the continued existence of the institution. His name and the names of two other founding committee members were inscribed on the front door of the yeshiva. The other two members were R' Nissim Nahum (see #437) and R' Mashiach Borochov.

יובל

השבוע לפני חמישים שנה, בראי עתונות התקופה * שבת פרשת כי תשא תש"ז *

הוקמה אגודה לעתיד בני עדות המזרח "אוצר התורה"

* נציג האגודה סולק מסוריה בצו הממשלה *

בזמן האחרון התעוררו עסקנים אחדים בארץ ובחו"ל לדאוג לעתיד בני עדות המזרח.

המצב הירוד בחינוך בארץ, ידוע. אבל העסקנים מתאוננים על הסכנה הצפויה לבני עדות המזרח במזרח הקרוב. המצב הוא כ"כ ירוד עד כי אין צורך במספרים. כולם רואים את הסכנה בעין, כי אין זו שאלה על העתיד אלא על ההווה.

עסקנים מבני עדות המזרח בירושלים ובאמריקה התארגנו, ואחרי שבאו בדברים בחליפת מכתבים וטלגרמות, באו לידי החלטה ליצור חברה בשם "אוצר התורה" במטרה ליסד בתי חנוך לבנים ולבנות עפ"י התורה והמסורה, לפתוח ישיבות ולדאוג לחינוך מורים. כי שאלת המורים היא שאלה הכי חשובה העומדת עתה על הפרק.

במקומות שונים מבקשים לשלוח להם מורים חרדים ואי אפשר למלא את הדרישה.

העסקן הנכבד מר יוסף שמעא בירושלים, אף הוא אחד מהעסקנים בחברה זו נסע לדמשק, בירות, וארם צובא. במטרה כפולה, ראשית לאסוף כספים למטרה זו ושנית לפתוח בתי ת"ת במקומות הדרושים ולחזק את הקיימים. מר שמעא היה מצליח בתפקידו הכפול לולא שהוכרח ע"פ צו הממשלה הסורית לעזוב את סוריה.

בשבוע שעבר עזב מר שמעא את ארצנו הקדושה בדרכו לאנגליה, משם יצא לאמריקה למצא את האמצעים הכספיים הדרושים להגשמת תכנית החברה.

1946 newspaper article of the Yovel reporting on Mr. Shamah's first trip on behalf of Ozar HaTorah.

To stimulate economic development, he built the first commercial business section outside the walls of of the Old City, known today as the Shamah Trade Center. In 1928 he acquired a large piece of land and raised money for the venture from investors abroad. Although delayed by the riots of 1929, R' Shamah succeeded in completing the project. It was an impressive structure for those years and served hundreds of Jerusalem merchants. However, in 1948 the War of Independence caused most of the merchants to abandon their stores and the building was used by small manufacturers.

Mr. Joseph Shamah with R' Yosef Ades

In addition to his management skills, R' Shamah was a studious person, who loved scholars and was constantly in their company. Sadly, he passed away in 1934 at the young age of 53. Everyone who knew him was shocked at the tragic loss of such a dynamic creative individual, a true builder of Jerusalem. His oldest son, Mr. Joseph Shamah (see #501), continued his father's holy work. One of his daughters, Rachel, married Hacham Shalom Harari-Raful (son of R' Ezra; see #304). They named their second son Eliyahu. He later became *Rosh Yeshiva* of *Neve Eretz*.

[501] **SHAMAH, Mr. Joseph**

מר יוסף שמאע הלוי

(— 1989)

Distinguished philanthropist and community leader of the Aram Soba community in *Eretz Yisrael*. He was born in Aram Soba, the son of R' Eliyahu Shamah (see #500), a highly respected leader who had dedicated himself to the development of education for the Jewish community in *Eretz Yisrael* and around the world. Joseph was raised and educated in Central and North America, but moved to *Eretz Yisrael* with his parents in the mid-1920's.

Unfortunately, Joseph's distinguished father passed away in 1934 at a young age, leaving Joseph the responsibility for caring for the family and continuing his holy work. Following in his father's footsteps, Joseph Shamah turned his sights toward helping Jewish communities and headed many Syrian community organizations including those in *Eretz Yisrael*. He created the *Sedakah U'Marpeh* foundation to support the poor and sick in need of hospital care, and was a leader of congregation *Magen David*.

One of Joseph Shamah's great accomplishments was his genius and foresight in recognizing the threat to the future of Sephardic Jewry.

One of Joseph Shamah's great accomplishments was his genius and foresight in recognizing the threat to the future of Sephardic Jewry. After the tumultuous results of World War II, Sephardic religious education had diminished to the point where its continuation was in jeopardy. Along with Mr. Isaac Shalom (see #497) he founded the famous *Ozar Hatorah* educational network, which at its height had over 50,000 students around the world. Primary areas of focus were the Jewish communities of Morocco and Iran, which were in dire poverty and whose religious life was disintegrating in the 1940's and 1950's. Mr. Shamah let nothing stand in his way. Over a period of many years, he established numerous religious schools and *yeshivot* throughout Morocco and Iran. These Torah institutions contributed the Torah leaders that lead Moroccan and Iranian Jewry to this very day.

In the mid-1950's following the influx of Jews from North Africa into France, the necessity for religious schooling was especially critical. Mr. Shamah worked particularly hard in establishing *Talmidei Torah* for young children and *yeshivot* for older students. Through these schools, the "forgotten million," as he called these Sephardim, would bring the Sephardic religious heritage back to its glory.

He was a nonmaterialistic, humble man, who hid from the limelight, and avoided discord. He was therefore respected and accepted by all, Ashkenazim and Sephardim. Until his last day, his only concern was the welfare of the entire Jewish people. He passed away on 25 Heshvan, 5750 (1989).

He left three sons: Elly, David, and Moshe. One of his daughters, Yaffa, married R' Moshe Shrem of *Mesilat HaTorah*.

[502] **SHAMAH, R' Yosef**

רבי יוסף שמאע הלוי

(19th century)

Worthy scholar of Aram Soba. He was born in Aram Soba to R' Eliyahu Shamah (see #499). R' Yosef worked on his father's manuscript for the book *Korban Isheh* and saw to its publishing in Livorno in 1821. The scholarly abilities and piety of R' Yosef were praised by the rabbis of Livorno in their approbation for the book. He was also lauded during the course of a eulogy delivered by R' Yitzhak Attiah (see #120) on the passing of R' Yosef's son-in-law, R' Yosef Marini (#408), as recorded in R' Attiah's book *Eikev Anavah*.

[503] **SHAMAH, Señor Yoshiyahu Yomtob**

סי יאשיהו יום טוב שמאע הלוי

(— 1975)

Last president of the dwindling Aram Soba community in Syria. His term of office was marked by a special concern for the needy of the city. As the administrator of the community's charity fund, he took an active role, seeking out poor people rather than waiting for them to come to him.

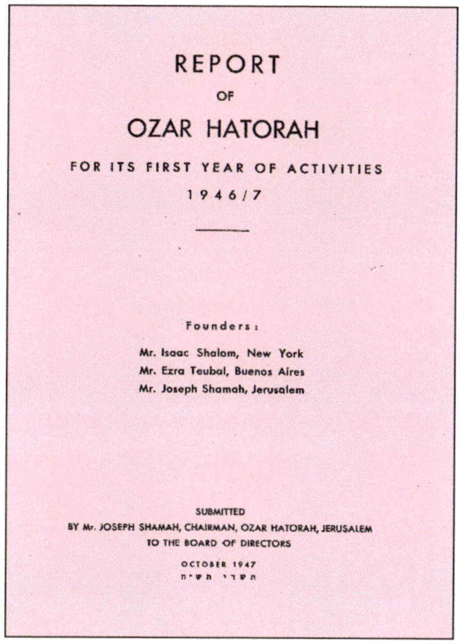

REPORT

OF

OZAR HATORAH

FOR ITS FIRST YEAR OF ACTIVITIES

1946/7

Founders:

Mr. Isaac Shalom, New York

Mr. Ezra Teubal, Buenos Aires

Mr. Joseph Shamah, Jerusalem

SUBMITTED

BY Mr. JOSEPH SHAMAH, CHAIRMAN, OZAR HATORAH, JERUSALEM

TO THE BOARD OF DIRECTORS

OCTOBER 1947

תשרי תש"ח

Title page of Ozar HaTorah's first year's report submitted by Mr. Joseph Shamah

He was a businessman of the highest integrity, who was respected by all who dealt with him, Jew and Arab alike. He was so trustworthy that people did not feel the need for paper documentation to back up verbal commitments.

During Israel's War of Independence, the Jewish community of Aram Soba was beset by rioting Arab mobs. Synagogues and other Jewish properties were destroyed. This was the final straw as far as Señor Shamah was concerned and he made up his mind to leave Syria, as so many others had done before him. When the vice president of the Aleppo Chamber of Commerce heard that Señor Shamah was planning to leave the city, he tried to prevent his departure, even going so far as to call in the police. For two hours they held up the train in which Señor Shamah was sitting, but he persevered and saw the last of his beloved city on that day in 1949. The train took him to Beirut where he lived until 1959, when he left for Italy. He passed away in Italy on 6 Heshvan, 5735 (1975) and was laid to rest on the Mount of Olives, Jerusalem. He was survived by scholarly grandchildren studying Torah in the *yeshivot* of Jerusalem.

When the vice president of the Aleppo Chamber of Commerce heard that Señor Shamah was planning to leave the city, he tried to prevent his departure.

[504] **SHAYO (ABADI), R' Edmond**

רבי אדמון שעיו (עבאדי)

(1923 — 1998)

Worthy scholar and rabbi of Jerusalem. He was born in Aram Soba in 1923, a son of R' Yosef Shayo (see #507) and a brother of R' Ezra Shayo (see #506). When he was 5 years old his family moved to Jerusalem where he studied in the yeshiva *Porat Yosef*. He excelled in his studies and used every opportunity to bask in the wisdom of the great Torah scholars and rabbis that embellished Jerusalem in those years. Ultimately, he was ordained to the rabbinate at the age of 24. He followed this up with continuing study into *halachah* and Kabbalah. He passed away in Jerusalem on 9 Tevet, 5758 (1998).

Señor Yoshiyahu Yomtob was the last president of the dwindling Aram Soba community in Syria.

R' Ezra Shayo (Abadi)

[505] SHAYO (ABADI), R' Ezra

רבי עזרא שעיו (עבאדי)

(1869 — 1939)

Distinguished scholar, *dayan* (judge), and educator of Aram Soba. He was born in Aram Soba in 1869, a son of R' Yosef and a grandson of R' Shalom Abadi-Shayo. His brother was R' Yeshuah Abadi and his son-in-law was R' Shalom Yitzhak Mizrahi (see #429), an eminent scholar and rabbi of Jerusalem.

As a boy, he studied in the Talmud Torah under R' Yaakob Alfia (see #45) and later in the yeshiva under R' Abraham Ades (see #37), R' Yomtob Yedid (see #593), and R' Ezra Hamway (see #272). He applied himself to his studies and quickly became known as a brilliant young scholar. While still a youngster he was asked by R' Yeshayah Dayan (see #203) and R' Nissim Lofez (see #396) to be a tutor to young men older than himself. Also, during the long winter nights he taught in-depth *halachah* to the scholarly merchants of Aram Soba. At the age of 16 he was formally appointed as a teacher in the General Talmud Torah of Aram Soba, a school which had about a thousand students at the time.

Also, during the long winter nights he taught in-depth halachah to the scholarly merchants of Aram Soba. At the age of 16 he was formally appointed as a teacher in the General Talmud Torah of Aram Soba, a school which had about a thousand students at the time.

Over the course of the years he became known as one of the primary educators of Aram Soba, teaching an in-depth approach to large numbers of students who would go on to be future leaders and scholars. In fact, most of Aram Soba's great scholars and rabbis of his generation were students of his. Especially noteworthy in this regard were R' Shaul Matloub Abadi (see #9), R' Shelomo Zafrani (see #598), R' Moshe Tawil (see #586), R' Eliyahu Lofez (see #394), R' Shaul Laniado (the son of R' Moshe Dib Laniado), and R' David Sutton (see #538). He once told his grandson, R' Ezra Abadi-Shayo, that it seemed he had taught as many students as there were hairs on his head.

He once told his grandson, R' Ezra Abadi-Shayo, that it seemed he had taught as many students as there were hairs on his head.

He was overjoyed to marry Frieda, the daughter of the eminent scholar and *Av Bet Din*, R' Yeshayah Dayan (see #203). Tragically, this most righteous woman passed away on 11 Tishrei, 5669 (1908), leaving her husband and small children. He remarried and his worthy second wife, Leah, helped him raise his children. She passed away some years later on 9 Tevet 5696 (1935) in Jerusalem, leaving him a widower for the remaining four years of his life.

He also served for a period of 30 years as a *dayan* on the *Bet Din* of Aram Soba together with R' Ezra Hamway (see #272), who was the *Av Bet Din* (Chief Judge), and with R' Moshe Ezra Mizrahi (see #424), who was to become the next *Av Bet Din*.

During World War I when all travel to and from Aram Soba was stopped, the survival of the city's Talmud Torah was threatened. R' Shayo put all his efforts into raising the funds needed to keep alive this critical institution of over a thousand students.

In 1935 he left Aram Soba to spend his final years in Jerusalem. He was a deeply committed scholar, who was engaged in Torah study at all hours, up to his final day, despite the illnesses and difficulties of old age. On his final day, 4 Shevat, 5699 (1939), he completed his morning prayers in his hospital room with a *minyan* of 10 people whom he had asked to be with him.

He then put away his *tallit* and *tefillin* and went down to sit in the courtyard of the hospital. There he said to R' Abraham Shrem, the principal of the yeshiva *Porat Yosef*, "I send my regards to all the scholars of the yeshiva." He then gave an inspirational talk to the people around him, ending with the words, "Let your garments always be white, and your head never lack oil" *(Kohelet* 9:8*)*. He called to a hospital attendant to clean the floor of the courtyard in which he was sitting. He then stood up to say *Viduy* (the deathbed confession) and recited the verse, "In Your hand I entrust my spirit; You redeemed me, O *Hashem*, G-d of truth" *(Tehillim* 31:6*)*, and gave his soul back to his Creator.

He was buried on the Mount of Olives and eulogized by the senior rabbis of Aram Soba and Jerusalem, and by his son R' Yosef Shayo (see #507).

Some of his *hiddushim* (original Torah thoughts) and responsa were published by his son R' Yosef in the book *Shaare Ezra* (Jerusalem 5722/1962). The eulogy which R' Yosef delivered for his father also appears there in addition to the eulogy which he delivered for his father's teacher R' Abraham Ades (see #37).

Some of his other *hiddushim* were included in the anthology *Otsarot Hachmei Aram Soba al HaRambam* (Jerusalem 5749/1989) that was published by the Aram Soba Foundation.

[506] **SHAYO (ABADI), R' Ezra**

רבי עזרא שעיו (עבאדי)

(1916 — 1986)

Eminent scholar and educator of Aram Soba and Jerusalem. He was born in Aram Soba in 1916, a son of R' Yosef Shayo (see #507) and a grandson of R' Ezra Shayo (see #505). When he was 12 years old his family moved to Jerusalem where he studied in the yeshiva *Porat Yosef* and later became a teacher. He was known for his clarity of thought and his ability to explain complex concepts to his students. Ultimately, he became a lecturer at *Porat Yosef* and rabbi of the Ades synagogue in Jerusalem. He was an expert scribe of Torah scrolls, *tefillin*, and *mezuzot*. He was also very active in charitable works.

In addition to his other talents he had a beautiful singing voice, and besides serving *as hazzan* (cantor) of the Ades Synagogue, he was much in demand as a guest *hazzan* in other synagogues.

He also led an organization in Jerusalem called *Sedakah U'Marpeh*, which was modeled on the organization with the same name in Aram Soba, whose purpose was to provide medical facilities for the sick. He passed away in Jerusalem on 24 Av, 5746 (1986) and was succeeded as rabbi of the Ades Synagogue by his son R' Yosef Shayo.

[507] **SHAYO (ABADI), R' Yosef**

רבי יוסף שעיו (עבאדי)

(1894 — 1976)

Eminent scholar and editor of Aram Soba and Jerusalem. He was born in Aram Soba in 1894 to R' Ezra Shayo (see #505). On his mother's side he was a grandson of R' Yeshayah Dayan (see #203). As a boy he studied Torah in the *Bet Midrash Etz Haim*, under his father and R' Shaul Matloub Abadi (see #9); he studied Kabbalah under R' Yosef Yedid (see #594). He also took on the responsibility of managing the *eruv* and the *mikvaot*, as well as the baking of matzah.

In 1935 he settled in Jerusalem and studied in the Kabbalist yeshiva *Oz Ve-Hadar*, adjacent to *Porat Yosef*. He later became head of the *yeshivot Nehar Shalom* and *Bet El*. He also became a *mohel* for the Jerusalem community.

R' Shayo was an expert in the history and genealogy of the scholars of Aram Soba. He worked on the manuscripts of earlier scholars and managed to publish many of their books. Many of his manuscript notes were adapted by R' Abraham Ezra Ades of Bnei Brak and added to this work. A particularly successful effort was the anthology *MeHalab Ha'Aretz* (Jerusalem 5726/1966), containing the *hiddushim* (original Torah thoughts) of many important *Hachamim* of Aram Soba, as well as complete copies of *sefarim* (scholarly

R' Ezra Shayo (Abadi)

Ultimately, he became a lecturer at Porat Yosef and rabbi of the Ades synagogue in Jerusalem. He was an expert scribe of Torah scrolls, tefillin, and mezuzot. He was also very active in charitable works.

בינ"ו עמ"י עש"ו וכס"ד

ספר

מחלב הארץ

חידושים וביאורים מכתבי יד חכמי ורבני וגאוני ארם צובה ראשונים ואחרונים שיש בהם עיון עמוק ופלפול. בסברה ישרה שהיו ת"י מפוזרים אחת הנה וכו' כתובים בניירות בלות ומטושטשות. קבצתים והעתקתים והגהתים וסדרתים עפ"י סדר הש"ס להקל על המעיינים בו. ונעשו כמן שיטה מקובצת. וחברתים ונעשו חיבור שלם אשר קובע ברכה לעצמו. וזכינו להוציאם לאור תעלומה ללמוד וליהנות מהם. וצרפתי אליהם מה שכתבו בהמאסף ז"ל ד' שנים ראשונות. ויהיו שפתותיהם דובבות ויהיה להם נ"ר בגן עדנם זצוק"ל וזיע"א.

וצרפנו אליהם פסק לר"מ ור"מ מאריה דאתרין הרה"ג הרש"ל ז"ל וזיע"א מחבר ב"ד ש"ש מספרו כסא שלמה סי' א'. ועוד קובץ כ"י ביאור על מס' אבות להרה"ג המעיי"ן זלה"ה ושמנו שמו מי מעיין. ועוד דרושים כ"י להרה"ג שלמה בכמה"ר מאיר לאנייאדו ז"ל ושמנו שמו חיי שלמה. וס' ויזרע יצחק להר' יצחק לאנייאדו (מלכי שובה) ז"ל דרושים על מלת בראשית בס"ו אופנים מיוסדים עפ"י האר"י זיע"א. ועוד קובץ כ"י להר' המקו' אברהם סאלם ז"ל ושמנו שמו חיי אברהם רמזים ומוסר עפ"י האר"י החי זצוק"ל וזיע"א.

וזכותם וזכות תורתם יעמוד לנו ויזכנו האל ית' ללמוד תורה לשמה לעשות נ"ר ליוצרנו לעשות רצון בוראנו ולעילוי שכינת עזינו. ונזכה אנחנו וזו"ז בבריאות שלימה וחיים טובים ארוכים ומתוקנים. ויתן לנו האל תקוה טובה ואחרית טובה וימלא את כל משאלות לבנו לטובה לעיתש"ל ונזכה ונחיה בבנין בית קדשינו ותפארתינו ולביאת גואלנו גואל צדק במהרה בימינו אכי"ר.

וגם לעילוי נר"ן בני הבחור השקדן בתורה יניק וחכים המר ונאנח ר' רחמים בן מזל ז"ל תנצב"ה.

הצעיר יוסף בכמהר"ר
עזרא עבאדי (שעיו)
בא סי' יש"ע ס"ט

נדפס

בעיה"ק ירושלים תובב"א

שנת שי"ם שלו"ם תשכ"ו

Title Page of MeHalab Ha'Aretz

R' Yosef Shayo (Abadi)

books), some of which were being published here for the first time.

He published some of his father's *hiddushim* and responsa in the book Shaare Ezra (Jerusalem 5722/1962). That book also included *hiddushim* of R' Moshe Swed (see #575) and R' Mordechai Abadi (see #8).

He passed away on 29 Kislev, 5737 (1976), leaving two scholarly sons: R' Ezra (see #506) and R' Admon (see #504), who held rabbinical positions in Jerusalem. His grandson R' Rahamim Shayo authored the book *Ginzei Aretz* (Jerusalem 5761/2001), in which he also included R' Yosef's work on the customs of Aram Soba.

Shrem Lineage. Rabbi Eliyahu Shrem (see #509) relates that years ago when each family had to choose an official last name they created the name Shrem as an acronym for the words, *Shabbat*, *Rosh Hodesh*, *Yom Tov*, and *Milah*. It is also an acronym for the phrase *"Ye'he Shme Raba Mevorach,"* **יהא שמה רבא מברך** (scrambled).

[508] SHREM, R' David

רבי דוד שרים

(— 1901)

Worthy scholar and rabbi of Aram Soba. He was the fourth son of R' Yitzhak Shrem (see #517). He passed away in Jerusalem on 28 Shevat, 5661 (1901), leaving two scholarly sons: R' Yitzhak Shrem (see #519) and R' Rahamim Shrem (see #514).

[509] SHREM, R' Eliyahu

רבי אליהו שרים

(1932 — 2002)

R' Eliyahu Shrem

Eminent scholar and educator of Tel Aviv and Givatayim. He was born in the Old City of Jerusalem in 1932 to R' Ezra (see #510) and Zarifa Shrem. His mother was a daughter of R' Yitzhak Shrem (see #519).

His Youth

He studied in the Talmud Torah *Bnai Sion* and in *Yeshivat Porat Yosef*. He excelled in his studies and was ordained to the rabbinate at the age of 21. He followed this up by continued study in *halachah* and Kabbalah.

He was known as one of the great *matmidim* (dedicated students) of *Porat Yosef*. A fellow student was once seen in R' Eliyahu's regular place in the *Bet Midrash* lighting a candle. When asked what he was doing, he answered, "Lighting a candle and saying *Tehillim* in the cave of Eliyahu," thereby connecting R' Eliyahu's learning spot to the Cave of Eliyahu in the Great Synagogue of Aleppo.

While still a young man, he was sent on missions to the great leaders of the Ashkenazic yeshiva world and developed personal bonds with the *Hazon Ish*, the *Ponevezher Rav*, and the *Brisker Rav*. When R' Eliyahu got married, the *Brisker Rav* sent his son to the wedding to wish him *mazal tov*.

In 1947 he married Rivkah, daughter of R' Raphael Abbu, who was the *Av Bet Din* (Chief Judge) of Tel Aviv and later major activist on behalf of *Ozar HaTorah* traveling to Morocco to set up Torah schools.

In 1951 he founded a Tel Aviv branch of *Porat Yosef*. Eight years later the yeshiva became independent under the name *"Torah VeHora'ah."* With that came the financial responsibilities. He traveled the world raising money for the yeshiva.

Rabbi and Educator of Tel Aviv

In 1960 he was accepted as the rabbi of the Commercial Center of Tel Aviv. In addition, he founded a yeshiva in Givatayim, a township in central Israel, between Tel Aviv and Ramat Gan. In this effort he received substantial assistance from Mr. Emil Hamway, a native of Aram Soba.

In 1987 R' Eliyahu Harari-Raful, the *Rosh Yeshiva of Neve Eretz,* and grandson of R' Ezra Harari–Raful (see #304), was involved in distributing money in Israel for the philanthropic Reichmann family of Canada and wanted R' Eliyahu to open a preschool and elementary school. R' Eliyahu refused, saying it required full-time involvement and he didn't have the time. R' Raful said, "Let's ask Rav Shach." They went to Rav Shach, who told him to take on the assignment, adding, "Rav Shrem, the Sephardim want to return to religion. They are only waiting for someone to call out to them. Call for them; make it easy for them and they will come. And they will turn over their families as well." A year later they had 110 students and the school continues to grow.

His Respect for Others

He once saw his son calling R' Ben-Sion Abba Shaul (see #24) on the phone with a *halachah* question. He told his son, "You think that he's your friend and that you can call him on the phone? Go to him and ask your questions."

His Final Years

He suffered from various maladies, forcing him to spend much time in hospitals. However, this did not stop his spiritual activities and he managed to bring many of his fellow patients closer to religious life.

He passed away on 4 Heshvan, 5762 (2002) and was laid to rest in Jerusalem. He was blessed with scholarly sons who continued his holy work in running the *yeshivot* which he founded. After his death his son R' Dvir Shrem published the book *Vaya'al Eliyahu* (Tel Aviv 5762/2002), containing the story of his life. This book also includes a lengthy introduction on the many generations of rabbis in the Shrem family.

[510] **SHREM, R' Ezra**

רבי עזרא שרים

(1895 — 1963)

Distinguished administrator and manager of the yeshiva *Porat Yosef* in Jerusalem. He was born in Aram Soba in 1895, a son of the Kabbalist R' Yitzhak Shrem (see #518). His parents brought him to Jerusalem the following year, accompanied by R' Abraham Ades (see #37). The three generations of this holy family (grandfather, father, son) were generally together, even at the Western Wall (*Kotel Ma'arabi*), where it was reported that they had a vision showing them the location of the Divine Presence (the *Shechinah*) at the top of the wall.

R' Ezra Shrem

As a boy, R' Ezra studied in a Talmud Torah in Jerusalem, after which he joined the yeshiva *Ohel Moed* (the forerunner of *Porat Yosef*) under the leadership of R' Raphael Shelomo Laniado (see #364). He also studied in the yeshiva *Tuvo Yisbe'u* under the leadership of R' Yosef Haim Cohen.

During the years of World War I he was forced to serve in the Turkish Army. Upon leaving the army he became a teacher in the *Magen David* Talmud Torah of the Aram Soba community in Jerusalem and then later in the yeshiva *Porat Yosef*. In the course of time he became one of the key administrators of the yeshiva, concerned with its development and success. After the War of Independence, the yeshiva needed to be reestablished outside the walls of the Old City and R' Shrem took an active role in this essential endeavor. Following this interruption he saw the yeshiva grow and prosper, becoming a network of *yeshivot* connected by a common approach to Torah education.

In the course of time he became one of the key administrators of the yeshiva, concerned with its development and success.

He was also a member of the managing board of the *Magen David* Talmud Torah and a vice chairman of the Bayit V'gan community board. His efforts had a great impact on the growth and prosperity of that community.

Distinguished administrator and manager of the yeshiva Porat Yosef in Jerusalem.

He worked on his father's manuscript commentaries on the book *Etz HaHaim* and saw to it that they were published under the title *Hiddushei Maharitz Shrem*, and included in the

זה השער לה׳ צדיקים יבואו בו

חלק שלישי

ספר

שערי דרך החיים

המחבר הצעיר רחמים בכמהר״ר דוד שרים הי״ו

שאו שערים ראשיכם והנשאו פתחי עולם ויבא מלך הכבוד

נדפס בעיה״ק ירושלם

דפוס הר׳ חיים בהר״ש הלוי ז״ל צוקרמן

Title Page of Shaare Derech Haim

book *Shaare Rahamim* by his cousin R' Rahamim Shrem *(see #514)*.

He passed away on 8 Tevet, 5723 (1963). His sons R' Abraham, R' Moshe, and R' Eliyahu (see #509) continued his holy work in the network of *yeshivot* associated with the name *Porat Yosef*.

[511] **SHREM, R' Halfon-Haim**

רבי חלפון־חיים שרים

(— 1912)

Eminent scholar and rabbi of Aram Soba. He was a son of R' Yitzhak Shrem (see #518), and was known for his brilliance in Torah learning. His grandfather R' Yosef Shrem (see #520), praises him in the introduction to the book *Pi HaBe'er* and thanks him for his help in getting the book published. Sadly, he passed away at a young age on 17 Heshvan, 5673 (1912), only four years after the death of his father.

[512] **SHREM, R' Moshe**

רבי משה שרים

(— 1868)

Worthy scholar and rabbi of Aram Soba. According to his grave marker, he passed away in the month of Nissan 5628 (1868). However, little else is known about him.

[513] **SHREM, R' Rahamim**

רבי רחמים שרים

(— 1900)

Worthy scholar and rabbi of Aram Soba. According to his grave marker he passed away on 21 Tishre, 5661 (1900). However, little else is known about him.

R' Rahamim Shrem

[514] **SHREM, R' Rahamim**

רבי רחמים שרים

(1859 — 1934)

Eminent Kabbalist of Jerusalem. He was born in 1859, possibly in Kilis, a small town near Aram Soba. His father was R' David Shrem (see #508). He was brought to Jerusalem as a young child. R' Shrem grew up with a strong commitment to the study of Kabbalah, which he studied in the yeshiva *Rehovot HaNahar*.

He wrote a book of responsa in two volumes, addressing issues related to the teachings of the *Rashash* (R' Shalom Sharabi) on *tefillah* and other *mitzvot*. This book was called *Shaare Rahamim* (Vol. I, Jerusalem 5686/1926; Vol. II, Jerusalem 5688/1928). He then wrote *Shaare Derech Haim* (Jerusalem 5691/1931), which was the third volume to *Shaare Rahamim* and whose responsa also addressed topics raised by the book *Etz HaHaim* of R' Haim Vital. He received approbations on these books from leading rabbis of Jerusalem, including R' Yosef Haim Sonnenfeld, R' Yosef Yedid (see #595), R' Haim Shaul Dweck (see #228), and R' Aharon Shelomo Maharil. He also wrote the book *Taamei HaMitzvot* (Jerusalem 5693/1933) giving the underlying meaning of the *mitzvot* from both the revealed and Kabbalistic standpoint.

He passed away on 22 Tevet, 5694 (1934), leaving one son, R' Raphael David Shrem, and two daughters.

[515] **SHREM, R' Shahud**

רבי שחוד שרים

(1915— 1999)

Worthy scholar and rabbi of Beirut and Sao Paulo. He was born in Aram Soba in 1915, the son of R' Moshe Shrem. However, he became orphaned at a young age. He studied Torah under R' Moshe Tawil (see #586) in the *Bet Midrash* known as *Bet Nasi*. For a time he was a teacher in the Talmud Torah of Jamileyé, after which he went to Beirut and took a position as rabbi of a congregation there. Later, he moved to Brazil, becoming the senior rabbi of the Aram Soba community. He passed away in Sao Paulo on 22 Tamuz, 5759 (1999). He was a man who strongly believed in teaching Torah to the people, giving classes until his very last day.

[516] **SHREM, R' Shalom**

רבי שלום שרים

(19th century)

Worthy Kabbalist of Aram Soba and Jerusalem. He was born in Aram Soba, the son of R' Yosef Shrem and the father of the famous Wandering Emissary *(HaSheliah HaNoded),* R' Yosef Haim Shrem (see #521). He got married in Jerusalem and became one of the select Kabbalists of the yeshiva *Bet El*. However, his wife passed away in 1855 and this experience apparently induced him to return to Aram Soba. There, in 1860, he married a divorcee, Sabtia, the daughter of R' Abraham Sutton-Azrak. The fruit of this marriage was a scholarly son, R' Shimon Shrem.

[517] **SHREM, R' Yitzhak**

רבי יצחק שרים

(— 1872)

Distinguished scholar and rabbi of Aram Soba. He was a son of R' Yosef Shrem. R' Yitzhak devoted himself to the study of Torah and the support of worthy causes. He wrote many holy books and expended his efforts and his funds in getting them published. His published works are as follows:

- *Be'er Yitzhak* (Livorno 5624/1864). Elucidation of *Ibn Ezra's* commentary on the Torah.
- *Hadar Ezer* (Izmir 5625/1865). Elucidation of *Ibn Ezra's* commentary on *Tanach*. The introduction was signed by seven leading rabbis of Aram Soba: R' Haim Mordechai Labaton (see #336), R' Moshe Sutton (see #554), R' Yitzhak Antebi (see #83), R' Raphael S. Nehmad, R' Abraham Laniado (see #348), R' Shaul Dweck (see #239), and R' Shalom Chasky (see #149).
- *Likutim MiPardes* (Aram Soba 5630/1873 and 5633/1873). Two volumes of teachings on spiritual development in accordance with all aspects of Torah *(Pshat, Remez, Drash,* and *Sod),* arranged in alphabetical sequence by topic. The introduction was written by R' Mordechai Abadi (see #8).
- *Likutim Amarim* (Aram Soba 5633/1873).
- *Mussar Hachamim* (Aram Soba 5633/1873). Collected teachings of spiritual guidance by the Sages on *Bereshit, Shemot,* and *Vayikra*.
- *Pi HaBe'er* (Jerusalem 5668/1878). Elucidation of R' Eliyahu Mizrahi's commentary on the Torah.

One of his responsa is included in the book *Shaare Rahamim* by R' Rahamim Yosef Franco, the rabbi of Hebron.

He passed away on 16 Tishrei, 5633 (1872), having been blessed with four scholarly sons to carry on his name: R' Rahamim, R' Yosef (see #520), R' Moshe, and R' David (see #508).

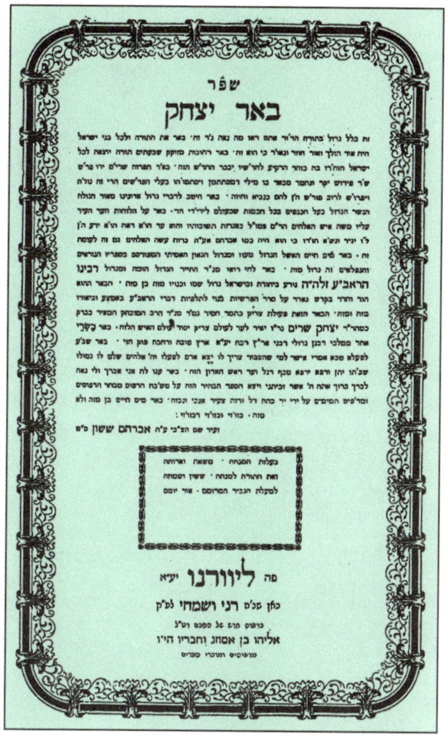
ספר
באר יצחק
פה ליוורנו יע"א
כאן מכ"ס רני ושמחי לפ"ק
אליהו בן אמוזג וחבריו הי"ו

Title Page of Be'er Yitzhak

[518] **SHREM, R' Yitzhak**

רבי יצחק שרים

(1860 — 1909)

Eminent Kabbalist and *dayan* (judge) of Aram Soba and Jerusalem. He was born in Aram Soba in 1860, the only son of R' Yosef Shrem (see #520). He was named after his scholarly grandfather R' Yitzhak Shrem (see #517). Following in the footsteps of his ancestors, he applied himself to his studies and quickly became known as a brilliant young scholar, excelling in both the revealed and the mystical approach to Torah.

R' Shahud Shrem (see # 515)

In 1896 he immigrated to Jerusalem and was appointed a *dayan* (judge) on the Sephardic *Bet Din*. He founded a yeshiva in the Mahane Yehudah section of Jerusalem, in the Obadiah Harari synagogue. R' Shrem continued in his spiritual growth and became one of the select members of the Kabbalist yeshiva *Bet El*. His father was surprised to see his colleagues refer to him for clarification of difficult topics in Kabbalah.

His father was surprised to see his colleagues refer to him for clarification of difficult topics in Kabbalah.

He wrote many *hiddushim* (original Torah thoughts) , most of which remained in manuscript form. One of his manuscripts was *Shemot HaGittin*, in which he listed new Jewish names that had not been identified by previous *halachic* (legal) authorities. Some of his *hiddushim* were incorporated into the published books of R' Yaakob Shaul Elyashar. His commentaries on the book *Etz HaHaim* by R' Haim Vital were published under the title *Hiddushei Maharis Shrem* (Jerusalem 5688/

R' Yosef Haim Shrem

1928). This book was combined with the book *Shaare Rahamim* by his nephew R' Rahamim Shrem (see #514) and published through the efforts of his son, R' Ezra Shrem (see #510).

In the introduction which R' Yaakob Shaul Elyashar wrote to the book *Tikkun Hatzot*, he praises R' Yitzhak in the highest terms. R' Yitzhak passed away on 21 Shevat, 5669 (1909), leaving two scholarly sons: R' Halfon-Haim (see #511) and R' Ezra (see #510).

[519] **SHREM, R' Yitzhak**

רבי יצחק שרים

(— 1932)

Eminent scholar and Kabbalist of Jerusalem. He was a son of R' David Shrem (see #508). Although an accomplished scholar he chose to earn his own livelihood, while maintaining a low profile and actively supporting Torah institutions. He was also knowledgeable in the mystical approach to Torah, and lived an austere life, fasting frequently, even when he was ill.

His brother, R' Rahamim Shrem (see #514), praises him in the introduction to his book *Shaare Rahamim*, making special note of his efforts in support of the yeshiva in which Kabbalah was being studied in his neighborhood. He passed away on 27 Nissan, 5693 (1932) in Jerusalem.

R' Yosef Haim Shrem was fluent in many languages, including Aramaic, Arabic, Georgian, Spanish, English, and French. He was an outstanding speaker, a charming singer, and made an excellent impression wherever he went.

On a visit to Baghdad, he so impressed the Chief Rabbi, R' Yosef Haim (the Ben Ish Hai), that the two men could be seen taking long walks through the city together.

(520) **SHREM, R' Yosef**

רבי יוסף שרים

(— 1914)

Eminent scholar and rabbi of Aram Soba and Jerusalem. He was the second son of R' Yitzhak Shrem (see #517). He is praised by R' Mordechai Abadi (see #8) in the introduction to R' Yitzhak's book *Likutim MiPardes*.

He wrote the introduction to R' Yitzhak's book *Pi HaBe'er* (Jerusalem 5668/1908) and published the book with the aid of his grandson, R' Halfon-Haim Shrem (see #511).

He left Aram Soba for Jerusalem in 1896 and passed away there on 3 Elul, 5675 (1914). He left one son, R' Yitzhak Shrem (see #518).

(521) **SHREM, R' Yosef Haim**

רבי יוסף חיים שרים

(1851 — 1948)

Eminent emissary of Jerusalem's Torah institutions to the lands of the Middle East. He was born in Aram Soba in 1851 to R' Shalom Shrem (see #516). He was a nephew of R' Yitzhak Shrem (see #519). In 1852 his family moved to Jerusalem, which is where he grew up. His mother passed away when he was a small child and his father passed away a few years later. He studied in the Talmud Torah *Doresh Sion* and in various *yeshivot*. At the age of 31 he took up the role of emissary to raise funds for the Sephardic institutions of Jerusalem and Hebron. He was fluent in many languages, including Aramaic, Arabic, Georgian, Spanish, English, and French. He was an outstanding speaker, a charming singer, and made an excellent impression wherever he went.

It was reported that in 1895 while in Georgia he composed two songs, one in honor of Czar Nicholas II, who had just been crowned, and the other in praise of the Jews of Georgia, who were generous in their donations to *Eretz Yisrael*. They were incorporated into the book of *pizmonim* (hymns) which the Georgian Jews sing at the conclusion of *Shabbat*.

On a visit to Baghdad, he so impressed the Chief Rabbi, R' Yosef Haim (the *Ben Ish Hai*), that the two men could be seen taking long walks through the city together. This sight had a positive effect on R' Shrem's fund-raising in Baghdad that year.

R' Shrem established a synagogue in his house on Nabon Street in Jerusalem, which continued to be in use long after his death. He passed away in Jerusalem in 1948 and was laid to rest in Givat Ram.

His inspirational lectures and other *hiddushim* (original Torah thoughts) were published under the title *Debar Yosef* (Jerusalem 5747/1987). The book also contains a number of eulogies, including one for the *Ben Ish Hai*.

Because of his successes in raising funds and his many adventures he became known as *HaSheliah HaNoded* (The Wandering Emissary) and a book with that title was written about him.

SHWEKY, see CHOUEKA

(522) SILVERA, Señor Aharon

סי' אהרן סלוירה

(— 1925)

Eminent philanthropist of Aram Soba and Jerusalem. He was a successful and learned merchant, who devoted himself and his wealth to holy causes. In Aram Soba, Señor Silvera served as administrator of the Talmud Torah and took special responsibility for the orphans among its students, personally providing for their food, clothing, and shelter. During World War I conditions were very difficult for the poor people of the city and he went to great lengths to help them.

In 1919 he left Aram Soba and moved to Jerusalem. There he rededicated himself to holy pursuits. He owned a two-story apartment building in the Mahane Yehudah section. On the upper floor he built a synagogue and *Bet Midrash*, open to all, day and night. The income from the rental of the apartments on the lower floor was assigned to provide support for the *shamosh* (sexton) and *hazzan* (cantor) and the upkeep of the *Bet Midrash,* which was named *Zechut Aharon* after its founder. He spared no effort in embellishing the synagogue with beautiful furniture and books. The complex continues to serve the needs of scholars and is named *Bet Aharon*. For many years the position of *shamosh* was held by the eminent scholar, R' David-Sion Laniado (see #352).

Since he was not blessed with children, Señor Silvera bequeathed all his assets to charities, with the exception of the money for his wife's *ketubah* (marriage contract). The two major institutions that he favored were the Sephardic Old Age Home and the *Magen David* Talmud Torah of Jerusalem, run by R' Aharon Harari-Raful (see #303), R' Haim Tawil (see #584), and R' Natan Salem (see #472). The bequest to the Talmud Torah was conditional upon the school continuing to follow the holy traditions of Aram Soba.

Silvera Synagogue in Aram Soba after Arab riots

The above provisions are spelled out in his will, which was witnessed by R' Yosef Yedid (see #594) and R' Abraham Ades (see #37). As executors he named R' Ezra Attiah (see #102), R' Eliyahu Shamah (see #500), and R' Ezra Harari-Raful (see #304), among others.

Once he had earmarked all his funds for holy purposes, he lived frugally. One of the rabbis who visited him when he was ill saw how he was scrimping on food and medicine and asked about it. Señor Silvera explained that since he had willed the bulk of his property for holy purposes, any penny that he did not spend in his lifetime would add merit to his account in the World to Come. Anyway, the money wasn't really his, but was holy money.

Once he had earmarked all his funds for holy purposes, he lived frugally.

He was a son of R' Shemuel Silvera (see #529) and passed away on 11 Adar, 5685 (1925), leaving no children of his own. However, R' David Laniado was privileged to live in his house and saw to it that the voice of Torah learning should continue to be heard in the *Bet Aharon* day and night, as was the wish of the deceased. R' Shalom Hedaya (see #310) praises him in his book *Shalom Le'Am* and attributed his own scholarly achievements to Señor Silvera and to

Since he was not blessed with children, Señor Silvera bequeathed all his assets to charities, with the exception of the money for his wife's ketubah.

He is mentioned with high praise by R' Yosef Yedid (see #593) in the book Torat Hacham and thanks him for his constant support and blesses him with continued sucsess.

his father. These men of vision recognized the potential of a destitute orphan boy and gave him the emotional and material support that would enable him to develop into a Torah scholar.

He is mentioned with high praise by R' Yosef Yedid (see #594) in the book *Torat Hacham* and thanks him for his constant support and blesses him with continued success.

At his funeral, he was eulogized by R' Yosef Yedid as recorded in *She'erit Yosef*, part 3 (Brooklyn 5737/1977).

[523] **SILVERA, R' David**

רבי דוד סלוירה

(— 1882)

Worthy scion of a noble Aram Soba family. Distinguished by his good works and devotion to scholarship. He passed away on 8 Tevet, 5642 (1882). His name appeared in the list of Aram Soba scholars receiving a weekly stipend from the special fund that had been set up for the support of worthy individuals who dedicate their lives to Torah study (see #267 and Document Section, Document No. 30).

[524] **SILVERA, R' Eliyahu**

רבי אליהו סלוירה

(— 1761)

Eminent scholar and philanthropist of Livorno and Aram Soba. He was a native of Livorno (Leghorn), who went to live in Aram Soba for business reasons. He loved the community and used his wealth and business skills for its benefit. One of his first initiatives was to establish a *Bikur Holim* fund with an associated pharmacy, which provided medicine to the poor. Subsequently, good people from his family and the Picciotto and Altaras families continued the holy work and *Bikur Holim* became a permanent organization.

One of his first initiatives was to establish a Bikur Holim fund with an associated pharmacy, which provided medicine to the poor.

R' Eliyahu supported many other causes and personally helped modest scholars and the needy poor. In the year 1730 he established a yeshiva with a huge library for the benefit of the scholars of the city. The yeshiva was known as *Midrash Bet Silvera* and was also called *Midrash R' Dabbah*, after the *Rosh Yeshiva*. His grandson R' Ezra Silvera wrote about an incident told to him by his father. R' Eliyahu had been sitting in his office at home when a blaze of light appeared to emanate from it. When people rushed to the place where he was sitting, they found nothing at all, just R' Eliyahu learning Torah in his normal way. The only possible explanation was that Eliyahu HaNabi (the prophet Elijah) had come to visit R' Eliyahu.

He was mentioned in glowing terms by R' Yitzhak Berachah in his book *Beirach Yitzhak* (see #129), and by R' Emanuel Hai Riki in his books *Hon Ashir* and *Aderet Eliyahu*. The name *Aderet Eliyahu* was chosen in honor of R' Eliyahu Silvera. R' Emanuel also named his book *Kiryat Hannah* for R' Eliyahu's wife.

It is reported in the book *Tov Re'i* (Tiberias 5694/1934) that in his later years R' Eliyahu Silvera moved to Tiberias and passed away there in 1761. The same book reports that R' Eliyahu wore an amulet containing a letter written by the great Kabbalist, the *Rashash* (R' Shalom Sharabi). In the letter, the *Rashash* responds point by point to criticisms of the yeshiva *Bet El*.

[525] **SILVERA, R' Ezra Raphael**

רבי עזרא רפאל סלוירה

Eminent scholar and philanthropist of Beirut. He earned his living as a merchant of the community, but was a highly respected scholar as well. He is mentioned in the book *Yisa Ish* by the *Rishon LeSion* (Chief Rabbi of *Eretz Yisrael*), R' Yaakob Shaul Elyashar (*Yorah Deah* 3) with reference to the laws of *ribit* (interest). On that topic, R' Silvera takes an active part in a learned discussion involving R' Yaakob Meir and R' Shalom Hedaya (see #310).

[526] **SILVERA, R' Meir**

רבי מאיר סלוירה

(— 1925)

Worthy scholar and philanthropist of Aram Soba. He was the treasurer of the Talmud Torah and always acted in the interest of the community. He passed away on 2 Heshvan, 5685 (1925).

[527] **SILVERA, R' Raphael**

רבי רפאל סלוירה

(— 1943)

Worthy scholar and rabbi of Aram Soba. He was the son of R' Shelomo Silvera (see #528). One of his *halachic* (legal) rulings is cited in the book *Torat Abraham* (New York 5764/2004) by his brother-in-law, Mr. Abraham D. Sutton (see #536). He passed away on 20 Kislev, 5703 (1943). There is also a reference to a special prayer which he composed and other *hiddushim* (original Torah thoughts).

[528] **SILVERA, R' Shelomo**

רבי שלמה סלוירה

(— 1892)

Eminent scholar and philanthropist of Tunis and Aram Soba. In the Jerusalem Archives (Griabski) there is an original promissory note in which a certain R' Shelomo Silvera of Tunis commits to send the yearly sum of 124 reales each year to R' Mordechai Haim Meyuhas of Jerusalem to enable him to learn Torah. The period of the document is measured from Sivan 5598 (1838). This appears to be the same R' Silvera who ultimately moved to Aram Soba, where he became the father-in-law of Mr. Abraham D. Sutton (see #536). He passed away on 17 Heshvan, 5652 (1892).

[529] **SILVERA, R' Shemuel**

רבי שמואל סלוירה

(— 1890)

Worthy scholar and philanthropist of Aram Soba. He was the father of Señor Aharon Silvera (see #522) and was especially known for his good works. He managed the Orphanage Home of Aram Soba and devoted himself to meeting the needs of the young orphans. He also did much to help young scholars continue their studies.

R' Shalom Hedaya (see #310) speaks of him with high praise in his book *Shalom Le'Am* (p. 45), thanking him for his personal support. He passed away on 26 Tevet, 5650 (1890).

[530] **SILVERA, R' Yehezkel**

רבי יחזקאל סלוירה

(— 1890)

Worthy scion of a noble Aram Soba family. Distinguished by his good works and piety. A good and gentle man, he passed away at a relatively young age on 4 Elul, 5650 (1890). His name appeared in the list of Aram Soba scholars receiving a weekly stipend from the special fund that had been set up for the support of worthy individuals who dedicate their lives to Torah study (see #267 and Document Section, Document No. 30).

[531] **SILVERA, R' Yitzhak Obadiah**

רבי יצחק עובדיה סלוירה

Worthy scholar and philanthropist of Aram Soba and Egypt. He was born in Aram Soba and moved to Egypt. His name is mentioned favorably in the introduction to *Torat Hacham* (Jerusalem 5671/1911) by R' Yosef Yedid (see #594). The author writes how grateful he is to R' Silvera for making it possible for him to devote his time to learning Torah.

[532] **SOFER, R' Yaakob Haim [Kaf HaHaim]**

רבי יעקב חיים סופר (כף החיים)

(1870 — 1939)

Known as the *Kaf HaHaim*; rabbinic authority and Kabbalist of Baghdad and Jerusalem. Although not of Syrian descent, he is included in this work because of his strong connection to the rabbis of Syria residing in Jerusalem and his relationship as a notable pupil and close aide of R' Haim Shaul Dweck (see #228).

R' Yaakob Haim Sofer (Kaf HaHaim)

He was born in Baghdad in about 1870 to R' Yitzhak Baruch Sofer (see #533). At the age of 34, with the blessing of the *Ben Ish Hai* (Chief Rabbi of Baghdad), the *Kaf HaHaim* moved to Jerusalem. In 1909, a small yeshiva called *Shoshanim LeDavid* opened in the Bukharan quarter. It was in this *Bet Midrash* that the *Kaf HaHaim* studied and wrote his books. His major work, *Kaf*

HaHaim, is a commentary on *Shulhan Aruch (Orah Haim* and part of *Yorah Deah).* It intertwines basic *halachic* (legal) explanations with a variety of mystical guidance. The final volume of his work was published with the help of the Brooklyn Syrian community, as described in the introduction.

Rav Chaim Kanievsky, the son of the Steipler, and a "Baki" (Torah expert) of our generation, said, "When you learn the laws of Sifrei Torah, you can't budge without using the Kaf HaHaim's book, Kol Yaakob."

The *Kaf HaHaim* also wrote an important book called *Kol Yaakob*, on the laws of *tefillin, mezuzot,* and *Sifrei Torah.* Rav Chaim Kanievsky, the son of the *Steipler*, and a *"Baki"* (Torah expert) of our generation, said, "When you learn the laws of *Sifrei Torah*, you can't budge without using the *Kaf HaHaim's* book, *Kol Yaakob.*"

He had tremendous knowledge of Kabbalah. The source of his mystic knowledge was the time he spent learning in *Rehovot HaNahar*, where Hacham Haim Shaul Dweck (see #228) was the *Rosh Yeshiva*. The *Kaf HaHaim* became a student of this great Kabbalist, and even helped put out one of his books. Hacham Haim Shaul writes a thank-you to the *Kaf HaHaim* in one of his books: "He is standing on my right hand, *Hashem* should give him the *zechut* (merit) to toil in Torah always, and the Torah should always be with his children, grandchildren, and great-grandchildren." Today, this blessing is an actualization; there are grandchildren and great-grandchildren of the *Kaf HaHaim* who are R*oshei Yeshivot*, including R' Eliyahu Sion Sofer and R' Yaakob Haim Sofer.

The Kaf HaHaim's humility kept him from revealing his dreams during his lifetime.

The *Kaf HaHaim* passed away in 1939. After the *Kaf HaHaim* passed away, his family found a notebook of dreams that he had carefully recorded. Many *hiddushim* (original Torah ideas) came to him during this time. Just as the *Bet Yosef* had an angel guiding him while writing his momentous work, the *Kaf HaHaim* also merited Divine inspiration. One could not produce such works without it. Each message he received in a dream was inscribed with the date. On the 14th of Nissan, he was told: "Be careful, don't eat the meat; something got mixed in with it and it's not kosher," and another time, "Don't buy the bread in the street; it has worms in it."

Just as the Bet Yosef had an angel guiding him while writing his momentous work, the Kaf HaHaim also merited Divine inspiration.

After he had published his first volume, his father appeared to him in a dream. The *Kaf HaHaim* asked him how they liked his book in the Heavens. His father ensured him that he would finish all of the *Orah Haim*. In another dream, he was told, *"Kaf HaHaim;* In the Heavens they are learning your book ... the *Ben Ish Hai* wrote the *haskamah* (approbation) in the Heavenly version."

The *Kaf HaHaim*'s humility kept him from revealing his dreams during his lifetime. Under the laws of *Tefillat Minhah* (the afternoon prayer) in the *Kaf HaHaim*, he wrote, "Start with *LaMenatze'ah* ... don't switch the order. This is what happened to a G-d-fearing man. Once he didn't say the beginning of the prayer, but started with *Ashrei*. That night, he was asked in a dream, 'Why was something missing from your prayer?'" The *Kaf HaHaim*'s family later found out from the journal that recorded his dreams that he was this anonymous "G-d-fearing man." In another instance, he recorded in his private journal being chided in a dream for missing the time for dropping three coins in the *kupah* (charity box) during the prayer *Vayivarech David*. The *Kaf HaHaim* noted in his book that one shouldn't be careless with these seemingly trivial items — in the Heavens it really makes a difference!

He was also told in his dreams when to correct something he had written in error. In the laws of *Yom Tov*, the *Kaf HaHaim* mentions that the right way to slice the bread for the blessing *HaMotzi* is to start from the upper right-hand corner. Why didn't he mention this earlier, perhaps in the laws of *Shabbat*? He explained, "This was told in the dream of a certain G-d-fearing man." Once again he was the G-d-fearing man and he hadn't had the dream until he was up to the volume dealing with *Yom Tov*, so it couldn't have been written earlier.

One Torah scholar had a question regarding the *kashrut* of a chicken. The *Kaf HaHaim* told him that it wasn't kosher. This man went to another rabbi, who told him it was kosher, but suggested he ask the *Kaf HaHaim's* permission out of respect. The *Kaf HaHaim* said, "If that rabbi said it's okay, then I will not argue." This man brought his chicken to the public ovens to be cooked, but he forgot it there, and when he finally returned, it was completely charred and no longer edible. He brought it back to the *Kaf HaHaim* who was not surprised by the outcome, "I told you it wasn't kosher." The *Kaf HaHaim's* merit had saved this man from eating unkosher food.

[533] SOFER, R' Yitzhak Baruch

רבי יצחק ברוך סופר

(— 1905)

Worthy scholar and rabbi of Baghdad, father of the *Kaf HaHaim* (see #532). At one point he was invited to be Chief Rabbi of Damascus, but declined out of humility. He passed away in 1905.

[534] SUKARY, R' Yaakob

רבי יעקב סוכרי

(— 1908)

Eminent scholar and rabbi of Damascus and Jerusalem. He was a son of R' Shelomo Sukary, who was *Av Bet Din* (Chief Judge) of the Damascus community. However, R' Yaakob moved to Jerusalem when he had the opportunity. On his mother's side he was a grandson of R' Yaakob Antebi (see #75) and was named after him. He authored two major works: *Vayikra Yaakob*, inspirational lectures (Livorno 5640/1880) and *Yoru Mishpatecha LeYaakob*, analogies and parables (Calcutta 5642/1882), at R' Eliyahu Moshe Dweck's press.

R' Yaakob was burdened with the care of a large family and was under great financial pressure. Accordingly, he was forced to go abroad to seek help, going as far as Egypt and India. He was well received wherever he went, but his difficult economic circumstances haunted him throughout his life. He passed away in Jerusalem on 6 Shevat, 5668 (1908) and was buried on the Mount of Olives.

Sutton Lineage. By tradition, the family name Sutton (**סתהון**) originated from two Arabic words: "siteh" and "hon." The Arabic "siteh" can mean the number six and "hon" means "here." Tradition has it that the census takers were visiting Aram Soba and came upon a tent in front of which children were playing. They asked the children how many people lived in that tent. The answer was "Six here!" And so the name Sutton was established.

However, the Arabic "siteh" can also means "grandmother," so that the name Sutton derives from the phrase, "My grandmother is here." A tradition behind this phrase has been reported by R' Ephraim Levy in the name of R' Shalom Sutton (see #557). It seems that a worthy member of the Aram Soba community became deathly ill and all hope for recovery was abandoned. However, he miraculously got better and described a dream that he had while in his comatose state. In the dream his grandmother came to him and assured him that he would recover and live out the rest of his days. As a commemoration of that miracle, he told people to call him Sutton, "My grandmother is here."

[535] SUTTON, R' Abraham

רבי אברהם סתהון

(— 1816)

Distinguished scholar and Chief Rabbi of Aram Soba. His father was R' Shelomo Sutton. He was a famous student of R' Yitzhak Berachah (see #129). R' Sutton is praised at length in the book *HaMa'alot LeShelomo* of R' Raphael Shelomo Laniado (see #363). There he is described as working one day out of the week to support himself and devoting the remaining six days to the study of Torah. Although his early life was lived in poverty, his fortune changed and he became well to do in his later years.

It appears that he was appointed to the position of Chief Rabbi after the death of R' Ephraim Laniado (see #355). R' Sutton's major book, *Malel Le'Abraham*

ספר
מלל לאברהם
פה ליוורנו יע"א
Con Approvazione.

Title Page of Malel Le'Abraham

(Livorno 5603/1843), was published by his grandson, R' Moshe Sutton (see #552), who wrote an introduction. It consists of inspirational lectures on *Bereshit* following a *halachic* (legal) approach, as well as eulogies for various great rabbis, among whom is the *Hida* (R' Haim Yosef David Azulai). R' Sutton passed away on 14 Kislev, 5574 (1813).

He apparently had two sons, one of whom was R' Yosef Sutton (see #566). He had a grandson named Abraham, as he writes in *Malel Le'Abraham* (Sermon No. 6), "My name is in him." That grandson became *Bar Mitzvah* on *Rosh Hodesh* Heshvan, 5567 (1807).

His other books, *Leket Shikchah*, *Dali Bepiskaya,* and *Leshonot BeHardal*, were spoken of in *HaMa'alot LeShelomo* and *Malel Le'Abraham* as having been left in manuscript form. Various other writings were tragically lost. In the book *Masveh Moshe* (p. 151) by R' Moshe Swed (see #573), the author writes that R' Abraham also wrote a book *Mi Yemalel*. In addition, R' Abraham wrote the introduction to *Zechor LeYitzhak* by R' Yitzhak Harari (see #295).

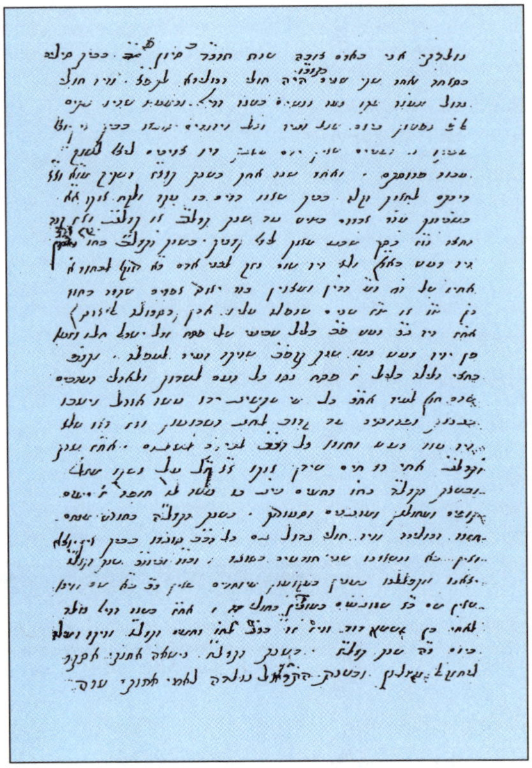

Mr. Sutton's manuscript diary

Mr. Abraham Sutton purchased the library of Shemaya Angel, a wealthy banker of Damascus.

One of R' Abraham's responsa appears in the book *Korban Isheh* by R' Eliyahu Shamah (see #499) (*Even HaEzer* 20). He joined other rabbis and scholars in signing the approbation to the book *Beirach Moshe* of R' Moshe Galante, the Chief Rabbi of Damascus.

In addition, one of his learned questions appears in the book *Bigdei Yesha* (p. 119b) of R' Yeshayah Attiah (see #119). In introducing the question, R' Attiah praises R' Abraham's brilliance and devotion to Torah. He then offers his analysis and responsum.

[536] **SUTTON, Mr. Abraham D.**
מר אברהם סתהון

(1864 — 1938)

Worthy scholar and merchant of Aram Soba. His father was R' David Sutton (see #537). R' Haim Tawil (see #584) praises him in his introduction to his father's book *Et Sofer*, thanking Mr. Sutton for his help in getting the book published. He also assisted in the publishing effort for the book *Karnot Sadik* by R' Eliyahu Mani of Hebron.

In 1884 Mr. Sutton married Salhah, the daughter of R' Shelomo Silvera (see #528), a scholarly merchant of an "aristocratic" family. Their first child was a girl, Nehamah. They were then blessed with five sons: David, Shelomo, Moshe Yehudah, Yosef Ezra, and Raphael Yeshayah.

Mr. Sutton was unusual in that he maintained a personal journal, recording the major events of his life and the details of his travels. On three separate occasions, starting at the age of 26, he traveled to *Eretz Yisrael* to pray at the graves of the righteous. Especially noteworthy was his visit to Meron in 1890 on *Lag Le'Omer*, the *Hilula* of *Rashbi* (R' Shimon bar Yochai).

In 1909 he and his 12-year-old son Shelomo (Sam A. Sutton) traveled to New York via Beirut, Alexandria, and Naples. They arrived safely despite the fact that the sailing from Naples to New York took 13 days and was jeopardized by a major storm that damaged the ship. He and his son remained alone in New York for two years when they were joined by David, the oldest son. It took another three years before his wife and other children were able to get to New York.

In 1922 he went back to Egypt for the wedding of his son Shelomo, who had become a learned scholar. During a subsequent trip to Syria he stopped off in Damascus where he purchased the library of Shemaya Angel, a wealthy banker of Damascus. The library contained about 1500 to 2000 volumes of holy books. For this he paid the equivalent of $3300, which represented a handsome yearly salary for a white-collar worker at that time. The notes and comments that he wrote in many of the books are an indication of the time he spent back in New York learning them.

In 1926 he precipitated a major crisis in the Aram Soba community in New York when a controversial rabbi from Syria was invited to speak at the *Magen David* synagogue on 67th Street in Brooklyn. Mr. Sutton rose up and shouted in Arabic, "Have you come to destroy us here as you did in Halab?" This courageous act was repaid with a visit the next day from the *shamosh* (sexton) of the synagogue, returning his *"koracha"* (*tallit* bag) as a sign that he was no longer welcome. As a result he founded his own synagogue, which became known as the Sutton Shul *(Knees Sithon)*.

He passed away on 15 Av, 5698 (1938). He was eulogized by his brother-in-law, R' Raphael Silvera (see #527), who spoke of his philanthropic support for various holy institutions, especially the Tashbar elementary schools in *Eretz Yisrael* and the Shevet Ahim fund for scholars in Syria.

His collected writings were published in January 2004 by his grandchildren in a book called *Torat Abraham*. This reflects his correspondence on *halachic* issues with the great rabbis of the day, including R' Yosef Yedid (see #594), R' Obadiah Hedaya (see #309), and R' Meyer Waknin, Chief Rabbi of Tiberias.

R' Abraham Harari-Raful (see #302) reported that on one occasion Mr. Sutton was seen weeping in a *shul* which he attended during the course of his travels. The rabbi of the *shul* asked him if he was experiencing a problem. Mr. Sutton explained that he was moved by the *Birchat HaTorah* in which we pray that that our children and grandchildren become Torah scholars. He said, "I know my children and try to educate them properly, but I might never meet my grandchildren. For them I can only shed tears that they follow the path of the Torah." In telling this story to one of Mr. Sutton's great-grandsons, R' Harari-Raful added, "If he has worthy grandchildren and great-grandchildren today, it is from those tears."

[537] SUTTON, R' David Ezra
רבי דוד עזרא סתהון

(— 1904)

Worthy scholar and rabbi of Aram Soba. He was the son of Ezra Sutton (not to be confused with R' Ezra Sutton, see #540). He moved to Jerusalem in his later years and passed away on 22 Tishrei, 5664 (1903). He was buried on the Mount of Olives. His son was Mr. Abraham D. Sutton (see #536).

R' David Sutton

[538] SUTTON, R' David
רבי דוד סתהון

(1888 — 1950)

Eminent *Av Bet Din* (Chief Judge) and Chief Rabbi of Buenos Aires. He was born in Aram Soba in 1888 to R' Moshe Sutton, a brilliant Torah scholar. On his father's side he was a grandson of R' Abraham Sutton (see #535) and on his mother's side he was a grandson of R' Hillel David Sutton (see #546). R' Moshe, his father, together with his oldest brother, R' Shaul, and his younger brother, R' Shelomo Sutton, were active in the founding of the *Sedakah U'Marpeh* organization, as well as members of the board of the general Talmud Torah of Aram Soba.

מצחף
שמירת שבת
חפט' אל סבת

בהי כתבת מקאלאת כתירה בשאן אל סבת ובעץ'
מקאלאת וקוואנין בשאן
מאכולאת אל חראם.

פאלפתהי בלגא אל ערביה לכי כל אחד יקרא
פיהי אל טאלב מוענת אל רב ורחמתתי
הצעיר דוד משה סתהון ס"ט

אנטבע פי קדם אל ש"יפי ש' תרפ"ט לב"ע
בםטבעת ציון ואביב הי"ו
אדרים: ח"ר דוד סתון קודס, בוכ"רליה.

רפוס "אביב", ירושלים.

Title Page of Matzhaf Shemirat Shabbat

R' David received his early education in the Talmud Torah and afterwards he studied in the *Bet Midrash* under R' Ezra Shayo (see #505). He developed into a fully rounded scholar in both the revealed and mystical aspects of Torah. He received special training in Kabbalah from R' Yomtob Yedid (see #593) and worked to raise himself to a high level of piety and self-denial.

In approximately 1910 he was appointed the rabbi of Kilis, a small town in Turkey, north of Aram Soba. One of his responsa had been sent to R' Eliyahu Hamway (see #271) who served before him as the rabbi of the town. It was subsequently published by his children in the book *Yaaleh HaDas* (pp. 105).

After World War I, he moved with his family to Jerusalem and in 1929 he was called to Buenos Aires by R' Shaul Sutton, who was the Chief Rabbi of the Sephardic community of Argentina. In that city he sat as *Av Bet Din* (Chief Judge), together with his colleagues R' Yaakob Abadi (Prassia) and R' Haim Yaakob Batias. As the *Av Bet Din*, he contributed greatly to the strengthening of religious life of Buenos Aires.

As the Av Bet Din, he contributed greatly to the strengthening of religious life of Buenos Aires.

After the death of R' Shaul Sutton, R' David was appointed as Chief Rabbi in his place. R' David was blessed with worthy and scholarly children. He passed away in Buenos Aires on 20 Av, 5710 (1950).

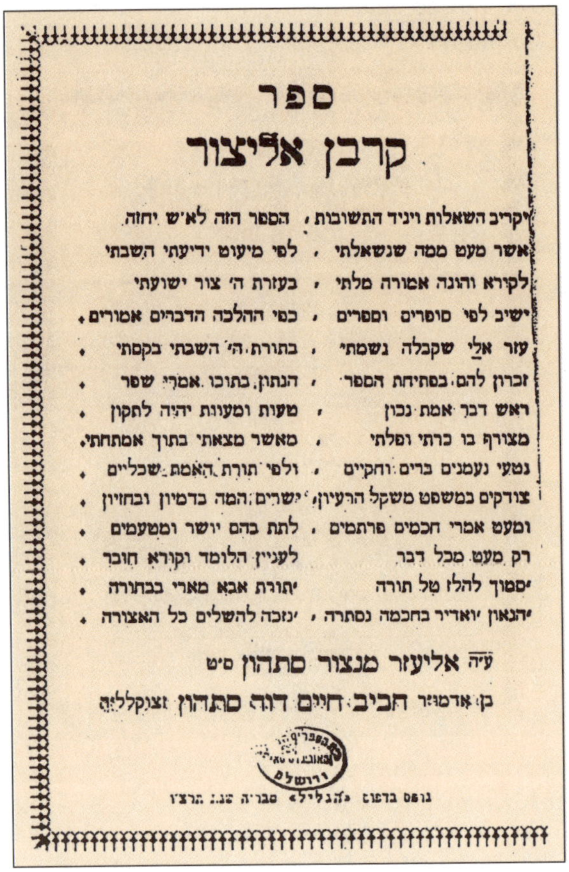
ספר

קרבן אליצור

יקריב השאלות ויגיד התשובות , הספר הזה לא״ש יחזה
אשר מעט ממה שנשאלתי , לפי מיעוט ידיעתי השבתי
לקורא והונה אמורה מלתי , בעזרת ה׳ צור ישועתי
ישיב לפי סופרים וספרים , כפי ההלכה הדברים אמורים .
עזר אלי שקבלה נשמתי , בתורת ה׳ השבתי בקשתי .
זכרון להם בפתיחת הספר , הנתון בתוכו אמרי שפר .
ראש דבר אמת נכון , טעות ומעוות יהיה לתקון .
מצורף בו כרתי ופלתי , מאשר מצאתי בתוך אמתחתי .
נטעי נעמנים ברים וחקיים , ולפי תורת האמת שכליים .
צודקים במשפט משקל הרעיון , ישרים המה בדמיון ובחזיון .
ומעט אמרי חכמים פרתמים , לתת בהם יושר ומטעמים .
רק מעט מכל דבר לעניין הלומד וקורא חובר .
יסמוך להלז טל תורה יתורת אבא מארי בבתורה .
יהגאון יואדיר בחכמה נסתרה , ינזכה להשלים כל האצורה .

ע״ה אליעזר מנצור סתהון ס״ט

בן אדמו״ר חביב חיים דוד סתהון זצוקללה״ה

נדפס בדפוס «הגליל» טבריה תב״ג תרצ״ו

Title Page Korban Elitzur

Even in a distant land he had never compromised on the intensity of his piety. A year prior to his death, his oldest son, R' Shaul Sutton, wanted to buy the privilege of leading the *Kol Nidrei* service for his saintly father. The bidding went up to an unusual high amount, until it reached the point that R' Shaul had to pay half of the money that he had in the bank. After R' David completed the service he blessed his son Shaul, praying to *Hashem* that R' Shaul should always find true religious devotion and that he should be worthy of receiving *Hashem's* bounty, "without limit." A year later, shortly after R' David passed away, his son achieved great financial success.

While still in Aram Soba, R' David worked on the publication of the book *Vayelaket Yosef* (Aram Soba 5675/1915) by R' Yosef Sutton (see #565). In addition, he worked with his brother R' Shalom Sutton (see #557) to publish the books *Aruchah U'Marpeh*, *Pirkei Abot*, and *Shemirat Shabbat* by their maternal grandfather R' Hillel David Sutton (see #546).

In 1928 while he was living in Jerusalem he published his own book *Matzhaf Shemirat Shabbat* (Jerusalem 5689), containing the *halachot* of *Shabbat* and of forbidden foods, written in Hebrew and Arabic. He also included responsa and *halachic* (legal) rulings related to the observance of *Shabbat*. The *hiddushim* (original Torah thoughts) and responsa of R' David Sutton were published in the book *Ya'aleh HaDas* (Jerusalem 5734/1974), through the efforts of his sons.

[539] **SUTTON, R' Eliezer Mansour**
רבי אליעזר מנצור סתהון

(1860 — 1937)

Distinguished scholar and Kabbalist of Aram Soba. He was born in Tiberias in 5620 (1860) to R' Habib David Haim Sutton (see #544) and authored the following books:

- *Notzar Adam* (Tiberias 5690/1930). Essays on spiritual development. A supplement *Hosafah Notzar Adam* was published in the same year, with its page numbers continuing the sequence of the original. He received approbations from the Chief Rabbi of Alexandria, R' Abraham Abukzer; the Chief Rabbi of the Ashkenazic community in Tiberias, R' Moshe Kliers; and the Chief Rabbi of the Sephardic community in Tiberias, R' Yaakob Hai Zerihan.
- *Korban Elitzur* (Tiberias 5696/1936). Responsa on a variety of topics such as going out with glasses or a watch tied to a chain. This book was bound with his father's book *Tal Torah*. He received

approbations from the Chief Rabbi of Israel and from the Chief Rabbi of the Sephardic community in Tiberias.

R' Sutton was also known to have expertise in mathematics and astronomy. He had two worthy sons: R' Gabriel Aharon and R' Nissim. He passed away on 2 Av, 5697 (1937).

[540] **SUTTON, R' Ezra**

רבי עזרא סתהון

(— 1891)

Worthy scholar and rabbi of Aram Soba. He passed away on 22 Tamuz, 5651 (1891).

[541] **SUTTON, R' Ezra Menashe**

רבי עזרא מנשה סתהון

(— 1854)

Worthy scholar and rabbi of Damascus. He was the father of R' Nissim Ezra Sutton (see #556). His name appeared in the list of Damascus scholars receiving a weekly stipend from the special fund that had been set up for the support of worthy individuals who dedicate their lives to Torah study. (See Document Section, Document No. 30.) He passed away on 8 Heshvan, 5615 (1854).

[542] **SUTTON, R' Gabriel**

רבי גבריאל סתהון

(— 1839)

Eminent scholar and rabbi of Aram Soba and Tiberias. He was born in Aram Soba and became a Torah scholar there, leaving many *hiddushim* (original Torah thoughts) in manuscript form. In 1820 he moved to Tiberias and became known as one of the respected scholars of the community.

R' Gabriel was the grandfather of R' Habib David Haim Sutton (see #544). Some background to that birth is given in the book *Yehudei HaMizrach Be'Eretz Yisrael* (Vol. II, page 486, note 2), where a remark by R' Moshe Hamway of Haifa may be found. R' Moshe reported that R' Gabriel had two sons: R' Habib and R' David Sutton. The first married Masudah, the daughter of R' Aharon Chabot (see #143), who was Chief Rabbi in Jerusalem. He passed away and his widow was then married (as a *yebamah*) to his brother David. However, David became ill and died shortly after the marriage. When Masudah gave birth, the little orphan child was named Habib David after his departed "fathers" and as protection they added the name Haim. R' Gabriel passed away in Tiberias in 1839 two years after the birth of his orphan grandchild.

[543] **SUTTON, R' Gabriel**

רבי גבריאל סתהון

(— 1893)

Eminent scholar and *dayan* (judge) of Aram Soba. He moved to Safed to practice an intensely pious approach to religious observance. He passed away in Safed on 25 Tevet, 5653 (1893). At the Ben-Zvi Institute (File No. 477) there is a manuscript of inspirational lectures, *Dorash Eliyahu,* by R' Eliyahu Rahamim Antebi. Sermon No. 5 is described as a memorial lecture for R' Gabriel Sutton, which the author delivered about a month after his burial. He mentions that he had also given a memorial lecture a week after the burial.

[544] **SUTTON, R' Habib David Haim**

רבי חביב דוד חיים סתהון

(1837 — 1906)

Distinguished scholar and *Av Bet Din* (Chief Judge) of Tiberias. On his father's side he was a grandson of R' Gabriel Sutton of Aram Soba (see #542) and on his mother's side he was a grandson of R' Aharon Chabot (see #143).

R' Sutton was born in Tiberias in 1837. He was born to his mother Masudah in her second marriage, which was a *yibum* (levirate marriage) after the death of her first husband R' Habib Sutton. Thus, his father was R' Habib's brother, R' David Sutton. However, shortly after he was born, R' David also died. He was named Habib David after his biological

זה השער לה' צדיקים יבאו בו :

ספר

תקפו של נס

חביב חיים דוד סתהון

Jüd. Gemeinde Berlin.

נדפס פעה"ק ירושלם תובב"א

Title Page of Takfo shel Ness

father R' David and his deceased uncle R' Habib, whose name he was meant to continue because of the *yibum*. As protection he was given the added name Haim. He was known as *Had BeDara*, literally, "The unique one of his generation," a play on the word *Had* (ח"ד), which is an acronym of "Habib David (חביב דוד)."

His noble mother, who raised him without a father, was the daughter of R' Aharon Chabot (see #143), who was born in Aram Soba, but settled in Tiberias.

It was not long before he became well known as one of the great scholars of the city and people called him simply Hacham David. His primary teachers were his grandfather, R' Aharon Chabot, and R' Haim Shemuel Kovarti, who was known as the Señor of Tiberias. In 1857 he joined other rabbis of Tiberias in signing the approbation for the founding of the yeshiva *Bet Yaakob* by R' Yitzhak Gouitta of Trieste, Italy.

R' Habib contributed greatly to the welfare of the Jewish community of Tiberias and often went to foreign countries to raise funds for the institutions of the city. In 1865 he made a trip to Morocco together with R' Abraham Sabah for the benefit of the *kollel* institutions of Tiberias. Again, in 1873 he traveled to the cities of the western Mediterranean to raise funds. He reported that when he arrived in the city of Fez, he was received with great honor and all of the senior rabbis of the city came out to greet him. Among them was the Chief Rabbi, R' Abner Yisrael HaSarfati, who in the past had never gone out to greet a visiting emissary. This amazed the scholars of the city, especially when the Chief Rabbi accompanied him to his lodging place and stayed with him there for a while. The Chief Rabbi explained that he saw a light shining above the head of Hacham David Sutton signaling his greatness in Torah and his holiness, and so how could he not give him honor?

Thus, he encouraged people to believe in the reality of miracles performed by sages, even though their explanation is cloaked in mystery.

The Chief Rabbi explained that he saw a light shining above the head of Hacham David Sutton signaling his greatness in Torah and his holiness.

He mentions a segulah (practice invoking a healing power), which is to put a cup of water under the Chair of Eliyahu during the ceremony.

In the course of time he was appointed as *Av Bet Din* (Chief Judge) of Tiberias by the Chief Rabbi, R' Yosef David Abulafia. He was an expert in the *Gemara* and the rulings of the *halachic* (legal) authorities, and was also well versed in mathematics and engineering. He earned his livelihood by dealing in the herbs used to make dyes.

Toward the end of his life he moved to Haifa, where he founded a yeshiva as a memorial to Eliyahu HaNabi. He was able to get support for the yeshiva from Señor Abraham Edrei, a wealthy Egyptian philanthropist. R' Habib remained at the helm of the yeshiva until the day he died on 12 Tevet, 5667 (1906). In that year he wrote an approbation to the book *Eretz HaHaim* by R' Haim Sutton (see #545). He left two scholarly sons: R' Eliezer Mansour (see #539) and R' Shelomo Yitzhak (see #560).

His published works are as follows:

- *Takfo shel Ness* (Jerusalem 5654/1894 and Vol. 2 5659/1899). Commentary on the teachings of R' Meir Baal Haness, in two volumes. He explained that what people perceive as the miracles and wonders of pious sages are actually quite normal. The laws of nature only apply to people whose primary orientation is to the world around them. However, great sages who disdain this world and orient themselves to the world of the spirit are able to draw upon the "laws" of that world, which supersede those of the material world. Thus, he encouraged people to believe in the reality of miracles performed by sages, even though their explanation is cloaked in mystery.
- *Shemesh U'Magen* (Jerusalem 5650/1890 and 5737/1977). Extracts from the teachings of R' Shimshon of Ostropolya, which were revealed to him in a dream.
- *Kursaya D'Eliyahu* (Jerusalem 5666/1906). Teachings from the *Gemara* in praise of Eliyahu HaNabi (the prophet Elijah). In this book he reviews many of the practices associated with the *mitzvah* of *brit milah* (circumcision). He mentions a *segulah* (practice invoking a healing power), which is to put a cup of water under the Chair

of Eliyahu during the ceremony. By tradition, the angel Raphael (the angel of healing) accompanies Eliyahu HaNabi at every *brit milah*.

- *Tal Torah* (Salonika 5637/1877). Commentary on the Torah. Published with the book *Korban Elitzur*, by his son R' Eliezer Mansour Sutton (see #539).

In addition he left various *hiddushim* (original Torah thoughts) in manuscript form, under the title *Taamei HaMitzvot*. One of his responsa was printed in the book *Shaare Rahamim* by R' Rahamim Yosef Franco (*Even Ha'Ezer* 10).

In the introduction to the second volume of his book *Takfo shel Ness* he describes his travels to Jerusalem to arrange for printing the first volume. He stopped off in the new town of Zichron Yaakob and stayed there five days because the heavy rains made the roads impassable. At the end of his stay, the people of the town saw him off with great ceremony, together with a horseman going to Jaffa. That trip, which should have taken 14 hours, lasted seven days because of all the difficulties and hazards that they encountered. While he was on the road he had a habit of continuously saying various portions of *Tehillim* which provide protection for travelers, such as, "Praiseworthy are those whose way is perfect" (*Tehillim* 119:1).

While reciting the holy verses, he realized that all of the next 15 chapters, beginning with the words, *"Shir HaMaalot"* (A Song of Ascents), are somehow related to moving from place to place and that most of them include some mention of Sion and Jerusalem. And he thought about the Jews in ancient times, who traveled to Jerusalem three times a year for the festivals. There were among them major caravans from Babylonia and it was said that the trip from Babylonia took 15 days. The people who made this trip surely said the Wayfarer's Prayer (*Tefillat HaDerech*), and said the verse, "Praiseworthy are those whose way is perfect," followed by one of the *"Shir HaMaalot,"* chapters, one for each day of the trip. He then discussed how the 15 chapters are connected to one another and concluded that it was the love of Jerusalem and the reciting of verses from *Tehillim* that protected him throughout all of the vicissitudes of a difficult trip.

[545] SUTTON, R' Haim

רבי חיים סתהון

(1871 — 1918)

Eminent scholar and rabbi of Safed. He was born in Safed in 1871 to R' Menashe Sutton (see #551). R' Menashe was then the Chief Rabbi of the town. However, R' Menashe passed away when Haim was 5 years old, and the child's stepfather R' Yitzhak Yaakob Salitzer faithfully saw to it that he was educated in the *yeshivot* of the city as his father would have wished. His teachers included R' Abraham Hai Shaki and R' Yosef Hakim.

In the introduction to the second volume of his book Takfo shel Ness he describes his travels to Jerusalem to arrange for printing the first volume.

In 1902 he was appointed to be Chief Rabbi of Safed, but his aversion to prestige and his intense desire to concentrate on the study of Torah led him to leave the rabbinate shortly thereafter. In the same year he wrote an approbation for the book *Ari Shaag* by R' Yehudah Seitlin of Safed.

אתהלך לפני ה' בארצות החיים (תהלים קט"ז)
ספר
ארץ חיים
כולל ענינים הנוגעים לארץ ישראל בדינים ומנהגים
ותקנות והסכמות של הראשונים והאחרונים
רבנן תקיפי וחסידי דארעא דישראל זלה"ה
אשר חיברתי בעזרת השם יתברך אנא זעירא
דמן חבריא ותלמידיהון
חיים סתהון
מעיה"ק צפת תובב"א
כנסיה לשם שמים
נדפס בשנת יגדיל תורה לפ"ק
פה עיה"ק ירושלם תובב"א
ונתתי צבי בארץ חיים (יחזקאל כ"ו)
EREZ HAIM
par
Rabbi Haim Sitehon
de SAFFED (Palestine)
Imprimerie AZRIEL Jerusalem

Title Page of Eretz Haim

Even as a youth he began to write down his *hiddushim* (original Torah thoughts) , which he managed to publish in the book *Eretz Haim* (Jerusalem 5668/1908). The book contains customs and practices applicable to *Eretz Yisrael*, arranged according to the *Shulhan Aruch*. He received approbations from the great rabbis of his time, including R' Yaakob Shaul Elyashar, R' Yitzhak Moshe Abulafia of Damascus, the *Radbaz* (R' David ben Zakai), and R' Chaim Berlin of Jerusalem. The book was completed on 18 Shevat, 5666 (1906), his 35th birthday.

He lived in great poverty and endured many painful illnesses, none of which deterred him from his continued commitment to Torah study. It was said that he habitually ate the herb "hablador," which benefits the faculty of memory. This contributed to his sharpness of mind, but may have caused harm as well. In 1918 he fell ill with typhus, which at that time was a deadly disease. While alone in his room, the illness overwhelmed him and he jumped out of bed in confusion. He ran out into the courtyard and fell into a water hole, which brought about his death on 6 Iyar 5678 (1918). He left a son Menashe and two daughters.

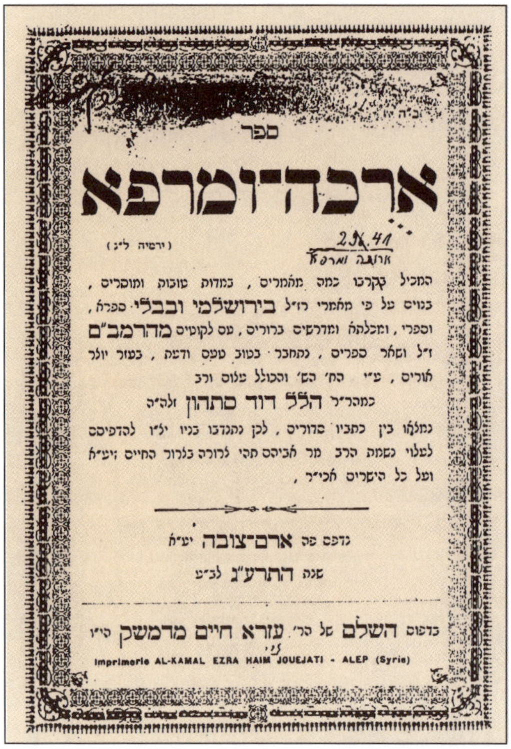

ספר
ארכה ומרפא
(ירמיה ל"ג)
המכיל בקרבו כמה מאמרים, במדות טובות ומוסרים,
בנוים על פי מאמרי רז"ל בירושלמי ובבלי ספרא,
וספרי, ומכלתא ומדרשים ברורים, עם לקוטים מהרמב"ם
ז"ל ושאר ספרים, נתחבר בטוב טעם ודעת, בעזר יוצר
אורים, ע"י החכם השלם והכולל עלוס ורב
כמהר"ר הלל דוד סתהון זלה"ה
נמצאו בין כתביו סדורים, לכן נתנדבו בניו יצ"ו להדפיסם
לעלוי נשמת הרב מר אביהם תהי לרוחה בצרור החיים זיע"א
ועל כל הישרים אכי"ר,
נדפס פה ארם־צובה יע"א
שנה התרע"ג לפ"ק
בדפוס השלם של הר' עזרא חיים מרמשק הי"ו
Imprimerie AL-KAMAL EZRA HAIM JOUEJATI - ALEP (Syrie)

Title Page of Aruchah U'Marpeh

[546] SUTTON, R' Hillel David

רבי הלל דוד סתהון

(— 1909)

Distinguished scholar and rabbi of Aram Soba, commonly known as "Hacham David Menashe." He was the son of R' Menashe Sutton (see #551) and the son-in-law of R' Shalom Chasky (see #149). He passed away on 17 Tishrei, 5669 (1908).

Among the noteworthy books, which he authored was *Aruchah U'Marpeh* (Aram Soba 5673/1913), which contains guidelines of ethics and morality based upon teachings of the Sages in the *Talmud Yerushalmi, Talmud Bavli*, and *Midrashim*. This material is accompanied by selections from the *Rambam* and other books, and is organized according to the *Aleph Bet*. The book was published through the efforts of the author's sons, R' Menashe, R' Ezra and R' Yaakob, who found the manuscript among the writings of their father. The book was reissued in 1965 through the efforts of the grandson of the author, R' Shalom Sutton (see #557).

He also authored *Masechet Abot* (Jerusalem 5690/1930), a collection of teachings from the *Gemara* and *Midrashim* that pertain to the topics raised in *Pirkei Abot*. This was published by the author's grandsons (from his daughter), R' David and R' Shalom Moshe Sutton, who also wrote an introduction.

Other *hiddushim* (original Torah thoughts) of R' Hillel David Sutton appeared in the journal *HaMe'asef* published by R' Ben-Sion Kouenka, and in the books *Maaseh Ha'Ish* and *Sh'al Ha'Ish* of R' Yaakob Shaul Elyashar. In addition, he joined R' Eliyahu Hamway (see #271) in providing a responsum for inclusion in the book *Shaare Rahamim* of R' Rahamim Yosef Franco. He also left a book in manuscript form entitled *LeHe'ir al HaShulhan*, dealing with the *halachot* of *Pesah*.

[547] SUTTON, R' Matloub

רבי מטלוב סתהון

(— 1834)

Worthy scholar of Aram Soba. He was the father of R' Menashe Sutton (see #551) and a descendant of R' Yosef Menashe Sutton who in 1525 signed a responsum of the *Maharalbach* (R' Levi ben Habib) (sect. 134), together with other rabbis of Aram Soba. He passed away on 1 Adar 2, 5594 (1834).

[548] SUTTON, R' Matloub

רבי מטלוב סתהון

(— 1885)

Eminent scholar and rabbi of Aram Soba. He was a grandson of the previously mentioned R' Matloub Sutton (see #547) and the oldest son of R' Menashe Sutton (see #551). Among his papers was found a eulogy for his father, which was subsequently published in his father's book *Pirhei Shoshanim* (Aram Soba 5670/1910). Unfortunately, his *hiddushim* (original Torah thoughts) have been lost. He passed away on 16 Av, 5645 (1885).

[549] SUTTON, R' Matloub Menashe

רבי מטלוב מנשה סתהון

(— 1929)

Eminent scholar of Aram Soba. R' Sutton was a grandson of the previously mentioned R' Matloub Sutton (see #547). He passed away at an early age, while his father was still living, on 8 Tamuz, 5689 (1929). He was eulogized by R' Yosef Yedid (see #594) (*Yemei Yosef*, Vol. II, page 515, Brooklyn 1974).

[550] **SUTTON, R' Menashe**

רבי מנשה סתהון

Worthy scholar of Aram Soba. He was the oldest son of R' Hillel David Sutton (see #546) and a grandson of R' Menashe Sutton (see #551). R' Menashe and his scholarly brothers R' Ezra and R' Yaakob jointly published their father's book *Aruchah U'Marpeh* (Aram Soba 5673/1913) and they dedicated the proceeds to the support of the general orphanage home of Aram Soba. R' Menashe also published his grandfather's book *Pirhei Shoshanim* (Aram Soba 5670/1910) and wrote an introduction to it. R' Menashe was blessed with four worthy sons: R' David, R' Shelomo, R' Nissim, and R' Eliyahu.

[551] **SUTTON, R' Menashe**

רבי מנשה סתהון

(— 1876)

Distinguished scholar and rabbi of Aram Soba and Safed. He was the son of R' Matloub Sutton (see #547) and was knowledgeable in all aspects of Torah learning, including the calendar and Hebrew grammar. In addition, he acquired general knowledge in astronomy, mathematics, and engineering. He supported himself through his initiatives in business. R' Menashe was known for his important work *Kenisiyah Leshem Shamayim* (Jerusalem 5734/1974), in which he argued fiercely against the practice of sorcery to banish evil spirits from a sickroom or maternity ward. This was unfortunately prevalent at the time and R' Menashe's campaign against it received encouragement from many other rabbis. Thus, a total of 36 rabbis and scholars signed the approbation to the book in 1852. He received support from the four major regions of the ancient *yishuv* in *Eretz Yisrael*: Jerusalem, Hebron, Tiberias, and Safed, from both the Sephardic and Ashkenazic communities, and from Damascus. (See Document Section, Document No. 31.)

He also wrote a number of other works, including the following:

- *Pirhei Shoshanim* (Aram Soba 5675/1915). Guidance to spiritual development through stories, poems, and songs. The book was published through the efforts of his grandson R' Menashe (see #550), who wrote a glowing and informative tribute in the introduction.
- *Klalei Dikdukei HaKriah* (Aram Soba 5674/1914). A tract on the rules of grammar that affect correct reading of the Torah. This was published at the end of the book *Peh Eliyahu* by R' Eliyahu Hamway (see #271).
- *Mateh Menashe*, consisting of three volumes of *hiddushim* (original Torah thoughts) on the *Gemara*, *Rambam*, and other authorities.
- *Siftei Sadik* on the four parts of the *Shulhan Aruch*.

He produced two additional works, which remained in manuscript form. In his later years, he decided to retire from his business activities and move to Jerusalem. However, in 1870 while passing through Safed he was invited by the community to serve as their Chief Rabbi. After living in Safed four years, he was called to serve as Chief Rabbi in Aram Soba. Two years later he succumbed to the entreaties of the people of No-Amon, Egypt to come and serve as their rabbi. However, while on the way, he fell ill in the city of Alexandria. The leaders of No-Amon went out to greet their new rabbi, but were sadly disappointed because he passed away in Alexandria on 24 Elul, 5636 (1876) and never made it to his new home. He was blessed with four sons: R' Matloub (see #548), R' Hillel David (see #546), R' Moshe (see #555), and R' Haim

R' Menashe was known for his important work Kenisiyah Leshem Shamayim (Jerusalem 5634/1974) in which he argued fiercely against the practice of sorcery to banish evil spirits from a sickroom or maternity ward.

ספר

כנסיה לשם שמים

בעיה"ק ירושלים תובב"א

תרל"ד

Title Page of Kenisiyah Leshem Shamayim

(see #545). R' Haim became known as the author of the book *Eretz HaHaim*.

[552] SUTTON, R' Moshe

רבי משה סתהון

(1797 — 1878)

ספר
קהלת משה
אשר אסף איש חיל רב פעלים : עדיתו הענוי ·
עוסק עם הצבור לש"ש מנהיג ודבר בעיר הזאת
נעמ"י ושמו הטוב מפורסם עד קצוי ארץ וים
רחוקים · איש חסד ומרבה להטיב עוזר וסומך
בגופו ובממונו אוהב התורה ולומדיה · עטרת
תפארת · גולת הכותרת · נזר החכמים · בכן של
קדושים · אראלים ותרשישים · הרב המופלא
ובכוד ס' מלא · בכוד גדולת כמוהר"ר
משה בכמהר"י סתהון נר"ו
יתן ה' לנצח לעד לעולם · ובירק יכון עולם כי"ר:
חלק ראשון
ארם צובה
בדפוס שיחו חי הי"ו ן' הרב כמהר"ר אברהם ששון זצ"ל
התר"לג

Title Page of Kehillat Moshe

Eminent scholar and rabbi of Aram Soba. He was known for the active role which he played in the life of the community and for his musical and poetic skills. He was a son of R' Yosef Sutton (see #566) and a grandson of R' Abraham Sutton (see #535), author of the book *Malel Le'Abraham*. In his grandfather's book there is a lecture on the topic of *tefillin* (lecture 21), which R' Abraham prepared for his grandson Moshe on the occasion of his *Bar Mitzvah* in the year 5570 (1810).

R' Moshe took it upon himself to publish his grandfather's book, but he was also an author in his own right. His books *Kehillat Moshe* (Aram Soba 5633/1873) and *Dibrei Moshe* (Livorno 5604/1844) contain elaborate poetic lectures. He also signed the approbation for the book *Hadar Ezer* of R' Yitzhak Shrem (see #517) and the book *Nochah HaShulhan* by R' Haim Mordechai Labaton (see #336).

In 1822 Aram Soba experienced a major earthquake, which caused much damage to the city. About a thousand Jews died in this calamity, including Señor Ezra Picciotto, the general consul of Austria. All of this was described by R' Moshe Sutton in *Kehillat Moshe* (see #58 for more details). He also composed a *kinah* (lamentation), which is customarily said on Tishah B'Av.

He served for many years as the spokesman for the community of Aram Soba and was active in the campaign to save the Jews of Damascus during the infamous Damascus Blood Libel in 1840.

He served for many years as the spokesman for the community of Aram Soba and was active in the campaign to save the Jews of Damascus during the infamous Damascus Blood Libel in 1840. For that purpose, he corresponded with Sir Moses Montefiore, Albert Cohen, the House of Rothschild, and the House of Sassoon. He passed away on 22 Tamuz, 5638 (1878).

[553] SUTTON, R' Moshe

רבי משה סתהון

(— 1881)

Worthy scholar and rabbi of Aram Soba. He moved to Baghdad and that is where he passed away on 3 Nissan, 5641 (1881).

[554] SUTTON, R' Moshe

רבי משה סתהון

Worthy scholar and rabbi of Aram Soba. He was a son of R' Yosef Sutton (see #565) and a son-in-law of R' Hillel David Sutton (see #546). Among his scholarly sons were R' David Sutton (see #538) and R' Shalom Sutton (see #557). In 1865 he signed the approbation to the book *Hadar Ezer* of R' Yitzhak Shrem (see #517).

[555] SUTTON, R' Moshe

רבי משה סתהון

Worthy scholar and rabbi of Aram Soba. He was the second son of R' Menashe Sutton (see #551). His brother R' Haim Sutton (see #545) pays tribute to him in the introduction to his book *Eretz HaHaim*. He moved to Safed and that is where he passed away.

[556] SUTTON, R' Nissim Ezra

רבי נסים עזרא סתהון

(— 1869)

Worthy scholar and rabbi of Damascus. His father was R' Ezra Menashe Sutton (see #541). He passed away at a relatively young age on 23 Heshvan, 5629 (1869).

[557] SUTTON, R' Shalom

רבי שלום סתהון

(— 1977)

Eminent scholar and rabbi of Jerusalem. He founded the Hafetz Haim orphanage home in Jerusalem and managed it for many years with total devotion.

He was a son of R' Moshe Sutton (see #554) and a brother of R' David Sutton (see #538). His father-in-law was R' Nissim Nahum (see #437).

His brother R' David pays tribute to him in his responsa, which were published in the appendix to the book *Vayelaket Yosef / Birchot Shamayim* (Aram Soba 5675/1915) by R' Yosef Sutton (see #565).

In his last years he endured the pain and suffering of ill health and finally passed away on 11 Av, 5737 (1977).

[558] **SUTTON, R' Shaul**

רבי שאול סתהון

(1851 — 1930)

Distinguished and influential *Av Bet Din* (Chief Judge) of Buenos Aires. He was born in Aram Soba in 1851 to R' David Sutton and at the age of 26 was appointed a member of the local *Bet Din*. After four years in the *Bet Din* he received an appointment to become the rabbi of Ein Tab, a position which he held for the next 10 years. In 1891 he returned to Aram Soba and founded a yeshiva designed to train rabbis for the next generation.

In 1913 he went to Buenos Aires to visit his sons, who had moved there 5 years before. While he was there he was invited to serve as rabbi and *Av Bet Din* for the Sephardic community of the city. In that capacity he contributed greatly to the strengthening of religious life of Buenos Aires, especially the reorganization of kosher-slaughtering practices. Also noteworthy was the founding of a Talmud Torah called *Yesod Daat* and a burial society, *Hesed shel Emet*. In addition he struggled successfully against improper conversions to Judaism and against the *brit milah* (circumcision) of children born from non-Jewish mothers.

Ultimately, he introduced a complete ban against accepting conversions in Buenos Aires. This became a matter of necessity because of the lack of community cohesion in the city at that time. It frequently happened that someone who wanted to marry a non-Jewish bride simply declared her Jewish, or made a declaration of conversion in the presence of unqualified laymen. The resulting children were presented to the community as having been born from Jewish parents even though they were non-Jewish according to the *halachah*. (See Document Section, Document No. 4.)

R' Shaul Sutton

The ruling against accepting converts was endorsed by the leading rabbis of the time including: the Chief Rabbi of Israel, R' Yaakob Meir; the *Bet Din* of the Ashkenazic communities in Jersualem, R' Tzvi Pesach Frank; the *Bet Din* of the Sephardic communities in Jersualem, R' Ezra Hamway (see #272), R' Haim Tawil (see #584), the rabbis of Aram Soba, and the *Av Bet Din* of Aram Soba, R' Moshe Mizrahi (see #424). Following in his footsteps, a similar ruling was made in the Syrian community of New York by R' Yaakob Kassin (see #330), R' Haim Tawil (see #584), R' Moshe Cohen (see #164), R' Mordechai Maslaton (see #411), and R' Moshe Gindi (see #266). (See Document Section, Document No. 4.)

He also wrote a book of responsa, called *Diber Shaul* (Jerusalem 5687/1927). R' Sutton passed away in Buenos Aires on 19 Sivan, 5690 (1930).

[559] **SUTTON, R' Shelomo**

רבי שלמה סתהון

(— 1918)

Worthy scholar of Aram Soba. He was born in Aram Soba and moved to Jerusalem to live out his remaining years. After a life devoted to Torah and *mitzvot* he passed away on 19 Av, 5678 (1918) and was buried on the Mount of Olives. He was blessed with three worthy sons: R' Raphael, R' Eliyahu, and R' Abraham Sutton.

R' Eliyahu was a son-in-law of R' Ben-Sion Kouenka, publisher of the journal *HaMe'asef*. Tragically, he was killed at a young age on 7 Iyar, 5700 (1940) by rioting Arab mobs in the Old City of Jerusalem.

Title Page of Diber Shaul

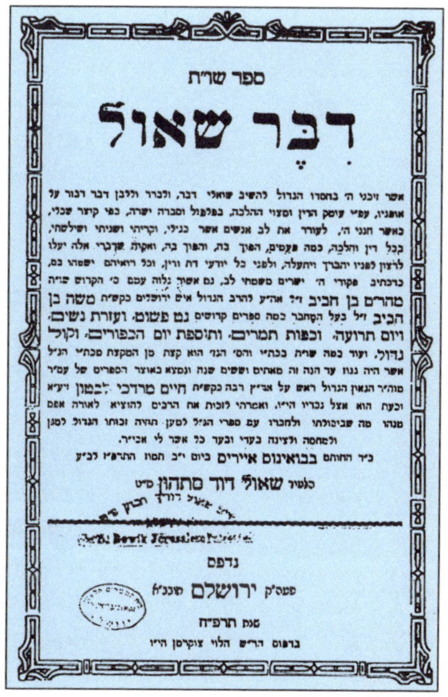

ספר שו"ת

דבר שאול

כלשיר שאול דוד סתהון ס"ט

נדפס

פעה"ק ירושלם תובב"א

שנת תרפ"ח

R' Raphael also died young, on 3 Tishrei, 5687 (1926). The gravestones of R' Shelomo and his sons R' Raphael and R' Eliyahu were restored after the Six Day War through the efforts of a granddaughter of R' Shelomo, Mrs. Fortune Cohen.

[560] **SUTTON, R' Shelomo Yitzhak**

רבי שלמה יצחק סתהון

(— 1931)

ספר
וילקט יוסף
וברכות שמים
מדבר בדינים הצריכים בזמן הזה מהלכות בשולי עכו"ם ומהלכות ברכות. מעשי ידי איש חיל יושר תמים וענו. הרב הכולל אור גולל כמהר"ר יוסף סתיהון ז"ל.
ואתו עמו איזה חדושים ממני נכדו המו"ל
דוד משה סתיהון הי"ו.
ארם צובה
שנת התרע"ה
בדפוס הרה"ג ישעיה דיין
על ידי בניו שאול שלמה ויצחק הע"י

Title Page of Vayelaket Yosef

Worthy scholar and merchant of Tiberias. He was born in Tiberias, the second son of R' Habib David Haim Sutton (see #544). In time he acquired a reputation as a man continually immersed in Torah studies. However, he chose not to profit from Torah pursuits and made his living as a merchant of Judaica. He still found the time to learn through the entire Talmud three times and write a *Sefer Torah*. In addition he authored two holy books, which were never published. He passed away on 24 Tishrei, 5691 (1931).

[561] **SUTTON, R' Yaakob**

רבי יעקב סתהון

(— 1929)

Worthy philanthropist of Aram Soba. He was a son of R' Yosef Sutton (see #567). R' Yaakob was a humble man, an honest merchant who was active in providing discreet help to people in need. He passed away on 3 Shevat, 5689 (1929).

[562] **SUTTON, R' Yaakob**

רבי יעקב סתהון

(early 20th century)

Eminent scholar and philanthropist of Buenos Aires. He was a son of R' Abraham Sutton and a son-in-law of R' Eliyahu Laniado (see #382). In about 1914 he moved to Buenos Aires to join his father-in-law. He became a successful and honorable merchant and worked closely with his father-in-law on fostering Torah life in the city. He was especially involved in building a synagogue and Talmud Torah for the Aram Soba community. He was also active in providing support for the poor of Buenos Aires and Jerusalem. Over a period of 28 years he put all his energies and resources into holy work.

[563] **SUTTON, R' Yitzhak**

רבי יצחק סתהון

(— 1935)

Worthy philanthropist of Aram Soba. His father was R' Haim Sutton. He passed away on 10 Adar, 5695 (1935) and was memorialized at the end of the book *Rei'ah Yitzhak* by R' Yitzhak Alfia (p. 172), who was his cousin. He was unique in the degree to which he showed respect and love to Torah scholars.

[564] **SUTTON, R' Yosef**

רבי יוסף סתהון

(— 1877)

Worthy scholar and rabbi of Damascus. He passed away on *Hoshana Rabbah* 21 Tishrei, 5638 (1877).

[565] **SUTTON, R' Yosef**

רבי יוסף סתהון

(1813 —)

Distinguished scholar and rabbi of Aram Soba. He was named after his grandfather, R' Yosef Sutton (see #566). His father's name was Abraham, as was his great-grandfather, the author of *Malel Le'Abraham* (see #535). R' Yosef was a prolific author, producing 10 major works over the course of his life:

- *Vayelaket Yosef* (Aram Soba 5675/1915). *Halachot* (laws) of forbidden foods and foods cooked by non-Jews. The book was published by the grandson of the author, R' David Sutton (see #538).
- *Birchot Shamayim*. *Halachot* (laws) on the blessings over food, drink, and fragrances. An abbreviated version of the book is included in *Vayelaket Yosef*.
- *Vayimatz'e Yosef* (Jerusalem 5734/1973). Allusions to all of the *mitz-*

vot of the Torah and the Sages in the words of *Perashat Haazinu*. The above three books have been reprinted as a set, together with *Yaaleh HaDas* by R' David Sutton, the grandson of R' Yosef (see #538).

- *Vayedaber Yosef.* On allusions to all of the *mitzvot* of the Torah and the Sages in the words of the Ten Commandments.
- *Vayizkor Yosef.* On allusions to all of the *mitzvot* of the Torah and the Sages in the words of *Tehillim*.
- *Vayivarech Yosef.* On the foods and situations in which there are uncertainties about the appropriate blessing.
- *Porat Yosef.* A commentary on the branches of *mitzvot*.
- *Edut BiYehosef.* On ethics and morality.
- *Diber Yosef.* On the *mitzvot* and ethical guidance for women, written in Arabic.
- *Tomru LeYosef.* Allusions from verses of the Torah and *Birkat Kohanim*.
- *Vayar Yosef.* Totals of words, letters, and notational marks in the *Tanach*, following the order introduced by R' Saadiah Gaon.

It appears that only the first three works were published. The rest remained in manuscript form. R' Yosef was blessed with three scholarly sons: R' Shaul, R' Moshe, and R' Shelomo.

[566] **SUTTON, R' Yosef**

רבי יוסף סתהון

Worthy scholar and rabbi of Aram Soba. He was a son of R' Abraham Sutton, the author of *Malel Le'Abraham* (see #535) and the father of R' Abraham Sutton and R' Moshe Sutton (see #552). R' Moshe speaks warmly of his father, R' Yosef, in the introduction to *Malel Le'Abraham*.

[567] **SUTTON, R' Yosef Menashe**

רבי יוסף מנשה סתהון

(— 1888)

Worthy scholar and rabbi of Aram Soba. He moved to Jerusalem, where he passed away on 14 Adar, 5648 (1888). At the Ben-Zvi Institute [file no. 302/29] there is an original document in which R' Yosef Menashe's name appears as the second signer, preceded by R' Yaakob Shaul Elyashar, the *Rishon LeSion* (Chief Rabbi of *Eretz Yisrael*). The document is dated 27 Av, 5641 (1881).

[568] **SUTTON-SHOMER, R' Yaakob**

רבי יעקב סתהון־שומר

(— 1917)

Worthy scholar and rabbi of Aram Soba. He passed away on 11 Tamuz, 5677 (1917).

[569] **SUTTON-SHOMER, R' Yeshayah**

רבי ישעיה סתהון־שומר

(— 1901)

Worthy scholar of Aram Soba. He was known for the brilliance of his reasoning. R' Yeshayah passed away on 9 Tevet, 5662 (1901).

[570] **SWED, R' Eliyahu**

רבי אליהו סוויד

Worthy scholar of Aram Soba. He was born to R' Moshe Swed (see #573), who mentions him in his book *Masveh Moshe* (p. 151). R' Eliyahu also had a son named R' Moshe Swed (see #574), who became a scribe and a *shohet* (ritual slaughterer).

[571] **SWED, R' Eliyahu**

רבי אליהו סוויד

Worthy scholar and rabbi of Aram Soba. He is spoken of highly by R' Yosef Yedid (see #594) in his book *She'erit Yosef* (Vol. I, *Even Ha'Ezer*, 1). The context is a question about a possible illegitimate birth, which R' Swed had posed.

[572] **SWED, R' Ezra**

רבי עזרא סוויד

(— 1884)

Worthy scholar and *dayan* (judge) of Aram Soba. He was a son of R' Moshe Swed (see #575) and a son-in-law of R' Haim Mordechai Labaton (see #336). In 1869 his name appeared in the list of Aram Soba scholars receiving a weekly stipend from the special fund that had been set up for the support of worthy individuals who dedicate their lives to Torah study (see #267 and

Document Section, Document No. 30). He composed a number of *pizmonim* (hymns), such as *"Anochi Eshal,"* which is part of the special prayers *(bakashot) of Aram Soba.*

He passed away at a relatively young age on 3 Av, 5644 (1884), while his father was still living. He was eulogized by R' Ezra Tawil (see #582). He was blessed with two sons: R' Moshe and R' Mordechai Nissim.

[573] **SWED, R' Moshe**

רבי משה סוויד

(— 1814)

Eminent scholar and *dayan* (judge) of Aram Soba. He is known for his important book *Masveh Moshe*, which remained for 200 years in its original manuscript form. Somehow the manuscript made its way to Mexico City, where it turned up in the possession of the Ashear family. R' Mordechai Attiah (see #109) discovered the manuscript and sent it to Jerusalem, where it was prepared for publication by his son R' Eliyahu Attiah (editor of the second edition to *LiKedoshim Asher Ba'Aretz*). It was finally printed in Jerusalem in 1967 (5727). The book covers 48 learned topics, including many responsa. He was also known to be a composer of *pizmonim* (hymns) for inclusion in the prayer service.

Somehow the manuscript made its way to Mexico City.

One night, after denouncing the Alliance in a synagogue lecture, he was attacked in his home and stabbed.

R' Moshe Swed was the son of R' Yosef Swed and the son-in-law of R' Ezra Sayagh (see #492). When R' Ezra passed away he was eulogized by R' Gabriel Ashkenazi (see #93), who mentioned R' Moshe as a phenomenal scholar and *dayan* (judge). He served as the secretary to the *Bet Din* during the time when R' Raphael Shelomo Laniado (see #363) was Chief Rabbi.

R' Moshe passed away on 25 Sivan, 5574 (1814) at the time of a terrible epidemic in Aram Soba. Shortly before his death he had delivered a eulogy for R' Eliyahu Shamah (see #499), who succumbed to the same epidemic. Later, other rabbis who eulogized R' Shamah also mentioned the tragic loss of R' Swed. He was blessed with five scholarly sons: R' Yosef (see #578), R' Eliyahu (see #570), R' Yitzhak, R' Nissim (see #577), and R' Yeshuah. Some scholarly grandsons were named after him (see #574 and #575).

[574] **SWED, R' Moshe**

רבי משה סוויד

(— 1888)

Worthy scribe and *shohet* (ritual slaughterer) of Aram Soba. He was a son of R' Eliyahu Swed (see #570). He passed away on 25 Tishrei, 5649 (1888).

[575] **SWED, R' Moshe**

רבי משה סוויד

(— 1889)

Eminent scholar and *dayan* (judge) of Aram Soba. He is believed to have been the son of R' Yosef Swed (see #578) and the grandson of the earlier R' Moshe Swed (see #573). In 1865 he joined other rabbis of Aram Soba in signing the approbation for the first book-printing initiative of the city (see Document Section, Document No.25), which was introduced by R' Abraham Sasson and his sons (see #476).

He was a tireless foe of the *"Kol Yisrael Haverim"* organization (Alliance Israelite Universelle) and its school system. One night, after denouncing the Alliance in a synagogue lecture, he was attacked in his home and stabbed. The perpetrators were apparently never identified.

He wrote the books *Emet U'Mishpat* (responsa) and *Shalom Ve'Emet* (inspirational lectures). Both remained in manuscript form. However, in 1857 R' Shalom Chasky (see #149) and R' Haim Shemuel Wazan from Ein Tab wrote highly complimentary reports on his efforts. Some of his inspirational lectures were printed in the book *Shaare Ezra* (Jerusalem 5722/1962) by R' Ezra Shayo (see #505).

R' Swed is also mentioned by R' Ezra Tawil (see #582) in his book *Et Sofer* (sect. 3). He speaks of showing his own manuscript to the "exceptionally brilliant scholar," R' Moshe Swed, for his approval. Another mention of R' Swed is found in the lecture which R' Yosef Yedid (see #594) gave on *Shabbat Shuvah* in 1929. R' Yedid quotes a Torah interpretation that he heard as a youth from the mouth of R' Swed (*She'erit Yosef,* Vol. I).

At the end of the introduction that some rabbis of Aram Soba wrote to the book *Sefat Emet* by R' Eliyahu Mishan (Jerusalem 5664/1904), they announce that they have in their possession the manuscripts of various responsa by the Chief Rabbi, R' Shaul Dweck, and by the second in holiness, the great rabbi, R' Moshe Swed. He passed away on 29 Iyar, 5649 (1889). His son was R' Ezra Swed (see #572). His daughter married R' Abraham Haim Ades (see #37), whose second son, R' Moshe (#39), was named after his maternal grandfather.

[576] **SWED, R' Nissim**

רבי נסים סוויד

(— 1888)

Worthy scholar and *dayan* (judge) of Aram Soba. He was a son of R' Yosef Swed (see #578) and a grandson of R' Moshe Swed (see #573), the author of *Masveh Moshe*. His brother was the *dayan* (judge) R' Moshe Swed (see #575). In 1852 he joined other rabbis of Aram Soba in signing the approbation to the book *Kenisiyah Leshem Shamayim* (see Document Section, Document No. 31) by R' Menashe Sutton (see #551). His signature also appears on an original document dated 1882, following the signature of R' Mordechai Labaton (see #339).

[577] **SWED, R' Nissim**

רבי נסים סוויד

(19th century)

Worthy scholar of Aram Soba. He was a son of R' Moshe Swed (see #573), the author of *Masveh Moshe*. His name appeared in the list of Aram Soba scholars receiving a weekly stipend from the special fund that had been set up for the support of worthy individuals who dedicate their lives to Torah study (see Document Section, Document No. 30).

שמח זבולן בצאתך וישכר באהלך

ספר

ישׂשכר וזבולון

כולל מאמרים מהזוה״ק ומתיקונים ור״ם ומדרשים בשבח המגיע למעלת המחזיק ביד לומדי תורה וכמה גדל מעלת הצדקה עם עמלי תורה ושבח חכמת הקבלה ושבחי האר״י הקדוש זצוק״ל וזיע״א ושבחי מו״ר הרב שר שלום שרעבי זלה״ה וזיע״א החרדים ישימו עיונם בספר הזה ובטח יתלהב לבם לאמרי קודש וכונתינו בזה רק לזכות הרבים ולזכות עצמינו לעשות נחת רוח לפניו אבי״ר.

נדפס פה

עיה״ק ירושלם ת״ו

שנת לחייו כערג״ת הבושם

בדפוס עזריאל – ירושלם

גל עיני ואביטה נפלאות מתורתך

עץ חיים היא למחזיקים בה ותומכיה מאשר

Title Page of Yisaschar U'Zevulun

[578] **SWED, R' Yosef**

רבי יוסף סוויד

Worthy scholar of Aram Soba. He was a son of R' Moshe Swed (see #573), the author of *Masveh Moshe*, and a father of the brothers R' Moshe Swed (see #575) and R' Nissim Swed (see #576).

Tawil Lineage. According to tradition, the Tawil family of *Kohanim* traces its origin back to Eli HaKohen, the *Kohen Gadol* in the time of the *Shoftim* (Judges). The *Gemara* in *Rosh Hashanah* (18a) describes a curse placed on Eli's family that would only be forgiven through Torah and *hesed* (benevolence). The name Tawil was given to serve as a good omen since it means "long" in Arabic, auguring long life.

[579] **TAWIL, R' Abraham**

רבי אברהם מעילי הכהן טוויל

(— 1907)

Worthy scholar, *darshan* (lecturer), and teacher of Aram Soba. He was a son of R' Eliyahu Tawil (see #581). He taught *Gemara* in the Talmud Torah of Aram Soba and gave many students their grounding in learning skills. However, he moved to Jerusalem while still relatively young, and died there on 4 Kislev, 5668 (1907). He was eulogized by R' Yaakob Haim Yisrael Alfia (see #45).

[580] **TAWIL, R' Aharon**

רבי אהרן מעילי הכהן טוויל

(— 1916)

Eminent scholar and Kabbalist of Aram Soba. He was a son of R' Eliyahu Tawil (see #581). One of his sons-in-law was R' Moshe Tawil (see #586). He left Aram Soba for Jerusalem at approximately the same time as his brother R' Abraham (see #579). In Jerusalem he became an active member of the local community of Kabbalists and contributed to the body of work in this field. He left many *hiddushim* (original Torah

R' Aharon Tawil

כי עזרא הכין לבבו לדרוש את

ספר

ע"ט סופר

שו"ת

נדפס

בעיה"ק ירושלם תובב"א

שנת תרפ"ח לפ"ק

דפוס הר"ש הלוי צוקרמן

Title Page of Et Sofer

thoughts) in manuscript form and also authored a treatise called *Yisaschar U'Zevulun* (Jerusalem 5673/1913), which is an inspirational work seeking to encourage the support of Torah scholars. He passed away on 26 Sivan, 5676 (1916).

[581] TAWIL, R' Eliyahu
רבי אליהו מעילי הכהן טוויל

(19th century)

Worthy scholar and Kabbalist of Aram Soba. He was the father of R' Abraham and R' Aharon Tawil (see #579 and #580), as well as of a third son named R' Nissim. R' Eliyahu was an avid student of the *Zohar*.

[582] TAWIL, R' Ezra
רבי עזרא מעילי הכהן טוויל

(1830 — 1890)

Eminent scholar and *Av Bet Din* (Chief Judge) of Aram Soba. He was born in 1830 and passed away on 27 of Adar 2, 5650 (1890). He wrote a book of responsa, which he called *Et Sofer* (Jerusalem 5688/1928). The book was published by his son R' Haim (see #584), who added an appendix called *Matza Haim*, consisting of inspirational lectures. He was blessed with four other sons: Moshe, Mordechai, Shelomo, and Shaul.

R' Haim Tawil

One of his responsa was published in the book *Maaseh Ish* by R' Yaakob Shaul Elyashar. It also appears that one of his responsa was included in the book *Shaare Rahamim* by R' Rahamim Yosef Franco (sect. 13) under the name R' Ezra Cohen from Aram Soba.

He studied Kabbalah with R' Shemuel Morsaya (see #434) and R' Shelomo Safdeyé (see #469). The outcome of this collaboration was the book *Emet Me'Aretz* (Jerusalem 5748/1988), published by the yeshiva *Ahabat Shalom*.

In 1869 his name appeared in the list of Aram Soba scholars receiving a weekly stipend from the special fund that had been set up for the support of worthy individuals who dedicate their lives to Torah study (see #267 and Document Section, Document No. 30). He was 39 years old at that time.

[583] TAWIL, R' Haim
רבי חיים מעילי הכהן טוויל

(— 1864)

Worthy scholar and rabbi of Damascus. He passed away at a relatively young age on 6 Av, 5624 (1864).

[584] TAWIL, R' Haim
רבי חיים מעילי הכהן טוויל

(— 1942)

Eminent scholar and *dayan* (judge) of Aram Soba, New York, and Jerusalem. He was born in Aram Soba, the son of R' Ezra Tawil (see #582). After becoming a learned Torah scholar in the *yeshivot* of Aram Soba, he was appointed to serve as a member of its *Bet Din*. In 1906, together with other scholars and rabbis of Aram Soba, he signed a *halachic* (legal) ruling directed against those who desecrate *Shabbat* (see Document Section, Document No. 27).

Between 1932 and 1936 a *Hevra Kadisha* (Burial Society) in Jerusalem started to change funeral customs and copy the ways of the gentiles. R' Haim joined R' Ezra Hamway (see #272) in issuing a proclamation against them (see Document Section, Document No. 5). He was also active in the *Magen David* Talmud Torah of Jerusalem.

In 1938 he joined R' Ezra Hamway and R' Ezra Shayo (see #505) in an approbation to the ruling of R' Shaul Sutton (see #558) of the Syrian community of Argentina not to accept converts due to the lack of religious sincerity on the part of the converts (see Document Section, Document No. 4).

Shortly before the outbreak of World War I he immigrated to New York, where he became a rabbi for the local Aram Soba community. While there, he also authored a book called *Masa Haim*, consisting of 10

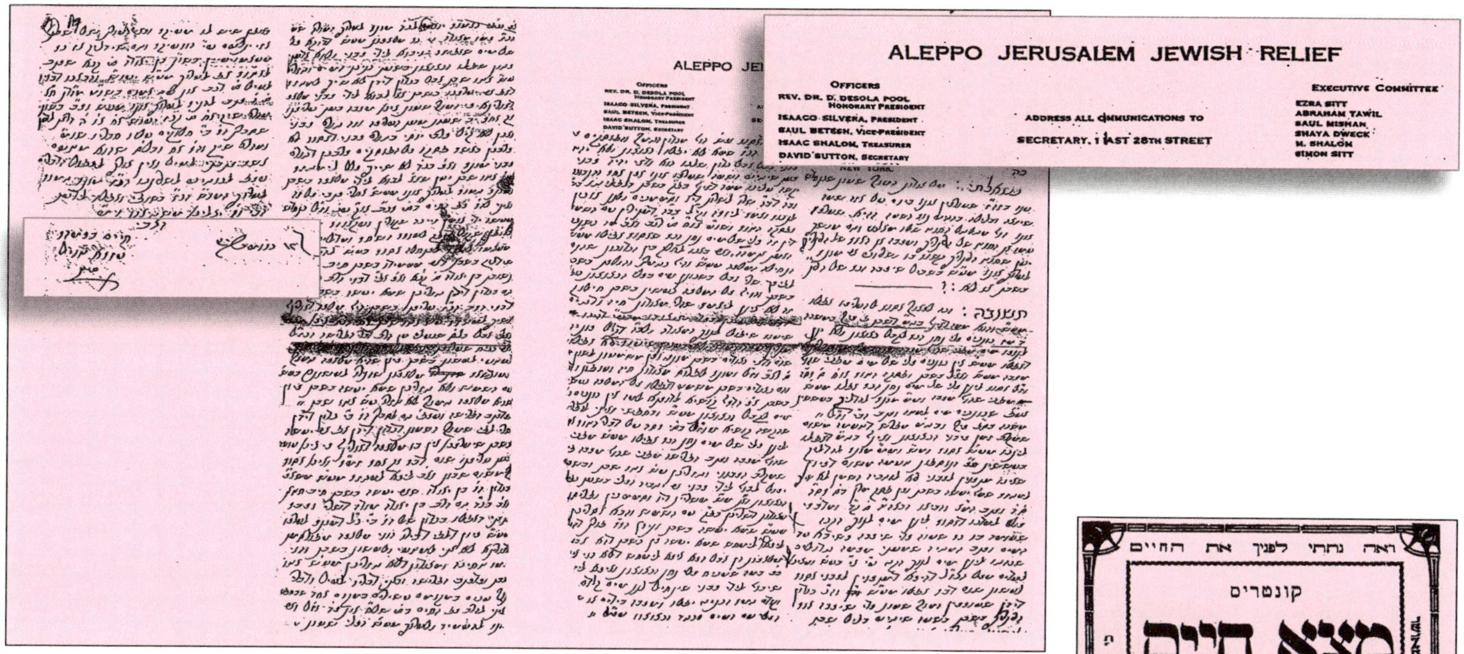

ALEPPO JERUSALEM JEWISH RELIEF

OFFICERS
REV. DR. D. DESOLA POOL, HONORARY PRESIDENT
ISAACO SILVERA, PRESIDENT
SAUL BETESH, VICE-PRESIDENT
ISAAC SHALOM, TREASURER
DAVID SUTTON, SECRETARY

ADDRESS ALL COMMUNICATIONS TO SECRETARY, 1 EAST 28TH STREET

EXECUTIVE COMMITTEE
EZRA SITT
ABRAHAM TAWIL
SAUL MISHAN
SHAYA DWECK
M. SHALOM
SIMON SITT

Responsum from R' Tawil to Mr. A. D. Sutton (see #536)

ראה נתתי לפניך את החיים

קונטרים

מצא חיים

לזכות הרבים וזכות התורה ההיה מגן בעדי ובעד ביתי ובעד בני, והי יזכנו לביאת משיחנו ולבנין בית מקדשינו במהרה בימינו אמן נצח סלה

חיים בכמהר״ר עזרא ע״לי הכהן ס״ט

נדפס

בעיה״ק ירושלם תובב״א

שנת תרפ״ח לפ״ק

דפוס הר״ש הלוי צוקרמן

כי מוצאי מצא חיים ויפק רצון מה׳

Title Page of Masa Haim

inspirational lectures related to important days of the year. He published this together with the book *Et Sofer* by his father (Jerusalem 5688/1928). At the end of the book he added a pamphlet titled, "The Way of Torah," a directive on proper education from the leading rabbis of Europe (see Document Section, Document No. 6). He explains that this pamphlet, printed originally in Europe, needs to be disseminated among Sephardic Jewry as well. In the beginning of his book he thanks Mr. Abraham D. Sutton (see #536) and Mr. Moshe Shalom for helping in the publishing effort.

In 1937 he moved to Jerusalem and served there as a *dayan* (judge) in the Sephardic

R' Moshe Tawil (#585) and family

Bet Din until his last days. He passed away there on 12 Tevet, 5702 (1942).

[585] TAWIL, R' Moshe

רבי משה מעילי הכהן טוויל

(— 1927)

Worthy scholar of Aram Soba. His father was R' Eliyahu, whose other sons were R' Abraham and Aharon Tawil (see #579 and #580). He was a very pious man who experienced much pain and suffering, including the loss of his eyesight. However, he was blessed with sons and grandsons who were notable Torah scholars. One of his sons, R' Yosef Tawil, was a rabbi in Brooklyn. He passed away on Friday afternoon, before *Shabbat*, 7 Adar II, 5687 (1927).

R' Moshe Tawil (#586)

[586] TAWIL, R' Moshe

רבי משה מעילי הכהן טוויל

(1896 — 1977)

Distinguished founder and *Rosh Yeshiva* of the yeshiva *Degel HaTorah* of Aram Soba and the yeshiva *Zichron Moshe* of Tel Aviv. He was a successful educator, nurturing hundreds of students, many of whom became rabbis and *dayanim* (judges) in various communities throughout the world. He was renowned for his depth and breadth of Torah knowledge. Thus, the rabbis and scholars of Aram Soba often turned to him with *halachic* (legal) questions and were happy to accept his rulings.

He was born in Aram Soba in approximately 1896 to R' Yosef and Rachel Tawil. However, when he was only a month old his father died, so Moshe grew up in his grandfather's house. He attended the Talmud Torah of Aram Soba and then entered the yeshiva, where he studied Torah under R' Abraham Antebi (see #64). After that he became the special pupil of R' Shaul Matloub Abadi (see #9), a renowned educator. When R' Abadi went to New York, R' Moshe continued his studies under R' Ezra Shayo (see #505), who was the primary teacher of all the scholars of that generation in Aram Soba.

He soon became known as a brilliant and capable scholar, and was ordained as a rabbi at the age of 20. He was then approached by leading members of the community and asked to start a new yeshiva for students who had graduated from the Talmud Torah. In response, he started the yeshiva *Degel Hatorah,* which was to become the major yeshiva of the city. During the years 1921 – 1956, hundreds of students passed through its doors. Among his noteworthy students were: R' Yitzhak Chehebar, the Chief Rabbi of Buenos Aires (see #152); R' Yitzhak Zafrani, the chairman of *Keter Torah*; R' Yaakob Attiah, Rabbi of the Aram Soba congregation of Bat Yam; and R' Sadek Harari, the Chief Rabbi of Mexico.

The yeshiva put great effort on developing the piety and character of its students. R' Tawil also ensured that there was an effective relationship with the philanthropists of the city, so as to ensure that financial help would be available to the students, many of whom came from poor homes.

The Doctor Can't Do It Alone. The wealthy people of Aram Soba appreciated the importance of Torah. Typically, when a member of the family became ill and it was necessary to see a doctor, the head of the family would set aside an amount of money equal to the doctor's fee. This additional amount would be given to two students of the yeshiva, who would recite *Tehillim* to help gain *Hashem's* blessing for a speedy recovery.

R' Moshe Tawil would select students for this purpose, according to their needs. He would also instruct selected students to have in mind when they are immersed in their studies (e.g., from 10 a.m. to 11 a.m.) that the merit of their learning should be dedicated to the recovery of a specific ill person. This was a way to help the students meet pressing family needs and would also make them more conscious of the importance of total dedication in their studies.

He was an active opponent of the *Kol Yisrael Haverim* organization (Alliance Israelite Universelle) and its secular school system. His tireless efforts bore fruit and the Alliance schools of Aram Soba finally closed their doors.

In the book *Meir Tov*, R' Yomtob J. Yedid speaks of the impact that R' Moshe Tawil had on his generation. He writes, "Who does not know what Moshe, the servant of *Hashem*, has done? Who does not remember when the *Kol Yisrael Haverim* organization (the Alliance) sought to influence the poor children of the Talmud Torah, the young lambs, to entice them with smooth arguments to leave the Talmud Torah and to join their lot, to drink from their poison, and to fill their basket with bitter grapes? Who does not remember that he was almost the only one who recognized the danger that was threatening to come from this? With a courageous heart he strengthened himself like a lion and waged a campaign against them. He overcame his enemies even though a few of the men of the community secretly assisted the organization. He did not accept favors from them and did not seek their favor, but fought them with a strong hand. He did not give them an opportunity to have an effect and his efforts were vindicated so that he nullified their counsel and voided their plans."

He also fought to preserve the modesty of Jewish women. One year, which happened to be a year of drought, some people organized a club for mixed dancing. The spiritual leaders of the community were unable to stop this breakdown in traditional moral standards, because the organizers were influential men, who felt free to disregard Torah guidance. When the drought continued to get worse, the community leaders decided to announce a fast day. Naturally, as a first step, they came to R' Moshe to ask for his concurrence. To their surprise, he refused; however he told his *shamosh* (sexton) to announce that women and girls were forbidden from going to the dance club on *Motza'e Shabbat*, which was when the dances were held. These words had their desired effect and the club closed down shortly after. On the following day, the rains came and the drought ended.

In 1947 when the Arab riots struck Aram Soba, and the mobs burned down Jewish homes, many of the wealthy people of the community fled to the city of Beirut. R' Moshe traveled to Beirut and conducted a fund-raising effort to provide help for the suffering people of Aram Soba.

His wife was Sarah, the daughter of R' Aharon Tawil (see #580). She was an important helpmate in his holy work. When people came to the house to ask his advice or ask *halachic* questions, she made them feel welcome. She did whatever she could to enhance the honor of the Torah and to help R' Moshe fulfill his holy mission.

His day was continually occupied with learning Torah for 16 hours a day. He could be found in the *Bet Midrash* at 2 a.m. teaching Torah to a group of his students. He never sought a vacation or rest from his labors in Torah.

In 1958 he moved to Tel Aviv, where he lived his remaining years. It was there that he founded the yeshiva *Zichron Moshe*, where young scholars study Torah following the approach of Aram Soba. His sons Yitzhak and Aharon continued in managing the yeshiva after he passed away on 8 Heshvan, 5737 (1977).

He was an active opponent of the Kol Yisrael Haverim organization (Alliance Israelite Universelle) and its secular school system.

He could be found in the Bet Midrash at 2 a.m. teaching Torah to a group of his students.

He also fought to preserve the modesty of Jewish women.

[587] **TAWIL, R' Moshe (the Elder)**
רבי משה מעילי הכהן טוויל (הזקן)

(— 1910)

Worthy scholar of Aram Soba. People called him "the elder" to distinguish him from R' Moshe ben Eliyahu Tawil (see #585). He passed away in Jerusalem on 10 Shevat, 5670 (1910) and was eulogized by the *Av Bet Din* (Chief Judge) of Jerusalem, R' Yosef Yedid (#594), as recorded in in the book *She'erit Yosef* (Section of Lectures, Number 12).

ספר

מנחת אליעזר

סובב הולך על דרך עץ החיים להרב המקובל
האלהי רבינו מהרח"ו זלה"ה, בו ידמו מאמר
א' מרבותינו בעלי התלמוד בק"ל דרכים כל חיך
המטעמ: אומרלי לי אשר אגב למודי דרכתי קצת"
וקבצתים לאחרים וראיתי כי יש בו שיעור בפ"ע
ולכן הוצאתים לאור להיות למזכרת כללים
לזכות את הרבים, אנכי שועל הויצא מקדשי
קדשים בנן של קדושים

הצעיר אליעזר ידיד הלוי ס"ט

פעה"ק ירושלם תובב"א

שנת וזאת תורת המנחה לפ"ק

בדפוס הר"ש הלוי צוקערמאן הי"ו

Title Page of Minhat Eliezer

[588] YAFET, R' Shet bar

רבי שת בר יפת

(13th century)

Eminent scholar of Aram Soba. He was an author of holy books, who lived in the 13th century, long before printing had been invented. Manuscripts were painstakingly copied by hand. He wrote an extensive commentary on the Torah and the *Haftarot*, which he called *Hemdat HaTe'udah LeBet Yisrael VeYehudah*. Afterwards he wrote an abbreviated version for the benefit of his young sons, which he called *Hemdat HaTe'udah*. He completed both books in 1284.

[589] YEDID, R' Aharon

רבי אהרן ידיד הלוי

(— 1871)

Worthy scholar and rabbi of Beirut. He was known to have a beautiful voice, which brought joy and inspiration to those who heard him. He passed away in Beirut on 20 Adar, 5631 (1871).

R' Eliezer (Rahamim) Yedid

[590] YEDID, R' Eliezer (Rahamim)

רבי אליעזר (רחמים) ידיד הלוי

(1885 — 1934)

Eminent scholar and Kabbalist of Jerusalem. He was one of the scholars and teachers of the yeshiva *Porat Yosef,* as well as the Kabbalist *yeshivot Rehovot HaNahar* and *Bet El.* He was known for his exceptional piety and devoutness.

R' Yedid was born in Aram Soba in 1885, the second son of R' Yomtob Yedid (see #593). His mother, Rachel, was a daughter of R' Yosef Labaton (see #341). In 1890 he moved with his parents to Jerusalem.

He was blessed with three sons: R' Yaakob, R' Yitzhak, and R' Abraham. He passed away on 24 Adar, 5694 (1934).

He published his father's book *Simhat Yomtob* (Jerusalem 5686/1926) and incorporated some of his own *hiddushim* (original Torah thoughts) on Kabbalah, which he called *Amar HaBen*. Other published works of R' Eliezer are:

- *Minhat Eliezer* (Jerusalem 5670/1910). Commentary on the Kabbalist book *Etz HaHaim* by R' Haim Vital.
- *Debar Eliezer* (Jerusalem 5670/1910). Guide to spiritual development in the areas of human reproduction, Torah study, and charity.
- *Aryeh Shaag* (Jerusalem 5683/1923). An anthology of selected teachings by Jewish Sages. Part II of this work contains *hiddushim* on spiritual development, such as what to learn at the table. It was bound with *Simhat Yomtob*.
- *Shivhei Maharam* (Jerusalem 5692/1932). Biography of R' Mordechai Haim Labaton (see #336) and biographical details of his father R' Yomtob Yedid. Also included is a presentation of 39 *mitzvot* related to lending money to the poor.

He also prepared the *siddur* of the *Rashash* (R' Shalom Sharabi) for publication (Jerusalem 5670/1910). This work is in nine volumes. (For further information see the section entitled, "Printing the Siddur of the *Rashash*," under the biography of R' Haim Shaul Dweck, #228.)

[591] YEDID, R' Mordechai

רבי מרדכי ידיד הלוי

(— 1912)

Worthy scholar and teacher of Aram Soba. He was a teacher of reading skills to young children and lived in great poverty. He was an expert in Hebrew grammar and composed a number of *piyutim* (poetic prayers), two of which were published in the book *Torat Hacham* by his renowned son, R' Yosef Yedid (see #594). He also knew *Tanach* by heart, together with its Arabic translation. Every day, he would recite the entire Book of *Tehillim* by heart, together with the associated prayers (*Yehi Ratzon*). When his son left Aram Soba to go to Jerusalem, R' Mordechai went along and remained there until he passed away on 18 Heshvan, 5673 (1912). Both for his own sake and as the father of a distinguished son, R' Mordechai's funeral attracted great respect and honor.

[592] **YEDID, R' Yitzhak**

רבי יצחק ידיד הלוי

(— 1917)

Worthy scholar and rabbi of Aram Soba. He authored a major book on the *halachot* of *shehitah*. During the latter part of his life he lived in Port Said, Egypt, where he was engaged as a rabbi and *shohet* (ritual slaughterer). He was the oldest son of R' Yomtob Yedid (see #593), but died at a relatively young age on 10 Elul, 5677 (1917) while his father was still alive. Six years later when his father passed away, his younger brother, R' Eliezer Yedid (see #590), memorialized him during the eulogy for his father (*Simhat Yomtob*, vol. 5, no. 5).

[593] **YEDID, R' Yomtob**

רבי יום טוב ידיד הלוי

(1856 — 1923)

Distinguished scholar, *dayan* (judge), and Kabbalist of Aram Soba and Jerusalem. He participated in the Chief Rabbinate of Aram Soba, together with the *Av Bet Din* (Chief Judge) R' Ezra Hamway (see #272), R' Moshe Mizrahi, and R' Ezra Shayo (see #505).

He was born in Aram Soba in 1856 and became known for his exceptional piety and devoutness, as well as for his greatness in Kabbalah. Through his warm and friendly approach to dealing with people he succeeded in promoting the study of Kabbalah in public and in bringing Jews back to religious observance.

His Family

He settled in Jerusalem in about 1910. On 28 Kislev, 5677 (1916), his wife Rachel passed away. She was the daughter of R' Yosef Labaton (see #341) and granddaughter of R' Haim Mordechai Labaton (see #336), author of *Nochah HaShulhan* and *Ben Yair*. In Elul of that year (1917), he returned to Aram Soba and was received with acclaim. There he took a second wife, the daughter of R' Menahem Gindi and granddaughter of R' Yaakob Gindi. From this second marriage he had a son and a daughter. The son, Menahem Yedid, became a leader of the Aram Soba community in Tel Aviv and established the *Moreshet Aram Soba*, a foundation dedicated to preserving the heritage of Aleppo. R' Yomtob passed away in Aram Soba on *Rosh Hodesh* Tamuz, 5683 (1923).

R' Mordechai Yedid also knew Tanach by heart, together with its Arabic translation.

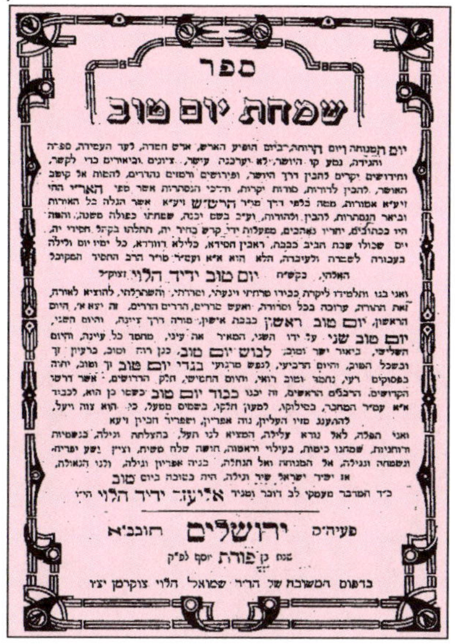
ספר
שמחת יום טוב
פעיה״ק ירושלים תובב״א
בדפוס המשכבת של הר״ר שמואל הלוי צוקרמן יצ״ו

Title Page of Simhat Yomtob

One of his daughters was married to R' Aharon Abitbol, who had come to Eretz Yisrael from Morocco. Sadly, he died young in 1908. In the last year of his life his wife gave birth to a son and he was able to participate in the *brit* (circumcision ceremony) as the *sandek*. He passed away one hour later.

His Writings

R' Yomtob's writings on Kabbalah were incorporated into the book *Simhat Yomtob* (Jerusalem 5686/1926), which was published by his son, R' Eliezer Yedid (see #590). That book consists of five parts, as follows:

- *Yomtob Rishon*. Commentary on the Kabbalist book *Etz HaHaim* by R' Haim Vital.
- *Yomtob Sheni*. Commentary on the book *Mamarei Rashbi*.
- *Levush Yomtob*. Additional commentary on the Kabbalist book *Etz HaHaim* by R' Haim Vital.
- *Bigdei Yomtob*. Commentary on *Tanach* and *Gemara*, following a Kabbalist approach.
- *Kebod Yomtob*. Ten eulogies delivered by various rabbis on the passing of R' Yomtob, including two by his son R' Eliezer. This part was also published separately in an expanded edition, which included biographical information concerning R' Mordechai Haim Labaton (see #336) and additional eulogies.

He also wrote a commentary on the *siddur* of the *Rashash* (R' Shalom Sharabi), consisting of nine volumes focusing on *kavanot* (recommended meditations on prayers and *mitzvot)*.

In addition, he joined with two other rabbis, R' Aharon Harari-Raful (see #303) and R' Haim ben Saadiah, to issue the book *Tzemach Tzaddik*, which extols the special virtues of studying Torah on Thursday nights (*Lel Shishi*) and provides a program for what to learn and what prayers to say on that night.

His Diligence

He devoted every spare minute to Torah study. In *Kebod Yomtob*, R' Eliezer Yedid related that even when his father was invited to officiate at a wedding or *brit milah* he would sit in a corner, engrossed in a holy book, refusing to be disturbed by the crowds of people.

R' Yosef Yedid

His Piety

When he partook of food it was with the purest and holiest of thoughts. Before eating he would meditate according to the applicable *kavanot* (meditations) specified in the *siddur* of the *Rashash* (R' Shalom Sharabi) even if this meant the food would get cold or an insufficient amount would be left over for him to eat.

He was a faithful participant in daily midnight prayer and study sessions *(Tikkun Hatzot*). He was also active together with R' Elazar Mizrahi in organizing a midnight study group called *Shomrim LaBoker*, as described by the *Rishon LeSion*, R' Yaakob Shaul Elyashar, in the introduction to the book *Tikkun Hatzot* by R' Nissim Harari-Raful (see #305). The group met in the synagogue called *Kollel HaSephardim*, which has a history going back to R' Yochanan ben Zakai, as described by the *Ramban*.

[594] **YEDID, R' Yosef**

רבי יוסף ידיד הלוי

(1867 — 1930)

Rabbinical authority, Kabbalist, and *dayan* (judge). He was born in Aram Soba in 1867 to R' Mordechai Yedid (see #591), who was a devoted teacher of young schoolchildren. He was a nephew of R' Yomtob Yedid (see #593), but it was only with the aid of R' Shaul Kassin (see #327) that young Yosef was able to fulfill his childhood dream of committing himself to intense Torah learning (see box). In Aram Soba he studied alongside R' Ezra Shayo (see #505) under R' Abraham Ades (see #37), ultimately becoming a *dayan* (judge).

Where There's a Will. When Yosef Yedid's father, a teacher of small children in Aram Soba, began to lose his vision, the young boy was required to help him continue to teach and manage the classroom (even though his father knew the Torah by heart). Yosef was very frustrated, it hurt him to spend his time teaching the basics, but his family was poor and he had to help his father. The school day was long, starting around 7 a.m. and lasting until after 4 p.m. After each day, Yosef would go to *shul* and approach the *Hechal* (Torah cabinet). In front of the Torah scrolls, he would cry, "*Hashem*, I want to learn. I want to learn *Shas*, I want to learn *Poskim*. I don't want to spend my life ignorant of spiritual depths; I want to reach great levels!"

On one of those days, R' Shaul Kassin (see #327) walked in and saw the boy crying. He waited until Yosef had completed his prayers, then approached the tear-stained boy and asked him why he was so troubled. Yosef poured out his heart again, telling R' Kassin of his desire to learn and excel in Torah. R' Kassin was taken by the boy's drive and said, "If that's the case, you will learn and we will find someone else to help your father." He raised money from wealthy men in Syria, and sent Yosef to yeshiva.

Sure enough, R' Yosef proved that Torah was his destiny. He became an accomplished scholar in Syria and a respected Kabbalist when he was older.

In 1890 he settled in Safed learning Torah day and night, and living in poverty. Ten years later, when he traveled to Jerusalem to publish his first book, *Torat Hacham*, his uncle R' Yomtob Yedid (see #593) urged him to move to Jerusalem and told him of a synagogue that was looking for a rabbi. After accepting the position at the Bukharan Shul, R' Yedid moved to Jerusalem and was asked to serve on the Syrian *Bet Din* with R' Yaakob Ades (see #41) and R' Raphael Shelomo Laniado (see #364). Eventually he became the *Av Bet Din* (Chief Judge). In that position Syrian communities worldwide contacted him for the final word on *halachah* and *hashkafah* issues.

He fought tirelessly against the winds of secularism that had begun to blow through the Sephardic community. He wrote a strong letter condemning those who teach Torah as a history exercise without referring to the classic commentaries, such as *Rashi*, *Ramban*, and the *Midrashim* (see Document Section, Document No. 6). This was an addendum to a large pamphlet titled, "The Way of the Torah," originally published in Europe in 1920 and later reprinted by R' Haim Tawil (see #584) in Jerusalem in 1923. He also signed on the letter to Agudat Yisrael protesting the appointment of a principal with the title Dr. (see Document Section, Document No. 7).

Jewish education in Aram Soba was traditionally conducted in Arabic, the language of the people. In the early 20th century various educators promoted the idea of conducting classes in Hebrew, especially in Argentina. The Syrian scholars and rabbis of Argentina were very much against this because Hebrew had become the means by which Zionists introduced antireligious ideas and vulgar language into common speech. At first they turned to R' Haim Shaul Dweck, the renowned Kabbalist and founder of the yeshiva *Rehovot HaNahar* of Jerusalem (see #228). R' Dweck agreed with what they were trying to do, but said he was already too old and weak to take a leading role in this fight. He suggested that they refer the matter to the *Bet Din* of R' Yosef Chaim Sonnenfeld. In the end they went to R' Yosef Yedid, who took up the matter with all of his energy and fought vigorously to forbid the use of Hebrew as a teaching tool. Instead the Sephardic communities around the world were asked to keep to their ancient traditions and teach in the common language of the place in which they lived (see Document Section, Document No. 8).

He fought tirelessly against the winds of secularism that had begun to blow through the Sephardic community.

In 1924 he became concerned about the B'nai B'rith organization, which was seeking to make inroads in Syria. He corresponded with R' Ezra Hamway (see #272) about this and strongly urged him to stay away from the B'nai B'rith movement (see Document Section, Document No. 23).

A Dream of Heaven. In 1930, at the age of 63, R' Yosef became seriously ill. He gave R' Natan Salem (see #472) instructions on the burial and personal affairs to tend to after his passing. In return for carrying out the holy task, R' Natan asked R' Yosef for two things: (1) to come to him in a dream and tell him about what goes on in Heaven and (2) to get help from *Hashem* so that he may finally have a child. At the time R' Natan was well into his 50's and his wife into her 40's.

After R' Yosef's passing, R' Natan went to pray at his grave. The following Friday night, R' Natan had a dream in which he saw his departed teacher, R' Yosef, learning in the *Bet Midrash*. In the dream, R' Natan kissed him on the hand and R' Yosef proceeded to recount for him the experience, "They went through my daily schedule ... *Tikkun Hatzot* (midnight prayer), getting up early in the morning for prayers, breakfast, learning all day, the *Bet Din*, a Torah class ... ". After going through the details in final judgment, a trivial lapse was revealed from which R' Yosef had to be cleansed through a very short stint in *Gehinom* (purgatory) thereby perfecting his soul. When he arrived at the first gate to *Gehinom*, the angel refused to let him in. At the second, third, and all subsequent gates, the angels continued to refuse him entry. R' Yosef asked, "Why aren't they letting me in? I want to be purified! Why won't they complete my judgment?" An angel answered, "At the first gate, all the *Masechtot* (books) of *Gemara* came and blocked the entrance. At the second gate, the *Poskim* (rabbinical authorities) came. At each successive gate more Torah came to deny you access. Finally, we realized that because of all your merit, it would be impossible for you to enter."

R' Yosef continued to speak to R' Natan through the dream. "People who learn Torah have a unique appearance in Heaven. Learning Torah guards one's spirit. The light of the Torah cleanses the soul." R' Yosef opened a *sefer* and showed R' Natan a page that had a stain on the corner. "There are two ways you can take this stain out. You can rip the page, or you can take a chemical and rub it on the stain to erase it, so there is no need to tear anything. Learning Torah takes the stain off the soul and purifies it so *yisurim* (experiences of penitent suffering) aren't necessary. Learn Torah with all your strength, because only that will save you in judgment." R' Yosef continued, "I've also taken care of your second request: You will have a child."

The dream made a deep impression on R' Natan and he consulted with the Kabbalist R' Yehudah Fetaya, who told him the dream was true. Inevitably, not longer afterwards, R' Natan had a boy, Abraham, his only child. That child grew up to be a Torah scholar and the *Rosh Yeshiva* of *Meor HaTalmud* in Jerusalem.

ספר

תורת חכם

ח"א

יוסף מרדכי ידיד הלוי ס"ט

פעה"ק ירושלם תובב"א

שנת אעת"ר לפ"ק

Title Page of Torat Hacham

Among R' Yedid's noted students were R' Yehudah Aryeh Haimoff, R' Ezra Attiah (see #102), and R' Yaakob Kassin (see #330), the son of R' Shaul Kassin who first gave him the ability to pursue Torah. He lived in great poverty and lost four sons and a daughter in their infancy. Three other sons and one daughter passed away in early childhood. He had one surviving son, R' Shelomo, who moved to America and published many of his father's books, working from original manuscripts.

He passed away on *Shabbat,* 8 Adar, 5690 (1930) at the age of 63, a week after surgery in Shaare Zedek hospital in Jerusalem.His published works are as follows:

- *Torat Hacham* (Jerusalem 5671/1911). *Halachot* (laws) relating to the respect owed to Torah scholars and the behavior expected of Torah scholars.
- *Yemei Yosef* (Part I, Jerusalem 5673/1913). Responsa on a variety of topics including putting on a *tallit* at night and combing hair on *Shabbat*. Part 2 (Brooklyn 5734/1974) was bound with Volume I of *She'erit Yosef.*
- *Birkat Yosef* (Jerusalem 5685/1925). Two volumes on the laws of *berachot,* organized according to the *Alef Bet.* A third volume on the same topic, focusing on *Hanukah*, was published in Jerusalem in 1973 (5733), which replaced a defective edition published two years earlier. R' Shelomo included a biography of his father in this volume.
- *Vayehi Yosef* (Jerusalem 5689/1929). The *halachot* (laws) of divorce with a detailed exposition on how specific names of men and women are to be written on a *get* (divorce document).
- *Yemei Yosef Batra* (Brooklyn 5732/1972). Responsa on a variety of topics, such as wearing a watch on *Shabbat*, shaving on *Hol HaMoed*, and eating grasshoppers (by the Jews of Yemen).
- *She'erit Yosef.* Volume I (Brooklyn 5734/1974) contains responsa on a variety of topics including the case of a bad odor occurring in the synagogue and a case of desertion from the army. This volume, which also includes a number of eulogies, was bound together with Part II of *Yemei Yosef.* Volume II (Brooklyn 5737/1977) contains responsa on a variety of topics including women making *tefillin*, smoking in the synagogue, and shaving with cutting implements.

Volume III (Brooklyn 5737/1977) also contains responsa on a variety of topics including calling up additional people to the Torah, paying a *hazzan* (cantor) for *Shabbat* services, and teaching secular subjects in a Talmud Torah. This volume also contains inspirational lectures and eulogies. Volume IV (Jerusalem 5739/1979) deals primarily with the *halachic* (legal) dispute related to the selling of land to a non-Jew in the *shemittah* year.

[595] YEDID, R' Yosef

רבי יוסף ידיד הלוי

(— 1923)

Worthy scholar and teacher of *Gemara*. He lived in Tedef, a town near Aram Soba, which is known as being the burial place of Ezra HaSofer. He passed away on 24 Tevet, 5683 (1923).

[596] ZAFRANI, R' Moshe

רבי משה זעפראני

(— 1815)

Worthy scholar and *dayan* (judge) of Jerusalem. He built the *Bnei Moshe Bet Midrash*, which was named after him. R' Moshe passed away on 22 Iyar, 5575 (1815).

[597] ZAFRANI, R' Shalom

רבי שלום זעפראני

(19th century)

Worthy *darshan* (lecturer) and *shohet* (ritual slaughterer) of Aram Soba. He worked as an expert *shohet* alongside R' Moshe Swed (see #574).

[598] ZAFRANI, R' Shelomo

רבי שלמה זעפראני

(1891 — 1965)

Eminent scholar and *dayan* (judge) of Aram Soba. He was born in Aram Soba in 1891 to R' Abraham Selim Zafrani, who was a *shamosh* (sexton) of the *Bet Din* (religious court). This position was apparently a tradition in the family, as his grandfather, R' Mordechai, had also been a *shamosh* of the *Bet Din*.

His primary teacher was R' Ezra Shayo (see #505), but he also studied under R' Yeshayah Dayan (see #202), R' Shelomo Safdeyé (see #469), R' Yaakob Dweck (see #248), and R' Yitzhak Bekhor Mizrahi (see #432). His preferred place of study was the *Bet Midrash* adjacent to the Great Synagogue of Aram Soba.

R' Shelomo Zafrani

His wife, Latifa of the worthy Cabasso family, faithfully managed his household during good times and bad. During periods of economic hardship she did what she could to hide their situation from prying eyes of neighbors.

He occupied a variety of positions within the Aram Soba community. Among others, he served as a manager of the *mikvaot* of the city. He also managed the preparation of *ketubot* (marriage contracts) together with R' Yitzhak Dayan (see #208). In addition, he taught *Gemara* in the yeshiva *Degel Torah LeTalmidim* over a period of fifty years, together with his colleague, R' Moshe Tawil (see #586). For a time he also served as a *dayan* (judge) on the *Bet Din* of Aram Soba.

He also served as the *hazzan* (cantor) for *Shabbat* and holiday services in the Great Synagogue. In this capacity he combined musical talent with his knowledge of the inner meaning of the *tefillot*, the applicable *halachah*, and the ability to express heartfelt emotion in the prayers.

> *He combined musical talent with his knowledge of the inner meaning of the tefillot, the applicable halachah, and the ability to express heartfelt emotion in the prayers.*

One of his challenges during the period of the First World War was the secular school system of the *Kol Yisrael Haverim* organization (Alliance Israelite Universelle). Unfortunately, its intentions of undermining religious beliefs and practices were not immediately apparent. The school authorities initially pretended that they were also concerned with teaching Torah. One of their subterfuges was to engage a *"Hacham"* to assist in the education of the youth. R' Zafrani accepted this position in all innocence, thinking that he would have the opportunity to guide the children in accordance with Jewish tradition. He was glad to have a paying job in difficult economic times. However, after a short while he realized that he had been misled. The students were oriented to their secular studies and were not interested in getting up on time for *tefillot* (prayers). In fact, they did not pay much attention to religious subjects altogether. When he raised these issues with the principal of the school, he was told in a harsh tone, "This institution is not a *Bet Midrash*. The reason we have a *Hacham* is to overcome the reluctance of of religious families to send their children here." When he heard this, R' Zafrani immediately resigned his position, confident that with the help of *Hashem*, he would find a living elsewhere.

Something Doesn't Smell Right. R' Abraham Zafrani, son of R' Shelomo, related the following story in connection with the Alliance. One of the new teachers came from France to teach in the Alliance acting like a religious man. People suspected that it was an act, but at first were unable to prove it. Finally, someone put a piece of raw meat in his *koracha* (*tallit* and *tefillin* bag), which he stored in the school. After a week a terrible stench was noticed and it was quickly traced to the *koracha*. That was ample proof that he hadn't put on *tallit* or *tefillin* for a week and he was thereby exposed.

During the Arab riots of 1948 he was one of the rescuers of the Keter Aram Soba.

During the Arab riots of 1948 he was one of the rescuers of the *Keter Aram Soba*, the ancient manuscript containing the entire text of the *Tanach*, including the Torah. After the Great Synagogue was destroyed, he was one of those who went in to seek the *Keter*, which had been kept there in an iron safe. They found the charred and damaged pages of the *Keter* scattered about the ruins of the synagogue and tearfully gathered them up. They then managed to hide the *Keter* in a series of secret locations until 1957, when he and R' Moshe Tawil turned the *Keter* over to Mordechai Faham who smuggled it out of Syria to *Eretz Yisrael*, by way of Turkey.

In 1959 he settled in Tel Aviv, but almost immediately was struck by a series of misfortunes. In the first year upon his arrival in Tel Aviv he was badly injured in a traffic accident. In 1962 he came down with a serious illness and was bedridden for many months. Despite his ailments he did not spare himself and founded a *Hachnasat Kallah* fund to help young Torah scholars with their wedding expenses. In 1965 he was injured in another road accident and after 8 days of severe pain he passed away on 22 Adar I 5725 (1965). He left four scholarly sons: R' Abraham, R' Yitzhak, R' Yaakob, and R' Moshe. R' Yitzhak became principal of the Talmud Torah *Keter Torah* and head of the *Keter Torah* organization in Tel Aviv. His daughter Azize married R' Yaakob Attiah, who served as a rabbi in Beirut and then went on to become rabbi of the Syrian-Lebanese congregation of Bat Yam.

In his final days he accepted his misfortunes upon himself as the will of G-d, which is not to be questioned. He rejected any hint of complaint that his fate was unfair and undeserved. He instructed his sons in his final will and testament that they should not remember him as a *Hacham* or Rabbi, and that they should not eulogize him. They should simply sound the shofar at his funeral and say a brief prayer.

[599] ZONANA, R' David

רבי דוד זוננה

(— 1950)

Worthy scholar of Aram Soba. He was the brother of R' Eliyahu Zonana (see #600). Their father was apparently R' Haim Zonana. Shortly before the outbreak of World War I he escaped to Mexico where he went into business. However, he kept up his connection with the scholarly life of Aram Soba, conducting a weekly *shiur* and supporting institutions of learning. In 1937 he moved to Jerusalem, ultimately passing away on 4 Sivan, 5710 (1950).

[600] ZONANA, R' Eliyahu

רבי אליהו זוננה

(1878 — 1914)

Worthy scholar and rabbi of Aram Soba. He was born in 1878, apparently to R' Haim Zonana. His father-in-law was R' Natan Marcus and he was a brother of R' David Zonana (see #599). R' Eliyahu passed away at a young age on 8 Tamuz, 5674 (1914).

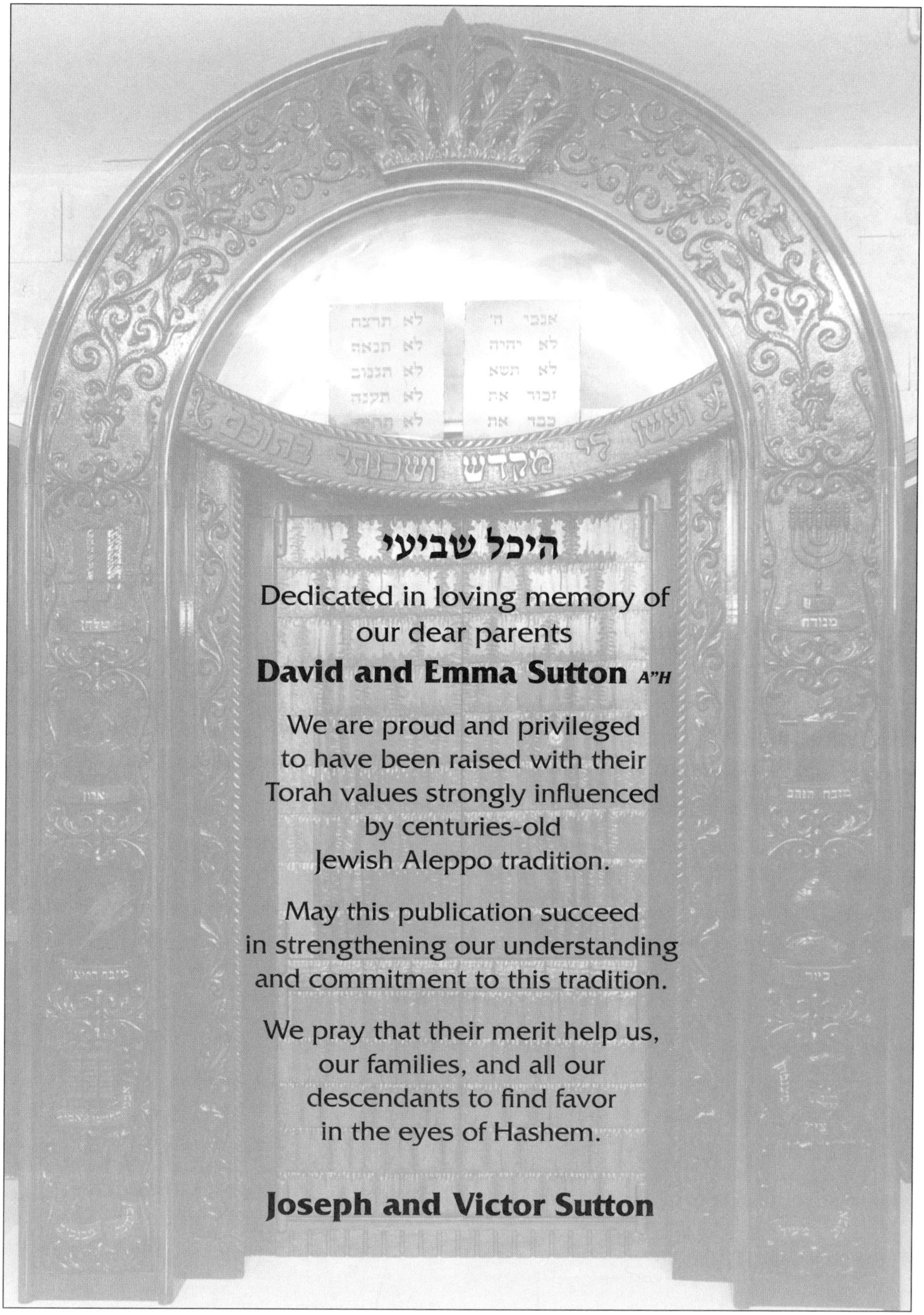

היכל שביעי

Dedicated in loving memory of
our dear parents

David and Emma Sutton *A"H*

We are proud and privileged
to have been raised with their
Torah values strongly influenced
by centuries-old
Jewish Aleppo tradition.

May this publication succeed
in strengthening our understanding
and commitment to this tradition.

We pray that their merit help us,
our families, and all our
descendants to find favor
in the eyes of Hashem.

Joseph and Victor Sutton

Section Seven

Document Section

Section VII – INDEX OF DOCUMENTS

CHARITY

(1) Appointment of Administrator for Rabbinical Funds (1927)

(2) Letter Concerning Distribution of Charity (1944)

CONVERSION

(3) Proclamation Against Accepting Converts in Brooklyn, New York (1935)

(4) Approbation on Ruling Against Conversion in Argentina (1938)

CUSTOMS

(5) Letter Against Changing Burial Customs (1941)

EDUCATION

(6) Halachic Ruling on Jewish Education (1926)

(7) Letter to Agudat Yisrael Regarding Education (1926)

(8) Letter Regarding the Use of the Hebrew Language in Education (1928)

(9) Letter Against the Works of Amozeg (1860's)

KABBALAH

(10) Halachic Ruling in Defense of the Ari'zal (1715)

(11) Declaration in Support of Kaballah (1914)

(12) Approbation on Book Defending Kabbalah (1938)

KASHRUT

(13) Letter Concerning Grape Leaves (1700's)

(14) Takanot of Shohatim (1853)

KETER ARAM SOBA

(15) Letters from Syrian Rabbis on Authenticity of the Keter (1995)

(16) Letter from Ashkenazi Rabbis on Authenticity of the Keter (2003)

MODESTY

(17) Approbation on Covering Hair with a Wig (1889)

(18) Recommendation to Wearing Veils (1848-1858)

(19) Proclamation Against Mixed Seating at Weddings (1906)

(20) Admonition against Mixed Seating at Weddings (1848-1858)

MUSIC

(21) Rambam's Ruling Against Gentile Music (1100's)

(22) Letter Against Gentile Music (1928)

ORGANIZATIONS OF CONCERN

(23) Proclamation about B'nai B'rith (1924)

(24) Proclamation Against Participation in the Secular Zionist Party (1926)

PRINTING

(25) Proclamation Concerning Printing Press (1865)

SHABBAT

(26) Waiting 72 Minutes after Sunset to End Shabbat (1700's)

(27) Resolution against the Desecration of Shabbat (Aleppo 1906)

(28) Resolution against the Desecration of Shabbat (Jerusalem 1907)

(29) Excommunication of the Cheesemakers Who Desecrate Shabbat (1876)

TORAH SUPPORT

(30) Letter Concerning Kollel (1891)

WITCHCRAFT

(31) Resolution against Witchcraft (1857)

YESHIVOT AND OTHER HOLY ASSOCIATIONS

(32) Study Group Contract (circa 1800)

(33) Prayer Group Contract (1910, 1933)

(34) Letter by Rabbi Eliezer Silver After Visit to Porat Yosef (1964)

(35) Rabbinical Association Group Contract (1885)

(36) Aliyah Contract (1737)

(37)Letter from Rabbis of Porat Yosef against the study of philosophy and college (1942).

Introduction to Documents

The vibrancy of the religious life of the Jews of Aleppo is evident in the many documents which were produced by its rabbis over the centuries to advocate and interpret authentic religious practices. A diverse sampling of the actual documents is presented here to give the reader a better sense of the issues that our ancestors faced. Variations of these concerns re-appeared in successive generations and many of them are reflected in the challenges facing the observant community of today. However, it should be noted that these documents are being provided for their historical significance, not for *halachah* purposes. As with all matters of *halachah,* consult your rabbi.

CHARITY

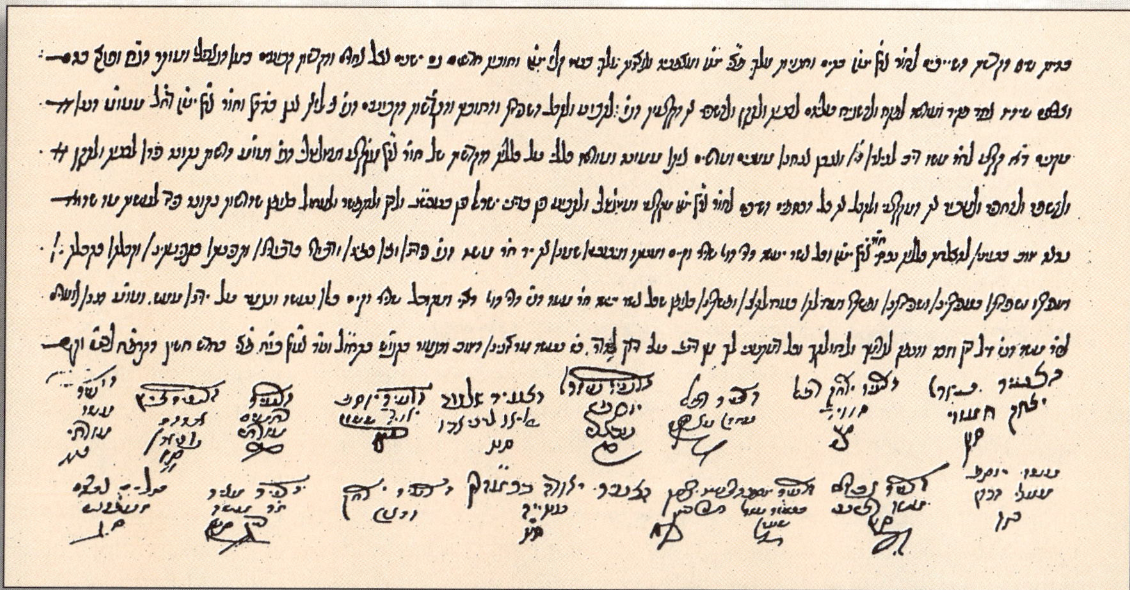

(1) Appointment of Administrator for Rabbinical Funds (1927)

In 1928, R' Moshe (Dib) Laniado (see #359) was appointed by the *Bet Din* of Aram Soba to manage the assets that had been donated over the years to provide support for rabbis and scholars of the community. See Document No. 30 for details of original establishing of Rabbinical trust funds. The document of appointment is presented below:

> Since there are holy properties set aside for the rabbis and scholars of Aleppo (may *Hashem* guard it forever), there are houses and stores in Aleppo and storehouses in Kilis, and debts owed for both new and old pledges and the monthly dues and the like, we need one person who will be the administrator of these properties, to watch over them and guard them, to build and repair, to rent and collect the rent.
>
> Therefore we, the rabbis of the *Bet Din* of Aleppo and the rabbis signed below, have agreed willingly to transfer four cubits of land to R' Moshe (Dib) Laniado and with it we appoint him and empower him to be the general administrator of all the

rabbinical properties of Aleppo. He is authorized to build, repair, rent, sublease, or sell any of the properties and to receive any money that is due the rabbis of Aleppo, including land and movable properties. He is authorized to represent us in Jewish or gentile courts and to make a compromise if necessary and even to forgive claims. In short, he is authorized to do whatever seems correct in his eyes to bring succcess to the finances of the rabbis of Aleppo and whatever he does is legally binding. From here on his hand is our hand, his mouth is our mouth, his word is our word, his claim is our claim, his acceptance is our acceptance, his sale is our sale, and his rental is our rental. Whatever he does is as if it was done by us all.

This was done willingly with a full *kinyan* [procedure of transaction] according to the laws of our rabbis.

We, the undersigned, Heshvan 5688 (1927)

Ezra Hamway
Yitzhak Swed
Raphael Marcus
Ezra Abadi
Shelomo Laniado
Yosef Sasson
Rahamim Mizrahi
Sion Abraham Laniado
Moshe Mizrahi
Moshe Tawil
Abraham Rabia
Yosef Shayo
Yitzhak Dayan
Yehudah Attiah
Yitzhak Hedaya
Meir Dayan
Selim Abraham Zafrani
Moshe Tawil

(2) Letter Concerning Distribution of Charity (1944)

In the year 1944, Syrian rabbis in Israel wrote a letter concerning the appropriation of funds donated in memory of Rav Meir Baal Haness. The issue was whether the funds must go to schools in Tiberias only or whether they should be sent all over *Eretz Yisrael*. The Syrian rabbis argued that the custom in Aleppo over the generations had been to use the money donated for Rav Meir Baal Haness for local causes, whereas Tiberias causes had a separate *kupah* (collection box) marked Tiberias.They listed the treasurers of the Rav Meir Baal Haness fund over the years, noting that all of them used the proceeds to buy holy books and to support the dissemination of Torah by means of classes on *Shabbat*. The following rabbis were listed as treasurers: R' Haim Zonana, R' Michael Mishan (#419), R' Nissim Shalom, and R' Abraham Missry. The letter continued:

The treasurers would put out trays on *Purim* and *Erev Yom Kippur* and make an announcement requesting donations for Rav Meir Baal Haness [and all the money went to local Torah study]. Furthermore many holy books have stamped in them "Holy to Rav Meir." However, with all of the confusion due to wars and immigration the money has [now] gone to Tiberias only and this is a mistake. We have many Syrian institutions in Israel and *halachah* dictates that the poor of your own city comes first. There is *Yeshivat Torat Moshe* in Tel Aviv with over 400 students. In Jerusalem we have *Yeshivat Magen David*, an orphanage, and *Yeshivat Porat Yosef*, the majority of whose rabbinical staff, *kollel* rabbis, and students are from Aleppo. There are also many poverty-stricken elderly and widows who need financial help. Therefore the money coming from Aleppo should go for the causes of Aleppo. Tiberias on the other hand is getting smaller and has very few rabbis. It does not even have a yeshiva for higher learning. They send their children to *Porat Yosef* and they only have one or two poor Syrian families.

In conclusion, we, the rabbis of Aleppo living in *Eretz Yisrael,* have agreed, after investigating the *halachic* works of Aleppo rabbis, that according to the *halachah* all donations coming from Aleppo should go to the needy of Aleppo only, for the Talmud Torah, for *kollel* rabbis in the yeshiva, and for poor Torah scholars, as was the custom throughout the generations, and with this the holy name of Rav Meir Baal Haness will become greater and he will guard over us and will bring pride and glory to the Aleppo community. May the merit of Rav Meir guard over all the donors, may the blessings of the Torah come upon them, and may they succeed in their endeavors.

Signed in Jerusalem and Tel Aviv, Nissan 5704 (1944)

Yitzhak Dayan
Meir Dayan
Yitzchak Alfia
Ezra Husny
Abraham Rabia
Ezra son of Abraham Ades
Nissim Eney
Yosef the son of Ezra Shayo
Obadiah Antar
Yitzhak Hedaya
Yaakob Sardar
Shalom Mizrahi
Mordechai Attiah
Shaul Antebi

An additional letter was written by the Syrian rabbis residing in Jerusalem on the above topic. They cite precedents from earlier rabbis, namely Rabbi Shemuel Laniado, Rabbi Abraham Antebi, Rabbi Mordechai Labaton, and Rabbi Mordechai Abadi. They state:

Each of these rabbis gave the donations for Rav Meir Baal Haness to local causes and bought books with it. We saw the same practice with our own eyes, as performed by Rabbi Yeshaya Dayan, Rabbi Ezra Hamway, and Rabbi Moshe Mizrahi. The collectors would sit at the entrance to the synagogue and raise funds in memory of Rav Meir and give the proceeds to Torah scholars. We hereby appoint Rav Yitzhak Dayan, Mr. Yosef Missry, and Mr. Edmond Shamah to distribute these funds in *Eretz Yisrael*.

Signed in Jerusalem

Abraham Antebi ***Yehudah Attiah*** ***Aharon Harari-Raful***

[Note: This letter is quoted in *Ginzei Aretz* of R' Rahamim Shayo on page 100.]

CONVERSION

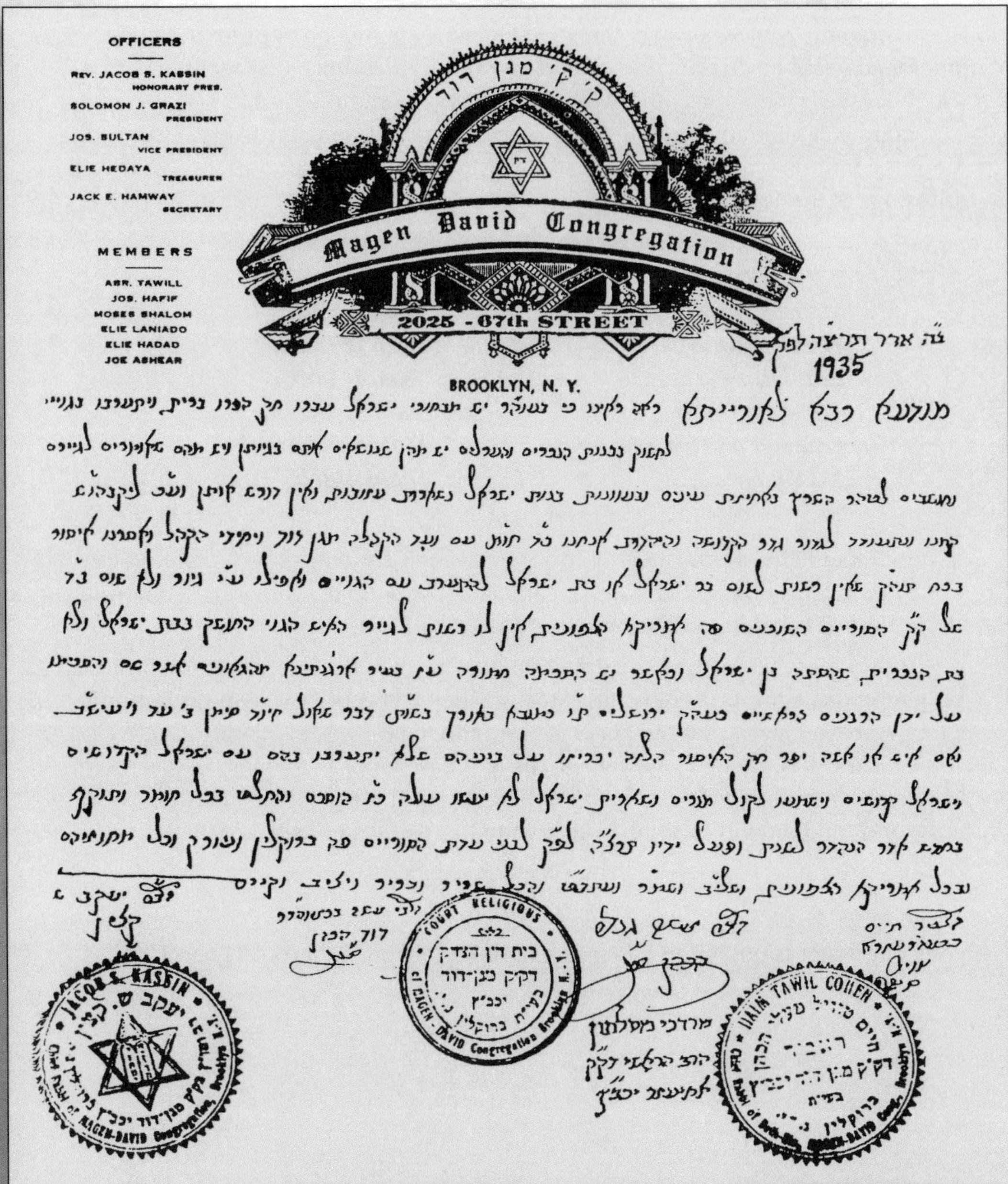

OFFICERS

REV. JACOB S. KASSIN
HONORARY PRES.

SOLOMON J. GRAZI
PRESIDENT

JOS. SULTAN
VICE PRESIDENT

ELIE HEDAYA
TREASURER

JACK E. HAMWAY
SECRETARY

MEMBERS

ABR. TAWILL
JOS. HAFIF
MOSES SHALOM
ELIE LANIADO
ELIE HADAD
JOE ASHEAR

ק"ק מגן דוד

Magen David Congregation

2025 - 67th STREET

BROOKLYN, N. Y.

1935

(3) Proclamation Against Accepting Converts in Brooklyn, New York (1935)

(3) Proclamation Against Accepting Converts in Brooklyn, New York (1935)

In 1935, shortly after assuming his new position in New York, R' Yaakob Kassin (see #330) issued an edict that no converts would be accepted into the Syrian community under any circumstances. This bold initiative served as a firm bulwark against assimilation, which was increasing at an alarming rate across the United States. Not only were conversions discontinued, but even those who had been converted at other places were not accepted. Today, his edict is famous — its benefits are acknowledged, and it is recognized as one of his most significant and timely actions, which helped promote a perfect and harmonious communal unity.

This decree was first enacted during the month of Adar in 5695 (1935). A revised and even stronger version was promulgated in Sivan of the year 5744 (1984). **The following is a translation of the text of the first enactment, which was written in R' Yaakob Kassin's own handwriting:**

> We have seen to our sorrow that, on account of our many sins, some of the young men of Israel have transgressed the Divine statute that the Holy Covenant must never be uprooted. They have mingled with the nations, and have desired the daughters of alien and uncircumcised peoples. Some of our sons marry them as gentiles, while others have the notion to convert their non-Jewish partners, in the belief that one can purify himself while still grasping the source of the impurity.
>
> Therefore, for the sake of the unification of the Holy One, Blessed be He and His Presence, we stand firm in our determination to erect a holy barrier against the erosion of our sacred values. We, the members of the *Bet Din* whose signatures appear below, in association with the Board of the *"Magen David"* Community and its leaders, absolutely forbid, with all the force of the Holy Torah, any man or woman of the House of Israel to marry a gentile, even after the conversion of the party concerned. The *Bet Din* of the holy community of Syrian Jews residing in North America has no authority whatsoever to convert a gentile man who desires a Jewish woman, or a non-Jewish woman who incites the passion of a Jewish man. This is in accordance with a strict ruling currently being enforced in a city in Argentina by the local rabbis, as well as with the rabbinical consensus in the holy city of Jerusalem, as discussed at length in the book of responsa *Diber Shaul* by R' Shaul Sutton (see #558).
>
> If a man or woman violates the above prohibition, the community shall proclaim that it is forbidden to marry their children. The people of Israel, who are holy, will surely obey their teachers, and the remnant of Israel will not tolerate evil.
>
> All the above has been agreed and decided, in full severity and with all the power at our command, in the month of Adar in the year 5685, by the members of the Community of Syrians here in Brooklyn, New York and all its districts and the whole of North America. Those who obey the words of this edict shall dwell in security and tranquility, without fear, and they shall be blessed with all that is good. Everything is established and confirmed ...".

Rabbi Yaakob Kassin — ***R' Moshe Dweck (Kassab)***
R' Haim Tawil — ***R' Mordechai Maslaton***
R' Moshe Gindi

(4) Approbation on Ruling Against Conversion in Argentina (1938)

Early in the 20th century, the rabbis of Argentina led by Rabbi Shaul Sutton (see #558) made a bold move to prohibit the acceptance of converts under all circumstances. They did this out of concern that people were converting for reasons of marriage only and without any religious sincerity. The measure was very effective in helping prevent intermarriage. However, in 1938 people began to question the decision and so the rabbis of Argentina turned to their colleagues in Jerusalem for support. The following is a translation of the approval.

Many years ago the great rabbis of Argentina, shepherds of the community, constructed a barrier to guard the purity of the Jewish family. They acted courageously and prohibited the accepting of converts. They further prohibited circumcising children born from such marriages because they have the *halachic* status of gentiles. This is because it was discovered that the motive of the converts was to fulfill their lustful desires and not to come under the shelter of G-d. In truth after they converted they did not accept upon themselves the yoke of G-d. They violated the laws of the Torah in public.

The Chief Rabbis of Jerusalem of that time agreed with [the rabbis of Argentina]. This was an important ruling to guard the purity of Israel and it prevented us from being assimilated (Heaven forbid) in the lands of freedom. All of this is discussed at length in the book *Diber Shaul* [by Rabbi Shaul Sutton].

It has come to our attention that some people want to breach this ruling. We are shocked and amazed that at times of trouble for the Jewish people such people exist. Rather than unify and guard Israel against assimilation (Heaven forbid), are they not concerned to be likened to Balaam the wicked, who promoted promiscuity in Israel? They are like Zimri, who publicly took a Midianite woman to give birth to idolatrous children.

We have therefore gathered to affirm the ruling. This is a decree of the Torah that no court and surely no individual rabbi is permitted to perform conversions in Argentina.

And surely in the case of those who have married converts and have had children from them, we may not accept them or circumcise their children. Anyone who transgresses this is making a breach in the wall of our religion and we will banish him from our community and pursue him to destruction.

We are confident that people concerned with G-d and the holiness of the Jewish people will abide by the ruling and that no one will even contemplate otherwise. May G-d hasten our redemption and gather in all those who are scattered.

Signed, the judges of Aleppo currently residing in Jerusalem,

Ezra (son of) Yitzhak Hamway ***Haim Tawil*** ***Ezra (son of) Yosef Shayo***

[Note: This letter is quoted in *Yismach Ezra* of R' Ezra Hamway (see #272), page 21.]

CUSTOMS

(5) Letter Against Changing Burial Customs (1941)

During the period between 1932 and 1936, a burial society in Jerusalem wanted to adopt new customs based on those of the gentile world. In 1941 R' Yitzhak Alfia (see #46) wrote his book *Ahavat Hashem* to combat this aberration and received the approbations of over 100 rabbis.

The following is the approbation of the rabbis of Aram Soba residing in Jerusalem, R' Ezra Yitzhak Hamway (see #272) and R' Haim Tawil (see #584):

> We the rabbis of Aleppo currently residing in Jerusalem have seen the words of the great rabbis clearly portraying that it is forbidden to change any customs that were instituted by the previous generations who are like angels. Who would have the audacity to change them in the slightest way? We know the *halachic* ramifications of our customs and anyone who changes them is a trangressor. We are confident that all Jews are holy and they will remain with the customs of their holy fathers. Those who heed our words will dwell securely protectd from any evil. May G-d bless His nation with peace, Amen.
>
> Signed,
>
> ***Ezra Yitzhak Hamway***
> *Previously head of the Rabbinical Court of Aleppo, currently head of the Rabbinical Court of the Aleppo community of Jerusalem*
>
> ***Haim Tawil***
> *Author of Masa Haim, previously head of the Aleppo Court of New York, currently head of the Sephardic Rabbinical Court of Jerusalem*

[Note: This letter is quoted in *Yismach Ezra* by Ezra Hamway page 23.]

EDUCATION

(6) Halachic Ruling on Jewish Education (1926)

In 1926, R' Yosef Yedid (see #594), who was *Av Bet Din* (Chief Judge) of the Syrian *Bet Din* in Jerusalem, issued the following ruling against the non-traditional approach to Jewish education.

> I have seen the pamphlet called *"The Way of Torah"* that was issued by certain eminent, holy, and distinguished rabbis on the subject of teaching Jewish children the Hebrew language and the associated curriculum of new studies.
>
> These practices are totally forbidden as anyone who investigates their ways can see. Truthfully there is no need for more proof, but nevertheless I must write a little to make known that anyone who identifies with Judaism and who who truly believes with a full heart that our Holy Torah, both the Written and Oral, was given at Mount Sinai by G-d, must educate his children with the heritage of our Sages, the curriculum of old.
>
> Anyone who speaks, explains or teaches in accordance with his own views as he might teach chronicles and history with his own views, in effect denies the Torah of Moshe. Such a person is a heretic and an apostate and has no part in the World to Come. When one finds narratives in the Holy Torah, it is sacrilege to say that they are just stories. There is no such thing as a story or narrative in our Holy Torah that is not founded on wisdom and ethics. There no story that doesn't teach us ways to come

closer to G-d, to help us understand his constant supervision, to make known the concept of reward and punishment and many deep and lofty secrets.

How else are we able to make a blessing when we are called up to read in the *Sefer Torah*? Should we bring a storybook to bless upon, Heaven forbid? There is definitely no part of even the smallest letter of our Holy Torah from which many sets of Laws are not derived and secrets revealed, as the Sages have said.

Anyone who does not teach and explain the Torah to youngsters in accordance with the views of the early Rabbis such as *Rashi* and the *Ramban*, which have consistently been in compliance with the teachings of the *Gemara* and the *Midrashim* of our Sages, is in effect teaching them heresy and dissension. Abstaining from study altogether is better than such instruction, for it is better to be a total ignoramus than to be a heretic and an apostate.

All of Israel are upright … and may good blessings be bestowed upon them, Amen.

I sign with a blessing to the Month of Mercy (Elul), the year 5686 (1926), the servant who serves the One Lord,

Yosef Mordechai Yedid Halevi
Chief Justice in the Congregations of Halab

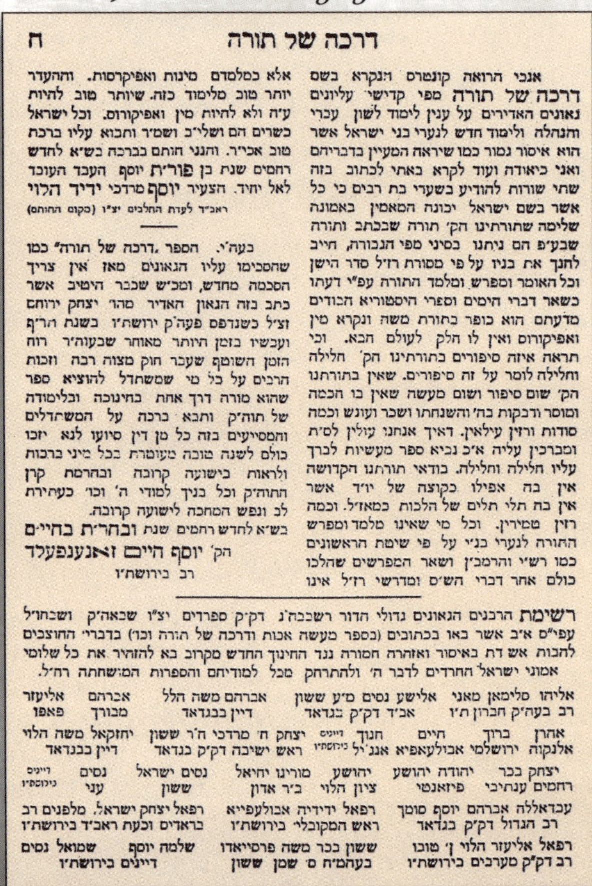

דרכה של תורה ח

אנכי הרואה קונטרס הנקרא בשם **דרכה של תורה** מפי קדישי עליונים גאונים האדירים על ענין לימוד לשון עברי והנהלה ולימוד חדש לנערי בני ישראל אשר הוא איסור גמור כמו שיראה המעיין בדבריהם ואני כיאודה ועוד לקרא באתי לכתוב בזה שתי שורות להודיע בשערי בת רבים כי כל אשר בשם ישראל יכונה המאמין באמונה שלימה שתורתינו הק' תורה שבכתב ותורה שבע"פ הם ניתנו בסיני מפי הגבורה, חייב לחנך את בניו על פי מסורת רז"ל סדר הישן וכל האומר ומפרש ומלמד התורה עפ"י דעתו כשאר דברי הימים וספרי היסטוריא הבודים מדעתם הוא כופר בתורת משה ונקרא מין ואפיקורוס ואין לו חלק לעולם הבא. וכי תראה איזה סיפורים בתורתינו הק' חלילה וחלילה לומר על זה סיפורים. שאין בתורתנו הק' שום סיפור ושום מעשה שאין בו חכמה ומוסר ודבקות בה' והשנחתו ושכר ועונש וכמה סודות ורזין עילאין. דאיך אנחנו עולין לס"ת ומברכין עליה א"כ נביא ספר מעשיות לברך עליו חלילה וחלילה. בודאי תורתנו הקדושה אין בה אפילו כקוצה של יו"ד אשר אין בה תלי תלים של הלכות כמאז"ל. וכמה רזין טמירין. וכל מי שאינו מלמד ומפרש התורה לנערי בנ"י על פי שיטת הראשונים כמו רש"י והרמב"ן ושאר המפרשים שהלכו כולם אחר דברי הש"ס ומדרשי רז"ל אינו אלא כמלמדם מינות ואפיקרסות. וההעדר יותר טוב מלימוד כזה. שיותר טוב להיות ע"ה ולא להיות מין ואפיקורוס. וכל ישראל כשרים הם ושלי"כ ושמ"ר ותבוא עליו ברכת טוב אכי"ר. והנני חותם בברכה בש"א לחדש רחמים שנת בן **פור"ת** יוסף העבד העוכד לאל יחיד. הצעיר **יוסף** מרדכי **ידיד הלוי**
ראב"ד לעדת החלבים יצ"ו (מקום החותם)

———

בעה"י. הספר "דרכה של תורה" כמו שהסכימו עליו הגאונים מאז אין צריך הסכמה מחדש, ומכ"ש שכבר היטיב אשר כתב בזה הגאון האדיר מהר' יצחק ירוחם זצ"ל כשנדפס פעה"ק ירושת"ו בשנת הר"ף ועכשיו בזמן היותר מאוחר שבעוה"ר רוח הזמן השוטף שעבר חוק מצוה רבה וזכות הרבים על כל מי שמשתדל להוציא ספר שהוא מורה דרך אחת בחינוכה ובלימודה של תוה"ק ותבא ברכה על המשתדלים והמסייעים בזה כל מן דין סיועו לנא יזכו כולם לשנה טובה מעוטרת בכל מיני ברכות ולראות בישועה קרובה ובהרמת קרן התוה"ק וכל בניך למודי ה' וכו' כעתירת לב ונפש המחכה לישועה קרובה.
בש"א לחדש רחמים שנת **ובחר"ת בחיים**
הק' **יוסף חיים זאנענפעלד**
רב בירושת"ו

רשימת הרבנים הגאונים גדולי הדור רשבבה"ג דק"ק ספרדים יצ"ו שבאה"ק ושבחו"ל עפי"ם א"ב אשר באו בכתובים (בספר מעשה אבות ודרכה של תורה וכו') בדברי' החוצבים להבות אש דת באיסור ואזהרה חמורה נגד החינוך החדש מקרוב בא להזהיר את כל שלומי אמוני ישראל החרדים לדבר ה' ולהתרחק מכל למודיהם והספרות המשחתה רח"ל.

אליהו סלימאן מאני, רב בעה"ק חברון ת"ו — אלישע נסים מ"ע ששון, אב"ד דק"ק בגדאד — אברהם משה הלל, דיין בבגדאד — אברהם מבורך — אליעזר פאפו

אהרן אלנקוה — ברוך ירושלמי — חיים אבולעאפיא — חנוך אנג'יל (דיינים בירושת"ו) — יצחק ח' מרדכי ח"ר ששון, ראש ישיבה דק"ק בגדאד — יחזקאל משה הלוי, דיין בבגדאד

יצחק בכר רחמים ענתיבי — יהודה יהושע פיזאנטי — יהושע ציון הלוי — מורינו יחיאל ב"ר אדון — נסים ישראל ששון — נסים עני (דיינים בירושת"ו)

עבדאללה אברהם יוסף סומך, רב הגדול דק"ק בגדאד — רפאל ידידיה אבולעפייא, ראש המקובלי' בירושת"ו — רפאל יצחק ישראל. מלפנים רב בבראדים וכעת ראב"ד בירושת"ו

רפאל אליעזר הלוי ן' טובו, רב דק"ק מערבים בירושת"ו — ששון בכר משה פרסייאדו, בעהמ"ת ס' שמן ששון — שלמה יוסף — שמואל נסים, דיינים בירושת"ו

(6) Halachic Ruling on Jewish Education (1926)

(7) Letter to Agudat Yisrael Regarding Education (1926)

In 1926 the *Agudat Yisrael* organization sent an educator from Frankfurt, named Dr. Auerbach, to lead the Talmud Torah schools of the Sephardim in Jerusalem. This elicited strong objections from many of the Jerusalem rabbis who sent a letter of protest to the leaders of the *Agudat Yisrael*. In the letter they asked that every effort be made to cancel the appointment of Dr. Auerbach as that would be an opening to a change from traditional teaching methods. Furthermore, they objected to anyone with the West European title of "Dr." being appointed in a position of spiritual leadership. They were concerned that this might harm the souls of the students and implant the poison of the *Haskalah* (Enlightenment) and liberalism. Among the signers to this letter were R' Yosef Yedid, the head of the Sephardic *Bet Din* (see #594), R' Ezra Harari-Raful, founder of the Sephardic yeshiva *Ohel Moed* (see #304), and Y' Yaakob Haim Sofer, the *Kaf HaHaim* (see #532). The text of the letter is given below.

Adar 10, 1926, Jerusalem

After the proper greetings we are turning to you concerning the news that *Agudat Yisrael* plans on sending Dr. Auerbach to be the principal of the Talmud Torah *Bnei Sion*. We would like you to know that this Talmud Torah is the only one of its kind among Sephardic Jewry, which follows the educational system of old, a tradition handed down over generations. It has one goal and that is to make the Torah great and glorious, and to plant the fear of G-d in the hearts of the children. They are the last remnant to whom we can look for the raising of the banner of Torah among Sephardim which as of late has dropped so drastically in a shocking manner due to the new schooling that has been introduced. From our Talmud Torah we have seen many boys who continue in *Porat Yosef*. These boys are outstanding in Torah and the fear of G-d.

We thank all of our brethren who have supported our institutions and are saving Sephardic Jewry from spiritual destruction, as is said, "If there are no baby goats there will be no adult goats."

Experience has shown us that if a principal has the title Dr., there is a great danger for the spirit of the school, besides the internal changes that will be made based on new approaches. We have seen that any place that has a Dr. as principal changes from a Talmud Torah to a "school." In addition to that danger, the title Dr. itself has a negative impact on the students as we have seen. They view the principal as a symbol and will dedicate themselves to secular studies so that they themselves will receive the title Dr. They will then not devote themselves solely to Torah and the fear of G-d as did the rabbis of old. This can bring about the destruction of Torah, especially among the Sephardic community, whose number of Torah scholars is diminishing.

What a disgrace this is to the rabbis of Jerusalem, a city full of scholars with great ability to educate boys and girls on the correct path! We are amazed! Does the pure education in the spirit of our grandfather Yaakob, based on Torah and the fear of G-d without any secularism, need an educator from Germany with the title Dr.? That title alone damages the boys and girls of Jerusalem! Who knows how deep the damage will go?

We are asking you to stand in this time of weakness and to save the remnants of the Sephardic Talmud Torah. We don't have other *Talmudei Torah* as the Ashkenazim do. Let *Agudat Yisrael* know that we are strongly opposed and adamantly refuse a principal with the title Dr. It is known that the [new] schools have destroyed our youth to the point that we have almost lost Torah learners amongst our youth. We hope you will stand firm and save these pure souls, the pure lambs, from the strange winds. It is the merit of the breath emanating from the mouths of schoolchildren on which the world stands (*Shabbat* 119b). May we be worthy to see the building of Sion and Jerusalem, the uplifting of Torah, and the coming of the righteous redeemer speedily in our days.

Haim Shaul Dweck ***Yosef Yedid*** ***Ezra Harari-Raful***
(The Aram Soba Court of Jerusalem)

Yaakob Haim Sofer
(Yeshivat Shoshanim L'David of the Iraqi Community In Jerusalem)

Abraham Aminoff ***Shelomo Sofioff***
(Bukharan Court of Jerusalem)

Eliyahu Maarabi
(Yeshivat Yagdil Torah of the Damascus Community of Jerusalem)

[Note: The above letter is quoted in the book *He'ir HaMizrach by R' Binyamin Gilkrov*, page 163.]

(8) Letter Regarding the Use of the Hebrew Language in Education (1928)

Jewish education in Aram Soba was traditionally conducted in Arabic, the language of the people. In the early 20th century various educators promoted the idea of conducting classes in Hebrew, especially in Argentina. The Syrian scholars and rabbis of Argentina were very much against this because Hebrew had become the means by which Zionists introduced antireligious ideas and vulgar language into common speech.

At first they turned to R' Haim Shaul Dweck, the renowned Kabbalist and founder of the yeshiva *Rehovot HaNahar* of Jerusalem (see #228). R' Dweck agreed with what they were trying to do, but said he was already too old and weak to take a leading role in this fight. He suggested that they refer the matter to the *Bet Din* of R' Yosef Chaim Sonnenfeld.

In the end they went to R' Yosef Yedid (see #594), the head of the *Bet Din* of the Aram Soba Community in Jerusalem. R' Yedid took up the matter with all of his energy and fought vigorously to forbid the use of Hebrew as a teaching tool. Instead the Sephardic communities around the world were asked to keep to their ancient traditions and teach in the common language of the place in which they lived.

Bless G-d, Jerusalem, 18 Iyar, 5688 (1928)

To the Honorable Master, who loves Torah and its mitzvot, who engages himself in holy work, Rabbi Yaakob Abraham Sutton:

To the Director of the Foundation of Religion, with the help of G-d, Buenos Aires, Argentina.

Your clear letter has reached me and in it you go to great lengths to expound on the subject of teaching the Hebrew language to schoolchildren. Woe to me if I say anything and woe to me if I don't say anything.

If I should say that the study of the Hebrew language, which is the language of our holy forefathers, is prohibited, how embarrassing and shaming it would be for us. If I should not say anything, behold we have seen with our own eyes how much damage has resulted from teaching Hebrew as a language. This is because new ideas have come from those within our circles who have published books in Hebrew; they speak in Hebrew, yet they transgress the Torah. All of their publications are of heresy and dissension, of carnality and disgrace. They are of the opinion that in order to be called a Jew it is enough to speak Hebrew and to be a Jew without religion. We have seen here in the schools — due to our own sins — that they educate thousands of children with wretched culture, teaching them public desecration of *Shabbat* and total denial of G-d. It is well known to everyone that they care only for the language and for the land of Israel [not its holiness]. Because of our sins, the verse has come true for us, "And into it will come lawless people and profane it" (*Yehezkel* 7:22).

It is well known that this is the time to act for G-d. It is even allowed to transgress the Torah in return for assurance that it will be observed properly in the future. The episode of the Prophet Elijah at Mount Carmel attests to this concept.

Anyhow, I do not know why there is such a problem if we choose not to teach in Hebrew. Is it such a great *mitzvah* to use specifically the Hebrew language? It is sufficient to expound the Torah, each one in his own language, as we have always studied and taught in the entire Jewish nation from the time of the destruction of the Temple throughout the exile until now. The entire Talmud was written in Aramaic, as that was the language of the time. The *Rambam* and other great Rabbis wrote their works in Arabic. They saw no dishonor or disgrace to the Holy Language because that is what the people spoke. What we should be particular about is to explain the Torah in accordance with what was handed down to us, with commentators such as *Rashi* and the *Ramban*.

The language is not called the Holy Language for any reason other than that it was the language in which the Torah was given, as the *Ramban* writes. Even in the bathrooms and bathhouses one may speak of mundane things in the Holy Language. It is only words of Torah which are not allowed in these places, even in other languages. Therefore, the main emphasis is not on the Holy Language specifically but rather in the content of what is spoken. The holiness of the Holy Language is only because of the Torah.

Those who put tremendous emphasis on Hebrew have caused the desecration of the Torah and the religion. Had your Honor seen with his own eyes even some of the terrible things that have been done, surely you would have said that we must tear our clothing and bless the Truthful Judge, as do the mourners. Those that have studied Hebrew can now use books that are alien to our culture. In addition to all that has been mentioned so far, they cause the schoolchildren to be interrupted from their holy study of the Torah, the study upon which the whole world exists. Instead they encumber them with emptiness and with bad and prohibited things, things that we cannot even mention here. The greatest danger is that when the children learn to speak Hebrew well, it draws them to study the new books that are filled with lechery and heresy, and to read their newspapers which taint the soul of the young.

If Your Honor is concerned that the children are being anyway drawn to read the Spanish newspapers which are also filled with these things, and they pursue their desires which cause them to transgress the Torah, you should know that in Hebrew it is different. When they study in Hebrew, the danger is much greater, for besides the fact that they learn to pursue their desires, they learn to transgress intentionally and become full-fledged heretics.

Therefore my advice is that you should not introduce any changes in the language that is used for teaching; rather they should study in Arabic or the national language, Spanish. By doing so you will prevent the possibility of new, inappropriate ideas from contaminating their education. In one moment you can lose many years of hard work. Be strong and courageous in your work to disseminate and glorify Torah. Do not hold yourself back from this great matter for there is no way to measure the greatness of guiding a school of 300 students with the Torah and the fear of the Heaven. May the will of G-d be successful in your hands, Amen.

These are the words of the undersigned, for the honor of the Torah, with intense dedication and peace,

Yosef Yedid HaLevi

We have seen what was written above by his Honor, the Great Rabbi, and Chief Judge for our brothers the *Halabi* community, R' Yosef Yedid. His words are a remedy for our eyes and from them we will not budge an inch. Praiseworthy is the one who walks in the holy path, the path which is well worn from use throughout the generations. May the merit of the schoolchildren stand with those who contend with this, and may they merit seeing consolation for Zion and the building of the Temple speedily in our days, Amen.

We write and sign for the glory of Torah, may it be elevated.

Court of Justice for the Ashkenazi communities in Jerusalem,

Mordechai Leib Rubin ***Yitzchak Frankel*** ***Dov Tzvi Karlenstein***

The issue was also presented to R' Haim Shaul Dweck, Rosh Yeshiva of Yeshivat Rechovot HaNahar, who referred the matter to the Ashkenazi Bet Din of Jerusalem, as indicated below.

He replied: "I am weak and many problems have beset me. Therefore I gave your letter to the righteous and pious Rav Yosef Chaim Sonnenfeld and his *Bet Din*, as it says and you shall do as they direct you' (referring to the *Bet Din* of Jerusalem). They have more expertise on these issues and have more experience, and the Heavens above agree with them. See what they do and follow them."

Haim Shaul Dweck

Rosh Yeshiva of Yeshivat Rechovot HaNahar

I have seen the letter from his Honor the great Rabbi Yosef Yedid and the great Rabbis of the Court of Justice and it would be sacrilege to deviate from their words.

Signed,

Yosef Chaim Sonnenfeld

[Note: The above letter is quoted from *Mara D'Ara Yisrael*, pages 188-190.]

מרן הגאון רבי מרדכי עבאדי זצ״ל
ראב״ד ארם צובה

סימן ח׳

בענין איסור לימוד בספרים שכתב אפיקורס

מורי ורבותי השרידים אשר ה׳ קורא. מהודעין אנחנו לכך שאיך לעת עתה קרא מקרה בלתי טהור. שיש אחד בעיר ליוורנו זה שמו אליהו בן אמוזג. הוא המדפיס אשר בעיר ליוורנו הנז׳ שעכשיו חיבר פירוש על החומש וקרא שמו אם למקרא והדפיס הפירוש הנז׳ סביב לחומש. וגם הוא עשה שחיבר פירוש אחר וקרא שמו אם למסורת. ואנן בדידן לא הגיע לידינו רק ספר אם למקרא שסביב לחומש, וראה ראינו שבפירושו עירב קודש בחול ונזרקה בו מינות ואפיקורסות ורוח טומאה עוכרתו. והפך דברי אלהים חיים ללענה ורוש. וגלה פנים בתורה שלא כהלכה בדרשות של דופי שדרש, ובפירושים של הבל שפירש. וכפי הדין הגמור שהספר ההוא טעון שריפה כדין ס״ת שכתבו מין ישרף.

והנה אם באנו להגיד את כל הקורות ואת כל הכפירות היוצאים מתוך פירושו יאריך הסיפור. על כן בשבטי ישראל הודענו נאמנה שאין רשות לשום בר ישראל לא לקנותו ולא לקרות בו ואפי׳ אם ירצה לקרות בו המקרא דוקא בלתי פירוש עם כל זה אסור, וכן לא יניחנו שום אדם בביתו, וכמו שאמר הכתוב ולא ידבק בידך מאומה מן החרם.

האמנם זאת לדעת כי שאר ספרים שמדפיסם אליהו בן אמוזג הנז׳, הן חומשים הן סידורים או ספרי רז״ל הן שאר ספרים שמדפיס, ואין עליהם שום פירוש ממנו בעצמו אלא רק מודפסים בבית הדפוס שלו, הנה אלו מותרים לקרות בהם כשאר ספרי הקודש וזה ברור.

והא לך איזה דוגמאות טעויות מדברי המחבר.

א. בפרשת נח דף ל״ב ע״ב על פסוק וירח ה׳ את ריח הניחוח כי אחר שהביא דעת המשתדל בטעם למה הגדילה התורה מעלת הקרבנות, פיחת מעלתם והכה על קדקודו וכתב שהלך אחרי ההבל שהמציאו הכופרים בתורה מן השמים. והוא כתב וז״ל ואם כנגד זה לא מצינו בתורה מליצות על הקרבנות אשר תואר להם כתואר מליצות

(9) Letter Against the Works of Amozeg (1860's)

(9) Letter Against the Works of Amozeg (1860's)

In the mid-1860's Rabbi Mordechai Abadi (see #8) wrote a letter condemning the work of the Italian philosopher Eliyahu ben Amozeg (b.1822, d.1900), who was a professor of theology at the Rabbinical Seminary of Livorno. The letter is quoted in the book *Ginzei Aretz* of R' Rahamim Shayo, son of R' Edmon Shayo (see #504), page 86.

Our masters and rabbis,

We want you to know of a spiritually polluted situation that has occurred. There is a man from Livorno whose name is Eliyahu ben Amozeg and who is a printer by trade. He has written a commentary on the *Humash* titled *Em LeMikra*.He has also put out a book called *Em LeMesoret* which hasn't reached us. [Editor's note : It seems the second book was only in manuscript form at that point and due to the pressure put on Amozeg from the rabbis of Aleppo it never appeared in print.]

His commentary mixes the holy and the mundane [by quoting secular sources] and a spirit of heresy has possessed him. He has turned the words of the living G-d into bitter wormwood. He has distorted the Torah with nonsensical approaches and inane ideas that he has thought up. According to the Absolute Law his book must be burned like a *Sefer Torah* written by a heretic.

If we would delineate all the heresy that he has written, we would run out of space. Therefore we are making it known in the tribes of Israel that no one has permission to buy his book or to read it. You may not even use it for the *Humash* section, without using his commentary. No one should have it in his home, as the Torah says [concerning idolatry]: "No part of the banned property may adhere to your hand" [*Debarim* 13:18].

Let us make known that the books of others which are printed in his printing press whether they be *siddurim* or *humashim* or books of *Hazal* without any commentary of his may be used like any other holy book and this is clear.

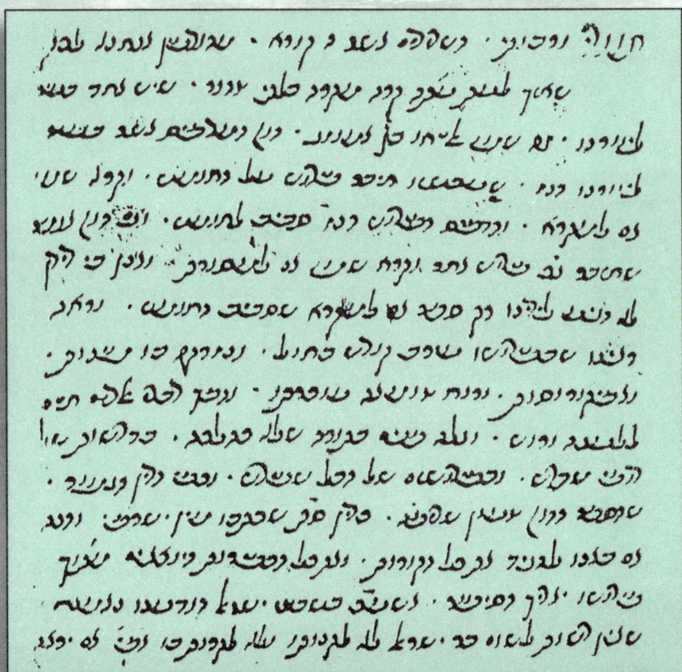

R' Mordechai Abadi's handwritten letter against the works of Amozeg

KABBALAH

(10) Halachic Ruling in Defense of the Ari'zal (1715)

In the year 5475 (1715) R' Yosef Irgis of Livorno posed a question to the rabbis of Aleppo, which was occasioned by a controversy challenging the traditional approach to Kabbalah. The text of the insertion *"Zachrenu L'Haim"* that we say in the *Amidah* during the ten days of *Teshubah* is based on the teachings of the *Ari'zal* (R' Yitzhak Luria), who showed how Kabbalah can add new depths of meaning to our prayers. A man got up in the synagogue and attacked the students of Kabbalah and the *Ari'zal* in particular. Others joined him in his attack, arguing that they should revert to the text used before the *Ari'zal*.

The rabbis of Aleppo answered the query with the following words:

> First, who are we to get involved in the deciding of this text that rabbis of old argued about (see the *Bet Yosef* on *Orach Haim* 582), but now that our master the holy *Ari'zal* decided on the text, who has the courage to do otherwise? There is no question that the man in question should be excommunicated and defamed the world over. We have only the words of the holy *Ari'zal* and we follow his decisions. Eliyahu HaNabi spoke to him and we have accepted his word. Anyone who argues with him is arguing with G-d Almighty himself. Surely this wicked man has separated himself from the Jewish people by denying the fundamentals of our faith and speaking out against students of Kabbalah and our holy master the *Ari'zal*. That man is a sinner and has caused others to sin with him. Those renegades who came to his aid have no remedy for their disease.

The rabbis of Aleppo continue by quoting from the words of Rav Moshe Kordevero concerning one who questions Kabbalah. They then conclude by saying that the wicked man should be excommunicated until he returns to G-d and begs forgiveness of the rabbis whom he disrespected. They then sign the ruling as follows:

> All that we have written is simple and does not need to be drawn out. Signed in Aleppo (G-d guard it), 5475 [1715]

Moshe Harari ***Shemuel Dweck***
Shemuel Pinto ***Yosef son of Elisha Nawi***
Shemuel son of Shelomo Laniado

[Note: The above responsa is quoted from *Dibrei Yosef* by R' Yosef Irgis, Chapter 3.]

(11) Declaration in Support of Kabbalah (1914)

In 1914 the Jewish community of Yemen was confronted by a dissident group which questioned the validity of the *Zohar*, the ancient text of Jewish mysticism. When the matter came to the attention of the Rabbis of Aram Soba, they became very concerned and signed the following proclamation:

NOT A TIME TO BE QUIET!

> In the newspaper *Herut* we have read the details of a frightening occurrence that recently took place in Yemen. A group of nonbelievers brought false accusations to

government officials against the people that uphold our holy Torah and the words of our *Hazal* (Holy Rabbis of Blessed Memory) and the words of the holy *Zohar* of the godly Rav Shimon bar Yochai. It has caused pain to our ears to hear these words of blasphemy from this new group which attacked the *Zohar* and all learning of mysticism. This has caused a tremendous *Hilul Hashem* [desecration of G-d's name].

We have also read in the *Herut* newspaper that the rabbis of Sanaa [Yemen] were brought before the government officials. The rabbis testified about the truth of the Torah and said the government could verify their testimony [as to the validity of the *Zohar*] with the rabbis of Jerusalem. We waited impatiently for the rabbis of Jerusalem to come forward in their defense and to protest against the sinners. According to our great rabbi, the *Ramban* (in *perashat Aharei Mot*), sinners who are wise in their own eyes [questioning what they can't see with their eyes] are called heretics. The *Ramak* (Rav Moshe Kordevero) writes that those who deny the hidden spheres of Kabbalah because of their bad nature, due to being accustomed to secular thinking and gentile ways, are deemed heretics and are deniers of the oral law.

To our surprise we have not seen any reaction from the rabbis of Jerusalem. Therefore we, the rabbis of Aleppo, have risen against this terrible abomination and we are making a strong protest aganst these sinners who have sabotaged the respect of our Torah and our people in the eyes of the nations. As long as thay do not turn back from their evil path, they have no portion in the Jewish people nor an inheritance in the house of Jacob. Everyone should pay attention to these words and be in awe; they should not sin again and publicly desecrate G-d's name and may the honor of our Torah and nation grow in the eyes of the nations.

Signed in Aleppo

Hizkiah Shabbetai, Chief Rabbi
Yaakob Shaul Dweck
Ezra Hamway
Moshe Ezra Mizrahi
Reuben Ancona
Yehuda Dweck
Shelomo Eliyahu Laniado
Ezra Yitzhak Dweck
Yitzhak Raphael Swed
Yitzhak Moshe Avigdor
Yaakob Sutton Shomer
Yitzhak Dayan
Yehudah Attiah
Eliyahu Hamway
Rahamim Cohen
Ezra Abadi
Abraham Hamway
Shemuel Chasky
Yosef Sasson
Rahamim Mizrahi

[Note: The above document is quoted from *Vayismach Ezra* by R' Ezra Hamway (#272), page 3.]

הסכמת הרה״ג יושבי עַל מדין מאירים לארץ ולדרים
ראשי אבות בי דינא רבא
דק״ק ספרדים בירושלם ת״ו

זה ספר אשר חובר ע״י אנשי שם חו״ר מעיר תימן יע״א שומרי משמרת תורת ה׳ הנקרא בשם **אמונת ה׳** כשמו כן הוא להורות את הדרך ילכו בה בחוקי האלקים ותורותיו, תורה שבכתב ותורה שבע״פ בנסתר ובנגלה ולבאר קדושת ספר ה׳זהר הקדוש עיקר ושרש הקבלה מהתנא הקדוש הרשב״י ז״ל זיע״א באשר כל קורא תחזינה משרים. ולבטל דברי נרגן אדם בליעל הקפ״ח ותלמידיו הפריצים ואפיקורסים החכמים בעיניהם אשר לפי דעתם השפל באו למישדי ביה נרגא ושתו בשמים פיהם לדבר על ה׳ ועל משיחו, ועליהם נאמר (בזוהר ח״ג דר״צ ודרצ״ב ע״א) מאן דלא עאל ונפק טב ליה דלא איברי ונאמר (תהלים י״ב) יכרת ה׳ כל שפתי חלקות לשון מדברת גדולות. ועל אנשים כאלה וחבריהם נאמר שלא להשיב על דבריהם כי הם הבל ודבריהם הבל כמ״ש (אבות פ״ב מי״ד) ודע מה שתשיב לאפיקורוס ואמרו (בסנהדרין דל״ח ע״ב) הני מילי באפיקורוס גוי אבל לא באפיקורוס ישראל וכבר נגמר דיניהו כמ״ש (בר״ה י״ז ובסנהדרין צ״ט) האפיקורסים שכפרו בתורה שחטאו והחטיאו את הרבים כגון ירבעם בן נבט וחבריו יורדין לגהינם ונדונין בה לדורי דורות כמש״ה (ישעיה ס״ו) כי תולעתם לא תמות ואשם לא תכבה וגו׳ והיה מן הדין שלא לענות להם, אמנם צדקו במעשיהם להשיב להם תשובה כמש״ה (משלי כ״ו ה׳) ענה כסיל וגו׳ פן יהיה חכם וגו׳ ולמען הסר המכשלה מאנשים תמימים וישרים בדרכם לבל יפלו ברשת אשר טמנו לרגלי אנשים כשרים ותמימי דרך שלא יטעו בדברי שקר ואפיקורסות. **ובכן אנן בדידן ראשי אבות ב״ד ק״ק הספרדים דעה״ק ירושלם ת״ו** מזהירים ומצהירים בזה שכל איש אשר הלך ח״ו אחרי דרכי המסית האפיקורוס הנז״ל וחפץ יחפוץ בחיים ולזכות לראות באור החיים הוא שתכף ומיד יבקש תקון לנפשו לעזוב דרכו שהלך עד היום ולא יהיה כקרח וכעדתו ובזה יציל נפשו ונפש כל ב״ב מרדת שחת. ואם יקשו לבבם ולא ישמעו את דברינו אלה הרי הם מובדלים מקהל ישראל תקולל אלקם בארץ החיים וסופם ירשו גהינם ולנצח לא יראו אור רח״ל. והאיש אשר ישמע את דברינו אלה ואת מוסרנו יטו אזן קשבת לחזור אל אלקינו כי ירבה לסלוח יראו זרע ויאריכו ימים ושנים ותחזינה עינינו ועיני כל ישראל בבנין הבית ושלום על כל ישראל. שנת א׳ ר׳ צ׳ ו׳ ת׳ החיים והשלום.

כלב״י **חזקיה שבתי**	כלע״ר **אברהם עזריאל**	כ״ג **שלום הדאיה**
ס״ט	ס״ט	ס״ט

(12) Approbation on Book Defending Kabbalah (1938)

(12) Approbation on Book Defending Kabbalah (1938)

In 1938 a Yemenite rabbi anonymously published a book *Emunat Hashem* (*Faith in G-d*). He was later revealed to be R' Yosef Subari, who authored it at the age of 17. The book was intended as a response to a book, *Milhemet Hashem* (War of G-d), that a heretic from Yemen by the name of Yihye Kepah had published. That book contained blasphemous words and arrogant arguments questioning the authenticity of the *Zohar*.

R' Shalom Hedaya (see #310) and his colleagues on the Sephardic *Bet Din* (court) of Jerusalem wrote a letter of approbation to R' Subari that reads as follows:

> This book was written by one of the rabbis of Yemen, a guardian of the Torah. The book's title (*Emunat Hashem*) befits its nature, which is to direct the reader to the path of the Torah and its laws, including the Written and Oral Law, the hidden and the revealed. He also describes the holiness of the *Zohar* and demolishes the words of the contentious, evil man, Kepah, and his students who are violators of the faith and heretics.
>
> In truth, we are not supposed to answer people like this because they are worthless and their words are futile. Judgment has already been passed upon them by the *Gemara* (*Sanhedrin* 99b), as it states, "Those who deny the Torah and cause others to sin like Yeraboam shall go to the depths of *Gehinom* [Purgatory] for generations." Even so it is proper to answer in order to remove a stumbling block from uninformed people to prevent these innocents from falling into the trap that [Kepah and his students] have set and to save the innocents from being misled by their lies and heresy.
>
> Therefore we the chief judges of the Sephardic court of Jerusalem caution any person who has followed them and wants life, and wants to be worthy to see the light of life, should immediately look for a remedy for his soul and leave the evil ways that he has trodden until now. He should not be like Korach and his company, and with this he will save himself and his family from descending to the depths of the abyss.
>
> If he chooses to harden his heart and doesn't heed our words, he will be separated from the Jewish people and will lose his portion in the world to come. The ones that heed our words and listen to our admonition will be forgiven because G-d forgives. They will be found worthy to have children and live a long life. May we all be worthy to see the rebuilding of the *Bet HaMikdash* and peace on the Jewish people.
>
> ***Hizkiah Shabbetai*** ***Abraham Uziel*** ***Shalom Hedaya***

The *Emunat Hashem* controversy was also the catalyst for R' Yaakob Kassin (see #330) to write his book *Yesod Emunah* (*Foundations of Faith*). In the first chapter he speaks of the repentance necessary and describes the appropriate punitive measures as follows:

> He should fast 301 fasts corresponding to the numerical value of fire [אש] to save himself from the fires of *Gehinom* [Purgatory]. He should wear sackcloth and constantly confess his sins. He should refrain from meat and wine except on *Shabbat* and holidays, and should try to bring others back to Judaism. If he can't fast, he should redeem the fasts with money.

KASHRUT

(13) Letter Concerning Grape Leaves (1700's)

In the early 1700's a great controversy broke out in Aram Soba concerning the consumption of grape leaves used in the delicacy referred to as *yebra*. The concern was over worms that were not easily discernable and therefore impossible to check. Eventually the rabbis of Aram Soba banned the consumption of the grape leaves. R' Matloub Abadi (see #9) discusses the topic at length in his book *Magen Ba'adi* (pp. 101-102) and explains the need to be aware of these decrees:

> I wrote out all the specifics of the agreement of the rabbis of Aleppo to warn our holy congregation in America to uphold the tradition of their fathers and not to eat grape leaves that come from Syria but rather buy those that are grown in America that have not been established to be wormy and can be checked.

He refers the reader to the book *Hanan Elokim* of Rav Haim Abulafia, which discusses the entire episode at length. (For further research see *Mahzik Berachah* of the *Hida* (*Yoreh Deah* 84-24) and *Kaf HaHaim* (ibid. 84-94.)

The rabbis of Aram Soba turned to Rabbi Abulafia to aid them in controlling the issue, which had gotten out of hand. The letter and *halachic* ruling, which they sent to him, was signed by the leading scholars and rabbis of city. A shortened version of the letter is given here: (The original version is over fifteen pages and goes into the *halachic* intricacies at length.)

> The following has occurred in Aleppo. We have found that grape leaves contain many thin worms that can barely be seen and most people checking them will not see them.
>
> The matter was brought to the attention of the court, but [the judges] didn't find anything in the grape leaves. They therefore assumed it was a one-time occurrence and were going to dismiss it. However, the leaves were then shown to younger rabbis with better vision and the result was that they did see [the worms]. The [judges] continued to check and the same thing happened again. Some people saw and others did not. When the rabbis realized the severity of the issue, they decreed that no one may partake of the grape leaves. As it happened, the final decision was taken late Friday afternoon and they did not have time to make it known before *Shabbat*. Therefore, they made announcements in the synagogues after *Arbit* on Friday night. The holy Jews spilled out their bubbling pots and some gave [the food] to their gentile neighbors. [The Jews] accepted the prohibition upon themselves without objecting.

One rabbi, who was not involved in the decision-making process, became upset that he was not involved (as he told the Chief Rabbi) and began to argue that the rabbis made an unnecessary prohibition. He explained that all that was needed was to heat the leaves over a flame and the worms would leave. We tried that approach and it was not successful. He then claimed the worms would dissolve in the cooking process. His words had an impact and his followers complied with his decision. One day he was sitting with Chief Rabbi Shemuel Laniado at a *Seudat Mitzvah* [festive meal] on a terrace with grape vines dangling overhead. This rabbi challenged Rabbi Laniado to find worms. Inevitably, when they looked closely they did find worms. Rabbi Laniado said, "If so, we must reaffirm the proclamation since you are in agreement," and so it was.

A year passed, summer came, and some people missed the taste of the *yebra*. People began to taunt this rabbi saying, "How is it that you gave in?" He then sat down and wrote a long *halachic* dissertation to permit the consumption of *yebra*. We went through his analysis and found many faults in his argument. We presented them to him and he continues to stand by his work. We sent him our response in writing and without even opening it he took out a grape leaf and said a loud *berachah* (blessing) and ate it. Our messenger reacted saying, "It is forbiddden to answer, 'Amen.'"

All of this has caused a *Hillul Hashem* (desecration of G-d's name) in the eyes of the people and we can no longer control the situation. Please save us.

Shemuel son of Rav Shelomo Laniado
Mordechai son of Yitzchak Atzban
Yosef son of R' Mordechai Dayan
Yehudah son of R' Yomtob Kassin
Sadkah Houssin
Gabriel son of R' David Cohen
Yeshayah son of R' Yitzhak Dabbah
Moshe Harari
Michael Harari
Yitzhak Berachah
Shelomo son of R' Shemuel Laniado

[Note: This letter is quoted from the book *Hanan Elokim* by R' Haim Abulafia at the end of the response section.]

(14) Takanot of Shohatim (1853)

All of the procedures involved in preparing kosher meat were strictly observed in Aram Soba. To ensure that the complex requirements of kosher slaughtering were consistently met, all practitioners of this craft were licensed and supervised under direction of the *Bet Din*. In 1853 certain regulations governing the practices of the *shohatim* (kosher slaughterers) and *bodekim* (knife examiners) were formally adopted by the *Bet Din*. A copy of the document may be found in the Biographies section of this book under the entry for R' Yitzhak Yeshayah Alfia (see #47), who was mentioned in the document as the *Mashgiach* (supervisor) of slaughtering practices in the city. A translation of the document is given below.

These are the *takanot* [regulations] which we have drawn up in conjunction with the *shohatim* (kosher slaughterers) of Aram Soba. They have all accepted these rules of practice without reservation and have obligated themselves by swearing an oath to *Hashem*.

1. At the end of each normal workday when the *shohatim* prepare to leave for home, one *shohet* and one *bodek* must stay behind to be available for the additional slaughtering that may be necessary. However, on Fridays, both summer and winter, all of the *shohatim* must remain on duty until all slaughtering has been completed. The [*shohet*] whose responsibility is to check the lung [of each slaughtered animal]

must give his knife to the *bodek* in order not to have a [possibly unexamined] knife in his hand to slaughter [the next animal]. The same rule must be followed by the last *shohet* of the day [even if he is not planning to slaughter additional animals].

2. The *shohatim* must meet each day to sharpen their knives and to show them to one another so that each knife will be approved by three experts. This meeting will take place in the home of **R' David Kassin** [see #322].

3. Anyone who acts as a *bodek* (responsible for examining the knife) may not be involved in checking the lung [as it may interfere with his concentration because of the different sensitivities involved].

4. The current practice of informal understandings involving gratuities [tips for extra attention in the checking process] must be discontinued. All gratuities for *shohatim* are to be based on the standard agreements, unless a specific question has arisen about the knife or the lung.

5. Every *shohet* must be accompanied by a young man [apprentice] who will apply the [special] stamp that distinguishes Jewish from non-Jewish slaughtering. This young man must stay with the *shohet* until the slaughtering is complete. The *shohet* may not dispute with the young man and may surely not sell him the gratuities (that is, certain parts of the animals that are usually given to the *shohet*).

6. Those who stamp the meat [marking it as kosher] must work together in order that they observe [their responsibilities] meticulously. This is especially the case on Thursdays in the winter and on Fridays in the summer. They must not divert their attention to the right or left and must not become occupied in the selling of the gratuities.

All of these conditions and obligations have been adopted by the *shohatim* of Aram Soba. The *bodekim* are **R' David Kassin** [see #322], **R' Shalom Salem**, **R' Yosef Dweck** [see #252], and **R' Yedidyah Dayan** [see #201]. The *shohatim* are: **R' Abraham Chabot** [see #142], **R' Moshe Swed** [see #574], **R' Yitzhak Alfia** [see #47], and the steadfast young man **Moshe Dayan**.

All these have formally committed themselves without reservation and with a solemn oath to Hashem, here in the city of Aram Soba, the 11th day of the month Tamuz, in the year 5613 [1853] of Creation. This is firm, right, and abiding, and so we the Great *Bet Din* have set our signature.

In addition, among those who have signed below is **R' Yitzhak Alfia** [see #47], who has committed to us that he will act as *Mashgiach* (supervisor) over all the matters stated above, lest any one of the *shohatim* or *bodekim* should violate (Heaven forbid!) any of these particulars. If he should observe that any individual is in violation, whether intentional or unintentional, he is obligated to immediately inform one or two of the leading rabbis of Aram Soba. And furthermore, if he should see any hint of prohibited behavior (Heaven forbid!) in any one of [the *shohatim* or *bodekim*] he is obliged to report it without any delay whatsoever. He has formally committed himself without reservation and with a sacred promise to Hashem on this date, and we, the Great *Bet Din* have confirmed it.

KETER ARAM SOBA

(15) Letters from Syrian Rabbis on Authenticity of the Keter (1995)

In recent years, some secular scholars have raised questions about the authenticity of the *Keter Aram Soba* (the Aleppo Codex). In response, R' David Yitzhaki has written a book, titled *Nebiyei Emet V'Sedek,* to refute the arguments of the skeptics and to demonstrate the contrary. His work received a letter of approbation from two great rabbis of Aram Soba involved in the rescue of the *Keter,* including a description of its final days. A translation of the letter is provided below. (See the end of Section III for the original of the letter.)

Addressed to Rabbi David Yitzhaki.

Concerning your investigation into the authenticity of the *Keter* and the relevance to *halachah* to know the proper [method of] writing of *Nebi'im* [Prophets] and *Ketubim* [Scriptures] for those who want to write them on parchment:

Truths that are publicized don't need to be proven. It was known and publicized in Aleppo, a city of scholars and scribes, as is mentioned by the early rabbis and through our tradition from generation to generation, that the manuscript of the Torah, *Nebi'im,* and *Ketubim* known as the *Keter Aram Soba* that resided in honor in our community for hundreds of years is the book of the well-known *Baal HaMesorah*.

After part of the *Keter* was lost and damaged in the Arab riots against the Jews of Aleppo in 1948, I had the merit to be among those who rescued the *Keter*. We gathered the scrolls and eventually it was taken to Israel.

The following are the details of the above story. After the United Nations decided on the separation of Israel in the winter of 1947, angry Arabs rioted in the streets of Aleppo with knives and axes in their hands and instilled fear into the Jewish inhabitants. Thank G-d, no lives were lost.

In the process they burned the synagogues and *Talmudei Torah*. The holy books were burnt or torn and strewn everywhere. Three days after the riots I entered the old synagogue with my master, my father-in-law, the *Gaon* R' Shelomo Zafrani, and R' Sadek Harari. We found the *Keter* on the floor, with missing [pages] from the beginning of the Torah until *Perashat Ki Tabo*. We did not see any sign of burning on the *Keter* and we don't know where the missing section ended up. One day on the way out of the yeshiva an Arab police officer approached me with a section of the *Keter* in his hands and he asked me if it was indeed from the *Keter*. It was part of *Tehillim*, containing Chapter 15.

The *Keter* was guarded with great diligence in the ancient old synagogue of Aleppo in the Cave of Eliyahu HaNabi in our community for hundreds of years. Due to the great holiness of the *Keter* it was locked in a large solid iron cabinet. It had two locks with two different keys and each key was held by a trusted officer of the congregation so that it was not possible to open it without both officers being present.

You have asked whether it is possible for the *Keter* to have been switched with another manuscript that was there. That is unthinkable since the *Keter* is so well known to us so that there is no concern at all. Its writing is distinctive in size and style, and I know that firsthand.

The lengths to which the community went in guarding the *Keter* can be learned from the following anecdote. In the winter of 1943 a man came to Aleppo to check the *Keter*. (I later learned that his name was Professor Moshe David Cassuto.) After two weeks they finally allowed him to look at it. I was asked with two other great rabbis from the community to sit with him and supervise him. We sat for four-hour periods during the days he was allotted to view the *Keter*. They warned us to watch him "with seven eyes" to ensure that he didn't photograph any pages or tear out a page and hide it.

Respectfully yours,

Yaakob R. Attiah

I endorse all the above.

Yitzhak son of Rav Shelomo Zafrani

The testimony of the great rabbis signed above does not need any strengthening. Anyone who sees what they have written understands that publicized and well known truths do not have to be proven. I am merely attesting to the fact that whatever these rabbis write is with extreme accuracy.

Yehudah Ades, Rosh Yeshiva of Kol Yaakob

Another letter of approbation was sent by R' Abraham Zafrani on 24 Tevet, 5756 (1995). The text reads as follows:

Addressed to Rabbi David Yitzhaki.

Concerning your question on the status of the *Keter Aram Soba*:

It is well known and has been public knowledge of the entire community of Aleppo throughout all generations until today that the *Tanach* known as the *Keter Aram Soba* is the *Keter* that the *Rambam* discusses in the laws of *Sefer Torah* (8:4), saying that he depends on it because "it is the *Keter,* checked and marked with *nekudot* [pronunciation notations] by Ben-Asher with great care over many years."

Our fathers told us that their fathers told them that they have a tradition over generations that this *sefer* is, without question, very holy to the entire community and its rabbis treated it with great holiness. No one was permitted to leaf through it to check from it or even to look at it. The *Keter* was locked in an iron safe with two different keys in the hands of two great men of the community.

I remember when I was young on Friday night after *Arbit* we would go into the Cave of Eliyahu HaNabi (may his merit guard over us, Amen); that is the place in which the safe with the *Keter* was kept. We would sit there and recite *Shir HaShirim*. When we finished we would kiss the safe and return home. This holy place was usually locked. However, when a public or private trouble arose, we would enter to light candles in a special corner in memory of Eliyahu HaNabi (may his merit guard over us, Amen). The safe itself was never opened. Not one of the community of Aleppo dared to transgress the command of the rabbis. (It is well known that all of the members of the Syrian community are G-d-fearing people, *Shabbat* observers, and guardians of religion with simple faith, who heed to the word of their rabbis without question on all religious matters, especially concerning the opening of the above-mentioned safe.)

We have been told that a certain professor from Jerusalem visited and, after much pressure and repeated requests from the rabbis of the congregation, was allowed to look at the *Keter* under strict supervision of the rabbis. It never entered anyone's mind that someone would have the audacity to try to switch the *Keter*, let alone be successful at it. To our sorrow in the year 1948 the Arabs (may their names and memory be blotted out) burnt the synagogue. On the 8th of Kislev they broke open the safe thinking there was money inside and damaged the *Keter*. From then until 1956 the *Keter* (what remained of it) was guarded secretly by the rabbis of Aleppo. In the year 1956 I remember that my father, my master, the crown of my head, Hacham Shelomo Zafrani *zt'l*, together with my teacher, my master, the crown of my head, the *Gaon Hacham* Moshe Tawil *zt'l*, handed over the *Keter*, in my presence, to Mr. Mordechai Faham *zt'l* to rescue it and bring it to Israel. That was the first time I had the opportunity to see the manuscript. Years later when I moved to New York, I saw a copy of the *Keter* and I recognized it to be the duplicate of the *Keter* I had seen in 1948.

In summary, concerning your question I stress and reiterate: It is clear to me beyond a doubt that the *Keter* that is today in Jerusalem, according to the transmission from our fathers and the tradition in our hands, is the very same *Keter* that the *Rambam* depended on because Ben-Asher checked it, put in the *nekudot*, etc.

Abraham Zafrani

(16) Letter from Ashkenazi Rabbis on Authenticity of the Keter (2003)

In addition to the letters of approbation described above, R' David Yitzhaki received the following letter of approbation from great rabbis of the Ashkenazi Torah world for his book *Nebiyei Emet V'Sedek*.

Tradition of Writing Nebi'im and Ketubim

1. The Ashkenazim have no *Mesorah* for the method of writing the *Nebi'im* [Prophets] and the four *Megillot*.
2. The only tradition [that has been handed down] from generation to generation is the *Mesorah* of Aram Soba. The famous *Keter* that they possessed was the *sefer* checked by Ben-Asher, on which the *Rambam* depended. This tradition is based on Torah scholarship of the past 500 years. The many proofs that Rabbi Yitzhaki brought appear to be correct.
3. Concerning the claim of the secular scholars that the *Keter* and Ben-Asher have connections to the Karaites, it is unthinkable to undo an established tradition

based on the claims of their research. Their way from then to now has been to put blemishes on holy things based on questionable proofs and theories. It is known that this is done maliciously, as is their way.

4. On topics like these, in which only few are expert, it is easy to fool the less knowledgeable. However, to those who are familiar with the topic, the contrary is true. All the proofs against the authenticity of the *Keter* only strengthen its validity. Anyone who is not familiar with the topic and starts to analyze it will most likely come out with a distorted view, especially if he is only privy to part of the relevant information.

Michael Yehudah Lefkowitz	***Zvi Rotberg***
Nissim Karelitz	***Yehudah Shapira***
Chaim Kanievski	***Yaacob Meir Stern***

[Note: This letter is quoted from *Nebiyei Emet V'Sedek* by R' David Yitzhaki.]

On issuance of this letter, much controversy arose. Many questioned the practical implications the letter entailed. Rabbi Tzvi Goldberg of Jerusalem, in his book *Masoratenu*, clarified the opinions of the above signatures.

Although most halachic authorities agree to the authenticity of the *Keter* they do not agree that one should change the age-old customs of writing *Nebi'im* or *Ketubim* based on the *Keter*. In the year 2003 Rabbi Tzvi Goldberg of Jerusalem printed a book, *Masoratenu (Our Tradition)*, in which he goes to great lengths to prove the validity of the traditions other than the *Keter* and brings letters from many halachic authorities.

The following is a translation from a letter by Rabbi Reuven Feinstein, son of Rav Moshe Feinstein, *Rosh Yeshiva* of the Staten Island Yeshiva:

1st of Elul 5762

I have seen the pamphlet written by Rabbi Goldberg clarifying the *Mesorah* of the *Tanach*. He brings solid proof against changing from the text of the *Tanach* that has been passed down over the generations. I was happy to see that he acted selflessly in clarifying this issue and making it known that the group of people that chose to change the writing of the *Tanach* based on the *Keter* is a contradiction to the concept of "Tradition " which is the foundation of our religion. It is well known that my master, my father (Rav Moshe), was very strict about any sort of change even in cases of strong proof and logic if it contradicts our tradition. I am signing to strenghthen his words, especially since I saw that the great *halachic* authorities of our holy land have agreed with him. May it be His will that this breach be fixed and the crown of old returned.

Reuven Feinstein

Typical clothing in Aleppo, 1873. Left to right: Married Jewish woman, Arab man, Arab woman Photo taken by famed Arab historian and photographer Hamdy-Bey, who states: "The [Jewish woman's] headdress is peculiar to Aleppo. In many parts of the Orient when Jewish women cut off their hair after marriage, it was the practice to ornament their headdress with cock's feathers or white fringes. Only in Aleppo did they wear a wig. This woman wears a kind of miter of striped silk to which is attached a trimming of false hair and long tresses."

(17) Approbation on Covering Hair with a Wig (1889)

In the year 1889 Rabbi Yitzhak Abulafia, Chief Rabbi of Damascus (see #35), issued a ruling permitting women to use wigs to cover their hair instead of the standard kerchiefs. The text of his *halachic* dissertation is included in his book *Pnei Yitzhak* (*Even Ha'Ezer*, Vol. VI, Chap. 6). The responsum is also quoted in the book, *Yabia Omer*, Vol. IV (*Even Ha'Ezer,* Chap. 3). At the time this was a controversial issue since most women did not use the new and more fashionable wigs. He also turned to the court of Aram Soba to obtain its agreement. [Editor's note: Since this is a question of *halachah,* no one should come to a conclusion based on the information presented here, but should seek the advice of his rabbinical authority.]

הסכמת רבני צובה יע״א על הפס״ד הנז״ל ח״ל

מענותנותיה דמני״ר הרב הגדול מוה״ר רב״י אב״א נר״ו הנז׳ עליון למעלה אוהבו ליוה והוא פקד עלינו לבא עה״ח ולבלתי סור מן המלוה פ״ק לא מרינו ועברנו בכל דב״ק בהשו׳ הרמתה לאורכה ולרחבה וניחזי אכן שכל דבריו אמו״ן וא״ל חיזוק ויפה דן את הדין אמת לאמיתו רה״ה ויתר לבית יעקב אלו הנשים ללבוש פאה נכרית וכולהו טעמי דיהיב בשיטתא הלכתא נינהו ומפיו אנו חיים ומי כמוהו מורה והכי נהיגי נשי דידן בפני רבנן קמאי ובתראי וע״ד אמת ולדק באנו כיאודס ועוד לקרא ות״ש פה אר״ן יע״א בחדש זיו איר דהאי שתא שנת והחכמ״ה תע״ז לחכ״ס לפ״ק ברוב עוז ושלום.

הצעיר	הצעיר	הצעיר
בכור מזרחי	משה ח״ר יצחק הררי	יצחק לבטון
ס״ט	ס״ט	ס״ט

וכה דיבר אלי חד מנייהו מלכי הרבנים הנז׳ הי״ו בתוך כתבו הטהור ששלח לי עם הסכמתם הרמתה הנז״ל וז״ל גם הפס״ד בענין פאה נכרית מאפס הפנאי לא למדתי בו באורכה כי זכורני מימי קדם בימי מהר״א סתהון ומהר״א שמאע ז״ל המחבר ס׳ קרבן אשר היינו פלוגתייהו ונהגו להיתרא וכעת הסכימו הב״ד יל״ו כוותיה דמר יל״ו וש״ש

הצעיר **משה ח״ר יצחק הררי** ס״ט

(17) Approbation on Covering Hair with a Wig (1889)

Agreement of Rabbis of Aleppo to the above-mentioned decision [of Rabbi Abulafia]

In his humility the great Rabbi has sought our approval for his above-mentioned decision. We are obeying his command and we have examined his ruling, which has discussed the matter at great length. All his words are true and right, and do not need any affirmation. His ruling is a true judgment in the matter of allowing the House of Yaakob [referring to the women] to wear wigs. All of the reasons that he gives are in accordance with *halachah* and we live by his words. Who knows how to come to a decision in *halachah* like him?

Furthermore our women have worn them in front of rabbis of the present and rabbis of old and they have never protested.

We sign here in Aleppo in the month of Iyar 5649 (1889)

Bekhor Mizrahi ***Moshe son of Yitzhak Harari*** ***Yitzhak Labaton***

Rabbi Moshe Harari added some separate words of his own:

I did not have time to analyze the entire ruling on the topic of wigs. However, there is no need to do so because I remember from the days of old in the days of R' Abraham Sutton (see #536) and Rabbi Eliyahu Shamah (see #500), author of the book *Korban*

Isheh, that argued about this topic and the practice was adopted according to the lenient opinion. The court has continued to agree with the decision of our master.

Moshe son of Yitzhak Harari

(18) Recommendation to Wearing Veils (1848-1858)

Rabbi Abraham Antebi (see #63), in his book *Hochmah U'Mussar* (Jerusalem edition 1981, page 106), bemoaned the fall of modesty occurring in his generation and expresses concern about the fact that the Jewish women of Allepo didn't wear veils to cover their faces. He writes the following:

> How could it be that the gentile women wear veils and the Jewish women do not? Furthermore, how could it be that the rabbis don't say anything, not in this generation and not in previous generations?
>
> Actually, the custom of not wearing a veil stemmed from the extreme modesty of the generations of old. Women generally did not go out into the streets but remained in their homes and courtyards. And so, if they needed to go out, the scarf around their head sufficed; they would wrap the scarf around their faces and let only one eye show. But today most women do go into the public area. They cover their head with a scarf, but their faces are revealed. Therefore, we should decree that all women must wear veils besides the scarves to cover their faces.

מודעה ואזהרה

מאת רבותינו מארי דארעא דישראל

ורבנן קשישאי ובתי הדינים

ספרדים ואשכנזים פרושים וחסידים

לזאת ראינו לנו לחובה להודיע בשער בת רבים דעת תוה"ק
לאפרושי מאיסורא, וכפי מה שכבר נתבאר החומר שבדבר בדברי
רבותינו בעלי השו"ע ושאר פוסקים מובהקים זכרונם לברכה שמוטל
חוב קדוש להשגיח בסעודות חתונה וכיוצא בהן, שלא יאכלו אנשים
ונשים בחדר אחד, כי אם האנשים בחדר מיוחד והנשים בחדר
מיוחד, בין בש"ק ובין בחול. וישראל קדושים יתאמצו בכל תוקף
ועוז להעמיד גדרי הצניעות על תלם ולחזק דת משה ויהודית.

(19) Proclamation Against Mixed Seating at Weddings (1906)

(19) Proclamation Against Mixed Seating at Weddings (1906)

In 1906 the rabbis of Jerusalem issued a strongly worded proclamation against mixed seating at weddings. This practice was an obvious indication of a lowering in moral standards in *Eretz Yisrael*, as was the case worldwide. Thirty-five rabbis signed the document. Among the rabbis who were asked to sign were the Aram Soba *Bet Din* of Jerusalem, consisting of R' Haim Shaul Dweck (see #228), R' Yosef Yedid (see #594), and R' Ezra Harari-Raful (see #304). R' Yaacob Haim Sofer (see #532) was also asked to sign.

An Announcement and Warning

From the Rabbis of Israel and the elders of the high courts of Ashkenazim, Sephardim, Perushim, and Hasidim.

Ethics and modesty are the foundation of Jewish life throughout the generations. They are our glory, in which we pride ourselves among all other nations. How much have our rabbis of blessed memory warned us about watching and guarding to avoid mingling of men and women in any situation, whether it be at happy gatherings or otherwise. They constantly made resolutions so as not to breach the fence of morality and to be on guard against all evil. But due to our great sins, we have heard and seen that the people are becoming lenient in this grave sin, especially at happy gatherings. Men and women gather to celebrate in one hall. They turn the happiness of bride and groom into the sin of improper thoughts and a breach in the walls of modesty and proper ethics (Heaven forbid). This is happening publicly; one sin brings along another and this results in single boys and girls mingling in levity and foolishness. This is causing G-d's name and the holiness of Israel to be profaned.

Therefore we have seen that it is our obligation to make known publicly the opinion of our holy Torah to prevent people from sinning. We have previously spoken of the severity of the matter as explained in the words of our rabbis, the *Shulhan Aruch,* and other *halachic* authorities. And we have explained that it is our holy responsibility to take care at wedding feasts and the like that men and women do not eat in one room; rather men in one room and women in another, whether on *Shabbat* or weekdays. Jews are holy and they will try with all of their ability to hold firm the safeguards of modesty and to strengthen the religion. In this merit may we see the full redemption and an immedite salvation in our days, Amen.

By the request of the undersigned, for the honor of G-d during the days of *Shobabim,* 5666 [1906], Jerusalem.

(20) Admonition Against Mixed Seating at Weddings (1848-1858)

R' Abraham Antebi (see #63), in his book *Hochmah U'Mussar* (Jerusalem edition — 1981, page 107), bemoans the fall in modesty occurring in his generation and writes the following:

A new disease has arisen in our day that never was heard of before. It was always the custom that on the night of the wedding, female musicians would play on the ladies' side and male musicians on the men's side. Today the musicians playing on the ladies' side are men and the ladies are dancing in front of the male musicians without realizing what they are doing.

Furthermore, people are accustoming themselves to mixed seating at the wedding celebration and although I have publicly protested this and some G-d-fearing people heeded, many did not. I can testify that from the day these new customs were introduced we have not had a day of rest, only sorrow and pain. We are having economic problems and it is going from bad to worse. How is it that people don't have pity on their livelihood?

The ladies who are modest should speak to their husbands on these issues. Learn from the great women of old who gained so much from their modesty. Learn from the wife of R' Akiba and the many stories recounted in the *Gemara*.

MUSIC

(21) Rambam's Ruling Against Gentile Music (1100's)

The issue of listening to Arabic music goes back to the time of the *Rambam*, who was asked about this problem by the Syrian community. The following is the translation of responsum No. 244 of the *Rambam*:

Question from Aleppo: Is it permissible to listen to Arabic songs and music?

Answer: All music is forbidden, even without words, as it says in the *Gemara Sota* (48a), "The ear that listens to music should be uprooted." The *Gemara* in *Gittin* (7a) explains that there is no difference in the type of instruments used. Any sound that brings pleasure to the soul and stirs the emotions is prohibited. They base themselves on the verse from the prophet (*Hoshea* 9:1) "Rejoice not, Israel, like the exultation of the nations." The reason for this is obvious; this desire must be controlled and held in check so as not to arouse it. [Editor's note: The romantic qualities of music and its potential to stimulate immoral desire are well known.]

We cannot concern ourselves here with individuals who get a spiritual boost from music and get closer to G-dly thinking, and so become humbled. The Torah was written for the majority of people and the norm. As has been said, "Rabbis speak for the general case."

We have already explained in the commentary to *Pirkei Abot* (1:17) that there is no difference between words spoken in Hebrew or Arabic. Words are not permitted or prohibited based on the language in which they are spoken, rather on the content they possess. In truth, words of stupidity should not be listened to even when not in the form of a song. If they are played on an instrument, three sins are transgressed: first, listening to words of nonsense and vulgarity; second, listening to songs; third, listening to instruments; and if people are drinking wine a fourth prohibition is involved as the prophet states, "There are harp and lyre and drum and flute at their drinking parties" (*Yeshayah* 5:12). And if a woman is singing, a fifth sin is involved — that of hearing the voice of a woman, as is stated in *Gemara Berachot* (24a), "A woman's voice is equivalent to an immodest exposure, surely when she is singing."

We have explained and proven clearly that the purpose of the Jewish people is to become a holy nation and we should not involve ourselves in actions or speech unless they are bringing us to perfection or a step towards perfection. We should not arouse drives within us that bring us to no good and make us uninhibited in foolishness and merriment. We have explained this already in the book *Moreh Nevuchim*.

The music that the *Geonim* (Rabbis of the era before the *Rishonim*) have permitted is that of hymn and praise [to G-d]. Heaven forbid to include mundane song in that category. Such a statement could not be said by the Jewish people, not by a *gaon* or a simple person. It is impossible to say that these songs are sung among worthy people. I don't believe worthy people would be in such places where alcoholic beverages are consumed. We have explained all of this in *Moreh Nevuchim*. And they surely are not worthy if they are listening to instruments besides the songs.

With wishes of peace, Moshe

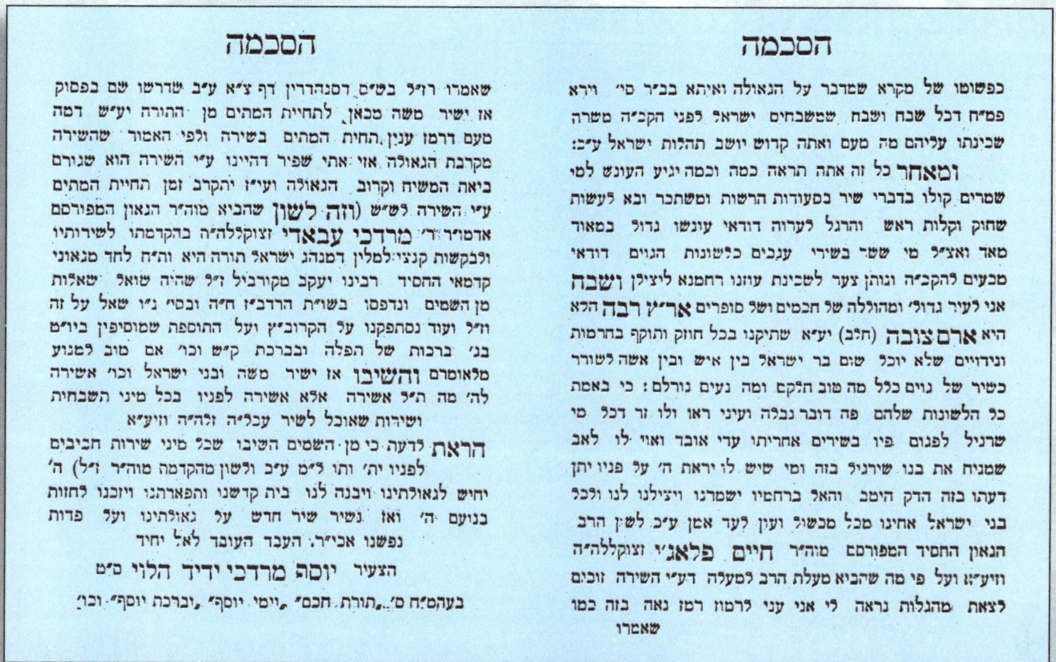

הסכמה

כפשוטו של מקרא שמדבר על הגאולה ואיתא בב״ר סי׳ וירא פמ״ח דכל שבח ושבח שמשבחים ישראל לפני הקב״ה משרה שכינתו עליהם מה מעם ואתה קדוש יושב תהלות ישראל ע״כ:

ומאחר כל זה אתה תראה כמה וכמה יגיע העונש למי שמרים קולו בדברי שיר בסעודות הרשות ומשתכר ובא לעשות שחוק וקלות ראש והרגל לערוה דודאי עונשו גדול במאוד מאד ואצ״ל מי ששר בשירי עגבים כלשונות הגוים דודאי מכעים להקב״ה וגוהן צער לשכינת עוזנו רחמנא ליצילן ושבח אני לעיר גדול׳ ומהוללה של חכמים ושל סופרים אר״ץ רבה הלא היא ארם צובה (ח״ב) יע״א שתיקנו בכל חוזק ותוקף בחרמות ונידויים שלא יוכל שום בר ישראל בין איש ובין אשה לשורר כשיר של גוים כלל מה טוב חלקם ומה נעים גורלם: כי באמת כל הלשונות שלהם פה דובר נבלה ועיני ראו ולו זר דכל מי שרגיל לפגום פיו בשירים אחריתו עדי אובד ואוי לו לאב שמניח את בנו שירגיל בזה ומי שיש לו יראת ה׳ על פניו יתן דעתו בזה הדק היטב והאל ברחמיו ישמרנו ויצילנו לנו ולכל בני ישראל אחינו מכל מכשול ועון לעד אמן ע״כ לש״ן הרב הגאון החסיד המפורסם מוה״ר חיים פלאג״י זצוקללה״ה וזיע״א ועל פי מה שהביא מעלת הרב למעלה דע״י השירה זוכים לצאת מהגלות נראה לי אני עני לרמוז רמז נאה בזה כמו שאמרו

הסכמה

שאמרו רז״ל בש״ס דסנהדרין דף צ״א ע״ב שדרשו שם בפסוק אז ישיר משה מכאן לתחיית המתים מן ההורה יע״ש דמה טעם דרמז ענין תחית המתים בשירה ולפי האמור שהשירה מקרבת הגאולה אזי אתי שפיר דהיינו ע״י השירה הוא שגורם ביאת המשיח וקרוב הגאולה ועי״ז יתקרב זמן תחיית המתים ע״י השירה לש״ש (וזה לשון שהביא מוה״ר הגאון המפורסם אדמו״ר ר׳ מרדכי עבאדי זצוקללה״ה בהקדמתו לשירותיו ולבקשות קנצי למלין דמנהג ישראל תורה היא והי״ח לחד מגאוני קדמאי החסיד רבינו יעקב מקורביל ז״ל שהיה שואל שאלות מן השמים ונדפסו בשו״ת הרדב״ז ח״ה ובסי׳ נ״ו שאל על זה וז״ל ועוד נסתפקנו על הקרוב״ץ ועל התוספת שמוסיפין ביו״ט בג׳ ברכות של הפלה ובברכת ק״ש וכו׳ אם טוב למנוע מלאומרם והשיבו אז ישיר משה ובני ישראל וכו׳ אשירה לה׳ מה ה״ל אשירה אלא אשירה לפניו בכל מיני השבחות ושירות שאוכל לשיר עכל״ה זלה״ה וזיע״א

הראת לדעה כי מן השמים השיבו שכל מיני שירות חביבים לפניו ית׳ ותו ל״מ ע״כ ולשון מהקדמה מוה״ר ז״ל) ה׳ יחיש לגאולתינו ויבנה לנו בית קדשנו ותפארתנו ויזכנו לחזות בנועם ה׳ ואז נשיר שיר חדש על גאולתינו ועל פדות נפשנו אכי״ר. העבד העובד לאל יחיד

הצעיר יוסף מרדכי ידיד הלוי ס״ט

בעהמ״ח ס׳ ,,תורת חכם״ ,,ימי יוסף״ ,,וברכת יוסף״ וכו׳

(22) Letter Against Gentile Music (1928)

(22) Letter Against Gentile Music (1928)

Many rabbis expressed concern over the years with the negative effects of gentile music. R' Haim Palagi (see #449) in his book *Nefesh Haim* mentions a ban on such music that originated in Aleppo. This is quoted by R' Yosef Yedid (see #594) in his introduction to the first printing of R' Moshe Ashear's book of *pizmonim* (hymns) titled *Hallel VeZimrah* (see #88):

After all that has been written about singing songs of praise to G-d you realize the great punishment that will befall anyone who raises his voice in song at a party that is not for the purpose of a *mitzvah* and becomes drunk. Eventually this brings to foolishness, levity, and promiscuity and then surely his punishment will be great.

It goes without saying that someone who sings love songs in the gentile tongue is definitely angering G-d and causes pain to His Divine Presence.

I praise the great city of rabbis and scribes, the great city of Aram Soba, which made strong resolutions with threats of bans and excommunication against any Jew, man or woman, who sings gentile songs. Fortunate is their portion and sweet is their lot. In truth all gentile songs are vulgarities.

I saw with my own eyes that whoever accustomed himself to defile his mouth was destined for destruction. Woe to the father that permits his son to get involved in such music. Even if he is going to a wedding, it is sinful to permit his young son to go. A man who is G-d fearing will take great care in this area. May G-d in His mercy protect us and save us and the entire nation of Israel from sin.

ORGANIZATIONS OF CONCERN

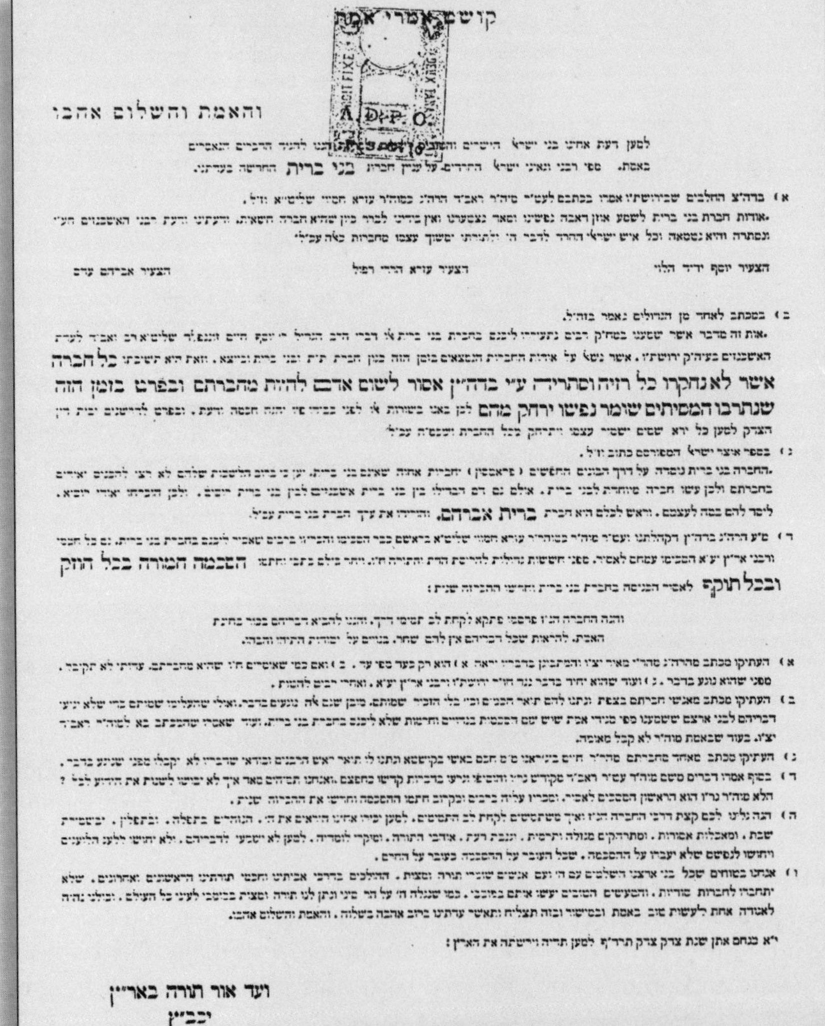

קושט אמרי אמת

והאמת והשלום אהבו

הצעיר יוסף ידיד הלוי — הצעיר עזרא הררי רפול — הצעיר אברהם עדס

ועד אור תורה בארי"ן

יכב"ץ

(23) Proclamation About B'nai B'rith (1924)

[Editor's Note: This letter has no reference to the B'nai B'rith activities of today, rather to a religious concern in Aleppo.]

(23) Proclamation About B'nai B'rith (1924)

In 5684 (1924), eighty years after the B'nai B'rith organization had been founded in New York, B'nai B'rith's main branch in the Middle East decided to open Bnai Brith branches in Aleppo and Damascus.

Among B'nai B'rith's avowed goals were: "mutual aid, charity, promoting ethics, and strengthening ties and fraternity between Jews and their neighbors." Today, one hears of the association's activities, most of which are concentrated in its Anti-Defamation League which fights anti-Semitism and promotes human rights.

However, the last of B'nai B'rith's goals — "strengthening ties and fraternity between Jews and their neighbors" — had the potential of causing serious damage to people's commitment to Judaism. Perceptive Torah sages foresaw the organization's danger and the future tragedies it might inflict on the Jewish people. They warned against the spiritual danger lying in wait for anyone who came in contact with them.

Like other faithful Jewish communities, the holy community of Aram Soba didn't permit B'nai B'rith to gain a foothold in their community. Dr. Yosef Yakir Behar led a group of officials from B'nai B'rith's Middle East office which arrived from Constantinople looking for representatives among Aleppo's Jews. After an exhausting search, they found several naive Jews who were willing to head B'nai B'rith's new office.

The launching of the Aleppo branch led to a huge conflict in the community. When the heads of the *Bet Din*, chief among them R' Ezra Hamway (see #272), heard about its formation, they fiercely fought the new initiative. R' Ezra published a fiery announcement in which he assailed and denounced the establishment of the organization. He explained that the leaders of B'nai B'rith were not revealing their true motives, which were the introduction of foreign ideas that were likely to make the people stray from the way of G-d. They might even aim to blur the boundaries between a Jew and a non-Jew, thereby leading to intermarriage.

The result of Hacham Ezra's admonitions and fierce protests was that the initial support and sympathy that had greeted the Bnai Brith representatives faded away completely. Those community leaders who had agreed to establish the branch were unable to brush off the views of the Aleppo *Bet Din* and public opinion. They withdrew their membership from the B'nai B'rith organization.

When the organization's representatives and founders saw how difficult it was to get a foothold in Aleppo, they decided to go all out to prove that they were "kosher." At first, they approached the *Rishon LeSion* (Chief Rabbi of *Eretz Yisrael)*, R' Yaakov Meir. They sent him a detailed letter in which they listed the suspicions of the Aleppo rabbis and scholars against them, and asked him to write his opinion of them to the heads of the community.

This is the contents of the letter which they sent to Jerusalem:

B"H, Aleppo, 27 Tamuz 5784 (1924)

B'nai B'rith Association

Adar II during *Purim*

The honored Dr. Yakir, the chief executive of the B'nai B'rith office in Constantinople, came to our city to found a branch in Aleppo. This matter is new and strange in the eyes of our community, and the *hachamim, rabbanim,* and *dayanim* have suspicions about whether this association will in some way oppose Judaism, G-d forbid. We therefore ask the great *Rav* and *gaon* of Jerusalem, the *Rishon LeSion,* Yaakov Meir, to inform us his words of truth.

The *Rishon LeSion*, R' Yaakov Meir, sent the following message in a telegram from Jerusalem to the head of the community: "I recommend Dr. Yakir Behar of the B'nai B'rith association with all my heart as being faithful to our holy religion."

When the head of the local B'nai B'rith community board received the telegram, he assembled all the community board members for a special meeting in which they decided, "We accept with favor and good will the founding of the honored association, according to its conditions, to uphold and uplift our nation both physically and spiritually, which is its sole purpose."

The community board published an announcement containing the telegram it received from R' Yaakov Meir, in addition to letters sent to the *Rosh Av Bet Din* of Aleppo from various rabbis throughout the world who fully supported the association. Their intention was to soften the *Rosh Av Bet Din's* views and convince him of the innocent goals of the association. In this way they hoped he would remove his staunch opposition to it.

But this tactic didn't succeed, and R' Ezra continued to fiercely oppose the B'nai B'rith branch in Aleppo. B'nai B'rith then responded by getting letters of approval from rabbis in other cities and even claiming that R' Ezra had retracted his position.

At this point, the honor of Torah was defended by a committee of Aram Soba sages, organized as the *Torah Ohr Committee*. They issued a proclamation in which they recounted the developments of the affair together with the resolute opinion of the *Rosh Av Bet Din*. They also publicized the letters which several Aleppo rabbis living in Jerusalem had sent to R' Ezra expressing their negative opinion of B'nai B'rith, consisting of R' Yosef Yedid (see #594), R' Ezra Harari-Raful, and R' Abraham Ades (see #37).

The Jerusalem sages had also sent to Aleppo the letter of the Ashkenazic Chief Rabbi of Jerusalem, R' Yosef Chaim Sonnenfeld, who had issued a warning against the association. He had written, "No one may join any association, whose open and covert agenda was not investigated by the *Bet Din*, particularly in these days when those who incite [against Judaism] have increased. One who cares about his soul should keep distant from them."

Due to the far-reaching wisdom and courage of R' Ezra and the other Aleppo sages, the attempt to found a B'nai B'rith branch in the city failed. The association's representatives were forced to return to their cities and countries, and the Aleppo Jews were saved from their detrimental influence.

The proclamation by the sages of the *Torah Ohr Committee* of Aleppo is presented below::

The Adorned Words of Truth
Love Truth and Peace

To make it known to our Jewish brothers that are upright, good to G-d and good to people, we hereby present the words of truth from our rabbis concerning the new chapter of B'nai B'rith that was started in our community.

1. The *Bet Din* of Aleppo in Jerusalem wrote the following to the head of our court, the crown of our head, R' Ezra Hamway *shlit'a*:

"The news concerning the B'nai B'rith organization has pained our souls and hurt us greatly. We do not have the ability to analyze their ways because they are a secret organization. Our opinion and the opinion of the Ashkenazi rabbis (may G-d guard over them) is that "whatever is in hiding is contaminated." [Editor's note: The literal application of this principle is in reference to a married woman secluded with another man. It is being used figuratively here to indicate that any covert organization whose motives are not clear must be assumed to have hidden contaminants.] Any G-d fearing Jew who is concerned with the word of G-d and his Torah must remove himself from such organizations.

Yosef Yedid ***Ezra Harari-Raful*** ***Abraham Ades***

2. Rav Yosef Chaim Sonnenfeld was asked about organizations like B'nai B'rith that are currently common. His reply was that it is forbidden to join any organization whose secrets and hidden practices have not been checked with the *Bedatz* (Rabbinical High Court). Especially in our times, when the enticers have increased, anyone concerned about his soul should distance himself from them. It is the obligation of public speakers and rabbinical courts to make this known so that all G-d-fearing people will distance themselves.

3. In the encyclopedia of Jewish topics called *Otzar Yisrael* it is written: The *Bnai Brith* organization was founded on the principles of the Free Masons, which were clubs that did not allow Jews. Therefore they started a group called *B'nai B'rith.* [Editor's note: Literally, "sons of the *brith*" or covenant, referring to the *brit milah*.]

4. The rabbis of our Rabbinical Court and their leader, the crown of our head, R' Ezra Hamway, have proclaimed a prohibition against joining B'nai B'rith and all the other rabbis of Aleppo have agreed with them. This was due to their great concern over the destruction to our Torah and religion, Heaven forbid. They have jointly signed a strong agreement and published a second proclamation of the same nature.

The B'nai B'rith organization has issued a poster to attract uninformed people. We will quote their information and analyze it:

A) They quote a letter from R' Yaacob Meir. If one read his words carefully, he himself says he is basing his opinion on secondhand information. Furthermore, if he belongs to the organization as they claim, he is biased and his testimony can't be accepted. Lastly, his opinion is an individual opinion against the many respected rabbis of Jerusalem and Aleppo, and the majority overrides an individual.

B) They quote a letter from members of their organization in Safed and they give them the title "Rabbi" without mentioning their names. Obviously as members of the organization they are biased. Perhaps they concealed their names because thay don't want their community to know of their involvement. It has been told to us by reliable sources that many communities have strong bans against joining B'nai B'rith to the point of excommunication. They also claim that they sent their letter to R' Hamway and he received it, but the fact of the matter is that he didn't receive anything.

C) They quote from a member of the group, Haim Bigarno of Constantinople, and they have even given him the title Chief Rabbi. His words are also not acceptable because he is biased as well.

D) At the end they misquote R' Hamway. We are amazed at the lack of shame on their part. How can they attempt to contradict what is well known? R' Hamway was the first to come out against them. He publicly proclaims his opposition and has recently signed a second letter.

5. We have revealed a few examples of the ways of this organization and how they prey on the hearts of the uninformed. We have done this so that G-d-fearing Jews who are careful with prayer, *tefillin*, *Shabbat,* and *kashrut*, who keep away from unethical business practices, and who love Torah and respect those who study it should not pay attention to them. Do not be concerned with their taunting; be more concerned with your soul and do not disobey the ruling [of the rabbis] as it states, "Whoever disobeys a rabbinical ruling is as though he transgresses an excommunication."

6. We are confident that all of our people — who are at peace with G-d, who observe the Torah and *mitzvot,* and who walk in the path of our forefathers and our Torah scholars of today and yesteryear — will not join any secret clubs. All good deeds should be done publicly just as G-d publicly revealed himself on Mount Sinai and gave us the Torah and *mitzvot*.

May we all become united in recognizing what is good, true, and upright and with this we will see success and our community will be blessed with peace and tranquility. Peace and truth shall be loved.

11th of the month of comfort (Av) 5684

The "Light of Torah" Committee, Aleppo

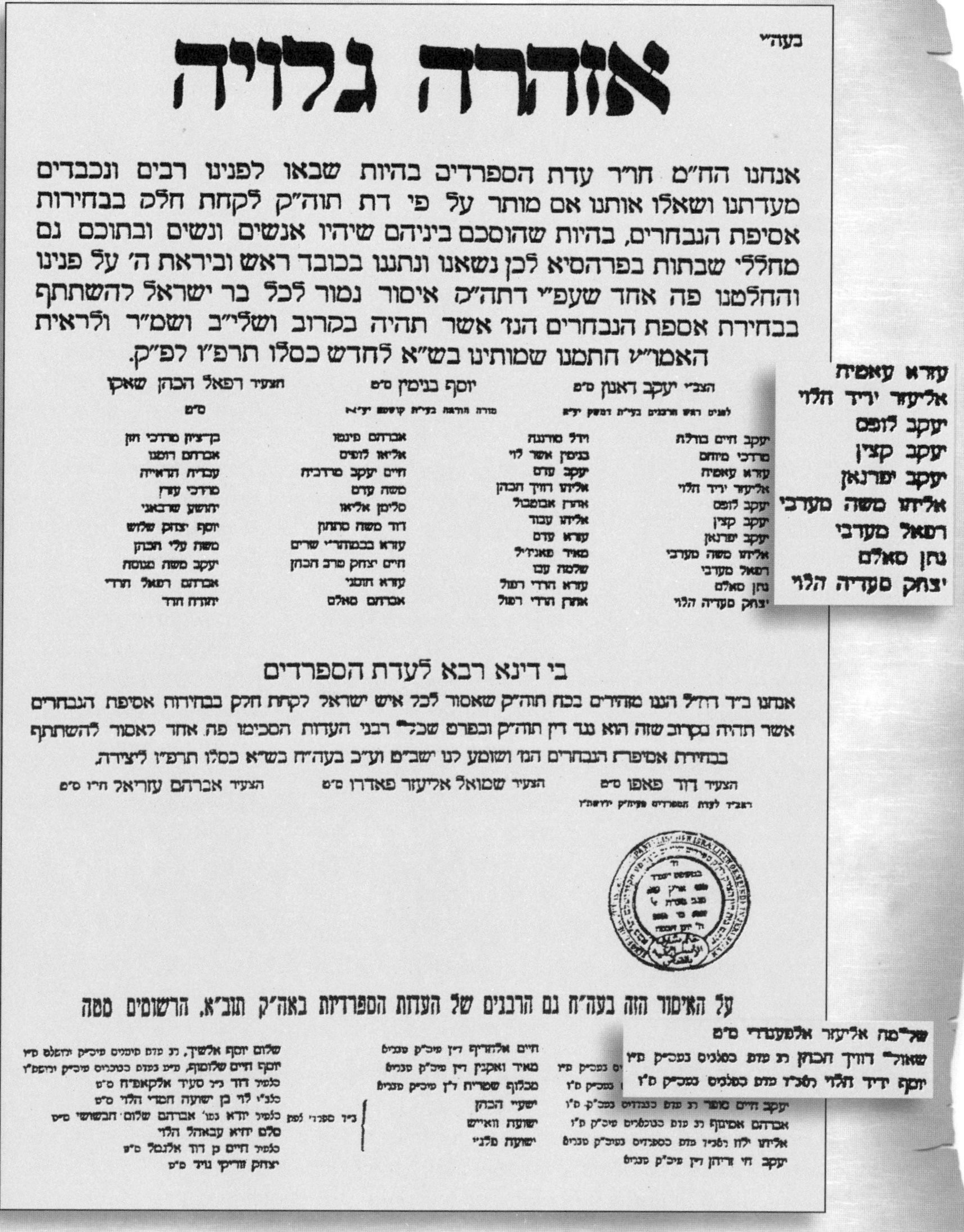

בעה"י

אזהרה גלויה

אנחנו הח"מ חו"ר עדת הספרדים בהיות שבאו לפנינו רבים ונכבדים מעדתנו ושאלו אותנו אם מותר על פי דת תוה"ק לקחת חלק בבחירות אסיפת הנבחרים, בהיות שהוסכם ביניהם שיהיו אנשים ונשים ובתוכם גם מחללי שבתות בפרהסיא לכן נשאנו ונתננו בכובד ראש וביראת ה' על פנינו והחלטנו פה אחד שעפ"י דתה"ק איסור נמור לכל בר ישראל להשתתף בבחירת אספת הנבחרים הנז' אשר תהיה בקרוב ושלי"ב ושמ"ר ולראית האמו"ע חתמנו שמותינו בש"א לחדש כסלו תרפ"ו לפ"ק.

הצב"י יעקב דאנון ס"ט — יוסף בנימין ס"ט — הצעיר רפאל הכהן שאקו ס"ט

יעקב חיים בולת	וידל סורנגה	אברהם פינטו	בן־ציון מרדכי חזן
מרדכי מיוחס	בנימין אשר לוי	אליאו לופיס	אברהם רוסנו
עזרא עאמיח	יעקב עדס	חיים יעקב מרדכיה	עבדיה הדאייה
אליעזר יריד הלוי	אליהו רוויך הכהן	משה עדס	מרדכי עדן
יעקב לופס	אהרן אבומבול	סלימן אליאו	יהושע שרבאני
יעקב קצין	אליהו עבוד	דוד משה מתתון	יוסף יצחק שלוש
יעקב יפרנאן	עזרא עדס	עזרא בבמוהרר"י שרים	משה עלי הכהן
אליהו משה מערבי	מאיר פאניז'ל	חיים יצחק מרב הכהן	יעקב משה מנוסה
רפאל מערבי	שלמה עבו	עזרא חומסי	אברהם רפאל הודי
נתן סאלם	עזרא הודי רפול	אברהם סאלם	יהודה הוד
יצחק סעדיה הלוי	אהרן הודי רפול		

עזרא עאמיח
אליעזר יריד הלוי
יעקב לופס
יעקב קצין
יעקב יפרנאן
אליהו משה מערבי
רפאל מערבי
נתן סאלם
יצחק סעדיה הלוי

בי דינא רבא לעדת הספרדים

אנחנו ב"ד הח"ל הננו מזהירים בכח תוה"ק שאסור לכל איש ישראל לקחת חלק בבחירות אסיפת הנבחרים אשר תהיה בקרוב שזה הוא נגד דין תוה"ק וכפרט שכל" רבני העדות הסכימו פה אחד לאסור להשתתף בבחירת אסיפת הנבחרים הנז' ושומע לנו ישב"ט וע"ב בעה"ח בש"א כסלו תרפ"ו ליצירה.

הצעיר דוד פאפו ס"ט — הצעיר שמואל אליעזר פאדרו ס"ט — הצעיר אברהם עוזיאל חיו ס"ט

על האיסור הזה בעה"ח גם הרבנים של העדות הספרדיות באה"ק תוב"א, הרשומים מטה

שלמה אליעזר אלפאנדרי ס"ט
שאול רוויך הכהן
יוסף יריד הלוי
יעקב חיים סופר
אברהם אפינוף
אליהו ילוז
יעקב חי זריהן

חיים אלהדיף
מאיר ואקנין
מכלוף שטרית
ישעיי הכהן
ישועה וואייש
ישועה פלג'י

שלום יוסף אלשיך
יוסף חיים שלוסוף
דוד אלקאפח
לוי בן ישועה חמדי הלוי
יודא נסו' אברהם שלום חבשושי
סלם יודא עבאהל הלוי
חיים בן דוד אלנמל
יצחק זריקי נויד

(24) Proclamation Against Participation in the Secular Zionist Party (1926)

(24) Proclamation Against Participation in the Secular Zionist Party (1926)

In the year 1926 the secular Zionists organized a political party known as the *Vaad Leumi*. The Sephardic rabbis of Israel signed a proclamation against participating in it due to the irreligious practices of the candidates. An English translation of the proclamation is provided here.

An Open Warning

We the undersigned rabbis of the Sephardic community are responding to the question posed to us by many respectable people of our congregation concerning whether it is permissible based on the laws of our holy Torah to take part in the voting (by the *Vaad Leumi*) for their candidates. Our considerations are: first, they have decided to have men and women together as candidates; second, some among them desecrate *Shabbat* publicly.Therefore we have discussed the matter very seriously and with the fear of G-d and have decided that it is absolutely forbidden for any Jew to participate in the voting that will take place in the near future. We have signed below in the month of Kislev 5686 (1926).

Yaakob Danun
Yosef Binyamin
Raphael Shako
Yaakob Burla
Mordechai Meyuchas
Ezra Attiah
Eliezer Yedid
Yaakob Lofez
Yaakob Kassin
Yaakob Ifergan
Eliyahu Ma'arabi
Ezra Ades
Meir Panigel
Shelomo Abu
Ezra Harari-Raful
Aharon Harari-Raful
Abraham Pinto
Eliyahu Lofez
Raphael Ma'arabi
Natan Salem
Yitzchak Saadiah Levy
Vidal Sorgona
Binyamin Asher Levy
Yaacob Ades
Eliyahu Dweck
Aharon Abotbol
Eliyahu Aboud
Haim Mordebeya
Moshe Ades
Suleman Eliyahu
David Moshe Sutton
Ezra Shrem
Haim Yitzhak Tarab
Ezra Husney
Abraham Salem
Ben-Sion Hazan
Abraham Dumano
Obadiah Hedaya
Mordechai Ezran
Yehoshua Shaharbani
Yosef Shalush
Moshe Tawil
Yaakob Mounsa
Abraham Harari
Yaakob Hadad

Over 20 additional rabbis signed, among them, R' Shelomo Eliezer Alfandri, R' Shaul Dweck, R' Yosef Yedid, and R' Yaakob Haim Sofer.

PRINTING

(25) Proclamation Concerning Printing Press (1865)

In 1865 R' Abraham Sasson (see #475) and his sons, R' Eliyahu Hai (see #477) and R' Moshe Hai, opened the first Jewish printing press in Aram Soba. This was seen as a great benefit to the community and so, to help the Sasson family protect their investment, 52 rabbis of Aram Soba issued an official endorsement of the new venture. The proclamation prohibited anyone from starting a competing press over a period of 20 years. This was upheld to the extent that even after the Sassons moved the press to *Eretz Yisrael* seven years after its inception, R' Yeshayah

Dayan (see #203) waited another 13 years before starting his own press, in compliance with the ban. The document is as follows:

> Eliyahu the son of Abraham Sasson has decided to open a printing press to benefit the Jewish community and to glorify the Torah. He traveled out of town for a year to learn the trade and he invested much time and effort to learn the intricate process involved in this holy work. Great expenses were involved besides the payment to the printers to teach him the trade. He also had no income during that time to support his family. Additional expenses were incurred in the purchasing of all the printing equipment.
>
> Rav Eliyahu [Sasson] has expressed concern that others not go into competition with him and cause him great financial loss. He has asked us to protect him from such an occurrence. We the undersigned are responding to a proper request and are hereby making a firm decision to forbid anyone from opening a competing press. Anyone who does so will be considered transgressing against a *herem* [ban] and liable to excommunication. This ban includes those who dwell in our country and those who don't. It includes Jew and gentile, even with government permission. It includes men or women. There is no difference between large or small letters whether in block letters or *Rashi* script. If a Moslem or Christian on his own decides to open a printing press, no Jew is permitted to work there or to print books there.
>
> All this has been decided with the force of a Torah ban. If anyone should violate it, there will come down upon him all the curses of the Torah and he will be bitten by the bite of the rabbis, which has no healing. Anyone who maliciously ignores the ban will be pursued to destruction.
>
> This ban is for 20 years from this day. Whoever listens to us will dwell in peace and tranquility protected from all fears. Those that listen to us will be blessed with sweetness and all good. All Jews are holy and should be blessed tenfold by G-d Almighty and should blossom like roses.
>
> We the undersigned, Aleppo, 9 Iyar 5625 (1865)

Haim Mordechai Labaton
Shalom Chasky
Raphael Shelomo Nehmad
Moshe Sutton
Ezra Chasky
Yitzhak Shrem
Shaul Dweck
Abraham Dayan
Shalom Lahmi
Haim Shaul Abadi
Abraham Laniado
Ezra Attiah
Eliyahu Mishan
David Kassin
Ezra Abadi
Michael Ashkenazi
Yitzhak Harari
Yitzhak Antebi
Shalom Mizrahi
Yaacob Abadi
Mordechai Abadi
Shelomo Safdeyé
Aharon Choueka
Raphael Moshe Sasson
Eliezar Labaton
Haim Ashkenazi
Yosef Labaton
Yitzhak Dayan
Yedidyah Dayan
Moshe Eliyahu Swed
Shmuel Dweck
Moshe Cohen
Moshe Swed
Menashe Matloub Sutton
Nissim Yeshayah Harari
Ezra Tawil
Yisrael Sasson
Mordechai Labaton
Yitzchak Labaton
Ephraim Abadi
Shimon Mizrahi
Yehudah Attiah
Eliyahu Hamway
Moshe Abraham Dayan
Moshe Tawil
Abraham Kassin
Eliyahu Sasson
Shaul Dayan
Hiyya Harari
Eliyahu Dweck
Nissim Swed
Yeshayah Chasky

[Note : The above document is quoted from the book *Hebrew printing in Middle Eastern Lands* by Abraham Yeiri (Jerusalem 1936) pages 36-37.]

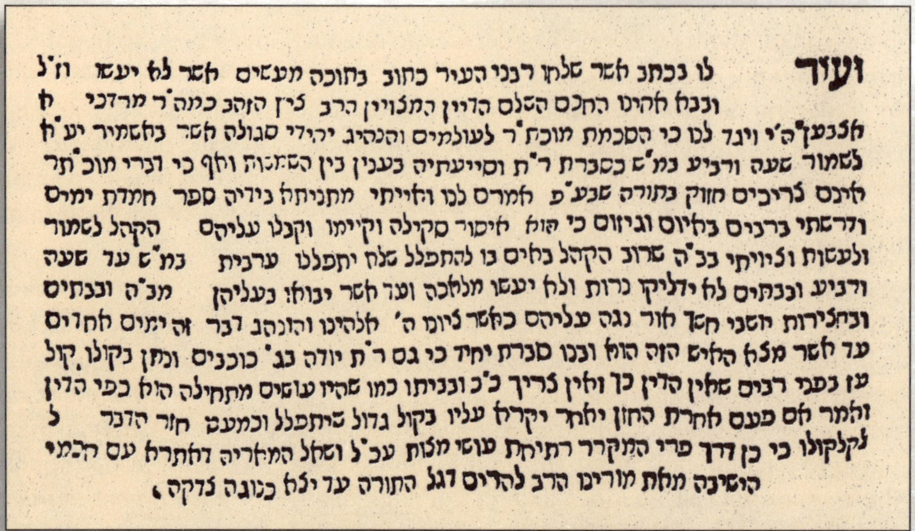

ועוד לו נכתב אשר שלחו רבני העיר כחוב בתוכה מעשים אשר לא יעשו וז"ל
ובנא אחינו החכם השלם הדיין המצויין הרב כליל הזהב כמה"ר מרדכי א
אצבען ה"י ויגד לנו כי הסכמת מוכת"ר לעולמים והנהיג יחידי סגולה אשר באזמיר יע"א
לשמור שעה ורביע במ"ש כסברת ר"ת וסייעתיה בענין בין השמשות ואף כי דברי מוכ"תר
אינם צריכים חזוק בתורה שבע"פ אמרם לנו ואייתי מתניתא בידיה ספר חמדת ימים
ודרשתי ברבים באיום וגיזום כי הוא איסור סקילה וקיימו וקבלו עליהם הקהל לשמור
ולעשות וצויתי בב"ה שרוב הקהל באים בו להתפלל שלא יתפללו ערבית במ"ש עד שעה
ורביע ובבתים לא ידליקו נרות ולא יעשו מלאכה ועד אשר יבואו בעליהן מב"ה ובבתים
ובאפירות חשכי חשך אור נגה עליהם כאשר צוה ה' אלהינו והונהג דבר זה ימים אחדים
עד אשר מצא האיש הזה הוא ובנו סברת יחיד כי גם ר"ת יודה בג' כוכבים ונתן בקולו קול
עז נפני רבים שאין הדין כן ואין צריך כ"כ ובניתו כמו שהיו עושים מתחילה הוא כפי הדין
והאמר אם פעם אחרת החזן יאחר יקרא עליו בקול גדול שיתפלל וכמעט חזר הדבר ל
קלקולו כי כן דרך פרי המקרר רתיחת עושי מצות עכ"ל ושאל המורה דאתרא עם הבמי
הושיבה מאת מורינו הרב להרים דגל התורה עד יצא כנוגה צדקה ׃

(26) Waiting 72 Minutes After Sunset to End Shabbat (1700's)

(26) Waiting 72 Minutes After Sunset to End Shabbat (1700's)

R' Shemuel Laniado (see #372) was the Chief Rabbi of Aram Soba for more than 40 years. On more than one occasion of religious turmoil in his community, he requested the help of R' Haim Abulafia, Chief Rabbi of Tiberias, previously of Izmir, Turkey, and considered the leading Sephardic authority of his generation.

R' Laniado had heard of a measure for enhanced religious observance instituted by R' Abulafia and tried to do the same. However, he encountered some resistance. The following is a translation of the letter which he wrote to R' Abulafia on this issue. [Editor's note: As with all matters of *halachah,* consult your rabbi. These documents are being provided for their historical signifigance, not for *halachah* purposes.]

> Some time ago the great rabbi and judge, the golden crown, Rabbi Mordechai Atzban (see #122), told us about the observance that you instituted in your congregation in Izmir to wait an hour and a quarter on *Motza'e Shabbat*, following the opinion of Rabbeinu Tam concerning twilight. Although your words do not need strengthening, I announced them publicly and admonished the people, reminding them that [the desecration of *Shabbat*] is a sin with the punishment of stoning. They all accepted upon themselves to fulfill this *halachah*. I directed that in the main synagogue, where the majority of people pray, they should not start the *Arbit* service until an hour and a quarter has passed and that no fire be lit in the homes or any forbidden activity be done until the husbands return. With the houses cloaked in darkness, the holy light will shine upon them as our G-d has commanded us.
>
> We were successful in accustoming the people to this for a short time until a particular individual and his son found a minority opinion, which holds that even

Rabbeinu Tam agrees to [ending *Shabbat* after] three stars [are visible]. He publicly announced in a loud voice in the synagogue that the law is not such [to wait an hour and a quarter] and the way we had done it previously is the proper law. He threatened that if the *hazzan* waits to start he will scream at him. We have almost returned to the previous custom, which is the way of those people who throw cold water on others who want to do a *mitzvah*. We request of you to uplift the flag of Torah and clarify the matter.

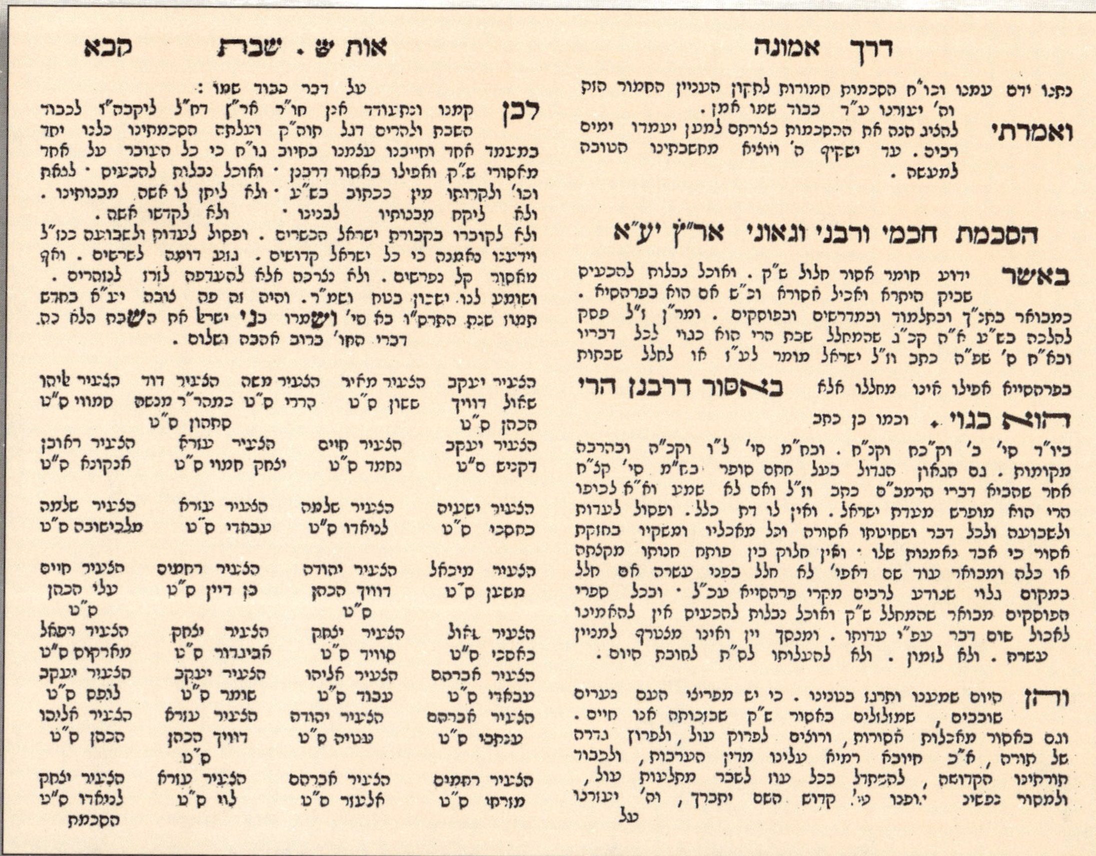

דרך אמונה

אות ש. שבת קכא

הסכמת חכמי ורבני וגאוני אר״ץ יע״א

(27) Resolution Against the Desecration of Shabbat (1906)

(27) Resolution Against the Desecration of Shabbat (Aleppo 1906)

In 1906 the scholars and rabbis of Aram Soba gathered together and approved strong measures to be taken against those who desecrated *Shabbat*. This initiative was under the leadership of the Chief Rabbi of Aram Soba, R' Yaakob Dweck (see #248). The resolution was subsequently adopted by the leading scholars and rabbis of the entire region.

The text of the Aram Soba resolution is given below. It has also been published in R' Dweck's book *Derech Emunah*.

It is well known that the desecration of the holy *Shabbat* and the intentional eating of nonkosher meat are serious violations, as detailed in the *Tanach, Gemara,*

Midrashim, and *Poskim [halachic* authorities]. Furthermore, the *Shulhan Aruch (Orach Chaim*, sec. 123) states that a person who descrates *Shabbat* is effectively a non-Jew and should be treated as such in all matters. The *Shulhan Aruch* also states (*Orach Chaim*, sec. 385) that any Jew who practices heathen religions or publicly violates the laws of *Shabbat*, even those which are Rabbinical in origin, is to be treated as a non-Jew. This ruling also appears in various other locations within the *Shulhan Aruch*, including *Yoreh Deah* (sec. 2, 128, and 158) and *Hoshen Mishpat* (sec. 36 and 125).

Furthermore, the great rabbi, *Chatam Sofer,* writes (in *Hoshen Mishpat* sec. 198, after quoting the *Rambam*): "If it is not possible to coerce him, he must be isolated from the Jewish community and treated as though he has no religion. He is ineligible to testify or swear in a Jewish court or for any legal action, any animal that he has slaughtered is nonkosher, and any food or drink that he provides is assumed to be nonkosher because he can no longer be trusted. And this applies whether his store is open [and visible], partially or completely." He also states that even if the desecration of *Shabbat* was not in the presence of ten people, as long as it occurred in a place that was visible and known to the public, it is considered to be a public desecration.

It is clear from the writings of all the *halachic* authorities that any person who desecrates the holy *Shabbat* or knowingly eats nonkosher meat cannot be trusted to attest to the *kashrut* of any food. Also his contact with wine makes it *nesech* [nonkosher] and he cannot be counted into the ten people who are needed for a *minyan* [in a religious service], or into the three people needed for *zimun* [group blessing after a meal], or to be called up to the Torah reading [in the synagogue] for any of the required blessings.

We have recently heard and are outraged that there are in our midst transgressors and delinquents who scorn the restrictions of *Shabbat* (whose merit justifies our very existence), who scorn the prohibitions against eating nonkosher foods, and who would like to throw off their constraints and break out of the framework of Torah. Accordingly, the honor of the holy Torah and the principle of communal responsibility make it our duty to expend every effort to stop these offensive practices, and to sacrifice our very lives for the honor of *Hashem*'s holy Name, and may *Hashem* help us in this.

Therefore, we, the scholars and rabbis of Aram Soba (for the sake of the Unification of the Holy One, Blessed is He, and His Presence) are taking a stand for the honor of *Shabbat* and for the flag of our holy Torah. And we hereby join together in a united front to commit ourselves with firmness, but with love, that anyone who violates any of the prohibitions of the holy *Shabbat*, including prohibitions that are Rabbinical in origin, and anyone who knowingly eats nonkosher food, will be called a heretic as described in the *Shulhan Aruch*, and we will not let him marry our daughters, nor will we accept his daughters for our sons, nor will we marry a woman to him, nor will we allow him to be buried among the graves of observant Jews, and he will be ineligible to testify or swear in a Jewish court or for any legal action as mentioned above. However, we are confident that all Jews are holy, the branch is like the roots, and they avoid even a minor violation. And so it is only necessary to improve the responsiveness of those [who are basically] observant. And whoever listens to us [and obeys] shall dwell in security and without fear.

And we are here in Soba (may *Hashem* build our city) in the month of Tamuz 5666 (1906), the 24th day, as indicated in [the *gematria* of the verse] "And the Children of Yisrael shall keep the *Shabbat*" (*Shemot* 31:16).

And here are the [names] of the scholars and rabbis, with [wishes of] great love and peace.

Ezra Levi	***Yeshayah Chasky***	***Eliyahu Aboud***
Moshe Harari	***Shelomo Malki Shuba***	***Abraham Abadi***
Meir Sasson	***Ezra Abadi***	***Yaakob Lofez***
Yaakob Shaul Dweck	***Yehudah Dweck***	***Yaakob Shomer***
Eliyahu Hamway	***Michael Mishan***	***Yehudah Attiah***
David Menashe Sutton	***Haim Cohen***	***Abraham Antebi***
Haim Nehmad	***Rahamim Ben Dayan***	***Eliyahu Cohen***
Yaakob Daknes	***Yitzhak Swed***	***Ezra Dweck***
Reuven Ancona	***Yeshayah Chasky***	***Abraham Elazar***
Ezra Yitzhak Hamway	***Raphael Marcus***	***Rahamim Mizrahi***
Shelomo Laniado	***Yitzhak Avigdor***	***Yitzhak Laniado***

[Derech Emunah, Jerusalem Edition, pages 227-228]

(28) Resolution Against the Desecration of Shabbat (Jerusalem 1907)

In the year 5667 (1907) the proclamation concerning *Shabbat* was sent to the Syrian rabbis of Jerusalem for their approval. They responded by regretting the fact that the holy city of Aleppo, their birthplace, was being obliged to deal with such issues. They then proceeded to affirm all that was said by the rabbis of Aleppo and added the following strong words:

We will go to the Western Wall, the place which G-d's presence has never left, and ask him to seek vengeance against anyone who disobeys the proclamation concerning *Shabbat* and *Kashrut*. We pray that G-d causes them to repent and when they repent they will once again be our brothers, may G-d forgive them. Our strong hope is that since all Jews are holy they will listen to their teachers and be blessed with all the blessings of the Torah, Amen.

Signing in Jerusalem in honor of the Torah and its students, and in honor of G-d
8th of Shevat 5667

Yitzhak Labaton	***Yosef Shrem***
Yomtob Yedid	***Yomtob Sasson***
Abraham Antebi	***Abraham Salem***
Meir Laniado	***Yitzhak Abadi***
Shaul Kassin	

(29) Excommunication of the Cheesemakers Who Desecrate Shabbat (1876)

In the year 5636 (1876), the scholars and rabbis of Aram Soba signed a public letter of excommunication against the makers of cheese who were desecrating *Shabbat* by working a seven-day week. The proclamation was as follows:

> This is to make known that we, the scholars and rabbis of Aleppo (G-d guard over it), the elders and the judges, have seen the great stumbling block and the severe transgression of *Shabbat* that is being perpetrated constantly by the cheese producers. They get milk and make cheese on *Shabbat* just as they do during the week and in so doing they transgress many prohibitions. They perform the prohibited acts of squeezing, constructing, sewing the bags, and sealing them, before sending them to the city.
>
> We are making it known that from here on we are decreeing upon them with the power of the holy Torah and with the power of excmomunication that all the cheesemakers and their workers should turn away from thier evil path and not return to it again. Separate yourselves from the sin of transgressing *Shabbat* that is the equivalant to the sin of idolatry. No cheesemaker has permission to buy milk on Friday afternoon or Saturday. However, if the Arabs want to make butter on their own you can buy that butter.
>
> Whoever breaches this *herem* [ban] will be bit by a *nahash* [literally, a snake, but also an acronym for *niduy, shamta,* and *herem*, which are all words meaning excommunication]. Anyone who disobeys this, besides violating the Torah and the *herem*, will be publicly identified by name in the synagogue. He will be prohibited to sell to any Jew and we will pursue him until his destruction. Those who obey us will dwell in safety, secure from all fears.
>
> The words of the undersigned, 5636 (1876)
>
> ***Moshe Sutton***
> ***Moshe Cohen***
> ***Moshe Swed***
> ***Abraham Dayan***
> ***Eliyahu Mishan***
> ***Abraham Shabbetai***
> ***Moshe Sasson***
> ***David Kassin***
> ***Menashe Matloub Sutton***
> ***Shaul Haim Abadi***

[Note: This document is quoted from *LiKedoshim Asher Ba'Aretz* page 167.]

TORAH SUPPORT

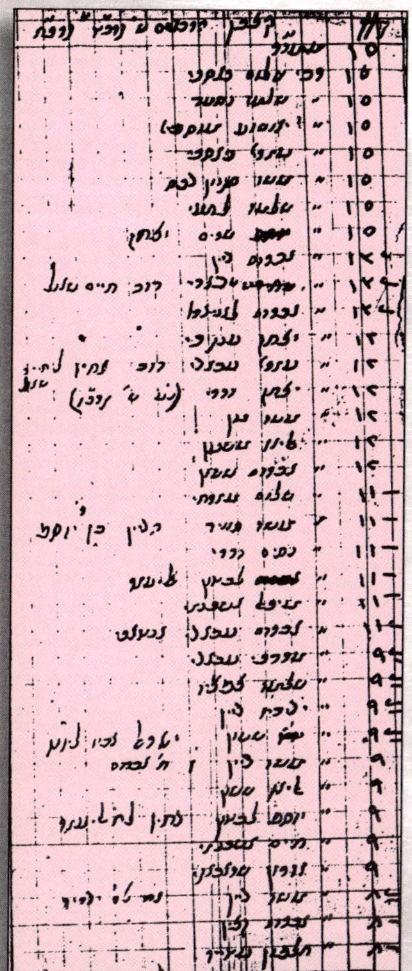

Weekly Stipend List for Torah Scholars (1928)

(30) Letter Concerning Kollel (1891)

In the year 1891 the rabbis of the community recommitted themselves to the support of Torah scholars. They issued the following public letter:

> For many years the Jewish people, the vineyard of G-d, blossomed beautifully. We refer here to the Torah scholars and their students who were enabled to flourish through the support of the community leaders. This enabled serious learning with devotion and the blossoms became fruit, referring to the students who developed into grape clusters. From them Torah emanates throughout Israel.
>
> As time went on the supporters became weak and the rabbis were left helpless. In the meantime the number of Torah scholars dwindled because they were forced to

fend for themselves and find their own means of support. Because of this, Torah has become weak and is relegated to the sidelines. Students refrain from committing themselves to a life of studying because they don't see a source of livelihood and if there are no young students there will be no elderly Torah scholars.

We realize that if we are quiet at this point Aleppo will become desolate of Torah. Therefore we have gathered together to strengthen the weary limbs of the Torah scholars. We have come to a strong agreement that all leftover funds in the *Gemilut Hesed* fund [Editor's note: similar to *Bikur Holim* of today], which is under the control of the trusted treasurer Mr. Sasson Gabay, be used toward the support of the rabbis and scholars. They should buy property and use the income toward their support. They should receive a weekly stipend. The funds should also support young scholars because as we have just said, if there are no young people learning there will be no older scholars.

Whoever questions or disputes our decision will find his position difficult indeed. He will need to bear the blame for causing *Bitul Torah* [neglect of the Torah during the time when it should be studied] and the responsibility for the consequences will be his.

We are sure that G-d will bring success to our endeavors for it [the Torah] is a tree of life to those who cling to it and its supporters are fortunate. Whoever strenghthens this principle will be fortunate. Fortunate is the nation that has such. May the sweetness of G-d be upon us.

Signing for the honor of G-d and his Torah 5651 [1891]

Shelomo Safdeyé Yitzhak Labaton Yitzhak Bekhor Mizrahi Eliyahu Hamway

The Chief Rabbi, Abraham Dweck, added the following words:

I have seen all that was written above, whereby the rabbis have affirmed the support of Torah. Fortunate are they and fortunate is their lot. There is no *mitzvah* that compares to [that of supporting Torah scholars]. The world stands on it, especially our city. Therefore, I lend my hand to their project of supporting Torah scholars and whoever wishes to differ will need to defend his case. Anyone who stands in the way will end up with a disease for which there is no cure. All those who support this project will live a long life, both they and their children. Wealth and honor will not leave their tents.

Signed Adar 1, 5651

The authors of the letter also stated the bylaws and particulars of the fund, which was set up to support Torah scholars, and added the following:

It is well known that from time immemorial, there have been generous people who have set aside funds for a foundation to support the Torah scholars of our community of Aleppo. The system was set up that only the profits are distributed and the principal must remain intact. If under extreme cicumstances the principal is used, it must be replenished immediately.The rabbis who are supported must be on an approved list and if one of them leaves he will be replaced by another rabbi that is worthy of this funding.The newest rabbi starts at a lower stipend amount and each rabbi moves up a level until the maximum of 10 grush. [They then list 43 rabbis of that time, with a starting stipend of 4 grush going up to 10 grush.]

[Note: The above documents are quoted on *LiKedoshim Asher Ba'Aretz*, pages 184-186.]

WITCHCRAFT

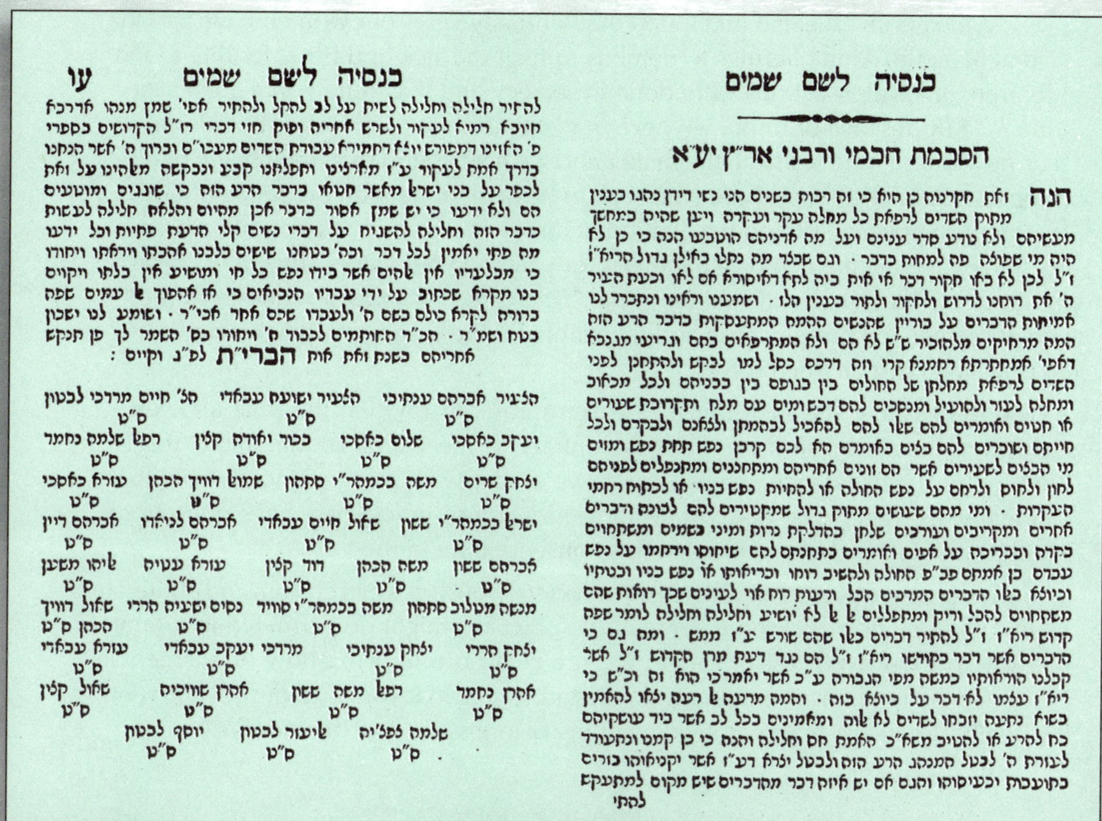

כניסיה לשם שמים

הסכמת חכמי ורבני אר"ץ יע"א

כניסיה לשם שמים עו

(31) Resolution Against Witchcraft (1857)

(31) Resolution Against Witchcraft (1857)

In the year 5617 (1857) a proclamation was signed by over 30 rabbis of Aleppo against a practice that had become common among many Jewish women, that of making offerings to demons so that they would heal the sick and bring fertility to the barren. The proclamation was spearheaded by Rabbi Menashe Sutton (see #551). He eventually wrote an entire book on the topic, titled *Kenisiyah Leshem Shamayim*. The topic is also dicussed at length by R' Haim Palagi (see #449) in his book, *Haim B'Yad* (section 34).

R' Sutton went on to send letters around the world to get the approval of rabbis in distant places.He found a favorable reception and received approbations from over 300 rabbis, among them the high courts of Jerusalem, Acre, Hebron, Safed, and Tiberias. The court of Damascus signed as well. He also received letters from individual rabbis, including R' Haim Palagi of Izmir, R' Yaakob Boka'i (see #139), and R' Heller of Safed.

Here is the proclamation signed by the rabbis of Aleppo:

> We have investigated and found that for many years our women have had the practice of making offerings to demons to heal the sick and bring fertility to the barren. Since their actions were done in secrecy and thay relied on a great sage, the *Riaz* (R' Yeshaya of Trani), we never had occasion to look into it. But *Hashem* has now stirred us to research the matter and we have found that none of the practitioners of this custom or those who seek to be healed mention the name of G-d. Their foolish practice is to pour a libation of honey or water, or to offer salt, wheat, and barley and tell the demons that this is for you and your cattle. They then crack eggs and say, "Accept this, a soul for a soul." They then make their requests. Some even go further and burn incense and set a table for the demons and light candles, and bow and prostrate themselves.
>
> Woe to eyes that see such things, Heaven forbid, to say that the *Riaz* allowed such practices and even if he did it is contrary to the words of *Maran* [R' Yosef Karo in the *Shulhan Aruch*], whose words we acccept like those of Moshe from the Almighty. But surely the *Riaz* never allowed it. These practioners have gone from bad to worse; they believe more in this nonsense than in the truth.
>
> Therefore we have strengthened ourselves to abolish this evil custom and obliterate this spirit of idolatry. Even if some of the practices might be permitted in a limited way to those who resist change, we say Heaven forbid to allow any leniencies, since the Torah says concerning an idolatrous tree that you must destroy the roots as well; surely this practice of worshipping demons is worse than idolatry.

We thank G-d for having directed us on the correct path to uproot this idolatry from our land. We pray to G-d that He bring atonement to us, since those that sinned were unaware of the severity of their acts. But from now on, Heaven forbid that anyone follows such practices or allows his household to. We pray to G-d that He instills in our hearts His love and awe and the belief in His Oneness, that only He grants life and death and only He is our savior. May the following words of the prophet be fulfilled upon us, "Then He will turn the language of all nations to one clear tongue calling in the name of G-d." All those who heed us will dwell peacefully and be protected from all evil.

We the undersigned 5617

Abraham Antebi
Yeshuah Abadi
Haim Mordechai Labaton
Yaakob Chasky
Shalom Chasky
Yehudah Kassin
Raphael Nehmad
Yitzhak Shrem
Moshe Sutton
Shemuel Dweck
Ezra Chasky
Yisrael Sasson
Shaul Abadi
Abraham Laniado
Abraham Dayan
Abraham Sasson
Moshe Cohen
David Kassin

Ezra Attiah
Eliyahu Mishan
Menashe Matloub Sutton
Moshe Swed
Nissim Yeshayah Harari
Shaul Dweck
Yitzhak Harari
Yitzhak Antebi
Mordechai Abadi
Ezra Abadi
Aharon Nehmad
Raphael Moshe Sasson
Aharon Choueka
Shaul Kassin
Shelomo Safdeyé
Eliezer Labaton
Yosef Labaton

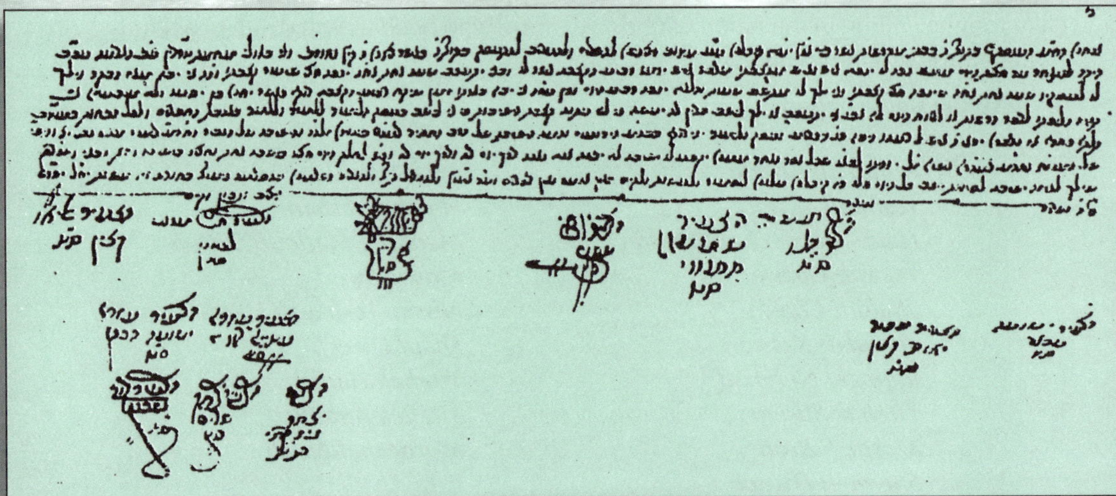

(32) Study Group Contract (circa 1800)

(32) Study Group Contract (circa 1800)

A common practice among scholars over the ages in Aram Soba was to organize themselves into study groups. This practice promoted steady and reliable attendance and participation in study sessions at designated locations. Some study groups were sponsored by wealthy individuals who donated stipends for the support of the scholars. As an additional level of commitment some study groups set up a "contract of connection" (*Shtar Hitkashrut*) by which the members formalized their responsibilities to the group and to each other. An example of such a contract is shown below.

We the undersigned who involve ourselves with the study of G-d's Torah in the *Batei Midrash* of Aleppo (may *Hashem* protect it) have accepted upon ourselves with good will to awake early and remain late to involve ourselves in *Hashem*'s Torah as He commands us during all seasons.

If anyone of us is late because of wordly issues and comes after midday he will lose from his pay and if he is an hour late he will lose accordingly.

These fines are not only for wordly matters, but even if he is late due to responsibilities in the *Bet Din* or the like, because money given for *yeshivot* is for those learning in the yeshiva together with the group. The learning must be in the known houses of study, namely the yeshiva of the pious R' Moshe Picciotto of blessed memory (see #458), the yeshiva of the philanthropist R' Meir Gabai (see #265), and the yeshiva of the late *Nasi* [it is not clear who this refers to]. It is also understood that you choose a set spot and not move from place to place and surely not learn half a day in one yeshiva and half a day in another.

All of this we have accepted upon ourselves to raise our Torah and make it greater.

(circa 5560)

Moshe Levy	***Yehudah Kassin***
Shimon Hamway	***Ezra Attiah***
Yosef Sasson	***Ezra Cohen***
Yeshayah Dayan	***Yitzhak Mizrahi***
Chaim Mordechai Labaton	***Yitzhak Shrem***
Eliyahu Kassin	***David Ashkenazi***
Yeshuah Abadi	

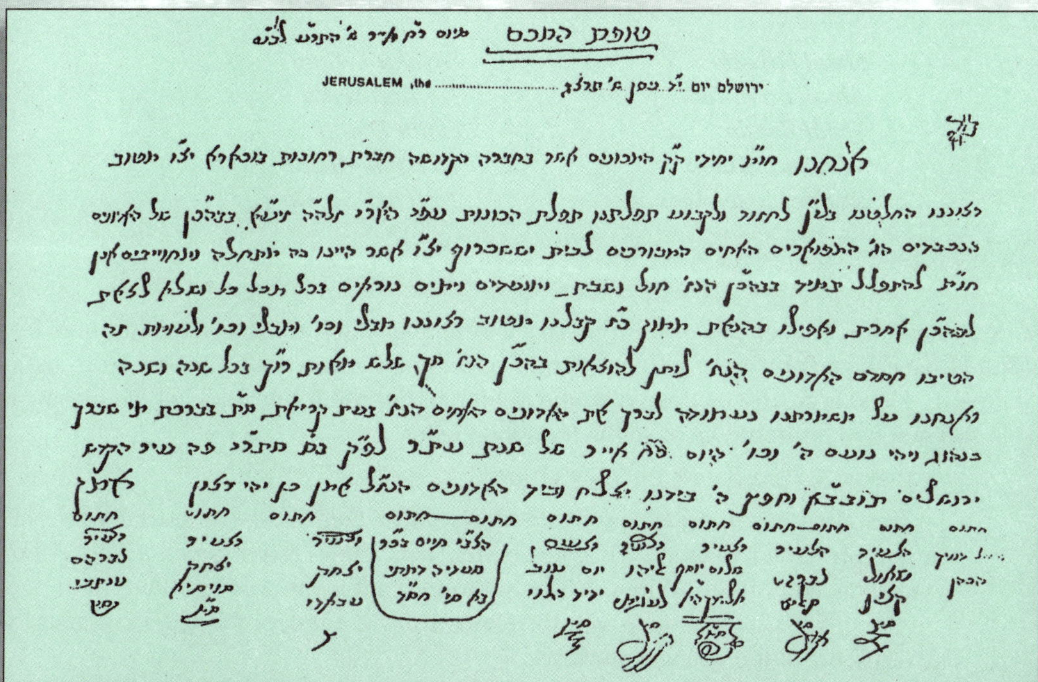

(33) Prayer Group Contract (1910, 1933)

(33) Prayer Group Contract (1910, 1933)

The model of the *Shtar Hitkashrut* (contract of connection) used for study groups was also adapted for Kabbalah prayer groups, in which the great demands of meditative prayer were reinforced by the sense of comradeship and mutual support that occurred when the same pious scholars prayed together on a regular basis. The following *Shtar Hitkashrut* of *Yeshivat Rehovot HaNahar* in Jerusalem was handwritten by Rabbi Yaakob Kassin (see #330).

Rosh Hodesh Iyar 1910 (original contract) Nissan 14, 1933 (second signing)

We, the undersigned of the Congregation of *Mekavnim* of the holy group of *Rehovot HaNahar* of Bukhara, out of our own goodwill, have decided to restablish the prayers with the *kavanot* [meditations] of the *Ari'zal*. The prayer group is located in the synagogue of the honorable philanthropists the Yissacharoff brothers, in which we have always been located. We the undersigned obligate ourselves to pray in the above-mentioned synagogue on weekdays, *Shabbat*, holidays, and high holidays, all inclusive, and we will not pray in another synagogue even for financial considerations. We have accepted this all in goodwill. The above-mentioned brothers with their goodness and kindness have reciprocated and agreed to support this institution with 300 ruble sterling annually. We will bless these brothers in the "*Mi sheberach*" [blessing] at the *Sefer Torah* as is customary.

May the sweetness of G-d be upon us. Jerusalem.
May *Hashem* bring success to us and the brothers. Amen.

Shaul Dweck
Abraham Antebi
Shaul Kassin
Abraham Salem
Shalom Yosef Alshich
Eliyahu L'Agmi
Yomtob Yedid
Haim Damti
Yitzchak Abadi
Yitzchak Suisse

(34) Letter by Rabbi Eliezer Silver After Visit to Porat Yosef (1964)

In 1964 Rabbi Eliezer Silver, the renowned American rabbinical personality and leader, visited the yeshiva *Porat Yosef* in Jerusalem. (See Biographies section, #24, for a discussion of that visit.) He was greatly impressed by the quality of intense Torah study which he saw there. He summarized his impressions in the following letter.

Thursday, *Perashat Re'eh* 5724 (1964)

This afternoon I visited the Sephardic yeshiva *Porat Yosef* in Jerusalem. I gave a complex *shiur* [lecture] for three hours, with topics from *Gemara* and *Poskim* (*halachic* authorities). With G-d's help I found that I was able to converse in depth in the entire *shas* [Talmud] with the *Rosh Yeshiva*, a few of the older students, and even some of the younger students.

I found that they are great in Torah with vast knowledge and analytic ability in a variety of topics in the *Gemara*. They know how to find distinctions and explain [complex topics] no less than most of the rabbis of Lithuania that are in Israel today.

I am confident that since most of them are diligent about their learning even in vacation time (contrary to other *yeshivot*) and since they are learning day and night even now, that they will surely become *Gedolim* (great Torah scholars) and some of them will even be worthy of becoming *Geonim* (geniuses of Torah scholarship) in Israel. [Editor's note: Traditionally, Torah studies were not interrupted in *Porat Yosef* during the widely accepted three-week summer break known as *ben hazemanim*.]

I enjoyed it there more than in most of the *yeshivot* I visited in our holy land. I gave them my blessing that their greatness should receive worldwide recognition and the student body of *Porat Yosef* should increase and grow. They should influence other *yeshivot* to be like them. They should all be blessed with physical well being and be written and sealed to a long life befitting Torah scholars of their stature.

Eliezer the son of Bunim Tzemach Silver,
Chief of the Presidium of the Union of Orthodox Rabbis of America and Canada

(35) Rabbinical Association Group Contract (1885)

In the era of R' Shelomo Safdeyé (#469) the following document was signed by 26 rabbis of Aleppo. The document is brought by Rabbi David Laniado (in *LiKedoshim Asher Ba'Aretz,* page 160), although he doesn't mention the rabbis by name:

Shtar Hitkashrut Among Rabbis of Aleppo to Stand Up Against Evildoers and to Supervise Community Matters

We the undersigned rabbis and scholars of Aleppo have joined to strengthen ourselves to uplift the banner of Torah. We have committed ourselves as a group to stand up against any issue that is contrary to our Torah. And we obligate ourselves to negate that issue whether it is a public or private issue. We will uproot it from its source as we see fit.

We will discuss the matter with the general commitee and with the Chief Rabbi. Once the majority agrees to combat the issue, no one has the right to evade his responsibility. When an issue has been chosen we will fight with all our strength for the honor of G-d and his Torah. Once the majority has decided on an issue, everyone must follow even if it is not his opinion; furthermore, he may not reveal his contrary opinion to the public. If a Torah scholar is insulted in the slightest way it is our obligation to do what we can to regain the respect due him according to the Torah and to strengthen ourselves with all our souls and resources.

Every Sunday at noon we shall meet to discuss community matters and to deal with all outstanding issues involving practices which are forbidden as well as those which are permissible but require correction. If an urgent issue arises we can call an emergency meeting and all must attend even in the middle of the week. If anyone retracts from his commitment he will be fined as the group sees fit. This agreement is binding for two years from the date below. We have obligated ourselves to follow the above commitment, but without a vow, for the honor of our holy Torah and its *mitzvot.*

May G-d support activities that bring honor to His name.

8 Sivan, 5655 (1885)

(36) Aliyah Contract (1737)

In his research for the classic book *LiKedoshim Asher Ba'Aretz*, R' David-Sion Laniado came across the following fascinating 18th century document. It was a *Shtar Hitkashrut* (commitment contract) between two scholars who guaranteed to each other that they would both immigrate to *Eretz Yisrael* within three years. R' Laniado found the document to be a wonderful demonstration of the great yearning that the rabbis of old had for the sacred air of *Eretz Yisrael*. He wrote, "Any person who reads this document today will surely be moved to go up to Zion, to Jerusalem, the holy city which Hashem chose as His dwelling place, and especially in these days when people with financial means can earn a livelihood there, because it is a land of opportunity, whose air is pure, and it grants wisdom to those who reside there. May we worthy to see it rebuilt!"

Whereas with the help of G-d we have become aware of the teachings of our holy sages on the great virtue of residing in *Eretz Yisrael* and that to live in *Eretz Yisrael* is equivalent in importance to all the *mitzvot* of the Torah, we the undersigned, Moshe Roshit and Abraham Laniado, are ashamed and embarrassed, and we must go up to the mountain [*Eretz Yisrael*] to ingratiate ourselves to its soil and to find favor with its stones and the masses of its ruins, to stand and minister before Hashem in the place of which He has said, "I will give it to you." And so we have joined together in bonds of love for *Eretz Yisrael* and its holiness to go up there, with no thought given to the possibility of changing our minds or backing out in any way.

And since we have been encumbered and constrained with superficial and passing matters, which have disturbed our peace of mind, and subjected us to circumstances from which we cannot easily extricate ourselves, and since each of us has limited means, we do not have the wherewithal to undertake the journey because the way is long and we are pressed to support our families. Accordingly, we have resolved to set a deadline which we will not violate, lest we be diverted by extraneous circumstances. We have taken it upon ourselves to remain here no more than three consecutive years, counted from *Rosh Hodesh* Nissan that has passed, and in three months after the end of the three years we will be obligated to immediately go with our wives and children, without any delay whatsoever, except for a truly unavoidable, circumstance that happens to one of us and is evident to another.

And we have take an oath by the Torah and the sanctity of *Eretz Yisrael*, that either of us who will not agree to go at that time despite the departure of his fellow and our master, our teacher, R' Yaakob Obadiah, that man shall as of now be obliged to pay a penalty of 2500 pounds as a true gift when the above-mentioned Rabbi Yaakob requests it. And to ensure that our righteousness precedes us, we have agreed that each one of us will advance to the above-mentioned Rabbi Yaakob the sum of 2500 pounds so that between the two of us there will be 5000 pounds, and the money will be a loan to him, and he will have the benefit of any profit he can make with it. And we will either do business with the money and give him the profit or put it in his hands and he will do as is fitting in his eyes, and the profit will be used to sustain his household. And the term of this loan shall be for a period of 10 years in the Glorious Land [*Eretz Yisrael*], counted from the day it comes into his hand; and during that time it will be like a gift to him that we will not take it from him nor from the one to whom he gives it for safekeeping, either all or part.

And all this we have sworn and we have executed a contract each one with the other, and with the above-mentioned Rabbi Yaakob, with no reservations. And likewise, the above-mentioned Rabbi Yaakob obligates himself to go with us or with one of us at that time, and he has sworn to repay the 2500 pounds if one of us does not go, Heaven forfend, Hashem in His mercy will recognize his good intentions and give him salvation for the sake of His Name.

And this is the second day of the week, the fourth day of Sivan in the year 5497 (1737)

[Note: This document appears in *LiKedoshim Asher Ba'Aretz*, page 89.]

כ"ו סיון תש"ב

לכבוד מעלת הרה"ג והאדונים הנכבדים חברי ועד הישיבה פורת יוסף תכב"ץ (תכון בצדק) הע"א (השם עליהם יחיו אמן)

רבנים ואדונים נכבדים אנחנו החותמים מטה חכמי ורבני ישיבת פורת יוסף נודע לנו כי אחדים מתלמידי ישיבתנו הוגים בספרי מחקר ופילוספיה , ולא כל מוחא סביל דא כאשר כתב הרב משפט צדק בשם גדולי ראשונים ואחרונים . שבזה נמשכים גם ללמוד בספרי השכלה חדשים המלאים כפירה ומינות . ודין גרמא שרוצים לעזוב את התורה הקדושה והישיבה ואמורים להכנס לאוניברסיטה המקנה מדות ודעות חילוניות לחניכיה כידוע. ושמענו כי ועד עדת הספרדים מוכן לעזור בעזרה כספית להשגת מטרה זו . והיות וענינים אלו מהוים פרצה גדולה בחומת התורה ומזיקים הרבה לישיבתנו הקדושה ולתלמידיה , לכן ראינו חובה לנפשנו לכבוד ה' ולתורה הקדושה לעורר בזה תשומת לבכם למצב . ואנו מבקשים מרו"מ בכל לשון של בקשה כי תואילו נא לעמוד על המשמר ולהשתדל בכל כוחם לתקן כל המעוות תיקון , למען בנין ישיבתנו וקיום התורה והמצות. כי אם חס ושלום ימשך כך המצב - תורה מה תהא עליה ? וביחוד בדור יתום זה , שזו היא הישיבה היחידה בין הספרדים והיא כל תקוותנו. כי ממנה תצא תורה ואורה ליהדות הספרדית בכל העולם כולו. אי לזאת הננו מבקשים בזה מרו"מ כי תשתדלו להשפיע בכל דרכי השפעה הן על התלמידים הן על המסייעים המחזיקים בידם לאחוז בכל האמצעים לגדור את הפירצה הנוראה הזאת . ושלא יכנס שום תלמיד ישיבה לאונברסטיה והשם יהיה בעזרכם לתקן תקנות גדולות למנוע התלמידים שלא יקראו עוד בספרי פילוספיה למיניהם כי אם לחנכם בתמימות עם השם ובאמונה טהורה בלי שום ספיקות ושאלות חס ושלום .וגם למנעם מן ההגיון בכל מיני ספרים העלולים להשפיע השפעה זרה להם בתורה וביראה . אנו בטוחים כי ...... עד אשר יתקנו הדברים למען עדת השם ועמו בעת צרה . והשם יתברך יגדור פירצותנו , וישיב לב בנים על האבות , ונזכה לראות בהרמת קרן התורה ובביאת משיח במהרה בימינו אמן.

נאום:

עזרא עדס | יוסף טוויל | שלום לופס | אפרים מנשה כהן

בן ציון אטון | נסים עזראן | רפאל ביטון | עזרא שרים

אברהם רפול | מנצור בן שמעון | יוסף שהרבני | ששון לוי

שלום סתהון | יוסף חיים בן פינחס | נסים ענתבי | אברהם ורקנין

יעקב כהן | ע. הדאיה | יהודה צדקה | דוד רפול

אברהם ענתבי

(37)Letter from Rabbis of Porat Yosef Against the Study of Philosophy and College (1942)

(37) Letter from Rabbis of Porat Yosef Against the Study of Philosophy and College (1942)

In the year 1942 one of the committee members of *Porat Yosef* suggested teaching the English language as a subject in the yeshiva. He explained, "If we are to produce rabbis for the Diaspora they must be fluent in English." The rabbis of the yeshiva were strongly opposed. The committee member was insistent; he said, "It will be taught in the evening and during lunch breaks. "Rabbi Shalom Lofez (#399) got wind of the plans and he immediately took action. He wrote the text of a "*Kol Koreh* (proclamation)" voicing the opinions of the rabbis and had it signed by the leading rabbis of the yeshiva. The following is the text of the proclamation:

To the honorable members of the committee of the yeshiva *Porat Yosef*,

We the undersigned rabbis and scholars of *Porat Yosef* have become aware that a small number of the students in our yeshiva are studying books of research and philosophy, something that most people can't handle. The *sefer Mishpat Sedek* writes in the name of the *Rishonim* (early rabbis) and *Aharonim* (later rabbis) that studying philosophy draws the reader to new books of *Haskalah* (Reform and Conservative movements) full of heresy and atheism. This is causing some of our students to leave our Holy Torah and yeshiva. They plan on entering a university that implants in those that are educated there irreligious traits and ideals, as is well known to all. We have heard that the Board of the Sephardic community is willing to give financial aid toward this goal. These issues will make a great breach in the wall of Torah and will damage our yeshiva and its students.

Therefore, it is our obligation, for the honor of G-d and His Torah, to bring this to your awareness. We ask you to please stand guard and try with all your strength to repair the situation for the sake of our yeshiva and for the sake of Torah and *mitzvot*.

If, Heaven forbid, the situation continues, what will become of Torah? Especially in our orphaned generation that this is the only Sephardic yeshiva. It is our only hope for the future. From here Torah and light will spread to Sephardic world Jewry. We are asking that you please do everything in your power to arouse world public opinion in our favor and to influence the students and the financial backers. Use all measures to repair this breach and to stop any students from going to university. May *Hashem* assist you to make rules and regulations to prevent the students from reading all types of philosophical works. Rather, they should be educated with simple pure faith without instilling doubts and questions, Heaven forbid. Prevent them as well from studying any books that might possibly bring foreign influences into their study of Torah and fear of G-d. We are sure that until you will repair the breaches for the sake of the community of G-d ... (illegible sentence in original document). May *Hashem* repair all our breaches and return the hearts of the sons to their fathers. We should merit to see the uplifting of the flag of Torah and the coming of Mashiah speedily in our days, Amen. Signed (26th of Sivan 5702)

Ezra Ades
Yosef Tawil
Shalom Lofes
Ephraim Menashe Cohen
Ben-Sion Atoon
Nissim Ezran

Raphael Bitton
Ezra Shrem
Abraham Raful
Mansour Ben-Shimon
Yosef Shaharbani
Sasson Levy

Shalom Sutton
Yosef Haim ben Pinhas
Nissim Antebi
Abraham Waknin
Yaakob Cohen
E. Hedayah

Yehudah Sadkah
David Raful
Abraham Antebi

In memory of

Tunie Sutton

by

Elie Sutton and Family

Family Roots

YOUR FAMILY TREE

After reading about the noble lives of our memorable ancestors, it is only natural to feel a great sense of duty to continue in their ways and to fulfill the saying, "The apple does not fall far from the tree." We have provided a blank genealogical table to enable the reader to connect to his or her own glorious past.

The *Gemara* (*Taanit* 5b) describes an occasion when two Talmudic Sages, Rav Nachman and Rav Yitzhak, were sharing a meal and enjoying each other's company. After eating, they exchanged some Torah thoughts. Finally, as they were getting up to leave, Rav Nachman asked Rav Yitzhak to give him a blessing. Rav Yitzhak began with a story about a man who was traveling in the desert. Hungry, tired, and thirsty, he came to a tree with very sweet fruit. The tree also cast a comfortable shade and there was a pleasant stream of water flowing under its spreading branches. The man ate from its fruit, drank from the water, and rested in its shade. When he was about to continue his journey, he said, "Tree, O tree, how can I bless you? Shall I say: May your fruits be sweet? They are sweet already. That your shade should be pleasant? It is already pleasant. That a stream of water may flow beneath you? A stream of water already flows beneath you. Therefore [I will say instead], May it be G-d's will, that all the saplings cut from you should be like you."

"You, too, Rav Nachman," said Rav Yitzhak. "With what shall I bless you? With the knowledge of the Torah? You already have the knowledge of Torah. With riches? You already have riches. With children? You already have children. Therefore, I say, May it be G-d's will that your offspring will be like you."

May the blessing of Rav Yitzhak be fulfilled in our community and may all of us be like our forebears in the family tree of which we ourselves are an essential part.

אילן היוחסין לשושלת ששון עג'מי
ARRIVED TO ALEPPO AND WERE MARRIED
YOUSIF SASSOON THE SON OF RAPHAEL FROM CITY HAMADAN IN 1704

PATERNAL GENEALOGY

GREAT GREAT GRANDFATHER
(Father's father's father's father)
HEBREW NAME
ENGLISH NAME
BORN (DATE/PLACE)
DIED (DATE/PLACE)

GREAT GREAT GRANDMOTHER
(Father's father's father's mother)
HEBREW NAME
ENGLISH NAME
BORN (DATE/PLACE)
DIED (DATE/PLACE)

MARRIED (DATE/PLACE)

GREAT GREAT GRANDFATHER
(Father's mother's father's father)
HEBREW NAME
ENGLISH NAME
BORN (DATE/PLACE)
DIED (DATE/PLACE)

GREAT GREAT GRANDMOTHER
(Father's father's mother's mother)
HEBREW NAME
ENGLISH NAME
BORN (DATE/PLACE)
DIED (DATE/PLACE)

MARRIED (DATE/PLACE)

GREAT GREAT GRANDFATHER
(Father's mother's father's father)
HEBREW NAME
ENGLISH NAME
BORN (DATE/PLACE)
DIED (DATE/PLACE)

GREAT GREAT GRANDMOTHER
(Father's mother's father's mother)
HEBREW NAME
ENGLISH NAME
BORN (DATE/PLACE)
DIED (DATE/PLACE)

MARRIED (DATE/PLACE)

GREAT GREAT GRANDFATHER
(Father's mother's mother's father)
HEBREW NAME
ENGLISH NAME
BORN (DATE/PLACE)
DIED (DATE/PLACE)

GREAT GREAT GRANDMOTHER
(Father's mother's mother's mother)
HEBREW NAME
ENGLISH NAME
BORN (DATE/PLACE)
DIED (DATE/PLACE)

MARRIED (DATE/PLACE)

GREAT GRANDFATHER
(Father's father's father)
HEBREW NAME
ENGLISH NAME
BORN (DATE/PLACE)
DIED (DATE/PLACE)

GREAT GRANDMOTHER
(Father's father's mother)
HEBREW NAME
ENGLISH NAME
BORN (DATE/PLACE)
DIED (DATE/PLACE)

MARRIED (DATE/PLACE)

GREAT GRANDFATHER
(Father's mother's father)
HEBREW NAME
ENGLISH NAME
BORN (DATE/PLACE)
DIED (DATE/PLACE)

GREAT GRANDMOTHER
(Father's mother's mother)
HEBREW NAME
ENGLISH NAME
BORN (DATE/PLACE)
DIED (DATE/PLACE)

MARRIED (DATE/PLACE)

GRANDFATHER'S SIBLINGS

GRANDFATHER
(Father's father)
HEBREW NAME
ENGLISH NAME
BORN (DATE/PLACE)

GRANDMOTHER
(Father's mother)
HEBREW NAME
ENGLISH NAME
BORN (DATE/PLACE)

MARRIED (DATE/PLACE)

GRANDMOTHER'S SIBLINGS

FATHER'S SIBLINGS

FATHER
HEBREW NAME
ENGLISH NAME
BORN (DATE/PLACE)
MARRIED (DATE/PLACE)

FATHER'S SIBLINGS

MATERNAL GENEALOGY

GREAT GREAT GRANDFATHER
(Mother's father's father's father)

HEBREW NAME
ENGLISH NAME
BORN (DATE/PLACE)
DIED (DATE/PLACE)

GREAT GREAT GRANDMOTHER
(Mother's father's father's mother)

HEBREW NAME
ENGLISH NAME
BORN (DATE/PLACE)
DIED (DATE/PLACE)

MARRIED (DATE/PLACE)

GREAT GREAT GRANDFATHER
(Mother's father's mother's father)

HEBREW NAME
ENGLISH NAME
BORN (DATE/PLACE)
DIED (DATE/PLACE)

GREAT GREAT GRANDMOTHER
(Mother's father's mother's mother)

HEBREW NAME
ENGLISH NAME
BORN (DATE/PLACE)
DIED (DATE/PLACE)

MARRIED (DATE/PLACE)

GREAT GREAT GRANDFATHER
(Mother's mother's father's father)

HEBREW NAME
ENGLISH NAME
BORN (DATE/PLACE)
DIED (DATE/PLACE)

GREAT GREAT GRANDMOTHER
(Mother's mother's father's mother)

HEBREW NAME
ENGLISH NAME
BORN (DATE/PLACE)
DIED (DATE/PLACE)

MARRIED (DATE/PLACE)

GREAT GREAT GRANDFATHER
(Mother's mother's mother's father)

HEBREW NAME
ENGLISH NAME
BORN (DATE/PLACE)
DIED (DATE/PLACE)

GREAT GREAT GRANDMOTHER
(Mother's mother's mother's mother)

HEBREW NAME
ENGLISH NAME
BORN (DATE/PLACE)
DIED (DATE/PLACE)

MARRIED (DATE/PLACE)

GREAT GRANDFATHER
(Mother's father's father)

HEBREW NAME
ENGLISH NAME
BORN (DATE/PLACE)
DIED (DATE/PLACE)

GREAT GRANDMOTHER
(Mother's father's mother)

HEBREW NAME
ENGLISH NAME
BORN (DATE/PLACE)
DIED (DATE/PLACE)

MARRIED (DATE/PLACE)

GREAT GRANDFATHER
(Mother's mother's father)

HEBREW NAME
ENGLISH NAME
BORN (DATE/PLACE)
DIED (DATE/PLACE)

GREAT GRANDMOTHER
(Mother's mother's mother)

HEBREW NAME
ENGLISH NAME
BORN (DATE/PLACE)
DIED (DATE/PLACE)

MARRIED (DATE/PLACE)

GRANDFATHER'S SIBLINGS

GRANDFATHER
(Mother's father)

HEBREW NAME
ENGLISH NAME
BORN (DATE/PLACE)

GRANDMOTHER
(Mother's mother)

HEBREW NAME
ENGLISH NAME
BORN (DATE/PLACE)

MARRIED (DATE/PLACE)

GRANDMOTHER'S SIBLINGS

MOTHER'S SIBLINGS

MOTHER

HEBREW NAME
ENGLISH NAME
BORN (DATE/PLACE)
MARRIED (DATE/PLACE)

MOTHER'S SIBLINGS

Bibliography

Ahuzat Eretz [Jerusalem 2004], R' Eliyahu Lofez (see #394), *Introduction by R' Rahamim Shayo*

Aleh Ezra [Lakewood 1999], R' Ezra Attiah (see #102), *Published by R' David Zafrani*

Aleppo Chronicles [Brooklyn 1988], Joseph A. D. Sutton

Amudei Shesh [Jerusalem 1891], R' Shmuel Boyarski

Avnai Zikaron [Jerusalem 1999], R' Abraham Salem (*Rosh Yeshivat Meor HaTorah*), *Memories of his father, R' Natan Salem* (see #472)

Avotenu Sipru Lanu, Moshe Rabi (Rabia –Sutton)

Be'er Yitzhak [Livorno 1864], R' Yitzhak Shrem (see #517) , *Introduction to Bnei Brak edition (1989), R' Eliyahu Shrem (#509)*

Ben David [Jerusalem 1929], R' Moshe Dweck Kassab (see #256)

Customs of the Great Synagogue,
(Appendix to *Holech Tamim U'Poel Sedek*) R' Shelomo Zafrani (see #598)

Derech Emunah, R' Yaakob Dweck (see #248)

Dibrei Moshe [Jerusalem 2002], R' Moshe Ezra Mizrahi (see #424), *Introduction by R' Rachamim Shayo*

Dibrei Shalom [Jerusalem 1994], R' Shalom Yitzhak Mizrahi (see #429), *Introduction by his son, R' Yaakob Mizrahi*

Dignity, Edmond J. Safra Philanthropic Foundation

Eved Ne'eman [Jerusalem 2003], R' Aryeh Drillman, *Biography of R' Shalom Lofez (see #399)*

Even Safir [Lik-Megenza1866], R' Yaacov Safir

Gedolim Sadikim (Appendix to *Shalom Le'Am,* R' Shalom Chasky) [Jerusalem1982], R' Saadiah Manir

Ginzei Eretz [Jerusalem 2001], R' Rahamim Shayo, *Anthology of Aleppine Rabbis*

Hachmei HaMizrach [Jerusalem 1982], Shraga Weiss

Hachmei HaSephardim Be'Eretz Yisrael [Jerusalem 1981], Shraga Weiss

HaKeter [Jerusalem 1987], Amnon Shamosh

HaMoreh Miri Peer, *Biography of R' Ezra Attiah (see #102)*

Hanan Elokim [Izmir 1737], R' Haim Abulafia

Hazon Yeshayah [Jerusalem 1998], R' Yeshayah Dayan (see #203), *Introduction by R' Rahamim Shayo*

Hebrew Printing in Middle Eastern Lands [Jerusalem 1936], Abraham Yeiri

Hedvat Yaakob [Jerusalem 2000], R' Yaakob Ades (see #41)

Heir HaMizrach, [Jerusalem 2002], R' Binyamin Gilkrav

Hochmah U'Mussar [Jerusalem 1981], R' Abraham Antebi (see #63)

Holech Tamim U'Poel Sedek [Jerusalem 1979], R' Abraham Dayan (see #173), *Appendix — Zichron Dibrei Eretz*

Keter Aram Soba [Jerusalem 1933], R' Meir Rahamim Nehmad (#446)

Kevod Yom Tob, *Memorial Book on the Life of R' Yomtob Yedid (see #593)*

Kenisiyah Leshem Shamayim [Jerusalem 1874], R' Menashe Sutton (see #551)

Kuntras Hechin Ezra [Jerusalem 1982], R' Abraham Harari-Raful (see #302)

Nahalat Ezra [Jerusalem 1984], R' Ezra Hedaya (see #307), *Machon HaKtav edition, Introduction*

LiKedoshim Asher Ba'Aretz [Jerusalem 1932, 1952], R' David-Sion Laniado (see #352)

LiKedoshim Asher Ba'Aretz [Jerusalem 1980], R' David-Sion Laniado, *Published by R' David Sharikaz, R' Eliyahu Attiah, R' Ephraim Levi, and the author's sons*

LiKedoshim Asher Ba'Aretz, R' Abraham E. Ades, R' Ephraim Levi [*Unpublished*] *manuscript for upcoming revision to LiKedoshim Asher Ba'Aretz*

Likutei David [Jerusalem 1967], R' David-Sion Laniado

Ma'ayan Ganim [Jerusalem 1958], R' Mordechai Abadi (see #8), *Machon HaKtav edition, Introduction*

Ma'ayan HaShevuah [Jerusalem 2004], R' Wallach

Mahzor Bet Din, R' Abraham Hamway (see #269), *Machon HaKtav edition, Introduction*

Magen Ba'adi [Brooklyn 1970], R' Matloub Abadi (see #9)

Mara D'Ara Yisrael [Jerusalem 2003], *Biography of R' Yosef Chaim Sonnenfeld,* Yosef Moshe Sofer

Masaot Yerushalayim Muncaz

Masoratenu [Jerusalem 2003], R' Tzvi Goldberg, *on the Keter Aram Soba*

Men of Faith and Vision [New York 2003], Sam Catton

Minhat Aharon [Jerusalem 1980], R' Aharon Choueka (see #154), *Introduction by his son R' Yaakob Choueka*

Moshe Haya Roeh [Jerusalem 2003] *Biography of R' Moshe Pardo by R' Wallach*

Nebei Emet V'Sedek [Bnei Brak 2003], R' David Yitzhaki, *on the Keter Aram Soba*

Ner Yom Tob, *Journal published by Yeshivat Simhat Yom Tob (volumes 1-12)*

Nochah HaShulhan, R' Haim Mordechai Labaton (see #336), *Machon HaKtav edition, i Introduction*

Ohel Yesharim [Livorno 1822], R' Abraham Antebi (see #63)

Ohr LeSion [Jerusalem 1995], R' Ben-Sion Abba Shaul (see #24)

Orot HaMizrach [Bnei Brak: 1974], R' Aharon Surasky

Pada Et Abraham, R' Abraham Mounsa

Pe'at HaSadeh [Jerusalem 1998], R' Haim Shaul Dweck (see #228), *Introduction by R' Yaakob Hillel, Rosh Yeshiva of Yeshivat Ahavat Shalom*

Peri Etz HaGan [Jerusalem 1931], R' Yaakob Kassin (see #330)

Princely Wisdom [Jerusalem 1995], *Published by Yeshivat Ahavat Shalom, Biography of R' Yaakob Kassin (*see #330*)*

Shalom Avdo [Jerusalem 1996], R' Obadiah Hedaya (see #309), *Articles on author included at the end of the book*

Shalom Le'Am [Jerusalem 2004], R' Shalom Hedaya (see #310), *Introduction by Avinoam Kahn*

She'erit Yaakob [Aram Soba 1925, Jerusalem 2000], R' Yaakob Dweck (see #248), *Introduction by A. Yisrael*

Shir U'Shevahah Hallel VeZimrah [New York 1983], *Introduction by Sam Catton*

Tiferet Sion [Jerusalem 2000], *Biography of R' Ben-Sion Abba Shaul (see #24)*

Torat Abraham [New York 2004], Abraham D. Sutton (see #536), *Introduction by his grandson, Leon S. Sutton*

Treasures of the Aleppo Community, Israel Museum

VaYa'al Eliyahu [Tel Aviv 2002], R' Dvir Shrem, *Biography of his father, R' Eliyahu Shrem (#509)*

Yismach Ezra [Jerusalem 2005], R' Asher Hamway, *Biography of R' Ezra Hamway* (#272)

VaYizra Yitzhak [Jerusalem 2001], R' Haim Levi, *Biography of R' Yitzhak Chehebar (see #152)*

Visions of the Rav [New York 2003**]**, Avraham Birnbaum, *Biography of Rabbi Abraham Kalmanowitz*

VaYisa Yaakob [Jerusalem 1957], R' Yaakob (Jack) Maleh (see #402)

Yaskil Abdi, R' Obadiah Hedaya (see #309), *Introduction*

Yesod HaEmunah [New York 1981], R' Yaakob Kassin (see #330)

Yimalet Nafsho [Jerusalem 1990], R' Abraham Hamway, *Introduction by R' Yosef Cohen*

Yitzhak Yeranen [Buenos Aires 1991], R' Yitzhak Chehebar (see #152)

Photo Credits

These are the photos with copyrights. All others are mentioned in Acknowledgments.

Outdoor Tebah — *Washington, Freer Gallery of Art, Arthur M. Sackler Gallery Archives, front cover, title page*

Aleppo citadel — *Israel Museum. p. 1*

View of Aleppo — *Sephardic Community Center Archives (courtesy Adelle Marcus and Sadie Safdie), p. 8*

Bab al Faraj — *Sephardic Community Center Archives (courtesy Adelle Marcus and Sadie Safdie), p. 8*

Suq —*Sephardic Community Center Archives (courtesy Adelle Marcus), p. 9*

Aleppo citadel — *Sephardic Community Center Archives, p. 10*

Founders of Magen David Synagogue and Talmud Torah —*Sephardic Community Center Archives (courtesy Chalom Family), p. 16*

Torah cases in the Great Synagogue — *courtesy Sarah Shamah, Jerusalem, p. 18*

Rabbis of Aleppo — *Joseph Segal, p. 23*

Interior view of the old western wing — *Beth Hatefusoth, Tel Aviv, p. 24*

Model of the summer courtyard — *Beth Hatefusoth, Tel Aviv, p. 24*

Hechal HaTekiah — *courtesy Sarah Shamah, Jerusalem, p. 25*

Outdoor Tebah — *Washington, Freer Gallery of Art, Arthur M. Sackler Gallery Archives, p. 25*

Cave of Eliyahu HaNabi —*Beth Hatefusoth, Tel Aviv. p. 35*

Asher Baghdedi — *Moreshet Aram Soba, p. 35*

List of donors for stipends — *Archives of Mier Beneyahu p. 47*

List of scholars receiving stipends — *Archives of Mier Beneyahu p. 48*

The Orphanage Home Band —*Moreshet Aram Soba, p. 49*

Rules of the Talmud Torah —*Moreshet Aram Soba, p. 50*

Alphabet Chart — *Moreshet Aram Soba, p. 50*

Talmud Torah financial report — *Moreshet Aram Soba, p. 51*

Alliance Teachers — *Moreshet Aram Soba. p. 52*

Arab woman with Sefer Torah scrolls — *J. Philip, p. 67*

R' Ben-Sion Hazzan in Jordanian custody — *J. Philip, p. 67*

Title pages — *Dr. Yaron Harel from " Books of Aleppo"*

Registry of Ketubot — *Archives of Mier Beneyahu p. 159*

Registry of Britot — *Archives of Mier Beneyahu p. 160*

Charity document — *Moreshet Aram Soba, p. 363*

Jewish married woman with a Moslem couple — Aleppo, Syria
Jewish National and University Library, Jerusalem, p. 388

Weekly Stipend List fot Torah Scholars — *Archives of Mier Beneyahu p. 407*

Study group contract — *Karlin Stolin from the Bais Aharon V' Yisrael Journal, p. 412*

Index

How This Index Works

When last name is entirely in capital letters, this indicates one of the 600 personalities listed in the Biographies Section: VI. The number in brackets — following the names — refers to sequence where biography is listed. The number following that refers to page where biography can be found. For cross-references, see individual entry. All other names in the index refer to personalities or pla es that are discussed throughout the book. Numbers refer to pages where they are mentioned.

A

E

I

J

K

L

M

N

O

P